Hakluyt's Voyages

Books by Irwin R. Blacker

———◆———

TAOS

THE GOLDEN CONQUISTADORES

CONQUEST: THE DISPATCHES OF CORTES
FROM THE NEW WORLD

Edited by Irwin R. Blacker

PRESCOTT'S HISTORIES: THE RISE AND
DECLINE OF THE SPANISH EMPIRE

THE

THIRD AND LAST
VOLVME OF THE VOY-
AGES, NAVIGATIONS, TRAF-
fiques, and Difcoueries of the *Englifh Nation*, and in
fome few places, where they haue not been, of ftrangers, performed within and before the time of thefe hundred yeeres, to all
parts of the *Newfound* world of *America*, or the *Weft Indies*, from 73.
degrees of Northerly to 57. of Southerly latitude:

As namely to *Engronland*, *Meta Incognita*, *Eftotiland*,
Tierra de Labrador, *Newfoundland*, vp *The grand bay*, the gulfe of S. *Lau-*
rence, and the Riuer of *Canada* to *Hochelaga* and *Saguenay*, along the coaft of *Aram-*
bec, to the fhores and maines of *Virginia* and *Florida*, and on the Weft or backfide of them
both, to the rich and pleafant countries of *Nueua Bifcaya*, *Cibola*, *Tignex*, *Cicuic*,
Quiuira, to the 15. prouinces of the kingdome of *New Mexico*, to the
bottome of the gulfe of *California*, and vp the
Riuer of *Buena Guia:*

And likewife to all the yles both fmall and great lying before the
cape of *Florida*, *The bay* of *Mexico*, and *Tierra firma*, to the coafts and Inlands
of *Newe Spaine*, *Tierra firma*, and *Guiana*, vp the mighty Riuers of *Orenoque*,
Deffekebe, and *M.zannon*, to euery part of the coaft of *Brefil*, to the Riuer of *Plate*,
through the Streights of *Magellan* forward and backward, and to the
South of the faid Streights as farre as 57. degrees:

And from thence on the backfide of *America*, along the coaftes, harbours,
and capes of *Chili*, *Peru*, *Nicaregua*, *Nueua Efpanna*, *Nueua Galicia*, *Culiacan*,
California, *Noua Albion*, and more Northerly as farre as 43. degrees:

Together with the two renowmed, and profperous voyages of Sir *Francis Drake*
and *M.Thomas Candifh* round about the circumference of the whole earth, and
diuers other voyages intended and fet forth for that courfe.

Collected by Richard Haklvyt *Preacher, and fometimes*
ftudent of Chrift-Church in Oxford.

¶ Imprinted at London by *George Bifhop*, *Ralfe*
Newberie, and Robert Barker.
Anno Dom, 1600.

HAKLUYT'S VOYAGES

*The Principal
Navigations Voyages
Traffiques & Discoveries
of the English Nation*

*Made by Sea or Over-land to the
Remote and Farthest Distant Quarters
of the Earth at any time within the
compasse of these 1600 Yeeres*

BY RICHARD HAKLUYT
*Preacher, and sometime Student of
Christ-Church in Oxford*

Selected and Edited and with an Introduction by
IRWIN R. BLACKER

NEW YORK · THE VIKING PRESS

910
H12h

51273
Nov. '65

To Max and Sally Gartenberg

Contents

Chronology of Hakluyt's Life and Major Work

c. 1552   Born. Probably in London

1560–70   Attended Westminster School. Probably came under professional influence of Richard Hakluyt, Lawyer, about 1568

1570–78   Attended Christchurch, Oxford, receiving B.A. and M.A. degrees

c. 1578   Ordained deacon and priest by Bishop of Salisbury

1580   Arranged for Florio's translation of Cartier's first two American voyages. Corresponded with Mercator concerning Russian Company's expedition in search of Northeast Passage

1582   May 21. Licensed to publish *Divers Voyages,* dedicated to Philip Sidney. Consulted with principals of Gilbert's American colony

1583   March. On Walsingham's instructions, sought support for Gilbert's colony

1583–88   Attached as chaplain to English Ambassador to France, Sir Edward Stafford

1584   October 13. Presented Queen the *Discourse on Western Planting*

1585–86   Involved in publication of Pigafetta's *Itinerario,* interviews with Pedro Dias concerning Spanish pilots, Drake's return from West Indies, publication of

French translation of Espejo's journey into New Mexico

1587   February 22. Dedicated own edition of Martyr's *Decades*
        May 1. Dedicated English version of French Florida
        Probably married in this year to Duglasse Cavendish, niece of the circumnavigator

1589   March 7. One of nineteen to whom Ralegh assigned his rights to the Virginia Colony. Published *Voyages and Discoveries*

1590   Installed as rector of Wetheringsette and Blockford, Suffolk

1597   August 8. Wife buried. Consulted by Sir Robert Cecil concerning Guiana colonization

1598   October 7. Dedicated first volume of *Voyages* to Lord Charles Howard, First Lord

1599   October 16. Participated in organization of East India Company in which he remained active
        October 24. Dedicated second volume of *Voyages* to Sir Robert Cecil

1600   September 1. Dedicated third volume of *Voyages* to Sir Robert Cecil

1602   May 4. Installed as prebendary of Westminster, a post he held until death

1604   March 30. Married Frances Smithe, a widow of fifty

1609   Involved in organization of second Virginia Company

1616   July 5. Hakluyt Island, northwest coast of Greenland, named by William Baffin
        November 23. Died
        November 26. Buried in Westminster Abbey

A Note on the
Selection and Organization

The principle of selection in the present edition has been to offer the greatest possible variety from the materials which comprise Hakluyt's collection, and at the same time to reveal the multi-faceted nature of the *Voyages*. For this reason such disparate elements as letters, ruttiers, navigational training techniques, reports of great sea battles, official correspondence, diaries, logs, etc., have been included. There is no other way to show the complex nature and purpose of the *Voyages*. However, every effort has been made to include those documents and reports which are basic to English Renaissance history and economics as well as to the growth of geographic knowledge. For this latter reason the decision was taken to include Richard Thorne's summary of geographic knowledge, one of the first significant works of Tudor geography. While many of these papers are slight, fugitive documents—such as the correspondence between Elizabeth and foreign monarchs, the two letters of Walsingham, the almost vague references to the Cabots, the charters for foreign companies which laid the groundwork for investment and exploration—they reveal the breadth of the enterprise.

The order of the selections is basically chronological, with variations when it was felt that a body of materials concerning one person or series of voyages should best be kept together to show completely the nature of a single endeavor. However, the activities of Drake and Hawkins covered so great a span of time, that the accounts of these have been kept in their chronological positions. Hakluyt's original plan of working chronologically within geographic areas could not be applied to a selection from his materials, and he himself departed from this pattern when he included the account of the Armada in the first of his three volumes, the one dedicated to Lord Howard, who had been in command of the operations against the Armada. His personal and political reasons for placing it there, out of order, could not justify doing so in an abridged modern edition.

The text is that of the Glasgow 1903–1905 edition, which reproduced the original exactly except for following modern usage in words containing i, j, u, and v; in the elimination of contracted forms such as m̄ for mm, ñ for nn, ū for um, q for que; and in correcting obvious printers' errors.

Introduction

HAKLUYT'S *Voyages and Discoveries* is basically an anthology, a collection of materials written by others. However, probably no similar materials ever assembled have had greater purpose or impact on the history of their own time and upon the understanding of an age. When Richard Hakluyt, the younger, began to prepare his collected papers for publication, they had already been used for years by the persons for whom they were intended—the businessmen, geographers, explorers, and seamen of England.

The *Voyages* was no casual collection of exciting stories to intrigue and entertain—though they are both intriguing and entertaining. The *Voyages* are the very papers of empire. When Richard Hakluyt the elder began to collect the fugitive documents of the first English sailors who probed the far seas beyond England's shores, the island kingdom was a small parochial state involved in its own internal politics and wars. It is true that some few Englishmen had made their way to the Holy Land and the Continent of Europe, though the eastern portions of that continent were only vague notions. There was some slight knowledge about the discoveries of Columbus and the sea ventures of the Portuguese and Spanish. Columbus himself had tried to interest Henry VII in a voyage of discovery, but nothing had come of this. England's own participation in the enterprise of the sea had been limited and generally fruitless, and the few ventures made had been under the guidance of foreigners.

However, by the time the last volume of the *Voyages* was published in 1600, the English empire had become a reality. English seamen had sailed around the world, had sought the passage to India and China by the northeast route and established trade with Russia, had sought the Northwest Passage and died in the Arctic wastes, had taken the Southwest Passage to harass the Spaniards, and finally had settled upon the south-eastern route around Africa, plundering the trade of Portugal. They had probed Russia to Persia, had raped the Spanish colonies in the New World, raided the Spanish ports, and smashed the Armada. And during these same years they had begun the Western Planting, establishing their own colonies in the New World.

In keeping with a tradition that was to dominate England through most of its history, the aim of the voyages was trade. As much as anything else, the *Voyages* must be read as economic history. The two Richard Hakluyts, cousins and friends, collected their information to inform the government and businessmen about the possibilities of trade in the more remote parts of the world. When a group of merchants sat down to plan a voyage, purchase ships, hire crews to sail them, and buy cargoes to fill them, they wanted to know not only where they would find the best opportunities for profit, but what cargoes to purchase, what merchandise they might find at the end of the voyage, the kinds of people with whom they were going to deal, and the nature of the climate and land their captains would encounter. When the merchant venturers formed their companies to trade with Russia, the East Indies, the Levant, or establish the new colonies of North America, they sought the necessary information from the Hakluyts. And so, while compiling their records of voyages made by other captains and for other countries, the Hakluyts gathered in the economic picture of the world with which the Elizabethans expected to trade.

Trade being their purpose, their goal, the wealthy merchants of London, Plymouth, and Bristol did not want to invest without the specific knowledge then available. Nor did the government. And so, while the Hakluyts were never a part of the Tudor government, they worked closely with it. Lord Burghley, his son Robert Cecil, and Francis Walsingham were by turns in contact with the Hakluyts, upon whom they depended for information.

The *Voyages* reveals not only the economic world of the Tudor Age, but its geography. Without the energies the Hakluyts expended in meeting with returned sailors, seeking out the logs of past voyages, the very sailing orders, the correspondence between Elizabeth and her ambassadors, between the great captains and their financial backers, the articles which governed colonization, the ruttiers (route directions) by which the captains sailed, many of the records might have been lost. Aside from the collection of the papers, the *Voyages* provides an insight into the physical and cultural worlds beyond England's horizons as the Tudor Englishman understood those worlds. Richard Hakluyt sought those records which described in detail the peoples met, the land they lived in, the sailing direction, because there were no handy maps to guide the English captains. In many instances, these had to be drawn from the very papers he was collecting.

But more than geography charted, the *Voyages* is geography revealed, the map unrolled, the light breaking across the unknown corners. It is Davis in the Arctic Straits; it is Willoughby seeking a route to China above the Scandinavian peninsula; it is Jenkinson seeking one through Russia and into Persia. It is Ralegh coasting Guinea, Drake probing the "backside" of America. It is geographic revelation—something which would never again happen on such a scale or make such an impact upon the minds of a generation.

Because of the impact of this knowledge and its usefulness, the *Voyages* must be read as propaganda. This does not mean, however, that Richard Hakluyt tampered with his texts to distort the facts. He was much too careful a scholar to have attempted anything of the sort. But he could not have avoided knowing that his materials were often treated as more than a source of economic and geographic information, that the merchant venturers were using these papers to solicit investors, and the government to promote the emerging nationalism of England. No literate contemporary of Shakespeare working on the London scene could have failed to be aware of the growing stature of England, and no patriot would have failed to add to that stature. Hakluyt's *Voyages* are propaganda: they praise England, promote colonization, rally support for the growing naval forces, hail the achievements of the great captains, and at the same time reveal the weaknesses of England's great enemy, Spain. A few of the pieces selected for inclusion are nothing more or less than a real-estate promoter's descriptions of lands he wants to develop. Praises are sung of the opportunities to be gained by investment. The climate is praised, the natives hailed

as friends, the land described as rich and abundant. One Hakluyt or the other helped to write many of these, and, in helping,
committed himself to a program of empire. If investment and
trade were the goals of the Elizabethan merchant venturers,
empire was obviously the best way to achieve this goal. Empire
would assure British monopoly and control as it had assured the
Spanish and Portuguese monopoly which the British were trying
to break down. The *Voyages* contributed in no small way to
preparing the English—the Queen, her ministers, her merchants, and her captains, as well as the people—psychologically
for empire.

At the same time as it propagandized for and justified the
emerging empire and the planting of the English flag in the
remote corners of the world, the *Voyages* recorded that very act
as history. Hakluyt went beyond the political, economic, and
geographic history which the records of voyages and negotia-
tions comprised, to the relationships between the developing
might of England and the determined stand of Spain to hold onto
her control of the world's waterways. In this relationship, this
series of conflicts, Hakluyt not only shows international relations
and waves the flag, but also records in the many reports of
battles, from the destruction of Hawkins' third fleet to the destruction of the Armada, the international history of his time.
The *Voyages* provides the reader with a sense of history stronger
than that given by almost any other book.

While it is large, almost overwhelmingly so, the *Voyages* re-
mains surprisingly personal. In most instances, the writers were
eyewitnesses to the events they recorded; in many, they were
the very men who controlled history. This aspect has long
caught the imagination and fancy of the general reader and fre-
quently of the very young. The great men of an age make their
way through these pages, revealed by their actions, what they
said about themselves, and what men who knew them said
about them. Here Drake raises his flag and Hawkins his. Here
Ralegh dreams and Willoughby freezes to death in the Arctic.
Here Jenkinson notes that he has travelled far for his queen and
is ready to rest. Here Davis describes his probings of the north
and Frobisher his. Here Lancaster records what was in a sense
the final victory for all who came before him, because he was
the man who determined the British route of empire to the

Orient, even though he lost his ship in Brazil and came home aboard a French vessel. Here the great captains fight the colorful and tragic battles—Grenville outnumbered but determined to protect his men ashore, Howard sailing to meet the Armada. These are not the accounts of novelists or historians attempting to re-create a past they have explored; they are the reports of the very men who made the journeys, fought the battles. The *Voyages* is eyewitness drama.

Of scarcely less significance is an aspect of which the reader becomes aware as he reads the *Voyages*: Hakluyt is reporting the growth of the British Navy, which for the next three centuries was to dominate the world's oceans. Hawkins may be remembered for his slaving voyages, but he was also working to establish a navy. The same is true of Drake and the others who sailed with them; because of their efforts, England became a power on the seas. It was during the lifetimes of the two Richard Hakluyts that the small insular nation emerged as an empire whose power lay in her navy.

If the captains and the navy they created appear significant in the reading of the *Voyages*, so too do the English seamen who began as fishermen out of Bristol and capped their age as world travelers. They suffered greatly, and, as in the case of their captains, very few of them died at home. The *Voyages* is the story of the courage and determination of these seamen as much as it is the tale of the glory and imagination of their captains. That this smaller world of the men in the masts and at the capstans comes through so vividly in any reading of Hakluyt's *Voyages* is probably less intentional than any other aspect of the collection. The economics, geography, propaganda, history, and naval growth—the very enterprise of the sea as undertaken by England—were all part of a great plan. No man sat down and said, "We will do this thing." But many sat down and determined that they would find a way to the East, break the Spanish monopoly, cripple the Spanish might, establish trade and colonies. From this interwoven set of aims the empire emerged, and the Hakluyts recorded that emergence.

The *Voyages* may be read in many ways, but they must be read as literature. This is not the self-conscious literature of the creative artist, but the matter-of-fact reporting of men of action, whose account of what they had accomplished, given the lan-

guage of Shakespeare and his contemporaries, captured the
vitality of an age. The *Voyages* is often referred to as an epic.
There is no question that it is the epic of the English people as
they told it themselves. Some of the captains, such as Ralegh,
were accomplished and educated men. Others, such as Jenkinson, were less literate, but certainly no less observant and no
less capable of reporting what they had seen and done. The
Voyages has an energy and scope which involves the reader,
catches him up and takes him away in spite of the writers' lack
of conscious artistry. Perhaps its greatest achievement is in that
very lack of artistry—in its simplicity.

The simplicity is that of the common seaman, the officers
who stood on the decks beside Drake, Hawkins, and Cavendish.
Most of them had no literary pretensions. They wrote the story
they knew so that others might understand it. Some of these
stories are imaginative and vital, but not all. In the account of
the last voyage of Drake and Hawkins—a voyage memorable
if for no other reason than that both of these great captains died
in the course of it—the narrator's ineptness is overcome only by
the significance and color of his materials. Poorly told accounts
are rare, however; and some are as dramatic as James Lancaster's narration of 1594, in which the explorer inserted set
speeches in the classical manner.

The *English Voyages* developed slowly in the form it now
has. It is not certain at what point the younger Richard Hakluyt
decided to create the book from the materials he and his older
cousin had been collecting for years. The two Richard Hakluyts
are distinguished from each other by the professions for which
they were trained. The older cousin is known as the Lawyer,
and the younger, who prepared the *Voyages*, was educated for
the clergy and has been called the Preacher. While the work is
completely that of the Preacher, the younger Richard Hakluyt
admits that his interest and inspiration in part stemmed from his
older relative's involvement with geography.

I do remember that being a youth, and one of her Majesties
scholars at Westminster that fruitful nurserie, it was my happe to
visit the chamber of M. Richard Hakluyt my cosin, a Gentleman of
the Middle Temple, well knowen unto you, at a time when I found
lying upon his boord certeine bookes of Cosmographie, with an

universall Mappe: he seeing me somewhat curious in the view thereof, began to instruct my ignorance, by shewing me the division of the earth into three parts after the olde account, and then according to the latter, & better distribution, into more: he pointed with his wand to all the knowen Seas, Gulfs, Bayes, Straights, Capes, Rivers, Empires, Kingdomes, Dukedomes, and Territories of ech part, with declaration also of their speciall commodities & particular wants, which by the benefit of traffike, & entercourse of merchants, are plentifully supplied. From the Mappe he brought me to the Bible, and turning to the 107 Psalme, directed mee to the 23 & 24 verses, where I read, that they which go downe to the sea in ships, and occupy by the great waters, they see the works of the Lord, and his woonders in the deepe, &c. Which words of the Prophet together with my cousins discourse (things of high and rare delight to my yong nature) tooke in me so deepe an impression, that I constantly resolved, if ever I were preferred to the University, where better time, and more convenient place might be ministred for these studies, I would by Gods assistance prosecute that knowledge and kinde of literature, the doores whereof (after a sort) were so happily opened before me.

The apprenticeship of the younger Hakluyt began at Oxford, where, he says, "I fell to my intended course and by degrees read over whatsoever printed or written discoveries and voyages I found extant either in the Greeke, Latine, Italian, Spanish, Portugall, French, or English languages, and in my publike lectures was the first, that produced and shewed both the olde imperfectly composed, and the new lately reformed Mappes, Globes, Spheares, and other instruments of this Art for demonstration in the common schooles, to the singular pleasure, and generall contentment of my auditory. In continuance of time, and by reason principally of my insight in this study, I grew familiarly acquainted with the chiefest Captaines at sea, the greatest Merchants, and the best Mariners of our nation. . . ."

In the years that followed, the younger Hakluyt was responsible in part for the publication of a number of volumes in the field of geography, among them Cartier's first two American voyages as translated by John Florio, famed as the translator of Montaigne, and even a French edition of Espejo's Journey into New Mexico. In 1582, at the age of thirty, Hakluyt published the *Diverse Voyages Touching the Discovery of America.* Smaller and much less significant than his later works, this collection of materials about what was then known concerning America set the pattern for what was to come.

The next year, 1583, and during the four years that followed, Hakluyt worked in France. Here he learned more about the New World and the great experience of his century than he had been able to learn in isolated England. Here, as has been said, Hakluyt discovered America. French contacts with the new geography were more extensive than England's as French ships had sailed over more of the known oceans. In addition, the Spanish papers which were so rigidly kept from English perusal were available in France. Hakluyt did not visit France as a spy, but there is little question that the Dutch and Portuguese did have spies in France working against Spain. Hakluyt brought back to England from his five years on the Continent an entirely new perspective on the voyaging of the sixteenth century.

However, it is possible that his absence from England, as well as a shortage of funds, cost him a chance to observe at first hand the colonization of Virginia. When Ralegh sailed for America in 1585 he took with him Thomas Hariot of Oxford as observer. It is difficult to say whether Hakluyt would have learned more about the enterprise of the sea if he had sailed with Ralegh than he did by remaining in France. With the care of an eager scholar, one who has that necessary quality of acquisitiveness generally attributed to a pack rat, Hakluyt gathered as much information as he could find in France about the Portuguese efforts in Africa and Asia. He also learned of the French activities in the West Indies—information which was to be important to English seamen—and the practices of the Breton fishermen on the Newfoundland coast. He learned of the fur market created by New France and of the silver strikes made in Mexico and New Mexico by the Spaniards. He learned the nature of the land loosely known as Florida and of the efforts at Brazilian settlement and exploitation. But, as important as anything else, Hakluyt learned that England's efforts at sea had been slight, her rewards—compared to those of her European neighbors—small, her knowledge of the world neglected, and her own reputation as a world power generally ignored.

In 1588 Hakluyt returned home, and by 1589 he was prepared to publish what might be considered the first draft of his major work, which was to take into account all that he had learned abroad. This volume, a full seven hundred thousand words of geographical materials, was described on its title page as *The Principall Navigations, Voiages and Discoveries of the English nation, made by Sea or over Land, to the remote and farthest distant Quarters of the earth at any time within the compasse of these 1500 yeeres: By Richard Hakluyt Master of Arts, and Student sometime of Christchurch in Oxford.*

The *Principall Navigations,* large and impressive as it was, followed the pattern of a significant predecessor of which Hakluyt was very much aware. In 1550 Gian Battista Ramusio, a Venetian official, published *Delle Navigazioni e Viaggi,* which contains many reports of exploration that can be found nowhere else. In all, three volumes of Ramusio's collection were published between 1550 and 1559, the last two posthumously. As an editor, Ramusio was as careful as Hakluyt and as discriminating. The very nature and structure of the Venetian's work must have had great influence on the young English preacher.

While his title promised much, Hakluyt was able to fulfill only a part of that promise; less than one-tenth of the book was devoted to medieval texts and pre-Columbian voyages, and the greater part of this small portion was made up of Mandeville's dubious account of a journey to the Far East. All the other accounts were eyewitness reports of English endeavors. Where the materials were to be found only in a foreign language, Hakluyt printed the original and followed it with a translation of his own. In the case of large undertakings, he did not hesitate to use more than one account of the voyage, thus preserving supplemental information and rounding out the story as fully as possible.

Except in his introduction to the collection as a whole, Hakluyt makes no comment upon his materials. He allows the reader to evaluate them for his own needs. A large portion of the volume was given over to Peter Martyr's *Decades*; five hundred thousand of the seven hundred thousand words were derived from manuscripts, and about seventeen thousand were translated.

The basic source material collected in the *Principall Navigations* consisted of documents, both governmental and business,

letters of all kinds, commissions, naval instructions, the private
records of the merchant companies, the reports from agents
traveling abroad, the logs of ships' captains, all kinds of private
correspondence, including some which the two Richard Hakluyts had sent or received. In addition, Hakluyt included the
large propaganda tracts which campaigned for colonization in
America.

The materials available to him about activities prior to 1550
were limited, but among activities after that date he was able
to locate accounts of the Levant and Russian trade, as well as
correspondence between Elizabeth and the Sultan of Turkey.
Some accounts of African voyages were made available, but
others seem to have been overlooked or suppressed. At that
moment in its history, England had established a *rapproche-
ment* with Portugal in their mutual conflict with Spain, and any
detailed accounts of English voyages into Portugal's overseas
empire would not have been well received.

A careful reading of the *Principall Navigations* indicates that
the Russian Company had opened its files to Hakluyt, because
the account of the Russian trade is one of the most complete.
At the same time, the records of the Cabot voyages of 1536,
which laid the foundation for the English claims to North
America, are clearly of a secondary nature, and the details of
the venture remain vague. The number of western voyages
covered is large. Hawkins' three voyages along a triangular
route, from England to Africa to the Spanish West Indies and
home, are included, as is Davis's voyage to the northwest and
Drake's circumnavigation.

Published the year after the defeat of the Spanish Armada,
the *Principall Navigations* appears a monument to that victory,
with so many of the events which led up to that conflict carefully recorded in the collection. However, it was an unfinished
monument, because in 1598 Richard Hakluyt began to publish
the *Voyages*, a new and revised version of the earlier work.

By this time many of the great personalities of the story—
Hawkins, Drake, Frobisher, Cavendish, Jenkinson, Hatton, Walsingham, Burghley, and even their great antagonist, Philip II of
Spain—were gone from the scene. The intellectual and political
climate of England had changed with the defeat of the Armada,
and England was looking at both itself and the world in a new

way. The small island had become the center of an empire; its navy had defeated the greatest in the world; its maritime ventures no longer needed to be curtailed for fear of angering another power. The extent to which England had emerged is reflected in the difference between the *Principall Navigations* and the *Voyages*.

In his final effort, Richard Hakluyt strove to achieve a complete text, one that would include everything that could be considered of value on his subject. And his subject was larger now. By the time he published the third volume of the *Voyages* in 1600, he had added a hundred years to the period covered, reaching toward the end of the sixteenth century. In addition, he extended his plan backward in time, more than tripling the amount of medieval materials utilized in the 1589 edition. The new medieval documents reveal a greater awareness of economic history. A considerable body of information was now added to cover the relationship of the early English kings to the German and Scandinavian trade. Without comment, Hakluyt dropped Sir John Mandeville entirely, and included instead several narratives of actual journeys to the East. Marco Polo's was not among these, but his work was readily available, as the other texts were not. Even though the medieval portions of the book were enlarged, they remained a small part of the entire project, now expanded from the original seven hundred thousand words to over one million seven hundred thousand words.

The size of the task was enormous and its scope astonishing. In addition to adding the sixteenth century to achieve completeness, Hakluyt laid primary emphasis on the English sea voyages made during his own lifetime. He pushed the English claims of priority in the north and northeast and, by placing the accounts of this accomplishment at the front of the book, emphasized its importance to his entire plan. The papers of the Russian Company were once again utilized, and the nature of the Russian trade, with its new problems, was explored more fully. With the emphasis on completeness, the New World came in for an increased share of attention, and the colonizing ventures there were reported more thoroughly this time. Ralegh's sad and fruitless efforts were carefully documented, as were those of his half-brother, Sir Humphrey Gilbert.

Hakluyt also in this edition set out to establish England's

reputation as the naval power she had so recently proved her-
self. Whereas the earlier version of the collection dealt mostly
with trade and travel, in the new version he did not hesitate to
add the reports of the sea battles which were being waged on all
the oceans. The privateers had become respectable; the navy
had come of age. The Spanish conflicts were certainly the most
significant, and many clashes were reported—England against
Spain in Africa, in the West Indies, in the Pacific, in the Spanish
coastal waters; and, of course, the defeat of the Armada.

Hakluyt's increased interest in history and economics did not
detract from his primary purpose in the *Voyages*—the creation
of a practical geography. He was so fully convinced his book
achieved this end that he was prepared to claim: "There is no
chief river, no port, no town, no city, no province of any reckoning in the West Indies that hath not here some good description
thereof." To buttress this claim, he did not hesitate to use the
papers of non-Englishmen; Spanish, French, Italian, and Dutch
travel accounts were included. However, the foreign materials
used were much less extensive than the English accounts. Reports of the Spanish voyages were available in Ramusio and in
numerous individual small volumes. Accounts of the English
voyages were not.

While later historians were to criticize Hakluyt for making his
final *Voyages* too inclusive, it is difficult to imagine what sub-
sequent histories of England would have been like had his collection not possessed this very quality. In reading the *Voyages*
one must remember that Hakluyt not only reflected his own
time but was a part of it. While he embodies as a scholar all
the strengths and weaknesses of his era, there is one significant
difference between him and his contemporaries. He appears to
have had a better understanding of the importance of primary
sources than any other historian of his period. The early English
historians were basically antiquarians without the methods of
the archivist and completely without the ability to conceive of
the proper use of their materials in large plans and patterns.
And they could not separate myth from fact. Hakluyt surpassed
his contemporaries in this respect; the *Voyages* does have a pattern, was conceived on a scale that extends far beyond the confines of mere chronology, and is based solidly upon docu-
mentary sources. The difference between his judgment in the

selection and use of materials and that of his contemporaries can be seen in *Purchas, His Pilgrimes,* prepared by the heir to Hakluyt's papers. Purchas was a mere compiler who worked without any profound sense of history or of how to utilize his materials. Hakluyt's sense of organization is revealed, by contrast, in his detailed title-page descriptions.

An analysis of the final text of the *Voyages,* prepared by George B. Parks, indicates the relative weight of the medieval and contemporary materials. The former covered three major areas: north and northeast, totaling 175,000 words—171,000 more than the 1589 edition; south and southeast, 65,500 words; and west and southwest, only 7350. The contemporary text for the north and northeast contained 315,000 words, or 50 per cent more than in the earlier edition. The south and southeastern voyages account for 325,000 words, more than double that of the earlier edition. And the west and southwestern documents comprise 812,000 words, as compared to less than 300,000 words in the 1589 edition. Thus, Hakluyt remained faithful in large part to the concept of his first book—*Diverse Voyages*—in emphasizing the New World enterprises.

Obviously, the *Voyages* was not a complete record even of the English voyages, partly because that would have been an impossible task, partly because Hakluyt did not understand the nature of economic history, and partly because certain business reports and state papers of necessity had to remain confidential. The lack of understanding of economic history kept him from including actual financial records, account books, and ledgers. No sixteenth-century historian could imagine anyone's being interested in what had been traded for what on a particular voyage, let alone the itemized value of a particular cargo.

One difference between modern and Elizabethan editing may be seen in the way in which Hakluyt treated the actual texts of his accounts. The modern scholar would not trim away the beginning statements or headnotes which might reveal the character and motives of the reporter. And while this trimming might be considered unwise by the modern scholar, for Hakluyt's purposes one is not altogether certain that it is a flaw. The character and motives of the writer not only did not interest him, but had no place in the design he had established for the *Voyages.* The basic texts did interest him and, with a reserve amazing for his time, he refrained from tampering with the accounts. He did not cut, rewrite, or interpret. He delivered the documents to us exactly as he found them. He was a strange cross between the sixteenth-century antiquarian, ingathering for the sake of curiosity, and the modern archivist, collecting in the belief that there will eventually be a use for his acquisitions. In his own case, Hakluyt was convinced, quite rightly, that there was a use, in fact, there were many uses, and those immediate, for what he had gathered together.

Hakluyt's *Voyages* is the prose epic of the English people. As Shakespeare's characters are giants, so too are Hakluyt's. As Shakespeare's language is vigorous and colorful, so too is the language of the *Voyages*. As Shakespeare's plays reflect the mind and spirit of his age, so too does Hakluyt's monumental work. The collection is Elizabethan in its vitality and scope, with all the greatness attributable to that age; at the same time it is more—in its panorama of the revealed birth of an empire and the opening of the globe, the *Voyages* has no equivalent in the English language.

Hakluyt's Voyages

1

The Letters Patents of king Henry the
seventh granted unto John Cabot and his
three sonnes, Lewis, Sebastian, and Sancius for
the discoverie of new and unknowen lands

HENRY by the grace of God, king of England and France,
and lord of Ireland, to all to whom these presents shall come,
Greeting.

Be it knowen that we have given and granted, and by these
presents do give and grant for us and our heires, to our welbeloved John Cabot citizen of Venice, to Lewis, Sebastian, and
Santius, sonnes of the sayd John, and to the heires of them, and
every of them, and their deputies, full and free authority, leave,
and power to saile to all parts, countreys, and seas of the East,
of the West, and of the North, under our banners and ensignes,
with five ships of what burthen or quantity soever they be, and
as many mariners or men as they will have with them in the
sayd ships, upon their owne proper costs and charges, to seeke
out, discover, and finde whatsoever isles, countreys, regions or
provinces of the heathen and infidels whatsoever they be, and
in what part of the world soever they be, which before this time
have bene unknowen to all Christians: we have granted to them,
and also to every of them, the heires of them, and every of
them, and their deputies, and have given them licence to set up
our banners and ensignes in every village, towne, castle, isle, or
maine land of them newly found. And that the aforesayd John
and his sonnes, or their heires and assignes may subdue, occupy
and possesse all such townes, cities, castles and isles of them
found, which they can subdue, occupy and possesse, as our vassals, and lieutenants, getting unto us the rule, title, and jurisdiction of the same villages, townes, castles, & firme land so found.
Yet so that the aforesayd John, and his sonnes and heires, and

their deputies, be holden and bounden of all the fruits, profits, gaines, and commodities growing of such navigation, for every their voyage, as often as they shall arrive at our port of Bristoll (at the which port they shall be bound and holden onely to arrive) all maner of necessary costs and charges by them made, being deducted, to pay unto us in wares or money the fift part of the capitall gaine so gotten. We giving and granting unto them and to their heires and deputies, that they shall be free from all paying of customes of all and singular such merchandize as they shall bring with them from those places so newly found. And moreover, we have given and granted to them, their heires and deputies, that all the firme lands, isles, villages, townes, castles and places whatsoever they be that they shall chance to finde, may not of any other of our subjects be frequented or visited without the licence of the foresayd John and his sonnes, and their deputies, under paine of forfeiture aswell of their shippes as of all and singuler goods of all them that shall presume to saile to those places so found. Willing, and most straightly commanding all and singuler our subjects aswell on land as on sea, to give good assistance to the aforesayd John and his sonnes and deputies, and that as well in arming and furnishing their ships or vessels, as in provision of food, and in buying of victuals for their money, and all other things by them to be provided necessary for the sayd navigation, they do give them all their helpe and favour. In witnesse whereof we have caused to be made these our Letters patents. Witnesse our selfe at Westminster the fift day of March, in the eleventh yeere of our reigne.

2

An extract taken out of the map of Sebastian Cabot, cut by Clement Adams, concerning his discovery of the West Indies, which is to be seene in her Majesties privie gallerie at Westminster, and in many other ancient merchants houses

The king upon the third day of February, in the 13 yeere of his reigne, gave licence to John Cabot to take sixe English ships in any haven or havens of the realme of England, being of the burden of 200 tunnes, or under, with all necessary furniture, and to take also into the said ships all such masters, mariners, and subjects of the king as willingly will go with him, &c.

I N the yere of our Lord 1497 John Cabot a Venetian, and his sonne Sebastian (with an English fleet set out from Bristoll) discovered that land which no man before that time had attempted, on the 24 of June, about five of the clocke early in the morning. This land he called Prima vista, that is to say, First seene, because as I suppose it was that part whereof they had the first sight from sea. That Island which lieth out before the land, he called the Island of S. John upon this occasion, as I thinke, because it was discovered upon the day of John the Baptist. The inhabitants of this Island use to weare beasts skinnes, and have them in as great estimation as we have our finest garments. In their warres they use bowes, arrowes, pikes, darts, woodden clubs, and slings. The soile is barren in some places, & yeeldeth litle fruit, but it is full of white beares, and stagges farre greater then ours. It yeeldeth plenty of fish, and those very great, as seales, and those which commonly we call salmons: there are soles also above a yard in length: but especially there is great abundance of that kinde of fish which the Savages call baccalaos. In the same Island also there breed hauks, but they are so blacke that they are very like to ravens, as also their partridges, and egles, which are in like sort blacke.

3

A discourse of Sebastian Cabot touching his discovery of part of the West India out of England in the time of king Henry the seventh, used to Galeacius Butrigarius the Popes Legate in Spaine, and reported by the sayd Legate in this sort

D O E you not understand sayd he (speaking to certaine Gentlemen of Venice) how to passe to India toward the Northwest, as did of late a citizen of Venice, so valiant a man, and so well practised in all things pertaining to navigations, and the science of Cosmographie, that at this present he hath not his like in Spaine, insomuch that for his vertues he is preferred above all other pilots that saile to the West Indies, who may not passe thither without his licence, and is therefore called Piloto mayor, that is, the grand Pilot. And when we sayd that we knew him not, he proceeded, saying, that being certaine yeres in the city of Sivil, and desirous to have some knowledge of the navigations of the Spanyards, it was tolde him that there was in the city a valiant man, a Venetian borne named Sebastian Cabot, who had the charge of those things, being an expert man in that science, and one that coulde make Cardes for the Sea with his owne hand, and that by this report, seeking his acquaintance, hee found him a very gentle person, who intertained him friendly, and shewed him many things, and among other a large Mappe of the world, with certaine particuler Navigations, as well of the Portugals, as of the Spaniards, and that he spake further unto him to this effect.

When my father departed from Venice many yeeres since to dwell in England, to follow the trade of marchandises, hee tooke mee with him to the citie of London, while I was very yong, yet having neverthelesse some knowledge of letters of humanitie, and of the Sphere. And when my father died in that time when

newes were brought that Don Christopher Colonus Genuese had
discovered the coasts of India, whereof was great talke in all the
Court of king Henry the 7. who then raigned, insomuch that all
men with great admiration affirmed it to be a thing more divine
then humane, to saile by the West into the East where spices
growe, by a way that was never knowen before, by this fame
and report there increased in my heart a great flame of desire to
attempt some notable thing. And understanding by reason of
the Sphere, that if I should saile by way of the Northwest, I
should by a shorter tract come into India, I thereupon caused
the King to be advertised of my devise, who immediately commanded two Carvels to bee furnished with all things appertayning to the voyage, which was as farre as I remember in the yeere
1496. in the beginning of Sommer. I began therefore to saile
toward the Northwest, not thinking to finde any other land then
that of Cathay, & from thence to turne toward India, but after
certaine dayes I found that the land ranne towards the North,
which was to mee a great displeasure. Neverthelesse, sayling
along by the coast to see if I could finde any gulfe that turned,
I found the lande still continent to the 56. degree under our
Pole. And seeing that there the coast turned toward the East,
despairing to finde the passage, I turned backe againe, and
sailed downe by the coast of that land toward the Equinoctiall
(ever with intent to finde the saide passage to India) and came
to that part of this firme lande which is nowe called Florida,
where my victuals failing, I departed from thence and returned
into England, where I found great tumults among the people,
and preparation for warres in Scotland: by reason whereof there
was no more consideration had to this voyage.

Whereupon I went into Spaine to the Catholique king, and
Queene Elizabeth, which being advertised what I had done,
intertained me, and at their charges furnished certaine ships,
wherewith they caused me to saile to discover the coastes of
Brasile, where I found an exceeding great and large river named
at this present Rio de la plata, that is, the river of silver, into
the which I sailed and followed it into the firme land, more then
sixe score leagues, finding it every where very faire, and inhabited with infinite people, which with admiration came running dayly to our ships. Into this River runne so many other
rivers, that it is in maner incredible.

After this I made many other voyages, which I nowe pretermit, and waxing olde, I give my selfe to rest from such travels, because there are nowe many yong and lustie Pilots and Mariners of good experience, by whose forwardnesse I doe rejoyce in the fruit of my labours, and rest with the charge of this office, as you see.

4

The booke made by the right worshipful M. Robert
Thorne in the yeere 1527. in Sivil, to Doctour Ley,
Lord ambassadour for king Henry the eight, to
Charles the Emperour, being an information of the
parts of the world, discovered by him and the king
of Portingal: and also of the way to the Moluccaes
by the North

RIGHT noble and reverend in &c. I have received your letters, and have procured and sent to know of your servant, who,
your Lordship wrote, should be sicke in Merchena. I cannot
there or els where heare of him, without he be returned to you,
or gone to S. Lucar, and shipt. I cannot judge but that of some
contagious sicknesse hee died, so that the owner of the house
for defaming his house would bury him secretly, and not be
knowen of it. For such things have often times happened in this
countrey.

Also to write unto your Lordshippe of the new trade of
Spicery of the Emperour, there is no doubt but that the Islands
are fertile of Cloves, Nutmegs, Mace, and Cinnamom: and that
the said Islands, with other there about, abound with golde,
Rubies, Diamondes, Balasses, Granates, Jacincts, and other
stones & pearles, as all other lands, that are under and neere the
Equinoctiall. For we see, where nature giveth any thing, she is
no nigard. For as with us and other, that are aparted from the
said Equinoctiall, our mettals be Lead, Tinne, and Iron, so
theirs be Gold, Silver, and Copper. And as our fruits and
graines bee Apples, Nuts, and Corne, so theirs be Dates, Nutmegs, Pepper, Cloves, and other Spices. And as we have Jeat,
Amber, Cristall, Jasper, and other like stones, so have they
Rubies, Diamonds, Balasses, Saphyres, Jacincts, and other like.

And though some say that of such precious mettals, graines, or kind of spices, and precious stones, the abundance and quantity is nothing so great, as our mettals, fruits or stones above rehearsed: yet if it be well considered, how the quantitie of the earth under the Equinoctiall to both the Tropicall lines, (in which space is found the sayd Golde, spices and precious stones) is as much in quantity, as almost all the earth from the Tropickes to both the Poles; it cannot be denied but there is more quantity of the sayd mettals, fruites, spices, and precious stones, then there is of the other mettals and other things before rehearsed. And I see that the preciousnes of these things is measured after the distance that is between us, and the things that we have appetite unto. For in this navigation of the Spicerie was discovered, that these Islands nothing set by golde, but set more by a knife and a nayle of iron, then by his quantitie of Golde: and with reason, as the thing more necessary for mans service. And I doubt not but to them should be as precious our corne and seedes, if they might have them, as to us their spices: & likewise the pieces of glasse that here we have counterfeited are as precious to them, as to us their stones: which by experience is seene daylie by them that have trade thither. This of the riches of those countries is sufficient.

Touching that your Lordship wrote, whether it may bee profitable to the Emperor or no? it may be without doubt of great profite: if, as the king of Portingal doth, he would become a merchant, and provide shippes and their lading, and trade thither alone, and defend the trade of these Islands for himselfe. But other greater businesse withholdeth him from this. But still, as now it is begunne to be occupied, it would come to much. For the shippes comming in safetie, there would thither many every yere, of which to the Emperour is due of all the wares and jewels that come from thence the fift part for his custome cleare without any cost. And besides this hee putteth in every flote a certaine quantitie of money, of which hee enjoyeth of the gaines pound and pounds like as other adventurers doe. In a fleete of three shippes and a Caravel that went from this citie armed by the marchants of it, which departed in Aprill last past, I and my partener have one thousand foure hundred duckets that we employed in the sayd fleete, principally for that two English men, friends of mine, which are somewhat learned in Cosmographie,

should goe in the same shippes, to bring me certaine relation of
the situation of the countrey, and to be expert in the navigation
of those seas, and there to have informations of many other
things, and advise that I desire to knowe especially. Seeing in
these quarters are shippes, and mariners of that countrey, and
cardes by which they saile, though much unlike ours, that they
should procure to have the said cards, and learne how they
understand them, and especially to know what navigation they
have for those Islands Northwards, and Northeastward.

For if from the sayd Islands the sea did extend, without inter-
position of land, to saile from the North point to the Northeast
poynt one thousand seven hundred or one thousand eight hundred leagues, they should come to the New found Islands that
we discovered, and so we should be neerer to the sayd Spicerie
by almost two thousand leagues then the Emperour, or the king
of Portingal are. And to advise your Lordship whether of these
Spiceries of the king of Portingal or the Emperours is neerer,
and also of the titles that either of them hath, and howe our
New found lands are parted from it, (for that by writing without some demonstration, it were hard to give any declaration of
it) I have caused that your Lordship shall receive herewith a
little Mappe or Carde of the world: the which, I feare me, shall
put your Lordship to more labour to understand, then me to
make it, onely for that it is made in so litle roome that it cannot
be but obscurely set out, that is desired to be seene in it, and
also for that I am in this science little expert: Yet to remedy in
part this difficulty, it is necessary to declare to your Lordship
my intent, with which I trust you shall perceive in this Card
part of your desire, if, for that I cannot expresse mine intent,
with my declaration I doe not make it more obscure.

First, your Lordship knoweth that the Cosmographers have
divided the earth by 360 degrees in latitude, and as many in
longitude, under the which is comprehended all the roundnes
of the earth: the latitude being divided into foure quarters,
ninetie degrees amount to every quarter, which they measure by
the altitude of the Poles, that is the North and South starres,
being from the line Equinoctiall till they come right under the
North starre the said ninetie degrees: and as much from the
sayd line Equinoctiall to the South starre be other ninety
degrees. And as much more is also from either of the sayd

starres agayne to the Equinoctiall. Which imagined to bee round, is soone perceived thus, 360 degrees of latitude to be consumed in the said foure quarters of ninetie degrees a quarter: so that this latitude is the measure of the worlde from North to South, and from South to North. And the longitude, in which are also counted other 360, is counted from West to East, or from East to West, as in the Card is set.

The sayd latitude your Lordship may see marked and divided in the ende of this Card on the left hand: so that if you would know in what degrees of latitude any region or coast standeth, take a compasse, and set the one foot of the same in the Equinoctial line right against the said region, & apply the other foote of the compasse to the said region or coast, & then set the sayd compasse at the end of the Card, where the degrees are divided. And the one foote of the compasse standing in the line Equinoctial, the other will shew in the scale the degrees of altitude or latitude that the said region is in. Also the longitude of the world I have set out in the nether part of the Card, conteining also 360 degrees: which begin to be counted after Ptoleme and other Cosmographers from an headland called Capo Verde, which is over against a little crosse made in the part Occidental, where the division of the degrees beginneth, and endeth in the same Capo Verde.

Now to know in what longitude any land is, your Lordship must take a ruler or a compasse, and set the one foot of the compasse upon the land or coast whose longitude you would know, and extend the other foot of the compasse to the next part of one of the tranversall lines in the Orientall or Occidental part: which done, set the one foot of the compasse in the said transversal line at the end of the nether scale, the scale of longitude, and the other foot sheweth the degree of longitude that the region is in. And your Lordship must understand that this Card, though little, conteineth the universall whole world betwixt two collaterall lines, the one in the Occidentall part descendeth perpendicular upon the 175 degree, & the other in the Orientall on the 170 degree, whose distance measureth the scale of longitude. And that which is without the two said transversall lines, is onely to shew how the Orientall part is joined with the Occident, and Occident with the Orient. For that that is set without the line in the Orientall part, is the same that is set within the

other line in the Occidentall part: and that that is set without the
line in the Occidentall part, is the same that is set within the line
in the Orientall part, to shew that though this figure of the
world in plaine or flatte seemeth to have an end, yet one imagining that this sayd Card were set upon a round thing, where
the endes should touch by the lines, it would plainely appeare
howe the Orient part joyneth with the Occident, as there without the lines it is described and figured.

And for more declaration of the said Card, your Lordship
shall understand, that beginning on the part Occidental within
the line, the first land that is set out, is the maine land and Islands of the Indies of the Emperour. Which maine land or
coast goeth Northward, and finisheth in the land that we found,
which is called here Terra de Labrador. So that it appeareth
the sayd land that we found, and the Indies to be all one maine
land.

The sayd coast from the sayd Indies Southward, as by the
Card your Lordshippe may see, commeth to a certaine straight
Sea, called Estrecho de todos Santos: by which straight Sea
the Spaniards goe to the Spiceries, as I shall declare more at
large: the which straight Sea is right against three hundred fifteene degrees of longitude, and is of latitude or altitude from
the Equinoctiall three and fifty degrees. The first land from
the sayd beginning of the Card toward the Orient are certaine
Islands of the Canaries, and Islandes of Capo verde. But the
first maine land next to the line Equinoctial is the sayd Capo
verde, and from thence Northward by the straight of this sea
of Italie. And so followeth Spayne, France, Flanders, Almaine,
Denmarke, and Norway, which is the highest parte toward the
North. And over against Flanders are our Islands of England
and Ireland. Of the landes and coastes within the streights I
have set out onely the Regions, dividing them by lines of their
limits, by which plainely I thinke your Lordship may see, in
what situation everie region is, and of what highnesse, and
with what regions it is joyned. I doe thinke few are left out of
all Europe. In the parts of Asia and Affrica I could not so wel
make the sayd divisions: for that they be not so wel knowen,
nor need not so much. This I write because in the said Card
be made the said lines & strikes, that your Lordship should understand wherefore they doe serve. Also returning to the fore-

said Capo verde, the coast goeth Southward to a Cape called
Capo de buona speransa: which is right over against the 60. &
65. degree of longitude. And by this Cape go the Portingals
to their Spicerie. For from this Cape toward the Orient, is the
land of Calicut, as your Lordship may see in the headland over
against the 130. degree. From the sayd Cape of Buona speransa
the coast returneth toward the line Equinoctial, and passing
forth entreth the red sea, & returning out, entreth again into the
gulfe of Persia, and returneth toward the Equinoctiall line, till
that it commeth to the headland called Calicut aforesayd, and
from thence the coast making a gulfe, where is the river of Gan-
ges, returneth toward the line to a headland called Malaca,
where is the principall Spicerie: & from this Cape returneth and
maketh a great gulfe, and after the coast goeth right toward the
Orient, and over against this last gulfe and coast be many Islands, which be Islandes of the Spiceries of the Emperour.
Upon which the Portingals and he be at variance.

The sayd coast goeth toward the Orient, and endeth right
against the 155. degrees, and after returneth toward the Occident Northward: which coast not yet plainely knowen, I may
joine to the New found lande found by us, that I spake of before. So that I finish with this briefe declaration of the Card
aforesayd. Well I know I should also have declared how the
coasts within the straights of the Sea of Italie runne. It is playne
that passing the streights on the North side of that Sea after the
coast of Granado, and with that which pertaines to Spaine, is
the coast of that which France hath in Italie. And then followeth in one piece all Italie, which land hath an arme of the Sea,
with a gulfe which is called Mare Adriaticum. And in the bottome of this gulfe is the citie of Venice. And on the other part
of the sayd gulfe is Sclavonia, and next Grecia, then the streits
of Constantinople, and then the sea called Euxinus, which is
within the sayd streights: and comming out of the sayd
streights, followeth Turcia major (though now on both sides it
is called Turcia.) And so the coast runneth Southward to Syria,
and over against the sayd Turcia are the Islands of Rhodes,
Candie, and Cyprus. And over against Italie are the Islands
of Sicilia and Sardinia. And over against Spaine is Majorca and
Minorca. In the ende of the gulfe of Syria is Judea. And from
thence returneth the coast toward the Occident, till it commeth

to the streights where we began, which all is the coast of Affrike
and Barbarie. Also your Lordship shall understand that the
coastes of the Sea throughout all the world, I have coloured
with yellow, for that it may appeare that all that is within the
line coloured yellow, is to be imagined to be maine land or
Islands: and all without the line so coloured to bee Sea: whereby it is easie and light to know it. Albeit in this little roome
any other description would rather have made it obscure then
cleere. And the sayd coasts of the Sea are all set justly after the
maner and forme as they lie, as the navigation approveth them
throughout all the Card, save onely the coastes and Isles of the
Spicerie of the Emperour which is from over against the 160.
to the 215. degrees of longtitude, For these coastes and situations of the Islands, every of the Cosmographers and pilots of
Portingal & Spayne do set after their purpose. The Spaniards
more towards the Orient, because they should appeare to ap-
pertain to the Emperour: & the Portingals more toward the
Occident, for that they should fal within their jurisdiction. So
that the pilots and navigants thither, which in such cases should
declare the truth, by their industrie do set them falsly every one
to favour his prince. And for this cause can be no certaine situation of that coast and Islands, till this difference betwixt them
be verified. Now to come to the purpose of your Lordships demaund touching the difference between the Emperour and the
king of Portingal, to understand it better, I must declare the
beginning of this discoverie. Though peradventure your Lordship may say that in that I have written ought of purpose, I fall
in the proverbe, A gemino ovo bellum: But your Lordship commanded me to be large, and I take licence to be prolixious,
and shalbe peradventure tedious, but your Lordship knoweth
that Nihil ignorantia verbosius.

In the yeere 1484 the king of Portingal minded to arme certaine Carvels to discover this Spicerie. Then forasmuch as he
feared that being discovered, every other prince woulde sende
and trade thither, so that the cost and perill of discovering
should be his, and the profite common: wherefore first hee gave
knowledge of this his minde to all princes Christened, saying
that hee would seeke amongst the infidels newe possessions of
regions, and therefore would make a certaine armie: and that
if any of them would helpe in the cost of the sayd armie, he

should enjoy his part of the profite or honour that should come of it. And as then this discovering was holden for a strange thing and uncertaine. Nowe they say, that all the Princes of Christendome answered, that they would be no part of such an armie, nor yet of the profit that might come of it. After the which he gave knowledge to the Pope of his purpose, and of the answere of all the Princes, desiring him that seeing that none would helpe in the costes, that he would judge all that should bee found and discovered to be of his jurisdiction, and commannd that none other princes should intermeddle therewith. The Pope sayd not as Christ saith, Quis me constituit judicem inter vos? He did not refuse, but making himselfe as Lord and Judge of all, not onely granted that all that should be discovered from Orient to Occident, should be the kings of Portingal, but also, that upon great censures no other Prince should discover but he. And if they did, all to bee the kings of Portingal. So he armed a fleete, and in the yeere 1497 were discovered the Islands of Calicut, from whence is brought all the spice he hath.

After this in the yere 1492 the king of Spaine willing to discover lands toward the Occident without making any such diligence, or taking licence of the king of Portingal, armed certaine Carvels, and then discovered this India Occidentall, especially two Islands of the sayd India, that in this Card I set forth, naming the one la Dominica, and the other Cuba, and brought certaine golde from thence. Of the which when the king of Portingal had knowledge, he sent to the king of Spaine, requiring him to give him the sayd Islands. For that by the sentence of the Pope all that should be discovered was his, and that hee should not proceede further in the discoverie without his licence. And at the same time it seemeth that out of Castil into Portingal had gone for feare of burning infinite number of Jewes that were expelled out of Spaine, for that they would not turne to be Christians, and carried with them infinite number of golde and silver. So that it seemeth that the king of Spaine answered, that it was reason that the king of Portingal asked, and that to be obedient to that which the Pope had decreed, he would give him the sayd Islands of the Indies. Nowe for as much as it was decreed betwixt the sayde kings, that none should receive the others subjects fugitives, nor their goods,

therfore the king of Portingal should pay and returne to the
king of Spaine a million of golde or more, that the Jewes had
caryed out of Spaine to Portingal, & that in so doing, he would
give these Islands, and desist from any more discovering. And
not fulfilling this, he would not onely not give these Islands,
but procure to discover more where him thought best. It seemeth that the king of Portingal would not, or could not with his
ease pay this money. And so not paying, that he could not let
the king of Spaine to discover: so that he enterprised not toward the Orient where he had begun & found the Spicerie. And
consented to the king of Spaine, that touching this discovering
they should divide the worlde betweene them two. And that all
that should be discovered from Cape Verde, where this Card
beginneth to be counted in the degrees of longitude, to 180 of
the sayd scale of longitude, which is halfe the world toward the
Orient, & finisheth in this Card right over against a litle crosse
made at the said 180 degrees, to be the king of Portingals. And
all the land from the said Crosse towarde the Occident, untill it
joyneth with the other Crosse in the Orient, which conteineth
the other hundreth and eightie degrees, that is the other halfe
of the worlde, to be the king of Spaines. So that from the land
over against the said hundreth & eighty degrees untill it finish
in the three hundred and sixtie on both the ends of the Card,
is the jurisdiction of the king of Spaine. So after this maner
they divided the world betweene them.

Now for that these Islands of Spicery fall neere the terme
and limites betweene these princes (for as by the sayd Card
you may see they begin from one hundred and sixtie degrees of
longitude, and ende in 215) it seemeth all that falleth from
160 to 180 degrees, should be of Portingal: and all the rest of
Spaine. And for that their Cosmographers and Pilots coulde
not agree in the situation of the sayde Islandes (for the Portingals set them all within their 180 degrees, and the Spaniards
set them all without:) and for that in measuring, all the Cosmographers of both partes, or what other that ever have bene cannot give certaine order to measure the longitude of the worlde,
as they doe of the latitude: for that there is no starre fixed
from East to West, as are the starres of the Poles from North
to South, but all mooveth with the mooving divine: no maner
can bee founde howe certainely it may bee measured, but by

conjectures, as the Navigants have esteemed the way they have gone. But it is manifest that Spaine had the situation of al the lands from Cape Verde, toward the Orient of ye Portingals to their 180 degrees. And in all their Cardes they never hitherto set the saide Islands within their limitation of the sayd 180 degrees, (though they knewe very well of the Islands,) till now that the Spaniards discovered them. And it is knowen that the king of Portingal had trade to these Islands afore, but would never suffer Portingal to go thither from Calicut: for so much as he knew that it fell out of his dominion: least by going thither there might come some knowledge of those other Islands of the king of Spaine, but bought the cloves of Marchants of that countrey, that brought them to Calicut, much deerer then they would have cost, if he had sent for them, thinking after this maner it would abide alwayes secret. And now that it is discovered he sendes and keepes the Spaniards from the trade all that he can.

Also it should seeme that when this foresaid consent of the division of the worlde was agreed of betweene them, the king of Portingal had already discovered certaine Islandes that lie over against Cape Verde, and also certaine part of the maine land of India toward the South, from whence he fette Brasill, and he called it the land of Brasil. So for that all should come in his terme and limites, hee tooke three hundred and seventie leagues beyond Cape Verde: and after this, his 180 degrees, being his part of the worlde, should begin in the Carde right over against the 340 degrees, where I have made a little compasse with a crosse, and should finish at the 160 degree, where also I have made another little marke. And after this computation without any controversie, the Islands of the spicery fal out of the Portingals domination. So that nowe the Spaniards say to the Portingals, that if they would beginne their 180 degrees from the sayde Cape Verde, to the intent they should extende more toward the Orient, and so to touch those Islandes of the Spicerie of the Emperour, which is al that is betweene the two crosses made in this Card, that then the Islands of Cape Verde and the lande of Brasil that the Portingals nowe obtaine, is out of the sayd limitation, and that they are of the Emperours. Or if their 180 degrees they count from the 370 leagues beyond the said Cape Verde, to include in it the said Islands and lands of Brasil, then plainely appeareth the said 180 degrees should finish long before they come to these Islands of the Spicerie of the Emperour: As by this Carde your Lordship may see. For their limits should begin at the 340 degrees of this Carde, and ende at the 160 degrees, where I have made two little markes of the compasse with crosses in them.

So that plainely it should appeare by reason, that the Portingals should leave these Islands of Cape Verde and land of Brasil, if they would have part of the Spicerie of the Emperours: or els holding these, they have no part there. To this the Portingals say, that they will beginne their 180 degrees from the selfe same Cape Verde: for that it may extende so much more toward the Orient, and touch these Islandes of the Emperours: and would winne these Islandes of Cape Verde and land of Brasil neverthelesse, as a thing that they possessed before the consent of this limitation was made.

So none can verely tell which hath the best reason. They be not yet agreed, Quare sub Judice lis est.

But without doubt (by all conjectures of reason) the sayd Islands fall all without the limitation of Portingal, and pertaine to Spaine, as it appeareth by the most part of all the Cardes made by the Portingals, save those which they have falsified of late purposely.

But now touching that your Lordship wrote, whether that which we discovered toucheth any thing the foresayd coastes: once it appeareth plainely, that the Newefound land that we discovered, is all a maine land with the Indies Occidentall, from whence the Emperour hath all the gold and pearles: and so continueth of coast more then 5000 leagues of length, as by this Carde appeareth. For from the said New lands it proceedeth toward the Occident to the Indies, and from the Indies returneth toward the Orient, and after turneth Southward up till it come to the Straits of Todos Santos, which I reckon to be more then 5000 leagues.

So that to the Indias it should seeme that we have some title, at least that for our discovering we might trade thither as other doe. But all this is nothing neere the Spicerie.

Now then if from the sayd New found lands the Sea be navigable, there is no doubt, but sayling Northward and passing the Pole, descending to the Equinoctial line, we shall hit these

Islands, and it should be a much shorter way, then either the Spaniards or the Portingals have. For we be distant from the Pole but thirty and nine degrees, and from the Pole to the Equinoctiall be ninetie, the which added together, bee an hundred twenty and nine degrees, leagues 2489. and miles 7440: Where we should find these Islands. And the Navigation of the Spaniards to the Spicerie is, as by this Carde you may see, from Spaine to the Islandes of Canarie, and from these Islandes they runne over the line Equinoctiall Southwarde to the Cape of the maine land of the Indians, called the Cape of Saint Augustine, and from this Cape Southwards to the straites of Todos Santos, in the which navigation to the said straites is 1700. or 1800 leagues; and from these Straites being past them, they returne towarde the line Equinoctiall to the Islands of Spicerie, which are distant from the saide Straites 4200. or 4300. leagues.

The navigation of the Portingals to the said Islandes is departing from Portingall Southward towarde the Cape Verde, and from thence to another Cape passing the line Equinoctial called Capo de bona speransa, and from Portingal to the Cape is 1800 leagues, and from this Cape to the Islands of Spicerie of the Emperour is 2500. leagues.

So that this navigation amounteth all to 4300. leagues. So that (as afore is sayd,) if between our New found lands or Norway, or Island, the seas toward the North be navigable, we should goe to these Islands a shorter way by more then 2000. leagues.

And though we went not to the sayd Islandes, for that they are the Emperours or kings of Portingal, wee shoulde by the way and comming once to the line Equinoctiall, finde landes no lesse riche of golde and Spicerie, as all other landes are under the sayd line Equinoctiall: and also should, if we passe under the North, enjoy the navigation of all Tartarie. Which should be no lesse profitable to our commodities of cloth, then these Spiceries to the Emperour, and king of Portingal.

But it is a generall opinion of all Cosmographers, that passing the seventh clime, the sea is all ice, and the colde so much that none can suffer it. And hitherto they had all the like opinion, that under the line Equinoctiall for much heate the land was unhabitable.

Yet since (by experience is proved) no land so much habitable nor more temperate. And to conclude, I thinke the same should be found under the North, if it were experimented. For as all judge, Nihil fit vacuum in rerum natura: So I judge, there is no land unhabitable, nor Sea innavigable. If I should write the reason that presenteth this unto me, I should be too prolixe, and it seemeth not requisite for this present matter. God knoweth that though by it I should have no great interest, yet I have had and still have no litle mind of this businesse: So that if I had facultie to my will, it should be the first thing that I woulde understand, even to attempt, if our Seas Northward be navigable to the Pole, or no. I reason, that as some sickenesses are hereditarious, and come from the father to the sonne, so this inclination or desire of this discoverie I inherited of my father, which with another marchant of Bristow named Hugh Eliot, were the discoverers of the New found lands, of the which there is no doubt, (as nowe plainely appeareth) if the mariners would then have bene ruled, and followed their Pilots minde, the lands of the West Indies (from whence all the gold commeth) had bene ours. For all is one coast, as by the Carde appeareth, and is aforesayd.

Also in this Carde by the coastes where you see C. your Lordship shall understand it is set for Cape or headland, where I. for Iland, where P. for Port, where R. for River. Also in all this little Carde I thinke nothing be erred touching the situation of the land, save onely in these Ilands of Spicerie: which, for that (as afore is sayd) every one setteth them after his minde, there can be no certification how they stand. I doe not denie, that there lacke many things, that a consummate Carde should have, or that a right good demonstration desireth. For there should be expressed all the mountaines and Rivers that are principall of name in the earth, with the names of Portes of the sea, the names of all principall cities, which all I might have set, but not in this Carde, for the litle space would not consent.

Your Lordship may see that setting onely the names almost of every Region, and yet not of all, the roome is occupied. Many Islands are also left out, for the said lack of roome, the names almost of all Portes put to silence, with the roses of the windes or points of the compasse: For that this is not for Pilots to sayle by, but a summary declaration of that which your Lordship commanded. And if by this your Lordship cannot wel perceive the meaning of this Card, of the which I would not marveile, by reason of the rude composition of it, will it please your Lordship to advise mee to make a bigger and a better Mappe, or els that I may cause one to be made. For I know my selfe in this and all other nothing perfect, but Licet semper discens, nunquam tamen ad perfectam scientiam perveniens. Also I know, to set the forme Sphericall of the world in Plano after the true rule of Cosmographie, it would have bene made otherwise then this is: howbeit the demonstration should not have bene so plaine.

And also these degrees of longitude, that I set in the lower part of this card, should have bin set along by the line Equinoctiall, & so then must be imagined. For the degrees of longitude neere either of the poles are nothing equall in bignesse to them in the Equinoctiall. But these are set so, for that setting them a long the Equinoctial, it would have made obscure a great part of the map. Many other curiosities may be required, which for the nonce I did not set downe, as well for that the intent I had principally was to satisfie your doubt touching the spicerie, as for that I lack leasure and time. I trust your Lordship correcting that which is erred, will accept my good will, which is to doe any thing that I may in your Lordships service. But from henceforth I knowe your Lordship will rather commaund me to keepe silence, then to be large, when you shall be wearied with the reading of this discourse. Jesus prosper your estate and health.

Your Lordships
Robert Thorne 1527

Also this Carde and that which I write touching the variance betweene the Emperour and the king of Portingall, is not to be shewed or communicated there with many of that court. For though there is nothing in it prejudiciall to the Emperour, yet it may be a cause of paine to the maker: as well for that none may make these Cardes, but certaine appointed and allowed for masters, as for that peradventure it would not sound well to them, that a stranger should know or discover their secretes: and would appeare worst of all, if they understand that I write touching the short way to the spicerie by our Seas. Though peradventure of troth it is not to be looked to, as a thing that by all opinions is unpossible, and I thinke never will come to effect: and therefore neither here nor else where is it to be spoken of. For to move it amongst wise men, it should bee had in derision. And therefore to none I would have written nor spoken of such things, but to your Lordship, to whom boldly I commit in this all my foolish fantasie as to my self. But if it please God that into England I may come with your Lordship, I will shew some conjectures of reason, though against the generall opinion of Cosmographers, by which shall appeare this that I say not to lacke some foundation. And till that time I beseeche your Lordship let it be put to silence: and in the meane season it may please God to send our two Englishmen, that are gone to the Spicerie, which may also bring more plaine declaration of that which in this case might be desired.

Also I knowe I needed not to have beene so prolixe in the declaration of this Carde to your Lordship, if the sayd Carde had bene very well made after the rules of Cosmographie. For your Lordship would soone understand it better then I, or any other that could have made it: and so it should appeare that I shewed Delphinum natare. But for that I have made it after my rude maner, it is necessary that I be the declarer or gloser of mine own worke, or els your Lordship should have had much labour to understand it, which now with it also cannot be excused, it is so grossely done. But I knew you looked for no curious things of mee, and therefore I trust your Lordship will accept this, and hold me for excused. In other mens letters that they write they crave pardon that at this present they write no larger: but I must finish, asking pardon that at this present I write so largely. Jesus preserve your Lordship with augmentation of dignities.

Your servant Robert
Thorne, 1527

5

A brief relation of two sundry voyages made by the worshipful M. William Haukins of Plimmouth, father to Sir John Haukins knight, late Treasurer of her Majesties Navie, in the yeere 1530 and 1532

OLDE M. William Haukins of Plimmouth, a man for his wisedome, valure, experience, and skill in sea causes much esteemed, and beloved of K. Henry the 8, and being one of the principall Sea-captaines in the West parts of England in his time, not contented with the short voyages commonly then made onely to the knowne coasts of Europe, armed out a tall and goodly shippe of his owne of the burthen of 250 tunnes, called the Paule of Plimmouth, wherwith he made three long and famous voyages unto the coast of Brasil, a thing in those dayes very rare, especially to our Nation. In the course of which voyages he touched at the river of Sestos upon the coast of Guinea, where hee traffiqued with the Negros, and tooke of them Elephants teeth, and other commodities which that place yeeldeth: and so arriving on the coast of Brasil, he used there such discretion, and behaved himself so wisely with those savage people, that he grew into great familiarity and friendship with them. Insomuch that in his second voyage, one of the savage kings of the countrey of Brasil, was contented to take ship with him, and to be transported hither into England: whereunto M. Haukins agreed, leaving behinde in the Countery as a pledge for his safetie and returne againe, one Martin Cockeram of Plimmouth. This Brasilian king being arrived, was brought up to London and presented to K. Henry the 8, lying as then at White-hall: at the sight of whom the King and all the Nobilitie did not a litle marvaile, and not without cause: for in his cheekes were holes made according to their savage maner, and therein small bones were planted, standing an inch out from the said holes, which in his owne Countrey was reputed for a great braverie. He had also another hole in his nether lip, wherein was set a precious stone about the bignes of a pease: All his apparel, behaviour, and gesture, were very strange to the beholders.

Having remained here the space almost of a whole yeere, and the king with his sight fully satisfied, M. Hawkins according to his promise and appointment, purposed to convey him againe into his countrey: but it fell out in the way, that by change of aire and alteration of diet, the said Savage king died at sea, which was feared would turn to the losse of the life of Martin Cockeram his pledge. Neverthelesse, the Savages being fully perswaded of the honest dealing of our men with their prince, restored againe the said pledge, without any harme to him, or any man of the company: which pledge of theirs they brought home againe into England, with their ship fraighted, and furnished with the commodities of the countrey. Which Martin Cockeram, by the witnesse of Sir John Hawkins, being an officer in the towne of Plimmouth, was living within these fewe yeeres.

6

The originall of the first voyage for traffique
into the kingdom of Marocco in Barbarie, begun in
the yeere 1551. with a tall ship called the Lion
of London, whereof went as captaine Master Thomas
Windam, as appeareth by this extract of a letter of
James Aldaie, to the worshipfull master Michael
Locke, which Aldaie professeth himselfe to have
bene the first inventer of this trade

WORSHIPFUL Sir, having lately bene acquainted with
your intent to prosecute the olde intermitted discoverie for
Catai, if therein with my knowledge, travell or industrie I may
doe you service, I am readie to doe it, and therein to adventure
my life to the uttermost point. Trueth it is, that I have bene
by some men (not my friends) evill spoken of at London, saying that although I be a man of knowledge in the Arte of Navigation and Cosmographie, and that I have bene the inventer of
some voyages that be now growen to great effect; yet say they
maliciously and without just cause, that I have not bene willing
at any season to proceed in those voyages that I have taken in
hand, taking example especially of two voyages. The one was
when I was master in the great Barke Aucher for the Levant,
in which voyage I went not, but the causes they did not know
of my let from the same, nor of the other. But first the very
trueth is, that I was from the same voyage letted by the Princes
letters, which my Master Sebastian Gabota had obtained for
that purpose, to my great griefe. And as touching the second
voyage which I invented for the trade of Barbarie, the living
God knoweth that I say most true, that when the great sweate
was, (whereon the chiefe of those with whom I joyned in that
voyage died, that is to say, Sir John Lutterell, John Fletcher,

Henry Ostrich and others) I my selfe was also taken with the same sweate in London, and after it, whether with evill diet in keeping, or how I know not, I was cast into such an extreame fever, as I was neither able to ride nor goe: and the shippe being at Portesmouth, Thomas Windam had her away from thence, before I was able to stand upon my legges, by whom I lost at that instant fourescore pound. Besides I was appointed by them that died (if they had lived) to have had the whole government both of shippe and goods, because I was to them the sole inventer of that trade.

In the first voyage to Barbary there were two Moores, being noble men, whereof one was of the Kings blood, convayed by the said Master Thomas Windham into their Countrey out of England.

Yours humble at your commandement,

James Alday

7

The second voyage to Barbary in the yeere
1552. Set foorth by the right worshipfull Sir
John Yorke, Sir William Gerard, Sir Thomas Wroth,
Master Frances Lambert, Master Cole, and
others; Written by the relation of Master
James Thomas then Page to Master Thomas
Windham chiefe Captaine of this voyage

THE shippes that went on this voyage were three, whereof
two were of the River of Thames, That is to say, the Lyon of
London, whereof Master Thomas Windham was Captaine and
part owner, of about an hundred & fiftie tunnes: The other was
the Buttolfe about fourescore tunnes, and a Portugall Caravel
bought of certain Portugals in Newport in Wales, and
fraighted for this voyage, of summe sixtie tunnes. The number
of men in the Fleete were an hundred and twentie. The master
of the Lyon was one John Kerry of Mynhed in Somersetshire,
his Mate was David Landman. The chiefe Captaine of this
small Fleete was Master Thomas Windham a Norffolke gentleman borne, but dwelling at Marshfield-parke in Somerset shire.
This Fleete departed out of King-rode neere Bristoll about the
beginning of May 1552. being on a Munday in the morning:
and the Munday fortnight next ensuing in the evening came to
an ancker at their first port in the roade of Zafia, or Asafi on
the coast of Barbarie, standing in 32. degrees of latitude, and
there put on land part of our marchandise to be conveied by
land to the citie of Marocco: which being done, and having refreshed our selves with victuals and water, we went to the
second port called Santa Cruz, where we discharged the rest of
our goods, being good quantitie of linnen and woollen cloth,
corall, amber, Jet, and divers other things well accepted by the

Moores. In which road we found a French ship, which not knowing whether it were warre or peace betweene England and France, drewe her selfe as neere under the towne wals as she could possible, craving aide of the towne for her defence, if need were, which in deed seeing us draw neere, shot at us a piece from the wals, which came over the Lion our Admirall, betweene the maine mast & her foremast. Whereupon we comming to an anker, presently came a pinnes aboord us to know what we were, who understanding that we had bene there the yere before, & came with the good leave of their king in marchant wise, were fully satisfied, and gave us good leave to bring our goods peaceably on shore, where the Viceroy, whose name was Sibill Manache, within short time after came to visite us, and used us with all curtesie. But by divers occasions we spent here very neere three moneths before we could get in our lading, which was Sugar, Dates, Almonds, and Malassos or sugar Syrrope. And for all our being here in the heate of the Sommer, yet none of our company perished by sicknesse. Our ships being laden, wee drew into the Sea for a Westerne wind for England. But being at sea, a great leake fell upon the Lion, so that we were driven to Lancerota, and Forteventura, where, betweene the two Ilands, we came to a road, whence wee put on land out of our sayd ship 70. chestes of Sugar upon Lancerota, with some dozen or sixteene of our company, where the inhabitants supposing we had made a wrongfull prize of our caravell, suddenly came with force upon our people, among whom I my selfe was one, tooke us prisoners, and spoiled the sugars: which thing being perceived from our ships, they manned out three boates, thinking to rescue us, and drave the Spaniards to flight, whereof they slew eighteene, and tooke their governour of the Iland prisoner, who was a very aged gentleman about 70. yeeres of age. But chasing the enemie so farre, for our recoverie, as pouder and arrowes wanted, the Spaniards perceiving this, returned, and in our mens retire they slew sixe of them. Then a Parle grew, in the which it was agreed, that we the prisoners should be by them restored, and they receive their olde governour, giving us a testimonie under his and their hands, what damages wee had there received, the which damages were here restored, and made good by the king of Spaine his marchants upon our returne into England. After wee had searched and mended our leake, being returned aboord, we came under saile, and as wee were going to the sea on the one side of the Iland, the Cacafuego and other ships of the king of Portugals Armada entered at the other, and came to anker in the road from whence we were but newly departed, and shot off their great ordinance in our hearing. And here by the way it is to bee understood that the Portugals were much offended with this our new trade into Barbarie, and both in our voiage the yeere before, as also in this they gave out in England by their marchants, that if they tooke us in those partes, they would use us as their mortall enemies, with great threates and menaces. But by God and good providence wee escaped their handes. From this Iland shaping our course for England, we were seven or eight weekes before we could reach the coast of England. The first port wee entered into was the haven of Plimmouth, from whence within short time wee came into the Thames, and landed our marchandise at London, about the ende of the moneth of October, 1552.

8

Ordinances, instructions, and advertisements of and
for the direction of the intended voyage for Cathay,
compiled, made, and delivered by the right worshipfull
M. Sebastian Cabota Esquier, governour of the
mysterie and companie of the Marchants adventurers
for the discoverie of Regions, Dominions, Islands
and places unknowen, the 9. day of May, in the yere
of our Lord God 1553. and in the 7. yeere of the
reigne of our most dread soveraigne Lord Edward the 6.
by the grace of God, king of England, Fraunce and
Ireland, defender of the faith, and of the Church of
England and Ireland, in earth supreame head

FIRST the Captaine general, with the pilot major, the masters, marchants & other officers, to be so knit and accorded in
unitie, love, conformitie, and obedience in every degree on all
sides, that no dissention, variance, or contention may rise or
spring betwixt them and the mariners of this companie, to the
damage or hinderance of the voyage: for that dissention (by
many experiences) hath overthrown many notable intended and
likely enterprises and exploits.

2 Item, for as much as every person hath given an othe to
be true, faithfull, and loial subjects, and liege men to the kings
most excellent Majestie, his heires and successors, and for the
observation of all lawes & statutes, made for the preservation
of his most excellent Majestie, & his crown Imperiall of his
realmes of England and Ireland, and to serve his grace, the
Realme, and this present voyage truely, and not to give up, intermit, or leave off the said voyage and enterprise untill it shalbe
accomplished, so farre forth as possibilitie and life of man may

serve or extend: Therfore it behoveth every person in his degree, as well for conscience, as for dueties sake to remember his said charge, and the accomplishment thereof.

3 Item, where furthermore every mariner or passenger in his ship hath given like othe to bee obedient to the Captaine generall, and to every Captaine and master in his ship, for the observation of these present orders contained in this booke, and all other which hereafter shalbe made by the 12. counsailers in this present book named, or the most part of them, for the better conduction, and preservation of the fleete, and atchieving of the voyage, and to be prompt, ready and obedient in all acts and feates of honesty, reason, and duetie to be ministred, shewed & executed, in advancement and preferment of the voyage and exploit: therfore it is convenient that this present booke shall once every weeke (by the discretion of the Captaine) be read to the said companie, to the intent that every man may the better remember his othe, conscience, duetie and charge.

4 Item, every person by vertue of his othe, to doe effectually & with good wil (as farre forth as him shall complie) all, and every such act and acts, deede and deeds, as shalbe to him or them from time to time commanded, committed and enjoyned (during the voyage) by the Captain generall, with the assent of the Counsell and assistants, as well in and during the whole Navigation and voyage, as also in discovering and landing, as cases and occasions shall require.

5 Item, all courses in Navigation to be set and kept, by the advice of the Captaine, Pilot major, masters, & masters mates, with the assents of the counsailers and the most number of them, and in voyces uniformely agreeing in one to prevaile, and take place, so that the Captaine generall, shall in all counsailes and assemblies have a double voyce.

6 Item, that the fleete shal keep together, and not separate themselves asunder, as much as by winde & weather may be done or permitted, & that the Captaines, Pilots & masters shall speedily come aboord the Admiral, when and as often as he shall seeme to have just cause to assemble them for counsaile or consultation to be had concerning the affaires of the fleete and voyage.

7 Item, that the marchants, and other skilful persons in writ-

ing, shal daily write, describe, and put in memorie the Navigation of every day and night, with the points, and observation
of the lands, tides, elements, altitude of the sunne, course of
the moon and starres, and the same so noted by the order of
the Master and pilot of every ship to be put in writing, the captaine generall assembling the masters together once every weeke
(if winde and weather shal serve) to conferre all the observa-
tions, and notes of the said ships, to the intent it may appeare
wherein the notes do agree, and wherein they dissent, and upon
good debatement, deliberation, and conclusion determined, to
put the same into a common leger, to remain of record for the
company: the like order to be kept in proportioning of the
Cardes, Astrolabes, and other instruments prepared for the voyage, at the charge of the companie.

8 Item, that all enterprises and exploits of discovering or
landing to search Iles, regions, and such like, to be searched,
attempted, and enterprised by good deliberation, and common
assent, determined advisedly. And that in all enterprises, notable ambassages, suites, requests, or presentment of giftes, or
presents to Princes, to be done and executed by the captaine
generall in person or by such other, as he by common assent
shall appoint or assigne to doe or cause to be done in the same.

9 Item, the steward and cooke of every ship, and their associats, to give and render to the captaine and other head
officers of their shippe weekely (or oftner) if it shall seeme
requisite, a just or plaine and perfect accompt of expenses of
the victuals, as wel flesh, fish, bisket, meate, or bread, as also
of beere, wine, oyle, or vineger, and all other kinde of victuall-
ing under their charge, and they, and every of them so to order
and dispende the same, that no waste or unprofitable excesse
be made otherwise then reason and necessitie shall command.

10 Item, when any inferiour or meane officer of what degree
or condition he shalbe, shalbe tried untrue, remisse, negligent,
or unprofitable in or about his office in the voyage, or not to
use him selfe in his charge accordingly, then every such officer
to be punished or removed at the discretion of the captaine
and assistants, or the most part of them, and the person so removed not to be reputed, accepted, or taken from the time of
his remove, any more for an officer, but to remaine in such condition and place, as hee shall be assigned unto, and none of the

companie, to resist such chastisement or worthie punishment, as shalbe ministred unto him moderately, according to the fault or desert of his offence, after the lawes and common customes of the seas, in such cases heretofore used and observed.

11 Item, if any Mariner or officer inferiour shalbe found by his labour not meete nor worthie the place that he is presently shipped for, such person may bee unshipped and put on lande at any place within the kings Majesties realme & dominion, and one other person more able and worthy to be put in his place, at the discretion of the captaine and masters, & order to be taken that the partie dismissed shalbe allowed proportionably the value of that he shall have deserved to the time of his dismission or discharge, & he to give order with sureties, pawn, or other assurance, to repay the overplus of that he shall have received, which he shall not have deserved, & such wages to be made with the partie newly placed as shalbe thought reasonable, and he to have the furniture of al such necessaries as were prepared for the partie dismissed, according to right and conscience.

12 Item, that no blaspheming of God, or detestable swearing be used in any ship, nor communication of ribaldrie, filthy tales, or ungodly talke to be suffred in the company of any ship, neither dicing, carding, tabling, nor other divelish games to be frequented, whereby ensueth not onely povertie to the players, but also strife, variance, brauling, fighting, and oftentimes murther to the utter destruction of the parties, and provoking of Gods most just wrath, and sworde of vengeance. These and all such like pestilences, and contagions of vices, and sinnes to bee eschewed, and the offenders once monished, and not reforming, to bee punished at the discretion of the captaine and master, as appertaineth.

13 Item, that morning and evening prayer, with other common services appointed by the kings Majestie, and lawes of this Realme to be read and saide in every ship daily by the minister in the Admirall, and the marchant or some other person learned in other ships, and the Bible or paraphrases to be read devoutly and Christianly to Gods honour, and for his grace to be obtained, and had by humble and heartie praier of the Navigants accordingly.

14 Item, that every officer is to be charged by Inventorie

with the particulars of his charge, and to render a perfect accompt of the diffraying of the same together with modest &
temperate dispending of powder, shot, and use of all kinde of
artillery, which is not to be misused, but diligently to be preserved for the necessary defence of the fleete and voyage, together with due keeping of all instruments of your Navigation,
and other requisites.

15 Item, no liquor to be spilt on the balast, nor filthines to
be left within boord: the cook room, and all other places to be
kept cleane for the better health of the companie, the gromals
& pages to bee brought up according to the laudable order and
use of the Sea, as well in learning of Navigation, as in exercis-
ing of that which to them appertaineth.

16 Item, the liveries in apparel given to the mariners be to
be kept by the marchants, and not to be worne, but by the order
of the captaine, when he shall see cause to muster or shewe
them in good aray, for the advancement and honour of the
voyage, and the liveries to bee redelivered to the keeping of the
marchants, untill it shal be thought convenient for every person
to have the ful use of his garment.

17 Item, when any mariner or any other passenger shal
have neede of any necessarie furniture of apparell for his body,
and conservation of his health, the same shall bee delivered him
by the Marchant, at the assignement of the captaine and Master
of that shippe, wherein such needie person shall be, at such
reasonable price as the same cost, without any gaine to be ex-
acted by the marchants, the value therof to be entred by the
marchant in his booke, and the same to be discounted off the
parties wages, that so shal receive, and weare the same.

18 Item the sicke, diseased, weake, and visited person within
boord, to be tendered, relieved, comforted, and holpen in the
time of his infirmitie, and every maner of person, without respect, to beare anothers burden, and no man to refuse such
labour as shall be put to him, for the benefite, and publike
wealth of the voyage, and enterprise, to be atchieved exactly.

19 Item if any person shal fortune to die, or miscary in the
voyage, such apparell, and other goods, as he shall have at the
time of his death, is to be kept by the order of the captaine and
Master of the shippe, and an inventorie to be made of it, and
conserved to the use of his wife, and children, or otherwise ac-

cording to his mind, and wil, and the day of his death to be entred in the Marchants and Stewards bookes: to the intent it may be knowen what wages he shall have deserved to his death, and what shall rest due to him.

20 Item, that the Marchants appointed for this present voyage, shall not make any shew or sale of any kind of marchandizes, or open their commodities to any forrein princes, or any of their subjects, without the consent, privitie, or agreement of the Captaines, the cape Marchants and the assistants, or foure of them, whereof the captaine generall, the Pilot Major, the cape marchant to be three, and every of the pettie marchants to shewe his reckoning to the cape marchant, when they, or any of them shall be required: and no commutation or trucke to be made by any of the petie marchants, without the assent abovesaid: and all wares, and commodities trucked, bought or given to the companie, by way of marchandise, trucke, or any other respect, to be booked by the marchants, and to be wel ordred, packed, and conserved in one masse entirely, and not to be broken or altered, until the shippes shall returne to the right discharges, and inventorie of al goods, wares, and marchandises so trucked, bought, or otherwise dispended, to be presented to the Governor, Consuls, and Assistants in London, in good order, to the intent the Kings Majestie may be truly answered of that which to his grace by his grant of corporation is limited, according to our most bound dueties, and the whole companie also to have that which by right unto them appertaineth, and no embezelment shall be used, but the truth of the whole voyage to bee opened, to the common wealth and benefite of the whole companie, and mysterie, as appertaineth, without guile, fraude, or male engine.

21 Item, no particular person, to hinder or prejudicate the common stocke of the company, in sale or preferment of his own proper wares, and things, and no particular emergent or purchase to be employed to any severall profite, untill the common stocke of the companie shall be furnished, and no person to hinder the common benefite in such purchases or contingents, as shal fortune to any one of them, by his owne proper policie, industrie, or chance, nor no contention to rise in that behalfe, by any occasion of jewel, stone, pearles, precious mettals, or other things of the region, where it shall chance the same to

rise, or to be found, bought, trucked, permuted, or given: but every person to be bounden in such case, and upon such occasion, by order, and direction, as the generall captaine, and the Councell shall establish and determine, to whose order and discretion the same is left: for that of things uncertaine, no certaine rules may or can be given.

22 Item not to disclose to any nation the state of our religion, but to passe it over in silence, without any declaration of it, seeming to beare with such lawes, and rites, as the place hath, where you shall arrive.

23 Item for as much as our people, and shippes may appeare unto them strange and wonderous, and theirs also to ours: it is to be considered, how they may be used, learning much of their natures and dispositions, by some one such person, as you may first either allure, or take to be brought aboord your ships, and there to learne as you may, without violence or force, and no woman to be tempted, or intreated to incontinencie, or dishonestie.

24 Item the person so taken, to be well entertained, used, and apparelled, to be set on land, to the intent that he or she may allure other to draw nigh to shewe the commodities: and if the person taken may be made drunke with your beere, or wine, you shal know the secrets of his heart.

25 Item our people may not passe further into a lande, then that they may be able to recover their pinnesses, or ships, & not to credit the faire words of the strange people, which be many times tried subtile, and false, nor to be drawen into perill of losse, for the desire of golde, silver, or riches, and esteeme your owne commodities above al other, and in countenance shew not much to desire the forren commodities: neverthelesse take them as for friendship, or by the way of permutation.

26 Item every nation and region is to be considered advisedly, & not to provoke them by any disdaine, laughing, contempt, or such like, but to use them with prudent circumspection, with all gentlenes, and curtesie, and not to tary long in one place, untill you shall have attained the most worthy place y^t may be found, in such sort, as you may returne w^t victuals sufficient prosperously.

27 Item the names of the people of every Island, are to be taken in writing, with the commodities, and incommodities of

the same, their natures, qualities, and dispositions, the site of the same, and what things they are most desirous of, & what commodities they wil most willingly depart with, & what mettals they have in hils, mountaines, streames, or rivers, in, or under the earth.

28 Item if people shal appeare gathering of stones, gold, mettall, or other like, on the sand, your pinnesses may drawe nigh, marking what things they gather, using or playing upon the drumme, or such other instruments, as may allure them to harkening, to fantasie, but keepe you out of danger, and shewe to them no poynt or signe of rigour and hostilitie.

29 Item if you shall be invited into any Lords or Rulers house, to dinner, or other parliance, goe in such order of strength, that you may be stronger then they, and be warie of woods and ambushes, and that your weapons be not out of your possessions.

30 Item if you shall see them weare Lyons or Beares skinnes, having long bowes, and arrowes, be not afraid of that sight: for such be worne oftentimes more to feare strangers, then for any other cause.

31 Item there are people that can swimme in the sea, havens, & rivers, naked, having bowes and shafts, coveting to draw nigh your ships, which if they shal finde not wel watched, or warded, they wil assault, desirous of the bodies of men, which they covet for meate: if you resist them, they dive, and so will flee, and therefore diligent watch is to be kept both day & night, in some Islands.

32 Item if occasion shal serve, that you may give advertisements of your proceedings in such things as may correspond to the expectation of the company, and likelihood of successe in the voyage, passing such dangers of the seas, perils of ice, intollerable coldes, and other impediments, which by sundry authors & writers, have ministred matter of suspition in some heads, that this voyage could not succede for the extremitie of the North pole, lacke of passage, & such like, which have caused wavering minds, and doubtful heads, not onely to withdraw themselves from the adventure of this voyage, but also disswaded others from the same, the certaintie wherof, when you shall have tried by experience, (most certaine Master of all worldly knowledge) then for declaration of the trueth, which

you shall have experted, you may by common assent of counsell, sende either by land, or otherwaies, such two or one person, to bring the same by credite, as you shal think may passe
in safetie: which sending is not to be done, but upon urgent
causes, in likely successe of the voyage, in finding of passage, in
towardlines of beneficiall traffike, or such other like, whereby
the company being advertised of your estates and proceedings,
may further provide, foresee, and determine that which may
seeme most good and beneficiall for the publike wealth of the
same: either providing before hand such things, as shall bee
requisite for the continuance of the voyage, or else otherwise to
dispose as occasion shall serve: in which things your wisedomes
and discretions are to be used, and shewed, and the contents
of this capitule, by you much to be pondred, for that you be
not ignorant, how many persons, as well the kings Majestie,
the Lords of his honorable Counsel, this whole companie, as
also your wives, children, kinsfolkes, allies, friends and famil-
iars, be replenished in their hearts with ardent desire to learne
and know your estates, conditions, and welfares, and in what
likelihood you be in, to obtain this notable enterprise, which is
hoped no lesse to succeed to you, then the Orient or Occident
Indias have to the high benefite of the Emperour, and kings of
Portingal, whose subjects industries, and travailes by sea, have
inriched them, by those lands and Islands, which were to all
Cosmographers, and other writers both unknowne, and also by
apparances of reason voide of experience thought and reputed
unhabitable for extremities of heates, and colds, and yet indeed
tried most rich, peopled, temperate, and so commodious, as all
Europe hath not the like.

33 Item no conspiracies, parttakings, factions, false tales, untrue reports, which be the very seedes, and fruits of contention,
discord, & confusion, by evill tongues to be suffered, but the
same, & all other ungodlines to be chastened charitably with
brotherly love, and alwaies obedience to be used and practised
by al persons in their degrees, not only for duetie and conscience sake towards God, under whose mercifull hand navigants above all other creatures naturally bee most nigh, and
vicine, but also for prudent and worldly pollicie, and publike
weale, considering and alwaies having present in your mindes
that you be all one most royall kings subjects, and naturals, with

daily remembrance of the great importance of the voyage, the honour, glorie, praise, and benefite that depend of, and upon the same, toward the common wealth of this noble Realme, the advancement of you the travailers therein, your wives, and children, and so to endevour your selves as that you may satisfie the expectation of them, who at their great costs, charges, and expenses, have so furnished you in good sort, and plentie of all necessaries, as the like was never in any realme seene, used, or knowen requisite and needful for such an exploit, which is most likely to be atchieved, and brought to good effect, if every person in his vocation shall endevour himselfe according to his charge, and most bounden duetie: praying the living God, to give you his grace, to accomplish your charge to his glorie, whose merciful hand shal prosper your voyage, and preserve you from all dangers.

In witnes whereof I Sebastian Cabota, Governour aforesaide, to these present ordinances, have subscribed my name, and put my seale, the day and yeere above written.

The names of the twelve Counsellors appointed in this voyage.

1. Sir Hugh Willoughby Knight, Captaine generall.
2. Richard Chancelour Captaine of the Edward Bonaventure, and Pilot generall of the fleete.
3. George Burton Cape marchant.
4. Master Richard Stafford Minister.
5. Thomas Langlie Marchant.
6. James Dalabere Gentleman.
7. William Gefferson Master of the Bona Speranza Admirall.
8. Stephen Borrough Master of the Edward Bonaventure.
9. Cornelius Durfurth Master of the Confidentia.
10. Roger Wilson.
11. John Buckland.   Masters mates.
12. Richard Ingram.

9

[The Voyage of sir Hugh Willoughby, knight]

*The true copie of a note found written in one of the two ships,
to wit, the Speranza, which wintred in Lappia, where sir Hugh
Willoughby and all his companie died, being frozen to death.
Anno 1553*

THE voiage intended for the discoverie of Cathay, and divers
other regions, dominions, Islands, and places unknowen, set
forth by the right worshipful, master Sebastian Cabota Esquire, and Governour of the mysterie and company of the
Marchants Adventurers of the citie of London: which fleete
being furnished, did set forth the tenth day of May, 1553, and
in the seventh yeere of our most dread Soveraigne Lord, and
King, Edward the sixt.

*The names of the shippes of the fleete, and of their burden,
together with the names of the Captaines, and Counsellors,
Pilot Major, Masters of the ships, Marchants, as hereafter followeth.*

The Bona Esperanza, Admirall of the fleete, of 120. tunnes,
having with her a pinnesse, and a boate.
Sir Hugh Willoughby, knight, Captaine generall of the fleete.
William Gefferson, Master of the shippe.
Roger Wilson, his Mate.
William Gittons, Charles Barret, Gabriel Willoughby, John
Andrews, Alexander Woodfoord, Ralph Chatterton, Mar-
chants. . . .

The Edward Bonaventure, of 160. tunnes, with her a pinnesse, and a boate.
Richard Chancelor, Captaine, and Pilot major of the fleete.

Stephen Borowgh, Master of the ship.

John Buckland, his Mate.

George Burton, Arthur Edwards, Marchants.

John Stafford, Minister.

James Dallaber, Nicholas Newborrow, John Segswike, Thomas Francis, John Hasse, Richard Johnson, William Kempe. . . .

The Bona Confidentia of 90. tunnes, having with her a pinnesse, and a boate.

Cornelius Durfoorth, Master of the shippe.

Richard Ingram, his Mate.

Thomas Langlie, Edward Kever, Henrie Dorset, Marchants. . . .

The *Juramentum, or othe, ministred to the Captaine*

You shall sweare to be a faithfull, true, and loyal subject in all points, and duties, that to a subject appertaineth, to our soveraigne Lord the kings Majestie, his heires, and successors: and that you shall wel and truely to the uttermost of your capacitie, wit, & knowledge, serve this present voiage, committed to your charge, and not to give up, nor sooner intermit the same, until you shall have atchieved the same, so farre foorth, as you may without danger of your life, and losse of the fleete: you shall give good, true, and faithful counsell to the said societie, and to such as shal have the charge with or under you, and not to disclose the secrets, or privities of the same to any person by any maner of meane, to the prejudice, hurt, or damage of it. You shal minister justice to all men under your charge, without respect of person, or any affection, that might move you to decline from the true ministration of justice. And further, you shal observe, and cause to be observed, as much as in you lieth, all and singular rules, articles, provisions hitherto made, or heereafter to be made for the preservation or safeconduct of the fleete and voyage, and benefit of the company. You shall not permit nor suffer the stocke or goods of the company to be wasted, imbezeled, or consumed, but shall conserve the same whole and entire, without diminishment, untill you shall have delivered, or cause to be delivered the same, to the use of the companie. And finally you shal use your selfe in all points, sorts, and conditions, as to a faithfull captaine, and brother of this companie shall belong and appertaine: So helpe you God, &c.

The othe ministred to the Maister of the ship, &c.

You shall sweare by the holy contents in that booke, that you according and to the uttermost of your knowledge, and good understanding in mariners science and craft, shall in your vocation doe your best to conduct the good shippe called the N. &c. whereof you nowe are Maister under God, both unto and from the portes of your discoverie, and so use your indevour and faithfull diligence, in charging, discharging, lading againe, and roomaging of the same shippe, as may be most for the benefite and profite of this right woorshipfull fellowship: and you shall not privately bargein, buy, sell, exchange, barter, or distribute any goods, wares, merchandize, or things whatsoever (necessary tackles and victuals for the shippe onely excepted) to or for your owne lucre, gaine or profit, neither to nor for the private lucre, gaine, or profit of any other person or persons whatsoever. And further, If you shall know any boatswaine, mariner, or any other person or persons whatsoever, to buy, sell, barter, trucke, or exchange any goods, wares, marchandizes, or things for private account, reckoning, or behalfe, you shall doe your best to withstand and let the same: and if you cannot commodiously so doe, that then before the discharge of such goods bought for privat account, you shal give knowledge therof to the cape marchant of this said fellowship for the time being. And you shal not receive nor take, nor suffer to be received or taken into your said ship during this voyage any maner person or persons whatsoever, going or returning, but onely those mariners which without fraud or guile shall be hired to be of your company, and to serve in mariners craft and science onely: So helpe you God, &c.

These foresaid shippes being fully furnished with their pinnesses and boates, well appointed with al maner of artillerie, and other things necessary for their defence with al the men aforesaid, departed from Ratcliffe, and valed unto Detford, the 10. day of May, 1553.

The 11. day about two of the clocke, we departed from Detford, passing by Greenwich, saluting the kings Majesty then being there, shooting off our ordinance, & so valed unto Blackwall, and there remained until the 17. day, and that day in the morning we went from Blackwall, and came to Woolwich by nine of the clocke, and there remained one tide, and so the same night unto Heyreth.

The 18. day from Heyreth unto Gravesend, and there remained until the twentieth day: that day being Saterday, from Gravesend unto Tilberie Hope, remaining there untill the two and twentieth day.

The 22. day from Tilbery Hope to Hollie haven.

The 23. day from Hollie Haven, till we came against Lee, and there remained that night, by reason that the winde was contrary to us.

The 24. day the winde being in the Southwest in the morning, we sailed along the coast over the Spits, untill we came against S. Osyth, about sixe of the clocke at night, and there came to anker, and abode there all that night.

The 25. day about tenne of the clocke we departed from S. Osyth, and so sailed forward unto the Nase, and there abode that night for winde and tide.

The 26. day at five of the clock in the morning, we weyed our anker, and sailed over the Nase, the winde being at the Southwest, untill wee came to Orwell wands, and there came to an anker, and abode there untill the 28. day.

The same day being Trinitie Sunday about 7. of the clocke before noone we weyed our ankers, and sailed til we came athwart Walsursye, and there came to an anker.

The 29. day from thence to Holmehead, where we stayed that day, where we consulted which way, and what courses were best to be holden for the discoverie of our voyage, and there agreed.

The 30. day of May at five of the clocke in the morning wee set saile, and came against Yermouth about three leagues into the sea, riding there at anker all that night.

The last of May into the sea six leagues Northeast, and there taried that night, where the winde blew very sore.

The first of June the winde being at North contrary to us, wee came backe againe to Orwell, and remained there untill the 15. day, tarying for the winde, for all this time the winde was contrary to our purpose.

The 15 day being at Orwel in the latitude of 52 degrees, in

the morning wee weyed our ankers, and went forth into the wands about two miles from the towne, and lay there that night.

The 16 day at eight of the clocke we set forward, and sayled untill we came athwart Alburrough, and there stayed that night.

The 17 day about five of the clocke before noone we went backe unto Orfordnesse, and there remained untill the 19 day.

The 19 day at eight of the clocke in the morning we went backe to Orwel, and abode there three dayes tarying for the winde.

The 23 day of June the wind being faire in the Southwest we hailed into the seas to Orfordnesse, and from thence into the seas ten leagues Northeast: then being past the sands, we changed our course sixe leagues Northnortheast: about midnight we changed our course againe, and went due North, continuing in the same unto the 27 day.

The 27 day about seven of the clocke Northnorthwest 42 leagues to the ende to fall with Shotland: then the wind veared to the West, so that we could lie but North and by West, continuing in the same course 40 leagues, whereby we could not fetch Shotland: then we sayled North 16 leagues by estimation, after that North and by West, & Northnorthwest, then Southeast, with divers other courses, traversing and tracing the seas, by reason of sundry and manifolde contrary windes, untill the 14 day of July: and then the sunne entring into Leo, we discovered land Eastward of us, unto the which we sayled that night as much as we might: and after wee went on shore with our Pinnesse, & found little houses to the number of 30, where we knew that it was inhabited, but the people were fled away, as we judged, for feare of us.

The land was all full of little Islands, and that innumerable, which were called (as we learned afterwards) Ægeland, and Halgeland, which lieth from Orfordnesse North and by East, being in the latitude of 66 degrees. The distance betweene Orfordnesse and Ægeland 250 leagues. Then we sailed from thence 12 leagues Northwest, and found many other Islandes, and there came to anker the 19 day, and manned our Pinnesse, and went on shore to the Islands, and found people mowing and making of hay, which came to the shore and welcomed us. In which place were an innumerable sort of Islands, which were called the Isles of Rost, being under the dominion of the king of Denmarke: which place was in latitude 66 degrees, and 30 minutes. The winde being contrary, we remayned there three dayes, & there was an innumerable sort of foules of divers kindes, of which we tooke very many.

The 22 day the winde comming fayre, we departed from Rost, sailing Northnortheast, keeping the sea untill the 27 day, and then we drew neere unto the land, which was still East of us: then went foorth our Pinnesse to seeke harborow, & found many good harbours, of the which we entred into one with our shippes, which was called Stanfew, and the land being Islands, were called Lewfoot, or Lofoot, which were plentifully inhabited, and very gentle people, being also under the king of Denmarke: but we could not learne how farre it was from the maine land: and we remained there until the 30 day, being in latitude 68 degrees, and from the foresaid Rost about 30 leagues Northnortheast.

The 30 day of July about noone we weyed our ankers, and went into the Seas, and sayled along these Islands Northnortheast, keeping the land still in sight untill the second day of August: then hailing in close aboord the land, to the entent to knowe what land it was, there came a skiffe of the Island aboord of us, of whom we asked many questions, who shewed unto us, that the Island was called Seynam, which is the latitude of seventy degrees, and from Stanfew thirtie leagues, being also under the king of Denmarke, and that there was no merchandise there, but onely dryed fish, and traine oyle. Then we being purposed to goe unto Finmarke, inquired of him, if we might have a pilot to bring us unto Finmarke, & he said, that if we could beare in, we should have a good harbour, and on the next day a pilot to bring us to Finmarke, unto the wardhouse, which is the strongest holde in Finmarke, and most resorted to by report. But when wee would have entred into an harbour, the land being very high on every side, there came such flawes of winde and terrible whirlewinds, that we were not able to beare in, but by violence were constrained to take the sea agayne, our Pinnesse being unshipt: we sailed North and by East, the wind increasing so sore that we were not able to beare any saile, but tooke them in, and lay a drift, to the end to let the storme over passe. And that night by violence of winde, and thickenesse of mists, we were not able to keepe together within sight, and then about midnight we lost our pinnesse, which was a discomfort unto us. Assoone as it was day, and the fogge overpast, we looked about, and at the last we descried one of our shippes to Leeward of us: then we spred an hullocke of our foresaile, and bare roome with her, which was the Confidence, but the Edward we could not see. Then the flaw something abating, we and the Confidence hoysed up our sailes the fourth day, sayling Northeast and by North, to the end to fall with the Wardhouse, as we did consult to doe before, in case we should part company. Thus running Northeast and by North, and Northeast fiftie leagues, then we sounded, and had 160 fadomes, whereby we thought to be farre from land, and perceived that the land lay not as the Globe made mention. Wherfore we changed our course the sixt day, and sailed Southeast and by South eight and fortie leagues, thinking thereby to find the Wardhouse.

The eight day much winde rising at the Westnorthwest, we not knowing how the coast lay, strook our sayles, and lay a drift, where we sounded and found 160 fadomes as afore.

The ninth day, the wind vearing to the South Southeast, we sailed Northeast 25 leagues.

The tenth day we sounded, and could get no ground, neither yet could see any land, wherat we wondered: then the wind comming at the Northeast, we ran Southeast about 48 leagues.

The 11 day, the wind being at South, we sounded, and found 40 fadoms, and faire sand.

The 12 day the winde being at South and by East, we lay with our saile East, and East and by North 30 leagues.

The 14 day early in the morning we descried land, which land we bare with all, hoising out our boat to discover what land it might be: but the boat could not come to land the water was so shoale, where was very much ice also, but there was no similitude of habitation, and this land lyeth from Seynam East and by North 160 leagues, being in latitude 72 degrees. Then we plyed to the Northward the 15, 16 and 17 day.

The 18 day, the winde comming at the Northeast, and the Confidence being troubled with bilge water, and stocked, we thought it good to seeke harbour for her redresse: then we bare roome the 18 day Southsoutheast, about 70 leagues.

The 21 day we sounded, and found 10 fadome, after that we sounded againe, and found but 7 fadome, so shoalder and shoalder water, and yet could see no land, where we marveiled greatly: to avoide this danger, we bare roomer into the sea all that night Northwest and by West.

The next day we sounded, and had 20. fadoms, then shaped our course, and ran West Southwest untill the 23. day: then we descried Low land, unto which we bare as nigh as we could, and it appeared unto us unhabitable. Then wee plyed Westward along by that lande, which lyeth West Southwest, and East Northeast, and much winde blowing at the West, we haled into the sea North and by East 30 leagues. Then the winde comming about at the Northeast, we sailed West Northwest: after that, the winde bearing to the Northwest, we lay with our sailes West southwest, about 14. leagues, and then descried land, and bare in with it, being the 28. day, finding shoale water, and bare it till we came to 3. fadome, then perceiving it to be shoale water, and also seeing drie sands, we haled out againe Northeast along that land until we came to the point therof. That land turning to the Westwarde, we ran along 16. leagues Northwest: then comming into a faire bay, we went on land with our boat, which place was unhabited, but yet it appeared unto us that the people had bin there, by crosses, and other signes: from thence we went all along the coast Westward.

The fourth day of September we lost sight of land, by reason of contrary winds, and the eight day we descried land againe. Within two dayes after we lost the sight of it: then running West and by South about 30. leagues, we gat the sight of land againe, and bare in with it untill night: then perceiving it to be a lee shore, we gat us into the sea, to the end to have sea roome.

The 12. of September we hailed to shoareward againe, having then indifferent winde and weather: then being neere unto the shoare, and the tide almost spent, wee came to an anker in 30. fadoms water.

The 13. day we came along the coast, which lay Northwest and by West and Southeast and by East.

The 14. day we came to an anker within two leagues of the shoare, having 60. fadoms.

There we went a shore with our boat, & found two or three good harboroughs, the land being rocky, and high, but as for people could we see none. The 15 day we ran still along the coast untill the 17 day: then the winde being contrary unto us,

we thought it best to returne unto the harbor which we had
found before, and so we bare roomer with the same, howbeit
we could not accomplish our desire that day. The next day
being the 18 of September, we entred into the haven, and there
came to an anker at 6 fadoms. This haven runneth into the
maine, about two leagues, and is in bredth halfe a league,
wherein were very many seale fishes, & other great fishes, and
upon the maine we saw beares, great deere, foxes, with divers
strange beasts, as *guloines, and such other which were to us
unknowen, and also wonderfull. Thus remaining in this haven
the space of a weeke, seeing the yeare farre spent, & also very
evill wether, as frost, snow, and haile, as though it had beene
the deepe of winter, we thought best to winter there. Wherefore
we sent out three men Southsouthwest, to search if they could
find people, who went three dayes journey, but could finde
none: after that, we sent other three Westward foure daies
journey, which also returned without finding any people. Then
sent we three men Southeast three dayes journey, who in like
sorte returned without finding of people, or any similitude of
habitation.

*These two notes following were written upon the
outside of this Pamphlet, or Booke.*

1   The proceedings of Sir Hugh Willoughbie after he was
    separated from the Edward Bonaventure.
2   Our shippe being at an anker in the harbour called Sterfier
    in the Island Lofoote.

The river or haven wherein Sir Hugh Willoughbie with the
companie of his two ships perished for cold, is called Arzina in
Lapland, neere unto Kegor. But it appeareth by a Will found
in the ship that Sir Hugh Willoughbie and most of the company
were alive in January 1554.

---

* Or, Ellons.

10

The newe Navigation and discoverie of the kingdome of Moscovia, by the Northeast, in the yeere 1553: Enterprised by Sir Hugh Willoughbie knight, and perfourmed by Richard Chancelor Pilot major of the voyage: Written in Latine by Clement Adams

The Testimonie of M. Richard Eden in his Decades, concerning the Booke following

And whereas (saith he) I have before made mention howe Moscovie was in our time discovered by Richard Chanceler in his voyage toward Cathay, by the direction and information of M. Sebastian Cabota, who long before had this secret in his minde: I shall not neede here to describe that voyage, forasmuch as the same is largely and faithfully written in the Latine tongue, by that learned yong man Clement Adams, schoolemaster to the Queenes henshmen, as he received it at the mouth of the said Richard Chanceler.

A T what time our Marchants perceived the commodities and wares of England to bee in small request with the countreys and people about us, and neere unto us, and that those Marchandizes which strangers in the time and memorie of our auncesters did earnestly seeke and desire, were nowe neglected, and the price thereof abated, although by us carried to their owne portes, and all forreine Marchandises in great accompt, and their prises wonderfully raised: certaine grave Citizens of London, and men of great wisedome, and carefull for the good of their Countrey, began to thinke with themselves, howe this mischiefe might bee remedied. Neither was a remedie (as it then appeared) wanting to their desires, for the avoyding of so great an inconvenience: for seeing that the wealth of the Spaniards

and Portingales, by the discoverie and search of newe trades
and Countreys was marveilously increased, supposing the same
to be a course and meane for them also to obteine the like, they
thereupon resolved upon a newe and strange Navigation. And
whereas at the same time one Sebastian Cabota, a man in those
dayes very renowmed, happened to bee in London, they began
first of all to deale and consult diligently with him, and after
much speech and conference together, it was at last concluded
that three shippes should bee prepared and furnished out, for
the search and discoverie of the Northerne part of the world,
to open a way and passage to our men for travaile to newe and
unknowen kingdomes.

And whereas many things seemed necessary to bee regarded
in this so hard and difficult a matter, they first make choyse of
certaine grave and wise persons in maner of a Senate or companie, which should lay their heads together, and give their
judgements, and provide things requisite and profitable for all
occasions: by this companie it was thought expedient, that a
certaine summe of money should publiquely bee collected to
serve for the furnishing of so many shippes. And lest any private
man should bee too much oppressed and charged, a course was
taken, that every man willing to be of the societie, should dis-
burse the portion of twentie and five pounds a piece: so that
in short time by this meanes the summe of sixe thousand
pounds being gathered, the three shippes were bought, the most
part whereof they provided to be newly built and trimmed. But
in this action, I wote not whether I may more admire the care
of the Marchants, or the diligence of the Shipwrights: for the
Marchants, they get very strong and well seasoned plankes for
the building, the Shippewrights, they with daily travaile, and
their greatest skill doe fitte them for the dispatch of the shippes:
they calke them, pitch them, and among the rest, they make one
most stanch and firme, by an excellent and ingenious invention.
For they had heard that in certaine parts of the Ocean, a kinde
of wormes is bredde, which many times pearceth and eateth
through the strongest oake that is: and therfore that the Mariners, and the rest to bee imployed in this voyage might bee free
and safe from this danger, they cover a piece of the keele of the
shippe with thinne sheetes of leade: and having thus built the

ships, and furnished them with armour and artillerie, then followed a second care no lesse troublesome and necessarie then
the former, namely, the provision of victuals, which was to be
made according to the time and length of the voyage. And
whereas they afore determined to have the East part of the
world sayled unto, and yet that the sea towards the same was
not open, except they kept the Northren tract, whereas yet it
was doubtfull whether there were any passage yea or no, they
resolved to victuall the ships for eighteene moneths, which they
did for this reason. For our men being to passe that huge and
colde part of the world, they wisely foreseeing it, allowe them
sixe moneths victuall to saile to the place, so much more to remaine there if the extremitie of the winter hindered their returne, and so much more also for the time of their comming
home.

Nowe this provision being made and caried aboord, with
armour and munition of all sorts, sufficient Captaines and governours of so great an enterprise were as yet wanting: to which
office and place, although many men, (and some voyde of experience) offered themselves, yet one Sir Hugh Willoughbie a
most valiant Gentleman, and well borne, very earnestly requested to have that care and charge committed unto him: of
whom before all others, both by reason of his goodly personage
(for he was of a tall stature) as also for his singular skill in the
services of warre, the company of the Marchants made greatest
accompt: so that at the last they concluded and made choyce of
him for the Generall of this voyage, and appoynted to him the
Admirall with authoritie and commaund over all the rest. And
for the governement of other ships although divers men seemed
willing, and made offers of themselves thereunto, yet by a common consent one Richard Chanceler, a man of great estimation
for many good partes of wit in him, was elected, in whom alone
great hope for the performance of this businesse rested. This
man was brought up by one Master Henry Sidney, a noble
young Gentleman and very much beloved of King Edward, who
at this time comming to the place where the Marchants were
gathered together, beganne a very eloquent speech or Oration,
and spake to them after this maner following.

My very worshipfull friends, I cannot but greatly commend

your present godly and vertuous intention, in the serious enter-
prising (for the singular love you beare to your Countrey) a
matter, which (I hope) will proove profitable for this nation,
and honourable to this our land. Which intention of yours wee
also of the Nobilitie are ready to our power to helpe and
further: neither doe wee holde any thing so deare and precious
unto us, which wee will not willingly forgoe, and lay out in so
commendable a cause. But principally I rejoyce in my selfe,
that I have nourished and maintained that witte, which is like
by some meanes and in some measure, to profite and steede you
in this worthy action. But yet I would not have you ignorant
of this one thing, that I doe now part with Chanceler, not be
cause I make little reckoning of the man, or that his maintenance is burdenous and chargeable unto mee, but that you
might conceive and understand my good will and promptitude
for the furtherance of this businesse, and that the authoritie and
estimation which hee deserveth may be given him. You know
the man by report, I by experience, you by wordes, I by deedes,
you by speech and companie, but I by the daily triall of his life
have a full and perfect knowledge of him. And you are also to
remember, into howe many perils for your sakes, and his countreys love, he is nowe to runne: whereof it is requisite that wee
be not unmindefull, if it please God to send him good successe.
Wee commit a little money to the chaunce and hazard of Fortune: He commits his life (a thing to a man of all things most
deare) to the raging Sea, and the uncertainties of many dangers.
We shall here live and rest at home quietly with our friends,
and acquaintance: but hee in the meane time labouring to keepe
the ignorant and unruly Mariners in good order and obedience,
with howe many cares shall hee trouble and vexe himselfe? with
how many troubles shall he breake himselfe? and howe many
disquietings shall hee bee forced to sustaine? We shall keepe our
owne coastes and countrey: Hee shall seeke strange and unknowen kingdomes. He shall commit his safetie to barbarous
and cruell people, and shall hazard his life amongst the monstrous and terrible beastes of the Sea. Wherefore in respect of
the greatnesse of the dangers, and the excellencie of his charge,
you are to favour and love the man thus departing from us: and
if it fall so happily out that hee returne againe, it is your part
and duetie also, liberally to reward him.

After that this noble yong Gentleman had delivered this or some such like speech, much more eloquently then I can possiblie report it, the companie then present beganne one to looke upon another, one to question and conferre with another: and some (to whom the vertue and sufficiencie of the man was knowen) began secretly to rejoyce with themselves, and to conceive a speciall hope, that the man would proove in time very rare and excellent, and that his vertues already appearing and shining to the world would growe to the great honour and advancement of this kingdome.

After all this, the companie growing to some silence, it seemed good to them that were of greatest gravity amongst them, to inquire, search and seeke what might be learned & knowen, concerning the Easterly part or tract of the world. For which cause two Tartarians, which were then of the kings Stable, were sent for, & an interpreter was gotten to be present, by whom they were demaunded touching their Countrey and the maners of their nation. But they were able to answere nothing to the purpose: being in deede more acquainted (as one there merily and openly said) to tosse pottes, then to learne the states and dispositions of people. But after much adoe and many things passed about this matter, they grewe at last to this issue, to set downe and appoynt a time for the departure of the shippes: because divers were of opinion, that a great part of the best time of the yeere was already spent, and if the delay grewe longer, the way would bee stopt and bard by the force of the Ice, and the colde climate: and therefore it was thought best by the opinion of them all, that by the twentieth day of May, the Captaines and Mariners should take shipping, and depart from Radcliffe upon the ebbe, if it pleased God. They having saluted their acquaintance, one his wife, another his children, another his kinsfolkes, and another his friends deerer then his kinsfolkes, were present and ready at the day appoynted: and having wayed ancre, they departed with the turning of the water, and sailing easily, came first to Greenewich. The greater shippes are towed downe with boates, and oares, and the mariners being all apparelled in Watchet or skie coloured cloth, rowed amaine, and made way with diligence. And being come neere to Greenewich, (where the Court then lay) presently upon the newes therof, the Courtiers came running out, and the common people flockt together, standing very thicke upon the shoare: the privie Counsel, they lookt out at the windowes of the Court, and the rest ranne up to the toppes of the towers: the shippes hereupon discharge their Ordinance, and shoot off their pieces after the maner of warre, and of the sea, insomuch that the tops of the hilles sounded therewith, the valleys and the waters gave an Eccho, and the Mariners, they shouted in such sort, that the skie rang againe with the noyse thereof. One stoode in the poope of the ship, and by his gesture bids farewell to his friendes in the best maner hee could. Another walkes upon the hatches, another climbes the shrowds, another stands upon the maine yard, and another in the top of the shippe. To be short, it was a very triumph (after a sort) in all respects to the beholders. But (alas) the good King Edward (in respect of whom principally all this was prepared) hee onely by reason of his sickenesse was absent from this shewe, and not long after the departure of these ships, the lamentable and most sorowfull accident of his death followed.

But to proceede in the matter.

The shippes going downe with the tyde came at last to Woolwich, where they stayed and cast ancre, with purpose to depart therehence againe, as soone as the turning of the water, and a better winde should drawe them to set saile. After this they departed and came to Harwich, in which porte they stayed long, not without great losse and consuming of time: yet at the last with a good winde they hoysed up saile, and committed themselves to the sea, giving their last adieu to their native Countrey, which they knewe not whether they should ever returne to see againe or not. Many of them looked oftentimes backe, and could not refraine from teares, considering into what hazards they were to fall, and what uncertainties of the sea they were to make triall of.

Amongst the rest, Richard Chanceler, the Captaine of the Edward Bonaventure, was not a little grieved with the feare of wanting victuals, part whereof was found to be corrupt and putrified at Harwich, and the hoggesheads of wine also leaked, and were not stanch: his naturall and fatherly affection also somewhat troubled him, for he left behinde him his two little sonnes, which were in the case of Orphanes if he spedde not well: the estate also of his companie mooved him to care, being in the former respects after a sort unhappie, and were to abide with himselfe every good or badde accident: but in the meane time while his minde was thus tormented with the multiplicitie of sorowes and cares, after many dayes sayling, they kenned land afarre off, whereunto the Pilots directed the ships: and being come to it, they land, and finde it to be Rost Island, where they stayed certaine dayes, and afterwards set saile againe, and proceeding towards the North, they espied certaine other Islands, which were called the Crosse of Islands. From which places when they were a litle departed, Sir Hugh Willoughby the General, a man of good foresight and providence in all his actions, erected and set out his flagge, by which hee called together the chiefest men of the other shippes, that by the helpe and assistance of their counsels, the order of the governement, and conduction of the shippes in the whole voyage might bee the better: who being come together accordingly, they conclude and agree, that if any great tempest should arise at any time, and happen to disperse and scatter them, every shippe should indevour his best to goe to Wardhouse, a haven or castell of some name in the kingdome of Norway, and that they that arrived there first in safetie should stay and expect the comming of the rest.

The very same day in the afternoone, about foure of the clocke, so great a tempest suddenly arose, and the Seas were so outragious, that the ships could not keepe their intended course, but some were perforce driven one way, and some another way, to their great perill and hazard: The generall with the lowdest voyce cried out to Richard Chanceler, and earnestly requested him not to goe farre from him: but hee neither would nor could keepe companie with him, if he sailed still so fast: for the Admirall was of better saile then his shippe. But the said Admirall (I knowe not by what meanes) bearing all his sailes, was caried away with so great force and swiftnesse, that not long after hee was quite out of sight, and the third ship also with the same storme and like rage was dispersed and lost us.

The shippe boate of the Admirall (striking against the shippe,) was overwhelmed in the sight and viewe of the Mariners of the Bonaventure: and as for them that are already returned and arrived, they know nothing of the rest of the ships what was become of them.

But if it be so, that any miserable mishap have overtaken them, If the rage and furie of the Sea have devoured those good men, or if as yet they live, and wander up and downe in strange Countreys, I must needs say they were men worthy of better fortune, and if they be living, let us wish them safetie and a good returne: but if the crueltie of death hath taken holde of them, God send them a Christian grave and Sepulchre.

Nowe Richard Chanceler with his shippe and company being thus left alone, and become very pensive, heavie, and sorowfull, by this dispersion of the Fleete, hee (according to the order before taken,) shapeth his course for Wardhouse in Norway, there to expect and abide the arrivall of the rest of the shippes. And being come thither, and having stayed there the space of 7. dayes, and looked in vaine for their comming, hee determined at length to proceede alone in the purposed voyage. And as hee was preparing himselfe to depart, it happened that hee fell in company and speech with certaine Scottishmen: who having understanding of his intention, and wishing well to his actions, beganne earnestly to disswade him from the further prosecution of the discoverie, by amplifying the dangers which hee was to fall into, and omitted no reason that might serve to that purpose. But hee holding nothing so ignominious and reprochfull, as inconstancie and levitie of minde, and perswading himselfe that a man of valour coulde not commit a more dishonourable part then for feare of danger to avoyde and shunne great attempts, was nothing at all changed or discouraged with the speeches and words of the Scots, remaining stedfast and immutable in his first resolution: determining either to bring that to passe which was intended, or els to die the death.

And as for them which were with Master Chanceler in his shippe, although they had great cause of discomfort by the losse of their companie (whom the foresaid tempest had separated from them,) and were not a little troubled with cogitations and perturbations of minde, in respect of their doubtfull course: yet notwithstanding, they were of such consent and agreement of minde with Master Chanceler, that they were resolute, and prepared under his direction and government, to make proofe and triall of all adventures, without all feare or mistrust of future dangers. Which constancie of minde in all the companie did exceedingly increase their Captaines carefulnesse: for hee being swallowed up with like good will and love towards them, feared lest through any errour of his, the safetie of the companie should bee indangered. To conclude, when they sawe their desire and hope of the arrivall of the rest of the shippes to be every day more and more frustrated, they provided to sea againe, and Master Chanceler held on his course towards that unknowen part of the world, and sailed so farre, that hee came at last to the place where hee found no night at all, but a continuall light and brightnesse of the Sunne shining clearely upon the huge and mightie Sea. And having the benefite of this perpetuall light for certaine dayes, at the length it pleased God to bring them into a certaine great Bay, which was of one hundreth miles or thereabout over. Whereinto they entred, and somewhat farre within it cast ancre, and looking every way about them, it happened that they espied a farre off a certaine fisher boate, which Master Chanceler, accompanied with a fewe of his men, went towards to common with the fishermen that were in it, and to knowe of them what Countrey it was, and what people, and of what maner of living they were: but they being amazed with the strange greatnesse of his shippe, (for in those partes before that time they had never seene the like) beganne presently to avoyde and to flee: but hee still following them at last overtooke them, and being come to them, they (being in great feare, as men halfe dead) prostrated themselves before him, offering to kisse his feete: but hee (according to his great and singular courtesie,) looked pleasantly upon them, comforting them by signes and gestures, refusing those dueties and reverences of theirs, and taking them up in all loving sort from the ground. And it is strange to consider howe much favour afterwards in that place, this humanitie of his did purchase to himselfe. For they being dismissed spread by and by a report abroad of the arrivall of a strange nation, of a singular gentlenesse and courtesie: whereupon the common people came together offering to these newe-come ghests victuals freely, and not refusing to traffique with them, except they had bene bound by a certaine religious use and custome, not to buy any forreine commodities, without the knowledge and consent of the king.

By this time our men had learned that this Countrey was

called Russia, or Moscovie, and that Ivan Vasiliwich (which was at that time their Kings name) ruled and governed farre and wide in those places. And the barbarous Russes asked like-wise of our men whence they were, and what they came for: whereunto answere was made, that they were Englishmen sent into those coastes, from the most excellent King Edward the sixt, having from him in commandement certaine things to deliver to their King, and seeking nothing els but his amitie and friendship, and traffique with his people, whereby they doubted not, but that great commoditie and profit would grow to the subjects of both kingdomes.

The Barbarians heard these things very gladly, and promised their aide and furtherance to acquaint their king out of hand with so honest and a reasonable request.

In the meane time Master Chanceler intreated victuals for his money of the governour of that place (who together with others came aboord him) and required hostages of them likewise for the more assurance of safetie to himselfe and his company. To whom the Governours answered, that they knewe not in that case the will of their king, but yet were willing in such things as they might lawfully doe, to pleasure him: which was as then to affoord him the benefit of victuals.

Nowe while these things were a doing, they secretly sent a messenger unto the Emperour, to certifie him of the arrivall of a strange nation, and withall to knowe his pleasure concerning them. Which message was very welcome unto him, insomuch that voluntarily hee invited them to come to his Court. But if by reason of the tediousnesse of so long a journey, they thought it not best so to doe, then hee graunted libertie to his subjects to bargaine, and to traffique with them: and further promised, that if it would please them to come to him, hee himselfe would beare the final charges of poste horses. In the meane time the governours of the place differed the matter from day to day, pretending divers excuses, and saying one while that the consent of all the governours, and another while, that the great and waightie affaires of the kingdome compelled them to differ their answere: and this they did of purpose, so long to protract the time, untill the messenger (sent before to the king) did returne with relation of his will and pleasure.

But Master Chanceler, (seeing himselfe held in this suspense with long and vaine expectation, and thinking that of intention to delude him, they posted the matter off so often,) was very instant with them to performe their promise: Which if they would not doe, hee tolde them that hee would depart and proceede in his voyage. So that the Moscovites (although as yet they knew not the minde of their king) yet fearing the departure in deede of our men who had such wares and commodities as they greatly desired, they at last resolved to furnish our people with all things necessarie, and to conduct them by land to the presence of their king. And so Master Chanceler beganne his journey, which was very long and most troublesome, wherein hee had the use of certaine sleds, which in that Countrey are very common, for they are caried themselves upon sleds, and all their carriages are in the same sort, the people almost not knowing any other maner of carriage, the cause wherof is the exceeding hardnesse of the ground congealed in the winter time by the force of the colde, which in those places is very extreme and horrible, whereof hereafter we will say something.

But now they having passed the greater part of their journey, mette at last with the Sleddeman (of whom I spake before) sent to the king secretly from the Justices or governours, who by some ill happe had lost his way, and had gone to the Sea side, which is neere to the Countrey of the Tartars, thinking there to have found our ship. But having long erred and wandered out of his way, at the last in his direct returne, hee met (as hee was comming) our Captaine on the way. To whom hee by and by delivered the Emperours letters, which were written to him with all courtesie and in the most loving maner that could be: wherein expresse commandement was given, that post horses should bee gotten for him and the rest of his company without any money. Which thing was of all the Russes in the rest of their journey so willingly done, that they began to quarrell, yea, and to fight also in striving and contending which of them should put their post horses to the sledde: so that after much adoe and great paines taken in this long and wearie journey, (for they had travailed very neere fifteene hundred miles) Master Chanceler came at last to Mosco the chiefe citie of the kingdome, and the seate of the king: of which citie, and of the

Emperour himselfe, and of the principall cities of Moscovie, wee will speake immediatly more at large in this discourse.

Of Moscovie, which is also called Russia

Moscovie, which hath the name also of Russia the white, is a very large and spacious Countrey, every way bounded with divers nations. Towards the South and the East, it is compassed with Tartaria: the Northren side of it stretcheth to the Scytian Ocean: upon the West part border the Lappians, a rude and savage nation, living in woods, whose language is not knowen to any other people: next unto these, more towards the South, is Swecia, then Finlandia, then Livonia, and last of all Lituania. This Countrey of Moscovie, hath also very many and great rivers in it, and is marish ground in many places: and as for the rivers, the greatest and most famous amongst all the rest, is that, which the Russes in their owne tongue call Volga, but others know it by the name of Rha. Next unto it in fame is Tanais, which they call Don, and the third Boristhenes which at this day they call Neper. Two of these, to wit, Rha, and Boristhenes yssuing both out of one fountaine, runne very farre through the land: Rha receiving many other pleasant rivers into it, & running from the very head or spring of it towards the East, after many crooked turnings and windings, dischargeth it selfe, and all the other waters and rivers that fall into it by divers passages into the Caspian Sea. Tanais springing from a fountaine of great name in those partes, and growing great neere to his head, spreds it selfe at length very largely, and makes a great lake: and then growing narrowe againe, doth so runne for certaine miles, untill it fall into another lake, which they call Ivan: and therehence fetching a very crooked course, comes very neere to the river Volga: but disdaining as it were the company of any other river, doth there turne it selfe againe from Volga, and runnes toward the South, and fals at last into the Lake of Mœotis. Boristhenes, which comes from the same head that Rha doth, (as wee sayde before) carieth both it selfe, and other waters that are neere unto it, towards the South, not refusing the mixture of other small rivers: and running by many great and large Countreys fals at last into Pontus Euxinus. Besides these rivers, are also in Moscovie certaine lakes, and pooles, the lakes breede fish by the celestiall influence: and amongst them all, the chiefest and most principall is called Bealozera, which is very famous by reason of a very strong towre built in it, wherein the kings of Moscovie reserve and repose their treasure in all time of warre and danger.

Touching the Riphean mountaines, whereupon the snow lieth continually, and where hence in times past it was thought that Tanais the river did spring, and that the rest of the wonders of nature, which the Grecians fained and invented of olde, were there to be seene: our men which lately came from thence, neither sawe them, nor yet have brought home any perfect relation of them, although they remained there for the space of three moneths, and had gotten in that time some intelligence of the language of Moscovie. The whole Countrey is plaine and champion, and few hils in it: and towards the North it hath very large & spacious woods, wherein is great store of Firre trees, a wood very necessarie, and fit for the building of houses: there are also wilde beastes bred in those woods, as Buffes, Beares, and blacke Wolves, and another kinde of beast unknowen to us, but called by them Rossomakka: and the nature of the same is very rare and wonderfull: for when it is great with yong, and ready to bring foorth, it seeketh out some narrow place betweene two stakes, and so going through them, presseth it selfe, and by that meanes is eased of her burden, which otherwise could not be done. They hunt their buffes for the most part a horsebacke, but their Beares a foot, with woodden forkes. The north parts of the Countrey are reported to be so cold, that the very ice or water which distilleth out of the moist wood which they lay upon the fire is presently congealed and frozen: the diversitie growing suddenly to be so great, that in one and the selfe same firebrand, a man shall see both fire and ice. When the winter doth once begin there it doth still more & more increase by a perpetuitie of cold: neither doth that colde slake, untill the force of the Sunne beames doth dissolve the cold, and make glad the earth, returning to it againe. Our mariners which we left in the ship in the meane time to keepe it, in their going up onely from their cabbins to the hatches, had their breath oftentimes so suddenly taken away, that they eftsoones fell downe as men very neere dead, so great is the sharpeness of that colde

climate: but as for the South parts of the Countrey, they are
somewhat more temperate.

Of Mosco the chiefe Citie of the kingdome, and of the Emperour thereof

It remaineth that a larger discourse be made of Mosco, the principall Citie of that Countrey, and of the Prince also, as before
we have promised. The Empire and government of the king is
very large, and his wealth at this time exceeding great. And because the citie of Mosco is the chiefest of al the rest, it seemeth
of it selfe to challenge the first place in this discourse. Our men
say, that in bignesse it is as great as the Citie of London, with
the suburbes thereof. There are many and great buildings in it,
but for beautie and fairenes, nothing comparable to ours.
There are many Townes and Villages also, but built out of
order, and with no hansomnesse: their streets and wayes are
not paved with stone as ours are: the walles of their houses are
of wood: the roofes for the most part are covered with shingle
boords. There is hard by the Citie a very faire Castle, strong,
and furnished with artillerie, whereunto the Citie is joyned directly towards the North, with a bricke wall: the walles also of
the Castle are built with bricke, and are in breadth or thickenesse eighteene foote. This Castle hath on the one side a drie
ditch, on the other side the river Moscua, whereby it is made
almost inexpugnable. The same Moscua trending towards the
East doth admit into it the companie of the river Occa.

In the Castle aforesaide, there are in number nine Churches,
or Chappels, not altogether unhansome, which are used and
kept by certaine religious men, over whom there is after a sort,
a Patriarke, or Governour, and with him other reverend
Fathers, all which for the greater part, dwell within the Castle.
As for the kings Court and Palace, it is not of the neatest, onely
in forme it is foure square, and of lowe building, much surpassed and excelled by the beautie and elegancie of the houses
of the kings of England. The windowes are very narrowly built,
and some of them by glasse, some other by lettisses admit the
light: and whereas the Palaces of our Princes are decked, and
adorned with hangings of cloth of gold, there is none such
there: they build and joyne to all their wals benches, and that

not onely in the Court of the Emperour, but in all private mens houses.

Nowe after that they had remained about twelve dayes in the Citie, there was then a Messenger sent unto them, to bring them to the Kings house: and they being after a sort wearied with their long stay, were very ready, and willing so to doe: and being entred within the gates of the Court, there sate a very honorable companie of Courtiers, to the number of one hundred, all apparelled in cloth of golde, downe to their ankles: and therehence being conducted into the chamber of presence, our men beganne to wonder at the Majestie of the Emperour: his seate was aloft, in a very royall throne, having on his head a Diademe, or Crowne of golde, apparelled with a robe all of Goldsmiths worke, and in his hand hee held a Scepter garnished, and beset with precious stones: and besides all other notes and apparances of honour, there was a Majestie in his countenance proportionable with the excellencie of his estate: on the one side of him stood his chiefe Secretarie, on the other side, the great Commander of silence, both of them arayed also in cloth of gold: and then there sate the Counsel of one hundred and fiftie in number, all in like sort arayed, and of great state. This so honorable an assemblie, so great a Majestie of the Emperour, and of the place might very well have amazed our men, and have dasht them out of countenance: but notwithstanding Master Chanceler being therewithall nothing dismaied saluted, and did his duetie to the Emperour, after the maner of England, and withall, delivered unto him the letters of our king, Edward the sixt. The Emperour having taken, & read the letters, began a litle to question with them, and to aske them of the welfare of our king: whereunto our men answered him directly, & in few words: hereupon our men presented some thing to the Emperour, by the chiefe Secretary, which at the delivery of it, put of his hat, being before all the time covered: and so the Emperour having invited them to dinner, dismissed them from his presence: and going into the chamber of him that was Master of the Requests to the Emperour, & having stayed there the space of two howres, at the last, the Messenger commeth, and calleth them to dinner: they goe, and being conducted into the golden Court, (for so they call it, although not very faire) they finde the Emperour sitting upon an high and stately seate, apparelled

with a robe of silver, and with another Diademe on his head:
our men being placed over against him, sit downe: in the middes
of the roome stoode a mightie Cupboord upon a square foote,
whereupon stoode also a round boord, in manner of a Diamond,
broade beneath, and towardes the toppe narrowe, and every
steppe rose up more narrowe then another. Upon this Cup-
boorde was placed the Emperours plate, which was so much,
that the very Cupboord it selfe was scant able to sustaine the
waight of it: the better part of all the vessels, and goblets, was
made of very fine gold: and amongst the rest, there were foure
pots of very large bignesse, which did adorne the rest of the
plate in great measure: for they were so high, that they thought
them at the least five foote long. There were also upon this
Cupbord certaine silver caskes, not much differing from the
quantitie of our Fyrkins, wherein was reserved the Emperours
drinke: on each side of the Hall stood foure Tables, each of
them layde and covered with very cleane table clothes, whereunto the company ascended by three steps or degrees: all which
were filled with the assemblie present: the ghests were all apparelled with linnen without, and with rich skinnes within, and
so did notably set out this royall feast. The Emperour, when hee
takes any bread or knife in his hand, doth first of all crosse himselfe upon his forehead: they that are in speciall favour with the
Emperour sit upon the same bench with him, but somewhat
farre from him: and before the comming in of the meate, the
Emperour himselfe, according to an ancient custome of the
kings of Moscovy, doth first bestow a piece of bread upon every
one of his ghests, with a loud pronunciation of his title, and
honour, in this manner: The great Duke of Moscovie, and
chiefe Emperour of Russia, John Basiliwich (& then the officer
nameth the ghest) doth give thee bread. Whereupon al the
ghests rise up, and by & by sit downe againe. This done, the
Gentleman Usher of the Hall comes in, with a notable company
of servants, carying the dishes, and having done his reverence to
the Emperour, puts a yong Swanne in a golden platter upon the
table, and immediatly takes it thence againe, delivering it to the
Carver, and seven other of his fellowes, to be cut up: which
being perfourmed, the meate is then distributed to the ghests,
with the like pompe, and ceremonies. In the meane time, the
Gentleman Usher receives his bread, and tasteth to the Em-

perour, and afterward, having done his reverence, he departeth. Touching the rest of the dishes, because they were brought in out of order, our men can report no certaintie: but this is true, that all the furniture of dishes, and drinking vessels, which were then for the use of a hundred ghests, was all of pure golde, and the tables were so laden with vessels of gold, that there was no roome for some to stand upon them.

We may not forget, that there were 140. servitors arayed in cloth of gold, that in the dinner time, changed thrise their habit and apparell, which servitors are in like sort served with bread from the Emperour, as the rest of the ghests. Last of all, dinner being ended, and candles brought in, (for by this time night was come) the Emperour calleth all his ghests and Noble men by their names, in such sort, that it seemes miraculous, that a Prince, otherwise occupied in great matters of estate, should so well remember so many and sundry particular names. The Russes tolde our men, that the reason thereof, as also of the bestowing of bread in that maner, was to the ende that the Emperour might keepe the knowledge of his owne houshold: and withal, that such as are under his displeasure, might by this meanes be knowen.

Of the discipline of warre among the Russes

Whensoever the injures of their neighbours doe call the King foorth to battell, hee never armeth a lesse number against the enemie, then 300. thousand soldiers, 100. thousand whereof hee carieth out into the field with him, and leaveth the rest in garison in some fit places, for the better safetie of his Empire. He presseth no husbandman, nor Marchant: for the Countrey is so populous, that these being left at home, the youth of the Realme is sufficient for all his wars. As many as goe out to warfare doe provide all things of their owne cost: they fight not on foote, but altogether on horsebacke: their armour is a coate of maile, & a helmet: the coate of maile w^tout is gilded, or els adorned with silke, although it pertaine to a common soldier: they have a great pride in shewing their wealth: they use bowes, and arrowes, as the Turks do: they cary lances also into the field. They ride with a short stirrop, after the maner of the Turks: They are a kinde of people most sparing in diet, and most patient in extremitie of cold, above all others. For when the ground is covered with snowe, and is growen terrible and hard with the frost, this Russe hangs up his mantle, or souldiers coate, against that part from whence the winde and Snowe drives, and so making a little fire, lieth downe with his backe towards the weather: this mantle of his serves him for his bed, wall, house and all: his drinke is colde water of the river, mingled with oatemeale, and this is all his good cheere, and he thinketh himselfe well, and daintily fedde therewith, and so sitteth downe by his fire, and upon the hard ground, rosteth as it were his wearie sides thus daintily stuffed: the hard ground is his feather bed, & some blocke or stone his pillow: and as for his horse, he is as it were a chamberfellow with his master, faring both alike. How justly may this barbarous, and rude Russe condemne the daintinesse and nicenesse of our Captaines, who living in a soile & aire much more temperate, yet commonly use furred boots, and clokes? But thus much of the furniture of their common souldiers. But those that are of higher degrees come into the field a little better provided. As for the furniture of the Emperour himselfe, it is then above all other times, most notable. The coverings of his tent for the most part, are all of gold, adorned with stones of great price, and with the curious workemanship of plumasiers. As often as they are to skirmish with the enemie, they goe forth without any order at all: they make no wings, nor militarie divisions of their men, as we doe, but lying for the most part, in ambush, doe suddenly set upon the enemie. Their horses can well abstaine two whole daies from any meate. They feede upon the barkes of trees, and the most tender branches, in all the time of warre. And this scant and miserable maner of living, both the horse and his Master can well endure, sometimes for the space of two moneths, lustie, and in good state of body. If any man behave himselfe valiantly in the fielde, to the contentation of the Emperour, he bestoweth upon him in recompense of his service, some farme, or so much ground as he and his may live upon, which notwithstanding after his death, returneth againe to the Emperour, if he die without a male issue. For although his daughters be never so many, yet no part of that inheritance comes to them, except peradventure the Emperour of his goodnesse, give some portion of the land amongst them, to bestowe them withall. As for the man, whosoever he be, that is in this sort rewarded by the Emperours liberalitie, hee is bound in a great summe, to maintaine so many souldiers for the warre, when need shall require, as that land, in the opinion of the Emperour, is able to maintaine. And all those, to whom any land fals by inheritance, are in no better condition: for if they die without any male issue, all their lands fall into the hands of the Emperour. And moreover, if there be any rich man amongst them, who in his owne person is unfit for the warres, and yet hath such wealth, that thereby many Noble men and warriours might be maintained, if any of the Courtiers present his name to the Emperour, the unhappy man is by and by sent for, and in that instant, deprived of all his riches, which with great paines and travell all his life time he had gotten together: except perhaps some small portion thereof be left him, to maintaine his wife, children and familie. But all this is done of all the people so willingly at the Emperours commandement, that a man would thinke, they rather make restitution of other mens goods, then give that which is their owne to other men. Nowe the Emperour having taken these goods into his hands, bestoweth them among his Courtiers, according to their deserts: and oftener that a man is sent to the warres, the more the favour he thinketh is borne to him by the Emperour, although he goe upon his owne charge, as I said before. So great is the obedience of all men generally to their Prince.

Of the Ambassadors of the Emperour of Moscovie

The Moscovite, with no lesse pompe, and magnificence then that which we have spoken of, sends his Ambassadors to forren Princes, in the affaires of estate. For while our men were abiding in the Citie of Mosco, there were two Ambassadors sent to the King of Poland, accompanied with 500. notable horses, and the greater part of the men were arayed in cloth of gold, and of silke, and the worst apparell was of garments of blewe colour, to speake nothing of the trappings of the horses, which were adorned with gold and silver, and very curiously embrodered: they had also with them one hundred white and faire spare horses, to use them at such times, as any wearinesse came upon them. But now the time requireth me to speake briefly of other Cities of the Moscovites, and of the wares and commodities that the Countrey yeeldeth.

Novogorode

Next unto Mosco, the Citie of Novogorode is reputed the chiefest of Russia: for although it be in Majestie inferior to it, yet in greatnesse it goeth beyond it. It is the cheifest and greatest Marte Towne of all Moscovie: and albeit the Emperours seate is not there, but at Mosco, yet the commodiousnesse of the river, falling into that gulfe, which is called Sinus Finnicus, whereby it is well frequented by Marchants, makes it more famous then Mosco it selfe. This towne excels all the rest in the commodities of flaxe and hempe: it yeeldes also hides, honie, and waxe. The Flemings there sometimes had a house of Marchandize, but by reason that they used the like ill dealing there, which they did with us, they lost their privileges, a restitution whereof they earnestly sued for at the time that our men were there. But those Flemings hearing of the arrivall of our men in those parts, wrote their letters to the Emperour against them, accusing them for pirats and rovers, wishing him to detaine, and imprison them. Which things when they were knowen of our men, they conceived feare, that they should never have returned home. But the Emperour beleeving rather the Kings letters, which our men brought, then the lying and false suggestions of the Flemings, used no ill intreatie towards them.

Yeraslave

Yeraslave also is a Towne of some good fame, for the commodities of hides, tallow, and corne, which it yeeldes in great abundance. Cakes of waxe are there also to bee solde, although other places have greater store: this Yeraslave is distant from Mosco, about two hundred miles: and betwixt them are many populous villages. Their fields yeeld such store of corne, that in convaying it towards Mosco, sometimes in a forenoone, a man shall see seven hundred or eight hundred sleds, going and comming, laden with corne and salt fish: the people come a thousand miles to Mosco, to buy that corne, and then cary it away upon sleds: and these are those people that dwell in the North parts, where the colde is so terrible, that no corne doth growe there, or if it spring up, it never comes to ripenesse. The commodities that they bring with them, are saltfish, skinnes, and hides.

Vologda

Vologda being from Mosco, 550. miles yeeldes the commodities of Hempe and Flaxe also: although the greatest store of Flaxe is solde at Novogrode.

Plesco

The Towne of Plesco, is frequented of Marchants for the good store of Honie and Waxe that it yeeldeth.

Colmagro

The North parts of Russia yeelde very rare and precious skinnes: and amongst the rest, those principally, which we call Sables, worne about the neckes of our Noble women and Ladies: it hath also Martins skinnes, white, blacke, and red Foxe skinnes, skinnes of Hares, and Ermyns, and others, which they call and terme barbarously, as Bevers, Minxes, and Minivers. The sea adjoyning, breedes a certaine beast, which they call the Mors, which seeketh his foode upon the rockes, climing up with the helpe of his teeth. The Russes use to take them, for the great vertue that is in their teeth, whereof they make as great accompt, as we doe of the Elephants tooth. These commodities they cary upon Deeres backes to the towne of Lampas: and from thence to Colmagro, and there in the winter time, are kept great Faires for the sale of them. This Citie of Colmagro, serves all the Countrey about it with salt, and salt fish. The Russians also of the North parts, send thither oyle, which they call traine, which they make in a river called *Una, although it be also made elsewhere: and here they use to boile the water of the sea, whereof they make very great store of salt.

Of controversies in Lawe, and how they are ended

Having hitherto spoken so much of the chiefest Cities of Russia, as the matter required: it remaineth that we speake somewhat of the lawes, that the Moscovits doe use, as farre foorth

---

* Or, Dwina.

as the same are come to our knowledge. If any controversie arise among them, they first make their Landlords Judges in the matter, and if they cannot end it, then they preferre it to the Magistrate. The plaintif craveth of the said Magistrate, that he may have leave to enter law against his adversarie: and having obtained it, the officer fetcheth the defendant, and beateth him on the legges, till he bring forth a suretie for him: but if he be not of such credite, as to procure a surety, then are his hands by an officer tied to his necke, and he is beaten all the way, till he come before the Judge. The Judge then asketh him (as for example in the matter of debt) whether he oweth any thing to the plaintife. If he denies it, then saith the Judge, How canst thou deny it? the defendant answereth, By an othe: thereupon the officer is commaunded to cease from beating of him, untill the matter be further tried. They have no Lawyers, but every man is his owne Advocate, and both the complaint of the accuser, and the answere of the defendant, are in maner of petition delivered to the Emperour, intreating justice at his hands. The Emperour himselfe heareth every great controversie, and upon the hearing of it, giveth judgement, and that with great equitie, which I take to be a thing worthy of speciall commendation, in the Majestie of a Prince. But although he doe this with a good purpose of mind, yet the corrupt Magistrates do wonderfully pervert the same: but if the Emperour take them in any fault, he doeth punish them most severely. Now at the last, when ech partie hath defended his cause with his best reasons, the Judge demandeth of the accuser, whether he hath any more to say for himselfe: he answereth, that he will trie the matter in fight by his Champion, or else intreateth, that in fight betwixt themselves the matter may be ended: which being graunted, they both fight it out: or if both of them, or either of them seeme unfit for that kinde of triall, then they have publike Champions to be hired, which live by ending of quarrels. These Champions are armed with yron axes, and speares, and fight on foote, and he whose Champion is overcome, is by and by taken, and imprisoned, and terribly handled, untill he agree with his adversarie. But if either of them be of any good calling, and degree, and doe challenge one another to fight, the Judge granteth it: in which case they may not use publike Champions. And he that is of any good birth, doth contemne the other, if he be basely borne, and wil not fight with him. If a poore man happen to grow in debt, his Creditor takes him, & maketh him pay the debt, in working either to himselfe, or to some other man, whose wages he taketh up. And there are some among them, that use willingly to make themselves, their wives, and children, bondslaves unto rich men, to have a little money at the first into their hands, and so for ever after content themselves with meate and drinke: so little accompt doe they make of libertie.

Of punishments upon theeves

If any man be taken upon committing of theft, he is imprisoned, and often beaten, but not hanged for the first offence, as the manner is with us: and this they call the lawe of mercie. He that offendeth the second time hath his nose cut off, and is burnt in the forehead with a hot yron. The third time, he is hanged. There are many cutpurses among them, and if the rigour of the Prince did not cut them off, they could not be avoyded.

Of their religion

They maintaine the opinions of the Greeke Church: they suffer no graven images of saints in their Churches, but their pictures painted in tables they have in great abundance, which they do adore and offer unto, and burne waxe candles before them, and cast holy water upon them, without other honour. They say that our images which are set up in Churches, and carved, have no divinitie in them. In their private houses they have images for their household saints, and for the most part, they are put in the darkest place of the house: hee that comes into his neighbours house doth first salute his saints, although he see them not. If any foorme or stoole stand in his way, hee oftentimes beateth his browe upon the same, and often ducking downe with his head, and body, worshippeth the chiefe Image. The habite, and attire of the Priests, and of the Lay men, doth nothing at all differ: as for marriage, it is forbidden to no man: onely this is received and held amongst them for a rule, and custome, that if a Priests wife doe die, he may not marry againe, nor take a second wife: and therefore they of secular Priests, as they call them, are made Monkes, to whom then chastitie for ever is commanded. Their divine service is all done

and said in their owne language, that every man may understand it: they receive the Lords Supper with leavened bread,
and after the consecration, they carry it about the Church in
a saucer, and prohibite no man from receiving and taking of
it, that is willing so to doe. They use both the Olde and the
Newe Testament, and read both in their owne language, but so
confusedly, that they themselves that doe reade, understand not
what themselves doe say: and while any part of either Testament is read, there is libertie given by custome to prattle, talke,
and make a noise: but in the time of the rest of the service
they use very great silence and reverence and behave themselves very modestly, and in good sort. As touching the Lords
praier, the tenth man amongst them knowes it not: and for the
articles of our faith, and the ten commandements, no man, or at
the least very fewe of them doe either know them or can say
them: their opinion is, that such secrete and holy things as they
are should not rashly and imprudently be communicated with
the common people. They holde for a Maxime amongst them,
that the olde Lawe, and the commandements also are abolished
by the death and blood of Christ: all studies and letters of
humanitie they utterly refuse: concerning the Latine, Greeke,
and Hebrew tongues, they are altogether ignorant in them.

Every yeere they celebrate foure severall fastes, which they
call according to the names of the Saints: the first beginnes
with them, at the time that our Lent beginnes. The second is
called amongst them the fast of S. Peter. The third is taken
from the day of the Virgin Marie. And the fourth and last be-
gins upon S. Philips day. But as we begin our Lent upon Wednesday, so they begin theirs upon the Sunday. Upon the Saturday they eate flesh: whensoever any of those fasting feastes doe
drawe neere, looke what weeke doth immediatly goe before
them, the same weeke they live altogether upon white meates,
and in their common language they call those weekes, the fast
of Butter.

In the time of their fasts, the neighbours every where goe
from one to another, and visite one another, and kisse one
another with kisses of peace, in token of their mutuall love and
Christian concord: and then also they doe more often then at
any other time goe to the holy Communion. When seven dayes
are past, from the beginning of the fast, then they doe often

either goe to their Churches, or keepe themselves at home, and use often prayer: and for that sevennight they eate nothing but hearbes: but after that sevennights fast is once past, then they returne to their old intemperancie of drinking, for they are notable tospots. As for the keeping of their fasting dayes, they doe it very streightly, neither doe they eate any thing besides hearbes, and salt fish, as long as those fasting dayes doe endure: but upon every Wednesday and Friday, in every weeke throughout the yeere, they fast.

There are very many Monasteries of the order of S. Benedict, amongst them, to which many great livings, for their maintenance, doe belong: for the Friers and the Monkes doe at the least possesse the third part of the livings, throughout the whole Moscovite Empire. To those Monkes that are of this order, there is amongst them a perpetuall prohibition, that they may eate no flesh: and therefore their meate is onely salt fish, milke, and butter: neither is it permitted them by the lawes, and customes of their religion, to eate any fresh fish at all: and at those foure fasting times, whereof we spake before, they eate no fish at all: onely they live with hearbes, and cucumbers, which they doe continually for that purpose cause and take order to grow and spring, for their use and diet.

As for their drinke, it is very weake, and small. For the discharge of their office, they do every day say service, and that early in the mornings before day: and they doe in such sort, and with such observation begin their service, that they will be sure to make an ende of it, before day: and about nine of the clocke in the morning they celebrate the Communion. When they have so done, they goe to dinner, and after dinner they goe againe to service, and the like also after supper: and in the meane time while they are at dinner there is some exposition or interpretation of the Gospel used.

Whensoever any Abbot of any monasterie dieth, the Emperour taketh all his housholde stuffe, beastes, flockes of sheepe, golde, silver, and all that he hath: or els hee that is to succeede him in his place and dignitie doth redeeme all those things, and buyeth them of the Emperour for money.

Their churches are built of timber, and the towers of their churches for the most part are covered with shingle boordes. At the doores of their churches, they usually build some en-

trance or porch as we doe, and in their churchyardes they erect
a certaine house of wood, wherein they set up their bels, wherein sometimes they have but one, in some two, and in some also
three.

There is one use and custome amongst them, which is strange
and rare, but yet it is very ridiculous, and that is this: when any
man dyeth amongst them, they take the dead body and put it
in a coffine or chest, and in the hand of the corps they put a litle
scroule, & in the same there are these wordes written, that the
same man died a Russe of Russes, having received the faith,
and died in the same. This writing or letter they say they send
to S. Peter, who receiving it (as they affirme) reades it, and by
and by admits him into heaven, and that his glory and place is
higher and greater then the glory of the Christians of the Latine
church, reputing themselves to be followers of a more sincere
faith and religion then they: they hold opinion that we are but
halfe Christians, and themselves onely to be the true and perfect church: these are the foolish and childish dotages of such
ignorant Babarians.

Of the Moscovites that are Idolaters, dwelling neere to Tartaria

There is a certaine part of Moscovie bordering upon the countreys of the Tartars, wherein those Moscovites that dwell are
very great idolaters: they have one famous idole amongst them,
which they call the Golden old wife: & they have a custome
that whensoever any plague or any calamitie doth afflict the
countrey, as hunger, warre, or such like, then they goe to consult with their idol, which they do after this maner: they fall
down prostrate before the idol, & pray unto it, & put in the
presence of the same, a cymbal: & about the same certaine
persons stand, which are chosen amongst them by lot: upon
their cymball they place a silver tode, and sound the cymball,
and to whomsoever of those lotted persons that tode goeth, he
is taken, and by and by slaine: and immediately, I know not
by what illusions of the devill, or idole, he is againe restored to
life, & then doth reveale and deliver the causes of the present
calamitie. And by this meanes knowing how to pacifie the
idole, they are delivered from the imminent danger.

Of the forme of their private houses, and of the apparell of the people

The common houses of the countrey are every where built of beames of Firre tree: the lower beames doe so receive the round holownesse of the uppermost, that by the meanes of the building thereupon, they resist, and expell all winds that blow, and where the timber is joined together, there they stop the chinks with mosse. The forme & fashion of their houses in al places is foure square, with streit and narrow windowes, whereby with a transparent casement made or covered with skinne like to parchment, they receive the light. The roofes of their houses are made of boords covered without with ye barke of trees: within their houses they have benches or griezes hard by their wals, which commonly they sleepe upon, for the common people knowe not the use of beds: they have stooves wherein in the morning they make a fire, and the same fire doth either moderately warme, or make very hote the whole house.

The apparell of the people for the most part is made of wooll, their caps are picked like unto a rike or diamond, broad beneath, and sharpe upward. In the maner of making whereof, there is a signe and representation of nobilitie: for the loftier or higher their caps are, the greater is their birth supposed to be, and the greater reverence is given them by the common people.

The Conclusion to Queene Marie

These are the things most excellent Queene, which your Subjects newly returned from Russia have brought home concerning the state of that countrey: wherfore if your majestie shall be favourable, and grant a continuance of the travell, there is no doubt but that the honour and renowme of your name will be spred amongst those nations, whereunto three onely noble personages from the verie creation have had accesse, to whom no man hath bene comparable.

11

A compendious and briefe declaration of the journey of M. Anth. Jenkinson, from the famous citie of London into the land of Persia, passing in this same journey thorow Russia, Moscovia, and Mare Caspium, aliâs Hircanum, sent and imployed therein by the right worshipfull Societie of the Merchants Adventurers, for discoverie of Lands, Islands, &c. Being begun the foureteenth day of May, Anno 1561, and in the third yere of the reigne of the Queenes Majestie that now is: this present declaration being directed and written to the foresayd Societie

FIRST imbarking my selfe in a good shippe of yours, named the Swallow, at Gravesend, having a faire and good winde, our anker then weyed, and committing all to the protection of our God, having in our sailing diversitie of windes, & thereby forced to direct and observe sundry courses (not here rehearsed, because you have bene thereof heretofore amply informed) on the fourteenth day of July, the yere aforesayd I arrived in the bay of S. Nicholas in Russia: and the sixe and twentieth day of the same moneth, after conference then had with your Agents there, concerning your worships affaires, I departed from thence passing thorow the countrey of Vago, and on the eight day of August then following, I came to Vologda, which is distant from Colmogro, seven hundred miles, where I remained foure dayes, attending the arrivall of one of your boats, wherein was laden a chest of jewels with the present, by your worships appointed for the Emperors Majesty: which being arrived, and the chest received, I therewith departed toward the city of Mosco, and came thither the twentieth day of the same moneth, where I immediatly caused my comming to be signified unto the Secretary of the Imperiall Majesty, with the Queenes Highnesse letters addressed unto the same his Majestie, who informed the Emperour thereof. But his Highnesse having great affaires, and being at that present ready to be married unto a Ladie of Chircassi, of the Mahometicall law, commanded that no stranger, Ambassadour, nor other, should come before him for a time, with further streight charge, that during the space of three dayes that the same solemne feast was celebrating, the gates of the citie should be shut, and that no person, stranger or native (certeine of his household reserved) should come out of their said houses during the said triumph, the cause thereof unto this day not being knowen.

The sixt of September following, the Emperour made a great feast, whereunto were called all Ambassadours and strangers being of reputation, and having affaires: amongst whom I was one, but being willed by the Secretary first to come, and to shew him the Queenes Majesties letters, I refused so to doe, saying I would deliver the same unto the Emperours owne hands, and not otherwise: which heard, the Secretarie answered, that unlesse he might first peruse the sayd letters, I should not come into the Emperours presence, so that I was not at the feast. Neverthelesse, I was advertised by a noble man that I was inquired for by the Emperours Majestie, although the cause of my absence was to his Majestie unknowen. The next day following, I caused a supplication to be made, and presented it to his Highnesse owne hands, and thereby declared the cause of my comming, signified by the Queenes Majesties letters, and the answere of his sayd Secretary, most humbly beseeching his Grace that he would receive and accept the same as her Highnesse letters, with such honour and friendship, as his letters sent by Osep Napea were received by the hands of our late Sovereigne Lady Queene Mary, or els that it would please his Highnes to dismisse me, saying that I would not deliver the said letters but unto his owne hands, for that it is so used in our countrey. Thus the matter being pondered, and the effect of my supplication well disgested, I was foorthwith commaunded to come with the said letters before his Majestie, and so delivered the same into his owne hands (with such presents as by you were appointed) according to my request, which were gratefully accepted, & the same day I dined in his Graces presence, with great entertainment. Shortly after, I desired to know whether I should be licenced to passe thorow his Highnesse dominions into the land of Persia, according to the Queenes Majesties request: hereunto it was answered, that I should not passe thither, for that his Majestie meant to send an armie of men that way into the land of Chircassi, whereby my journey should be both dangerous & troublesome, and that if I should perish therein, it would be much to his Graces dishonour, but he doubted other matters, although they were not expressed. Thus having received his answere, neither to my expectation, nor yet contentation, and there remaining a good part of the yere, having in that time solde the most part of your kersies and other wares appointed for Persia, when the time of the yeere required to returne for England, I desired pasport, and post horses for money, which was granted: but having received my pasport, ready to depart, there came unto our house there Osep Napea, who perswaded me that I should not depart that day, saying that the Emperor was not truely informed, imputing great fault to the frowardnesse of the Secretary, who was not my friend: before whom comming againe the next day, and finding the same Secretary and Osep Napea together, after many allegations and objections of things, and perceiving that I would depart, I was willed to remaine untill the Emperours Majestie were spoken with againe touching my passage: wherewith I was content, & within three dayes after sending for me, he declared that the Emperours pleasure was, that I should not onely passe thorow his dominions into Persia, but also have his Graces letters of commendations to forren princes, with certaine his affaires committed to my charge, too long here to rehearse: whereupon I appointed my selfe for the voyage, & the 15 day of March, the yeere aforesaid, I dined againe in his Majesties presence in company of an Ambassadour of Persia and others, and receiving a cup of drinke at his Majesties hands, I tooke my leave of his Highnesse, who did not onely give me letters, as aforesayd, but also committed matter of importance and charge unto me, to be done when I should arrive in those countreys whither I intended to go, and having all things in readinesse for the same voyage, I departed from the city of Mosco the 27 day of April 1562, downe by the great river of

Volga, in company of the said Ambassadour of Persia, with whom I had great friendship and conference all the way downe the same river unto Astracan, where we arrived all in health the 10 day of June.

And as touching the situations of the cities, townes, castles and countreys, aswell of Mahometans as also of Gentils adjoyning to the same, whereby I passed from Mosco unto Astracan, I omit in this breviat to rehearse, for that I heretofore have declared the same most amply unto you in my voyage to Boghar. Thus being arrived at Astracan, as is aforesayd, I repaired unto the captaine there, unto whom I was commended from the Emperours Majesty, with great charge that he not only should ayd and succor me with all things needfull during my abode there, but also to safeconduct me with 50 gunners wel appointed in two stroogs or brigantines into the Caspian sea, until I had passed certaine dangerous places which pirats & rovers do accustome to haunt, and having prepared my barke for the sea, the Ambassador of Persia being before departed in a barke of his owne the 15 day of July, the yeere aforesayd, I and my company tooke our voyage from the sayd Astracan, and the next day at a West sunne, passed the mouth of the said river being twenty miles distant, lying next Southeast. The 18 at a Southwest sunne, we passed by three Islands being distant nine miles from the said mouth of Volga, and Southsouthwest from thence, sailing Southsouthwest the next day, at a West & by North sun we fel with the land called Challica Ostriva, being foure round Islands together, distant from the said three Islands forty miles. From thence sailing the said course the next day, we had sight of a land called Tuke, in the countrey of Tumen, where pirats and rovers do use: for feare of whom we haled off into the sea due East forty miles, and fell upon shallowes out of the sight of land, and there were like to have perished, escaping most hardly: then the 22 day we had sight of a goodly Island called Chatalet, distant from the said Challica Ostriva an hundred miles, the winde being contrary, and a stiffe gale, we were not able to seize it: but were forced to come to an anker to the leeward of the same sixe miles off in three or foure fathom water, being distant from the maine land to the Westward of us, which was called Skafcayl or Connyk a countrey of Mahometans, about   miles, and so riding at two ankers a head, having no other provision, we lost one of them, the storme and sea being growen very sore, and thereby our barke was so full of leaks, that with continuall pumping we had much adoe to keepe her above water, although we threw much of our goods overboard, with losse of our boat, and our selves thereby in great danger like to have perished either in the sea or els upon the lee shore, where we should have fallen into the hands of those wicked infidels, who attended our shipwracke: and surely it was very unlike that we should have escaped both the extremities, but onely by the power and mercy of God, for the storme continued seven dayes, to wit, untill the thirtieth day of the same moneth: and then the winde comming up at the West with faire weather, our anker weyed, and our saile displayed, lying South, the next day haling to the shore with a West sunne, we were nie a land called by the inhabitants Shyrvansha, and there we came againe to an anker, having the winde contrary, being distant from the said Chatalet 150 miles, and there we continued untill the third day of August, then having a faire winde, winding Southsoutheast, and sailing threescore miles, the next day at a Southeast sunne we arrived at a city called Derbent in the king of Hircans dominion, where comming to land, and saluting the captaine there with a present, he made to me and my company a dinner, and there taking fresh water I departed.

This city of Derbent is an ancient towne having an olde castle therein, being situated upon an hill called Castow, builded all of free stone much after our building, the walles very high and thicke, and was first erected by king Alexander the great, when he warred against the Persians and Medians, and then hee made a wall of a woonderfull height and thicknesse, extending from the same city to the Georgians, yea unto the principall city thereof named Tewflish, which wall though it be now rased, or otherwise decayed, yet the foundation remaineth, & the wall was made to the intent that the inhabitants of that countrey then newly conquered by the said Alexander should not lightly flee, nor his enemies easily invade. This city of Derbent being now under the power of the Sophy of Persia, bordereth upon the sea, adjoyning to the foresaid land of Shalfcall, in the latitude of 41 degrees. From thence sailing Southeast and Southsoutheast about 80 miles, the sixt day of August, the yere aforesaid, we arrived at our landing place called Shabran, where my barke discharged: the goods layd on shore, and there being in my tent keeping great watch for feare of rovers, wherof there is great plenty, being field people, the governor of the said countrey named Alcan Murcy, comming unto me, entertained me very gently, unto whom giving a present, he appointed for my safe-gard forty armed men to watch & ward me, until he might have newes from the king of Shirvan. The 12 day of the same moneth newes did come from the king, with order that I should repaire unto him with all speed: and for expedition, aswell camels to the number of five and forty to cary my goods, as also horses for me and my company were in readinesse, so that the goods laden, and taking my journey from thence the said twelft day, on the 18 of the same moneth I came to a city called Shamaky, in the said countrey of Hircan, otherwise called Shir-van, and there the king hath a faire place, where my lodging being appointed, the goods were discharged: the next day being the 19 day, I was sent for to come to the king, named Obdolow-can, who kept his court at that time in the high mountaines in tents, distant from the said Shamaki twentie miles, to avoyd the injury of the heat: and the 20 day I came before his presence, who gently interteined me, and having kissed his hands, he bad me to dinner, and commanded me to sit downe not farre from him. This king did sit in a very rich pavillion, wrought with silke & golde, placed very pleasantly, upon a hill side, of six-teene fathom long, and sixe fathom broad, having before him a goodly fountaine of faire water: whereof he & his nobility did drinke, he being a prince of a meane stature, and of a fierce countenance, richly apparelled with long garments of silke, and cloth of gold, imbrodred with pearles and stone: upon his head was a tolipane with a sharpe ende standing upwards halfe a yard long, of rich cloth of golde, wrapped about with a piece of India silke of twentie yards long, wrought with golde, and on the left side of his tolipane stood a plume of fethers, set in a trunke of golde richly inameled, and set with precious stones: his eare-rings had pendants of golde a handfull long, with two great rubies of great value, set in the ends thereof: all the ground within his pavilion was covered with rich carpets, & under him-selfe was spred a square carpet wrought with silver & golde, and therupon was layd two sutable cushions. Thus the king with

his nobility sitting in his pavilion with his legs a crosse, and perceiving that it was painfull for me so to sit, his highnesse caused
a stoole to be brought in, & did will me to sit thereupon, after
my fashion. Dinner time then approaching, divers clothes were
spred upon the ground, and sundry dishes served, and set in a
ranke with divers kindes of meats, to the number of 140 dishes,
as I numbred them, which being taken away with the table
clothes, and others spred, a banket of fruits of sundry kindes,
with other banketting meates, to the number of 150 dishes, were
brought in: so that two services occupied 290 dishes, and at the
end of the sayd dinner & banket, the king said unto me, Quoshe
quelde, that is to say, Welcome: and called for a cup of water
to be drawen at a fountaine, and tasting thereof, did deliver me
the rest, demanding how I did like the same, and whether there
were so good in our countrey or not: unto whom I answered
in such sort, that he was therewith contented: then he pro-
poned unto me sundry questions, both touching religion, and
also the state of our countreys, and further questioned whether
the Emperor of Almaine, the Emperor of Russia, or the great
Turke, were of most power, with many other things too long
here to rehearse, to whom I answered as I thought most meet.
Then he demanded whether I intended to goe any further, and
the cause of my comming: unto that I answered, that I was
sent with letters from the Queenes most excellent Majesty of
England unto the great Sophy, to intreat friendship and free
passage, and for his safeconduct to be granted unto English
merchants to trade into his Segniories, with the like also to be
granted to his subjects, when they should come into our countreys, to the honour and wealth of both realmes, and commodity of both their subjects, with divers other words, which I
omit to rehearse. This sayd king much allowing this declaration
sayd, that he would not onely give me passage, but also men
to safeconduct me unto the sayd Sophy, lying from the foresayd citie of Shamaki thirtie dayes journey, up into the land of
Persia, at a castle called Casbin: so departing from the king at
that time, within three dayes after, being the foure and twentieth day of August the yere aforesaid, he sent for me againe:
unto whom I repaired in the morning, and the king not being
risen out of his bed (for his maner is, that watching in the night,
and then banketting with his women, being an hundred and

forty in number, he sleepeth most in the day) did give one commandement that I should ride on hawking with many Gentlemen of his Court, and that they should shew me so much game
and pastime as might be: which was done, and many cranes
killed. We returned from hawking about three of the clocke
at the afternoone: the king then risen, and ready to dinner, I
was invited thereunto, and approching nigh to the entring in
of his tent, and being in his sight, two gentlemen incountered
me with two garments of that countrey fashion, side, downe
to the ground, the one of silke, and the other of silke and golde,
sent unto me from the king, and after that they caused me to
put off my upper garment, being a gowne of blacke velvet
furred with Sables, they put the sayd two garments upon my
backe, and so conducted me unto the king, before whom doing
reverence, and kissing his hand, he commanded me to sit not
farre from him, and so I dined in his presence, he at that time
being very mery, and demanding of me many questions, and
amongst other, how I like the maner of their hawking. Dinner
so ended, I required his highnesse safeconduct for to depart
towards the Sophy, who dismissing me with great favour, and
appointing his Ambassadour (which returned out of Russia)
and others, to safe-conduct me, he gave me at my departure a
faire horse with all furniture, and custome free from thence
with all my goods. So I returned to Shamaki againe, where I
remained untill the sixt of October, to provide camels, horses,
and other necessaries for my sayd intended journey.

But now before I proceed further, I purpose to write something of this countrey of Hircan, now called Shirvan, with the
townes and commodities of the same. This countrey of Hircan
in times past was of great renowme, having many cities, townes,
and castles in it: and the kings thereof in time of antiquity were
of great power, able to make wars with the Sophies of Persia:
but now it is not onely otherwise (for that the cities, townes,
and castles be decayed) but also the king is subject to the sayd
Sophie (although they have their proper king) and be at the
commandement of the sayd Sophy, who conquered them not
many yeeres passed, for their diversity in religion, and caused
not onely all the nobility & gentlemen of that countrey to be
put to death, but also over and besides, rased the walles of the
cities, townes, and castles of the said realme, to the intent that

there should be no rebellion, and for their great terror, caused a turret of free stone and flints to be erected in the sayd city called Shamaki, and in a ranke of flints of the sayd turret, did set the heads of the sayd nobility and gentlemen, then executed. This city is distant from the sea side, with camels, seven dayes journey, but now the same being much decayed, & chiefly inhabited with Armenians, another city called Arrash, bordering upon the Georgians, is the chiefest and most opulent in the trade of merchandise, & thereabouts is nourished the most abundant growth of raw silke, and thither the Turks, Syrians, and other strangers do resort and trafficke. There be also divers good and necessary commodities to be provided & had in this sayd realme: viz. galles rough and smooth, cotton wooll, allome, and raw silke of the naturall growth of that countrey: besides, nere all kinde of spices and drugges, and some other commodities, which are brought thither from out of East India, but in the lesse quantity, for that they be not assured to have vent or utterance of the same: but the chiefest commodities be there, raw silks of all sorts, whereof there is great plenty. Not farre from the sayd city of Shamaki, there was an olde castle called Gullistone, now beaten downe by this Sophy, which was esteemed to be one of the strongest castles in the world, and was besieged by Alexander the great, long time before he could win it. And not farre from the sayd castle was a Nunry of sumptuous building, wherein was buried a kings daughter, named Ameleck Channa, who slew herselfe with a knife, for that her father would have forced her (she professing chastity) to have married with a king of Tartarie: upon which occasion the maidens of that countrey do resort thither once every yere to lament her death.

Also in the sayd countrey there is an high hill called Quiquifs, upon the toppe whereof (as it is commonly reported) did dwell a great Giant, named Arneoste, having upon his head two great hornes, and eares, and eyes like a Horse, and a taile like a Cow. It is further sayd, that this monster kept a passage thereby, untill there came an holy man, termed Haucoir Hamshe, a kinseman to one of the Sophies, who mounted the sayd hill, and combating with the sayd Giant, did binde not onely him in chaines, but also his woman called Lamisache with his sonne named After: for which victory they of that countrey have this holy man in great reputation, and the hill at this day (as it is bruited) savoureth so ill, that no person may come nigh unto it: but whether it be true or not, I referre it to further knowledge.

Now to returne to the discourse of the proceeding in my voyage towards the great Sophie. The 6 of October in the yeere aforesayd, I with my company departed from Shamachi aforesaid, and having journeyed threescore miles, came to a towne called Yavate, wherein the king hath a faire house, with orchards and gardens well replenished with fruits of all sorts. By this towne passeth a great river called Cor, which springeth in the mountaines of the Georgians, & passing thorow the countrey of Hircania aforesayd, falleth into the Caspian or Hircan sea, at a place betweene two ancient townes called Shabran and Bachu, situate within the realme of Hircane, and from thence issueth further, passing thorow a fruitfull countrey, inhabited with pasturing people, which dwell in the Summer season upon mountaines, and in Winter they remoove into the valleyes without resorting to townes or any other habitation: and when they remoove, they doe journey in carravans or troops of people and cattell, carrying all their wives, children and baggage upon bullocks. Now passing this wilde people ten dayes journey, comming into no towne or house, the sixteenth day of October we arrived at a citie called Ardouill, where we were lodged in an hospitall builded with faire stone, and erected by this Sophies father named Ismael, onely for the succour and lodging of strangers and other travellers, wherein all men have victuals and feeding for man and horse, for three dayes and no longer. This foresayd late prince Ismael lieth buried in a faire Meskit, with a sumptuous sepulchre in the same, which he caused to be made in his life time. This towne Ardouill is in the latitude of eight and thirtie degrees, an ancient citie in the province of Aderravgan, wherein the Princes of Persia are commonly buried: and there Alexander the great did keepe his Court when he invaded the Persians. Foure dayes journey to the Westward is the citie Tebris in olde time called Tauris, the greatest citie in Persia, but not of such trade of merchandise as it hath bene, or as others be at this time, by meane of the great invasion of the Turke, who hath conquered from the Sophie almost to the sayd citie of Tauris, which the sayd Turke once sacked, and thereby caused the Sophie to forsake the same, and to keepe his court ten dayes journey from thence, at the sayd citie of Casbin.

The 21 day we departed from Ordowil aforesayd, travelling for the most part over mountaines all in the night season, and resting in the day, being destitute of wood, and therefore were forced to use for fewell the dung of horses & camels, which we bought deare of the pasturing people. Thus passing ten dayes journey the yere aforesayd, the second day of November we arrived at the foresayd citie of Casbin, where the sayd Sophie keepeth his court, and were appointed to a lodging not farre from the kings pallace, and within two dayes after the Sophie commanded a prince called Shalli Murzey, sonne to Obdolowcan king of Shirvan aforesayd, to send for me to his house, who asked me in the name of the said Sophy how I did, and whether I were in health, and after did welcome me, and invited me to dinner, whereat I had great enterteinment, and so from thence I returned to my lodging. The next day after I sent my interpreter unto the Sophies Secretarie, declaring that I had letters directed from our most gracious Sovereigne ladie the Queenes most excellent Majestie of the Realme of England, unto the sayd Sophy, and that the cause of my comming was expressed in the same letters, desiring that at convenient time I might come into his Majesties presence, who advertising the Sophy thereof, shortly after answered me that there were great affaires in hand: which being finished, I should come before his presence, willing me in the meane time to make ready my present if I had any to deliver.

At this time, the great Turkes Ambassadour arrived foure dayes before my comming, who was sent thither to conclude a perpetuall peace betwixt the same great Turke and the Sophie, and brought with him a present in golde, and faire horses with rich furnitures, and other gifts, esteemed to be woorth forty thousand pound. And thereupon a peace was concluded with joyfull feasts, triumphs and solemnities, corroborated with strong othes, by their law of Alkaron, for either to observe the same, and to live alwayes after as sworne brethren, ayding the one the other against all princes that should warre against them, or either of them. And upon this conclusion the Sophy caused the great Turkes sonne named Baiset Soltan, a valiant

Prince (who being fled from his father unto the Sophie, had remained in his Court the space of foure yeeres) to be put to death. In which time the sayd Turkes sonne had caused mortall warres betwixt the sayd Princes, and much prevailed therein: the Turke demanded therefore his sonne to be sent unto him, & the Sophy refused thereunto to consent. But now being slaine according to the Turks will, the Sophy sent him his head for a present, not a litle desired, and acceptable to the unnaturall father. Discoursing at my first arrivall with the king of Shirvan of sundry matters, and being intertained as hath bene before declared, the sayd king named Obdolocan, demaunding whether that we of England had friendship with the Turks or not: I answered, that we never had friendship with them, and that therefore they would not suffer us to passe thorow their countrey into the Sophy his dominions, and that there is a nation named the Venetians, not farre distant from us, which are in great league with the sayd Turks, who trade into his dominions with our commodities, chiefly to barter the same for raw silks, which (as we understand) come from thence: and that if it would please the sayd Sophy and other Princes of that countrey, to suffer our merchants to trade into those dominions, and to give us pasport and safe conduct for the same, as the sayd Turke hath granted to the sayd Venetians, I doubted not but that it should grow to such a trade to the profit of them as never before had beene the like, and that they should be both furnished with our commodities, and also have utterance of theirs, although there never came Turke into their land, perswading with many other wordes for a trade to be had. This king understanding the matter liked it marveilously, saying, that he would write unto the Sophy concerning the same: as he did in very deed, assuring me that the Sophy would graunt my request, and that at my returne unto him he would give me letters of safe conduct, and priviledges. The Turks Ambassadour was not then come into the land, neither any peace hoped to be concluded, but great preparation was made for warre, which was like much to have furthered my purpose, but it chanced otherwise. For the Turks Ambassadour being arrived, and the peace concluded, the Turkish merchants there at that time present, declared to the same Ambassadour, that my comming thither (naming me by the name of Franke) would in great part destroy their trade, and that it should be good for him to perswade the Sophy not to favour me, as his Highnesse meant to observe the league and friendship with the great Turke his master, which request of the Turkish merchants the same Ambassadour earnestly preferred, and being afterwards dismissed with great honour, he departed out of the Realme with the Turks sonnes head as aforesayd, and other presents.

The 20 day of November aforesayd, I was sent for to come before the sayd Sophy, otherwise called Shaw Thomas, and about three of the clocke at afternoone I came to the Court, and in lighting from my horse at the Court gate, before my feet touched the ground, a paire of the Sophies owne shoes termed in the Persian tongue Basmackes, such as hee himselfe weareth when he ariseth in the night to pray (as his maner is) were put upon my feet, for without the same shoes I might not be suffred to tread upon his holy ground, being a Christian, and called amongst them Gower, that is, unbeleever, and uncleane: esteeming all to be infidels and Pagans which do not beleeve as they do, in their false filthie prophets, Mahomet and Murtezalli. At the sayd Court gate the things that I brought to present his Majestie with, were devided by sundry parcels to sundry servitors of the Court, to cary before me, for none of my company or servants might be suffered to enter into the Court with me, my interpreter onely excepted. Thus comming before his Majestie with such reverence as I thought meete to be used, I delivered the Queenes Majesties letters with my present, which hee accepting, demaunded of mee of what countrey of Franks I was, and what affaires I had there to doe? Unto whom I answered that I was of the famous Citie of London within the noble Realme of England, and that I was sent thither from the most excellent and gracious soveraigne Lady Elizabeth Queene of the saide Realme for to treate of friendship, and free passage of our Merchants and people, to repaire and traffique within his dominions, for to bring in our commodities, and to carry away theirs to the honour of both princes, the mutuall commoditie of both Realmes, and wealth of the Subjects, with other wordes here omitted. He then demaunded me in what language the letters were written, I answered, in the Latine, Italian and Hebrew: well said he, we have none within our Realme that understand those tongues. Whereupon I answered that such a famous and worthy prince (as hee was) wanted not people of all nations within his large dominions to interprete the same. Then he questioned with me of the state of our Countreys, and of the power of the Emperour of Almaine, king Philip, and the great Turke, and which of them was of most power: whom I answered to his contentation, not dispraysing the great Turke, their late concluded friendship considered. Then he reasoned with mee much of Religion, demaunding whether I were a Gower, that is to say, an unbeleever, or a Muselman, that is, of Mahomets lawe. Unto whom I answered, that I was neither unbeleever nor Mahometan, but a Christian. What is that, said he unto the king of the Georgians sonne, who being a Christian was fled unto the said Sophie, and he answered that a Christian was he that beleeveth in Jesus Christus, affirming him to be the Sonne of God, and the greatest Prophet. Doest thou beleeve so, said the Sophie unto me? Yea that I do, said I: Oh thou unbeleever, said he, we have no neede to have friendship with the unbeleevers, and so willed me to depart. I being glad thereof did reverence and went my way, being accompanied with many of his gentlemen and others, and after me followed a man with a Basanet of sand, sifting all the way that I had gone within the said pallace, even from the said Sophies sight unto the court gate.

Thus I repaired againe unto my lodging, and the said night Shally Murzey sonne to the king of Hircan aforesaid, who favoured me very much for that I was commended unto him from his father, willed mee not to doubt of any thing, putting mee in hope that I should have good successe with the Sophie, and good intertainment.

Thus I continued for a time, dayly resorting unto me divers gentlemen sent by the Sophie to conferre with me, especially touching the affaires of the Emperour of Russia, and to know by what way I intended to returne into my countrey, either by the way that I came, or by the way of Ormus, and so with the Portingals ships. Unto whom I answered, that I durst not returne by the way of Ormus, the Portingals and wee not being friendes, fully perceiving their meaning: for I was advertised that the saide Sophie meant to have warres with the Portingals, and would have charged mee that I had bene come for a spie to passe through his dominions unto the saide Portingals, thinking them and us to be all one people, and calling all by the name of Franks, but by the providence of God this was prevented.

After this the said Sophie conferred with his nobilitie and counsel concerning me, who perswaded that he should not entertaine me wel, neither dismisse me with letters or gifts, considering that I was a Franke, and of that nation that was enemie to the great Turke his brother, perswading that if he did otherwise, and that the newes thereof should come to the knowledge of the Turke, it should be a meane to breake their new league and friendship lately concluded: disswading further because he had no neede, neither that it was requisite for him to have friendship with unbeleevers, whose Countreys lay farre from him, and that it was best for him to send me with my letters unto the said great Turke for a present, which he was fully determined to have done at some meet time, meaning to send his Ambassadour unto the said great Turke very shortly after.

But the king of Hircanes sonne aforesaide, understanding this deliberation, sent a man in post unto his father, for to declare and impart the purpose unto him, who as a gracious prince, considering that I had passed through his dominions, and that I had journeyed for a good intent, did write to the Sophie al that which he understood of his said determination, & that it should not stand with his Majesties honour to doe mee any harme or displeasure, but rather to give mee good entertainment, seeing I was come into his land of my free will, and not by constraint, and that if hee used mee evil, there would few strangers resort into his countrey, which would bee greatly unto his hinderance, with many other perswasions: which after that the saide Sophie had well and throughly pondered and disgested (much esteeming the same king of Hircane, being one of the valiantest princes under him and his nigh kinseman) changed his determined purpose, and the twentieth of March 1562. he sent to me a rich garment of cloth of golde, and so dismissed me without any harme.

During the time that I sojourned at the sayde City of Casbin, divers merchants out of India came thither unto mee, with whom I conferred for a trade of spices: whereunto they answered that they would bring of all sorts so much as we would have, if they were sure of vent, whereof I did promise to assure them, so that I doubt not but that great abundance thereof may from time to time be there provided and had.

The same twentieth day of March I returned from the saide Citie of Casbin where I remayned all the Winter, having sent away all my Camels before, and the thirtieth day I came to the saide Citie of Ardouil, and the fifteenth of April unto Zavat aforesayd, where king Obdolowcan was at that present, who immediatly sent for me, and demaunding of me many questions, declared that if it had not bene for him, I had bene utterly cast away, and sent to the great Turke for a present by the Sophie, through the evill perswasion of his wicked counsell, that the Zieties and holy men were the chiefe and principal procurers and moovers thereof: but the Sophie himselfe ment mee much good at the first, and thought to have given me good entertainment, and so had done, had not the peace and league fortuned to have bene concluded betweene them and the great Turke. Neverthelesse, sayd he, the Sophie hath written unto me to entertaine you well, and you are welcome into my Countrey, and so he intreated mee very gently, in whose Court I remained seven dayes, and obtained of him letters of safe conductes and priviledges in your names to bee free from paying custome, which I delivered unto your servants Thomas Alcocke and George Wrenne, at their departure towards Persia for your affaires: and his highnesse did give mee two garments of silke, and so dismissed me with great favour, sending with me his Ambassadour againe unto the Emperour of Russia, and committed the chiefest secret of his affaires unto me, to declare the same unto the Emperours Majestie at my returne: and thus departing the tenth day of April, I came to the City of Shamachi, and there remayning certaine dayes for provision of Camels downe to the Sea side, I sent from thence before men to repaire my Barke, and to make her in a readinesse. And during my abode in Shammachi, there came unto me an Armenian sent from the king of Georgia, who declared the lamentable estate of the same king, that being enclosed betwixt those two cruell tyrants and mightie princes, the said great Turke and the Sophie, hee had continuall warres with them, requiring for the love of Christ and as I was a Christian, that I would send him comfort by the said Armenian, and advise how he might send his Ambassadour to the sayd Emperour of Russia, and whether I thought that he would support him or no: and with many other wordes required me to declare his necessitie unto the same Emperour at my returne: adding further that the said king would have written unto me his minde, but that hee doubted the safe passage of his messenger. Unto whom I did likewise answere by word of mouth, not onely perswading him to sende his Ambassadour to Russia, not doubting but that he should finde him most honourable and inclined to helpe him, but also I directed him his way how the sayde king might send by the Countrey of Chircassi, through the favour of Teneruk king of the sayd Countrey, whose daughter the said king had lately married. And thus dismissing the saide Armenian, within two dayes after I sent Edward Cleark your servaunt unto the Citie of Arrash, where the most store of Silkes is to be had, giving him Commission to have passed further into the saide Countrey of Georgia, and there to have repaired unto the sayde king. And after my commendations premised, and my minde declared to have pursued for safeconduct of the same Prince for our Merchants to trade into his dominions, and that obtained to have returned againe with speede. The same your servaunt journeying to the sayd Citie of Arrash, and there finding certaine Merchants Armenians, which promised to goe to the sayd City of Georgia, comming to the borders thereof, was perceived by a Captaine there, that he was a Christian, and thereupon demaunded whither he went, and understanding that he could not passe further without great suspition, answered that he came thither to buy Silkes, and shewed the king of Hircanes letters which hee had with him, and so returned backe againe, and the fifteenth of April came to Shamachi: from whence I departed the sixteene of the same moneth, and the one and twentie thereof comming to the Seaside, and finding my barke in a readinesse, I caused your goods to be laden, and there attended a faire winde.

But before I proceede any further to speake of my returne, I intend with your favours somewhat to treate of the countrey of Persia, of the great Sophie, and of his countrey, lawes and religion.

This land of Persia is great and ample, devided into many kingdomes and provinces, as Gillan, Corasan, Shirvan, and many others having divers Cities, townes and castles in the same. Every province hath his severall King, or Sultan, all in obedience to the great Sophie. The names of the chiefest Cities be these: Teveris, Casbin, Keshan, Yesse, Meskit, Heirin, Ardouill, Shamachi, Arrash with many others. The countrey for the most part toward the sea side is plaine and full of pasture, but into the land, high, full of mountaines, and sharpe. To the South it bordereth upon Arabia and the East Ocean. To the North upon the Caspian sea and the lands of Tartaria. To the East upon the provinces of India, and to the West upon the confines of Chaldea, Syria, and other the Turkes lands. All within these dominions be of the Sophies, named Shaw Thamas, sonne to Ismael Sophie. This Sophie that now raigneth is nothing valiant, although his power be great, and his people martiall: and through his pusillanimitie the Turke hath much invaded his countreys, even nigh unto the Citie of Teveris, wherein hee was wont to keepe his chiefe court. And now having forsaken the same, is chiefly resident at Casbin aforesaide, and alwayes as the said Turke pursueth him, he not being able to withstand the Turke in the fielde, trusting rather to the mountaines for his safegard, then to his fortes and castles, hath caused the same to bee rased within his dominions, and his ordinance to be molten, to the intent that his enemies pursuing him, they should not strengthen themselves with the same.

This prince is of the age of fiftie yeeres, and of a reasonable stature, having five children. His eldest sonne he keepeth captive in prison, for that he feareth him for his valiantnesse and activitie: he professeth a kinde of holynesse, and saith that hee is descended of the blood of Mahomet and Murtezalli: and although these Persians bee Mahometans, as the Turkes and Tartars bee, yet honour they this false fained Murtezalli, saying that hee was the chiefest disciple that Mahomet had, cursing and chiding dayly three other disciples that Mahomet had called Ovear, Usiran, and Abebeck, and these three did slay the saide Murtezalli, for which cause and other differences of holy men and lawes, they have had and have with the Turkes and Tartars mortall warres. To intreat of their religion at large, being more or lesse Mahomets lawe and the Alkaron, I shall not need at this present. These persons are comely and of good complexion,

proude and of good courage, esteeming themselves to bee best
of all nations, both for their religion and holinesse, which is
most erroneous, and also for all other their fashions. They be
martial, delighting in faire horses and good harnesse, soone
angrie, craftie and hard people. Thus much I have thought
good to treate of this nation, and nowe I returne to discourse
the proceeding of the rest of my voyage.

My barke being ready at the Caspian sea as aforesaide, having a faire winde, and committing our selves unto God the 30.
day of May 1563. we arrived at Astracan, having passed no
lesse dangers upon the Sea in our returne, then wee sustained
in our going foorth, and remayning at the said Astracan, untill
the tenth day of June, one hundred gunners being there admitted unto mee for my safegard up the river Volga, the
fifteenth of July I arrived at the Citie of Cazan, where the
Captaine entertained me well, and so dismissing mee, I was conducted from place to place unto the Citie of Mosco, where I
arrived the twentieth day of August 1563. in safetie, thankes
bee to God, with all such goods, merchandizes, and jewels, as
I had provided as well for the Emperours stocke and accompt,
as also of yours, all which goods I was commaunded to bring
into the Emperours treasurie before it was opened, which I did,
and delivered those parcels of wares which were for his Majesties accompt, videlicet, precious stones, and wrought silkes of
sundry colours and sortes, much to his highnesse contentation,
and the residue belonging to you, viz. Crasko, and rawe silkes,
with other merchandizes, (as by accompt appeareth) were
brought unto your house, whereof part there remained, and the
rest was laden in your shippes lately returned.

Shortly after my comming to the Mosco, I came before the
Emperours Majestie, and presented unto him the apparell given
unto me by the Sophie, whose highnesse conferred with mee
touching the princes affaires which he had committed to my
charge: and my proceedings therein it pleased him so to accept,
that they were much to his contentation, saying unto mee, I
have perceived your good service, for the which I doe thanke
you, and will recompence you for the same, wishing that I
would travell againe in such his other affaires, wherein hee was
minded to employ mee: to whom I answered, that it was to my

heartie rejoycing that my service was so acceptable unto his highnesse, acknowledging all that I had done to bee but of duetie, humbly beseeching his grace to continue his goodnesse unto your worships, and even at that instant I humbly requested his Majestie to vouchsafe to graunt unto you a newe priviledge more ample then the first, which immediately was graunted, and so I departed. And afterwards having penned a briefe note howe I meant to have the same priviledges made, I repaired dayly to the Secretary for the perfecting of the same, and obtained it under his Majesties broade seale, which at my departure from thence, I delivered unto the custody of Thomas Glover your Agent there. The copy whereof, and also of the other priviledges graunted and given by the king of Hircan, I have already delivered unto you. Sojourning all that winter at Mosco, and in the meane time having bargained with the Emperours Majestie, I sent away your servant Edward Clarke hither overland with advise, and also made preparation for sending againe into Persia in meete time of the yeere. And committing the charge thereof unto your servants Thomas Alcocke, George Wrenne, and Richard Cheinie, the 28. of June last, I departed in poste from the said Mosco, and comming to Colmogro and so downe to the Sea side, I found your ships laden and ready to depart, where I embarked my selfe in your good ship called the Swallow, the 9. of July, one thousand five hundred sixtie foure, and having passed the Seas with great and extreme dangers of losse of shippe, goods and life, the 28. day of September last (God be praised) we arrived here at London in safetie.

Thus knowing that the couragious and valiant souldier, which adventureth both fame, member and life, to serve faithfully his soveraigne, esteemeth not the perils and dangers passed (the victorie once obtained) neither for his guerdon desireth any thing more, then that his service bee well taken of him for whom he enterprised it: So I perceiving your favourable benevolence to me extended in accepting my travels in good part to your contentations, do thinke my selfe therewith in great part recompensed: beseeching Almightie God so to prosper your adventures, from time to time hereafter to be made for reaping the fruits of my travels (at your great charges, and to my no small dangers) that ye may plentifully gather in and enjoy the same, to the illustrating of the Queenes most excellent Majestie, the honour and commoditie of this her highnesse Realme, and to the ample benefit and abundant enriching of you and your succession, & posteritie for ever.

12

The first voyage of the right worshipfull and valiant
knight sir John Hawkins, sometimes treasurer of
her Majesties navie Roial, made to the
West Indies 1562

MASTER John Haukins having made divers voyages to the
Iles of the Canaries, and there by his good and upright dealing
being growen in love and favour with the people, informed himselfe amongst them by diligent inquisition, of the state of the
West India, whereof hee had received some knowledge by the
instructions of his father, but increased the same by the ad-
vertisments and reports of that people. And being amongst
other particulars assured, that Negros were very good marchandise in Hispaniola, and that store of Negros might easily bee
had upon the coast of Guinea, resolved with himselfe to make
triall thereof, and communicated that devise with his worshipfull friendes of London: namely with Sir Lionell Ducket, sir
Thomas Lodge, M. Gunson his father in law, sir William Winter, M. Bromfield, and others. All which persons liked so well
of his intention, that they became liberall contributers and adventurers in the action. For which purpose there were three
good ships immediatly provided: The one called the Salomon
of the burthen of 120. tunne, wherein M. Haukins himselfe
went as Generall: The second the Swallow of 100. tunnes,
wherein went for Captaine M. Thomas Hampton: and the third
the Jonas a barke of 40. tunnes, wherein the Master supplied
the Captaines roome: in which small fleete M. Hawkins tooke
with him not above 100. men for feare of sicknesse and other
inconveniences, whereunto men in long voyages are commonly
subject.

With this companie he put off and departed from the coast
of England in the moneth of October 1562. and in his course

touched first at Teneriffe, where hee received friendly intertainement. From thence he passed to Sierra Leona, upon the coast of Guinea, which place by the people of the countrey is called Tagarin, where he stayed some good time, and got into his possession, partly by the sworde, and partly by other meanes, to the number of 300. Negros at the least, besides other merchandises which that countrey yeeldeth. With this praye hee sayled over the Ocean sea unto the Iland of Hispaniola, and arrived first at the port of Isabella: and there hee had reasonable utterance of his English commodities, as also of some part of his Negros, trusting the Spaniards no further, then that by his owne strength he was able still to master them. From the port of Isabella he went to Puerto de Plata, where he made like sales, standing alwaies upon his guard: from thence also hee sayled to Monte Christi another port on the North side of Hispaniola, and the last place of his touching, where he had peaceable traffique, and made vent of the whole number of his Negros: for which he received in those 3. places by way of exchange such quantitie of merchandise, that hee did not onely lade his owne 3. shippes with hides, ginger, sugars, and some quantitie of pearles, but he fraighted also two other hulkes with hides and other like commodities, which hee sent into Spaine. And thus leaving the Iland, he returned and disemboqued, passing out by the Ilands of the Caycos, without further entring into the bay of Mexico, in this his first voyage to the West India. And so with prosperous successe and much gaine to himselfe and the aforesayde adventurers, he came home, and arrived in the moneth of September 1563.

13

The voyage made by M. John Hawkins Esquire, and afterward knight, Captaine of the Jesus of Lubek, one of her Majesties shippes, and Generall of the Salomon, and other two barkes going in his companie, to the coast of Guinea, and the Indies of Nova Hispania, begun in An. Dom. 1564

MASTER John Hawkins with the Jesus of Lubek, a shippe of 700. and the Salomon a shippe of 140. the Tiger a barke of 50. and the Swallow of 30. tunnes, being all well furnished with men to the number of one hundreth threescore and tenne, as also with ordinance and victuall requisite for such a voyage, departed out of Plymmouth the 18. day of October, in the yeere of our Lord 1564. with a prosperous winde: at which departing, in cutting the foresaile, a marveilous misfortune happened to one of the officers in the shippe, who by the pullie of the sheat was slaine out of hand, being a sorowfull beginning to them all. And after their setting out ten leagues to the sea, he met the same day with the Minion a ship of the Queenes Majestie, whereof was Captaine David Carlet, and also her consort the John Baptist of London, being bounde to Guinea also, who hailed one the other after the custome of the sea with certaine pieces of ordinance for joy of their meeting: which done, the Minion departed from him to seeke her other consort the Merlin of London, which was a sterne out of sight, leaving in M. Hawkins companie the John Baptist her other consort.

Thus sayling forwards on their way with a prosperous winde untill the 21. of the same moneth, at that time a great storme arose, the winde being at Northeast about nine a clocke in the night, and continued so 23. houres together, in which storme M. Hawkins lost the companie of the John Baptist aforesayd, and of his pinnesse called the Swallow, his other 3. shippes being sore beaten with a storme. The 23. day the Swallow to his no small rejoycing, came to him againe in the night, 10. leagues to the Northward of Cape Finister, he having put roomer, not being able to double the Cape, in that there rose a contrary winde at Southwest. The 25. the wind continuing contrary, hee put into a place in Galicia, called Ferroll, where hee remained five dayes, and appointed all the Masters of his shippes an order for the keeping of good companie in this manner: The small shippes to bee alwayes ahead and aweather of the Jesus, and to speake twise a day with the Jesus at least: if in the day the Ensigne bee over the poope of the Jesus, or in the night two lights, then shall all the shippes speake with her: If there bee three lights aboord the Jesus, then doeth she cast about: If the weather bee extreme, that the small shippes cannot keepe companie with the Jesus, then all to keepe companie with the Salomon, and foorthwith to repaire to the Iland of Teneriffe, to the Northward of the road of Sirroes; If any happen to any misfortune then to shew two lights, and to shoote off a piece of ordinance. If any lose companie, and come in sight againe, to make three yawes, and strike the Myson three times: Serve God daily, love one another, preserve your victuals, beware of fire, and keepe good companie.

The 26. day the Minion came in also where hee was, for the rejoycing whereof hee gave them certaine pieces of ordinance, after the courtesie of the sea for their welcome: but the Minions men had no mirth, because of their consort the Merline, whome at their departure from Master Hawkins upon the coast of England they went to seeke, and having met with her, kept companie two dayes together, and at last by misfortune of fire (through the negligence of one of their gunners) the powder in the gunners roome was set on fire, which with the first blast strooke out her poope, and therewithall lost three men, besides many sore burned (which escaped by the brigandine being at her sterne) and immediatly, to the great losse of the owners, and most horrible sight to the beholders, she sunke before their eyes.

The 20. day of the moneth M. Hawkins with his consorts and companie of the Minion, having nowe both the brigandines at her sterne, wayed anker, and set saile on their voyage, having a prosperous winde thereunto.

The fourth of November they had sight of the Iland of Madera, and the sixt day of Teneriffe, which they thought to have beene the Canarie, in that they supposed themselves to have beene to the Eastward of Teneriffe, and were not: but the Minion being three or foure leagues ahead of us, kept on her course to Teneriffe, having better sight thereof then the other had, and by that meanes they parted companie. For M. Hawkins and his companie went more to the West, upon which course having sayled a while, hee espied another Iland, which hee thought to bee Teneriffe, and being not able by meanes of the fogge upon the hils, to discerne the same, nor yet to fetch it by night, went roomer untill the morning, being the seventh of November, which as yet hee could not discerne, but sayled along the coast the space of two houres, to perceive some certaine marke of Teneriffe, and found no likelyhood thereof at all, accompting that to bee, as it was in deede, the Ile of Palmes: and so sayling forwards, espied another Iland called Gomera, and also Teneriffe, with the which hee made, and sayling all night, came in the morning the next day to the port of Adecia, where he found his pinnesse which had departed from him the sixt of the moneth, being in the weather of him, and espying the pike of Teneriffe all a high, bare thither. At his arrivall somewhat before hee came to anker, hee hoysed out his shippes pinnesse rowing a shoare, intending to have sent one with a letter to Peter de ponte, one of the governours of the Iland, who dwelt a league from the shoare: but as hee pretended to have landed, suddenly there appeared upon the two points of the roade, men levelling of bases and harguebuzes to them, with divers others to the number of fourescore, with halberds, pikes, swordes and targets, which happened so contrary to his expectation, that it did greatly amaze him, and the more, because hee was nowe in their danger, not knowing well howe to avoyde it without some mischiefe. Wherefore hee determined to call to them for the better appeasing of the matter, declaring his name, and professing himselfe to bee an especiall friend to Peter de ponte, and that he had sundry things for him which he greatly desired. And in the meane time, while hee was thus talking with them, whereby hee made them to holde their hands, hee willed the marriners to rowe away, so that at last he gat out of their danger: and then asking for Peter de ponte, one of his sonnes being Sennor Nicolas de Ponte, came forth, whom hee perceiving, desired to put his men aside, and hee himselfe would leape a shoare and commune with him, which they did: so that after communication had betweene them of sundry things, and of the feare they both had, master Hawkins desired to have certaine necessaries provided for him. In the meane space, while these things were providing, hee trimmed the maine mast of the Jesus which in the storme afore-sayd was sprung: here he sojourned 7. dayes, refreshing him-selfe and his men. In the which time Peter de ponte dwelling at S. Cruz, a citie 20. leagues off, came to him, and gave him as gentle intertainment as if he had bene his owne brother. To speake somewhat of these Ilands, being called in olde time Insulæ fortunatæ, by the meanes of the flourishing thereof, the fruitfulnesse of them doeth surely exceede farre all other that I have heard of: for they make wine better then any in Spaine, they have grapes of such bignesse, that they may bee compared to damsons, and in taste inferiour to none: for sugar, suckets, raisins of the Sunne, and many other fruits, abundance: for rosine & raw silke, there is great store, they want neither corne, pullets, cattell, nor yet wilde foule: they have many Camels also, which being young, are eaten of the people for victuals, and being olde, they are used for caryage of necessaries: whose propertie is as hee is taught to kneele at the taking of his loade, and unlading againe: his nature is to ingender backward con-trary to other beastes: of understanding very good, but of shape very deformed, with a little bellie, long misshapen legges, and feete very broad of flesh, without a hoofe, all whole, saving the great toe, a backe bearing up like a molehill, a large and thin necke, with a little head, with a bunch of hard flesh, which nature hath given him in his breast to leane upon. This beast liveth hardly, and is contented with strawe and stubble, but of force strong, being well able to carrie 500. weight. In one of these Ilands called Fierro, there is by the reports of the inhabi-tants, a certaine tree that raineth continually, by the dropping whereof the inhabitants and cattell are satisfied with water, for other water have they none in all the Iland. And it raineth in such abundance, that it were incredible unto a man to beleeve such a vertue to bee in a tree, but it is knowen to be a divine matter, and a thing ordeined by God, at whose power therein wee ought not to marvell, seeing he did by his providence as we read in the Scriptures, when the children of Israel were going into the land of promise, feede them with Manna from heaven, for the space of 40. yeeres. Of the trees aforesaid wee saw in Guinie many, being of great height, dropping continually, but not so abundantly as the other, because the leaves are narrower, and are like the leaves of a peare tree. About these Ilands are certaine flitting Ilands, which have beene oftentimes seene, and when men approched neere them, they vanished: as the like hath bene of these Ilands nowe knowen by the report of the inhabitants, which were not found of long time one after the other: and therefore it should seeme hee is not yet borne to whom God hath appoynted the finding of them. In this Iland of Teneriffe there is a hill called The Pike, because it is piked, which is in heigth by their reports twentie leagues, having both winter and summer abundance of snowe in the top of it: this Pike may bee seene in a cleere day fiftie leagues off, but it sheweth as though it were a blacke cloude a great heigth in the element. I have heard of none to be compared with this in heigth, but in the Indias I have seene many, and in my judgement not inferiour to the Pike, and so the Spaniards write.

The 15. of November at night we departed from Teneriffe, and the 20. of the same wee had sight of ten Caravels, that were fishing at sea, with whome we would have spoken, but they fearing us, fled into a place of Barbarie, called Cape de las Barbas.

The twentieth, the ships pinnesse with two men in her, sayling by the ship, was overthrowen by the oversight of them that went in her, the winde being so great, that before they were espied, and the ship had cast about for them, she was driven half a league to leeward of the pinnesse, and had lost sight of her, so that there was small hope of recoverie, had not Gods helpe and the Captaines deligence bene, who having wel marked which way the pinnesse was by the Sunne, appointed 24 of the lustiest rowers in the great boate, to rowe to the wind-wardes, and so recovered, contrary to all mens expectations, both the pinnesse and the men sitting upon the keele of her.

The 25 he came to Cape Blanco, which is upon the coast of Africa, and a place where the Portugals do ride, that fish there in the moneth of November especially, and is a very good place of fishing, for Pargoes, Mullet, and Dogge fish. In this place the Portugals have no holde for their defence, but have rescue of the Barbarians, whom they entertaine as their souldiers, for the time of their being there and for their fishing upon that coast of Africa, doe pay a certaine tribute to the king of the Moores. The people of that part of Africa are tawnie, having long haire without any apparell, saving before their privie members. Their weapons in warres are bowes and arrowes.

The 26 we departed from S. Avis Baye, within Cape Blanco, where we refreshed our selves with fish, and other necessaries: and the 29 wee came to Cape Verde, which lieth in 14 degrees, and a halfe. These people are all blacke, and are called Negros, without any apparell, saving before their privities: of stature goodly men, and well liking by reason of their food, which passeth all other Guyneans for kine, goats, pullin, rise, fruits, and fish. Here wee tooke fishes with heads like conies, and teeth nothing varying, of a jolly thickenesse, but not past a foote long, and is not to be eaten without flaying or cutting off his head. To speake somewhat of the sundry sortes of these Guyneans: the people of Cape Verde are called Leophares, and counted the goodliest men of all other, saving the Congoes, which do inhabite on this side the cape de Buena Esperança. These Leophares have warres against the Ieloffes, which are borderers by them: their weapons are bowes and arrowes, targets, and short daggers, darts also, but varying from other Negros: for whereas the other use a long dart to fight with in their hands, they cary five or sixe small ones a peece, which they cast with. These men also are more civill then any other, because of their dayly trafficke with the Frenchmen, and are of nature very gentle and loving: for while we were there, we tooke in a Frenchman, who was one of the 19 that going to Brasile, in a Barke of Diepe, of 60 tunnes, and being a sea boord of Cape Verde, 200 leagues, the plankes of their Barke with a sea brake out upon them so suddenly, that much a doe they had to save themselves in their boats: but by Gods providence, the wind being Westerly, which is rarely seene there, they got to the shore, to the Isle Brava, and in great penurie gotte to Cape Verde, where they remained sixe weekes, and had meate and drinke of the same people. The said Frenchman having forsaken his fellowes, which were three leagues off from the shores, and wandring with the Negros too and fro, fortuned to come to the waters side: and communing with certaine of his countreymen, which were in our ship, by their perswasions came away with us: but his entertainement amongst them was such, that he desired it not: but through the importunate request of his Countreymen, consented at the last. Here we stayed but one night, and part of the day: for the 7 of December wee came away, in that pretending to have taken Negros there perforce, the Mynions men gave them there to understand of our comming, and our pretence, wherefore they did avoyde the snares we had layd for them.

The 8 of December wee ankered by a small Island called Alcatrarsa, wherein at our going a shore, we found nothing but sea-birds, as we call them Ganets, but by the Portugals, called Alcatrarses, who for that cause gave the said Island the same name. Herein halfe of our boates were laden with yong and olde fowle, who not being used to the sight of men, flew so about us, that we stroke them downe with poles. In this place the two shippes riding, the two Barkes, with their boates, went into an Island of the Sapies, called La Formio, to see if they could take any of them, and there landed to the number of 80 in armour, and espying certaine made to them, but they fled in such order into the woods, that it booted them not to follow: so going on their way forward till they came to a river, which they could not passe over, they espied on the otherside two men, who with their bowes and arrowes shot terribly at them. Whereupon we discharged certaine harquebuzes to them againe, but the ignorant people wayed it not, because they knewe not the danger thereof: but used a marveilous crying in their fight with leaping and turning their tayles, that it was most strange to see, and gave us great pleasure to beholde them. At the last, one being hurt with a harquebuz upon the thigh, looked upon his wound and wist not howe it came, because hee could not see the pellet. Here Master Hawkins perceiving no good to be done amongst them, because we could not finde their townes, and also not knowing how to goe into Rio grande, for want of a Pilote, which was the very occasion of our comming thither: and finding so many sholes, feared with our great ships to goe in, and therefore departed on our pretended way to the Idols.

The 10 of December, we had a Northeast winde, with raine and storme, which weather continuing two dayes together, was the occasion that the Salomon, and Tygre loste our companie: for whereas the Jesus, and pinnesse ankered at one of the Islands called Sambula, the twelfth day, the Salomon and Tygre came not thither till the 14. In this Island we stayed certaine daies, going every day on shore to take the Inhabitants, with burning and spoiling their townes, who before were Sapies, and were conquered by the Samboses, Inhabitants beyond Sierra Leona. These Samboses had inhabited there three yeres before our comming thither, and in so short space have so planted the ground, that they had great plentie of Mil, Rise, Rootes, Pompions, Pullin, goates, of small frye dried, every house full of the Countrey fruite planted by Gods providence, as Palmito trees, fruites like dates, and sundry other in no place in all that Countrey so aboundantly, whereby they lived more deliciously then other. These inhabitants have diverse of the Sapies, which they tooke in the warres as their slaves, whome onely they kept to till the ground, in that they neither have the knowledge thereof, nor yet will worke themselves, of whome wee tooke many in that place, but of the Samboses none at all, for they fled into the maine. All the Samboses have white teeth as we have, farre unlike to the Sapies which doe inhabite about Rio grande, for their teeth are all filed, which they doe for a braverie, to set out themselves, and doe jagge their flesh, both legges, armes, and bodies, as workemanlike, as a Jerkinmaker with us pinketh a jerkin. These Sapies be more civill then the Samboses: for whereas the Samboses live most by the spoile of their enemies, both in taking their victuals, and eating them also. The Sapies doe not eate mans flesh, unlesse in the warre they be driven by necessitie thereunto, which they have not used but by the example of the Samboses, but live onely with fruites, and cattell, whereof they have great store. This plentie is the occasion that the Sapies desire not warre, except they be therunto provoked by the invasions of the Samboses, whereas the Samboses for want of foode are inforced thereunto, and therefore are not woont onely to take them that they kill, but also keepe those that they take, untill such time as they want meate, and then they kill them. There is also another occasion that provoketh the Samboses to warre against the Sapies which is for covetousnes of their riches. For whereas the Sapies have an order to burie their dead in certaine places appointed for that purpose, with their golde about them, the Samboses digge up the ground, to have the same treasure: for the Samboses have not the like store of golde, that the Sapies have. In this Island of Sambula we found about 50 boates called Almadyes, or Canoas, which are made of one peece of wood, digged out like a trough but of a good proportion, being about 8 yards long, and one in breadth, having a beakhead and a sterne very proportionably made, and on the out side artifically carved, and painted red and blewe: they are able to cary twenty or thirty men, but they are about the coast able to cary threescore and upward. In these canoas they rowe standing upright, with an oare somewhat longer then a man, the ende whereof is made about the breadth and length of a mans hand, of the largest sort. They row very swift, and in some of them foure rowers and one to steere make as much way, as a paire of oares in the Thames of London.

Their Townes are pretily divided with a maine streete at the entring in, that goeth thorough their Towne, and another overthwart street, which maketh their townes crosse wayes: their houses are built in a ranke very orderly in the face of the street, and they are made round, like a dovecote, with stakes set full of Palmito leaves, in stead of a wall: they are not much more then a fathome large, and two of heigth, & thatched with Palmito leaves very close, other some with reede, and over the roofe thereof, for the better garnishing of the same, there is a round bundle of reede, pretily contrived like a louer: in the inner part they make a loft of stickes, whereupon they lay all their provision of victuals: a place they reserve at their enterance for the kitchin, and the place they lie in is devided with certaine mattes artifically made with the rine of Palmito trees: their bedsteades are of small staves layd along, and raysed a foote from the ground, upon which is layde a matte, and another upon them when they list: for other covering they have none. In the middle of the towne there is a house larger and higher then the other, but in forme alike, adjoyning unto the which there is a place made of foure good stancions of woode, and a round roofe over it, the grounde also raised round with claye a foote high, upon the which floore were strawed many fine mats: this is the Consultation-house, the like whereof is in all Townes, as the Portugals affirme: in which place, when they sitte in Counsell the King or Captaine sitteth in the midst, and the Elders upon the floore by him: (for they give reverence to their Elders) and the common sorte sitte round about them. There they sitte to examine matters of theft, which if a man be taken with, to steale but a Portugal cloth from another, hee is sold to the Portugals for a slave. They consult also, and take order what time they shall goe to warres: and as it is certainely reported by the Portugals, they take order in gathering of the fruites in the season of the yeere, and also of Palmito wine, which is gathered by a hole cut in the top of a tree, and a gourde set for the receiving thereof, which falleth in by droppes, and yeeldeth fresh wine againe within a moneth, and this devided part and portion-like to every man, by the judgement of the Captaine and Elders, every man holdeth himselfe contented: and this surely I judge to be a very good order: for otherwise, whereas scarsitie of Palmito is, every man would have the same, which might breed great strife: but of such things, as every man doeth plant for himselfe, the sower thereof reapeth it to his owne use, so that nothing is common, but that which is unset by mans hands. In their houses there is more common passage of Lizardes like Evats, and other greater, of blacke and blew colour, of neere a foote long, besides their tailes, then there is with us of Mise in great houses. The Sapies and Samboses also use in their warres bowes, and arrowes made of reedes, with heads of yron poysoned with the juyce of a Cucumber, whereof I had many in my handes. In their battels they have target-men, with broad wicker targets, and darts with heades at both endes, of yron, the one in forme of a two edged sworde, a foote and an halfe long, and at the other ende, the yron long of the same length made to counterpease it, that in casting it might flie level, rather then for any other purpose as I can judge. And when they espie the enemie, the Captaine to cheere his men, cryeth Hungry, and they answere Heygre, and with that every man placeth himselfe in order, for about every target man three bowemen will cover themselves, and shoote as they see advantage: and when they give the onset, they make such terrible cryes, that they may bee heard two miles off. For their beliefe, I can heare of none that they have, but in such as they themselves imagine to see in their dreames, and so worshippe the pictures, whereof wee sawe some like unto devils. In this Island aforesayde wee sojourned unto the one and twentieth of December, where having taken certaine Negros, and asmuch of their fruites, rise, and mill, as we could well cary away, (whereof there was such store, that wee might have laden one of our Barkes therewith) wee departed, and at our departure divers of our men being desirous to goe on shore, to fetch Pompions, which having prooved, they found to bee very good, certaine of the Tygres men went also, amongst the which there was a Carpenter, a yong man, who with his fellowes having fet many, and caryed them downe to their boates, as they were ready to depart, desired his fellow to tary while he might goe up to fetch a few which he had layed by for him selfe, who being more licorous then circumspect, went up without weapon, and as he went up alone, possibly being marked of the Negros that were upon the trees, espying him what hee did, perceaving him to be alone, and without weapon, dogged him, and finding him occupyed in binding his Pompions together, came behinde him, overthrowing him and straight cutte his throate, as hee afterwardes was found by his fellowes, who came to the place for him, and there found him naked.

The two and twentieth the Captaine went into the River, called Callowsa, with the two Barkes, and the Johns Pinnesse, and the Salomons boate, leaving at anker in the Rivers mouth the two shippes, the River being twenty leagues in, where the Portugals roade: hee came thither the five and twentieth, and dispatched his businesse, and so returned with two Caravels, loaden with Negros.

The 27. the Captaine was advertised by the Portugals of a towne of the Negros called Bymba, being in the way as they returned, where was not onely great quantitie of golde, but also that there were not above fortie men, and an hundred women and children in the Towne, so that if hee would give the adventure upon the same, hee might gette an hundreth slaves: with the which tydings hee being gladde, because the Portugals

shoulde not thinke him to bee of so base a courage, but that
hee durst give them that, and greater attempts: and being
thereunto also the more provoked with the prosperous successe
hee had in other Islands adjacent, where he had put them all
to flight, and taken in one boate twentie together, determined
to stay before the Towne three or foure houres, to see what
hee could doe: and thereupon prepared his men in armour
and weapon together, to the number of fortie men well appointed, having to their guides certaine Portugals, in a boat,
who brought some of them to their death: wee landing boat
after boat, and divers of our men scattering themselves, contrary to the Captaines will, by one or two in a company, for
the hope that they had to finde golde in their houses, ransacking
the same, in the meane time the Negros came upon them, and
hurte many being thus scattered, whereas if five or sixe had
bene together, they had bene able, as their companions did, to
give the overthrow to 40 of them, and being driven downe
to take their boates, were followed so hardly by a route of
Negros, who by that tooke courage to pursue them to their
boates, that not onely some of them, but others standing on
shore, not looking for any such matter by meanes that the
Negros did flee at the first, and our companie remained in the
towne, were suddenly so set upon that some with great hurt
recovered their boates; othersome not able to recover the same,
tooke the water, and perished by meanes of the oaze. While
this was doing, the Captaine who with a dosen men, went
through the towne, returned, finding 200 Negros at the waters
side, shooting at them in the boates, and cutting them in pieces
which were drowned in the water, at whose comming, they
ranne all away: so he entred his boates, and before he could
put off from the shore, they returned againe, and shot very
fiercely and hurt divers of them. Thus wee returned backe some
what discomforted, although the Captaine in a singular wise
maner caried himselfe, with countenance very cheerefull out-
wardly, as though hee did litle weigh the death of his men, nor
yet the great hurt of the rest, although his heart inwardly was
broken in pieces for it; done to this ende, that the Portugals
being with him, should not presume to resist against him, nor
take occasion to put him to further displeasure or hinderance
for the death of our men: having gotten by our going ten

Negros, and lost seven of our best men, whereof M. Field Captaine of the Salomon, was one, and we had 27 of our men
hurt. In the same houre while this was doing, there happened
at the same instant, a marveilous miracle to them in the shippes,
who road ten leagues to sea-ward, by many sharkes or Tibur-
ons, who came about the ships: among which, one was taken
by the Jesus, and foure by the Salomon, and one very sore
hurt escaped: and so it fell out of our men, whereof one of
the Jesus men, and foure of the Salomons were killed, and
the fift having twentie wounds was rescued, and scaped with
much adoe.

The 28 they came to their ships, the Jesus, and the Salomon,
and the 30 departed from thence to Taggarin.

The first of January the two barkes, and both the boates
forsooke the ships, and went into a river called the Casserroes,
and the 6 having dispatched their businesse, the two barkes returned, and came to Taggarin, where the two ships were at
anker. Not two dayes after the comming of the two ships
thither, they put their water caske a shore, and filled it with
water, to season the same, thinking to have filled it with fresh
water afterward: and while their men were some on shore, and
some at their boates, the Negros set upon them in the boates,
and hurt divers of them, and came to the caskes, and cut of
the hoopes of twelve buts, which lost us 4 or 5 dayes time,
besides great want we had of the same: sojourning at Taggarin,
the Swallow went up the river about her trafficke, where they
saw great townes of the Negros, and Canoas, that had threescore men in a piece: there they understood by the Portugals,
of a great battell betweene them of Sierra Leona side, and them
of Taggarin: they of Sierra Leona, had prepared three hundred
Canoas to invade the other. The time was appointed not past
six dayes after our departure from thence, which we would
have seene, to the intent we might have taken some of them,
had it not bene for the death and sickenesse of our men, which
came by the contagiousnes of the place, which made us to make
hast away.

The 18 of Januarie at night, wee departed from Taggarin,
being bound for the West Indies, before which departure certaine of the Salomons men went on shore to fill water in the
night, and as they came on shore with their boat being ready

to leape on land, one of them espied an Negro in a white coate, standing upon a rocke, being ready to have received them when they came on shore, having in sight of his fellowes also eight or nine, some in one place leaping out, and some in another, but they hid themselves streight againe: whereupon our men doubting they had bene a great companie, and sought to have taken them at more advantage, as God would, departed to their ships, not thinking there had bene such a mischiefe pretended toward them, as then was in deede. Which the next day we understood of a Portugal that came downe to us, who had trafficked with the Negros, by whom hee understood, that the king of Sierra Leona had made all the power hee could, to take some of us, partly for the desire he had to see what kinde of people we were, that had spoiled his people at the Idols, whereof he had newes before our comming, and as I judge also, upon other occasions provoked by the Tangomangos, but sure we were that the armie was come downe, by meanes that in the evening wee saw such a monstrous fire, made by the watring place, that before was not seene, which fire is the only marke for the Tangomangos to know where their armie is alwayes. If these men had come downe in the evening, they had done us great displeasure, for that wee were on shore filling water: but God, who worketh all things for the best, would not have it so, and by him we escaped without danger, his name be praysed for it.

The 29 of this same moneth we departed with all our shippes from Sierra Leona, towardes the West Indies, and for the space of eighteene dayes, we were becalmed, having nowe and then contrary windes, and some Ternados, amongst the same calme, which happened to us very ill, beeing but reasonably watered, for so great a companie of Negros, and our selves, which pinched us all, and that which was worst, put us in such feare that many never thought to have reached to the Indies, without great death of Negros, and of themselves: but the Almightie God, who never suffereth his elect to perish, sent us the sixteenth of Februarie, the ordinary Brise, which is the Northwest winde, which never left us, till wee came to an Island of the Canybals, called Dominica, where wee arrived the ninth of March, upon a Saturday: and because it was the most desolate place in all the Island, we could see no Canybals, but some of their houses where they dwelled, and as it should seeme forsooke the place for want of fresh water, for wee could finde none there but raine water, and such as fell from the hilles, and remained as a puddle in the dale, whereof wee filled for our Negros. The Canybals of that Island, and also others adjacent are the most desperate warriers that are in the Indies, by the Spaniardes report, who are never able to conquer them, and they are molested by them not a little, when they are driven to water there in any of those Islands: of very late, not two moneths past, in the said Island, a Caravel being driven to water, was in the night sette upon by the inhabitants, who cutte their cable in the halser, whereby they were driven a shore, and so taken by them, and eaten. The greene Dragon of Newhaven, whereof was Captaine one Bontemps, in March also, came to one of those Islands, called Granada, and being driven to water, could not doe the same for the Canybals, who fought with him very desperately two dayes. For our part also, if we had not lighted upon the desertest place in all that Island, wee could not have missed, but should have bene greatly troubled by them, by all the Spaniards reports, who make them devils in respect of me.

The tenth day at night, we departed from thence, and the fifteenth had sight of nine Islands, called the Testigos: and the sixteenth of an Island, called Margarita, where wee were entertayned by the Alcalde, and had both Beeves and sheepe given us, for the refreshing of our men: but the Governour of the Island, would neither come to speake with our Captaine, neither yet give him any licence to trafficke: and to displease us the more, whereas we had hired a Pilote to have gone with us, they would not onely not suffer him to goe with us, but also sent word by a Caravel out of hand, to Santo Domingo, to the Viceroy, who doeth represent the kings person, of our arrivall in those partes, which had like to have turned us to great displeasure, by the meanes that the same Vice-roy did send word to Cape de la Vela, and to other places along the coast, commanding them that by the vertue of his authoritie, no man should trafficke with us, but should resist us with all the force they could. In this Island, notwithstanding that wee were not within foure leagues of the Towne, yet were they so afraid, that not onely the Governour himselfe, but also all the inhabitants forsooke their Towne, assembling all the Indians to them and fled into the mountaines, as wee were partly certified, and also sawe the experience our selves, by some of the Indians comming to see us who by three Spaniards a horsebacke passing hard by us, went unto the Indians, having every one of them their bowes, and arrowes, procuring them away, who before were conversant with us.

Here perceiving no trafficke to be had with them, nor yet water for the refreshing of our men, we were driven to depart the twentieth day, and the 2 and twentieth we came to a place in the maine called Cumana, whither the Captaine going in his Pinnisse, spake with certaine Spaniards, of whom he demanded trafficke, but they made him answere, they were but souldiers newely come thither, and were not able to by one Negro: whereupon hee asked for a watring place, and they pointed him a place two leagues off, called Santa Fè, where we found marveilous goodly watering, and commodious for the taking in thereof: for that the fresh water came into the Sea, and so our shippes had aboord the shore twentie fathome water. Neere about this place, inhabited certaine Indians, who the next day after we came thither, came down to us, presenting mill and cakes of breade, which they had made of a kinde of corne called Maiz, in bignesse of a pease, the eare whereof is much like to a teasell, but a spanne in length, having thereof a number of granes. Also they brought down to us Hennes, Potatoes and Pines, which we bought for beades, pewter whistles, glasses, knives, and other trifles.

These Potatoes be the most delicate rootes that may be eaten, and doe farre exceed our passeneps or carets. Their pines be of the bignes of two fists, the outside whereof is of the making of a pine-apple, but it is soft like the rinde of a Cucomber, and the inside eateth like an apple, but it is more delicious then any sweet apple sugred. These Indians being of colour tawnie like an Olive, having every one of them both men and women, haire all blacke, and no other colour, the women wearing the same hanging downe to their shoulders, and the men rounded, and without beards, neither men nor women suffering any haire to growe in any part of their body, but dayly pull it off as it groweth. They goe all naked, the men covering no part of their body but their yard, upon the which they weare a gourd or piece of cane, made fast with a thrid about their loynes, leaving the other parts of their members uncovered, whereof they take no shame. The women also are uncovered, saving with a cloth which they weare a hand-breath, wherewith they cover their privities both before and behind. These people be very small feeders, for travelling they cary but two small bottels of gourdes, wherein they put in one the juice of Sorrell whereof they have great store, and in the other flowre of their Maiz, which being moist, they eate, taking sometime of the other. These men cary every man his bowe and arrowes, whereof some arrowes are poisoned for warres, which they keepe in a Cane together, which Cane is of the bignesse of a mans arme, other some with broad heades of iron wherewith they stricke fish in the water: the experience whereof we saw not once nor twise, but dayly for the time we taried there, for they are so good archers that the Spaniards for feare thereof arme themselves and their horses with quilted canvas of two ynches thicke, and leave no place of their body open to their enemies, saving their eyes which they may not hide, and yet oftentimes are they hit in that so small a scantling: their poyson is of such a force, that a man being stricken therewith dyeth within foure and twentie howers, as the Spaniards do affirme, & in my judgement it is like there can be no stronger poyson as they make it, using thereunto apples which are very faire and red of colour, but are a strong poyson, with the which together with venemous Bats, Vipers, Adders and other serpents, they make a medley, and therewith anoint the same.

The Indian women delight not when they are yong in bearing of children, because it maketh them have hanging breastes which they account to bee great deforming in them, and upon that occasion while they bee yong, they destroy their seede, saying, that it is fittest for olde women. Moreover, when they are delivered of childe, they goe straight to washe themselves, without making any further ceremonie for it, not lying in bed as our women doe. The beds which they have are made of Gossopine cotton, and wrought artificially of divers colours, which they cary about with them when they travell, and making the same fast to two trees, lie therein they and their women. The people be surely gentle and tractable, and such as desire to live peaceably, or els had it bene unpossible for the Spaniards to have conquered them as they did, and the more to live now peaceably, they being so many in number, and the Spaniards so few.

From hence we departed the eight and twentie, and the next day we passed betweene the maine land, and the Island called Tortuga, a very lowe Island, in the yeere of our Lorde God one thousande five hundred sixty five aforesaide, and sayled along the coast untill the first of Apiill, at which time the Captaine sayled along in the Jesus pinnesse to discerne the coast, and saw many Caribes on shore, and some also in their Canoas, which made tokens unto him of friendship, and shewed him golde, meaning thereby that they would trafficke for wares. Whereupon he stayed to see the maners of them, and so for two or three trifles they gave such things as they had about them, and departed: but the Caribes were very importunate to have them come on shore, which if it had not bene for want of wares to trafficke with them, he would not have denyed them, because the Indians which we saw before were very gentle people, and such as do no man hurt. But as God would have it, hee wanted that thing, which if hee had had, would have bene his confusion: for these were no such kinde of people as wee tooke them to bee, but more devilish a thousand partes and are eaters and devourers of any man they can catch, as it was afterwards declared unto us at Burboroata, by a Caravel comming out of Spaine with certaine souldiers, and a Captaine generall sent by the king for those Eastward parts of the Indians, who sayling along in his pinnesse, as our Captaine did to descry the coast, was by the Caribes called a shoore with sundry tokens made to him of friendshippe, and golde shewed as though they desired trafficke, with the which the Spaniard being mooved, suspecting no deceite at all, went ashore amongst them: who was no sooner ashore, but with foure or five more was taken, the rest of his company being invaded by them, saved themselves by flight, but they that were taken, paied their ransome with their lives, and were presently eaten. And this is their practise to toll with their golde the ignorant to their snares: they are bloodsuckers both of Spaniards, Indians, and all that light in their laps, not sparing their owne countreymen if they can conveniently come by them. Their policie in fight with the Spaniards is marveilous: for they chuse for their refuge the mountaines and woodes where the Spaniards with their horses cannot follow them, and if they fortune to be met in the plaine where one horseman may over-runne 100. of them, they have a devise of late practised by them to pitch stakes of wood in the ground, and also small iron pikes to mischiefe their horses, wherein they shew themselves politique warriers. They have more abundance of golde then all the Spaniards have, and live upon the mountaines where the Mines are in such number, that the Spaniards have much adoe to get any of them from them, and yet sometimes by assembling a great number of them, which happeneth once in two yeeres, they get a piece from them, which afterwards they keepe sure ynough.

Thus having escaped the danger of them, wee kept our course along the coast, and came the third of April to a Towne called Burboroata, where his ships came to an ancker, and hee him-selfe went a shore to speake with the Spaniards, to whom hee declared himselfe to be an Englishman, and came thither to trade with them by the way of marchandize, and therefore re-quired licence for the same. Unto whom they made answere, that they were forbidden by the king to trafique with any forren nation, upon penaltie to forfeit their goods, therfore they de-sired him not to molest them any further, but to depart as he came, for other comfort he might not looke for at their handes, because they were subjects and might not goe beyond the law. But hee replied that his necessitie was such, as he might not so do: for being in one of the Queens Armadas of England, and having many souldiours in them, hee had neede both of some refreshing for them, and of victuals, and of money also, without the which hee coulde not depart, and with much other talke perswaded them not to feare any dishonest part of his behalfe towards them, for neither would hee commit any such thing to the dishonour of his prince, not yet for his honest reputation and estimation, unlesse hee were too rigorously dealt withall, which hee hoped not to finde at their handes, in that it should as well redound to their profite as his owne, and also hee thought they might doe it without danger, because their princes were in amitie one with another, and for our parts wee had free trafique in Spain and Flanders, which are in his dominions, and therefore he knew no reason why he should not have the like in all his dominions. To the which the Spaniards

made answere, that it lay not in them to give any licence, for
that they had a governour to whom the government of those
parts was committed, but if they would stay tenne dayes, they
would send to their governour who was threescore leagues off,
and would returne answere within the space appointed, of his
minde.

In the meane time they were contented hee should bring his
ships into harbour, and there they would deliver him any victuals he would require. Whereupon the fourth day we went
in, where being one day and receiving all things according to
promise, the Captaine advised himselfe, that to remaine there
tenne dayes idle, spending victuals and mens wages, and perhaps in the ende receive no good answere from the governour,
it were meere follie, and therefore determined to make request
to have licence for the sale of certaine leane and sicke Negros
which hee had in his shippe like to die upon his hands if he
kept them ten dayes, having little or no refreshing for them,
whereas other men having them, they would bee recovered
well ynough. And this request hee was forced to make, because
he had not otherwise wherewith to pay for victuals & for necessaries which he should take: which request being put in writing
and presented, the officers and towne-dwellers assembled together, and finding his request so reasonable, granted him licence for thirtie Negros, which afterwards they caused the officers to view, to the intent they should graunt to nothing but
that were very reasonable, for feare of answering thereunto
afterwards. This being past, our Captaine according to their licence, thought to have made sale, but the day past and none
came to buy, who before made shewe that they had great neede
of them, and therefore wist not what to surmise of them,
whether they went about to prolong the time of the Governour
his answere because they would keepe themselves blamelesse,
or for any other pollicie hee knew not, and for that purpose
sent them worde, marveiling what the matter was that none
came to buy them. They answered, because they had granted
licence onely to the poore to buy those Negros of small price,
and their money was not so ready as other mens of more
wealth. More then that, as soone as ever they sawe the shippes,
they conveyed away their money by their wives that went into
the mountaines for feare, & were not yet returned, & yet asked

two dayes to seeke their wives and fetch their money. Notwithstanding, the next day divers of them came to cheapen, but
could not agree of price, because they thought the price too
high. Whereupon the Captaine perceiving they went about to
bring downe the price, and meant to buy, and would not confesse if hee had licence, that he might sell at any reasonable
rate, as they were worth in other places, did send for the principals of the Towne, and made a shewe hee would depart, declaring himselfe to be very sory that he had so much troubled
them, and also that he had sent for the governour to come
downe, seeing nowe his pretence was to depart, whereat they
marveiled much, and asked him what cause mooved him thereunto, seeing by their working he was in possibilitie to have his
licence.

To the which he replied, that it was not onely a licence that
he sought, but profit, which he perceived was not there to bee
had, and therefore would seeke further, and withall shewed
him his writings what he payed for his Negros, declaring also
the great charge he was at in his shipping, and mens wages,
and therefore to countervaile his charges, hee must sell his
Negros for a greater price then they offered. So they doubting
his departure, put him in comfort to sell better there then in
any other place. And if it fell out that he had no licence that
he should not loose his labour in tarying, for they would buy
without licence. Whereupon, the Captaine being put in comfort, promised them to stay, so that hee might make sale of his
leane Negros, which they granted unto. And the next day did
sell some of them, who having bought and payed for them,
thinking to have had a discharge of the Customer, for the custome of the Negros, being the Kings duetie, they gave it away
to the poore for Gods sake, and did refuse to give the discharge
in writing, and the poore not trusting their wordes, for feare,
least hereafter it might bee demaunded of them, did refraine
from buying any more, so that nothing else was done untill the
Governours comming downe, which was the fourteenth day,
and then the Captaine made petition, declaring that hee was
come thither in a shippe of the Queenes Majesties of England,
being bound to Guinie, and thither driven by winde and
weather, so that being come thither, hee had neede of sundry
necessaries for the reparation of the said Navie, and also great

need of money for the paiment of his Souldiours, unto whom hee had promised paiment, and therefore although hee would, yet would not they depart without it, & for that purpose he requested licence for the sale of certaine of his Negros, declaring that although they were forbidden to trafique with strangers, yet for that there was a great amitie betweene their princes, and that the thing perteined to our Queenes highnesse, he thought hee might doe their prince great service, and that it would bee well taken at his hands, to doe it in this cause. The which allegations with divers others put in request, were presented unto the Governour, who sitting in counsell for that matter, granted unto his request for licence. But yet there fell out another thing which was the abating of the kings Custome, being upon every slave 30. duckets, which would not be granted unto.

Whereupon the Captaine perceiving that they would neither come neere his price he looked for by a great deale, nor yet would abate the Kings Custome of that they offered, so that either he must be a great looser by his wares, or els compell the officers to abate the same kings Custome which was too unreasonable, for to a higher price hee coulde not bring the buyers: Therefore the sixteenth of April hee prepared one hundred men well armed with bowes, arrowes, harquebuzes and pikes, with the which hee marched to the townewards, and being perceived by the Governour, he straight with all expedition sent messengers to knowe his request, desiring him to march no further forward untill he had answere againe, which incontinent he should have. So our Captaine declaring how unreasonable a thing the Kings Custome was, requested to have the same abated, and to pay seven and a halfe per centum, which is the ordinarie Custome for wares through his dominions there, and unto this if they would not graunt, hee would displease them. And this word being caried to the Governour, answere was returned that all things should bee to his content, and thereupon hee determined to depart, but the souldiers and Mariners finding so little credite in their promises, demanded gages for the performance of the premisses, or els they would not depart. And thus they being constrained to send gages, wee departed, beginning our trafique, and ending the same without disturbance.

Thus having made trafique in the harborough untill the 28. our Captaine with his ships intended to goe out of the roade, and purposed to make shew of his departure, because nowe the common sort having imployed their money, the rich men were come to towne, who made no shew that they were come to buy, so that they went about to bring downe the price, and by this pollicie the Captaine knew they would be made the more eager, for feare least we departed, and they should goe without any at all.

The nine and twentie wee being at ancker without the road, a French ship called the Greene Dragon of Newhaven, whereof was Captaine one Bon Temps came in, who saluted us after the maner of the Sea, with certaine pieces of Ordinance, and we re-saluted him with the like againe: with whom having communication, he declared that hee had bene at the Mine in Guinie, and was beaten off by the Portugals gallies, and inforced to come thither to make sale of such wares as he had: and further that the like was happened unto the Minion: besides the Captaine Davie Carlet and a Marchant, with a dozen Mariners betrayed by the Negros at their first arrivall thither, and remayning prisoners with the Portugals; and besides other misadventures of the losse of their men, happened through the great lacke of fresh water, with great doubts of bringing home the ships: which was most sorrowfull for us to understand.

Thus having ended our trafique here the 4. of May, we departed, leaving the Frenchman behinde us, the night before the which the Caribes, whereof I have made mention before, being to the number of 200. came in their Canoas to Burboroata, intending by night to have burned the towne, and taken the Spaniards, who being more vigilant because of our being there, then their custome was, perceiving them comming, raised the towne, who in a moment being a horsebacke, by meanes their custome is for all doubts to keepe their horses ready sadled, in the night set upon them, & tooke one, but the rest making shift for themselves, escaped away. But this one, because he was their guide, and was the occasion that divers times they had made invasion upon them, had for his traveile a stake thrust through his fundament, and so out at his necke.

The sixt of May aforesaide, wee came to an yland called

Curaçao, where wee had thought to have anckered, but could
not find ground, and having let fal an ancker with two cables,
were faine to weigh it againe: and the seventh sayling along
the coast to seeke an harborow, and finding none, wee came
to an ancker where we rode open in the Sea. In this place we
had trafique for hides, and found great refreshing both of beefe,
mutton and lambes, whereof there was such plentie, that saving
the skinnes, we had the flesh given us for nothing, the plentie
whereof was so abundant, that the worst in the ship thought
scorne not onely of mutton, but also of sodden lambe, which
they disdained to eate unrosted.

The increase of cattell in this yland is marveilous, which from
a doozen of each sort brought thither by the governour, in 25.
yeres he had a hundreth thousand at the least, & of other cattel
was able to kill without spoile of the increase 1500. yeerely,
which hee killeth for the skinnes, and of the flesh saveth onely
the tongues, the rest hee leaveth to the foule to devoure. And
this I am able to affirme, not onely upon the Governours owne
report, who was the first that brought the increase thither, which
so remaineth unto this day, but also by that I saw my selfe in
one field, where an hundred oxen lay one by another all whole,
saving the skinne and tongue taken away. And it is not so
marveilous a thing why they doe thus cast away the flesh in all
the ylands of the West Indies, seeing the land is great, and more
then they are able to inhabite, the people fewe, having delicate
fruites and meates ynough besides to feede upon, which they
rather desire, and the increase which passeth mans reason to
beleeve, when they come to a great number: for in S. Domingo
an yland called by the finders thereof Hispaniola, is so great
quantitie of cattell, and such increase thereof, that notwithstanding the daily killing of them for their hides, it is not possible
to asswage the number of them, but they are devoured by wilde
dogs, whose number is such by suffering them first to range
the woods and mountaines, that they eate and destroy 60000.
a yeere, and yet small lacke found of them. And no marveile,
for the said yland is almost as bigge as all England, and being
the first place that was founde of all the Indies, and of long
time inhabited before the rest, it ought therefore of reason to be
most populous: and to this houre the Viceroy and counsell
royall abideth there as in the chiefest place of all the Indies, to

prescribe orders to the rest for the kings behalfe, yet have they but one Citie and 13. villages in all the same yland, whereby the spoile of them in respect of the increase is nothing.

The 15. of the foresaid moneth wee departed from Curaçao, being not a little to the rejoycing of our Captaine and us, that wee had there ended our trafique: but notwithstanding our sweete meate, wee had sower sauce, for by reason of our riding so open at sea, what with blastes whereby our anckers being a ground, three at once came home, and also with contrary windes blowing, whereby for feare of the shore we were faine to hale off to have anker-hold, sometimes a whole day and a night we turned up and downe; and this happened not once, but halfe a dozen times in the space of our being there.

The 16. wee passed by an yland called Aruba, and the 17. at night anckered six houres at the West ende of Cabo de la vela, and in the morning being the 18. weighed againe, keeping our course, in the which time the Captaine sailing by the shore in the pinnesse, came to the Rancheria, a place where the Spaniards use to fish for pearles, and there spoke with a Spaniard, who tolde him how far off he was from Rio de la Hacha, which because he would not overshoot, he ankered that night againe, & the 19. came thither; where having talke with the kings treasurer of the Indies resident there, he declared his quiet trafique in Burboroata, & shewed a certificate of the same, made by the governour thereof, & therefore he desired to have the like there also: but the treasurer made answere that they were forbidden by the Viceroy and councill of S. Domingo, who having intelligence of our being on the coast, did sende expresse commission to resist us, with all the force they could, insomuch that they durst not trafique with us in no case, alleaging that if they did, they should loose all that they did trafique for, besides their bodies at the magistrates commaundement. Our Captaine replied, that hee was in an Armada of the Queenes Majesties of England, and sent about other her affaires, but driven besides his pretended voyage, was inforced by contrary windes to come into those parts, where he hoped to finde such friendship as hee should doe in Spaine, to the contrary whereof hee knewe no reason, in that there was amitie betwixt their princes. But seeing they would contrary to all reason go about to withstand his trafique, he would it should not be said by him, that having the force he hath, to be driven from his trafique perforce, but he would rather put it in adventure to try whether he or they should have the better, and therefore willed them to determine either to give him licence to trade, or else to stand to their owne harmes: So upon this it was determined hee should have licence to trade, but they would give him such a price as was the one halfe lesse then he had sold for before, and thus they sent word they would do, and none otherwise, and if it liked him not, he might do what he would, for they were not determined to deale otherwise with him. Whereupon, the captaine waying their unconscionable request, wrote to them a letter, that they dealt too rigorously with him, to go about to cut his throte in the price of his commodities, which were so reasonably rated, as they could not by a great deale have the like at any other mans handes. But seeing they had sent him this to his supper, hee would in the morning bring them as good a breakefast. And therefore in the morning being the 21. of May, hee shot off a whole Culvering to summon the towne, and preparing one hundred men in armour, went a shore, having in his great boate two Faulcons of brasse, and in the other boates double bases in their noses, which being perceived by the Townesmen, they incontinent in battell aray with their drumme and ensigne displayed, marched from the Towne to the sands, of footemen to the number of an hundred and fiftie, making great bragges with their cries, and weaving us a shore, whereby they made a semblance to have fought with us in deed. But our Captaine perceiving them so bragge, commanded the two Faulcons to be discharged at them, which put them in no small feare to see, (as they afterward declared) such great pieces in a boate. At every shot they fell flat to the ground, and as wee approched neere unto them, they broke their aray, and dispersed themselves so much for feare of the Ordinance, that at last they went all away with their ensigne. The horsemen also being about thirtie, made as brave a shew as might be, coursing up and downe with their horses, their brave white leather Targets in the one hand, and their javelings in the other, as though they would have received us at our landing. But when wee landed, they gave ground, and consulted what they should doe, for little they thought wee would have landed so boldly: and therefore as the Captaine was putting his men in aray, and marched forward to have encountred with them, they sent a messenger on horsebacke with a flagge of truce to the Captaine, who declared that the Treasurer marveiled what he meant to doe to come a shore in that order, in consideration that they had granted to every reasonable request that he did demaund: but the Captaine not well contended with this messenger, marched forwards. The messenger prayed him to stay his men, and saide, if hee would come apart from his men, the Treasurer would come and speake with him, whereunto hee did agree to commune together. The Captaine onely with his armour without weapon, and the Treasurer on horsebacke with his javeling, was afraide to come neere him for feare of his armour, which he said was worse then his weapon, and so keeping aloofe communing together, granted in fine to all his requests. Which being declared by the Captaine to the company, they desired to have pledges for the performance of all things, doubting that otherwise when they had made themselves stronger, they would have bene at defiance with us: and seeing that now they might have what they would request, they judged it to be more wisedome to be in assurance then to be forced to make any more labours about it. So upon this, gages were sent, and we made our trafique quietly with them. In the mean time while we stayed here, wee watered a good breadth off from the shore, where by the strength of the fresh water running into the Sea, the salt water was made fresh. In this River we saw many Crocodils of sundry bignesses, but some as bigge as a boate, with 4. feete, a long broad mouth, and a long taile, whose skinne is so hard, that a sword wil not pierce it. His nature is to live out of the water as a frogge doth, but he is a great devourer, and spareth neither fish, which is his common food, nor beastes, nor men, if hee take them, as the proofe thereof was knowen by a Negro, who as hee was filling water in the River was by one of them caried cleane away, and never seene after. His nature is ever when hee would have his prey, to cry and sobbe like a Christian body, to provoke them to come to him, and then hee snatcheth at them, and thereupon came this proverbe that is applied unto women when they weepe, Lachrymæ Crocodili, the meaning whereof is, that as the Crocodile when hee crieth, goeth then about most to deceive, so doeth a woman most commonly when she weepeth. Of these the Master of the Jesus watched one, and by the banks side stroke him with a pike of a bill in the side, and after three or foure times turning in sight, hee sunke downe, and was not afterward seene. In the time of our being in the Rivers Guinie, wee sawe many of a monstrous bignesse, amongst the which the captaine being in one of the Barks comming downe the same, shot a Faulcon at one, which very narowly hee missed, and with a feare hee plunged into the water, making a streame like the way of a boate.

Now while we were here, whether it were of a feare that the Spaniards doubted wee would have done them some harme before we departed, or for any treason that they intended towards us, I am not able to say; but then came thither a Captaine from some of the other townes, with a dozen souldiers upon a time when our Captaine and the treasurer cleared al things betweene them, and were in a communication of a debt of the governors of Burboroata, which was to be payd by the said treasurer, who would not answer the same by any meanes. Whereupon certaine words of displeasure passed betwixt the Captaine and him, and parting the one from the other, the treasurer possibly doubting that our Captaine would perforce have sought the same, did immediately command his men to armes, both horsemen and footemen: but because the Captaine was in the River on the backe side of the Towne with his other boates, and all his men unarmed and without weapons, it was to be judged he ment him little good, having that advantage of him, that comming upon the sudden, hee might have mischieved many of his men: but the Captaine having understanding thereof, not trusting to their gentlenesse, if they might have the advantage, departed aboord his ships, and at night returned againe, and demanded amongst other talke, what they meant by assembling their men in that order, & they answered, that their Captaine being come to towne did muster his men according to his accustomed maner. But it is to be judged to bee a cloake, in that comming for that purpose hee might have done it sooner, but the trueth is, they were not of force untill then, whereby to enterprise any matter against us, by meanes of pikes and harquebuzes, whereof they have want, and were now furnished by our Captaine, and also 3. Faulcons, which having got in other places, they had secretly conveyed thither, which made them the bolder, and also for that they saw now a convenient

place to do such a feat, and time also serving thereunto, by the
meanes that our men were not onely unarmed and unprovided,
as at no time before the like, but also were occupied in hewing
of wood, and least thinking of any harme: these were occasions
to provoke them thereunto. And I suppose they went about to
bring it to effect, in that *I with another gentleman being in the
towne, thinking of no harme towards us, and seeing men assembling in armour to the treasurers house, whereof I marveiled, and revoking to minde the former talke betweene the
Captaine and him, and the unreadinesse of our men, of whom
advantage might have bene taken, departed out of the Towne
immediatly to give knowledge thereof, but before we came to
our men by a flight-shot, two horsemen riding a gallop were
come neere us, being sent, as wee did gesse, to stay us least wee
should cary newes to our Captaine, but seeing us so neere our
men they stayed their horses, comming together, and suffring
us to passe, belike because wee were so neere, that if they had
gone about the same, they had bene espied by some of our men
which then immediatly would have departed, whereby they
should have bene frustrate of their pretence: and so the two
horsemen ridde about the bushes to espie what we did, and
seeing us gone, to the intent they might shadow their comming
downe in post, whereof suspition might bee had, fained a simple
excuse in asking whether he could sell any wine, but that
seemed so simple to the Captaine, that standing in doubt of
their courtesie, he returned in the morning with his three boats,
appointed with Bases in their noses, and his men with weapons
accordingly, where as before he caried none: and thus dissembling all injuries conceived of both parts, the Captaine went
ashore, leaving pledges in the boates for himselfe, and cleared
all things betweene the treasurer and him, saving for the gov-
erners debt, which the one by no meanes would answere, and
the other, because it was not his due debt, woulde not molest
him for it, but was content to remit it untill another time, and
therefore departed, causing the two Barkes which rode neere
the shore to weigh and go under saile, which was done because
that our Captaine demanding a testimoniall of his good behaviour there, could not have the same untill hee were under

---

* The author of this storie.

saile ready to depart: and therefore at night he went for the
same againe, & received it at the treasurers hand, of whom very
courteously he tooke his leave and departed, shooting off the
bases of his boat for his farewell, and the townesmen also shot
off foure Faulcons and 30. harquebuzes, and this was the first
time that he knew of the conveyance of their Faulcons.

The 31. of May wee departed, keeping our course to Hispaniola, and the fourth of June wee had sight of an yland, which
wee made to be Jamaica, marveiling that by the vehement
course of the Seas we should be driven so farre to leeward: for
setting our course to the West end of Hispaniola we fel with
the middle of Jamaica, notwithstanding that to al mens sight it
shewed a headland, but they were all deceived by the clouds
that lay upon the land two dayes together, in such sort that we
thought it to be the head land of the said yland. And a Spaniard
being in the ship, who was a Marchant, and inhabitant in
Jamaica, having occasion to go to Guinie, and being by treason
taken of the Negros, & afterwards bought by the Tangomangos,
was by our Captaine brought from thence, and had his passage
to go into his countrey, who perceiving the land, made as
though he knew every place thereof, and pointed to certaine
places which he named to be such a place, and such a mans
ground, and that behinde such a point was the harborow, but
in the ende he pointed so from one point to another, that we
were a leeboord of all places, and found our selves at the West
end of Jamaica before we were aware of it, and being once to
leeward, there was no getting up againe, so that by trusting of
the Spaniards knowledge, our Captaine sought not to speake
with any of the inhabitants, which if he had not made himselfe
sure of, he would have done as his custome was in other places:
but this man was a plague not onely to our Captaine, who made
him loose by overshooting the place 2000. pounds by hides,
which hee might have gotten, but also to himselfe, who being
three yeeres out of his Countrey, and in great misery in Guinie,
both among the Negros and Tangomangos, and in hope to come
to his wife and friendes, as he made sure accompt, in that at
his going into the pinnesse, when he went to shore he put on his
new clothes, and for joy flung away his old, could not afterwards finde any habitation, neither there nor in all Cuba, which
we sailed all along, but it fell out ever by one occasion or other,

that wee were put beside the same, so that he was faine to be brought into England, and it happened to him as it did to a duke of Samaria, when the Israelites were besieged, and were in great misery with hunger, & being tolde by the Prophet Elizæus, that a bushell of flower should be sold for a sickle, would not beleeve him, but thought it unpossible: and for that cause Elizæus prophesied hee should see the same done, but hee should not eate thereof: so this man being absent three yeeres, and not ever thinking to have seene his owne Countrey, did see the same, went upon it, and yet was it not his fortune to come to it, or to any habitation, whereby to remaine with his friends according to his desire.

Thus having sailed along the coast two dayes, we departed the seventh of June, being made to beleeve by the Spaniard that it was not Jamaica, but rather Hispaniola, of which opinion the Captaine also was, because that which hee made Jamaica seemed to be but a piece of the land, and thereby tooke it rather to be Hispaniola, by the lying of the coast, and also for that being ignorant of the force of the current, he could not beleeve he was so farre driven to leeward, and therfore setting his course to Jamaica, and after certaine dayes not finding the same, perceived then certainly that the yland which he was at before was Jamaica, and that the cloudes did deceive him, whereof he marvelled not a little: and this mistaking of the place came to as ill a passe as the overshooting of Jamaica: for by this did he also overpasse a place in Cuba, called Santa Cruz, where, as he was informed, was great store of hides to be had: & thus being disappointed of two of his portes, where he thought to have raised great profite by his trafique, and also to have found great refreshing of victuals and water for his men, hee was now disappointed greatly, and such want he had of fresh water, that he was forced to seeke the shore to obteine the same, which he had sight of after certaine dayes overpassed with stormes and contrary windes, but yet not of the maine of Cuba, but of certaine ylands in number two hundred, whereof the most part were desolate of inhabitants: by the which ylands the Captaine passing in his pinnesse, could finde no fresh water untill hee came to an yland bigger then all the rest, called the yle of Pinas, where wee anckered with our ships the 16. of June, and found water, which although it were neither so toothsome as running water, by the meanes it is standing, and but the water of raine, and also being neere the Sea was brackish, yet did wee not refuse it, but were more glad thereof, as the time then required, then wee should have bene another time with fine Conduit water. Thus being reasonably watered we were desirous to depart, because the place was not very convenient for such ships of charge as they were, because there were many shoales to leeward, which also lay open to the sea for any wind that should blow: and therfore the captaine made the more haste away, which was not unneedfull: for little sooner were their anckers weyed, and foresaile set, but there arose such a storme, that they had not much to spare for doubling out of the shoales: for one of the barks not being fully ready as the rest, was faine for haste to cut the cable in the hawse, and loose both ancker and cable to save her selfe.

Thus the 17. of June, we departed and on the 20. we fell with the West end of Cuba, called Cape S. Antony, where for the space of three dayes wee doubled along, till wee came beyond the shoales, which are 20. leagues beyond S. Anthony. And the ordinary Brise taking us, which is the Northeast winde, put us the 24. from the shoare, and therefore we went to the Northwest to fetch wind, and also to the coast of Florida to have the helpe of the current, which was judged to have set to the Eastward: so the 29. wee found our selves in 27. degrees, and in the soundings of Florida, where we kept our selves the space of foure dayes, sailing along the coast as neere as we could, in tenne or twelve fadome water, having all the while no sight of land.

The fift of July we had sight of certeine Islands of sand, called the Tortugas (which is lowe land) where the captaine went in with his pinnesse, and found such a number of birds, that in halfe an houre he laded her with them; and if they had beene ten boats more, they might have done the like. These Islands beare the name of Tortoises, because of the number of them, which there do breed, whose nature is to live both in the water and upon land also, but breed onely upon the shore, in making a great pit wherein they lay egges, to the number of three or foure hundred, and covering them with sand, they are hatched by the heat of the Sunne; and by this meanes commeth the great increase. Of these we tooke very great ones, which have both backe and belly all of bone, of the thickness of an inch: the fish whereof we proved, eating much like veale; and finding a number of egges in them, tasted also of them, but they did eat very sweetly. Heere wee ankered six houres, and then a faire gale of winde springing, we weyed anker, and made saile toward Cuba, whither we came the sixt day, and weathered as farre as the Table, being a hill so called, because of the forme thereof: here we lay off and on all night, to keepe that we had gotten to wind-ward, intending to have watered in the morning, if we could have done it, or els if the winde had come larger, to have plied to wind-ward to Havana, which is an harborow whereunto all the fleet of the Spanyards come, and doe there tary to have one the company of another. This hill we thinking to have beene the Table, made account (as it was indeed) that Havana was but eight leagues to wind-ward, but by the perswasion of a French man, who made the captaine beleeve he knew the Table very well, and had beene at Havana, sayd that it was not the Table, and that the Table was much higher, and neerer to the sea side, and that there was no plaine ground to the Eastward, nor hilles to the Westward, but all was contrary, and that behinde the hilles to the Westward was Havana. To which persuasion credit being given by some, and they not of the woorst, the captaine was persuaded to goe to leeward, and so sailed along the seventh and eight dayes, finding no habitation, nor no other Table; and then perceiving his folly to give eare to such praters, was not a little sory, both because he did consider what time he should spend yer he could get so far to wind-ward againe, which would have bene, with the weathering which we had, ten or twelve dayes worke, & what it would have bene longer he knew not, and (that which was woorst) he had not above a dayes water and therfore knew not what shift to make: but in fine, because the want was such, that his men could not live with it, he determined to seeke water, and to goe further to leeward, to a place (as it is set in the card) called Rio de los puercos, which he was in doubt of, both whether it were inhabited, & whether there were water or not, and whether for the shoalds he might have such accesse with his ships, that he might conveniently take in the same. And while we were in these troubles, and kept our way to the place aforesayd, almighty God our guide, who would not suffer us to run into any further danger, which we had bene like to have incurred, if we had ranged the coast of Florida along as we did before, which is so dangerous (by reports) that no ship escapeth which commeth thither, (as the Spanyards have very wel proved the same) sent us the eight day at night a faire Westerly winde, whereupon the captaine and company consulted, determining not to refuse Gods gift, but every man was contented to pinch his own bellie, whatsoever had happened; and taking the sayd winde, the ninth day of July got to the Table, and sailing the same night, unawares overshot Havana; at which place wee thought to have watered: but the next day, not knowing that wee had overshot the same, sailed along the coast, seeking it, and the eleventh day in the morning, by certeine knowen marks, we understood that we had overshot it 20 leagues: in which coast ranging, we found no convenient watering place, whereby there was no remedy but to disemboque, and to water upon the coast of Florida: for, to go further to the Eastward, we could not for the shoalds, which are very dangerous; and because the current shooteth to the Northeast, we doubted by the force thereof to be set upon them, and therefore durst not approch them: so making but reasonable way the day aforesayd, and all the night, the twelfth day in the morning we fell with the Islands upon the cape of Florida, which we could scant double by the meanes that fearing the shoalds to the Eastwards, and doubting the current comming out of the West, which was not of that force we made account of; for we felt little or none till we fell with the cape, and then felt such a current, that bearing all sailes against the same, yet were driven backe againe a great pace: the experience whereof we had by the Jesus pinnesse, and the Salomons boat, which were sent the same day in the afternoone, whiles the ships were becalmed, to see if they could finde any water upon the Islands aforesaid; who spent a great part of the day in rowing thither, being further off then they deemed it to be, and in the meane time a faire gale of winde springing at sea, the ships departed, making a signe to them to come away, who although they saw them depart, because they were so neere the shore, would not lose all the labour they had taken, but determined to keepe their way, and see if there were any water to be had, making no account but to finde the shippes well enough: but they spent so much time in filling the water which they had found, that the night was come before they could make an end. And having lost the sight of the ships, they rowed what they could, but were wholly ignorant which way they should seeke them againe; as indeed there was a more doubt then they knew of: for when they departed, the shippes were in no current; and sailing but a mile further, they found one so strong, that bearing all sailes, it could not prevaile against the same, but were driven backe: whereupon the captaine sent the Salomon, with the other two barks, to beare neere the shore all night, because the current was lesse there a great deale, and to beare light, with shooting off a piece now and then, to the intent the boats might better know how to come to them.

The Jesus also bare a light in her toppe gallant, and shot off a piece also now and then, but the night passed, and the morning was come, being the thirteenth day, and no newes could be heard of them, but the ships and barkes ceased not to looke still for them, yet they thought it was all in vaine, by the meanes they heard not of them all the night past; and therefore determined to tary no longer, seeking for them till noone, and if they heard no newes, then they would depart to the Jesus, who perforce (by the vehemency of the current) was caried almost out of sight; but as God would have it, now time being come, and they having tacked about in the pinnesses top, had sight of them, and tooke them up: they in the boats, being to the number of one and twenty, having sight of the ships, and seeing them tacking about; whereas before at the first sight of them they did greatly rejoyce, were now in a greater perplexitie then ever they were: for by this they thought themselves utterly forsaken, whereas before they were in some hope to have found them. Truly God wrought marvellously for them, for they themselves having no victuals but water, and being sore oppressed with hunger, were not of opinion to bestow any further time in seeking the shippes then that present noone time; so that if they had not at that instant espied them, they had gone to the shore to have made provision for victuals, and with such things as they could have gotten, either to have gone for that part of Florida where the French men were planted (which would have bene very hard for them to have done, because they wanted victuals to bring them thither, being an hundred and twenty leagues off) or els to have remained amongst the Floridians; at whose hands they were put in comfort by a French man, who was with them, that had remained in Florida at the first finding thereof, a whole yeere together, to receive victuals sufficient, and gentle entertainment, if need were, for a yeere or two, untill which time God might have provided for them. But how contrary this would have fallen out to their expectations, it is hard to judge, seeing those people of the cape of Florida are of more savage and fierce nature, and more valiant then any of the rest; which the Spanyards well prooved, who being five hundred men, who intended there to land, returned few or none of them, but were inforced to forsake the same: and of their cruelty mention is made in the booke of the Decades, of a frier, who taking upon him to persuade the people to subjection, was by them taken, and his skin cruelly pulled over his eares, and his flesh eaten.

In these Islands they being a shore, found a dead man, dried in a maner whole, with other heads and bodies of men: so that these sorts of men are eaters of the flesh of men, aswel as the Canibals. But to returne to our purpose.

The foureteenth day the shippe and barks came to the Jesus, bringing them newes of the recovery of the men, which was not a little to the rejoycing of the captaine, and the whole company: and so then altogether they kept on their way along the coast of Florida, and the fifteenth day come to an anker, and so from sixe and twenty degrees to thirty degrees and a halfe, where the French men abode, ranging all the coast along, seeking for fresh water, ankering every night, because we would overshoot no place of fresh water, and in the day time the captaine in the ships pinnesse sailed along the shore, went into every creeke, speaking with divers of the Floridians, because hee would understand where the French men inhabited; and not finding them in eight and twenty degrees, as it was declared unto him, marvelled thereat, and never left sailing along the coast till he found them, who inhabited in a river, by them called the river of May, and standing in thirty degrees and better. In ranging this coast along, the captaine found it to be all an Island, and therefore it is all lowe land, and very scant of fresh water, but the countrey was marvellously sweet, with both marish and medow ground, and goodly woods among. There they found sorell to grow as abundantly as grasse, and where their houses were, great store of maiz and mill, and grapes of great bignesse, but of taste much like our English grapes. Also Deere great plentie, which came upon the sands before them. Their houses are not many together, for in one house an hundred of them do lodge; they being made much like a great barne, and in strength not inferiour to ours, for they have stanchions and rafters of whole trees, and are covered with palmito-leaves, having no place divided, but one small roome for their king and queene. In the middest of this house is a hearth, where they make great fires all night, and they sleepe upon certeine pieces of wood hewen in for the bowing of their backs, and another place made high for their heads, which they put one by another all along the walles on both sides. In their houses they remaine onely in the nights, and in the day they desire the fields, where they dresse their meat, and make provision for victuals, which they provide onely for a meale from hand to mouth. There is one thing to be marvelled at, for the making of their fire, and not onely they but also the Negros doe the same, which is made onely by two stickes, rubbing them one against another: and this they may doe in any place they come, where they finde sticks sufficient for the purpose. In their apparell the men onely use deere skinnes, wherewith some onely cover their privy members, othersome use the same as garments to cover them before and behind; which skinnes are painted, some yellow and red, some blacke & russet, and every man according to his owne fancy. They do not omit to paint their bodies also with curious knots, or antike worke, as every man in his owne fancy deviseth, which painting, to make it continue the better, they use with a thorne to pricke their flesh, and dent in the same, whereby the painting may have better hold. In their warres they use a sleighter colour of painting their faces, thereby to make themselves shew the more fierce; which after their warres ended, they wash away againe. In their warres they use bowes and arrowes, whereof their bowes are made of a kind of Yew, but blacker then ours, and for the most part passing the strength of the Negros or Indians, for it is not greatly inferior to ours: their arrowes are also of a great length, but yet of reeds like other Indians, but varying in two points, both in length and also for nocks and feathers, which the other lacke, whereby they shoot very stedy: the heads of the same are vipers teeth, bones of fishes, flint stones, piked points of knives, which they having gotten of the French men, broke the same, & put the points of them in their arrowes head: some of them have their heads of silver, othersome that have want of these, put in a kinde of hard wood, notched, which pierceth as farre as any of the rest. In their fight, being in the woods, they use a marvellous pollicie for their owne safegard, which is by clasping a tree in their armes, and yet shooting not-withstanding: this policy they used with the French men in their fight, whereby it appeareth that they are people of some policy: and although they are called by the Spanyards Gente triste, that is to say, Bad people, meaning thereby, that they are not men of capacity: yet have the French men found them so witty in their answeres, that by the captaines owne report, a counseller with us could not give a more profound reason.

The women also for their apparell use painted skinnes, but most of them gownes of mosse, somewhat longer then our mosse, which they sowe together artificially, and make the same surplesse wise, wearing their haire downe to their shoulders, like the Indians. In this river of May aforesayd, the captaine entring with his pinnesse, found a French ship of fourescore tun, and two pinnesses of fifteene tun a piece, by her, and speaking with the keepers thereof, they tolde him of a fort two leagues up, which they had built, in which their captaine Monsieur Laudon-niere was, with certeine souldiers therein. To whom our cap-taine sending to understand of a watering-place, where he might conveniently take it in, and to have licence for the same, he straight, because there was no convenient place but up the river five leagues, where the water was fresh, did send him a pilot for the more expedition thereof, to bring in one of his barks, which going in with other boats provided for the same purpose, ankered before the fort, into the which our captaine went; where hee was by the Generall, with other captaines and soul-diers, very gently enterteined, who declared unto him the time of their being there, which was fourteene moneths, with the extremity they were driven to for want of victuals, having brought very little with them; in which place they being two hundred men at their first comming, had in short space eaten all the maiz they could buy of the inhabitants about them, and therefore were driven certeine of them to serve a king of the Floridians against other his enemies, for mill and other victuals:

which having gotten, could not serve them, being so many, so
long a time: but want came upon them in such sort, that they
were faine to gather acorns, which being stamped small, and
often washed, to take away the bitternesse of them, they did
use for bread, eating withall sundry times, roots, whereof they
found many good and holesome, and such as serve rather for
medecines then for meates alone. But this hardnesse not contenting some of them, who would not take the paines so much
as to fish in the river before their doores, but would have all
things put in their mouthes, they did rebell against the captaine,
taking away first his armour, and afterward imprisoning him:
and so to the number of fourescore of them, departed with a
barke and a pinnesse, spoiling their store of victuall, and taking
away a great part thereof with them, and so went to the Islands
of Hispaniola and Jamaica a roving, where they spoiled and
pilled the Spanyards; and having taken two caravels laden with
wine and casavi, which is a bread made of roots, and much
other victuals and treasure, had not the grace to depart therewith, but were of such haughty stomacks, that they thought their
force to be such that no man durst meddle with them, and so
kept harborow in Jamaica, going dayly ashore at their pleasure.
But God which would not suffer such evill doers unpunished did
indurate their hearts in such sort, that they lingered the time so
long, that a ship and galliasse being made out of Santa Domingo
came thither into the harborow, and tooke twenty of them,
whereof the most part were hanged, and the rest caried into
Spaine, and some (to the number of five and twenty) escaped
in the pinnesse, and came to Florida; where at their landing
they were put in prison, and incontinent foure of the chiefest
being condemned, at the request of the souldiers, did passe the
harquebuzers, and then were hanged upon a gibbet. This lacke
of threescore men was a great discourage and weakening to the
rest, for they were the best souldiers that they had: for they had
now made the inhabitants weary of them by their dayly craving
of maiz, having no wares left to content them withall, and therefore were inforced to rob them, and to take away their victual
perforce, which was the occasion that the Floridians (not well
contented therewith) did take certeine of their company in the
woods, and slew them; wherby there grew great warres betwixt
them and the Frenchmen: and therefore they being but a few

in number durst not venture abroad, but at such times as they were inforced thereunto for want of food to do the same: and going twenty harquebuzers in a company, were set upon by eighteene kings, having seven or eight hundred men, which with one of their bowes slew one of their men, and hurt a dozen, & drove them all downe to their boats; whose pollicy in fight was to be marvelled at: for having shot at divers of their bodies which were armed, and perceiving that their arrowes did not prevaile against the same, they shot at their faces and legs, which were the places that the Frenchmen were hurt in. Thus the Frenchmen returned, being in ill case by the hurt of their men, having not above forty souldiers left unhurt, whereby they might ill make any more invasions upon the Floridians, and keepe their fort withall: which they must have beene driven unto, had not God sent us thither for their succour; for they had not above ten dayes victuall left before we came. In which perplexity our captaine seeing them, spared them out of his ship twenty barrels of meale, & foure pipes of beanes, with divers other victuals and necessaries which he might conveniently spare: and to helpe them the better homewards, whither they were bound before our comming, at their request we spared them one of our barks of fifty tun. Notwithstanding the great want that the Frenchmen had, the ground doth yeeld victuals sufficient, if they would have taken paines to get the same; but they being souldiers, desired to live by the sweat of other mens browes: for while they had peace with the Floridians, they had fish sufficient, by weares which they made to catch the same: but when they grew to warres, the Floridians tooke away the same againe, and then would not the Frenchmen take the paines to make any more. The ground yeeldeth naturally grapes in great store, for in the time that the Frenchmen were there, they made 20 hogsheads of wine. Also it yeeldeth roots passing good, Deere marvellous store, with divers other beasts, and fowle, serviceable to the use of man. These be things wherewith a man may live, having corne or maiz wherewith to make bread: for maiz maketh good savory bread, and cakes as fine as flowre. Also it maketh good meale, beaten and sodden with water, and eateth like pap wherewith we feed children. It maketh also good beverage, sodden in water, and nourishable; which the Frenchmen did use to drinke of in the morning, and it assuageth their thirst, so that they had no need to drinke all the day after. And this maiz was the greatest lacke they had, because they had no labourers to sowe the same, and therfore to them that should inhabit the land it were requisit to have labourers to till and sowe the ground: for they having victuals of their owne, whereby they neither rob nor spoile the inhabitants, may live not onely quietly with them, who naturally are more desirous of peace then of warres, but also shall have abundance of victuals profered them for nothing: for it is with them as it is with one of us, when we see another man ever taking away from us, although we have enough besides, yet then we thinke all too little for our selves: for surely we have heard the Frenchmen report, and I know it by the Indians, that a very little contenteth them: for the Indians with the head of maiz rosted, will travell a whole day, and when they are at the Spanyards finding, they give them nothing but sodden herbs & maiz: and in this order I saw three-score of them feed, who were laden with wares, and came fifty leagues off. The Floridians when they travell, have a kinde of herbe dried, who with a cane and an earthen cup in the end, with fire, and the dried herbs put together, doe sucke thorow the cane the smoke thereof, which smoke satisfieth their hunger, and therwith they live foure or five dayes without meat or drinke, and this all the Frenchmen used for this purpose: yet do they holde opinion withall, that it causeth water & fleame to void from their stomacks. The commodities of this land are more then are yet knowen to any man: for besides the land it selfe, whereof there is more then any king Christian is able to inhabit, it flourisheth with medow, pasture ground, with woods of Cedar and Cypres, and other sorts, as better can not be in the world. They have for apothecary herbs, trees, roots and gummes great store, as Storax liquida, Turpintine, Gumme, Myrrhe, and Frankinsence, with many others, whereof I know not the names. Colours both red, blacke, yellow, & russet, very perfect, where-with they so paint their bodies, and Deere skinnes which they weare about them, that with water it neither fadeth away, nor altereth colour. Golde and silver they want not: for at the Frenchmens first comming thither they had the same offered them for little or nothing, for they received for a hatchet two pound weight of golde, because they knew not the estimation thereof: but the souldiers being greedy of the same, did take it from them, giving them nothing for it: the which they perceiving, that both the Frenchmen did greatly esteeme it, and also did rigorously deale with them, by taking the same away from them, at last would not be knowen they had any more, neither durst they weare the same for feare of being taken away: so that saving at their first comming, they could get none of them: and how they came by this golde and silver the French men know not as yet, but by gesse, who having travelled to the Southwest of the cape, having found the same dangerous, by meanes of sundry banks, as we also have found the same: and there finding masts which were wracks of Spanyards comming from Mexico, judged that they had gotten treasure by them. For it is most true that divers wracks have beene made of Spanyards, having much treasure: for the Frenchmen having travelled to the capeward an hundred and fiftie miles, did finde two Spanyards with the Floridians, which they brought afterward to their fort, whereof one was in a caravel comming from the Indies, which was cast away foureteene yeeres ago, & the other twelve yeeres: of whose fellowes some escaped, othersome were slain by the inhabitants. It seemeth they had estimation of their golde & silver, for it is wrought flat and graven, which they weare about their neckes; othersome made round like a pancake, with a hole in the midst, to boulster up their breasts withall, because they thinke it a deformity to have great breasts. As for mines either of gold or silver, the Frenchmen can heare of none they have upon the Island, but of copper, whereof as yet also they have not made the proofe, because they were but few men: but it is not unlike, but that in the maine where are high hilles, may be golde and silver aswell as in Mexico, because it is all one maine. The Frenchmen obteined pearles of them of great bignesse, but they were blacke, by meanes of rosting of them, for they do not fish for them as the Spanyards doe, but for their meat: for the Spanyards use to keepe dayly afishing some two or three hundred Indians, some of them that be of choise a thousand: and their order is to go in canoas, or rather great pinnesses, with thirty men in a piece, whereof the one halfe, or most part be divers, the rest doe open the same for the pearles: for it is not suffered that they should use dragging, for that would bring them out of estimation, and marre the beds of them. The oisters which have the smallest sort of pearles are found in seven or eight fadome water, but the greatest in eleven or twelve fadome.

The Floridians have pieces of unicornes hornes which they weare about their necks, whereof the Frenchmen obteined many pieces. Of those unicornes they have many; for that they doe affirme it to be a beast with one horne, which comming to the river to drinke, putteth the same into the water before he drinketh. Of this unicornes horne there are of our company, that having gotten the same of the Frenchmen, brought home thereof to shew. It is therfore to be presupposed that there are more commodities aswell as that, which for want of time, and people sufficient to inhabit the same, can not yet come to light: but I trust God will reveale the same before it be long, to the great profit of them that shal take it in hand. Of beasts in this countrey besides deere, foxes, hares, polcats, conies, ownces, & leopards, I am not able certeinly to say: but it is thought that there are lions and tygres as well as unicornes; lions especially; if it be true that is sayd, of the enmity betweene them and the unicornes: for there is no beast but hath his enemy, as the cony the polcat, a sheepe the woolfe, the elephant the rinoceros; and so of other beasts the like: insomuch, that whereas the one is, the other can not be missing. And seeing I have made mention of the beasts of this countrey, it shall not be from my purpose to speake also of the venimous beasts, as crocodiles, whereof there is great abundance, adders of great bignesse, whereof our men killed some of a yard and a halfe long. Also I heard a miracle of one of these adders, upon the which a faulcon seizing, the sayd adder did claspe her tail about her; which the French captaine seeing, came to the rescue of the faulcon, and tooke her slaying the adder; and this faulcon being wilde, he did reclaim her, and kept her for the space of two moneths, at which time for very want of meat he was faine to cast her off. On these adders the Frenchmen did feed, to no little admiration of us, and affirmed the same to be a delicate meat. And the captaine of the Frenchmen saw also a serpent with three heads and foure feet, of the bignesse of a great spaniell, which for want of a harquebuz he durst not attempt to slay. Of fish also they have in the river, pike, roch, salmon, trout, and divers other small fishes, and of great fish, some of the length of a man and longer, being of bignesse accordingly, having a snout much like a sword

of a yard long. There be also of sea fishes, which we saw comming along the coast flying, which are of the bignesse of a smelt,
the biggest sort whereof have foure wings, but the other have
but two: of these wee sawe comming out of Guinea a hundred
in a company, which being chased by the gilt-heads, otherwise
called the bonitos, do to avoid them the better, take their flight
out of the water, but yet are they not able to flie farre, because
of the drying of their wings, which serve them not to flie but
when they are moist, and therefore when they can flie no further
they fall into the water, and having wet their wings, take a new
flight againe. These bonitos be of bignesse like a carpe, and in
colour like a makarell, but it is the swiftest fish in swimming
that is, and followeth her prey very fiercely, not onely in the
water, but also out of the water: for as the flying fish taketh
her flight, so doeth this bonito leape after them, and taketh them
sometimes above the water. There were some of those bonitos,
which being galled by a fisgig, did follow our shippe comming
out of Guinea 500. leagues. There is a sea-fowle also that
chaseth this flying fish aswell as the bonito: for as the flying fish
taketh her flight, so doth this fowle pursue to take her, which to
beholde is a greater pleasure then hawking, for both the flights
are as pleasant, and also more often then an hundred times: for
the fowle can flie no way, but one or other lighteth in her
pawes, the number of them are so abundant. There is an innumerable yoong frie of these flying fishes, which commonly
keepe about the ship, and are not so big as butter-flies, and yet
by flying do avoid the unsatiablenesse of the bonito. Of the
bigger sort of these fishes wee tooke many, which both night
and day flew into the sailes of our ship, and there was not one
of them which was not woorth a bonito: for being put upon a
hooke drabling in the water, the bonito would leap thereat, and
so was taken. Also, we tooke many with a white cloth made
fast to a hooke, which being tied so short in the water, that it
might leape out and in, the greedie bonito thinking it to be a
flying fish leapeth thereat, and so is deceived. We tooke also
dolphins which are of very goodly colour and proportion to behold, and no lesse delicate in taste. Fowles also there be many,
both upon land and upon sea: but concerning them on the land
I am not able to name them, because my abode was there so
short. But for the fowle of the fresh rivers, these two I noted to

be the chiefe, whereof the Flemengo is one, having all red feathers, and long red legs like a herne, a necke according to the bill, red, whereof the upper neb hangeth an inch over the nether; and an egript, which is all white as the swanne, with legs like to an hearnshaw, and of bignesse accordingly, but it hath in her taile feathers of so fine a plume, that it passeth the estridge his feather. Of the sea-fowle above all other not common in England, I noted the pellicane, which is fained to be the lovingst bird that is; which rather then her yong should want, wil spare her heart bloud out of her belly: but for all this lovingnesse she is very deformed to beholde; for she is of colour russet: notwithstanding in Guinea I have seene of them as white as a swan, having legs like the same, and a body like a hearne, with a long necke, and a thick long beake, from the nether jaw whereof downe to the breast passeth a skinne of such a bignesse, as is able to receive a fish as big as ones thigh, and this her big throat and long bill doeth make her seem so ougly.

Here I have declared the estate of Florida, and the commodities therein to this day knowen, which although it may seeme unto some, by the meanes that the plenty of golde and silver, is not so abundant as in other places, that the cost bestowed upon the same will not be able to quit the charges: yet am I of the opinion, that by that which I have seene in other Islands of the Indians, where such increase of cattell hath bene, that of twelve head of beasts in five & twenty yeeres, did in the hides of them raise a thousand pound profit yerely, that the increase of cattel onely would raise profit sufficient for the same: for wee may consider, if so small a portion did raise so much gaines in such short time, what would a greater do in many yeres? and surely I may this affirme, that the ground of the Indians for the breed of cattell, is not in any point to be compared to this of Florida, which all the yeere long is so greene, as any time in the Summer with us: which surely is not to be marvelled at, seeing the countrey standeth in so watery a climate: for once a day without faile they have a shower of raine; which by meanes of the countrey it selfe, which is drie, and more fervent hot then ours, doeth make all things to flourish therein. And because there is not the thing we all seeke for, being rather desirous of present gaines, I doe therefore affirme the attempt thereof to be more requisit for a prince, who is of power able to go thorow with the same, rather then for any subject.

From thence wee departed the 28 of July, upon our voyage homewards, having there all things as might be most convenient for our purpose: and tooke leave of the Frenchmen that there still remained, who with diligence determined to make as great speede after, as they could. Thus by meanes of contrary windes oftentimes, wee prolonged our voyage in such manner that victuals scanted with us, so that we were divers times (or rather the most part) in despaire of ever comming home, had not God of his goodnesse better provided for us, then our deserving. In which state of great miserie, wee were provoked to call upon him by fervent prayer, which mooved him to heare us, so that we had a prosperous winde, which did set us so farre shot, as to be upon the banke of Newfound land, on Saint Bartholomews eve, and we sounded therupon, finding ground at an hundred and thirty fadoms, being that day somewhat becalmed, and tooke a great number of fresh codde-fish, which greatly relieved us: and being very glad thereof, the next day we departed, and had lingring little gales for the space of foure or five dayes, at the ende of which we sawe a couple of French shippes, and had of them so much fish as would serve us plentifully for all the rest of the way, the Captaine paying for the same both golde and silver, to the just value thereof, unto the chiefe owners of the saide shippes, but they not looking for any thing at all, were glad in themselves to meete with such good intertainement at sea, as they had at our hands. After which departure from them, with a good large winde the twentieth of September we came to Padstow in Cornewall, God be thanked, in safetie, with the losse of twentie persons in all the voyage, and with great profit to the venturers of the said voyage, as also to the whole realme, in bringing home both golde, silver, pearles and other jewels great store. His name therefore be praised for evermore. Amen.

The Register and true accounts of all herein expressed hath beene approoved by me John Sparke the younger, who went upon the same voyage, and wrote the same.

14

The third troublesome voyage made with the Jesus of
Lubeck, the Minion, and foure other ships, to the
parts of Guinea, and the West Indies, in the yeeres
1567 and 1568 by M. John Hawkins

THE ships departed from Plimmouth, the second day of October, Anno 1567 and had reasonable weather untill the seventh
day, at which time fortie leagues North from Cape Finister,
there arose an extreme storme, which continued foure dayes, in
such sort, that the fleete was dispersed, and all our great boats
lost, and the Jesus our chiefe shippe, in such case, as not
thought able to serve the voyage: whereupon in the same storme
we set our course homeward, determining to give over the
voyage: but the eleventh day of the same moneth, the winde
changed with faire weather, whereby we were animated to fol-
lowe our enterprise, and so did, directing our course with the
Ilands of the Canaries, where according to an order before
prescribed, all our shippes before dispersed, met at one of those
Ilands, called Gomera, where we tooke water, and departed
from thence the fourth day of November, towards the coast of
Guinea, and arrived at Cape Verde, the eighteenth of November: where we landed 150 men, hoping to obtaine some Negros,
where we got but fewe, and those with great hurt and damage
to our men, which chiefly proceeded of their envenomed arrowes: and although in the beginning they seemed to be but
small hurts, yet there hardly escaped any that had blood drawen
of them, but died in strange sort, with their mouthes shut some
tenne dayes before they died, and after their wounds were
whole; where I my selfe had one of the greatest woundes, yet
thankes be to God, escaped. From thence we past the time upon
the coast of Guinea, searching with all diligence the rivers from

Rio Grande, unto Sierra Leona, till the twelfth of Januarie, in which time we had not gotten together a hundreth and fiftie Negros: yet notwithstanding the sicknesse of our men, and the late time of the yeere commanded us away: and thus having nothing wherewith to seeke the coast of the West Indias, I was with the rest of our company in consultation to goe to the coast of the Mine, hoping there to have obtained some golde for our wares, and thereby to have defraied our charge. But even in that present instant, there came to us a Negro, sent from a king, oppressed by other Kings his neighbours, desiring our aide, with promise that as many Negros as by these warres might be obtained, aswell of his part as of ours, should be at our pleasure: whereupon we concluded to give aide, and sent 120 of our men, which the 15 of Januarie, assaulted a towne of the Negros of our Allies adversaries, which had in it 8000 Inhabitants, being very strongly impaled and fenced after their manner, but it was so well defended, that our men prevailed not, but lost sixe men and fortie hurt: so that our men sent forthwith to me for more helpe: whereupon considering that the good successe of this enterprise might highly further the commoditie of our voyage, I went my selfe, and with the helpe of the king of our side, assaulted the towne, both by land and sea, and very hardly with fire (their houses being covered with dry Palme leaves) obtained the towne, put the Inhabitants to flight, where we tooke 250 persons, men, women, & children, and by our friend the king of our side, there were taken 600 prisoners, whereof we hoped to have had our choise: but the Negro (in which nation is seldome or never found truth) meant nothing lesse: for that night he remooved his campe and prisoners, so that we were faine to content us with those few which we had gotten our selves.

Now had we obtained between foure and five hundred Negros, wherwith we thought it somewhat reasonable to seeke the coast of the West Indies, and there, for our Negros, and other our merchandize, we hoped to obtaine, whereof to countervaile our charges with some gaines, wherunto we proceeded with all diligence, furnished our watering, tooke fuell, and departed the coast of Guinea the third of Februarie, continuing at the sea with a passage more hard, then before hath bene accustomed till the 27 day of March, which day we had sight of an Iland, called Dominica, upon the coast of the West Indies, in fourteene degrees: from thence we coasted from place to place, making our traffike with the Spaniards as we might, somewhat hardly, because the king had straightly commanded all his Governors in those parts, by no meanes to suffer any trade to be made with us: notwithstanding we had reasonable trade, and courteous entertainement, from the Ile of Margarita unto Cartagena, without any thing greatly worth the noting, saving at Capo de la Vela, in a towne called Rio de la Hacha (from whence come all the pearles) the treasurer who had the charge there, would by no meanes agree to any trade, or suffer us to take water, he had fortified his towne with divers bulwarkes in all places where it might be entered, and furnished himselfe with an hundred Hargabuziers, so that he thought by famine to have inforced us to have put a land our Negros: of which purpose he had not greatly failed, unlesse we had by force entred the towne: which (after we could by no meanes obtaine his favour) we were enforced to doe, and so with two hundred men brake in upon their bulwarkes, and entred the towne with the losse onely of two men of our partes, and no hurt done to the Spaniards because after their voley of shot discharged, they all fled.

Thus having the town with some circumstance, as partly by the Spaniards desire of Negros, and partly by friendship of the Treasurer, we obtained a secret trade: whereupon the Spaniards resorted to us by night, and bought of us to the number of 200 Negros: in all other places where we traded the Spaniards inhabitants were glad of us and traded willingly.

At Cartagena the last towne we thought to have seene on the coast, we could by no meanes obtaine to deale with any Spaniard, the governour was so straight, and because our trade was so neere finished we thought not good either to adventure any landing, or to detract further time, but in peace departed from thence the 24 of July, hoping to have escaped the time of their stormes which then soone after began to reigne, the which they call Furicanos, but passing by the West end of Cuba, towards the coast of Florida there happened to us the 12 day of August an extreme storme which continued by the space of foure dayes, which so beat the Jesus, that we cut downe all her higher buildings, her rudder also was sore shaken, and withall was in so ex-

treme a leake that we were rather upon the point to leave her
then to keepe her any longer, yet hoping to bring all to good
passe, we sought the coast of Florida, where we found no place
nor Haven for our ships, because of the shalownesse of the
coast: thus being in greater dispaire, and taken with a newe
storme which continued other 3 dayes, we were inforced to take
for our succour the Port which serveth the citie of Mexico called
Saint John de Ullua, which standeth in 19 degrees: in seeking
of which Port we tooke in our way 3 ships which carried passengers to the number of an hundred, which passengers we
hoped should be a meane to us the better to obtaine victuals for
our money, & a quiet place for the repairing of our fleete.
Shortly after this the 16 of September we entered the Port of
Saint John de Ullua and in our entrie the Spaniardes thinking
us to be the fleete of Spaine, the chiefe officers of the Countrey
came aboord us, which being deceived of their expectation were
greatly dismayed: but immediatly when they sawe our demand
was nothing but victuals, were recomforted. I found also in the
same Port twelve ships which had in them by report two hundred thousand pound in gold & silver, all which (being in my
possession, with the kings Iland as also the passengers before
in my way thitherward stayed) I set at libertie, without the
taking from them the waight of a groat: onely because I would
not be delayed of my dispatch, I stayed two men of estimation
and sent post immediatly to Mexico, which was two hundred
miles from us, to the Presidentes and Councell there, shewing
them of our arrivall there by the force of weather, and the
necessitie of the repaire of our shippes and victuals, which
wantes we required as friends to king Philip to be furnished of
for our money: and that the Presidents and Councell there
should with all convenient speede take order, that at the arrivall
of the Spanish fleete, which was dayly looked for, there might
no cause of quarrell rise betweene us and them, but for the
better maintenance of amitie, their commandement might be
had in that behalfe. This message being sent away the sixteenth
day of September at night, being the very day of our arrivall, in
the next morning which was the seventeenth day of the same
moneth, we sawe open of the Haven thirteene great shippes,
and understanding them to bee the fleete of Spaine, I sent immediatly to advertise the Generall of the fleete of my being

there, doing him to understand, that before I would suffer them
to enter the Port, these should some order of conditions passe
betweene us for our safe being there, and maintenance of peace.
Now it is to be understood that this Port is made by a little
Iland of stones not three foote above the water in the highest
place, and but a bow-shoot of length any way, this Iland
standeth from the maine land two bow shootes or more, also it
is to be understood that there is not in all this coast any other
place for ships to arrive in safety, because the North winde hath
there such violence, that unlesse the shippes be very safely
mored with their ankers fastened upon this Iland, there is no
remedie for these North windes but death: also the place of
the Haven was so little, that of necessitie the shippes must ride
one aboord the other, so that we could not give place to them,
nor they to us: and here I beganne to bewaile that which after
followed, for now, said I, I am in two dangers, and forced to
receive the one of them. That was, either I must have kept out
the fleete from entring the Port, the which with Gods helpe I
was very well able to doe, or else suffer them to enter in with
their accustomed treason, which they never faile to execute,
where they may have opportunitie, to compasse it by any
meanes: if I had kept them out, then had there bene present
shipwracke of all the fleete which amounted in value to sixe
Millions, which was in value of our money 1800000. li. which
I considered I was not able to answere, fearing the Queenes
Majesties indignation in so waightie a matter. Thus with my
selfe revolving the doubts, I thought rather better to abide the
Jutt of the uncertainty, then the certaintie. The uncertaine
doubt I account was their treason which by good policie I
hoped might be prevented, and therefore as chusing the least
mischiefe I proceeded to conditions. Now was our first messenger come and returned from the fleete with report of the
arrivall of a Viceroy, so that hee had authoritie, both in all this
Province of Mexico (otherwise called Nueva Espanna) and in
the sea, who sent us word that we should send our conditions,
which of his part should (for the better maintenance of amitie
betweene the Princes) be both favourably granted, and faithfully performed, with many faire wordes how passing the coast
of the Indies he had understood of our honest behaviour
towardes the inhabitants where we had to doe, aswell elsewhere

as in the same Port, the which I let passe: thus following our demand, we required victuals for our money, and licence to sell as much ware as might furnish our wants, and that there might be of either part twelve gentlemen as hostages for the maintenance of peace: and that the Iland for our better safetie might be in our owne possession, during our abode there, and such ordinance as was planted in the same Iland which were eleven peeces of brasse: and that no Spaniard might land in the Iland with any kind of weapon: these conditions at the first he somewhat misliked, chiefly the guard of the Iland to be in our owne keeping, which if they had had, we had soone knowen our fare: for with the first North winde they had cut our cables and our ships had gone ashore: but in the ende he concluded to our request, bringing the twelve hostages to ten, which with all speede of either part were received, with a writing from the Viceroy signed with his hande and sealed with his seale of all the conditions concluded, & forthwith a trumpet blowen with commandement that none of either part should be meane to violate the peace upon paine of death: and further it was concluded that the two Generals of the fleetes should meete, and give faith ech to other for the performance of the premisses which was so done. Thus at the end of 3 dayes all was concluded & the fleete entered the Port, saluting one another as the maner of the sea doth require. Thus as I said before, thursday we entred the Port, Friday we saw the fleete, and on munday at night they entered the Port: then we laboured 2. daies placing the English ships by themselves & the Spanish ships by themselves, the captaines of ech part & inferiour men of their parts promising great amity of al sides: which even as with all fidelitie it was ment on our part, so the Spaniards ment nothing lesse on their parts, but from the maine land had furnished themselves with a supply of men to the number of 1000, and ment the next thursday being the 23 of September at dinner time to set upon us on all sides. The same Thursday in the morning the treason being at hand, some appearance shewed, as shifting of weapon from ship to ship, planting and bending of ordinance from the ships to the Iland where our men warded, passing too and fro of companies of men more then required for their necessary busines, & many other ill likelihoods, which caused us to have a vehement suspition, and therewithall sent to the Viceroy to enquire what was ment by it, which sent immediatly straight commandement to unplant all things suspicious, and also sent word that he in the faith of a Viceroy would be our defence from all villanies. Yet we being not satisfied with this answere, because we suspected a great number of men to be hid in a great ship of 900 tunnes, which was mored next unto the Minion, sent againe to the Viceroy the master of the Jesus which had the Spanish tongue, and required to be satisfied if any such thing were or not. The Viceroy now seeing that the treason must be discovered, foorthwith stayed our master, blew the Trumpet, and of all sides set upon us: our men which warded a shore being stricken with sudden feare, gave place, fled, and sought to recover succour of the ships; the Spainardes being before provided for the purpose landed in all places in multitudes from their ships which they might easily doe without boates, and slewe all our men a shore without mercie, a fewe of them escaped aboord the Jesus. The great ship which had by the estimation three hundred men placed in her secretly, immediatly fell aboord the Minion, but by Gods appointment, in the time of the suspicion we had, which was onely one halfe houre, the Minion was made readie to avoide, and so leesing her hedfasts, and hayling away by the sternefastes she was gotten out: thus with Gods helpe she defended the violence of the first brunt of these three hundred men. The Minion being past out, they came aboord the Jesus, which also with very much a doe and the losse of manie of our men were defended and kept out. Then there were also two other ships that assaulted the Jesus at the same instant, so that she had hard getting loose, but yet with some time we had cut our head-fastes and gotten out by the sterne-fastes. Nowe when the Jesus and the Minion were gotten about two shippes length from the Spanish fleete, the fight beganne so hotte on all sides that within one houre the Admirall of the Spaniards was supposed to be sunke, their Viceadmirall burned and one other of their principall ships supposed to be sunke, so that the shippes were little able to annoy us.

Then it is to be understood, that all the Ordinance upon the Ilande was in the Spaniardes handes, which did us so great annoyance, that it cut all the mastes and yardes of the Jesus, in such sort that there was no hope to carrie her away: also it

sunke our small shippes, wereupon we determined to place the
Jesus on that side of the Minion, that she might abide all the
batterie from the land, and so be a defence for the Minion till
night, and then to take such reliefe of victuall and other necessaries from the Jesus, as the time would suffer us, and to leave
her. As we were thus determining, and had placed the Minion
from the shot of the land, suddenly the Spaniards had fired two
great shippes which were comming directly with us, and having
no meanes to avoide the fire, it bredde among our men a marvellous feare, so that some sayd, let us depart with the Minion,
other said, let us see whither the winde will carrie the fire from
us. But to be short, the Minions men which had alwayes their
sayles in a readinesse, thought to make sure worke, and so
without either consent of the Captaine or Master cut their saile,
so that very hardly I was received into the Minion.

The most part of the men that were left alive in the Jesus,
made shift and followed the Minion in a small boat, the rest
which the little boate was not able to receive, were inforced to
abide the mercie of the Spaniards (which I doubt was very
little) so with the Minion only and the Judith (a small barke
of 50 tunne) we escaped, which barke the same night forsooke
us in our great miserie: we were now remooved with the Minion
from the Spanish ships two bow-shootes, and there rode all
that night: the next morning we recovered an Iland a mile from
the Spaniards, where there tooke us a North winde, and being
left onely with two ankers and two cables (for in this conflict we
lost three cables and two ankers) we thought alwayes upon
death which ever was present, but God preserved us to a longer
time.

The weather waxed reasonable, and the Saturday we set saile,
and having a great number of men and little victuals our hope
of life waxed lesse and lesse: some desired to yeeld to the Spaniards, some rather desired to obtaine a place where they might
give themselves to the Infidels, and some had rather abide with
a little pittance the mercie of God at Sea: so thus with many
sorowful hearts we wandred in an unknowen Sea by the space
of 14 dayes, till hunger inforced us to seek the land, for hides
were thought very good meat, rats, cats, mice and dogs, none
escaped that might be gotten, parrats and monkeyes that were
had in great price, were thought there very profitable if they

served the turne one dinner: thus in the end the 8 day of October we came to the land in the botome of the same bay of Mexico in 23 degrees and a halfe, where we hoped to have found inhabitants of the Spaniards, reliefe of victuals, and place for the repaire of our ship, which was so sore beaten with shot from our enemies and brused with shooting off our owne ordinance, that our wearie and weake armes were scarce able to defende and keepe out water. But all things happened to the contrary, for we found neither people, victuall, nor haven of reliefe, but a place where having faire weather with some perill we might land a boat: our people being forced with hunger desired to be set on land, whereunto I consented.

And such as were willing to land I put them apart, and such as were desirous to goe homewardes, I put apart, so that they were indifferently parted a hundred of one side and a hundred of the other side: these hundred men we set a land with all diligence in this little place beforesaid, which being landed, we determined there to take in fresh water, and so with our little remaine of victuals to take the sea.

The next day having a land with me fiftie of our hundreth men that remained for the speedier preparing of our water aboord, there arose an extreame storme, so that in three dayes we could by no meanes repaire aboord our ship: the ship also was in such perill that every houre we looked for shipwracke.

But yet God againe had mercie on us, and sent faire weather, we had aboord our water, and departed the sixteenth day of October, after which day we had faire and prosperous weather till the sixteenth day of November, which day God be praysed we were cleere from the coast of the Indies, and out of the chanell and gulfe of Bahama, which is betweene the Cape of Florida, and the Ilandes of Lucayo. After this growing neere to the colde countrey, our men being oppressed with famine, died continually, and they that were left, grew into such weakenesse that we were scantly able to manage our shippe, and the winde being alwayes ill for us to recover England, we determined to goe with Galicia in Spaine, with intent there to relieve our companie and other extreame wantes. And being arrived the last day of December in a place neere unto Vigo called Ponte Vedra, our men with excesse of fresh meate grew into miserable disseases, and died a great part of them. This matter was borne out as long as it might be, but in the end although there were none of our men suffered to goe a land, yet by accesse of the Spaniards, our feeblenesse was knowen to them. Whereupon they ceased not to seeke by all meanes to betray us, but with all speede possible we departed to Vigo, where we had some helpe of certaine English ships and twelve fresh men, wherewith we repaired our wants as we might, and departing the 20 day of January 1568 arrived in Mounts bay in Cornewall the 25 of the same moneth, praised be God therefore.

If all the miseries and troublesome affaires of this sorowfull voyage should be perfectly and throughly written, there should neede a painefull man with his pen, and as great a time as he had that wrote the lives and deathes of the Martyrs.

JOHN HAWKINS

15

The names of such countries as I Anthony Jenkinson have travelled unto, from the second of October 1546, at which time I made my first voyage out of England, untill the yeere of our Lord 1572, when I returned last out of Russia

FIRST, I passed into Flanders, and travelled through all the base countries, and from thence through Germanie, passing over the Alpes I travelled into Italy, and from thence made my journey through Piemont into France, throughout all which realme I have throughly journied.

I have also travelled through the kingdomes of Spaine and Portingal, I have sailed through the Levant seas every way, & have bene in all the chiefe Islands within the same sea, as Rhodes, Malta, Sicilia, Cyprus, Candie, and divers others.

I have bene in many partes of Grecia, Morea, Achaia, and where the olde citie of Corinth stoode.

I have travelled through a great part of Turkie, Syria, and divers other countries in Asia minor.

I have passed over the mountaines of Libanus to Damasco, and travelled through Samaria, Galile, Philistine or Palestine, unto Jerusalem, and so through all the Holy land.

I have bene in divers places of Affrica, as Algiers, Cola, Bona, Tripolis, the gollet within the gulfe of Tunis.

I have sailed farre Northward within the Mare glaciale, where we have had continuall day, and sight of the Sunne ten weekes together, and that navigation was in Norway, Lapland, Samogitia, and other very strange places.

I have travelled through all the ample dominions of the Emperour of Russia and Moscovia, which extende from the North sea, and the confines of Norway and Lapland, even to the Mare Caspium.

I have bene in divers countries neere about the Caspian sea, Gentiles, and Mahomeans, as Cazan, Cremia, Rezan, Cheremisi, Mordoviti, Vachin, Nagaia, with divers others of strange customes and religions.

I have sailed over the Caspian sea, & discovered all the regions thereabout adjacent, as Chircassi, Comul, Shascal, Shirvan, with many others.

I have travelled 40 daies journey beyond the said sea, towards the Oriental India, and Cathaia, through divers deserts and wildernesses, and passed through 5 kingdomes of the Tartars, and all the land of Turkeman and Zagatay, and so to the great citie of Boghar in Bactria, not without great perils and dangers sundry times.

After all this, in An. 1562, I passed againe over the Caspian sea another way, and landed in Armenia, at a citie called Derbent, built by Alexander the great, & from thence travelled through Media, Parthia, Hircania, into Persia to the court of the great Sophie called Shaw Tamasso, unto whom I delivered letters from the Queenes majestie, and remained in his court 8 moneths, and returning homeward, passed through divers other countries. Finally I made two voyages more after that out of England into Russia, the one in the yeere 1566, and the other in the yeere 1571. And thus being weary and growing old, I am content to take my rest in mine owne house, chiefly comforting my selfe, in that my service hath bene honourably accepted and rewarded of her majestie and the rest by whom I have bene imploied.

16

The first voyage attempted and set foorth by the expert and valiant captaine M. Francis Drake himselfe, with a ship called the Dragon, and another ship and a Pinnesse, to Nombre de Dios, and Dariene, about the yeere 1572, Written and recorded by one Lopez Vaz a Portugall borne in the citie of Elvas, in maner follow: which Portugale, with the discourse about him, was taken at the river of Plate by the ships set foorth by the Right Honourable the Earle of Cumberland, in the yeere 1586

THERE was a certaine English man named Francis Drake, who having intelligence how the towne of Nombre de Dios in Nueva Espanna, had but small store of people remaining there, came on a night, and entred the Port with foure Pinnesses, and landed about 150 men, & leaving 70 men with a trumpet, in a Fort which was there, with the other 80 he entred the towne, without doing any harme, till he came to the market place, and there discharged his calivers, & sounded a trumpet very loud, and the other which he had left in the Fort answered him after the same maner, with the discharging their calivers, and sounding their trumpets: the people hereupon not thinking of any such matter, were put in great feare, and waking out of their sleepe fled all into the mountaines, inquiring one of another what the matter should be, remaining as men amazed, not knowing what the uprore was which happened so suddenly in the towne. But 14 or 15 of them joyning together with their harquebuzes, went to the market place to know what they were that were in the towne, and in a corner of the market place they did discover the Englishmen, and seeing them to be but fewe, discharged their calivers at those Englishmen: their fortune was such that they killed the Trumpetter, and shot one of the principall men thorow the legge, who seeing himselfe hurt, retyred to the Fort, where the rest of their company was left: they which were in the Fort sounded their Trumpet, and seeing that they in the towne did not answere them, and hearing the calivers, thought that all they in the towne had bene slaine, and thereupon fled to their Pinnesses: the English captaine comming to the Fort, and not finding his men which he left there, he and his were in so great feare, that leaving their furniture behind them, and putting off their hose, they swamme, and waded all to their Pinnesses, and so went with their ships againe out of the Port.

Thus this English Captaine called Francis Drake, departed from Nombre de Dios, & slew onely one man in the towne which was looking out of a windowe to see what the matter was, and of his men had onely his Trumpetter slaine.

But he being discontented with the repulse which he had received there, came to the sound of Dariene, and having conference with certaine Negros which were fled from their masters of Panama, and Nombre de Dios, the Negros did tell him, that certaine Mules came laden with gold and silver from Panama to Nombre de Dios, who in companie of these Negros went thereupon on land, and stayed in the way where the treasure should come with an hundred shot, and so tooke two companies of mules, which came onely with their drivers mistrusting nothing, and he carried away the gold onely, for they were not able to carrie the silver through the mountaines. And two dayes after he came to the house of Crosses, where he killed sixe or seven marchants, but found no golde nor silver but much marchandize: so he fired the house, where was burnt above 200000 Duckets in marchandize, and so went to his ship againe: and within halfe an houre after he was a ship-boord, there came downe to the sandes three hundred shot of the Spaniards in the sight of his ships, of purpose to seeke him, but he cared little for them, being out of their reach, and so departed with his treasure.

17

The first Voyage of M. Martine Frobisher, to the Northwest, for the search of the straight or passage to China, written by Christopher Hall, Master in the Gabriel, and made in the yeere of our Lord 1576

THE 7. of June being Thursday, the two Barks, viz. the Gabriel, and the Michael & our Pinnesse set saile at Ratcliffe, and bare down to Detford, and there we ancred: the cause was, that our Pinnesse burst her boultsprit, and foremast aboard of a ship that rode at Detford, else wee meant to have past that day by the Court then at Grenewich.

The 8. day being Friday, about 12 of the clocke we wayed at Detford, and set saile all three of us, and bare downe by the Court, where we shotte off our ordinance and made the best shew we could: Her Majestie beholding the same, commended it, and bade us farewell, with shaking her hand at us out of the window. Afterward shee sent a Gentleman aboord of us, who declared that her Majestie had good liking of our doings, and thanked us for it, and also willed our Captaine to come the next day to the Court to take his leave of her.

The same day towards night M. Secretarie Woolly came aboorde of us, and declared to the company, that her Majestie had appointed him to give them charge to be obedient, and diligent to their Captaine, and governours in all things, and wished us happie successe.

The 12. day being over against Gravesend, by the castle or blockehouse, we observed the latitude, which was 51. degrees 33. min. And in that place the variation of the Compasse is 11. degrees and a halfe.

The 24. day at 2. of the clocke after noone, I had sight of Faire yle, being from us 6. leagues North and by East, and when I brought it Northwest and by North, it did rise at the Southermost ende with a litle hommocke, and swampe in the middes.

The 25. day from 4. to 8. a clocke in the forenoone, the winde at Northwest and by North a fresh gale, I cast about to the Westward, the Southermost head of Shotland called Swinborne head Northnorthwest from me, and the land of Faire yle, West Southwest from me. I sailed directly to the North head of that said land, sounding as I ranne in, having 60. 50. and 40. fathoms, and gray redde shels: and within halfe a mile of that Island, there are 36. fathoms, for I sailed to that Island to see whether there were any roadesteede for a Northwest winde, and I found by my sounding hard rockes, and foule ground, and deepe water, within two cables length of the shoare, 28. fathome, and so did not ancre but plied to and fro with my foresaile, and mizen till it was a high water under the Island. The tide setteth there Northwest and Southeast: the flood setteth Southeast, and the ebbe Northwest.

The 26. day having the winde at South a faire gale, sayling from Faire yle to Swinborne head, I did observe the latitude, the Island of Fowlay being West Northwest from me 6. leagues, and Swinborne head East southeast from me, I found my *elevation to be 37. degr. and my declination 22. degr. 46. min. So that my latitude was 59. degr. 46. min. At that present being neere to Swinborne head, having a leake which did trouble us, as also to take in fresh water, I plyed roome with a sound, which is called S. Tronions, and there did ancre in seven fathoms water, and faire sande. You have comming in the sounds mouth in the entring 17. 15. 12. 10. 9. 8. and 7. fathoms, and the sound lyeth in North northwest, and there we roade to a West sunne, & stopped our leake, and having refreshed our selves with water, at a North northwest sunne, I set saile from S. Tronions the winde at South Southest, and turned out till wee were cleare of the sound, and so sailed West to go cleare of the Island of Fowlay. And running off toward Fowlay, I sounded, having fiftie fathome, and streamie ground, and also I sounded Fowlay being North from mee one league off that Islande, having fiftie fathome at the South head, and streamie

---

* By elevation he meaneth the distance of the sunne from the zenith.

ground, like broken otmell, and one shell being redde and white like mackerell.

The 27. day at a South sunne I did observe the latitude, the Island of Fowlay being from me two leagues East Northeast: I found my selfe to be in latitude 59. degrees, 59. min. truly observed, the winde at South Southwest: I sailed West and by North.

From 12. to foure a clocke afternoone, the wind at South, a faire gale the shippe sailed West and by North 6. leagues, and at the ende of this watch, I sounded having 60. fathome, with little stones and shels, the Island from us 8. leagues East.

The first of July, from 4. to 8. a clocke, wee sailed West 4. glasses 4. leagues, and at that present we had so much winde that we spooned afore the sea Southwest 2. leagues.

The 3. day we found our Compasse to bee varied one point to the Westwards: this day from 4. to 8. a clocke we sailed West and by North 6. leagues.

From 8. to 12. a clocke at noone West and by North 4. leagues. At that present I found our Compasse to be varied 11. deg. and one 4. part to the Westwards, which is one point.

The 11 day at a Southeast sunne we had sight of the land of Friseland bearing from us West northwest 16. leagues, and rising like pinacles of steeples, and all covered with snowe. I found my selfe in 61. degr. of latitude. Wee sailed to the shoare and could finde no ground at 150. fathoms, we hoised out our boate, and the Captaine with 4. men rowed to the shoare to get on land, but the land lying full of yce, they could not get on land, and so they came aboord againe: We had much adoe to get cleare of the yce by reason of the fogge. Yet from Thursday 8. a clocke in the morning to Friday at noone we sailed Southwest 20. leagues.

The 18. day at a Southwest sunne I found the sunne to be elevated 33. deg. And at a Southsoutheast sunne 40. deg. So I observed it till I found it at the highest, and then it was elevated 52. deg. I judged the variation of the Compasse to be 2. points and a halfe to the Westward.

The 21. day we had sight of a great drift of yce, seeming a firme lande, and we cast Westward to be cleare of it.

The 26. we had sight of a land of yce: the latitude was 62. degrees, and two minutes.

The 28. day in the morning was very foggie: but at the
clearing up of the fogge, wee had sight of lande, which I supposed to be Labrador, with great store of yce about the land:
I ranne in towards it, and sownded, but could get no ground
at 100. fathom, and the yce being so thicke, I could not get to
the shoare, and so lay off, and came cleare of the yce. Upon
Munday we came within a mile of the shoare, and sought a
harborowe: all the sownd was full of yce, and our boate rowing
a shoare, could get no ground at 100. fathom, within a Cables
length of the shoare: then we sailed Eastnortheast along the
shoare, for so the lande lyeth, and the currant is there great,
setting Northeast, and Southwest: and if we could have gotten
anker ground, wee would have seene with what force it had
runne, but I judge a ship may drive a league and a halfe, in one
houre, with that tide.

This day at 4. of the cloke in the morning, being faire and
cleere, we had sight of a head land, as we judged, bearing from
us north, and by East, and we sailed Northeast, and by North
to that land, and when we came thither, wee could not get to
the lande for yce: for the yce stretched along the coast, so that
we could not come to the land, by five leagues.

Wednesday the first of August it calmed, and in the after
noone I caused my boate to be hoysed out, being hard by a
great Island of yce, and I and foure men rowed to that yce,
and sownded within two Cables length of it, and had sixteene
fathome, and little stones, and after that sownded againe within
a Minion shot, and had ground at an hundreth fathome, and
faire sand: we sownded the next day a quarter of a myle from
it, and had sixtie fathome rough ground, and at that present
being aboord, that great Island of yce fell one part from another
making a noyse as if a great cliffe had fallen into the Sea. And
at foure of the clocke I sownded againe, and had 90. fathome,
and small blacke stones, and little white stones, like pearles.
The tide here did set to the shoare.

The tenth I tooke foure men, and my selfe, and rowed to
shoare to an Island one league from the maine, and there the
flood setteth Southwest alongest the shoare, and it floweth as
neere as I could judge so too, I could not tarry to proove it,
because the ship was a great way from me, and I feared a fogge:
but when I came a shoare, it was a low water. I went to ye top

of the Island, and before I came backe, it was hied a foote water, and so without tarrying I came aboord.

The 11. we found our latitude to be 63. degr. and eight minutes, and this day we entred the streight.

The 12. wee set saile towardes an Island, called the Gabriels Island, which was 10. leagues then from us.

We espied a sound, and bare with it, and came to a sandie Baye, where we came to an anker, the land bearing East southeast off us, and there we rode al night in 8. fathome water. It floweth there at a Southeast Moone. We called it Priors sownd, being from the Gabriels Island, tenne leagues.

The 14. we waied, and ranne into another sownde, where wee ankered in 8. fathome water, faire sand, and blacke oaze, and there calked our ship, being weake from the wales upward, and tooke in fresh water.

The 15. day we waied, and sailed to Priors Bay, being a mile from thence.

The 16. day was calme, and we rode still, without yce, but presently within two houres it was frozen round about the ship, a quarter of an ynch thicke, and that day very faire, and calme.

The 17. day we waied, and came to Thomas Williams Island.

The 18. day we sailed North northwest, and ankered againe in 23. fathome, and tough oaze, under Burchers Island, which is from the former Island, ten leagues.

The 19. day in the morning, being calme, and no winde, the Captaine and I tooke our boate, with eight men in her, to rowe us a shoare, to see if there were there any people, or no, and going to the toppe of the Island, we had sight of seven boates, which came rowing from the East side, toward that Island: whereupon we returned aboord againe: at length we sent our boate with five men in her, to see whither they rowed, and so with a white cloth brought one of their boates with their men along the shoare, rowing after our boate, till such time as they sawe our ship, and then they rowed a shoare: then I went on shoare my selfe, and gave every of them a threadden point, and brought one of them aboord of me, where hee did eate and drinke, and then carried him on shoare againe. Whereupon all the rest came aboord with their boates, being nineteene persons, and they spake, but we understoode them not. They bee like to Tartars, with long blacke haire, broad faces, and flatte noses, and tawnie in colour, wearing Seale skinnes, and so doe the women, not differing in the fashion, but the women are marked in the face with blewe streekes downe the cheekes, and round about the eyes. Their boates are made all of Seales skinnes, with a keele of wood within the skin: the proportion of them is like a Spanish shallop, save only they be flat in the bottome, and sharpe at both ends.

The twentieth day wee wayed, and went to the Eastside of this Island, and I and the Captaine, with foure men more went on shoare, and there we sawe their houses, and the people espying us, came rowing towards our boate: whereupon we plied toward our boate: and wee being in our boate and they ashoare, they called to us, and we rowed to them, and one of their company came into our boate, and we carried him a boord, and gave him a Bell, and a knife: so the Captaine and I willed five of our men to set him a shoare at a rocke, and not among the company, which they came from, but their wilfulnesse was such, that they would goe to them, and so were taken themselves, and our boate lost.

The next day in the morning, we stoode in neere the shoare, and shotte off a fauconet, and sounded our trumpet, but we could heare nothing of our men: this sound wee called the five mens sound, and plyed out of it, but ankered againe in thirtie fathome, and oaze: and riding there all night, in the morning, the snow lay a foote thicke upon our hatches.

The 22. day in the morning we wayed, and went againe to the place where we lost our men, and our boate. We had sight of fourteene boates, and some came neere to us, but wee could learne nothing of our men: among the rest, we intised one boate to our ships side, with a Bell, and in giving him the Bell, we tooke him, and his boate, and so kept him, and so rowed downe to Thomas Williams Island, and there ankered all night.

The 26. day we waied, to come homeward, and by 12. of the clocke at noone, we were thwart of Trumpets Island.

The next day we came thwart of Gabriels Island, and at 8. of the clocke at night we had the Cape Labrador as we supposed West from us, ten leagues.

The 28. day we went our course Southeast.

We sailed Southeast, and by East, 22. leagues.

The first day of September in the morning we had sight of

the land of Friseland, being eight leagues from us, but we could not come neerer it, for the monstrous yce that lay about it. From this day, till the sixth of this Moneth, we ranne along Island, and had the South part of it at eight of the clocke, East from us ten leagues.

The seventh day of this moneth we had a very terrible storme, by force whereof, one of our men was blowen into the sea out of our waste, but he caught hold of the foresaile sheate, and there held till the Captaine pluckt him againe into the ship.

The 25. day of this moneth we had sight of the Island of Orkney, which was then East from us.

The first day of October we had sight of the Sheld, and so sailed about the coast, and ankered at Yarmouth, and the next day we came into Harwich.

18

The second voyage of Master Martin Frobisher, made to the West and Northwest Regions, in the yeere 1577. with a description of the Countrey, and people: Written by Master Dionise Settle

O N Whitsunday, being the sixe and twentieth of May, in the yeere of our Lord God 1577. Captaine Frobisher departed from Blacke Wall, with one of the Queenes Majesties ships, called The Aide, of nine score tunnes, or thereabouts: and two other little Barkes likewise, the one called The Gabriel, whereof Master Fenton, a Gentleman of my Lord of Warwikes, was Captaine: and the other, The Michael, whereof Master Yorke, a Gentleman of my Lord Admirals was Captaine, accompanied with seven score Gentlemen, souldiers, and sailers, well furnished with victuals, and other provision necessarie for one halfe yeere, on this his second voyage, for the further discovering of the passage to Cathay, and other Countreys, thereunto adjacent, by West and Northwest navigations: which passage or way, is supposed to bee on the North and Northwest part of America: and the said America to be an Island invironed with the sea, where through our Merchants may have course and recourse with their merchandize, from these our Northernmost parts of Europe, to those Orientall coasts of Asia, in much shorter time, and with greater benefite then any others, to their no little commoditie and profite that do or shall frequent the same. Our said Captaine and General of this present voyage and company having the yeere before, with two little pinnesses, to his great danger, and no small commendations given a worthy attempt towards the performance thereof, is also prest, when occasion shall be ministred (to the benefite of his Prince, and native Countrey) to adventure himselfe further therein. As for this second voyage, it seemeth sufficient, that he hath better explored and searched the commodities of those people and Countreys, which in his first voyage the yeere before he had found out.

Upon which considerations, the day and yeere before expressed, we departed from Blacke Wall to Harwich, where making an accomplishment of things necessary, the last of May we hoised up sailes, and with a merrie wind the 7. of June we arrived at the Islands called Orcades, or vulgarly Orkney, being in number 30. subject and adjacent to Scotland, where we made provision of fresh water; in the doing whereof our Generall licensed the Gentlemen and souldiers for their recreation, to goe on shore. At our landing, the people fled from their poore cottages, with shrikes and alarms, to warne their neighbours of enemies, but by gentle perswasions we reclamed them to their houses. It seemeth they are often frighted with Pirats, or some other enemies, that moove them to such sudden feare. Their houses are very simply builded with Pibble stone, without any chimneis, the fire being made in the middest thereof. The good man, wife, children, and other of their family eate and sleepe on the one side of the house, and the cattell on the other, very beastly and rudely, in respect of civilitie. They are destitute of wood, their fire is turffes, and Cowshards. They have corne, bigge, and oates, with which they pay their Kings rent, to the maintenance of his house. They take great quantitie of fish, which they dry in the wind and Sunne. They dresse their meat very filthily, and eate it without salt. Their apparell is after the rudest sort of Scotland. Their money is all base. Their Church and religion is reformed according to the Scots. The fisher men of England can better declare the dispositions of those people then I: wherefore I remit other their usages to their reports, as yeerely repaires thither, in their course to and from Island for fish.

We departed herehence the 8. of June, and followed our course betweene West and Northwest, untill the 4. of July: all which time we had no night, but that easily, and without any impediment we had when we were so disposed, the fruition of our bookes, and other pleasures to passe away the time: a thing of no small moment, to such as wander in unknowen seas, and long navigations, especially, when both the winds and raging surges do passe their common and wonted course. This benefite endureth in those parts not 6. weekes, while the sunne is neere the Tropike of Cancer: but where the pole is raised to 70. or 80. degrees, it continueth much longer.

All along these seas, after we were sixe dayes sailing from Orkney, we met floting in the sea, great Firre trees, which as we judged, were with the furie of great floods rooted up, and so driven into the sea. Island hath almost no other wood nor fuell, but such as they take up upon their coastes. It seemeth, that these trees are driven from some part of the New found land, with the current that setteth from the West to the East.

The 4. of July we came within the making of Frisland. From this shoare 10. or 12. leagues, we met great Islands of yce, of halfe a mile, some more, some lesse in compasse, shewing above the sea, 30. or 40. fathoms, and as we supposed fast on ground, where with our lead we could scarse sound the bottome for depth.

Here, in place of odoriferous and fragrant smels of sweete gums, & pleasant notes of musicall birdes, which other Countreys in more temperate Zones do yeeld, wee tasted the most boisterous Boreal blasts mixt with snow and haile, in the moneths of June and July, nothing inferior to our untemperate winter: a sudden alteration, and especially in a place or Parallele, where the Pole is not elevate above 61. degrees: at which height other Countreys more to the North, yea unto 70. degrees, shew themselves more temperate then this doth.

All along this coast yce lieth, as a continuall bulwarke, & so defendeth the Countrey, that those that would land there, incur great danger. Our Generall 3. dayes together attempted with the ship boate to have gone on shoare, which for that without great danger he could not accomplish, he deferred it untill a more convenient time. All along the coast lie very high mountaines covered with snow, except in such places, where through the steepenes of the mountaines of force it must needs fall. Foure dayes coasting along this land, we found no signe of habitation. Little birds, whiche we judged to have lost the shore, by reason of thicke fogges which that Countrey is much subject unto, came flying into our ships, which causeth us to suppose, that the Countrey is both more tollerable, and also habitable within, then the outward shore maketh shew or signification.

From hence we departed the eight of July: and the 16. of the same, we came with the making of land, which land our Generall the yeere before had named The Queenes foreland, being an Island as we judge, lying neere the supposed continent with America: and on the other side, opposite to the same, one other Island called Halles Isle, after the name of the Master of the ship, neere adjacent to the firme land, supposed continent with Asia. Betweene the which two Islands there is a large entrance or streight, called Frobishers streight, after the name of our Generall, the first finder thereof. This said streight is supposed to have passage into the sea of Sur, which I leave unknowen as yet.

It seemeth that either here, or not farre hence, the sea should have more large entrance, then in other parts within the frozen or untemperate Zone: and that some contrary tide, either from the East or West, with maine force casteth out that great quantity of yce, which commeth floting from this coast, even unto Friseland, causing that Countrey to seeme more untemperate then others, much more Northerly then the same.

I cannot judge that any temperature under the Pole, the time of the Sunnes Northerne declination being halfe a yere together, and one whole day, (considering that the Sunnes elevation surmounteth not 23. degrees and 30. minuts) can have power to dissolve such monstrous and huge yce, comparable to great mountaines, except by some other force, as by swift currents and tides, with the helpe of the said day of halfe a yeere.

Before we came within the making of these lands we tasted cold stormes, in so much that it seemed we had changed summer with winter, if the length of the dayes had not remooved us from that opinion.

At our first comming, the streights seemed to be shut up with a long mure of yce, which gave no litle cause of discomfort unto us all: but our Generall, (to whose diligence imminent dangers, and difficult attempts seemed nothing, in respect of his willing mind, for the commoditie of his Prince and Countrey,) with two little Pinnesses prepared of purpose, passed twise thorow them to the East shore, and the Islands thereunto adjacent: and the ship, with the two Barks lay off and on something further into the sea, from the danger of the yce.

Whilest he was searching the Countrey neere the shoare,

some of the people of the Countrey shewed themselves leaping and dauncing, with strange shrikes and cries, which gave no little admiration to our men. Our Generall desirous to allure them unto him by faire meanes, caused knives, and other things to be profered unto them, which they would not take at our hands: but being laid on the ground, and the party going away, they came and tooke up, leaving some thing of theirs to countervaile the same. At the length two of them leaving their weapons, came downe to our Generall and Master, who did the like to them, commanding the company to stay, and went unto them: who after certaine dumbe signes, and mute congratulations, began to lay handes upon them, but they deliverly escaped, and ranne to their bowes and arrowes, and came fiercely upon them, (not respecting the rest of our companie which were ready for their defence) but with their arrowes hurt divers of them: we tooke the one, and the other escaped.

Whilest our Generall was busied in searching the Countrey, and those Islands adjacent on the Eastshoare, the ship and barkes having great care, not to put farre into the sea from him, for that he had small store of victuals, were forced to abide in a cruell tempest, chancing in the night, amongst and in the thickest of the yce, which was so monstrous, that even the least of a thousand had bene of force sufficient, to have shivered our ship and barks into small portions, if God (who in all necessities, hath care upon the infirmitie of man) had not provided for this our extremitie a sufficient remedie through the light of the night, whereby we might well discerne to flee from such imminent dangers, which we avoyded with 14. Bourdes in one watch the space of 4 houres. If we had not incurred this danger amongst these monstrous Islands of yce, we should have lost our Generall and Master, and the most of our best sailers, which were on the shore destitute of victuals: but by the valure of our Master Gunner, Master Jackman, and Andrew Dier, the Masters Mates, men expert both in navigation, and other good qualities, wee were all content to incurre the dangers aforerehearsed, before we would with our owne safetie, runne into the seas, to the destruction of our sayd Generall, and his company.

The day following, being the 19. of Julie, our captaine returned to the ship with report of supposed riches, which shewed it selfe in the bowels of those barren mountaines, wherewith wee were all satisfied.

Within foure daies after we had bene at the entrance of the streights, the Northwest and West winds dispersed the yce into the sea, & made us a large entrance into the streights, so that without any impediment, on the 19. of Julie we entred them, and the 20. thereof, our Generall and Master with great diligence, sought out and sounded the West shoare, and found out a faire Harborough for the ship and barkes to ride in, and named it after our Masters mate, Jackmans sound, and brought the ship, barkes, and all their company to safe anker, except one man, which died by Gods visitation.

At our first arrivall, after the ship rode at anker, our generall, with such company as could well be spared from the ships, in marching order entred the lande, having speciall care by exhortations, that at our entrance thereinto, wee should all with one voyce, kneeling upon our knees, chiefly thanke God for our safe arrivall: secondly beseech him, that it would please his divine Majestie, long to continue our Queene, for whom he, and all the rest of our company in this order tooke possession of the Countrey: and thirdly, that by our Christian studie and endevour, those barbarous people trained up in Paganisme, and infidelitie, might be reduced to the knowledge of true religion, and to the hope of salvation in Christ our Redeemer. With other words very apt to signifie his willing mind, and affection toward his Prince and Countrey: whereby all suspicion of an undutifull subject, may credibly be judged to be utterly exempted from his mind. All the rest of the Gentlemen and other deserve worthily herein, their due praise and commendation.

These things in this order accomplished, our Generall commanded all the company to be obedient in things needfull for our owne safegard, to Master Fenton, Master Yorke, and Master Beast his Lieutenant, while he was occupied in other necessarie affaires, concerning our comming thither.

After this order we marched through the Countrey, with Ensigne displaied, so farre as was thought needfull, and now and then heaped up stones on high mountaines, and other places in token of possession, as likewise to signifie unto such as hereafter may chance to arrive there, that possession is taken in the behalfe of some other Prince, by those who first found out the Countrey.

Whoso maketh navigations to those Countreys, hath not onely extreme winds, and furious seas to encounter withall, but also many monstrous and great Islands of yce: a thing both rare, wonderfull, and greatly to be regarded.

We were forced sundry times, while the ship did ride here at anker, to have continuall watch, with boats & men ready with halsers to knit fast unto such yce, as with the ebbe & flood were tossed to and fro in the harborough, & with force of oares to hale them away, for endangering the ship.

Our Generall certaine dayes searched this supposed continent with America, and not finding the commodity to answere his expectation, after he had made triall thereof he departed thence with two little barks, and men sufficient to the East shore being the supposed continent of Asia, and left the ship with most of the Gentlemen, souldiers, and sailers, untill such time as he either thought good to send or come for them.

The stones of this supposed continent with America be altogether sparkled, and glister in the Sunne like gold: so likewise doth the sand in the bright water, yet they verifie the old Proverb: All is not gold that glistereth.

On this West shore we found a dead fish floating, which had in his nose a horne streight and torquet, of length two yards lacking two ynches, being broken in the top, where we might perceive it hollow, into the which some of our sailers putting spiders they presently died. I saw not the triall hereof, but it was reported unto me of a trueth: by the vertue whereof we supposed it to be the sea Unicorne.

After our Generall had found out good harborough for the ship and barks to anker in, and also such store of supposed gold ore as he thought himselfe satisfied withall, he returned to the Michael, whereof Master Yorke aforesaid was Captaine, accompanied with our master and his Mate: who coasting along the West shore not farre from whence the ship rode, they perceived a faire harborough, and willing to sound the same, at the entrance thereof they espied two tents of Seale skins, unto which the Captaine, our said Master, and other company resorted. At the sight of our men the people fled into the mountaines:

neverthelesse they went to their tents, where leaving certaine trifles of ours, as glasses, bels, knives, and such like things they departed, not taking any thing of theirs except one dogge. They did in like maner leave behind them a letter, pen, yncke, and paper, whereby our men whom the Captaine lost the yere before, and in that peoples custody, might (if any of them were alive) be advertised of our presence and being there.

On the same day after consultation had, all the Gentlemen, and others likewise that could be spared from the ship, under the conduct and leading of Master Philpot, (unto whom in our Generall his absence, and his Lieutenant Master Beast, al the rest were obedient) went a shore, determining to see, if by faire means we could either allure them to familiarity, or otherwise take some of them, and so attaine to some knowledge of those men whom our Generall lost the yeere before.

At our comming backe againe to the place where their tents were before, they had remooved their tents further into the said Bay or Sound, where they might if they were driven from the land, flee with their boates into the sea. We parting our selves into two companies, and compassing a mountaine came suddenly upon them by land, who espying us, without any tarying fled to their boates, leaving the most part of their oares behind them for haste, and rowed downe the bay, where our two Pinnesses met them and drove them to shore: but if they had had all their oares, so swift are they in rowing, it had bene lost time to have chased them.

When they were landed they fiercely assaulted our men with their bowes and arrowes, who wounded three of them with our arrowes: and perceiving themselves thus hurt, they desperatly leapt off the Rocks into the Sea, and drowned themselves: which if they had not done, but had submitted themselves, or if by any meanes we could have taken them alive (being their enemies as they judged) we would both have saved them, & also have sought remedy to cure their wounds received at our hands. But they altogether voyd of humanity, and ignorant what mercy meaneth, in extremities looke for no other then death: and perceiving they should fall into our hands, thus miserably by drowning rather desired death then otherwise to be saved by us: the rest perceiving their fellowes in this distresse, fled into the high mountaines. Two women not being so apt to escape as

the men were, the one for her age, and the other being incombred with a yong child, we tooke. The old wretch, whom divers
of our Saylers supposed to be eyther a devill, or a witch, had
her buskins plucked off, to see if she were cloven footed, and
for her ougly hew and deformity we let her goe: the yong woman and the child we brought away. We named the place where
they were slaine, Bloodie point: and the Bay or Harborough,
Yorks sound, after the name of one of the Captaines of the
two Barks.

Having this knowledge both of their fiercenesse and cruelty,
and perceiving that faire meanes as yet is not able to allure
them to familiarity, we disposed our selves, contrary to our inclination, something to be cruel, returned to their tents and
made a spoyle of the same: where we found an old shirt, a
doublet, a girdle, and also shooes of our men, whom we lost
the yeere before: on nothing else unto them belonging could
we set our eyes.

Their riches are not gold, silver or precious Drapery, but
their said tents and botes, made of the skins of red Deare and
Seale skins: also dogges like unto woolves, but for the most
part black, with other trifles, more to be wondred at for their
strangenesse, then for any other commoditie needefull for our
use.

Thus returning to our ship the 3. of August, we departed
from the West shore supposed firme with America, after we
had ankered there 13. dayes: and so the 4. thereof we came
to our Generall on the East shore, and ankered in a faire Harborough named Anne Warwickes sound, unto which is annexed
an Island both named after the Countesse of Warwicke, Anne
Warwickes sound and Isle.

In this Isle our Generall thought good for this voyage, to
fraight both the ship and barkes, with such stone or supposed
gold minerall, as he judged to countervaile the charges of his
first, and this his second navigation to these Countreys.

In the meane time of our abode here some of the countrey
people came to shew themselves unto us, sundry times on the
maine shore, neere adjacent to the said Isle. Our Generall desirous to have some newes of his men, whom he lost the yeere
before, with some company with him repaired with the ship
boat to common, or signe with them for familiaritie, where-

unto he is perswaded to bring them. They at the first shew made tokens, that three of his five men were alive, and desired penne, ynck, and paper, and that within three or foure dayes they would returne, and (as we judged) bring those of our men which were living, with them.

They also made signes or tokens of their King, whom they called Cacough, & how he was carried on mens shoulders, and a man farre surmounting any of our company, in bignesse and stature.

With these tokens and signes of writing, penne, yncke, and paper was delivered them, which they would not take at our hands, but being laid upon the shore, and the partie gone away, they tooke up: which likewise they do when they desire any thing for change of theirs, laying for that which is left so much as they thinke will countervaile the same, and not comming neere together. It seemeth they have bene used to this trade or traffique, with some other people adjoyning, or not farre distant from their Countrey.

After 4. dayes some of them shewed themselves upon the firme land, but not where they were before. Our General very glad thereof, supposing to heare of our men, went from the Island, with the boat, and sufficient company with him. They seemed very glad, and allured him about a certaine point of the land: behind which they might perceive a company of the crafty villaines to lye lurking, whom our Generall would not deale withall, for that he knew not what company they were, and so with few signes dismissed them and returned to his company.

An other time as our said Generall was coasting the Countrey with two little Pinnesses, whereby at our returne he might make the better relation thereof, three of the crafty villains, with a white skin allured us to them. Once againe our generall, for that he hoped to heare of his men, went towards them: at our comming neere the shore whereon they were, we might perceive a number of them lie hidden behind great stones, & those 3. in sight labouring by al meanes possible that some would come on land: and perceiving we made no hast by words nor friendly signes, which they used by clapping of their hands, and being without weapon, and but 3. in sight, they sought further meanes to provoke us thereunto. One alone laid flesh on the shore, which we tooke up with the Boat hooke, as necessary victuals for the relieving of the man, woman, and child, whom we had taken: for that as yet they could not digest our meat: whereby they perceived themselves deceived of their expectation, for all their crafty allurements. Yet once againe to make (as it were) a full shew of their craftie natures, and subtile sleights, to the intent thereby to have intrapped and taken some of our men, one of them counterfeited himselfe impotent and lame of his legs, who seemed to descend to the water side, with great difficulty: and to cover his craft the more, one of his fellowes came downe with him, and in such places where he seemed unable to passe, he tooke him on his shoulders, set him by the water side, and departed from him, leaving him (as it should seeme) all alone, who playing his counterfait pageant very well, thought thereby to provoke some of us to come on shore, not fearing, but that one of us might make our party good with a lame man.

Our Generall having compassion of his impotency, thought good (if it were possible) to cure him thereof: wherefore he caused a souldier to shoote at him with his Caleever, which grased before his face. The counterfeit villeine deliverly fled, without any impediment at all, and got him to his bow and arrowes, and the rest from their lurking holes, with their weapons, bowes, arrowes, slings, and darts. Our Generall caused some caleevers to be shot off at them, whereby some being hurt, they might hereafter stand in more feare of us.

This was all the answere for this time we could have of our men, or of our Generals letter. Their crafty dealing at these three severall times being thus manifest unto us, may plainely shew their disposition in other things to be correspondent. We judged that they used these stratagemes, thereby to have caught some of us, for the delivering of the man, woman and child whom we had taken.

They are men of a large corporature, and good proportion: their colour is not much unlike the Sunne burnt Countrey man, who laboureth daily in the Sunne for his living.

They weare their haire something long, and cut before either with stone or knife, very disorderly. Their women weare their haire long, and knit up with two loupes, shewing forth on either side of their faces, and the rest foltred upon a knot. Also some of their women race their faces proportionally, as chinne, cheekes, and forehead, and the wrists of their hands, whereupon they lay a colour which continueth darke azurine.

They eate their meat all raw, both flesh, fish, and foule, or something per boyled with blood and a little water which they drinke. For lacke of water they will eate yce, that is hard frosen, as pleasantly as we will do Sugar Candie, or other Sugar.

If they for necessities sake stand in need of the premisses, such grasse as the Countrey yeeldeth they plucke up and eate, not deintily, or salletwise to allure their stomacks to appetite: but for necessities sake without either salt, oyles or washing, like brute beasts devouring the same. They neither use table, stoole, or table cloth for comlines: but when they are imbrued with blood knuckle deepe, and their knives in like sort, they use their tongues as apt instruments to lick them cleane: in doing whereof they are assured to loose none of their victuals.

They frank or keepe certaine dogs not much unlike Wolves, which they yoke togither, as we do oxen & horses, to a sled or traile: and so carry their necessaries over the yce and snow from place to place: as the captive, whom we have, made perfect signes. And when those dogs are not apt for the same use: or when with hunger they are constrained for lacke of other victuals, they eate them: so that they are as needful for them in respect of their bignesse, as our oxen are for us.

They apparell themselves in the skins of such beasts as they kill, sewed together with the sinewes of them. All the foule which they kill, they skin, and make thereof one kind of garment or other, to defend them from the cold.

They make their apparel with hoods and tailes, which tailes they give when they thinke to gratifie any friendship shewed unto them: a great signe of friendship with them. The men have them not so side as the women.

The men and women weare their hose close to their legges, from the wast to the knee without any open before, as well the one kind as the other. Upon their legges they weare hose of leather, with the furre side inward two or three paire on at once, and especially the women. In those hose they put their knives, needles, and other things needfull to beare about. They put a bone within their hose, which reacheth from the foote to the knee, whereupon they draw their said hose, and so in place of garters they are holden from falling downe about their feete.

They dresse their skinnes very soft and souple with the haire on. In cold weather or Winter they weare the furre side inward: and in Summer outward. Other apparell they have none but the said skinnes.

Those beasts, fishes, and foules, which they kill, are their meat, drinke, apparell, houses, bedding, hose, shooes, threed, and sailes for their boates, with many other necessaries whereof they stand in need, and almost all their riches.

Their houses are tents made of Seale skins, pitched up with 4. Firre quarters foure square meeting at the top, and the skins sewed together with sinewes, and laid thereupon: they are so pitched up, that the entrance into them is alwayes South or against the Sunne.

They have other sorts of houses which we found not to be inhabited, which are raised with stones and Whale bones, and a skinne layd over them, to withstand the raine, or other weather: the entrance of them being not much unlike an Ovens mouth, whereto I thinke they resort for a time to fish, hunt, and foule, and so leave them untill the next time they come thither againe.

Their weapons are bowes, arrowes, darts, and slings. Their bowes are of wood of a yard long, sinewed at the back with strong sinewes, not glued too, but fast girded and tyed on. Their bow strings are likewise sinewes. Their arrowes are three pieces nocked with bone, and ended with bone, with those two ends, and the wood in the midst, they passe not in length halfe a yard or little more. They are fethered with two fethers the penne end being cut away, and the fethers layd upon the arrow with the broad side to the wood; insomuch that they seeme when they are tyed on, to have foure fethers. They have also three sorts of heads to those arrowes: one sort of stone or yron, proportioned like to a heart: the second sort of bone, much like unto a stopt head, with a hooke on the same: the third sort of bone likewise made sharpe at both sides, and sharpe pointed. They are not made very fast but lightly tyed to, or else set in a nocke, that upon small occasion the arrowes leave these heads behind them: and they are of small force, except they be very neere when they shoote.

Their Darts are made of two sorts: the one with many forkes of bones in the fore end and likewise in the midst: their proportions are not much unlike our toasting yrons but longer: these they cast out of an instrument of wood, very readily. The other sort is greater then the first aforesayd, with a long bone made sharpe on both sides not much unlike a Rapier, which I take to bee their most hurtfull weapon.

They have two sorts of boats made of leather, set out on the inner side with quarters of wood, artificially tyed together with thongs of the same: the greater sort are not much unlike our wherries, wherein sixteene or twenty men may sit: they have for a sayle drest the guts of such beasts as they kill very fine and thinne, which they sew together: the other boate is but for one man to sit and row in with one oare.

Their order of fishing, hunting, and fouling are with these said weapons: but in what sort, or how they use them we have no perfect knowledge as yet.

I can suppose their abode or habitation not to be here, for that neither their houses or apparell, are of such force to withstand the extremity of cold, that the Countrey seemeth to be infected with all: neither do I see any signe likely to performe the same.

Those houses or rather dennes which stand there, have no signe of footway, or any thing else troden, which is one of the chiefest tokens of habitation. And those tents which they bring with them, when they have sufficiently hunted and fished, they remove to other places: and when they have sufficiently stored them of such victuals, as the Countrey yeeldeth or bringeth forth, they returne to their winter stations or habitations. This conjecture do I make, for the infertility which I conjecture to be in that Countrey.

They have some yron whereof they make arrow heads, knives, and other little instruments, to worke their boates, bowes, arrowes, and darts withall, which are very unapt to doe any thing withall but with great labour.

It seemeth that they have conversation with some other people, of whom for exchange they should receive the same. They are greatly delighted with any thing that is bright, or giveth a sound.

What knowledge they have of God, or what Idoll they adore, we have no perfect intelligence, I thinke them rather Anthropophagi, or devourers of mans flesh then otherwise: for that there is no flesh or fish which they find dead (smell it never so filthily) but they will eate it, as they finde it without any other dressing. A loathsome thing, either to the beholders or hearers.

There is no maner of creeping beast hurtfull, except some Spiders (which as many affirme, are signes of great store of gold) and also certaine stinging Gnattes, which bite so fiercely, that the place where they bite shortly after swelleth and itcheth very sore.

They make signes of certaine people that weare bright plates of gold in their foreheads, and other places of their bodies.

The Countreys on both sides the streights lye very high with rough stony mountaines, and great quantitie of snow thereon. There is very little plaine ground and no grasse, except a little which is much like unto mosse that groweth on soft ground, such as we get Turffes in. There is no wood at all. To be briefe there is nothing fit or profitable for the use of man, which that Countrey with roote yeeldeth or bringeth forth: Howbeit there is great quantity of Deere, whose skins are like unto Asses, there heads or hornes doe farre exceede, as well in length as also in breadth, any in these our parts or Countreys: their feete likewise are as great as our oxens, which we measured to be seven or eight ynches in breadth. There are also hares, wolves, fishing beares, and sea foule of sundry sorts.

As the Countrey is barren and unfertile, so are they rude and of no capacitie to culture the same to any perfection: but are contented by their hunting, fishing, and fouling, with raw flesh and warme blood to satisfie their greedy panches, which is their only glory.

There is great likelihood of Earthquakes or thunder: for that there are huge and monstrous mountaines, whose greatest substance are stones, and those stones so shaken with some extraordinarie meanes that one is separated from another, which is discordant from all other Quarries.

There are no rivers or running springs, but such as through the heate of the Sunne, with such water as discendeth from the mountaines and hilles, whereon great drifts of snow do lie, are ingendred.

It argueth also that there should be none: for that the earth, which with the extremitie of the Winter is so frosen within, that that water which should have recourse within the same to maintaine springs, hath not his motion, whereof great waters have their originall, as by experience is seene otherwhere. Such valleis as are capable to receive the water, that in the Summer time by the operation of the Sunne descendeth from great abundance of snowe, which continually lyeth on the mountaines and hath no passage, sinketh into the earth and so vanisheth away, without any runnell above the earth, by which occasion or continuall standing of the said water, the earth is opened, and the great frost yeeldeth to the force thereof, which in other places foure or five fathoms within the ground for lacke of the said moisture, the earth (even in the very Summer time) is frosen, and so combineth the stones together, that scarcely instruments with great force can unknit them.

Also where the water in those valleis can have no such passage away, by the continuance of time in such order as is before rehearsed, the yeerely descent from the mountaines filleth them full, that at the lowest banke of the same, they fall into the valley, and so continue as fishing Ponds or Stagnes in Summer time full of water, and in the Winter hard frosen: as by skarres that remaine thereof in Summer may easily be perceived: so that the heat of Summer is nothing comparable or of force to dissolve the extremitie of cold that commeth in Winter.

Neverthelesse I am assured that below the force of the frost within the earth, the waters have recourse, and emptie themselves out of sight into the sea, which through the extremitie of the frost are constrained to doe the same: by which occasion the earth within is kept the warmer, and springs have their recourse, which is the onely nutriment of golde and Minerals within the same.

There is much to be sayd of the commodities of these Countreys, which are couched within the bowels of the earth, which I let passe till more perfect triall be made thereof.

The 24. of August, after we had satisfied our minds with fraight sufficient for our vessels, though not our covetous desires with such knowledge of the Countrey, people, and other commodities as are before rehearsed, we departed therehence. The 17. of September we fell with the lands end of England, and so sailed to Milford Haven, from whence our Generall rode to the Court for order, to what Port or Haven to conduct the ship.

We lost our two Barkes in the way homeward, the one the 29. of August, the other the 31. of the same moneth, by occasion of great tempest and fogge. Howbeit God restored the one to Bristowe, and the other made his course by Scotland to Yermouth. In this voyage we lost two men, one in the way by Gods visitation, and the other homeward cast over borde with a surge of the sea.

I could declare unto the Readers, the latitude and longitude of such places and regions as we have bene at, but not altogether so perfectly as our masters and others, with many circumstances of tempests and other accidents incident to Sea faring men, which seeme not altogether strange, but I let them passe to their reports as men most apt to set forth and declare the same. I have also left the names of the Countreys on both the shores untouched, for lacke of understanding the peoples language: as also for sundry respects, not needfull as yet to be declared.

Countreys new discovered where commoditie is to be looked for, doe better accord with a new name given by the discoverers, then an uncertaine name by a doubtfull Authour.

Our general named sundry Islands, Mountaines, Capes, and Harboroughs after the names of divers Noble men and other gentlemen his friends, aswel on the one shore as also on the other.

19

<hr/>

The third and last voyage unto Meta Incognita, made by M. Martin Frobisher, in the yeere 1578. Written by Thomas Ellis

THESE are to let you know, that upon the 25. of May, the Thomas Allen being Viceadmirall whose Captaine was M. Yorke, M. Gibbes Master, Christopher Hall Pilot, accompanied with the Reareadmiral named the Hopewel, whose Captaine was M. Henrie Carewe, the M. Andrewe Dier, and certaine other ships came to Gravesend, where wee ankred and abode the comming of certaine of our Fleete which were not yet come.

The 27. of the same moneth our Fleete being nowe come together, and all things prest in a readinesse, the wind favouring, and tide serving, we being of sailes in number eight, waied ankers and hoised our sailes toward Harwich to meete with our Admirall, and the residue which then and there abode our arrivall: where we safely arrived the 28. thereof, finding there our Admirall, whom we with the discharge of certaine pieces saluted, acording to order and duety, and were welcommed with the like courtesie: which being finished we landed: where our Generall continued mustering his souldiers and Miners, and setting things in order appertaining to the voyage untill the last of the said moneth of May, which day we hoised our sailes, and committing our selves to the conducting of Almightie God, we set forward toward the west Countrey in such luckie wise and good successe, that by the fift of June we passed the Dursies, being the utmost part of Ireland to the Westward.

And here it were not much amisse nor farre from our purpose, if I should a little discourse and speake of our adventures and chances by the way, as our landing at Plimmouth, as also the meeting certaine poore men, which were robbed and spoyled of all that they had by Pirates and Rovers: amongst whom was a man of Bristow, on whom our Generall used his liberality, and sent him away with letters into England.

But because such things are impertinent to the matter, I will returne (without any more mentioning of the same) to that from the which I have digressed and swarved, I meane our ships now sailing on the surging seas, sometime passing at pleasure with a wished Easterne wind, sometime hindered of our course againe by the Westerne blasts, untill the 20. day of the foresayd moneth of June, on which day in the morning we fell with Frizeland, which is a very hie and cragged land and was almost cleane covered with snow, so that we might see nought but craggie rockes and the tops of high and huge hilles, sometimes (and for the most part) all covered with foggie mists. There might we also perceive the great Isles of yce lying on the seas, like mountaines, some small, some big, of sundry kinds of shapes, and such a number of them, that wee could not come neere the shore for them.

Thus sailing alongst the coast, at the last we saw a place somewhat voyd of yce, where our Generall (accompanied with certaine other) went a shore, where they sawe certaine tents made of beasts skinnes, and boates much the like unto theirs of Meta Incognita. The tents were furnished with flesh, fish, skins, and other trifles: amongst the which was found a boxe of nailes: whereby we did conjecture, that they had either Artificers amongst them, or els a traffike with some other nation. The men ran away, so that wee could have no conference or communication with them. Our Generall (because hee would have them no more to flee, but rather incouraged to stay through his courteous dealing) gave commaundement that his men should take nothing away with them, saving onely a couple of white dogs, for the which he left pinnes, poynts, knives, and other trifling things, and departed without taking or hurting any thing, and so came abord, and hoysed sailes, and passed forwards.

But being scarce out of the sight thereof, there fell such a fogge and hidious mist that we could not see one another: whereupon we stroke our drums, and sounded our trumpets, to the ende we might keepe together: and so continued all that day and night till the next day that the mist brake up: so that we might easily perceive all the ships thus sailing together all that day, until the next day, being the 22. of the same: on which we cast about to shun the danger thereof.

But one of our small Barkes named the Michael, whose Captaine was Master Kinderslie, the Master Bartholomew Bull, lost our company, insomuch that we could not obteine the sight of her many dayes after, of whom I meane to speake further anon when occasion shall be ministred, and opportunitie serve. Thus we continued in our course untill the second of July, on which day we fell with the Queenes foreland, where we saw so much yce, that we thought it unpossible to get into the Straights: yet at the last we gave the adventure and entred the yce.

Being amongst it wee sawe the Michael, of whom I spake before, accompanied with the Judith, whose Captaine was Master Fenton, the Master Charles Jackman, bearing into the foresayd yce, farre distant from us, who in a storme that fell that present night, (whereof I will at large God willing, discourse hereafter) were severed from us, and being in, wandred up and downe the Straights amongst the yce many dayes in great perill, till at the last, (by the providence of God) they came safely to harbor in their wished Port. In the Countesse of Warwicks sound, the 20. of July aforesayd, tenne dayes before any of the other shippes: who going on shore found where the people of the Countrey had bene, and had hid their provision in great heapes of stones being both of flesh and fish, which they had killed; whereof wee also found great store in other places after our arrival. They found also divers engins, as bowes, slings, and darts. They found likewise certaine pieces of the Pinnesse which our Generall left there the yeere before, which Pinnesse he had sunke, minding to have it againe the next yeere.

Now seeing I have entreated so much of the Judith and the Michael: I will returne to the rest of the other ships, and will speake a little of the storme which fell, with the mishaps that we had, the night that we put into the yce: whereof I made mention before.

At the first entring into the yce in the mouth of the Straights, our passage was very narrow, and difficult but being once gotten in, we had a faire open place without any yce for the most part, being a league in compasse, the yce being round about us and inclosing us, as it were, within the pales of a parke. In which place, (because it was almost night) we minded to take in our sailes, and lie a hull all that night. But the storme so increased, and the waves began to mount aloft, which brought the yce so neere us, and comming on so fast upon us, that we were faine to beare in and out, where we might espie an open place. Thus the yce comming on us so fast, we were in great danger, looking every houre for death. And thus passed we on in that great danger, seeing both our selves and the rest of our ships so troubled and tossed amongst the yce, that it would make the strongest heart to relent.

At the last the Barke Dionyse being but a weake ship, and bruised afore amongst the yce, being so leake that no longer she could tarry above the water, sanke without saving any of the goods which were within her: which sight so abashed the whole Fleete, that we thought verily we should have tasted of the same sauce. But neverthelesse we seeing them in such danger, manned our boates and saved all the men in such wise, that not one perished: God be thanked.

The storme still increased and the yce inclosed us, so that we were faine to take downe top and top mastes: for the yce had so invironed us, that we could see neither land nor sea, as farre as we could kenne: so that we were faine to cut our cables to hang over boord for fenders, somewhat to ease the ships sides from the great and driry strokes of the yce: some with Capstan barres, some fending off with oares, some with plancks of two ynches thicke, which were broken immediatly with the force of the yce, some going out upon the yce to beare it off with their shoulders from the ships. But the rigorousnes of the tempest was such, and the force of the yce so great, that not onely they burst and spoyled the foresaid provision, but likewise so rased the sides of the ships, that it was pitifull to behold, and caused the hearts of many to faint.

Thus we continued all that dismall and lamentable night plunged in this perplexity, looking for instant death: but our God (who never leaveth them destitute which faithfully call upon him, although he often punisheth for amendements sake) in the morning caused the winds to cease, and the fogge which all that night lay on the face of the water to cleare: so that we might perceive about a mile from us, a certaine place cleare from any yce, to the which with an easie breath of wind which our God sent us, we bent our selves. And furthermore, hee provided better for us then we deserved or hoped for: for when we were in the foresaid cleare place, he sent us a fresh gale at West or at West Southwest, which set us cleare without all the yce. And further he added more: for he sent us so pleasant a day as the like we had not of a long time before, as after punishment consolation.

Thus we joyfull wights being at libertie, tooke in all our sailes and lay a hull, praysing God for our deliverance, and stayed to gather together our Fleete: which once being done, we seeing that none of them had any great hurt, neither any of them wanted, saving onely they of whom I spake before and the ship which was lost, then at the last wee hoised our sailes, and lay bulting off and on, till such time as it would please God to take away the yce that wee might get into the Straights.

And as we thus lay off and on we came by a marveilous huge mountaine of yce, which surpassed all the rest that ever we saw: for we judged it to be neere fourescore fathomes above water, and we thought it to be a ground for any thing that we could perceive, being there nine score fathoms deepe, and of compasse about halfe a mile.

Also the fift of July there fell a hidious fogge and mist, that continued till the nineteenth of the same: so that one shippe could not see another. Therefore we were faine to beare a small sayle and to observe the time: but there ran such a current of a tide, that it set us to the Northwest of the Queenes foreland the backside of all the Straights: where (through the contagious fogge having no sight either of Sunne or Starre) we scarce knew where we were. In this fogge the tenth of July we lost the company of the Viceadmirall, the Anne Francis, the Busse of Bridgewater, and the Francis of Foy.

The 16. day one of our small Barkes named the Gabriel was sent by our Generall to beare in with the land to descrie it, where being on land, they met with the people of the Countrey, which seemed very humane and civill, and offered to traffike with our men, profering them foules and skins for knives, and other trifles: whose courtesie caused us to thinke, that they had small conversation with other of the Straights.

Then we bare backe again to goe with the Queenes foreland: and the eighteenth day wee came by two Islands whereon we went on shore, and found where the people had bene: but we saw none of them. This day wee were againe in the yce, and like to be in as great perill as we were at the first. For through the darknesse and obscuritie of the foggie mist, we were almost run on rocks and Islands before we saw them: But God (even miraculously) provided for us, opening the fogges that we might see clearly, both where and in what danger we presently were, and also the way to escape: or els without faile we had ruinously runne upon the rocks.

When we knew perfectly our instant case, wee cast about to get againe on Sea-bord, which (God be thanked) by night we obtained and praised God. The cleare continued scarce an houre, but the fogge fell againe as thicke as ever it was.

Then the Rearadmirall and the Beare got themselves cleare without danger of yce and rocks, strooke their sailes and lay a hull, staying to have the rest of the Fleete come forth: which as yet had not found the right way to cleare themselves from the danger of rockes and yce, untill the next morning, at what time the Rearadmirall discharged certaine warning pieces to give notice that she had escaped, and that the rest (by following of her) might set themselves free, which they did that day.

Then having gathered our selves togither we proceeded on our purposed voyage, bearing off, and keeping our selves distant from the coast till the 19. day of July: at which time the fogges brake up and dispersed, so that we might plainely and clearely behold the pleasant ayre, which so long had bene taken from us, by the obscuritie of the foggie mists: and after that time we were not much encombred therewith untill we had left the confines of the Countrey.

Then we espying a fayre sound, supposed it to goe into the Straights betweene the Queenes foreland and Jackmans sound, which proved as we imagined. For our Generall sent forth againe the Gabriel to discover it, who passed through with much difficulty: for there ran such an extreme current of a tide, with such a horrible gulfe, that with a fresh gale of wind they were scarce able to stemme it: yet at the length with great travaile they passed it, and came to the Straights, where they met with the Thomas Allen, the Thomas of Ipswich, and the Busse of Bridgewater: who altogether adventured to beare into the yce againe, to see if they could obtaine their wished Port. But they were so incombred that with much difficultie they were

able to get out againe, yet at the last they escaping, the Thomas
Allen, and the Gabriel bare in with the Westerne shore, where
they found harbour, and there moared their ships untill the
fourth of August, at which time they came to us in the Countesse of Warwicks sound. The Thomas of Ipswich caught a
great leake which caused her to cast againe to Seabord and
so was mended.

We sailed along still by the coast untill we came to the
Queenes foreland, at the point whereof we met with part of
the gulfe aforesayd, which place or gulfe (as some of our
Masters doe credibly report) doeth flow nine houres, and ebs
but three. At that point wee discovered certaine lands Southward, which neither time nor opportunitie would serve to search.
Then being come to the mouth of the Straights we met with the
Anne Francis, who had laine bulting up and downe ever since
her departure alone, never finding any of her company. We met
then also the Francis of Foy, with whom againe we intended
to venture and get in: but the yce was yet so thicke, that we
were compelled againe to retyre and get us on Sea-bord.

There fell also the same day being the 26. of July, such an
horrible snow, that it lay a foot thick upon the hatches which
frose as it fell.

We had also at other times divers cruell stormes both of
snow and haile, which manifestly declared the distemperature
of the Countrey: yet for all that wee were so many times repulsed and put backe from our purpose, knowing that linger-
ing delay was not profitable for us, but hurtfull to our voyage,
we mutually consented to our valiant General once againe, to
give the onset.

The 28. day therefore of the same July we assayed, and with
little trouble (God be praysed) we passed the dangers by day
light. Then night falling on the face of the earth, wee hulled
in the cleare, til the chearefull light of the day had chased
away the noysome darkenesse of the night: at which time we
set forward towards our wished Port: by the 30. day wee obteined our expected desire, where we found the Judith, and
the Michael: which brought no smal joy unto the General,
and great consolation to the heavie hearts of those wearied
wights.

The 30. day of July we brought our ships into the Countesse

of Warwicks sound, and moared them, namely these ships,
The Admirall, the Rearadmiral, the Francis of Foy, the Beare
Armenel, the Salomon, and the Busse of Bridgewater: which
being done, our Generall commaunded us all to come a shore
upon the Countesses Iland, where he set his Miners to worke
upon the Mine, giving charge with expedition to dispatch with
their lading.

Our Generall himselfe, accompanied with his Gentlemen,
divers times made rodes into sundry partes of the Countrey,
as well to finde new Mines, as also to finde out and see the
people of the Countrey. He found out one Mine upon an
Island by Beares sound, and named it the Countesse of Sussex
Island. One other was found in Winters Fornace, with divers
others, to which the ships were sent sunderly to be laden. In
the same rodes he mette with divers of the people of the Countrey at sundry times, as once at a place called Davids sound:
who shot at our men, and very desperately gave them the onset,
being not above three or foure in number, there being of our
Countrey men above a dosen: but seeing themselves not able
to prevaile, they tooke themsleves to flight: whom our men pursued, but being not used to such craggie cliffes, they soone lost
the sight of them, and so in vaine returned.

We also saw of them at Beares sound, both by Sea and land
in great companies: but they would at all times keepe the water
betweene them and us. And if any of our ships chanced to be
in the sound (as they came divers times, because the Harbor
was not very good) the ship laded, and departed againe: then
so long as any ships were in sight, the people would not be
seene. But when as they perceived the ships to be gone, they
would not only shew themselves standing upon high cliffes, and
call us to come over unto them: but also would come in their
Botes very neere to us, as it were to brag at us: whereof our
Generall having advertisement, sent for the Captaines and Gentlemen of the Ships, to accompany and attend upon him, with
the Captaine also of the Anne Francis, who was but the night
before come unto us. For they, and the Fleebote having lost
us the 26. day in the great snowe, put into an harbour in the
Queenes foreland, where they found good Oare, wherewith they
laded themselves, and came to seeke the Generall: so that now
we had all our Shippes, saving one Barke, which was lost, and

the Thomas of Ipswich, who (compelled by what furie I knowe not) forsooke our company, and returned home without lading.

Our Generall accompanied with his Gentlemen, (of whom I spake) came all together to the Countesse of Sussex Island, neere to Beares sound: where he manned out certaine Pinnisses, and went over to the people: who perceiving his arrivall, fledde away with all speede, and in haste left certaine dartes and other engines behinde them, which we found: but the people we could not finde.

The next morning our Generall perceiving certaine of them in botes upon the Sea, gave chase to them in a Pinnesse under saile, with a fresh gale of winde, but could by no meanes come neere unto them: for the longer he sailed, the further off he was from them: which well shewed their cunning and activitie. Thus time wearing away, and the day of our departure approching, our Generall commaunded us to lade with all expedition, that we might be againe on Seaboard with our ships: for whilest we were in the Countrey, we were in continual danger of freezing in: for often snow and haile often falling, the water was so much frosen and congealed in the night, that in the morning we could scarce rowe our botes or Pinnesses, especially in Diers sound, which is a calme and still water: which caused our Generall to make the more haste, so that by the 30. day of August we were all laden, and made all things ready to depart.

But before I proceede any further herein, to shew what fortune befell at our departure, I will turne my penne a litle to M. Captaine Fenton, and those Gentlemen which should have inhabited all the yeere in those Countries, whose valiant mindes were much to be commended: For doubtlesse they had done as they intended, if lucke had not withstoode their willingnesse.

For the Barke Dionyse which was lost, had in her much of their house which was prepared and should have bene builded for them, with many other implements. Also the Thomas of Ipswich which had most of their provision in her, came not into the Streights at all: neither did we see her since the day we were separated in the great snow, of which I spake before. For these causes, having not their house, nor yet provision, they were disappointed of their pretence to tarie, and therefore laded their ships, and so came away with us.

But before we tooke shipping, we builded a litle house in the Countesse of Warwicks Island, and garnished it with many kinds of trifles, as Pinnes, Points, Laces, Glasses, Kombes, Babes on horsebacke and on foote, with innumerable other such fansies and toyes: thereby to allure and entice the people to some familiaritie against other yeeres.

Thus having finished all things we departed the Countrey, as I sayd before: but because the Busse had not lading enough in her, she put into Beares sound to take in a little more. In the meane while the Admirall, and the rest without at Sea stayed for her. And that night fell such an outragious tempest, beating on our ships with such vehement rigor, that anchor and cable availed nought: for we were driven on rockes and Islands of yce, insomuch that (had not the great goodnesse of God bene miraculously shewed to us) we had bene cast away every man. This danger was more doubtfull and terrible, then any that preceded or went before: for there was not any one shippe (I thinke) that escaped without damage. Some lost anchor and also cables, some botes, some Pinnesses: some anchor, cables, boates and Pinnisses.

This boystrous storme so severed us from one another, that one shippe knewe not what was become of another. The Admirall knewe not where to finde the Viceadmirall or Rearadmirall, or any other ship of our company. Our Generall being on land in Beares sound could not come to his Shippe, but was compelled to goe aboord the Gabriel where he continued all the way homeward: for the boystrous blasts continued so extreamely and so long a time, that they sent us homewarde (which was Gods favour towardes us) will we, nill we, in such haste, as not any one of us were able to keepe in company with other, but were separated. And if by chance any one Shippe did overtake other, by swiftnesse of sayle, or mette, as they often did: yet was the rigour of the wind so hidious, that they could not continue company together the space of one whole night.

Thus our journey outward was not so pleasant, but our comming thither, entering the coasts and countrey, by narrow Streights, perillous yce, and swift tides, our times of aboade there in snowe and stormes, and our departure from thence the 31. of August with dangerous blustering windes and tempests, which that night arose, was as uncomfortable: separating us so as wee sayled, that not any of us mette together, untill the 28. of September, which day we fell on the English coastes, betweene Sylley and the landes ende, and passed the channell, untill our arrivall in the river of Thames.

20

The Letters Patents graunted by her Majestie to Sir
Humfrey Gilbert knight, for the inhabiting and
planting of our people in America

ELIZABETH by the grace of God Queene of England, &c.
To all people to whom these presents shall come, greeting.
Know ye that of our especiall grace, certaine science and meere
motion, we have given and granted, and by these presents for
us, our heires and successours, doe give and graunt to our
trustie and welbeloved servaunt Sir Humfrey Gilbert of Comp-
ton, in our Countie of Devonshire knight, and to his heires and
assignes for ever, free libertie and licence from time to time and
at all times for ever hereafter, to discover, finde, search out,
and view such remote, heathen and barbarous lands, countreys
and territories not actually possessed of any Christian prince or
people, as to him, his heires & assignes, and to every or any of
them, shall seeme good: and the same to have, hold, occupie
and enjoy to him, his heires and assignes for ever, with all
commodities, jurisdictions and royalties both by sea and land:
and the sayd sir Humfrey and all such as from time to time
by licence of us, our heires and successours, shall goe and
travell thither, to inhabite or remaine there, to build and fortifie at the discretion of the sayde sir Humfrey, and of his heires
and assignes, the statutes or actes of Parliament made against
Fugitives, or against such as shall depart, remaine, or continue
out of our Realme of England without licence, or any other
acte, statute, lawe, or matter whatsoever to the contrary in
any wise notwithstanding. And wee doe likewise by these
presents, for us, our heires and successours, give full authoritie
and power to the saide Sir Humfrey, his heires and assignes, and
every of them, that hee and they, and every, or any of them,

shall and may at all and every time and times hereafter, have, take, and lead in the same voyages, to travell thitherward, and to inhabite there with him, and every or any of them, such and so many of our subjects as shall willingly accompany him and them, and every or any of them, with sufficient shipping, and furniture for their transportations, so that none of the same persons, nor any of them be such as hereafter shall be specially restrained by us, our heires and successors. And further, that he the said Humfrey, his heires and assignes, and every or any of them shall have, hold, occupy & enjoy to him, his heires or assignes, and every of them for ever, all the soyle of all such lands, countries, & territories so to be discovered or possessed as aforesaid, and of all Cities, Castles, Townes and Villages, and places in the same, with the rites, royalties and jurisdictions, as well marine as other, within the sayd lands or countreys of the seas thereunto adjoyning, to be had or used with ful power to dispose thereof, & of every part thereof in fee simple or otherwise, according to the order of the laws of England, as nere as the same conveniently may be, at his, and their will & pleasure, to any person then being, or that shall remaine within the allegiance of us, our heires and successours, paying unto us for all services, dueties and demaunds, the fift part of all the oare of gold and silver, that from time to time, and at all times after such discoverie, subduing and possessing shall be there gotten: all which lands, countreys and territories, shall for ever bee holden by the sayd Sir Humfrey, his heires and assignes of us, our heires and successours by homage, and by the sayd payment of the sayd fift part before reserved onely for all services.

And moreover, we doe by these presents for us, our heires and successours, give and graunt licence to the sayde Sir Humfrey Gilbert, his heires or assignes, and to every of them, that hee and they, and every or any of them shall, and may from time to time, and all times for ever hereafter, for his and their defence, encounter, expulse, repell, and resist, as well by Sea as by land, and by all other wayes whatsoever, all, and every such person and persons whatsoever, as without the speciall licence and liking of the sayd Sir Humfrey, and of his heires and assignes, shall attempt to inhabite within the sayd countreys, or any of them, or within the space of two hundreth leagues neere to the place or places within such countreys as aforesayd, if they shall not bee before planted or inhabited within the limites aforesayd, with the subjects of any Christian prince, being in amitie with her Majesty, where the said sir Humfrey, his heires or assignes, or any of them, or his or their, or any of their associates or companies, shall within sixe yeeres next ensuing, make their dwellings and abidings, or that shall enterprise or attempt at any time hereafter unlawfully to annoy either by Sea or land, the said sir Humfrey, his heires or assignes, or any of them, or his or their, or any of their companies: giving and graunting by these presents, further power and authoritie to the sayd sir Humfrey, his heires and assignes, and every of them from time to time, and at all times for ever hereafter to take and surprise by all maner of meanes whatsoever, all and every person and persons, with their shippes, vessels, and other goods and furniture, which without the licence of the sayd sir Humfrey, or his heires or assignes as aforesayd, shall be found traffiquing into any harborough or harboroughs, creeke or creekes within the limites aforesayd, (the subjects of our Realmes and dominions, and all other persons in amitie with us, being driven by force of tempest or shipwracke onely excepted) and those persons and every of them with their ships, vessels, goods, and furniture, to detaine and possesse, as of good and lawfull prize, according to the discretion of him the sayd sir Humfrey, his heires and assignes, and of every or any of them. And for uniting in more perfect league and amitie of such countreys, landes and territories so to bee possessed and inhabited as aforesayde, with our Realmes of England and Ireland, and for the better encouragement of men to this enterprise: wee doe by these presents graunt, and declare, that all such countreys so hereafter to bee possessed and inhabited as aforesayd, from thenceforth shall be of the allegiance of us, our heires, and successours. And wee doe graunt to the sayd sir Humfrey, his heires and assignes, and to all and every of them, and to all and every other person and persons, being of our allegiance, whose names shall be noted or entred in some of our courts of Record, within this our Realme of England, and that with the assent of the sayd sir Humfrey, his heires or assignes, shall nowe in this journey for discoverie, or in the second journey for conquest hereafter, travel to such lands, countreys and territories as aforesaid, and to their and every of their heires: that they and every or any of them being either borne within our sayd Realmes of England or Ireland, or within any other place within our allegiance, and which hereafter shall be inhabiting within any the lands, countreys and territories, with such licence as aforesayd, shall, and may have, and enjoy all the privileges of free denizens and persons native of England, and within our allegiance: any law, custome, or usage to the contrary notwithstanding.

And forasmuch, as upon the finding out, discovering and inhabiting of such remote lands, countreys and territories, as aforesayd, it shall be necessarie for the safetie of all men that shall adventure themselves in those journeys or voiages, to determine to live together in Christian peace and civill quietnesse each with other, whereby every one may with more pleasure and profit, enjoy that whereunto they shall attaine with great paine and perill: wee for us, our heires and successours are likewise pleased and contented, and by these presents doe give and graunt to the sayd sir Humfrey and his heires and assignes for ever, that he and they, and every or any of them, shall and may from time to time for ever hereafter within the sayd mentioned remote lands and countreys, and in the way by the Seas thither, and from thence, have full and meere power and authoritie to correct, punish, pardon, governe and rule by their, and every or any of their good discretions and pollicies, as well in causes capitall or criminall, as civill, both marine and other, all such our subjects and others, as shall from time to time hereafter adventure themselves in the sayd journeys or voyages habitative or possessive, or that shall at any time hereafter inhabite any such lands, countreys or territories as aforesayd, or that shall abide within two hundred leagues of any the sayd place or places, where the sayd sir Humfrey or his heires, or assignes, or any of them, or any of his or their associats or companies, shall inhabite within sixe yeeres next ensuing the date hereof, according to such statutes, lawes and ordinances, as shall be by him the said sir Humfrey, his heires and assignes, or every, or any of them devised or established for the better governement of the said people as aforesayd: so alwayes that the sayd statutes, lawes and ordinances may be as neere as conveniently may, agreeable to the forme of the lawes & pollicy of England: and also, that they be not against the true Christian faith or religion now professed in the church of England, nor in any wise to withdraw any of the subjects or people of those lands or places from the allegiance of us, our heires or successours, as their immediate Soveraignes under God. And further we doe by these presents for us, our heires and successours, give and graunt full power and authority to our trustie and welbeloved counseller, sir William Cecill knight, lord Burleigh, our high treasurer of England, and to the lord treasurer of England of us, for the time being, and to the privie counsell of us, our heires and successors, or any foure of them for the time being, that he, they, or any foure of them, shall, and may from time to time and at all times hereafter, under his or their handes or seales by vertue of these presents, authorize and licence the sayd sir Humfrey Gilbert, his heires and assignes, and every or any of them by him and themselves, or by their or any of their sufficient attorneys, deputies officers, ministers, factors and servants, to imbarke and transport out of our Realmes of England and Ireland, all, or any of his or their goods, and all or any the goods of his or their associates and companies, and every or any of them, with such other necessaries and commodities of any our Realmes, as to the said lord treasurer or foure of the privie counsell of us, our heires, or successours for the time being, as aforesayd, shall be from time to time by his or their wisedoms or discretions thought meete and convenient for the better reliefe and supportation of him the sayd sir Humfrey, his heires and assignes, and every or any of them, and his and their, and every or any of their said associates and companies, any act, statute, lawe, or other thing to the contrary in any wise notwithstanding.

Provided alwayes, and our will and pleasure is, and wee doe hereby declare to all Christian Kings, princes and states, that if the said Sir Humfrey, his heires or assignes, or any of them, or any other by their licence or appointment, shall at any time or times hereafter robbe or spoile by Sea or by land, or doe any act of unjust and unlawfull hostilitie to any of the Subjects of us, our heires, or successours, or any of the Subjects of any King, prince, ruler, governour or state being then in perfect league and amitie with us, our heires or successours: and that upon such injurie, or upon just complaint of any such prince, ruler, governour or state, or their subjects, wee our heires or successors shall make open proclamation within any the portes of our Realme of England commodious, that the said Sir Humfrey, his heires or assignes, or any other to whom these our Letters patents may extend, shall within the terme to be limited by such proclamations, make full restitution and satisfaction of all such injuries done, so as both we and the saide Princes, or others so complayning, may holde us and themselves fully contended: And that if the saide Sir Humfrey, his heires and assignes, shall not make or cause to bee made satisfaction accordingly, within such time so to be limited: that then it shall bee lawfull to us, our heires and successors, to put the said Sir Humfrey, his heires and assignes, and adherents, and all the inhabitants of the said places to be discovered as is aforesaide, or any of them out of our allegiance and protection, and that from and after such time of putting out of protection the saide Sir Humfrey, and his heires, assignes, adherents and others so to be put out, and the said places within their habitation, possession and rule, shal be out of our protection and allegiance, and free for all Princes and others to pursue with hostilitie as being not our Subjects, nor by us any way to bee advowed, maintained or defended, nor to be holden as any of ours, nor to our protection, dominion or allegiance any way belonging, for that expresse mention, &c. In witnesse whereof, &c. Witnesse our selfe at Westminster the 11. day of June, the twentieth yeere of our raigne. Anno Dom. 1578.

Per ipsam Reginam, &c.

21

The famous voyage of Sir Francis Drake into the South sea, and therehence about the whole Globe of the earth, begun in the yeere of our Lord 1577

THE 15. day of November, in the yeere of our Lord 1577. M. Francis Drake, with a fleete of five ships and barkes, and to the number of 164. men, gentlemen and sailers, departed from Plimmouth, giving out his pretended voyage for Alexandria: but the wind falling contrary, hee was forced the next morning to put into Falmouth haven in Cornewall, where such and so terrible a tempest tooke us, as few men have seene the like, and was in deed so vehement, that all our ships were like to have gone to wracke: but it pleased God to preserve us from that extremitie, and to afflict us onely for that present with these two particulars: The mast of our Admirall which was the Pellican, was cut over boord for the safegard of the ship, and the Marigold was driven ashore, and somewhat bruised: for the repairing of which damages wee returned againe to Plimmouth, and having recovered those harmes, and brought the ships againe to good state, we set forth the second time from Plimmouth, and set saile the 13. day of December following.

The 25. day of the same moneth we fell with the Cape Cantin, upon the coast of Barbarie, and coasting along, the 27. day we found an Island called Mogador, lying one mile distant from the maine, betweene which Island and the maine, we found a very good and safe harbour for our ships to ride in, as also very good entrance, and voyde of any danger.

On this Island our Generall erected a pinnesse, whereof he brought out of England with him foure already framed. While these things were in doing, there came to the waters side some of the inhabitants of the countrey, shewing foorth their flags of truce, which being seene of our Generall, hee sent his ships boate to the shore, to know what they would: they being willing to come aboord, our men left there one man of our company for a pledge, and brought two of theirs aboord our ship, which by signes shewed our General, that the next day they would bring some provision, as sheepe, capons and hennes, and such like: whereupon our Generall bestowed amongst them some linnen cloth and shooes, and a javeling, which they very joyfully received, and departed for that time.

The next morning they failed not to come againe to the waters side, and our Generall againe setting out our boate, one of our men leaping over rashly ashore, and offering friendly to imbrace them, they set violent hands on him, offering a dagger to his throte if hee had made any resistance, and so laying him on a horse, caried him away: so that a man cannot be too circumspect and warie of himselfe among such miscreants.

Our pinnesse being finished, wee departed from this place the 30. and last day of December, and coasting along the shore, wee did descrie, not contrary to our expectation, certaine Canters which were Spanish fishermen, to whom we gave chase and tooke three of them, and proceeding further we met with 3. Caravels and tooke them also.

The 17. day of January we arrived at Cape Blanco, where we found a ship riding at anchor, within the Cape, and but two simple Mariners in her, which ship we tooke and caried her further into the harbour, where we remained 4. dayes, and in that space our General mustered, and trayned his men on land in warlike maner, to make them fit for all occasions.

In this place we tooke of the Fishermen such necessaries as wee wanted, and they could yeeld us, and leaving heere one of our litle barkes called the Benedict, wee tooke with us one of theirs which they called Canters, being of the burden of 40. tunnes or thereabouts.

All these things being finished, wee departed this harbour the 22. of Januarie, carying along with us one of the Portugall Caravels which was bound to the Island of Cape Verde for salt, whereof good store is made in one of those Islands.

The master or Pilot of that Caravel did advertise our Generall that upon one of those Islands called Mayo, there was great store of dryed Cabritos, which a few inhabitants there dwelling did yeerely make ready for such of the kings Ships as did there touch, beeing bound for his countrey of Brasile or elsewhere. Wee fell with this Island the 27. of January, but the Inhabitants would in no case traffique with us, being thereof forbidden by the kings Edict: yet the next day our Generall sent to view the Island, and the likelihoodes that might be there of provision of victuals, about threescore and two men under the conduct and government of Master Winter and Master Doughtie, and marching towards the chiefe place of habitation in this Island (as by the Portugall wee were informed) having travailed to the mountaines the space of three miles, and arriving there somewhat before the day breake, we arrested our selves to see day before us, which appearing, we found the inhabitants to be fled: but the place, by reason that it was manured, wee found to be more fruitfull then the other part, especially the valleys among the hils.

Here we gave our selves a litle refreshing, as by very ripe and sweete grapes, which the fruitfulnesse of the earth at that season of the yeere yeelded us: and that season being with us the depth of Winter, it may seeme strange that those fruites were then there growing: but the reason thereof is this, because they being betweene the Tropike and the Equinoctiall, the Sunne passeth twise in the yeere through their Zenith over their heads, by meanes whereof they have two Summers, & being so neere the heate of the line, they never lose the heate of the Sunne so much, but the fruites have their increase and continuance in the midst of Winter. The Island is wonderfully stored with goates and wilde hennes, and it hath salt also without labour, save onely that the people gather it into heapes, which continually in great quantitie is increased upon the sands by the flowing of the sea, and the receiving heate of the Sunne kerning the same, so that of the increase thereof they keepe a continuall traffique with their neighbours.

Amongst other things we found here a kind of fruit called Cocos, which because it is not commonly knowen with us in England, I thought good to make some description of it.

The tree beareth no leaves nor branches, but at the very top the fruit groweth in clusters, hard at the top of the stemme of the tree, as big every severall fruite as a mans head: but hav-

ing taken off the uttermost barke, which you shall find to bee
very full of strings or sinowes, as I may terme them, you shall
come to a hard shell which may holde of quantitie in liquor a
pint commonly, or some a quart, and some lesse: within that
shell of the thicknesse of halfe an inch good, you shall have a
kinde of hard substance and very white, no lesse good and
sweete then almonds: within that againe a certaine cleare liquor,
which being drunke, you shall not onely finde it very delicate
and sweete, but most comfortable and cordiall.

After wee had satisfied our selves with some of these fruites,
wee marched further into the Island, and saw great store of
* Cabritos alive, which were so chased by the inhabitants, that
wee could doe no good towards our provision, but they had
layde out as it were to stoppe our mouthes withall, certaine
olde dryed Cabritos, which being but ill, and small and few,
wee made no account of.

Being returned to our ships, our Generall departed hence
the 31. of this moneth, and sayled by the Island of S. Iago,
but farre enough from the danger of the inhabitants, who shot
and discharged at us three peeces, but they all fell short of us,
and did us no harme. The Island is fayre and large, and as it
seemeth, rich and fruitfull, and inhabited by the Portugals, but
the mountaines and high places of the Island are sayd to be
possessed by the Moores, who having bin slaves to the Portugals, to ease themselves, made escape to the desert places of
the Island, where they abide with great strength.

Being before this Island, we espied two ships under sayle,
to the one of which wee gave chase, and in the end boorded
her with a ship-boat without resistance, which we found to be a
good prize, and she yeelded unto us good store of wine: which
prize our General committed to the custodie of Master Doughtie, and reteining the Pilot, sent the rest away with his Pinnesse,
giving them a Butte of wine and some victuals, and their wearing clothes, and so they departed.

The same night wee came with the Island called by the
Portugals, Ilha del fogo, that is, the burning Island: in the
Northside whereof is a consuming fire, the matter is sayde to
be of Sulphure, but notwithstanding it is like to bee a com-

* Or goates.

modious Island, because the Portugals have built, and doe
inhabite there.

Upon the South side thereof lyeth a most pleasant and sweete
Island, the trees whereof are always greene and faire to looke
upon, in respect whereof they call it Ilha Brava, that is, the
brave Island. From the bankes thereof into the sea doe run in
many places reasonable streames of fresh waters easie to be
come by, but there was no convenient roade for our ships: for
such was the depth, that no ground could bee had for anchoring, and it is reported, that ground was never found in that
place, so that the tops of Fogo burne not so high in the ayre,
but the rootes of Brava are quenched as low in the sea.

Being departed from these Islands, we drew towards the
line, where wee were becalmed the space of 3. weekes, but yet
subject to divers great stormes, terrible lightnings and much
thunder: but with this miserie we had the commoditie of great
store of fish, as Dolphins, Bonitos, and flying fishes, whereof
some fell into our shippes, wherehence they could not rise
againe for want of moisture, for when their wings are drie,
they cannot flie.

From the first day of our departure from the Islands of
Cape Verde, wee sayled 54. dayes without sight of land, and
the first land that we fell with was the coast of Brasil, which
we saw the fift of April in ye height of 33. degrees towards
the pole Antarctike, and being discovered at sea by the inhabitants of the countrey, they made upon the coast great fires
for a sacrifice (as we learned) to the devils, about which they
use conjurations, making heapes of sande and other ceremonies,
that when any ship shall goe about to stay upon their coast, not
onely sands may be gathered together in shoalds in every place,
but also that stormes and tempests may arise, to the casting
away of ships and men, whereof (as it is reported) there have
bene divers experiments.

The seventh day in a mightie great storme both of lightning,
rayne and thunder, wee lost the Canter which we called the
Christopher: but the eleventh day after, by our Generals great
care in dispersing his ships, we found her againe, and the place
where we met, our Generall called the Cape of Joy, where
every ship tooke in some water. Heere we found a good tempera-

ture and sweete ayre, a very faire and pleasant countrey with an exceeding fruitfull soyle, where were great store of large and mightie Deere, but we came not to the sight of any people: but traveiling further into the countrey, we perceived the footing of people in the clay-ground, shewing that they were men of great stature. Being returned to our ships, we wayed anchor, and ranne somewhat further, and harboured our selves betweene a rocke and the maine, where by meanes of the rocke that brake the force of the sea, we rid very safe, and upon this rocke we killed for our provision certaine sea-wolves, commonly called with us Seales.

From hence we went our course to 36. degrees, and entred the great river of Plate, and ranne into 54. and 55. fadomes and a halfe of fresh water, where wee filled our water by the ships side: but our Generall finding here no good harborough, as he thought he should, bare out againe to sea the 27. of April, and in bearing out we lost sight of our Flieboate wherein master Doughtie was, but we sayling along, found a fayre and reasonable good Bay wherein were many, and the same profitable Islands, one whereof had so many Seales, as would at the least have laden all our Shippes, and the rest of the Islands are as it were laden with foules which is wonderfull to see, and they of divers sortes. It is a place very plentifull of victuals, and hath in it no want of fresh water.

Our Generall after certaine dayes of his abode in this place, being on shore in an Island, the people of the countrey shewed themselves unto him, leaping and dauncing, and entred into traffique with him, but they would not receive any thing at any mans hands, but the same must bee cast upon the ground. They are of cleane, comely, and strong bodies, swift on foote, and seeme to be very active.

The eighteenth day of May our Generall thought it needfull to have a care of such Ships as were absent, and therefore indevouring to seeke the Flieboate wherein master Doughtie was, we espied her againe the next day: and whereas certaine of our ships were sent to discover the coast and to search an harbour, the Marygold and the Canter being imployed in that businesse, came unto us and gave us understanding of a safe harbour that they had found, wherewith all our ships bare, and entred it, where we watered and made new provision of victuals, as by Seales, whereof we slew to the number of 200. or 300. in the space of an houre.

Here our Generall in the Admirall rid close aboord the Flieboate, and tooke out of her all the provision of victuals and what els was in her, and halling her to the Lande, set fire to her, and so burnt her to save the iron worke: which being a doing, there came downe of the countrey certaine of the people naked, saving only about their waste the skinne of some beast with the furre or haire on, and something also wreathed on their heads: their faces were painted with divers colours, and some of them had on their heads the similitude of hornes, every man his bow which was an ell in length, and a couple of arrowes. They were very agill people and quicke to deliver, and seemed not to be ignorant in the feates of warres, as by their order of ranging a few men, might appeare. These people would not of a long time receive any thing at our handes; yet at length our Generall being ashore, and they dauncing after their accustomed maner about him, and hee once turning his backe towards them, one leapt suddenly to him, and tooke his cap with his golde band off his head, and ran a litle distance from him and shared it with his fellow, the cap to the one, and the band to the other.

Having dispatched all our businesse in this place, wee departed and set sayle, and immediatly upon our setting foorth we lost our Canter which was absent three or foure dayes: but when our General had her againe, he tooke out the necessaries, and so gave her over neere to the Cape of Good hope.

The next day after being the twentieth of June, wee harboured our selves againe in a very good harborough, called by Magellan Port S. Julian, where we found a gibbet standing upon the maine, which we supposed to be the place where Magellan did execution upon some of his disobedient and rebellious company.

The two and twentieth day our Generall went ashore to the maine, and in his companie, John Thomas, and Robert Winterhie, Oliver the Master gunner, John Brewer, Thomas Hood, and Thomas Drake, and entring on land, they presently met with the two or three of the countrey people, and Robert Winterhie having in his hands a bowe and arrowes, went about to make a shoote of pleasure, and in his draught his bowstring brake, which the rude Savages taking as a token of warre, began to bend the force of their bowes against our company, and drove them to their shifts very narrowly.

In this Port our Generall began to enquire diligently of the actions of M. Thomas Doughtie, and found them not to be such as he looked for, but tending rather to contention or mutinie, or some other disorder, whereby (without redresse) the successe of the voyage might greatly have bene hazarded: whereupon the company was called together and made acquainted with the particulars of the cause, which were found partly by master Doughties owne confession, and partly by the evidence of the fact, to be true: which when our Generall saw, although his private affection to M. Doughtie (as hee then in the presence of us all sacredly protested) was great, yet the care he had of the state of the voyage, of the expectation of her Majestie, and of the honour of his countrey did more touch him, (as indeede it ought) then the private respect of one man: so that the cause being thoroughly heard, and all things done in good order as neere as might be to the course of our lawes in England, it was concluded that M. Doughtie should receive punishment according to the qualitie of the offence: and he seeing no remedie but patience for himselfe, desired before his death to receive the Communion, which he did at the hands of M. Fletcher our Minister, and our Generall himselfe accompanied him in that holy action: which being done, and the place of execution made ready, hee having embraced our Generall and taken his leave of all the companie, with prayer for the Queenes majestie and our realme, in quiet sort laid his head to the blocke, where he ended his life. This being done, our Generall made divers speaches to the whole company, perswading us to unitie, obedience, love, and regard of our voyage; and for the better confirmation thereof, willed every man the next Sunday following to prepare himselfe to receive the Communion, as Christian brethren and friends ought to doe, which was done in very reverent sort, and so with good contentment every man went about his businesse.

The 17. day of August we departed the port of S. Julian, & the 20. day we fell with the streight or freat of Magellan going into the South sea, at the Cape or headland whereof we found the bodie of a dead man, whose flesh was cleane consumed.

The 21. day we entred The streight, which we found to have many turnings, and as it were shuttings up, as if there were no passage at all, by meanes whereof we had the wind often against us, so that some of the fleete recovering a Cape or point of land, others should be forced to turne backe againe, and to come to an anchor where they could.

In this streight there be many faire harbors, with store of fresh water, but yet they lacke their best commoditie: for the water is there of such depth, that no man shal find ground to anchor in, except it bee in some narow river or corner, or betweene some rocks, so that if any extreme blasts or contrary winds do come (whereunto the place is much subject) it carieth with it no small danger.

The land on both sides is very huge & mountainous, the lower mountains whereof, although they be monstrous and wonderfull to looke upon for their height, yet there are others which in height exceede them in a strange maner, reaching themselves above their fellowes so high, that betweene them did appeare three regions of cloudes.

These mountaines are covered with snow: at both the Southerly and Easterly partes of the streight there are Islands, among which the sea hath his indraught into the streights, even as it hath in the maine entrance of the freat.

This streight is extreme cold, with frost and snow continually; the trees seeme to stoope with the burden of the weather, and yet are greene continually, and many good and sweete herbes doe very plentifully grow and increase under them.

The bredth of the streight is in some place a league, in some other places 2. leagues, and three leagues, and in some other 4. leagues, but the narowest place hath a league over.

The 24. of August we arrived at an Island in the streights, where we found great store of foule which could not flie, of the bignesse of geese, whereof we killed in lesse then one day 3000. and victualled our selves throughly therewith.

The 6. day of September we entred the South sea at the Cape or head shore.

The seventh day wee were driven by a great storme from the entring into the South sea two hundred leagues and odde in longitude, and one degree to the Southward of the Streight: in which height, and so many leagues to the Westward, the fifteenth day of September fell out the Eclipse of the Moone at the houre of sixe of the clocke at night: but neither did the Eclipticall conflict of the Moone impayre our state, nor her clearing againe amend us a whit, but the accustomed Eclipse of the Sea continued in his force, wee being darkened more then the Moone seven fold.

From the Bay (which we called The Bay of severing of friends) wee were driven backe to the Southward of the streights in 57. degrees and a terce: in which height we came to an anker among the Islands, having there fresh and very good water, with herbes of singular vertue. Not farre from hence we entred another Bay, where wee found people both men and women in their Canoas, naked, and ranging from one Island to another to seeke their meat, who entered traffique with us for such things as they had.

We returning hence Northward againe, found the 3. of October three Islands, in one of which was such plentie of birdes as is scant credible to report.

The 8. day of October we lost sight of one of our Consorts wherein M. Winter was, who as then we supposed was put by a storme into the streights againe, which at our returne home wee found to be true, and he not perished, as some of our company feared.

Thus being come into the height of The streights againe, we ran, supposing the coast of Chili to lie as the generall Maps have described it, namely Northwest, which we found to lie and trend to the Northeast and Eastwards, whereby it appeareth that this part of Chili hath not bene truely hitherto discovered, or at the least not truely reported for the space of 12. degrees at the least, being set downe either of purpose to deceive, or of ignorant conjecture.

We continuing our course, fell the 29. of November with an Island called la Mocha, where we cast anchor, and our Generall hoysing out our boate, went with ten of our company to shore, where wee found people, whom the cruell and extreme dealings of the Spaniards have forced for their owne safetie and libertie to flee from the maine, and to fortifie themselves in this Island. We being on land, the people came downe to us to the water side with shew of great courtesie, bringing to us potatoes, rootes, and two very fat sheepe, which our Generall received and gave them other things for them, and had promised to have water there: but the next day repayring againe to the shore, and sending two men aland with barrels to fill water, the people taking them for Spaniards (to whom they use to shew no favour if they take them) layde violent hands on them, and as we thinke, slew them.

Our Generall seeing this, stayed here no longer, but wayed anchor, and set sayle towards the coast of Chili, and drawing towards it, we mette neere to the shore an Indian in a Canoa, who thinking us to have bene Spaniards, came to us and tolde us, that at a place called S. Iago, there was a great Spanish ship laden from the kingdome of Peru: for which good newes our Generall gave him divers trifles, wherof he was glad, and went along with us and brought us to the place, which is called the port of Valparizo.

When we came thither, we found indeede the ship riding at anker, having in her eight Spaniards and three Negros, who thinking us to have bene Spaniards and their friends, welcommed us with a drumme, and made ready a Bottija of wine of Chili to drinke to us: but as soone as we were entred, one of our company called Thomas Moone began to lay about him, and strooke one of the Spanyards, and sayd unto him, Abaxo Perro, that is in English, Goe downe dogge. One of these Spaniards seeing persons of that quality in those seas, all to crossed, and blessed himselfe: but to be short, wee stowed them under hatches all save one Spaniard, who suddenly and desperately leapt over boord into the sea, and swamme ashore to the towne of S. Iago, to give them warning of our arrivall.

They of the towne being not above 9. housholds, presently fled away and abandoned the towne. Our generall manned his boate, and the Spanish ships boate, and went to the Towne, and being come to it, we rifled it, and came to a small chappell which wee entred, and found therein a silver chalice, two cruets, and one altar-cloth, the spoyle whereof our Generall gave to M. Fletcher his minister.

We found also in this towne a warehouse stored with wine of Chili, and many boords of Cedar-wood, all which wine we brought away with us, and certaine of the boords to burne for fire-wood: and so being come aboord, wee departed the Haven, having first set all the Spaniards on land, saving one John Griego a Greeke borne whom our Generall caried with him for his Pilot to bring him into the haven of Lima.

When we were at sea, our Generall rifled the ship, and found in her good store of the wine of Chili, and 25000. pezoes of very pure and fine gold of Baldivia, amounting in value to 37000. ducats of Spanish money, and above. So going on our course, wee arrived next at a place called Coquimbo, where our Generall sent 14. of his men on land to fetch water: but they were espied by the Spaniards, who came with 300. horsemen and 200 footemen, and slewe one of our men with a piece, the rest came aboord in safetie, and the Spaniards departed: wee went on shore againe, and buried our man, and the Spaniards came downe againe with a flag of truce, but we set sayle and would not trust them.

From hence we went to a certaine port called Tarapaza, where being landed, we found by the Sea side a Spaniard lying asleepe, who had lying by him 13. barres of silver, which weighed 4000. ducats Spanish; we tooke the silver, and left the man.

Not farre from hence going on land for fresh water, we met with a Spaniard and an Indian boy driving 8. Llamas or sheepe of Peru which are as big as asses; every of which sheepe had on his backe 2. bags of leather, each bagge conteining 50. li. weight of fine silver: so that bringing both the sheepe and their burthen to the ships, we found in all the bags 800. weight of silver.

Here hence we sailed to a place called Arica, and being entred the port, we found there three small barkes which we rifled, and found in one of them 57 wedges of silver, each of them weighing about 20 pound weight, and every of these wedges were of the fashion and bignesse of a brickbat. In all these 3. barkes we found not one person: for they mistrusting no strangers, were all gone aland to the Towne, which consisteth of about twentie houses, which we would have ransacked if our company had bene better and more in number. But our Generall contented with the spoyle of the ships, left the Towne and put off againe to sea and set sayle for Lima, and by the way met with a small barke, which he boorded, and found in her good store of linnen cloth, whereof taking some quantitie, he let her goe.

To Lima we came the 13. day of February, and being entred the haven, we found there about twelve sayle of ships lying fast moored at an anker, having all their sayles caried on shore; for the masters and marchants were here most secure, having never bene assaulted by enemies, and at this time feared the approch of none such as we were. Our generall rifled these ships, and found in one of them a chest full of royals of plate, and good store of silkes and linnen cloth, and tooke the chest into his owne ship, and good store of the silkes and linnen. In which ship hee had newes of another ship called the Cacafuego which was gone toward Paita, and that the same shippe was laden with treasure: whereupon we staied no longer here, but cutting all the cables of the shippes in the haven, we let them drive whither they would, either to sea or to the shore, and with all speede we followed the Cacafuego toward Paita, thinking there to have found her: but before wee arrived there, she was gone from thence towards Panama, whom our Generall still pursued, and by the way met with a barke laden with ropes and tackle for ships, which hee boorded and searched, and found in her 80.li. weight of golde, and a crucifixe of gold with goodly great Emerauds set in it which he tooke, and some of the cordage also for his owne ship.

From hence we departed, still following the Cacafuego, and our Generall promised our company, that whosoever could first descrie her, should have his chaine of gold for his good newes. It fortuned that John Drake going up into the top, descried her about three of the clocke, and about sixe of the clocke we came to her and boorded her, and shotte at her three peeces of ordinance, and strake downe her Misen, and being entered, we found in her great riches, as jewels and precious stones, thirteene chests full of royals of plate, foure score pound weight of golde, and sixe and twentie tunne of silver. The place where we tooke this prize, was called Cape de San Francisco, about 150. leagues from Panama.

The Pilots name of this Shippe was Francisco, and amongst other plate that our Generall found in this ship, he found two very faire guilt bowles of silver, which were the Pilots: to whom our Generall sayd: Senior Pilot, you have here two silver cups, but I must needes have one of them: which the Pilot because hee could not otherwise chuse, yeelded unto, and gave the other to the steward of our General ships.

When this Pilot departed from us, his boy sayde thus unto our Generall: Captaine, our ship shall be called no more the Cacafuego, but the Cacaplata, and your shippe shall bee called the Cacafuego: which pretie speach of the Pilots boy ministred matter of laughter to us, both then and long after.

When our Generall had done what hee would with this Cacafuego, hee cast her off, and wee went on our course still towards the West, and not long after met with a ship laden with linnen and cloth and fine China-dishes of white earth, and great store of China-silks, of all which things wee tooke as we listed.

The owner himselfe of this shipe was in her, who was a Spanish Gentleman, from whom our Generall tooke a Fawlcon of golde, with a great Emeraud in the breast thereof, and the Pilot of the ship he tooke also with him, and so cast the ship off.

This Pilot brought us to the haven of Guatulco, the towne whereof, as he told us, had but 17. Spaniards in it. Assoone as we were entred this haven, wee landed, and went presently to the towne, and to the Towne-house, where we found a Judge sitting in judgement, being associate with three other officers, upon three Negros that had conspired the burning of the Towne: both which Judges & prisoners we tooke, and brought them a shipboord, and caused the chiefe Judge to write his letter to the Towne, to command all the Townesmen to avoid, that we might safely water there. Which being done, and they departed, we ransaked the Towne, and in one house we found a pot of the quantitie of a bushell, full of reals of plate, which we brought to our ship.

And here one Thomas Moone one of our company, tooke a Spanish Gentleman as hee was flying out of the towne, and searching him, he found a chaine of golde about him, and other jewels, which he tooke, and so let him goe.

At this place our General among other Spaniards, set ashore his Portugall Pilote, which hee tooke at the Islands of Cape Verde, out of a ship of S. Mary port of Portugall: and having set them ashore, we departed hence, and sailed to the Island of

Canno, where our Generall landed, and brought to shore his owne ship, and discharged her, mended, and graved her, and furnished our ship with water and wood sufficiently.

And while wee were here, we espied a shippe, and set saile after her, and tooke her, and found in her two Pilots, and a Spanish Governour, going for the Islands of the Philippinas: wee searched the shippe, and tooke some of her marchandizes, and so let her goe. Our Generall at this place and time, thinking himselfe both in respect of his private injuries received from the Spaniards, as also of their contempts and indignities offered to our countrey and Prince in generall, sufficiently satisfied, and revenged: and supposing that her Majestie at his returne would rest contented with this service, purposed to continue no longer upon the Spanish coasts, but began to consider and to consult of the best way for his Countrey.

He thought it not good to returne by the Streights, for two speciall causes: the one, lest the Spaniards should there waite, and attend for him in great number and strength, whose hands, hee being left but one ship, could not possibly escape. The other cause was the dangerous situation of the mouth of the streights in the South sea, where continuall stormes reigning and blustering, as he found by experience, besides the shoalds and sands upon the coast, he thought it not a good course to adventure that way: he resolved therefore to avoyde these hazards, to goe forward to the Islandes of the Malucos, and therehence to saile the course of the Portugals by the Cape of Buena Esperanza.

Upon this resolution, hee beganne to thinke of his best way to the Malucos, and finding himselfe where he now was becalmed, he saw that of necessitie hee must be forced to take a Spanish course, namely to sayle somewhat Northerly to get a winde. Wee therefore set saile, and sayled 600. leagues at the least for a good winde, and thus much we sailed from the 16. of April, till the 3. of June.

The 5. day of June, being in 43. degrees towards the pole Arctike, we found the ayre so colde, that our men being grievously pinched with the same, complained of the extremitie thereof, and the further we went, the more the colde increased upon us. Whereupon we thought it best for that time to seeke the land, and did so, finding it not mountainous, but low plaine land, till wee came within 38. degrees towards the line. In which height it pleased God to send us into a faire and good Baye, with a good winde to enter the same.

In this Baye we anchored, and the people of the Countrey having their houses close by the waters side, shewed themselves unto us, and sent a present to our Generall.

When they came unto us, they greatly wondred at the things that wee brought, but our Generall (according to his naturall and accustomed humanitie) courteously intreated them, and liberally bestowed on them necessary things to cover their nakednesse, whereupon they supposed us to be gods, and would not be perswaded to the contrary: the presents which they sent to our Generall, were feathers, and calles of net-worke.

Their houses are digged round about with earth, and have from the uttermost brimmes of the circle, clifts of wood set upon them, joyning close together at the toppe like a spire steeple, which by reason of that closenesse are very warme.

Their beds is the ground with rushes strowed on it, and lying about the house, have the fire in the midst. The men go naked, the women take bulrushes, and kembe them after the manner of hempe, and thereof make their loose garments, which being knit about their middles, hang down about their hippes, having also about their shoulders a skinne of Deere, with the haire upon it. These women are very obedient and serviceable to their husbands.

After they were departed from us, they came and visited us the second time, and brought with them feathers and bags of Tabacco for presents: And when they came to the top of the hill (at the bottome whereof we had pitched our tents) they staied themselves: where one appointed for speaker wearied himselfe with making a long oration, which done, they left their bowes upon the hill, and came downe with their presents.

In the meane time the women remaining on the hill, tormented themselves lamentably, tearing their flesh from their cheekes, whereby we perceived that they were about a sacrifice. In the meane time our Generall with his company went to prayer, and to reading of the Scriptures, at which exercise they were attentive, & seemed greatly to be affected with it: but when they were come unto us, they restored againe unto us those things which before we bestowed upon them.

The newes of our being there being spread through the Countrey, the people that inhabited round about came downe, and amongst them the King himselfe, a man of a goodly stature, & comely personage, with many other tall and warlike men: before whose comming were sent two Ambassadors to our Generall, to signifie that their King was comming, in doing of which message, their speach was continued about halfe an houre. This ended, they by signes requested our Generall to send some thing by their hand to their king, as a token that his comming might be in peace: wherein our Generall having satisfied them, they returned with glad tidings to their King, who marched to us with a princely majestie, the people crying continually after their manner, and as they drew neere unto us, so did they strive to behave themselves in their action with comelinesse.

In the fore-front was a man of a goodly personage, who bare the scepter or mace before the King, whereupon hanged two crownes, a lesse and a bigger, with three chaines of a marveilous length: the crownes were made of knit worke wrought artificially with fethers of divers colours: the chaines were made of a bonie substance, and few be the persons among them that are admitted to weare them: and of that number also the persons are stinted, as some ten, some 12. &c. Next unto him which bare the scepter, was the King himselfe, with his Guard about his person, clad with Conie skins, & other skins: after them followed the naked common sort of people, every one having his face painted, some with white, some with blacke, and other colours, & having in their hands one thing or another for a present, not so much as their children, but they also brought their presents.

In the meane time our Generall gathered his men together, and marched within his fenced place, making against their approching a very warre-like shew. They being trooped together in their order, and a generall salutation being made, there was presently a generall silence. Then he that bare the scepter before the King, being informed by another, whom they assigned to that office, with a manly and loftie voyce proclaymed that which the other spake to him in secrete, continuing halfe an houre: which ended, and a generall Amen as it were given, the King with the whole number of men and women (the children excepted) came downe without any weapon, who descending to the foote of the hill, set themselves in order.

In comming towards our bulwarks and tents, the scepter-bearer began a song, observing his measures in a daunce, and that with a stately countenance, whom the King with his Guarde, and every degree of persons following, did in like maner sing and daunce, saving onely the women, which daunced & kept silence. The General permitted them to enter within our bulwarke, where they continued their song and daunce a reasonable time. When they had satisfied themselves, they made signes to our General to sit downe, to whom the King, and divers others made several orations, or rather supplications, that hee would take their province and kingdome into his hand, and become their King, making signes that they would resigne unto him their right and title of the whole land, and become his subjects. In which, to perswade us the better, the King and the rest, with one consent, and with great reverence, joyfully singing a song, did set the crowne upon his head, inriched his necke with all their chaines, and offred unto him many other things, honouring him by the name of Hioh, adding thereunto as it seemed, a signe of triumph: which thing our Generall thought not meete to reject, because he knew not what honour and profit it might be to our Countrey. Wherefore in the name, and to the use of her Majestie he tooke the scepter, crowne, and dignitie of the said Countrey into his hands, wishing that the riches & treasure thereof might so conveniently be transported to the inriching of her kingdom at home, as it aboundeth in ye same.

The common sorte of people leaving the King and his Guarde with our Generall, scattered themselves together with their sacrifices among our people, taking a diligent viewe of every person: and such as pleased their fancie, (which were the yongest) they inclosing them about offred their sacrifices unto them with lamentable weeping, scratching, and tearing the flesh from their faces with their nailes, whereof issued abundance of blood. But wee used signes to them of disliking this, and stayed their hands from force, and directed them upwards to the living God, whom onely they ought to worship. They shewed unto us their wounds, and craved helpe of them at our hands, whereupon we gave them lotions, plaisters, and oyntments, agreeing to the state of their griefes, beseeching God to cure their diseases. Every third day they brought their sacrifices unto us, until they understood our meaning, that we had no pleasure in them: yet they could not be long absent from us, but dayly frequented our company to the houre of our departure, which departure seemed so greevous unto them, that their joy was turned into sorow. They intreated us, that being absent we would remember them, and by stealth provided a sacrifice, which we misliked.

Our necessarie businesse being ended, our Generall with his company travailed up into the Countrey to their villages, where we found herdes of Deere by 1000. in a company, being most large, and fat of body.

We found the whole Countrey to bee a warren of a strange kinde of Connies, their bodies in bignesse as be the Barbary Connies, their heads as the heads of ours, the feete of a Want, and the taile of a Rat being of great length: under her chinne is on either side a bag, into the which she gathereth her meate, when she hath filled her bellie abroad. The people eate their bodies, and make great accompt of their skinnes, for their Kings coate was made of them.

Our Generall called this Countrey Nova Albion, and that for two causes: the one in respect of the white bankes and cliffes, which lie towards the sea: and the other, because it might have some affinitie with our Countrey in name, which sometime was so called.

There is no part of earth heere to bee taken up, wherein there is not some probable shew of gold or silver.

At our departure hence our General set up a monument of our being there, as also of her Majesties right and title to the same, namely a plate, nailed upon a faire great poste, whereupon was ingraven her Majesties name, the day and yeere of our arrivall there, with the free giving up of the province and people into her Majesties hands, together with her highnesse picture and armes, in a peece of sixe pence of current English money under the plate, whereunder was also written the name of our Generall.

It seemeth that the Spaniards hitherto had never bene in this part of the Countrey, neither did ever discover the land by many degrees, to the Southwards of this place.

After we had set saile from hence, wee continued without sight of land till the 13. day of October following, which day in the morning wee fell with certaine Islands 8. degrees to the Northward of the line, from which Islands came a great number of Canoas, having in some of them 4. in some 6. and in some also 14. men, bringing with them cocos, and other fruites. Their Canoas were hollow within, and cut with great arte and cunning, being very smooth within and without, and bearing a glasse as if it were a horne daintily burnished, having a prowe, and a sterne of one sort, yeelding inward circle-wise, being of a great height, and full of certaine white shels for a braverie, and on each side of them lie out two peeces of timber about a yard and a halfe long, more or lesse, according to the smalnesse, or bignesse of the boate.

This people have the nether part of their eares cut into a round circle, hanging downe very lowe upon their cheekes, whereon they hang things of a reasonable weight. The nailes of their hands are an ynche long, their teeth are as blacke as pitch, and they renew them often, by eating of an herbe with a kinde of powder, which they alwayes carrie about them in a cane for the same purpose.

Leaving this Island the night after we fell with it, the 18. of October, we lighted upon divers others, some whereof made a great shew of Inhabitants.

Wee continued our course by the Islands of Tagulada, Zelon, and Zewarra, being friends to the Portugals, the first whereof hath growing in it great store of Cinnamom.

The 14. of November we fell with the Islands of Maluco, which day at night (having directed our course to runne with Tydore) in coasting along the Island of Mutyr, belonging to the King of Ternate, his Deputie or Vice-king seeing us at sea, came with his Canoa to us without all feare, and came aboord, and after some conference with our Generall, willed him in any wise to runne in with Ternate, and not with Tydore, assuring him that the King would bee glad of his comming, and would be ready to doe what he would require, for which purpose he himselfe would that night be with the King, and tell him the newes, with whom if he once dealt, hee should finde that as he was a King, so his word should stand: adding further, that if he went to Tydore before he came to Ternate, the King would have nothing to doe with us, because hee held the Portugall as his enemie: whereupon our General resolved to runne with Ternate, where the next morning early we came to anchor, at which time our Generall sent a messenger to the king with a velvet cloke for a present, and token of his comming to be in peace, and that he required nothing but traffique and exchange of marchandize, whereof he had good store, in such things as he wanted.

In the meane time the Vice-king had bene with the king according to his promise, signifying unto him what good things he might receive from us by traffique: whereby the King was mooved with great liking towards us, and sent to our Generall with speciall message, that hee should have what things he needed, and would require with peace and friendship, and moreover that hee would yeeld himselfe, and the right of his Island to bee at the pleasure and commandement of so famous a Prince as we served. In token whereof he sent to our Generall a signet, and within short time after came in his owne person, with boates, and Canoas to our ship, to bring her into a better and safer roade then she was in at present.

In the meane time, our Generals messenger beeing come to the Court, was met by certaine noble personages with great solemnitie, and brought to the King, at whose hands hee was most friendly and graciously intertained.

The King purposing to come to our ship, sent before 4. great and large Canoas, in every one whereof were certaine of his greatest states that were about him, attired in white lawne of cloth of Calicut, having over their heads from the one ende of the Canoa to the other, a covering of thinne perfumed mats, borne up with a frame made of reedes for the same use, under which every one did sit in his order according to his dignitie, to keepe him from the heate of the Sunne, divers of whom beeing of good age and gravitie, did make an ancient and fatherly shew. There were also divers yong and comely men attired in white, as were the others: the rest were souldiers, which stood in comely order round about on both sides, without whom sate the rowers in certaine galleries, which being three on a side all along the Canoas, did lie off from the side thereof three or foure yardes, one being orderly builded lower then another, in every of which galleries were the number of 4. score rowers.

These Canoas were furnished with warlike munition, every man for the most part having his sword and target, with his dagger, beside other weapons, as launces, calivers, darts, bowes and arrowes: also every Canoa had a small cast base mounted at the least one full yarde upon a stocke set upright.

Thus comming neere our shippe, in order they rowed about us, one after another, and passing by, did their homage with great solemnitie, the great personages beginning with great gravitie and fatherly countenances, signifying that ye king had sent them to conduct our ship into a better roade.

Soone after the King himselfe repaired, accompanied with 6. grave and ancient persons, who did their obeisance with marveilous humilitie. The king was a man of tall stature, and seemed to be much delighted with the sound of our musicke, to whom as also to his nobilitie, our Generall gave presents, wherewith they were passing well contented.

At length the King craved leave of our Generall to depart, promising the next day to come aboord, and in the meane time to send us such victuals, as were necessarie for our provision: so that the same night we received of them meale, which they call Sagu, made of the tops of certaine trees, tasting in the mouth like sowre curds, but melteth like sugar, whereof they make certaine cakes, which may be kept the space of ten yeeres, and yet then good to be eaten. We had of them store of rice, hennes, unperfect and liquid sugar, sugar canes, and a fruite which they call Figo, with store of cloves.

The King having promised to come aboord, brake his promise, but sent his brother to make his excuse, and to intreate our Generall to come on shoare, offring himself pawne aboord for his safe returne. Whereunto our Generall consented not, upon mislike conceived of the breach of his promise, the whole company also utterly refusing it. But to satisfie him, our General sent certaine of his Gentlemen to the Court, to accompany the King's brother, reserving the Vice-king for their safe returne. They were received of another brother of the kings, and other states, and were conducted with great honour to the Castle. The place that they were brought unto, was a large and faire house, where were at the least 1000. persons assembled.

The King being yet absent, there sate in their places 60. grave personages, all which were said to be of the kings

Counsel. There were besides 4. grave persons, apparelled all in red, downe to the ground, and attired on their heads like the Turkes, and these were said to be Romanes, and Ligiers there to keepe continual traffike with the people of Ternate. There were also 2. Turks Ligiers in this place, and one Italian. The king at last came in guarded with 12. launces covered over with a rich canopy, with embossed gold. Our men accompanied with one of their Captaines called Moro, rising to meete him, he graciously did welcome, and intertaine them. He was attired after the manner of the Countrey, but more sumptuously then the rest. From his waste downe to the ground, was all cloth of golde, and the same very rich: his legges were bare, but on his feete were a paire of shooes, made of Cordovan skinne. In the attire of his head were finely wreathed hooped rings of gold, and about his necke he had a chaine of perfect golde, the linkes whereof were great, and one folde double. On his fingers hee had six very faire jewels, and sitting in his chaire of estate, at his right hand stood a page with a fanne in his hand, breathing and gathering the ayre to the King. The fanne was in length two foote, and in bredth one foote, set with 8. saphyres, richly imbrodered, and knit to a staffe 3. foote in length, by the which the Page did hold, and moove it. Our Gentlemen having delivered their message, and received order accordingly, were licensed to depart, being safely conducted backe againe by one of the kings Counsell.

This Island is the chiefest of all the Islands of Maluco, and the King hereof is King of 70. Islands besides. The king with his people are Moores in religion, observing certaine new Moones, with fastings: during which fasts, they neither eat nor drinke in the day, but in the night.

After that our Gentlemen were returned, and that we had heere by the favour of the king received all necessary things that the place could yeeld us: our General considering the great distance, and how farre he was yet off from his Countrey, thought it not best here to linger the time any longer, but waying his anchors, set out of the Island, and sayled to a certaine litle Island to the Southwards of Celebes, where we graved our ship, and continued there in that and other businesses 26. dayes. This Island is throughly growen with wood of a large and high growth, very straight and without boughes, save onely in the head or top, whose leaves are not much differing from our broome in England. Amongst these trees night by night, through the whole land, did shew themselves an infinite swarme of fiery wormes flying in the ayre, whose bodies beeing no bigger then our common English flies, make such a shew and light, as if every twigge or tree had bene a burning candle. In this place breedeth also wonderfull store of Bats, as bigge as large hennes: of Crayfishes also heere wanted no plentie, and they of exceeding bignesse, one whereof was sufficient for 4. hungry stomacks at a dinner, beeing also very good, and restoring meate, whereof we had experience: and they digge themselves holes in the earth like Conies.

When wee had ended our businesse here, we waied, and set saile to runne for the Malucos: but having at that time a bad winde, and being amongst the Islands, with much difficultie wee recovered to the Northward of the Island of Celebes, where by reason of contrary winds not able to continue our course to runne Westwards, we were inforced to alter the same to the Southward againe, finding that course also to be very hard and dangerous for us, by reason of infinite shoalds which lie off, and among the Islands: whereof wee had too much triall to the hazard and danger of our shippe and lives. For of all other dayes upon the 9. of Januarie, in the yeere 1579. wee ranne suddenly upon a rocke, where we stucke fast from 8. of the clocke at night, til 4. of the clocke in the afternoone the next day, being indeede out of all hope to escape the danger: but our Generall as hee had alwayes hitherto shewed himselfe couragious, and of a good confidence in the mercie and protection of God: so now he continued in the same, and lest he should seeme to perish wilfully, both he, and we did our best indevour to save our selves, which it pleased God so to blesse, that in the ende we cleared our selves most happily of the danger.

We lighted our ship upon the rockes of 3. tunne of cloves, 8. peeces of ordinance, and certaine meale and beanes: and then the winde (as it were in a moment by the speciall grace of God) changing from the starreboord to the larboord of the ship, we hoised our sailes, and the happy gale drove our ship off the rocke into the sea againe, to the no litle comfort of all our hearts, for which we gave God such prayse and thanks, as so great a benefite required.

The 8. of Februarie following, wee fell with the fruitfull Island of Barateve, having in the meane time suffered many dangers by windes and shoalds. The people of this Island are comely in body and stature, and of a civil behaviour, just in dealing, and courteous to strangers, whereof we had the experience sundry wayes, they being most glad of our presence, and very ready to releeve our wants in those things which their Countrey did yeelde. The men goe naked, saving their heads and privities, every man having something or other hanging at their eares. Their women are covered from the middle downe to the foote, wearing a great number of bracelets upon their armes, for some had 8. upon each arme, being made some of bone, some of horne, and some of brasse, the lightest whereof by our estimation waied two ounces apeece.

With this people linnen-cloth is good marchandize, and of good request, whereof they make rols for their heads, and girdles to weare about them.

Their Island is both rich and fruitfull: rich in golde, silver, copper, and sulphur, wherein they seeme skilfull and expert, not onely to trie the same, but in working it also artificially into any forme and fashion that pleaseth them.

Their fruits be divers and plentiful, as nutmegs, ginger, long pepper, lemmons, cucumbers, cocos, figu, sagu, with divers other sorts: and among all the rest, wee had one fruite, in bignesse, forme, and huske, like a Bay berry, hard of substance, and pleasant of taste, which being sodden, becommeth soft, and is a most good and wholsome victuall, whereof we tooke reasonable store, as we did also of the other fruits and spices: so that to confesse a trueth, since the time that we first set out of our owne Countrey of England, we happened upon no place (Ternate onely excepted) wherein we found more comforts and better meanes of refreshing.

At our departure from Barateve, we set our course for Java major, where arriving, we found great courtesie, and honourable entertainment. This Island is governed by 5. Kings, whom they call Rajah: as Rajah Donaw, and Rajah Mang Bange, and

Rajah Cabuccapollo, which live as having one spirite, and one minde.

Of these five we had foure a shipboord at once, and two or three often. They are wonderfully delighted in coloured clothes, as red and greene: their upper parts of their bodies are naked, save their heads, whereupon they weare a Turkish roll, as do the Maluccians: from the middle downward they weare a pintado of silke, trailing upon the ground, in colour as they best like.

The Maluccians hate that their women should be seene of strangers: but these offer them of high courtesie, yea the kings themselves.

The people are of goodly stature, and warlike, well provided of swords and targets, with daggers, all being of their owne worke, and most artificially done, both in tempering their mettall, as also in the forme, whereof we bought reasonable store.

They have an house in every village for their common assembly: every day they meete twise, men, women, and children, bringing with them such victuals as they thinke good, some fruites, some rice boiled, some hennes roasted, some sagu, having a table made 3. foote from the ground, whereon they set their meate, that every person sitting at the table may eate, one rejoycing in the company of another.

They boile their rice in an earthen pot, made in forme of a sugar loafe, being ful of holes, as our pots which we water our gardens withall, and it is open at the great ende, wherein they put their rice dried, without any moisture. In the meane time they have ready another great earthen pot, set fast in a fornace, boiling full of water, whereinto they put their pot with rice, by such measure, that they swelling become soft at the first, and by their swelling stopping the holes of the pot, admit no more water to enter, but the more they are boiled, the harder and more firme substance they become, so that in the end they are a firme & good bread, of the which with oyle, butter, sugar, and other spices, they make divers sorts of meates very pleasant of taste, and nourishing to nature.

The French pocks is here very common to all, and they helpe themselves, sitting naked from ten to two in the Sunne, whereby the venemous humour is drawen out. Not long before our departure, they tolde us, that not farre off there were such great Ships as ours, wishing us to beware: upon this our Captaine would stay no longer.

From Java Major we sailed for the cape of Good Hope, which was the first land we fell withall: neither did we touch with it, or any other land, untill we came to Sierra Leona, upon the coats of Guinea: notwithstanding we ranne hard aboord the Cape, finding the report of the Portugals to be most false, who affirme, that it is the most dangerous Cape of the world, never without intolerable stormes and present danger to traveilers, which come neere the same.

This Cape is a most stately thing, and the fairest Cape we saw in the whole circumference of the earth, and we passed by it the 18. of June.

From thence we continued our course to Sierra Leona, on the coast of Guinea, where we arrived the 22. of July, and found necessarie provisions, great store of Elephants, Oisters upon trees of one kind, spawning and increasing infinitely, the Oister suffering no budde to grow. We departed thence the 24. day.

We arrived in England the third of November 1580. being the third yeere of our departure.

22

The relation of a Voyage made by a Pilot called Nuno
da Silva for the Vice-roy of new Spaine, the 20. of
May, in the yere of our Lord 1579. in the citie of
Mexico, from whence it was sent to the Vice-roy of
the Portugall-Indies: wherein is set downe the course
and actions passed in the Voyages of Sir Francis
Drake that tooke the aforesayd Nuno da Silva at S.
Iago one of the Island of Cabo Verde, and caried
him along with him through the Streights of
Magellan, to the Haven of Guatulco in new Spaine,
where he let him goe againe

NUNO DA SILVA borne in Porto, a Citizen and inhabitant
of Guaia, saith, that hee departed out of his house in the beginning of November in the yeere of our Lorde 1577. taking his
course to Cabo Verde, or The greene Cape, where he anchored
with his Shippe close by the Haven of the Island of Sant Iago,
one of the Islandes of Cabo Verde aforesayde, beeing the nineteenth of January in the yeere of our Lord 1578. And lying
there, there came six ships, which seemed to be Englishmen,
whereof the Admirall boorded his ship, and by force with his
men tooke him out of his ship, bringing him in the boate aboord
the Admirals shippe, leaving some of his best men aboord his
ship: and although the fortresse of the Island shot foure or five
times at them, yet they hurt not the Englishmen: who having
done, set saile from thence to the Island of Brava, taking with
them the ship of the sayd Nuno da Silva: being there, they filled
certaine vessels with fresh water: from thence holding their
course inward to sea, having first with a boat set the men of
Nuno da Silvas ship on land, onely keeping Nuno da Silva in

his ship, as also his ship with the wines that were therein. And Nuno da Silva saith, the cause why they kept him on boord was, because they knew him to bee a pilot for the coast of Brasilia, that hee might bring them to such places in those countreys as had fresh water.

Being put off from the Island of Brava, they helde their course to the land of Brasilia, which they descried upon the first of Aprill, under the height of thirtie degrees: and without landing or taking in fresh water, they helde on their course to Rio de la Plata, that is, The river of silver, lying under five and thirtie degrees, little more or lesse: where they went on land, and provided themselves of fresh water.

From thence they helde on their course till they came under nine and thirtie degrees, where they ankered: and beeing there they left two of their sixe shippes behinde them, and sailed but foure in companie (that of Nuno da Silva being one) till they came to the Bay called Baya de las Islas, that is, The Bay of the Ilands, lying under nine and fortie degrees, where it is sayde, that Magellan lay and wintered there with his shippe, when hee first discovered the Streight, which now holdeth his name. Into this Bay the twentieth of June they entred, and there ankered so close to the land, that they might send to it with a harquebuse shot: and there they sawe the land to bee inhabited with Indians, that were apparelled with skinnes, with their legges from the knees downeward, and their armes from the elbowes downeward naked, all the rest of their bodies beeing clothed, with bowes and arrowes in their handes, being subtill, great, and well formed people, and strong and high of stature: where sixe of the Englishmen went on land to fetch fresh water, and before they leapt on land, foure of the Indians came unto their boate, to whome the Englishmen gave bread and wine: and when the Indians had well eaten and drunke, they departed thence: and going somewhat farre from them, one of the Indians cryed to them, and sayde: Magallanes, Esta he minha Terra, that is, Magallanes, this is my countrey: and because the Englishmen followed them, it seemed the Indians fledde upward into the land, and beeing somewhat farre off, they turned backe againe, and with their arrowes slewe two of the English shippers, one being a Englishman, the other a Netherlander: the rest came backe againe and saved themselves in the boate,

wherewith they presently put off from the shore. Here they
stayed till the seventeenth of August, upon the which day they
set saile, running along by the coast about a league and a halfe
from the land, (for there it is all faire and good ground, at
twentie, and five and twentie fathome deepe) and were about
foure or five dayes before they came to the mouth or entrie of
the Streight: but because the wind was contrary, they stayed till
the 24 of August before they entred.

The entrie or mouth of the Streight is about a league broad,
on both sides being bare and flatte land: on the North side they
sawe Indians making great fires, but on the South side they
saw no people stirring. The foure and twentieth day aforesayd,
they beganne to enter into the Streight, with an Eastnortheast
wind. This Streight may bee about an hundred and tenne
leagues long, and in bredth a league. About the entry of the
Streight, and halfe way into it, it runneth right foorth without
any windings or turnings: and from thence about eight or tenne
leagues towards the ende, it hath some boutes and windings,
among the which there is one so great a hooke or headland,
that it seemed to runne into the other land: and there it is lesse
then a league broad from one land to the other: and from
thence forward it runneth straight out againe: And although you
finde some crookings, yet they are nothing to speake of. The
issue of the Streight lieth Westward, and about eight or tenne
leagues before you come to the ende, then the Streight beginneth to bee broader, and it is all high land to the ende
thereof, after you are eight leagues within the Streight, for the
first eight leagues after you enter is low flat land, as I sayd before: and in the entrie of the Streight you find the streame to
runne from the South sea to the North sea.

And after they began to saile in with the Eastnortheast wind,
being entred they passed along without any let or hinderance
either of wind or weather: and because the high land on both
sides lay covered with snow, and that all the Streight is faire and
cleare, they helde their course a harquebuse-shot in length
from off the North side, having nine and tenne fathome depth,
with good ground, as I said before, where (if neede require) a
man may anker: the hilles on both sides being full of trees,
some of the hilles and trees reaching downe to the sea side in
some places having plaine and even land: and there they sawe

not any great rivers, but some small rivers that issued out of the riffes and breaches of the land: and in the countrey where the great Cape or crooking is, on the South side they saw certaine Indian fishermen in their Canoas or skiffs, being such as they saw first on the North side, but more people they saw not on the South side.

Being out of the Streight on the other side, upon the sixt of September of the aforesaid yeere, they held their course Northwest for the space of three dayes, and the third day they had a Northeast wind, that by force drave them Westsouthwest, which course they held for the space of ten or twelve dayes with few sailes up: and because the wind began to be very great, they tooke in all their sailes, and lay driving till the last of September.

The 24 day of the same moneth having lost the sight of one of their shippes which was about an hundred tunne, then againe they hoised saile because the winde came better, holding their course Northeast for the space of seven dayes, and at the ende of the sayde seven dayes, they had the sight of certayne Islands, which they made towards for to anker by them, but the weather would not permit them: and being there, the wind fell Northwest: whereupon they sailed Westsouthwest.

The next day they lost the sight of another ship of their company, for it was very foule weather, so that in the ende the Admirals shippe was left alone, for the ship of Nuno da Silva was left in the Bay where they wintered before they entered into the Streights: and with this foule weather they ranne till they were under seven and fiftie degrees, where they entred into a haven of an Island, and ankered about the length of the shot of a great piece from the land, at twentie fathome deepe, where they stayed three or foure dayes, and the wind comming Southward, they weyed anker, holding their course Northward for the space of two daies, and then they espied a small unhabited Island, where being arrived, they stroke sailes, and hoised out their boate, and there they tooke many birds and Seales.

The next day they set saile againe, holding their course Northnortheast, and North, to another Island lying five or six leagues from the firme land, on the North side of the Streight, where they ankered about a quarter of a league from the land, in twelve fathome water. This Island is small and lowe land,

and full of Indians, the Island being altogether possessed and inhabited by them, where they hoysed out their boate, wherein the Admirall and twelve Englishmen entred, going to fetch fresh water, and to seeke for victuals: and being landed upon the Island, the Indians in exchange of other things, brought two Spanish sheepe, and a little Maiz or rootes whereof they make bread, and because it was late, they returned againe unto their ship, without doing any other thing for that day.

The next day the said Captaine with the aforesaid twelve men being harquebusiers, rowed to land againe, and set two of their company on shore with their vessels to fetch fresh water, and by the place where they should fill their water there lay certaine Indians secretly hidden, that fell upon the two Englishmen and tooke them: which they in the boat perceiving, went out to helpe them, but they were so assailed with stones & arrowes, that all or the most part of them were hurt, the Captaine himselfe being wounded with an arrow on the face, and with an other arrow in the head, whereby they were constrained to turne backe againe, without once hurting any of the Indians, and yet they came so neere the boate, that they tooke foure of their oares from them. This done, they set saile againe, running along the coast with a South winde, sailing so for the space of sixe dayes, passing by the haven called Sant Iago, and put into another haven, and there they tooke an Indian that lay fishing in a Canoa, giving him linnen and butchers chopping knives, with other trifles, and not long after there came another Indian aboord their shippe called Felippe, and he spake Spanish, he gave the English Captaine notice of a certaine shippe that lay in the haven of Sant Iago, which they had left sixe leagues behind them: with that intelligence the Indian being their guide, the next day they set saile and went to the aforesayd haven of S. Iago, and entring therein, they tooke the said shippe, wherein they found a thousand seven hundred and 70 Botijas or Spanish pots full of wine, and other things: which having done, they lept on land, where they tooke certaine sackes with meale, with whatsoever they could find; they tooke likewise the ornaments and the reliques out of the Church, wherewith they departed from thence, taking the aforesayd shippe, with two men (that they found in her) with them, and so departed from that haven, which lyeth under 32 degrees and a halfe, running along by the coast till they came under one and thirtie, and thirtie degrees: which was the place where they had appointed to meete, and there to stay for ech other, if by tempest or foule weather they chanced to be separated, and so loose eche others company.

And comming under thirtie degrees, they found a very good haven, whereinto they entred, and ankered at sixe fathome deepe, the shot of a great peece from the land, which was right over against a river, where they tooke in sixe pipes of fresh water: and to defend them that fetched the water, they set twelve men upon the land, and being busied in filling of their water, they espied a company of men comming towards them, whereof halfe of them were Spaniards, being about two hundred and fifty horsemen, and as many footemen, but they had no sooner espied them, but they presently entred into the boat, and escaped away, loosing but one man.

The same night they set saile againe with both their ships, running along the coast about ten leagues farther, where they tooke in some fresh water, but because they perceived certaine horsemen, they departed without lading any more water.

From thence they followed on their course along the coast for the space of 30. leagues, where they entred into a desert or unhabited haven: yet they went not on land, for every day they saw people upon the shore, & there they made out a smal pinnesse, the peeces wherof they brought ready framed out of England, and having prepared it, they launched it into the water, wherein the Captaine with fifteene men entred with the chiefe boatesman called John the Greeke, (being Master of the ship which they had taken in the haven of S. Iago,) wherewith they went to see if they could find the two shippes that they had lost by stormie weather, as I sayd before: and likewise thinking to goe on land to fill certaine vessels with fresh water, they durst not venture, for they saw people on all sides of the shore: so that in the ende they returned againe without hearing of the other ships: being there, they tooke all the ordinance out of their ship, and new dressed and rigged her: which done, they put a small peece of ordinance into the pinnesse, wherewith they set saile againe, following on their course.

Having sailed thirteene dayes, they came to an Island lying about the shotte of a base from the land, where they ankered, and there they found foure Indian fishermen in two Canoas who told them that on the firme land they might have fresh water, but they understanding that there was not much, and that it was somewhat within the land, would not spend any time about it, but set saile againe, leaving the fishermen with their Canoas, following on their course along by the shore.

The next day being somewhat further, they espied certaine Indian fishermen that were upon the land in their houses, which the English captaine perceiving, presently entred into his pinnesse, and rowed on land, where he tooke three of the said fishermen, taking with him halfe of the fish that lay packed upon the shore ready to be laden, with the which Indians and booty, they came on boord againe.

The next day following, they saw a barke laden with fish, that belonged to the Spaniards, with foure Indians in it. This barke with the Indians and the fish they tooke, and bound the Spanish ship to their sterne, and so drewe it after them, leaving the said Indians within it, who by night unbound the barke, and secretly made away with barke and fish, and were no more seene. The next day the Captaine went into the pinnesse, and because he saw certaine houses upon the shore, he made thither, and being on land, he found two men in them, one whereof he tooke, leaving the other behind, and there he found three thousand pezos of silver, (every pezo being the value of a ryall of eight,) and seven Indian sheepe, and hennes, & tooke al whatsoever they found: wherewith they departed from thence, following on their course. And two dayes after they came to the haven called Arica, where they found two ships, the one laden with goods and Spanish wares, out of the which they tooke only two hundred Botijas, or Spanish pots with wine, and out of the other seven and thirty barres of silver, which are peeces of ten or twelve pound eche barre, and thinking to leape on shore (with two barks that they found in the said haven, with about seven and thirty harquebuses and bowes) they perceived on the land certaine horsemen comming towards them, whereupon they left off their pretence, and tooke with them a Negro that they found in the barks, with whom they returned aboord.

The next day in the morning they burnt the ship, that was laden with the Spanish wares, and tooke the other with them, passing forward with it on their course, the Captaine sailing along the shore with his pinnesse, and the ship keeping about a league from him to seaward, to seeke for a ship wherof they had intelligence: and having in that maner sailed about five and forty leagues, they found the ship that lay at anker in a haven, who about two houres before had bene advertised of an English pirate or sea-rover, and had discharged eight hundred barres of silver out of her, and hidden it on the land, which silver belonged to the king of Spaine, of the which silver the Englishmen had received some intelligence, but they durst not go on land, because there were many Indians and Spaniards that stood to gard it, and they found nothing in the ship but three pipes of water: the ship they tooke with them, and being about a league in the sea, they hoysed up all her sailes and let her drive, doing the like with the ship that they had taken in Arica, as also the other of Sant Iago, which likewise they let drive, following on their course with their owne ship, and the pinnesse.

Being seven or eight leagues from the haven of Calao de Lyma, they espied three ships, and boording one of them, they tooke three men out of her, and so held on their course towards Calao de Lyma, where they entred, being about two or three houres within night, sailing in betweene all the ships that lay there, being seventeene in number: and being among the ships, they asked for the ship that had laden the silver, but when answere was made them, that the silver was layd on land, they cut the cables of the ships, and the masts of two of the greatest ships, and so left them. At the same time there arrived a ship from Panama laden with wares and merchandise of Spaine, that ankered close by the English ship, which was, while the English Captaine sought in the other ships for the silver. Assoone as the ship of Panama had ankered, there came a boat from the shore to search it: but because it was in the night, they let it alone till morning, and comming to the English ship, they asked what ship it was: whereupon one of the Spanish prisoners (by the English Captaines commandement) answered and said it was the ship of Michael Angelo, that came from Chili: which they of the boat hearing sent a man on board, who climing up, light upon one of the great peeces, wherewith he was afraid, and presently stept backe againe into the boat (because the shippes that lay there, and that sailed in those countreys, used to carry no great shot) and therewith they were abashed, and made from it: which the ship of Panama hearing, that was newly come in, shee judged it to be a rover, and therewith cutting her cables, shee put to sea, which the Englishmen perceiving, shipped certaine men in their pinnesse, and followed her: and being hard by her, they badde her strike, which they of the ship refused to doe, and with a harquebuse shot killed one of the Englishmen, wherewith they turned againe into their shippe, and presently set saile, following after the ship, which not long after they overtooke: which they of the shippe perceiving hoysed out their boate, and leaping into it, rowed to the land, leaving the shippe with all the goods, which the Englishmen presently tooke, and with her sayled on their course.

The next day they saw a boat with sailes making towards them, whereby they presently mistrusted it to be a spie, and not long after they perceived two great ships comming towards them, which the English thinke they came to fight with them, whereupon they let the shippe of Panama drive, therein leaving John the Greeke, with the two men that they had taken the same day that they entred into the Calao de Lyma, as I sayde before, and presently hoysed all their sailes, and sailed forward, not once setting eye againe upon the aforesayde ships, for they made towards the ship of Panama, which the Englishmen let drive. From thence they sailed againe along the coast, following on their course: and having sailed certaine dayes, they met a frigate that went towards Lyma, laden with wares and merchandises of the countrey, from whence the Englishmen tooke a lampe and a fountaine of silver, and asked the pilote being a Spaniard, if they met not with a ship, that they understood should be laden with silver, but the one Pilote saide he met her not, and the other said he saw her about three dayes before. This frigat came not to the ship, but to the pinnesse, wherein the Captaine sailed, for the pinnesse ranne close by the shore, and the ship kept a league and a halfe from the lande: whereupon they let the frigate goe, following on their course.

Two dayes after, they came to the haven called Payta, where they found a ship laden with Spanish wares, which the pinnesse boorded, and tooke without any resistance: for assoone as the Spaniards perceived the Englishmen, they presently made to land with their boate, and two of them lept into the sea, none staying in the shippe, but the Master, Pilote, and some Negros, out of the which shippe the Englishmen tooke the pilote, and all the bread, hennes and a hogge, and so sailed forward with the ship: but being about two harquebuse shot to seaward, they let it goe againe, not taking any thing out of it, and asking after the ship, which they sought for, they told them that about two dayes before she departed from that place, wherewith they followed on their course, and before night they met with a ship of Panama, which they presently boorded, but tooke nothing from her but onely a Negro, and so left it, holding on their course.

The next day being the first of Februarie, they met another ship that sailed to Panama, laden with fish and other victuals, and fortie barres of silver, and some gold, but I know not how much, which they tooke, and sent the passengers (with two friers that were in her) in a boate to land. The next day they hanged a man of the ship, because hee would not confesse two plates of golde that he had taken, which after they found about him: which done, they let the ship drive, following on their course.

The first of March towards noone, they espied the ship laden with silver, being about foure leagues to seaward from them: and because the English ship was somewhat heavie before, whereby it sailed not as they would have it, they tooke a company of Botijas or Spanish pots for oyle, and filling them with water, hung them by ropes at the sterne of the ship to make her sayle the better: and the shippe that sayled towards Panama made towards the English shippe to know what shee was, thinking it to bee one of the shippes that used to saile along the coastes, and to traffique in the countrey: and beeing hard by her, the English Captaine badde them strike, but the other refusing to doe it, with a great peece hee shotte her mast overboord, and having wounded the Master with an arrowe, the shippe presently yeelded, which they tooke, and sayled with her further into the sea, all that night and the next day and night, making all the way they could.

The third day being out of sight of the land, they beganne to search the ship, and to lade the goods out of her into their ship, which was a thousand three hundred barres or peeces of silver, and foureteene chestes with ryals of eight, and with gold: but what quantitie it was I know not, onely the passengers sayd that there was great store, and that three hundred barres of the silver belonged to the king, the rest belonged to certaine merchants. That done, they let the ship with the men saile on their course, putting the three pilots in her that they brought with them, so that as then they had none but their owne men aboord, being the sixt of March, and from thence they held their course towards the land of Nicaragua.

The thirteenth of March, either the day before or after, in the morning they descried land, not being very high, being a small Island two leagues from the firme land, and there they found a small Bay, wherein they ankered at five fathome deepe close by the land, and there they stayed till the twentie day. Upon the which day there passed a Frigate close by the Island, which with their pinnesse they followed, and taking her, brought her to the English ship, which frigat was laden with Salsaperilla, and Botijas or pots with butter and hony, and with other things. The English Captaine went on boord, and cast the Salsaperilla on the land, leaving all the rest of the wares in the frigate, and then he put all his peeces into the frigate, that so he might lay his ship on shore, to new calke and trimme her, which continued till the three and twentie or foure and twentie of March. Which done, and having made provision of wood and fresh water, they held on their course along by the coast, sayling Westward, taking the sayd frigate and her men with them, and having sailed two dayes, they tooke their men out of her, and set them in the pinnesse, among the which were foure sailers, that meant to sayle to Panama, and from thence to China, whereof one they tooke, with the letters and patents that hee had about him, among the which were the letters of the king of Spaine, sent to the governour of the Philippinas, as also the sea-cards wherewith they should make their voyage, and direct themselves in their course.

And so sailing untill the sixt of Aprill, about evening they discovered a shippe that held two leagues to seaward from the land: and before the next day in the morning they were hard by her, and suddenly fell upon her while her men slept, and presently made the men enter into their ship, among the which was one Don Francisco Xarate. Which done, they followed on their course with the sayd ship, out of the which they tooke certaine packes and other wares, but I know not what it was. They likewise tooke a Negro out of it, and three dayes after they both let the ship and men goe whether they woulde, setting therein the two saylers that should goe for China, which they had taken in the frigate, keeping onely one sailer to shewe them where they should find fresh water, to the which ende they tooke the emptie vessels with them to fill with water, and so kept on their course to the haven of Guatulco, where they put in, being upon Munday the thirteenth of Aprill, and having ankered, they stayed there till the sixe and twentie of Aprill: and about three or foure houres within the night, they set sayle, holding their course Westward, and an houre or two before they let Nuno da Silva goe, putting him into another ship, that lay in the haven of Guatulco.

From thence forward the Englishmen passed on their voyage, to the Islands of Malucos, and from thence they passed by the Cape de Buena Esperanza, and so to England, as it is well knowen, so that this is onely the description of the voyage that they made, while the said pilote Nuno da Silva was with them.

Hereafter followeth the copie of a letter written by sir Francis Drake (being in the South sea of New Spaine, in his ship called The Pellican or the Golden Hinde with the ship of Sant John de Anton, which hee had taken) to his companions in the other shippes that were of his company, and by foule weather separated from him, as I said before: The contents whereof were these:

Master Winter, if it pleaseth God that you should chance to meete with this ship of Sant John de Anton, I pray you use him well, according to my word and promise given unto them, and if you want any thing that is in this ship of Sant John de Anton, I pray you pay them double the value for it, which I will satisfie againe, and command your men not to doe her any hurt: and what composition or agreement we have made, at my returne into England I will by Gods helpe perfourme, although I am in doubt that this letter will never come to your hands: notwithstanding I am the man I have promised to be: Beseeching God, the Saviour of all the world, to have us in his keeping, to whom onely I give all honour, praise and glory. What I have written, is not only to you M. Winter, but also to M. Thomas, M. Charles, M. Caube, and M. Anthonie, with all our other good friendes, whom I commit to the tuition of him that with his blood redeemed us, and am in good hope, that we shal be in no more trouble, but that he will helpe us in adversitie, desiring you for the Passion of Christ, if you fall into any danger, that you will not despaire of Gods mercy, for hee will defend you and preserve you from all danger, and bring us to our desired haven, to whom bee all honour, glory, and praise for ever and ever. Amen. Your sorowfull Captaine, whose heart is heavy for you:

FRANCIS DRAKE

23

A Letter written from Goa, the principall City of all the East Indies, by one Thomas Stevens an English man, and sent to his father, M. Thomas Stevens: Anno 1579

AFTER most humble commendations: These shall be to crave your dayly blessing, with like commendations unto my mother; and withall, to certifie you of my being: according to your will and my duety. I wrote unto you taking my journey from Italy to Portugall, which letters I thinke are come to your hands, so that presuming thereupon, I thinke I have the lesse need at this time to tell you the cause of my departing, which neverthelesse in one word I may conclude, if I do but name obedience. I came to Lisbon toward the end of March, eight dayes before the departure of the shippes, so late that if they had not bene stayed about some weighty matters, they had bene long gone before our comming: insomuch that there were others ordained to goe in our places, that the kings provision and ours also might not be in vaine. Neverthelesse our sudden comming tooke place, and the fourth of Aprill five ships departed for Goa, wherein besides shipmen and souldiers, there were a great number of children which in the seas beare out better then men, and no marvell, when that many women also passe very well. The setting foorth from the port I need not to tell how solemne it is with trumpets, and shooting of ordinance, you may easily imagine it, considering that they go in the maner of warre. The tenth of the foresayd moneth we came to the sight of Porto Santo neere unto Madera, where an English shippe set upon ours (which was then also alone) with a few shots, which did no harme, but after that our ship had layed out her greatest ordinance, they straight departed as they came. The English shippe was very faire and great, which I

was sory to see so ill occupied, for she went roving about, so
that we saw her againe at the Canarian Iles, unto the which we
came the thirteenth of the sayd moneth, and good leisure we
had to woonder at the high mountaine of the Iland Tenerif,
for we wandred betweene that and great Canaria foure dayes
by reason of contrary windes: and briefly, such evill weather
we had untill the foureteenth of May, that they despaired, to
compasse the Cape of Good hope that yeere. Neverthelesse,
taking our voyage betweene Guinea and the Ilands of Capo
Verde, without seeing of any land at all, we arrived at length
unto the coast of Guinie, which the Portugals so call, chiefly
that part of the burning Zone, which is from the sixt degree
unto the Equinoctiall, in which parts they suffered so many
inconveniences of heats, and lacke of windes, that they thinke
themselves happy when the have passed it: for sometimes the
ship standeth there almost by the space of many dayes, sometime she goeth, but in such order that it were almost as good
to stand still. And the greatest part of this coast not cleare,
but thicke and cloudy, full of thunder and lightening, and raine
so unholesome, that if the water stand a little while, all is full
of wormes, and falling on the meat which is hanged up, it
maketh it straight full of wormes. Along all that coast we often
times saw a thing swimming upon the water like a cocks combe
(which they call a ship of Guinea) but the colour much fairer;
which combe standeth upon a thing almost like the swimmer
of a fish in colour and bignesse, and beareth underneath in the
water, strings, which save it from turning over. This thing is so
poisonous, that a man cannot touch it without great perill. In
this coast, that is to say, from the sixt degree unto the Equinoctiall, we spent no lesse then thirty dayes, partly with contrary
windes, partly with calme. The thirtieth of May we passed the
Equinoctiall with contentation, directing our course aswell as
we could to passe the promontory, but in all that gulfe, & in all
the way beside, we found so often calmes, that the expertest
mariners wondred at it. And in places where are alwayes woont
to be most horrible tempests, we found most quiet calmes which
was very troublesome to those ships which be the greatest of all
other, and cannot go without good windes. Insomuch, that when
it is tempest almost intollerable for other ships, and maketh
them maine all their sailes, these hoise up, and saile excellent

well, unlesse the waters be too too furious, which seldome happened in our navigation. You shall understand, that being
passed the line, they cannot straightway go the next way to the
promontory: but according the the winde, they draw always as
neere South as they can to put themselves in the latitude of the
point, which is 35 degrees and an halfe, and then they take their
course towards the East, and so compasse the point. But the
winde served us so, that at 33 degrees we did direct our course
toward the point or promontory of Good hope.

You know that it is hard to saile from East to West, or contrary, because there is no fixed point in all the skie, whereby
they may direct their course, wherefore I shall tell you what
helps God provided for these men. There is not a fowle that
appereth, or signe in the aire, or in the sea, which they have not
written, which have made the voyages heretofore. Wherfore,
partly by their owne experience, and pondering withall what
space the ship was able to make with such a winde, and such
direction, and partly by the experience of others, whose books
and navigations they have, they gesse whereabouts they be,
touching degrees of longitude, for of latitude they be always
sure: but the greatest and best industry of all is to marke the
variation of the needle or compasse, which in the Meridian of
the Iland of S. Michael, which is one of the Azores in the latitude of Lisbon, is just North, and thence swarveth towards the
East so much, that betwixt the Meridian aforesayd, and the
point of Africa it carrieth three or foure quarters of 32. And
againe in the point of Afrike, a little beyond the point that
is called Cape das Agulias (in English the needles) it returneth
againe unto the North, and that place passed, it swarveth againe
toward the West, as it did before proportionally. As touching
our first signes, the neerer we came to the people of Afrike, the
more strange kindes of fowles appeared, insomuch that when we
came within no lesse then thirty leagues (almost an hundred
miles) and six hundred miles as we thought from any Iland,
as good as three thousand fowles of sundry kindes followed our
ship: some of them so great that their wings being opened from
one point to the other, contained seven spannes, as the Mariners
sayd. A marvellous thing to see how God provided, so that in
so wide a sea these fowles are all fat, and nothing wanteth them.
The Portugals have named them all according to some propri-

ety which they have: some they call Rushtailes, because their
tailes be not proportionable to their bodies, but long and small
like a rush, some forked tailes because they be very broad and
forked, some Velvet sleeves, because they have wings of the
colour of velvet, and bowe them as a man boweth his elbow.
This bird is always welcome, for he appeareth neerest the
Cape. I should never make an end if I should tell all particulars: but it shall suffice briefly to touch a few, which yet shall
be sufficient, if you marke them, to give occasion to glorifie almighty God in his wonderfull works, and such variety in his
creatures. And to speake somewhat of fishes in all places of
calme, especially in the burning Zone, neere the line (for without we never saw any) there waited on our ship fishes as long
as a man, which they call Tuberones, they come to eat such
things as from the shippe fall into the sea, not refusing men
themselves if they light upon them. And if they finde any meat
tied in the sea, they take it for theirs. These have waiting on
them six or seven small fishes (which never depart) with gardes
blew and greene round about their bodies, like comely serving
men: and they go two or three before him, and some on every
side. Moreover, they have other fishes which cleave alwayes unto their body, and seeme to take such superfluities as grow
about them, and they are sayd to enter into their bodies also
to purge them if they need. The Mariners in time past have
eaten of them, but since they have seene them eate men their
stomacks abhorre them. Neverthelesse, they draw them up with
great hooks, & kill of them as many as they can, thinking that
they have made a great revenge. There is another kind of fish
as bigge almost as a herring, which hath wings and flieth, and
they are together in great number. These have two enemies, the
one in the sea, the other in the aire. In the sea the fish which is
called Albocore, as big as a Salmon, followeth them with great
swiftnesse to take them. This poore fish not being able to
swim fast, for he hath no finnes, but swimmeth with mooving
of his taile, shutting his wings, lifteth himselfe above the water,
and flieth not very hie: the Albocore seeing that, although he
have no wings, yet he giveth a great leape out of the water,
and sometimes catcheth him, or els he keepeth himselfe under
the water going that way on as fast as he flieth. And when the
fish being weary of the aire, or thinking himselfe out of danger,

returneth into the water, the Albocore meeteth with him: but
sometimes his other enemy the sea-crow, catcheth him before
he falleth. With these and like sights, but alwayes making our
supplications to God for good weather and salvation of the
ship, we came at length unto the point, so famous & feared of
all men: but we found there no tempest, only great waves,
where our Pilot was a little overseene: for whereas commonly
al other never come within sight of land, but seeing signes ordinary, and finding bottome, go their way sure and safe, he thinking himselfe to have winde at will, shot so nigh the land that
the winde turning into the South, and the waves being exceeding
great, rolled us so nere the land, that the ship stood in lesse
then 14 fadoms of water, no more then six miles from the
Cape, which is called Das Agulias, and there we stood as utterly cast away: for under us were rocks of maine stone so
sharpe, and cutting, that no ancre could hold the ship, the
shore so evill, that nothing could take land, and the land itselfe
so full of Tigers, and people that are savage, and killers of all
strangers, that we had no hope of life nor comfort, but onely
in God and a good conscience. Notwithstanding, after we had
lost ancres, hoising up the sailes for to get the ship a coast in
some safer place, or when it should please God, it pleased his
mercy suddenly, where no man looked for helpe, to fill our
sailes with wind from the land, & so we escaped, thanks be to
God. And the day following, being in the place where they are
alwayes wont to catch fish, we also fell a fishing, and so many
they tooke, that they served all the ship for that day, and part
of the next. And one of them pulled up a corall of great bignesse and price. For there they say (as we saw by experience)
that the corals doe grow in the maner of stalks upon the rocks
in the bottome, and waxe hard and red. The day of perill was
the nine and twentieth of July. And you shall understand that,
the Cape passed, there be two wayes to India: one within the
Ile of S. Laurence, which they take willingly, because they refresh themselves at Mosambique a fortnight or a moneth, not
without great need, and thence in a moneth more land in Goa.
The other is without the Ile of S. Laurence, which they take
when they set foorth so late, and come so late to the point, that
they have no time to take the foresayd Mosambique, and then
they goe heavily, because in this way they take no port. And

by reason of the long navigation, and want of food and water, they fall into sundry diseases, their gummes waxe great, and swell, and they are faine to cut them away, their legges swell, and all the body becommeth sore, and so benummed, that they can not stirre hand nor foot, and so they die for weakenesse, others fall into fluxes and agues, and die thereby. And this way it was our chance to make: yet though we had more then one hundred and fifty sicke, there died not past seven and twenty; which losse they esteemed not much in respect of other times. Though some of ours were diseased in this sort, yet, thanks be to God, I had my health all the way, contrary to the expectation of many: God send me my health so well in the land, if it may be to his honour and service. This way is full of privy rockes and quicke-sands, so that sometimes we durst not saile by night, but by the providence of God we saw nothing, nor never found bottome untill we came to the coast of India. When we had passed againe the line, and were come to the third degree or somewhat more, we saw crabs swimming on the water that were red as though they had bene sodden: but this was no signe of land. After, about the eleventh degree, the space of many dayes, more then ten thousand fishes by estimation followed round about our ship, whereof we caught so many, that for fifteene dayes we did eate nothing els, and they served our turne very well: for at this time we had neither meat nor almost any thing els to eate, our navigation growing so long that it drew neere to seven moneths, where as commonly they goe it in five, I meane when they saile the inner way. But these fishes were not signe of land, but rather of deepe sea. At length we tooke a couple of birds, which were a kinde of Hawks, whereof they joyed much, thinking that they had bene of India, but indeed they were of Arabia, as we found afterward. And we that thought we had bene neere India, were in the same latitude neere Zocotoro, an Ile in the mouth of the Red sea. But there God sent us great winds from the Northeast or Northnortheast, whereupon unwillingly they bare up toward the East, and thus we went tenne dayes without seeing signe of land, whereby they perceived their errour: for they had directed their course before alwayes Northeast, coveting to multiply degrees of latitude, but partly the difference of the Needle, and most of all the running seas, which at that time ran Northwest, had drawen us to this other danger, had not God sent us this winde, which at length waxed larger, and restored us to our right course. These running seas be so perillous that they deceive the most part of the governours, and some be so little curious, contenting themselves with ordinary experience, that they care not to seeke out any meanes to know when they swarve, neither by the compasse, nor by any other triall. The first signe of land were certaine fowles which they knew to be of India: the second, boughes of palmes and sedges: the third, snakes swimming on the water, and a substance which they call by the name of a coine of money, as broad and as round as a groat, woonderfully printed and stamped of nature, like unto some coine. And these two last signes be so certaine, that the next day after, if the winde serve, they see land, which we did to our great joy, when all our water (for you know they make no beere in those parts) and victuals began to faile us. And to Goa we came the foure and twentieth day of October, there being received with passing great charity. The people be tawny, but not disfigured in their lips & noses, as the Moores and Cafres of Ethiopia. They that be not of reputation, or at least the most part, goe naked, saving an apron of a span long, and as much in bredth before them, and a lace two fingers broad before them, girded about with a string and no more: and thus they thinke them as well as we with all our trimming. Of the fruits and trees that be here I cannot now speake, for I should make another letter as long as this. For hitherto I have not seene a tree here, whose like I have seene in Europe, the vine excepted, which neverthelesse here is to no purpose, so that all the wines are brought out of Portugall. The drinke of this countrey is good water, or wine of the Palme tree, or of a fruit called Cocos. And this shall suffice for this time. If God send me my health, I shall have opportunity to write to you once againe. Now the length of my letter compelleth me to take my leave: and thus I wish your most prosperous health. From Goa the tenth of November, 1579.

Your loving sonne Thomas Stevens

24

The interpretation of the letters, or privilege of the most mightie and Musumanlike Emperour Zuldan Murad Can, granted at the request of Elizabeth by the grace of the most mightie God, and only Creator of heaven and earth, of England, France and Ireland Queene, confirming a peace and league betwixt both the said Princes and their subjects

WE most sacred Musulmanlike Emperour, by the infinite and exceeding great power, by the everlasting and wonderfull clemencie, & by the unspeakable helpe of the most mighty & most holy God, creator of all things, to be worshipped and feared with all purenesse of minde, and reverence of speech, The prince of these present times, the onely Monarch of this age, able to give scepters to the potentates of the whole world, the shadow of the divine mercy and grace, the distributer of many kingdoms, provinces, townes and cities, Prince, and most sacred Emperour of Mecca, that is to say, of Gods house, of Medina, of the most glorious and blessed Jerusalem, of the most fertile Egypt, Jemen and Jovan, Eden and Canaan, of Samos the peaceable, and of Hebes, of Jabza, and Pazra, of Zeruzub and Halepia, of Caramaria and Diabekirvan, of Dulkadiria, of Babylon, and of all the three Arabias, of the Euzians and Georgians, of Cyprus the rich, and of the kingdomes of Asia, of Ozakior, of the tracts of the white and blacke Sea, of Grecia and Mesopotamia, of Africa and Goleta, of Alger, and of Tripolis in the West, of the most choise and principall Europe, of Buda and Temeswar, and of the kingdomes beyond the Alpes, and many others such like, most mightie Murad Can, the sonne of the Emperour Zelim Can, which was the sonne of Zoleiman Can, which was the sonne of Zelim Can, which was the sonne of Paiizid Can, which was the sonne of Mehemed Can, &c.

We most mightie prince Murad Can, in token of our Imperiall friendship, doe signifie and declare, that now of late Elizabeth Queene of England, France and Ireland, the most honourable Queene of Christendom (to whose marchants we wish happy successe) sent her letters by her worthy servant William Hareborne unto our stately and most magnificent Porch replenished with justice, which is a refuge and Sanctuary to all the princes of the world, by which letters her Majestie signified, that whereas heretofore certaine of her subjects had repaired to our saide stately Porche, and had shewed their obedience to the same, and for that cause had desired that leave and libertie might also be granted unto them, to come and goe for traffiques sake too and from our dominions, and that our Imperial commandement might be given, that no man should presume to hurt or hinder them, in any of their abodes or passages by sea or land, and whereas shee requested that we would graunt to all her subjects in generall, this our favour, which before wee had extended onely to a fewe of her people: therefore as wee have entred into amitie, and most holy league with the most excellent kings and princes our confederats, shewing their devotion, and obedience or services towards our stately Porch (as namely the French king, the Venetians, the king of Polonia and others) so also we have contracted an inviolable amitie, peace and league with the aforesaid Queene. Therefore wee give licence to all her people, and marchants, peaceably and safely to come unto our Imperiall dominions, with all their marchandise and goods without any impeachment, to exercise their traffique, to use their owne customes, and to buy and sell according to the fashions of their owne countrey.

And further her Majestie signified unto us, that certaine of her people had heretofore bene taken prisoners, and were detained in captivitie, and required that they might bee set at libertie, and that as we had graunted unto other Princes our confederats, priviledges, and Imperiall decrees, concerning our most inviolable league with them, so it would please our Imperial Majesty to graunt and confirme the like priviledges, and princely decrees to the aforesaid Queene.

Wherefore according to our humanitie and gracious ingraffed

disposition, the requests of her Majestie were accepted of us, and we have granted unto her Majestie this privilege of ours agreeable to reason & equitie. And we straightly command all our Beglerbegs, and Zanziacbegs our servants, and our Reyz, that is to say, our Judges, and all our customers in all places, havens and passages, that as long as this league and amitie with the conditions, and articles thereof, are kept and observed on the behalfe of the aforesaid Queene. 1 Our Imperiall commandement and pleasure is, that the people and subjects of the same Queene, may safely and securely come to our princely dominions, with their goods and marchandise, and ladings, and other commodities by sea, in great and smal vessels, and by land with their carriages and cattels, and that no man shall hurt them, but they may buy and sell without any hinderance, and observe the customes and orders of their owne countrey.

2 Item, if the aforesaid people and marchants shalbe at any time in the course of their journeis and dealings by any meanes taken, they shall be delivered and inlarged, without any excuse or cavillation.

3 Item, if their ships purpose to arive in any of our ports and havens, it shalbe lawfull for them so to do in peace, and from thence againe to depart, without any let or impediment.

4 Item, if it shall happen that any of their ships in tempestuous weather shall bee in danger of losse and perishing, and thereupon shall stand in need of our helpe, we will, and commaund that our men and ships be ready to helpe and succour them.

5 Item, if they shalbe willing to buy any victuals for their money, no person shall withstande them, but they shall buy the same without any disturbance to the contrary.

6 Item, if by any casualtie their shippes shall bee driven on shoare in perill of shipwracke, our Begs and Judges, and other our Subjects shall succour them, and such wares, and goods of theirs as shall bee recovered from the losse, shall bee restored to them, and no man shall wrong them.

7 Item, if the people of the aforesayd Queene, their interpreters and marchants, shall for trafique sake, either by lande or Sea repaire to our dominions paying our lawfull toll and custome, they shall have quiet passage, and none of our Captaines

or governours of the Sea, and shippes, nor any kinde of persons, shall either in their bodies, or in their goods and cattels, any way molest them.

8 Item, if any Englishman shall grow in debt, and so owe money to any other man, and thereupon doth absent himselfe that he can not be found, let no man be arrested or apprehended for any other mans debt, except he be the surety.

9 Item, if any Englishman shall make his will and testament, to whom soever by the same hee shall give his goods, the partie shall have them accordingly, and if hee die intestate, hee to whom the Consull or governour of the societie shall say the goods of the dead are to bee given, hee shall have the same.

10 Item, if the Englishmen or the marchants and interpreters of any places under the jurisdiction of England shall happen in the buying and selling of wares, by promises or otherwise to come in controversie, let them go to the Judge, and cause the matter to be entred into a booke, and if they wil, let them also take letters of the Judge testifying the same, that men may see the booke and letters, whatsoever thing shall happen, and that according to the tenour thereof the matter in controversie and in doubt may be ended: but if such things be neither entred in booke, nor yet the persons have taken letters of the Judge, yet he shall admit no false witnesse, but shall execute the Law according to justice, and shall not suffer them to be abused.

11 Item, if any man shall say, that these being Christians have spoken any thing to the derogation of our holy faith and religion, and have slandered the same, in this matter as in all others, let no false witnesses in any case be admitted.

12 Item, if any one of them shall commit any great crime, and flying thereupon cannot bee found, let no man be arrested, or detained for another mans fact, except he be his suretie.

13 Item, if any slave shall be found to be an Englishman, and their Consull or governour shall sue for his libertie, let the same slave be diligently examined, and if hee be found in deed to be English, let him be discharged and restored to the Englishmen.

14 Item, if any Englishman shall come hither either to dwel or trafique, whether hee be married or unmarried, he shall pay no polle or head money.

15 Item, if either in Alexandria, Damasco, Samos, Tunis,

Tripolis in ye west, the port townes of Ægypt, or in any other places, they purpose to choose to themselves Consuls or governours, let them doe so, and if they will alter them at any time, and in the roome of the former Consuls place others, let them do so also, and no man shall restraine them.

16 Item, if their interpreter shalbe at any time absent, being occupied in other serious matters, let the thing then in question bee stayed and differred till his comming, and in the meane time no man shall trouble them.

17 Item, if any variance or controversie shall arise among the Englishmen, and thereupon they shall appeale to their Consuls or governours, let no man molest them, but let them freely doe so, that the controversie begunne may be finished according to their owne customes.

18 Item, if after the time and date of this privilege, any pirats or other free governours of ships trading the Sea shall take any Englishman, and shall make sale of him, either beyonde the Sea, or on this side of the Sea, the matter shalbe examined according to justice, and if the partie shalbe found to be English, and shall receive the holy religion, then let him freely be discharged, but if he wil still remaine a Christian, let him then be restored to the Englishmen, and the buyers shall demaund their money againe of them who solde the man.

19 Item, if the ships of warre of our Imperiall highnesse shal at any time goe forth to Sea, and shall finde any English ships laden with marchandise, no man shall hinder them, but rather shall use them friendly, and doe them no wrong, even as wee have given and granted articles, and privileges to the French, Venetians, and other Kings and princes our confederats, so also wee have given the like to the English: and contrary to this our divine lawe and privilege, let no man presume to doe any thing.

20 Item, if either their great or small ships shall in the course of their voyage, or in any place to which they come, bee stayed or arrested, let no man continue the same arrest, but rather helpe and assist them.

21 Item, if any theeves and robbers shall by force take away any of their ships, and marchandise, let the same theeves and robbers be sought, and searched for with all diligence, and let them be punished most severely.

22 Last of all the Beglerbegs, and Zanziacbegs, our Captaines, our slaves and servants of Captaines using the sea, and
our Judges, customers and governours of ships called Reiz, and
free Reiz, all these, according to the tenor of this privilege
and articles, shalbe bound to doe accordingly: and, as long as
the Queene of England on her part shall duely keepe and observe this league and holy peace, expressed in this privilege, we
also for our Imperial part, do charge and commaund the same
so long to be straightly kept and observed.

Given at Constantinople, in the 988. yeere of our most holy
prophet, in the beginning of the moneth of June, And in the
yeere of JESUS 1580.

25

Her Majesties letter to the Turke or Grand Signior 1581. promising redresse of the disorders of Peter Baker of Ratcliffe, committed in the Levant

ELIZABETH by the divine grace of the eternall God, of England, France and Ireland most sacred Queene, and of the most Christian faith, against all the prophaners of his most holy Name the zealous and mightie defendour, &c. To the most re-nowned and Emperious Cæsar, Sultan Murad Can, Emperour of all the dominions of Turkie, and of all the East Monarchie chiefe above all others whosoever, most fortunate yeeres with the successe of al true happinesse. As with very great desire we wish and embrace the love and amitie of forreine Princes, and in the same by al good dueties and meanes we seeke to be confirmed: so to us there may bee nothing more grievous and disliking, then that any thing should happen through the de-fault of our Subjects, which any way might bring our faith and fidelitie into suspition: Although wee are not ignorant how many good princes by the like misadventure be abused, where the doings of the Subjects are imputed to the want of good government. But such matters of importance and so well ap-proved we may not omit: such is to us the sacred estimation of our honour, and of our Christian profession, as we would the same should appeare aswell in the concluding of our prom-ises and agreements, as in the faithful performing of the same.

The matter which by these our letters wee specially beholde, is a most injurious and grievous wrong which of late came unto our understanding, that should be done unto certaine of your subjects by certaine of our *Subjects, as yet not apprehended:

---

* This was Baker of Ratcliffe, who with the barke called the Roe, robbed certaine Grecians in the Levant.

but with all severitie upon their apprehension they are to be awarded for the same. And as the deede in it selfe is most wicked, so is it much more intollerable, by how much it doeth infringe the credit of our faith, violate the force of our authoritie, and impeach the estimation of our word faithfully given unto your Imperiall dignitie. In which so great a disorder if wee should not manifest our hatred towardes so wicked and evil disposed persons, we might not onely most justly be reproved in the judgement of all such as truely favour Justice, but also of all Princes the patrones of right and equitie, might no lesse be condemned. That therefore considered, which of our parts is ordained in this cause which may be to the good liking of your highnesse, we are most especially to request of your Imperiall Majestie, that through the default and disorder of a sort of evill and wicked disposed persons, you wil not withdraw your gratious favour from us, neither to hinder the trafique of our Subjects, which by vertue of your highnesse sufferance, and power of your licence are permitted to trade into your dominions & countreys, or that either in their persons or goods they be prejudiced in their traveyling by land or by water, promising unto your greatnesse most faithfully, that the goods whereof your subjects by great wrong and violence have bene spoyled, shall wholy againe be restored, if either by the lives or possessions of the robbers it may any way be brought to passe: And that hereafter (as now being taught by this evill example) wee will have speciall care that none under the title of our authoritie shall be suffered to commit any the like wrongs or injuries.

Neither they which have committed these evil parts had any power under your highnesse safeconduct graunted unto our subjects, but from some other safeconduct, whether it were true or fained, we knowe not, or whether they bought it of any person within the government of Marseils: but under the colour thereof they have done that, which the trueth of our dealing doeth utterly abhorre. Notwithstanding howsoever it be, wee will surely measure their evill proceedings with most sharpe and just correction, and that it shall repent them of the impeachment of our honours, as also it shalbe an example of our indignation, that others may dread at all times to commit the like offence. Wherefore that our amitie might be continued, as if this unfortunate hap had never chanced, and that the singuler affection of our Subjects towardes your Imperiall Majestie vowed, and dayly more and more desired, might be conserved and defended, we thereunto do make our humble suite unto your greatnesse: And for so great goodnesse towardes us and our people granted, doe most humbly pray unto the Almightie creatour of heaven and earth, ever to maintaine and keepe your most renowmed Majestie in all happinesse and prosperitie.

Dated at our palace of Greenewich the 26. of June, Anno 1581.

26

A Letter of Sir Francis Walsingham to M. Richard
Hakluyt then of Christchurch in Oxford, incouraging
him in the study of Cosmographie, and of furthering
new discoveries, &c.

I UNDERSTAND aswel by a letter I long since received
from the Maior of Bristoll, as by conference with Sir George
Pekham, that you have endevoured, & given much light for the
discovery of the Westerne partes yet unknowen: as your studie
in these things is very commendable, so I thanke you much for
the same; wishing you do continue your travell in these and
like matters, which are like to turne not only to your owne good
in private, but to the publike benefite of this Realme. And so I
bid you farewell. From the Court the 11. of March. 1582.

Your loving Friend,
FRANCIS WALSINGHAM

27

A letter of Sir Francis Walsingham to Master Thomas
Aldworth merchant, and at that time Maior of the
Citie of Bristoll, concerning their adventure in
the Westerne discoverie

AFTER my heartie commendations, I have for certaine
causes deferred the answere of your letter of November last till
now, which I hope commeth all in good time. Your good inclination to the Westerne discoverie I cannot but much commend. And for that sir Humfrey Gilbert, as you have heard
long since, hath bene preparing into those parts being readie to
imbarke within these 10. dayes, who needeth some further supply of shipping then yet he hath, I am of opinion that you shall
do well if the ship or 2. barkes you write of, be put in a readinesse to goe alongst with him, or so soone after as you may.
I hope this travell wil proove profitable to the Adventurers and
generally beneficiall to the whole realme: herein I pray you
conferre with these bearers, M. Richard Hackluyt, and M.
Thomas Steventon, to whome I referre you: And so bid you
heartily farewell. Richmond the 11. of March. 1582.

Your loving Friend,

FRANCIS WALSINGHAM

28

The Letters patents of the Queenes Majestie, granted to Master Adrian Gylbert and others, for the search and discovery of the Northwest Passage to China

E L I Z A B E T H by the grace of God of England, France, and Ireland Queene, defender of the faith, &c. To all, to whome these presents shall come, greeting: Forasmuch as our trustie and welbeloved subject Adrian Gylbert of Sandridge in the Countie of Devon, Gentleman, to his great costes and charges, hath greatly and earnestly travelled and sought, and yet doth travell and seeke, and by divers meanes indevoureth and laboureth, that the Passage unto China and the Iles of the Moluccas by the Northwestward, Northeastward, or Northward, unto which part or partes of the world, none of our loyall Subjects have hitherto had any traffique or trade, may be discovered, knowen, and frequented by the Subjects of this our Realme: Knowe yee therefore that for the considerations aforesayd and for divers other good considerations us thereunto specially mooving. We of our grace especiall, certaine knowledge, and meere motion, have given and granted, and by these presents for us, our heires and successors, doe give and grant free libertie, power, and full authoritie to the sayd Adrian Gylbert, and to any other person by him or his heires to be assigned, and to those his associates and assistants, whose names are written in a Scedule hereunto annexed, and to their heires, and to one assignee of each of them, and each of their heires at all times, and at any time or times after the date of these presents, under our Banners and Ensignes freely, without let, interruption, or restraint, of us, our heires or successors, any law, statute, proclamation, patent, charter, or proviso to the contrary notwithstanding, to saile, make voyage, and by any maner of meanes to passe and to depart out of this our Realme of England, or any our Realmes, Dominions, or Territories into all or any Isles, Countreys, Regions, Provinces, Territories, Seas, Rivers, Portes, Bayes, Creekes, armes of the Sea, and all Havens, and all maner of other places whatsoever, that by the sayde Northwestward, Northeastward, or Northward, is to be by him, his associates or assignes discovered, and for and in the sayde sayling, voyage, and passage, to have and use so many shippes, Barkes, Pinnesses, or other vessels of any quantitie or burthen, with all the furniture of men, victuals, and all maner of necessary provision, armour, weapons, ordinance, targets, and appurtinances whatsoever, as to such a voyage shall or may be requisite, convenient or commodious, any lawe, statute, ordinance or proviso to the contrary thereof notwithstanding. And also we doe give and grant to the sayde Adrian Gylbert, and his sayde associates, and to such assignee of him, and his heires, and to the heires and one assignee of every of his sayde associates for ever, full power and absolute authoritie to trade and make their resiance in any of the sayde Isles, Countreys, Regions, Provinces, Territories, Seas, Rivers, Portes, Bayes, and Havens, and all maner of other places whatsoever with all commodities, profites, and emoluments in the sayde places or any of them, growing and arising, with all maner of priviledges, prerogatives, jurisdictions and royalties both by sea and land whatsoever, yeelding and paying therefore unto us, our heires and successors, the tenth part of all such golde and silver oare, pearles, jewels, and precious stones, or the value thereof, as the sayd Adrian Gylbert and his sayd associates their heires and assignes, servants, factors, or workemen, and every or any of them shall finde, the sayd tenth to bee delivered duely to our Customer, or other officers by us, our heires or successors thereunto assigned, in the Portes of London, Dartmouth, or Plimmouth, at which three places onely the sayde Adrian Gylbert, and his sayde associates, their sayde heires and assignes, shall lade, charge, arrive, and discharge all maner of wares, goods, and merchandizes whatsoever to the sayde voyage, and newe trade belonging or appertaining. And moreover, wee have given, granted, and authorized, and by these presents for us, our heires and successors, of our grace especiall, certaine knowledge, and meere motion, doe give, graunt, and authorize the sayd Adrian Gilbert, and his sayd associats for ever, their heires and their said assignes & every of them, that if the aforesayd Iles, Countreys, Regions, Provinces, Territories, Seas, Rivers, Ports, Bayes, or Havens, or any other of the premisses by the sayd Adrian Gilbert or his associats, their heires and their said assignes or any of them, to be found by them, discovered and traffiqued unto by any trade as aforesayd, shall be by any other our subjects visited, frequented, haunted, traded unto or inhabited by the wayes aforesayd, without the special licence in writing of the said Adrian Gylbert and his associats, and their heires and assignes for ever, or by the most part of them, so that the sayd Adrian Gilbert, his heires or assignes be one of them, that then aswell their ship, or ships in any such voyage or voyages be used, as all and singuler their goods, wares, and marchandizes, or any other things whatsoever, from or to any of the places aforesayd transported, that so shall presume to visit, frequent, haunt, trade unto, or inhabite, shall be forfaited and confiscated, ipso facto, the one halfe of the same goods and marchandizes, or other things whatsoever, or the value thereof to be to the use of us, our heires or successours, and the other moytie thereof to be to the use of the sayd Adrian Gylbert and his sayd associats, their heires and assignes for ever: and unto the sayd Adrian Gylbert and his sayd associats, their heires and assignes wee impose, give, assigne, create and confirme this name peculiar to be named by, to sue and to be sued by, that is to wit, by the name of the Colleagues of the fellowship for the discoverie of the Northwest passage, and them for us, our heires and successours by that name doe incorporate, and doe erect and create as one body corporate to have continuance for ever. Moreover unto the sayd Adrian Gylbert, and his said associats, and unto their heires and their sayd assignes for ever, by name of the Colleagues of the fellowship, for the discoverie of the Northwest passage, we have given, granted, and confirmed, and doe by these presents give, grant, and confirme full power and authoritie from time to time, and at all times hereafter, to make order, decree and enact, constitute and ordeine, and appoynt all such ordinances, orders, decrees, lawes, and actes, as the sayd new corporation or body politique, Colleagues of the fellowship for the discoverie of the Northwest passage, shall thinke meete, necessary, and convenient, so that they or any of them be not contrary to the lawes of this realme, and of this our present graunt.

And we by our Royall prerogative, and fulnesse of our authority, of our grace especiall, certaine knowledge and meere motion, do establish, confirme & ratifie all such ordinances, orders, decrees, lawes and acts to be in so full and great power and authority, as we, our heires or successours may or can in any such case graunt, confirme, or ratifie. And further for the better incouragement of our loving subjects in this discoverie, we by our Royall prerogative, and fulnesse of authority for us, our heires and successours, doe give, graunt, establish, confirme, ordeine, ratifie and allow by these presents, to the sayd Adrian Gylbert and to his associates, and to the heires and assignes of them and every of them for ever, and to all other person or persons of our loving subjects whatsoever that shall hereafter travaile, sayle, discover, or make voyage as aforesayd to any the Iles, Mainelands, Countreys or Territories whatsoever, by vertue of this our graunt to be discovered, that the heires and assignes of them and every of them being borne within any of the Iles, Mainelands and Countreys, or Territories whatsoever before mentioned, shall have and injoy all the privileges of free Denizens, as persons native borne within this our Realme of England, or within our allegiance for ever, in such like ample maner and forme, as if they were or had bene borne and personally resiant within our sayd Realme, any law, statute, proclamation, custome or usage to the contrary hereof in any wise notwithstanding.

Moreover, for the consideration aforesayd by vertue hereof, we give and graunt unto the sayd Adrian Gylbert, his heires and assignes for ever, free libertie, licence and privilege, that during the space of five yeeres next and immediatly ensuing the date hereof, it shall not be lawfull for any person or persons whatsoever, to visit, haunt, frequent, trade, or make voyage to any Iles, Mainlands, Countreys, Regions, Provinces, Territories, Seas, Rivers, Ports, Bayes, and Havens, nor to any other Havens or places whatsoever hitherto not yet discovered by any of our subjects by vertue of this graunt to be traded unto, without the special consent and good liking of the said Adrian Gylbert, his heires or assignes first had in writing. And if any person or persons of the associats of the sayd Adrian, his heires or assignes, or any other person or persons whatsoever, free of this discovery, shall do any act or acts contrary to the tenour and true meaning hereof, during the space of the sayd five yeeres, that then the partie and parties so offending, they and their heires for ever shall loose (ipso facto) the benefite and privilege of this our graunt, and shall stand and remaine to all intents and purposes as persons exempted out of this graunt.

And further by vertue hereof wee give and graunt, for us, our heires and successours at all times during the space of five yeers next ensuing the date hereof, libertie and licence, and full authority to the sayd Adrian Gylbert, and his heires and as-signes, that if it shall happen any one or moe in any ship or ships sayling on their sayd voyage, to become mutinous, seditious, dis-ordered or any way unruly to the prejudice or hinderance of the hope for the successe in the attempt or prosecuting of this dis-coverie or trade intended, to use or execute upon him or them so offending, such punishment, correction, or execution, as the cause shall be found in justice to require by the verdict of twelve of the companie sworne thereunto, as in such a case ap-perteineth: That expresse mention of the certaintie of the prem-isses, or of other gifts or graunts by us to the sayd Adrian Gyl-bert and his associats before this time made is not mentioned in these presents, or any other lawe, act, statute, proviso, graunt, or proclamation heretofore made or hereafter to be made to the contrary hereof in any wise notwithstanding. In witnesse where-of we have made these our Letters to bee made patents: Wit-nesse our selfe at Westminster, the sixt day of Februarie, in the sixe and twenty yeere of our reigne.

29

The Letters patents, granted by the Queenes Majestie to M. Walter Ralegh, now Knight, for the discovering and planting of new lands and Countries, to continue the space of 6. yeeres and no more

ELIZABETH by the grace of God of England, France and Ireland Queene, defender of the faith, &c. To all people to whom these presents shal come, greeting. Know ye that of our especial grace, certaine science, & meere motion, we have given and granted, and by these presents for us, our heires and successors doe give and grant to our trusty and welbeloved servant Walter Ralegh Esquire, and to his heires and assignes for ever, free liberty & licence from time to time, and at all times for ever hereafter, to discover, search, finde out, and view such remote, heathen and barbarous lands, countreis, and territories, not actually possessed of any Christian prince, nor inhabited by Christian people, as to him, his heires and assignes, and to every or any of them shall seeme good, and the same to have, holde, occupy & enjoy to him, his heires and assignes for ever, with all prerogatives, commodities, jurisdictions, royalties, priviledges, franchises and pre-eminences, thereto or thereabouts both by sea and land, whatsoever we by our letters patents may grant, and as we or any of our noble progenitors have heretofore granted to any person or persons, bodies politique or corporate: and the saide Walter Ralegh, his heires and assignes, and all such as from time to time, by licence of us, our heires and successors, shal goe or travaile thither to inhabite or remaine, there to build and fortifie, at the discretion of the said Walter Ralegh, his heires & assignes, the statutes or act of Parliament made against fugitives, or against such as shall depart, remaine or continue out of our Realme of England without li-

cence, or any other statute, act, law, or any ordinance whatsoever to the contrary in any wise notwithstanding.

And we do likewise by these presents, of our especial grace,
meere motion, and certaine knowledge, for us, our heires and
successors, give and graunt full authoritie, libertie and power
to the said Walter Ralegh, his heires and assignes, and every
of them, that he and they, and every or any of them, shall and
may at all and every time and times hereafter, have, take, and
leade in the sayde voyage, and travaile thitherward, or to inhabite there with him or them, and every or any of them, such,
and so many of our subjects as shall willingly accompany him
or them, and every or any of them: and to whom also we doe
by these presents, give full libertie and authoritie in that behalfe, and also to have, take and employ, and use sufficient
shipping and furniture for the transportations, and Navigations
in that behalfe, so that none of the same persons or any of
them be such as hereafter shall be restrained by us, our heires
or successors.

And further that the said Walter Ralegh his heires and assignes, and every of them, shall have, holde, occupie and enjoy
to him, his heires and assignes, and every of them for ever, all
the soyle of all such landes, territories, and Countreis, so to be
discovered and possessed as aforesayd, and of all such Cities,
Castles, Townes, Villages, and places in the same, with the
right, royalties, franchises, and jurisdictions, as well marine
as other within the sayd landes, or Countreis, or the seas thereunto adjoyning, to be had, or used, with full power to dispose
thereof, and of every part in fee simple or otherwise, according
to the order of the lawes of England, as neere as the same conveniently may be, at his, and their wil and pleasure, to any
persons then being, or that shall remaine within the allegiance
of us, our heires and successors: reserving alwayes to us, our
heires and successors, for all services, dueties, and demaunds,
the fift part of all the oare of golde and silver, that from time
to time, and at all times after such discoverie, subduing and
possessing, shall be there gotten and obteined: All which lands,
Countries, and territories shall for ever be holden of the sayd
Walter Ralegh, his heires and assignes, of us, our heires and
successors, by homage, and by the sayd payment of the sayd
fift part, reserved onely for all services.

And moreover, we do by these presents, for us, our heires and successors, give and grant licence to the said Walter Ralegh, his heires, and assignes, and every of them, that he, and they, and every or any of them, shall and may from time to time, and at all times for ever hereafter, for his and their defence, encounter and expulse, repell and resist aswell by sea as by lande, and by all other wayes whatsoever, all and every such person and persons whatsoever, as without the especiall liking and licence of the sayd Walter Ralegh, and of his heires and assignes, shall attempt to inhabite within the sayde Countryes, or any of them, or within the space of two hundreth leagues neere to the place or places within such Countryes as afore-sayde (if they shall not bee before planted or inhabited within the limits as aforesayd with the subjects of any Christian Prince being in amitie with us) where the sayd Walter Ralegh, his heires, or assignes, or any of them, or his, or their, or any of their associats or company, shall within sixe yeeres (next en-suing) make their dwellings or abidings, or that shall enterprise or attempt at any time hereafter unlawfully to annoy, eyther by Sea or Lande the sayde Walter Ralegh, his heires or assignes, or any of them, or his or their, or any of his or their com-panies: giving, and graunting by these presents further power and authoritie to the sayd Walter Ralegh, his heires and as-signes, and every of them from time to time, and at all times for ever hereafter, to take and surprise by all maner of meanes whatsoever, all and every those person or persons, with their Shippes, Vessels, and other goods and furniture, which without the licence of the sayde Walter Ralegh, or his heires, or as-signes, as aforesayd, shalbe found traffiquing into any Harbour, or Harbours, Creeke, or Creekes, within the limits aforesayd, (the subjects of our Realmes and Dominions, and all other per-sons in amitie with us, trading to the Newfound lands for fish-ing as heretofore they have commonly used, or being driven by force of a tempest, or shipwracke onely excepted:) and those persons, and every of them, with their shippes, vessels, goods, and furniture to deteine and possesse as of good and lawfull prize, according to the discretion of him the sayd Wal-ter Ralegh, his heires, and assignes, and every, or any of them. And for uniting in more perfect league and amitie, of such Countryes, landes, and territories so to be possessed and inhabited as aforesayd with our Realmes of England and Ireland, and the better incouragement of men to these enterprises: we doe by these presents, graunt and declare that all such Countries, so hereafter to be possessed and inhabited as is aforesayd, from thencefoorth shall be of the allegiance to us, our heires and successours. And wee doe graunt to the sayd Walter Ralegh, his heires, and assignes, and to all, and every of them, and to all, and every other person and persons, being of our allegiance, whose names shall be noted or entred in some of our Courts of recorde within our Realme of England, that with the assent of the sayd Walter Ralegh, his heires or assignes, shall in his journeis for discoverie, or in the journeis for conquest hereafter travaile to such lands, countreis and territories, as aforesayd, and to their, and to every of their heires, and they, and every or any of them, being eyther borne within our sayde Realmes of England or Irelande, or in any other place within our allegiance, and which hereafter shall be inhabiting within any the Lands, Countryes, and Territories, with such licence, (as aforesayd) shall and may have all the priviledges of free Denizens, and persons native of England, and within our allegiance in such like ample maner and forme, as if they were borne and personally resident within our said Realme of England, any law, custome, or usage to the contrary notwithstanding.

And forasmuch as upon the finding out, discovering, or inhabiting of such remote lands, countries, and territories as aforesaid, it shalbe necessary for the safety of all men, that shall adventure themselves in those journeyes or voyages, to determine to live together in Christian peace, and civill quietnesse eche with other, whereby every one may with more pleasure and profit enjoy that whereunto they shall atteine with great paine and perill, wee for us, our heires and successors, are likewise pleased and contented, and by these presents doe give & grant to the said Walter Ralegh, his heires and assignes for ever, that he and they, and every or any of them, shall and may from time to time for ever hereafter, within the said mentioned remote lands and countries, in the way by the seas thither, and from thence, have full and meere power and authoritie to correct, punish, pardon, governe, and rule by their and every or any of their good discretions and policies, aswell in causes capitall, or criminall, as civil, both marine and other, all such our subjects, as shal from time to time adventure themselves in the said journeis or voyages, or that shall at any time hereafter inhabite any such lands, countreis, or territories as aforesayd, or that shall abide within 200. leagues of any of the sayde place or places, where the sayde Walter Ralegh, his heires or assignes, or any of them, or any of his or their associats or companies, shall inhabite within 6. yeeres next ensuing the date hereof, according to such statutes, lawes and ordinances as shall be by him the sayd Walter Ralegh, his heires and assignes, and every or any of them devised, or established, for the better government of the said people as aforesaid. So alwayes as the said statutes, lawes, and ordinances may be, as nere as conveniently may bee, agreeable to the forme of the lawes, statutes, governement, or pollicie of England, and also so as they be not against the true Christian faith, nowe professed in the Church of England, nor in any wise to withdrawe any of the subjects or people of those lands or places from the alleagance of us, our heires and successours, as their immediate Soveraigne under God.

And further, we doe by these presents for us, our heires and successors, give and grant ful power and authoritie to our trustie and welbeloved Counsailour Sir William Cecill knight, Lorde Burghley, or high Treasourer of England, and to the Lorde Treasourer of England for us, our heires and successors for the time being, and to the privie Counsaile of us, our heires and successors, or any foure or more of them for the time being, that he, they, or any foure or more of them, shall and may from time to time, and at all times hereafter, under his or their handes or Seales by vertue of these presents, authorise and licence the saide Walter Ralegh, his heires and assignes, and every or any of them by him, & by themselves, or by their, or any of their sufficient Atturneis, Deputies, Officers, Ministers, Factors, and servants, to imbarke & transport out of our Realme of England and Ireland, and the Dominions thereof, all or any of his or their goods, and all or any the goods of his and their associats and companies, and every or any of them, with such other necessaries and commodities of any our Realmes, as to the sayde Lorde Treasurer, or foure or more of the privie Counsaile, of us our heires and successors for the time being (as aforesaid) shalbe from time to time by his or their wisedomes, or discretions thought meete and convenient, for the better reliefe and supportation of him the sayde Walter Ralegh, his heires, and assignes, and every or any of them, and of his or their or any of their associats and companies, any act, statute, law, or any thing to the contrary in any wise notwithstanding.

Provided alwayes, and our wil and pleasure is, and we do hereby declare to all Christian kings, princes, and states, that if the sayde Walter Ralegh, his heires or assignes, or any of them, or any other by their licence or appointment, shall at any time or times hereafter robbe or spoile by sea or by land, or doe any acte of unjust or unlawfull hostilitie, to any of the subjects of us, our heires or successors, or to any of the subjects of any the kings, princes, rulers, Governours, or estates, being then in perfect league and amitie with us, our heires and successours, and that upon such injurie, or upon just complaint of any such Prince, Ruler, Governour or estate, or their subjects, wee, our heires and successors, shall make open Proclamation within any the portes of our Realme of England, that the saide Walter Ralegh, his heires and assignes, and adherents, or any to whom these our Letters patents may extende, shall within the termes to bee limited, by such Proclamation, make full restitution, and satisfaction of all such injuries done: so as both we and the said Princes, or other so complaining, may hold us and themselves fully contented: And that if the said Walter Ralegh, his heires and assignes, shall not make or cause to be made satisfaction accordingly within such time so to be limitted, that then it shal be lawful to us, our heires and successors, to put the sayde Walter Ralegh, his heires and assignes, and adherents, and all the inhabitants of the saide places to be discovered (as is aforesaid) or any of them out of our allegeance and protection, and that from and after such time of putting out of protection of the saide Walter Ralegh, his heires, assignes and adherents, and others so to be put out, and the said places within their habitation, possession and rule, shall be out of our allegeance and protection, and free for all Princes and others to pursue with hostilitie, as being not our subjects, nor by us any way to be avouched, maintained, or defended, nor to be holden as any of ours, nor to our protection, or dominion, or allegeance any way belonging: for that expresse mention of the cleere yeerely value of the certaintie of the premisses, or any part thereof, or of any other gift, or grant by us, or any our progenitors, or predecessors to the said Walter Ralegh, before this time made in these presents, bee not expressed, or any other grant, ordinance, provision, proclamation, or restraint to the contrary thereof, before this time, given, ordained, or provided, or any other thing, cause, or matter whatsoever, in any wise notwithstanding. In witnesse whereof, wee have caused these our letters to be made Patents. Witnesse our selves, at Westminster the five and twentie day of March, in the sixe and twentith yeere of our Raigne.

30

The first voyage made to the coasts of America, with two barks, where in were Captaines M. Philip Amadas, and M. Arthur Barlowe, who discovered part of the Countrey now called Virginia, Anno 1584. Written by one of the said Captaines, and sent to sir Walter Ralegh knight, at whose charge and direction, the said voyage was set forth

THE 27 day of Aprill, in the yeere of our redemption, 1584 we departed the West of England, with two barkes well furnished with men and victuals, having received our last and perfect directions by your letters, confirming the former instructions, and commandements delivered by your selfe at our leaving the river of Thames. And I thinke it a matter both unnecessary, for the manifest discoverie of the Countrey, as also for tediousnesse sake, to remember unto you the diurnall of our course, sayling thither and returning: onely I have presumed to present unto you this briefe discourse, by which you may judge how profitable this land is likely to succeede, as well to your selfe, (by whose direction and charge, and by whose servantes this our discoverie hath beene performed) as also to her Highnesse, and the Common wealth, in which we hope your wisedome wilbe satisfied, considering that as much by us hath bene brought to light, as by those smal meanes, and number of men we had, could any way have bene expected, or hoped for.

The tenth of May we arrived at the Canaries, and the tenth of June in this present yeere, we were fallen with the Islands of the West Indies, keeping a more Southeasterly course then was needefull, bcause wee doubted that the current of the Bay of Mexico, disbogging betweene the Cape of Florida and

Havana, had bene of greater force then afterwardes we found it to bee. At which Islands we found the ayre very unwholsome, and our men grew for the most part ill disposed: so that having refreshed our selves with sweet water, & fresh victuall, we departed the twelfth day of our arrivall there. These Islands, with the rest adjoyning, are so well knowen to your selfe, and to many others, as I will not trouble you with the remembrance of them.

The second of July, we found shole water, wher we smelt so sweet, and so strong a smel, as if we had bene in the midst of some delicate garden abounding with all kinde of odoriferous flowers, by which we were assured, that the land could not be farre distant: and keeping good watch, and bearing but slacke saile, the fourth of the same moneth we arrived upon the coast, which we supposed to be a continent and firme lande, and we sayled along the same a hundred and twentie English miles before we could finde any entrance, or river issuing into the Sea. The first that appeared unto us, we entred, though not without some difficultie, & cast anker about three harquebuz-shot within the havens mouth, on the left hand of the same: and after thankes given to God for our safe arrivall thither, we manned our boats, and went to view the land next adjoyning, and "to take possession of the same, in the right of the Queenes most excellent Majestie, as rightfull Queene, and Princesse of the same, and after delivered the same over to your use, according to her Majesties grant, and letters patents, under her Highnesse great Seale. Which being performed, according to the ceremonies used in such enterprises, we viewed the land about us, being, whereas we first landed, very sandie and low towards the waters side, but so full of grapes, as the very beating and surge of the Sea overflowed them, of which we found such plentie, as well there as in all places else, both on the sand and on the greene soile on the hils, as in the plaines, as well on every little shrubbe, as also climing towardes the tops of high Cedars, that I thinke in all the world the like abundance is not to be found: and my selfe having seene those parts of Europe that most abound, find such difference as were incredible to be written.

We passed from the Sea side towardes the toppes of those hilles next adjoyning, being but of meane higth, and from thence wee behelde the Sea on both sides to the North, and to the South, finding no ende any of both wayes. This lande lay stretching it selfe to the West, which after wee found to bee but an Island of twentie miles long, and not above sixe miles broade. Under the banke or hill whereon we stoode, we behelde the vallyes replenished with goodly Cedar trees, and having discharged our harquebuz-shot, such a flocke of Cranes (the most part white) arose under us, with such a cry redoubed by many ecchoes, as if an armie of men had showted all together.

This Island had many goodly woodes full of Deere, Conies, Hares, and Fowle, even in the middest of Summer in incredible abundance. The woodes are not such as you finde in Bohemia, Moscovia, or Hercynia, barren and fruitles, but the highest and reddest Cedars of the world, farre bettering the Ceders of the Açores, of the Indies, or Lybanus, Pynes, Cypres, Sassaphras, the Lentisk, or the tree that beareth the Masticke, the tree that beareth the rine of blacke Sinamon, of which Master Winter brought from the streights of Magellan, and many other of excellent smell and qualitie. We remained by the side of this Island two whole dayes before we saw any people of the Countrey: the third day we espied one small boate rowing towardes us having in it three persons: this boat came to the Island side, foure harquebuz-shot from our shippes, and there two of the people remaining, the third came along the shoreside towards us, and wee being then all within boord, he walked up and downe upon the point of the land next unto us: then the Master and the Pilot of the Admirall, Simon Ferdinando, and the Captaine Philip Amadas, my selfe, and others rowed to the land, whose comming this fellow attended, never making any shewe of feare or doubt. And after he had spoken of many things not understood by us, we brought him with his owne good liking, aboord the ships, and gave him a shirt, a hat & some other things, and made him taste of our wine, and our meat, which he liked very wel: and after having viewed both barks, he departed, and went to his owne boat againe, which hee had left in a little Cove or Creeke adjoyning: assoone as hee was two bow shoot into the water, he fell to fishing, and in lesse then halfe an houre, he had laden his boate as deepe, as it could swimme, with which hee came againe to the point of the lande, and there he devided his fish into two parts, pointing one part to the ship, and the other to the pinnesse: which, after he had (as much as he might) requited the former benefites received, departed out of our sight.

The next day there came unto us divers boates, and in one of them the Kings brother, accompanied with fortie or fiftie men, very handsome and goodly people, and in their behaviour as mannerly and civill as any of Europe. His name was Granganimeo, and the king is called Wingina, the countrey Wingandacoa, and now by her Majestie Virginia. The maner of his comming was in this sort: hee left his boates altogether as the first man did a little from the shippes by the shore, and came along to the place over against the ships, followed with fortie men. When he came to the place, his servants spread a long matte upon the ground, on which he sate downe, and at the other ende of the matte foure others of his companie did the like, the rest of his men stood round about him, somewhat a farre off: when we came to the shore to him with our weapons, hee never mooved from his place, nor any of the other foure, nor never mistrusted any harme to be offred from us, but sitting still he beckoned us to come and sit by him, which we performed: and being set hee made all signes of joy and welcome, striking on his head and his breast and afterwardes on ours, to shewe wee were all one, smiling and making shewe the best he could of all love, and familiaritie. After hee had made a long speech unto us, wee presented him with divers things, which hee received very joyfully, and thankefully. None of the company durst speake one worde all the time: onely the foure which were at the other ende, spake one in the others eare very softly.

The King is greatly obeyed, and his brothers and children reverenced: the King himselfe in person was at our being there, sore wounded in a fight which hee had with the King of the next countrey, called Wingina, and was shot in two places through the body, and once cleane through the thigh, but yet he recovered: by reason whereof and for that hee lay at the chiefe towne of the countrey, being six dayes journey off, we saw him not at all.

After we had presented this his brother with such things as we thought he liked, wee likewise gave somewhat to the other that sat with him on the matte: but presently he arose and tooke all from them and put it into his owne basket, making signes and tokens, that all things ought to bee delivered unto him, and the rest were but his servants, and followers. A day or two after this, we fell to trading with them, exchanging some things that we had, for Chamoys, Buffe, and Deere skinnes: when we shewed him all our packet of merchandize, of all things that he sawe, a bright tinne dish most pleased him, which hee presently tooke up and clapt it before his breast, and after made a hole in the brimme thereof and hung it about his necke, making signes that it would defende him against his enemies arrowes: for those people maintaine a deadly and terrible warre, with the people and King adjoyning. We exchanged our tinne dish for twentie skinnes, woorth twentie Crownes, or twentie Nobles: and a copper kettle for fiftie skins woorth fifty Crownes. They offered us good exchange for our hatchets, and axes, and for knives, and would have given any thing for swordes: but we would not depart with any. After two or three dayes the Kings brother came aboord the shippes, and dranke wine, and eat of our meat and of our bread, and liked exceedingly thereof: and after a few dayes overpassed, he brought his wife with him to the ships, his daughter and two or three children: his wife was very well favoured, of meane stature, and very bashfull: shee had on her backe a long cloake of leather, with the furre side next to her body, and before her a piece of the same: about her forehead shee had a bande of white Corall, and so had her husband many times: in her eares shee had bracelets of pearles hanging downe to her middle, (whereof we delivered your worship a little bracelet) and those were of the bignes of good pease. The rest of her women of the better sort had pendants of copper hanging in either eare, and some of the children of the kings brother and other noble men, have five or sixe in either eare: he himselfe had upon his head a broad plate of golde, or copper, for being unpolished we knew not what mettal it should be, neither would he by any meanes suffer us to take it off his head, but feeling it, it would bow very easily. His apparell was as his wives, onely the women weare their haire long on both sides, and the men but on one. They are of colour yellowish, and their haire black for the most part, and yet we saw children that had very fine aburne, and chestnut coloured haire.

After that these women had bene there, there came downe from all parts great store of people, bringing with them leather, corall, divers kindes of dies very excellent, and exchanged with us: but when Granganimeo the kings brother was present, none durst trade but himselfe: except such as weare red pieces of copper on their heads like himselfe: for that is the difference betweene the noble men, and the governours of countreys, and the meaner sort. And we both noted there, and you have understood since by these men, which we brought home, that no people in the worlde cary more respect to their King, Nobilitie, and Governours, then these doe. The Kings brothers wife, when she came to us (as she did many times) was followed with forty or fifty women alwayes: and when she came into the shippe, she left them all on land, saving her two daughters, her nurse and one or two more. The Kings brother alwayes kept this order, as many boates as he would come withall to the shippes, so many fires would hee make on the shore a farre off, to the end we might understand with what strength and company he approched. Their boates are made of one tree, either of Pine or of Pitch trees: a wood not commonly knowen to our people, nor found growing in England. They have no edge-tooles to make them withall: if they have any they are very fewe, and those it seemes they had twentie yeres since, which, as those two men declared, was out of a wrake which happened upon their coast of some Christian ship, being beaten that way by some storme and outragious weather, whereof none of the people were saved, but only the ship, or some part of her being cast upon the sand, out of whose sides they drew the nayles and the spikes, and with those they made their best instruments. The manner of making their boates is thus: they burne downe some great tree, or take such as are winde fallen, and putting gumme and rosen upon one side thereof, they set fire into it, and when it hath burnt it hollow, they cut out the coale with their shels, and ever where they would burne it deeper or wider they lay on gummes, which burne away the timber, and by this meanes they fashion very fine boates, and such as will transport twentie men. Their oares are like scoopes, and many times they set with long pooles, as the depth serveth.

The Kings brother had great liking of our armour, a sword, and divers other things which we had: and offered to lay a great boxe of pearle in gage for them: but we refused it for this time, because we would not make them knowe, that we esteemed thereof, untill we had understoode in what places of the countrey the pearle grew: which now your Worshippe doeth very well understand.

He was very just of his promise: for many times we delivered him merchandize upon his word, but ever he came within the day and performed his promise. He sent us every day a brase or two of fat Bucks, Conies, Hares, Fish the best of the world. He sent us divers kindes of fruites, Melons, Walnuts, Cucumbers, Gourdes, Pease, and divers rootes, and fruites very excellent good, and of their Countrey corne, which is very white, faire and well tasted, and groweth three times in five moneths: in May they sow, in July they reape, in June they sow, in August they reape: in July they sow, in September they reape: onely they cast the corne into the ground, breaking a little of the soft turfe with a wodden mattock, or pickeaxe: our selves prooved the soile, and put some of our Pease in the ground, and in tenne dayes they were of fourteene ynches high: they have also Beanes very faire of divers colours and wonderfull plentie: some growing naturally, and some in their gardens, and so have they both wheat and oates.

The soile is the most plentifull, sweete, fruitfull and wholsome of all the worlde: there are above foureteene severall sweete smelling timber trees, and the most part of their underwoods are Bayes and such like: they have those Okes that we have, but farre greater and better. After they had bene divers times aboord our shippes, my selfe, with seven more went twentie mile into the River, that runneth towarde the Citie of Skicoak, which River they call Occam: and the evening following, wee came to an Island, which they call Raonoak, distant from the harbour by which we entred, seven leagues: and at the North end thereof was a village of nine houses, built of Cedar, and fortified round about with sharpe trees, to keepe out their enemies, and the entrance into it made like a turne pike very artificially; when wee came towardes it, standing neere unto the waters side, the wife of Granganimo the kings brother came running out to meete us very cheerefully and friendly, her husband was not then in the village; some of her people shee commanded to drawe our boate on shore for the beating of the billoe: others she appointed to cary us on their backes to the dry ground, and others to bring our oares into the house for feare of stealing. When we were come into the utter roome, having five roomes in her house, she caused us to sit downe by a great fire, and after tooke off our clothes and washed them, and dryed them againe: some of the women plucked off our stockings and washed them, some washed our feete in warme water, and shee her selfe tooke great paines to see all things ordered in the best maner shee could, making great haste to dresse some meate for us to eate.

After we had thus dryed our selves, she brought us into the inner roome, where shee set on the boord standing along the house, some wheate like furmentie, sodden Venison, and roasted, fish sodden, boyled, and roasted, Melons rawe, and sodden, rootes of divers kindes, and divers fruites: their drinke is commonly water, but while the grape lasteth, they drinke wine, and for want of caskes to keepe it, all the yere after they drink water, but it is sodden with Ginger in it, and blacke Sinamon, and sometimes Sassaphras, and divers other wholesome, and medicinable hearbes and trees. We were entertained with all love and kindnesse, and with as much bountie (after their maner) as they could possibly devise. We found the people most gentle, loving, and faithful, voide of all guile and treason, and such as live after the maner of the golden age. The people onely care howe to defend themselves from the cold in their short winter, and to feed themselves with such meat as the soile affoordeth: there meate is very well sodden and they make broth very sweet and savorie: their vessels are earthen pots, very large, white and sweete, their dishes are wodden platters of sweet timber: within the place where they feede was their lodging, and within that their Idoll, which they worship, of whome they speake incredible things. While we were at meate, there came in at the gates two or three men with their bowes and arrowes from hunting, whom when we espied, we beganne to looke one towardes another, and offered to reach our weapons: but assoone as shee espied our mistrust, shee was very much mooved, and caused some of her men to runne out, and take away their bowes and arrowes and breake them, and withall beate the poore fellowes out of the gate againe. When we departed in the evening and would not tary all night, she was very sory, and gave us into our boate our supper halfe dressed, pottes and all, and brought us to our boate side, in which wee lay all night, remooving the same a prettie distance from the shoare: shee perceiving our jelousie, was much greived, and sent divers men and thirtie women, to sit all night on the banke side by us, and sent us into our boates five mattes to cover us from the raine, using very many wordes to intreate us to rest in their houses: but because wee were fewe men, and if wee had miscaried, the voyage had bene in very great danger, we durst not adventure any thing, though there was no cause of doubt: for a more kinde and loving people there can not be found in the worlde, as farre as we have hitherto had triall.

Beyond this Island there is the maine lande, and over against this Island falleth into this spacious water, the great river called Occam by the inhabitants on which standeth a towne called Pomeiock, & six dayes journey from the same is situate their greatest citie, called Skicoak, which this people affirme to be very great: but the Savages were never at it, only they speake of it by the report of their fathers and other men, whom they have heard affirme it to bee above one houres journey about.

Into this river falleth another great river, called Cipo, in which there is found great store of Muskles in which there are pearles: likewise there descendeth into this Occam, another river, called Nomopana, on the one side whereof standeth a great towne called Chawanook, and the Lord of that towne and countrey is called Pooneno: this Pooneno is not subject to the king of Wingandacoa, but is a free Lord: beyond this coun-try is there another king, whom they cal Menatonon, and these three kings are in league with each other. Towards the South-west, foure dayes journey is situate a towne called Sequotan, which is the Southermost towne of Wingandacoa, neere unto which, six and twentie yeres past there was a ship cast away, whereof some of the people were saved, and those were white people, whom the countrey people preserved.

And after ten dayes remaining in an out Island unhabited, called Wocokon, they with the help of some of the dwellers of Sequotan, fastened two boates of the countrey together & made mastes unto them, and sailes of their shirtes, and hav-ing taken into them such victuals as the countrey yeelded, they departed after they had remained in this out Island 3 weekes: but shortly after it seemed they were cast away, for the boates were found upon the coast, cast a land in another Island adjoyning: other then these, there was never any people apparelled, or white of colour, either seene or heard of amongst these people, and these aforesaid were seene onely of the inhabitantes of Secotan, which appeared to be very true, for they wondred marvelously when we were amongst them at the whitenes of our skins, ever coveting to touch our breasts, and to view the same. Besides they had our ships in marvelous admiration, & all things els were so strange unto them, as it appeared that none of them had ever seene the like. When we discharged any piece, were it but an hargubuz, they would tremble thereat for very feare, and for the strangenesse of the same: for the weapons which themselves use are bowes and arrowes: the arrowes are but of small canes, headed with a sharpe shell or tooth of a fish sufficient ynough to kill a naked man. Their swordes be of wood hardened: likewise they use wooden breastplates for their defence. They have besides a kinde of club, in the end whereof they fasten the sharpe hornes of a stagge, or other beast. When they goe to warres they cary about with them their idol, of whom they aske counsel, as the Romans were woont of the Oracle of Apollo. They sing songs as they march towardes the battell in stead of drummes and trumpets: their warres are very cruell and bloody, by reason whereof, and of their civill dissentions which have happened of late yeeres amongst them, the people are marvelously wasted, and in some places the countrey left desolate.

Adjoyning to this countrey aforesaid called Secotan beginneth a countrey called Pomovik, belonging to another king whom they call Piamacum, and this king is in league with the next king adjoyning towards the setting of the Sunne, and the countrey Newsiok, situate upon a goodly river called Neus: these kings have mortall warre with Wingina king of Wingandacoa: but about two yeeres past there was a peace made betweene the King Piemacum, and the Lord of Secotan, as these men which we have brought with us to England, have given us to understand: but there remaineth a mortall malice in the Secotanes, for many injuries & slaughters done upon them by this Piemacum. They invited divers men, and thirtie women

of the best of his countrey to their towne to a feast: and when
they were altogether merry, & praying before their Idol, (which
is nothing els but a meer illusion of the devil) the captaine or
Lord of the town came suddenly upon them, and slewe them
every one, reserving the women and children: and these two
have oftentimes since perswaded us to surprize Piemacum his
towne, having promised and assured us, that there will be found
in it great store of commodities. But whether their perswasion
be to the ende they may be revenged of their enemies, or for
the love they beare to us, we leave that to the tryall hereafter.

Beyond this Island called Roanoak, are maine Islands very
plentifull of fruits and other naturall increases, together with
many townes, and villages, along the side of the continent,
some bounding upon the Islands, and some stretching up further into the land.

When we first had sight of this countrey, some thought the
first land we saw to bee the continent: but after we entred into
the Haven, we saw before us another mighty long Sea: for
there lyeth along the coast a tracte of Islands, two hundreth
miles in length, adjoyning to the Ocean sea, and betweene the
Islands, two or three entrances: when you are entred betweene
them (these Islands being very narrow for the most part, as in
most places sixe miles broad, in some places lesse, in fewe
more) then there appeareth another great Sea, containing in
bredth in some places, forty, and in some fifty, in some twenty
miles over, before you come unto the continent: and in this
inclosed Sea there are above an hundreth Islands of divers
bignesses, whereof one is sixteene miles long, at which we
were, finding it a most pleasant and fertile ground, replenished
with goodly Cedars, and divers other sweete woods, full of
Corrants, of flaxe, and many other notable commodities, which
we at that time had no leasure to view. Besides this Island there
are many, as I have sayd, some of two, or three, of foure, of
five miles, some more, some lesse, most beautifull and pleasant
to behold, replenished with Deere, Conies, Hares and divers
beasts, and about them the goodliest and best fish in the world,
and in greatest abundance.

Thus Sir, we have acquainted you with the particulars of our
discovery, made this present voyage, as farre foorth as the
shortnesse of the time we there continued would affoord us

take viewe of: and so contenting our selves with this service at this time, which wee hope hereafter to inlarge, as occasion and assistance shalbe given, we resolved to leave the countrey, and to apply our selves to returne for England, which we did accordingly, and arrived safely in the West of England about the middest of September.

And whereas wee have above certified you of the countrey taken in possession by us, to her Majesties use, and so to yours by her Majesties grant, wee thought good for the better assurance thereof to record some of the particular Gentlemen, & men of accompt, who then were present, as witnesses of the same, that thereby all occasion of cavill to the title of the countrey, in her Majesties behalfe may be prevented, which otherwise, such as like not the action may use and pretend, whose names are:

> Master Philip Amadas,
> Master Arthur Barlow, } Captaines. . . .

We brought home also two of the Savages being lustie men, whose names were Wanchese and Manteo.

31

---◗◆◖---

The third voyage made by a ship sent in the yeere
1586, to the reliefe of the Colony planted in Virginia
at the sole charges of Sir Walter Ralegh

IN the yeere of our Lord 1586 Sir Walter Ralegh at his owne
charge prepared a ship of an hundred tunne, fraighted with all
maner of things in most plentifull maner, for the supply and
reliefe of his Colony then remaining in Virginia: but before
they set saile from England it was after Easter, so that our
Colony halfe despaired of the comming of any supply: wherefore every man prepared for himselfe, determining resolutely to
spend the residue of their life time in that countrey. And for
the better performance of this their determination, they sowed,
planted, and set such things as were necessary for their reliefe
in so plentifull a maner as might have sufficed them two yeeres
without any further labour. Thus trusting to their owne harvest,
they passed the Summer till the tenth of June: at which time
their corne which they had sowed was within one fortnight
of reaping: but then it happened that Sir Francis Drake in
his prosperous returne from the sacking of Sant Domingo, Cartagena, and Saint Augustine, determined in his way homeward
to visit his countreymen the English Colony then remaining
in Virginia. So passing along the coasts of Florida, he fell with
the parts where our English Colony inhabited: and having
espied some of that company, there he ankered and went aland,
where hee conferred with them of their state and welfare, and
how things had past with them. They answered him that they
lived all; but hitherto in some scarsity: and as yet could heare
of no supply out of England: therefore they requested him that
hee would leave with them some two or three ships, that if in
some reasonable time they heard not out of England, they might

then returne themselves. Which hee agreed to. Whilest some were then writing their letters to send into England, and some others making reports of the accidents of their travels ech to other, some on land, some on boord, a great storme arose, and drove the most of their fleet from their ankers to Sea, in which ships at that instant were the chiefest of the English Colony: the rest on land perceiving this, hasted to those three sailes which were appointed to be left there; and for feare they should be left behinde they left all things confusedly, as if they had bene chased from thence by a mighty army: and no doubt so they were; for the hand of God came upon them for the cruelty and outrages committed by some of them against the native inhabitants of that countrey.

Immediatly after the departing of our English Colony out of this paradise of the world, the ship abovementioned sent and set forth at the charges of Sir Walter Ralegh and his direction, arrived at Hatorask; who after some time spent in seeking our Colony up in the countrey, and not finding them, returned with all the aforesayd provision into England.

About fourteene or fifteene dayes after the departure of the aforesayd shippe, Sir Richard Grinvile Generall of Virginia, accompanied with three shippes well appointed for the same voyage, arrived there; who not finding the aforesayd shippe according to his expectation, nor hearing any newes of our English Colony there seated, and left by him anno 1585, himselfe travelling up into divers places of the countrey, aswell to see if he could heare any newes of the Colony left there by him the yeere before, under the charge of Master Lane his deputy, as also to discover some places of the countrey: but after some time spent therein, not hearing any newes of them, and finding the places which they inhabited desolate, yet unwilling to loose the possession of the countrey which Englishmen had so long held: after good deliberation, hee determined to leave some men behinde to reteine possession of the Countrey: whereupon he landed fifteene men in the Isle of Roanoak, furnished plentifully with all maner of provision for two yeeres, and so departed for England.

Not long after he fell with the Isles of Açores, on some of which Islands he landed, and spoiled the townes of all such things as were woorth cariage, where also he tooke divers Spanyards. With these and many other exploits done by him in this voyage, aswell outward as homeward, he returned into England.

32

The fourth voyage made to Virginia with three ships,
in the yere 1587. Wherein was transported
the second Colonie

IN the yeere of our Lord 1587. Sir Walter Ralegh intending
to persevere in the planting of his Countery of Virginia, prepared a newe Colonie of one hundred and fiftie men to be sent
thither, under the charge of John White, whom hee appointed
Governour, and also appointed unto him twelve Assistants, unto
whom hee gave a Charter, and incorporated them by the name
of Governour and Assitants of the Citie of Ralegh in Virginia.

April

Our Fleete being in number three saile, viz. the Admirall a
shippe of one hundred and twentie Tunnes, a Flie-boate, and a
Pinnesse, departed the sixe and twentieth of April from Portesmouth and the same day came to an ancker at the Cowes in
the Isle of Wight, where wee stayed eight dayes.

May

The fift of May, at nine of the clocke at night we came to Plimmouth, where we remained the space of two dayes.

The 8 we weyed anker at Plimmouth, and departed thence
for Virginia.

The 16 Simon Ferdinando, Master of our Admiral, lewdly
forsooke our Fly-boate, leaving her distressed in the Bay of
Portugal.

June

The 19 we fell with Dominica, and the same evening we sayled
betweene it, and Guadalupe: the 21 the Fly-boat also fell with
Dominica.

The 22 we came to an anker at an Island called Santa Cruz, where all the planters were set on land, staying there till the 25 of the same moneth. At our first landing on this Island, some of our women, and men, by eating a small fruit like greene Apples, were fearefully troubled with a sudden burning in their mouthes, and swelling of their tongues so bigge, that some of them could not speake. Also a child by sucking one of those womens breasts, had at that instant his mouth set on such a burning, that it was strange to see how the infant was tormented for the time: but after 24 houres, it ware away of it selfe.

Also the first night of our being on this Island, we tooke five great Torteses, some of them of such bignes, that sixteene of our strongest men were tired with carying of one of them but from the sea side to our cabbins. In this Island we found no watring place, but a standing ponde, the water whereof was so evill, that many of our company fell sicke with drinking thereof: and as many as did but wash their faces with that water, in the morning before the Sunne had drawen away the corruption, their faces did so burne and swell, that their eyes were shut up, and could not see in five or sixe dayes, or longer.

The second day of our abode there, we sent forth some of our men to search the Island for fresh water, three one way, and two another way. The Governour also, with six others, went up to the top of an high hill, to viewe the Island, but could perceive no signe of any men, or beastes, nor any goodnes, but Parots, and trees of Guiacum. Returning backe to our cabbins another way, he found in the discent of a hill, certaine potsheards of savage making, made of the earth of that Island: whereupon it was judged, that this Island was inhabited with Savages, though Fernando had told us for certaine the contrary. The same day at night, the rest of our company very late returned to the Governour. The one company affirmed, that they had seene in a valley eleven Savages, and divers houses halfe a mile distant from the steepe, or toppe of the hill where they stayed. The other company had found running out of a high rocke a very fayre spring of water, whereof they brought three bottels to the company: for before that time, we drank the stinking water of the pond.

The same second day at night Captaine Stafford, with the

Pinnesse, departed from our fleete, riding at Santa Cruz, to an Island, called Beake, lying neere S. John, being so directed by Ferdinando, who assured him he should there find great plenty of sheepe. The next day at night, our planters left Santa Cruz, and came all aboord, and the next morning after, being the 25 of June we weyed anker, and departed from Santa Cruz.

The seven and twentieth we came to anker at Cottea, where we found the Pinnesse riding at our comming.

The 28 we weyed anker at Cottea, and presently came to anker at S. Johns in Musketos Bay, where we spent three dayes unprofitable in taking in fresh water, spending in the meane time more beere then the quantitie of the water came unto.

Julie

The first day we weyed anker at Musketoes Bay, where were left behind two Irish men of our company, Darbie Glaven, and Denice Carrell, bearing along the coast of S. Johns till evening, at which time wee fell with Rosse Bay. At this place Ferdinando had promised wee should take in salte, and had caused us before, to make and provide as many sackes for that purpose, as we could. The Governour also, for that hee understood there was a Towne in the bottome of the Bay, not farre from the salt hils, appointed thirty shot, tenne pikes, and ten targets, to man the Pinnesse, and to goe aland for salt. Ferdinando perceiving them in a readines, sent to the Governour, using great perswasions with him, not to take in salt there, saying that hee knew not well whether the same were the place or not: also, that if the Pinnesse went into the Bay, she could not without great danger come backe, till the next day at night, and that if in the meane time any storme should rise, the Admirall were in danger to bee cast away. Whilest he was thus perswading, he caused the lead to be cast, and having craftily brought the shippe in three fadome and a halfe water, he suddenly began to sweare, and teare God in pieces, dissembling great danger, crying to him at the helme, beare up hard, beare up hard: so we went off, and were disappointed of our salt, by his meanes.

The next day sayling along the West end of S. John, the Governour determined to go aland in S. Germans Bay, to gather yong plants of Orenges, Pines, Mameas, and Plantanos, to set at Virginia, which we knew might easily be had, for that they grow neere the shore, and the places where they grew, well knowen to the Governour, and some of the planters: but our Simon denied it, saying: he would come to an anker at Hispaniola, & there land the Governour, and some other of the Assistants, with the pinnesse, to see if he could speake with his friend Alanson, of whom he hoped to be furnished both of cattel, and all such things as we would have taken in at S. John: but he meant nothing lesse, as it plainely did appeare to us afterwards.

The next day after, being the third of July, we saw Hispaniola, and bare with the coast all that day, looking still when the pinnesse should be prepared to goe for the place where Ferdinando his friend Alanson was: but that day passed, and we saw no preparation for landing in Hispaniola.

The 4 of July, sayling along the coast of Hispaniola, untill the next day at noone, and no preparation yet seene for the staying there, we having knowledge that we were past the place where Alanson dwelt, and were come with Isabella: hereupon Ferdinando was asked by the Governor, whether he meant to speake with Alanson, for the taking in of cattell, and other things, according to his promise, or not: but he answered that he was now past the place, and that Sir Walter Ralegh told him, the French Ambassador certified him, that the king of Spaine had sent for Alanson into Spaine: wherefore he thought him dead, and that it was to no purpose to touch there in any place, at this voyage.

The next day we left sight of Hispaniola, and haled off for Virginia, about foure of the clocke in the afternoone.

The sixt of July we came to the Island Caycos, wherein Ferdinando sayd were two salt pondes, assuring us if they were drie, we might find salt to shift with, untill the next supply: but it prooved as true as finding of sheepe at Baque. In this Island, whilest Ferdinando solaced himselfe ashore, with one of the company, in part of the Island, others spent the latter part of that day in other parts of the Island, some to seeke the salt ponds, some fowling, some hunting Swans, whereof we caught many. The next day early in the morning we weyed anker, leaving Caycos, with good hope, that the first land that we saw next should be Virginia.

About the 16 of July we fel with the maine of Virginia, which Simon Ferdinando tooke to be the Island of Croatoan, where we came to anker, and rode there two or three dayes: but finding himselfe deceived, he weyed, and bare along the coast, where in the night, had not Captaine Stafford bene more carefull in looking out, then our Simon Ferdinando, we had bene all cast away upon the breach, called the Cape of Feare, for we were come within two cables length upon it: such was the carelesnes, and ignorance of our Master.

The two and twentieth of July wee arrived safe at Hatorask, where our ship and pinnesse ankered: the Governour went aboord the pinnesse, accompanied with fortie of his best men, intending to passe up to Roanoak foorthwith, hoping there to finde those fifteene Englishmen, which Sir Richard Grinvile had left there the yeere before, with whom hee meant to have conference, concerning the state of the Countrey, and Savages, meaning after he had so done, to returne againe to the fleete, and passe along the coast, to the Bay of Chesepiok, where we intended to make our seate and forte, according to the charge given us among other directions in writing, under the hande of Sir Walter Ralegh: but assoone as we were put with our pinnesse from the ship, a Gentleman by the meanes of Ferdinando, who was appointed to returne for England, called to the sailers in the pinnesse, charging them not to bring any of the planters backe againe, but to leave them in the Island, except the Governour, & two or three such as he approved, saying that the Summer was farre spent, wherefore hee would land all the planters in no other place. Unto this were all the saylers, both in the pinnesse, and shippe, perswaded by the Master, wherefore it booted not the Governour to contend with them, but passed to Roanoak, and the same night at sunne-set went aland on the Island, in the place where our fifteene men were left, but we found none of them, nor any signe that they had bene there, saving onely wee found the bones of one of those fifteene, which the Savages had slaine long before.

The three and twentieth of July the Governour with divers of his company, walked to the North ende of the Island, where Master Ralfe Lane had his forte, with sundry necessary and decent dwelling houses, made by his men about it the yeere before, where wee hoped to find some signes, or certaine knowledge of our fifteene men. When we came thither, we found the fort rased downe, but all the houses standing unhurt, saving that the neather roomes of them, and also of the forte, were overgrowen with Melons of divers sortes, and Deere within them, feeding on those Melons: so wee returned to our company, without hope of ever seeing any of the fifteene men living.

The same day order was given, that every man should be employed for the repayring of those houses, which wee found standing, and also to make other newe Cottages, for such as should neede.

The 25 our Flyboate and the rest of our planters arrived all safe at Hatoraske, to the great joy and comfort of the whole company: but the Master of our Admirall Ferdinando grieved greatly at their safe comming: for hee purposely left them in the Bay of Portugal, and stole away from them in the night, hoping that the Master thereof, whose name was Edward Spicer, for that he never had bene in Virginia, would hardly finde the place, or els being left in so dangerous a place as that was, by meanes of so many men of warre, as at that time were abroad, they should surely be taken, or slaine: but God disappointed his wicked pretenses.

The eight and twentieth, George Howe, one of our twelve Assistants was slaine by divers Savages, which were come over to Roanoak, either of purpose to espie our company, and what number we were, or else to hunt Deere, whereof were many in the Island. These Savages being secretly hidden among high reedes, where oftentimes they find the Deere asleep, and so kill them, espied our man wading in the water alone, almost naked, without any weapon, save only a smal forked sticke, catching Crabs therewithall, and also being strayed two miles from his company, and shot at him in the water, where they gave him sixteen wounds with their arrowes: and after they had slaine him with their woodden swords, they beat his head in pieces, and fled over the water to the maine.

On the thirtieth of July Master Stafford and twenty of our men passed by water to the Island of Croatoan, with Manteo, who had his mother, and many of his kinred dwelling in that Island, of whom wee hoped to understand some newes of our fifteene men, but especially to learne the disposition of the people of the countrey towards us, and to renew our old friendship with them. At our first landing they seemed as though they would fight with us: but perceiving us begin to march with our shot towardes them, they turned their backes, and fled. Then Manteo their countrey man called to them in their owne language, whom, assoone as they heard, they returned, and threwe away their bowes and arrowes, and some of them came unto us, embracing and entertaining us friendly, desiring us not to gather or spill any of their corne, for that they had but little. We answered them, that neither their corne, nor any other thing of theirs, should be diminished by any of us, and that our comming was onely to renew the old love, that was betweene us and them at the first, and to live with them as brethren and friends: which answere seemed to please them well, wherefore they requested us to walke up to their Towne, who there feasted us after their maner, and desired us earnestly, that there might bee some token or badge given them of us, whereby we might know them to be our friends, when we met them any where out of the Towne or Island. They told us further, that for want of some such badge, divers of them were hurt the yeere before, being found out of the Island by Master Lane his company, whereof they shewed us one, which at that very instant lay lame, and had lien of that hurt ever since: but they sayd, they knew our men mistooke them, and hurt them in stead of Winginos men, wherefore they held us excused.

August

The next day we had conference further with them, concerning the people of Secotan, Aquascogoc, & Pomeiok, willing them of Croatoan to certifie the people of those townes, that if they would accept our friendship, we would willingly receive them againe, and that all unfriendly dealings past on both parts, should be utterly forgiven and forgotten. To this the chiefe men of Croatoan answered, that they would gladly doe the best they could, and within seven dayes, bring the Wiroances and chiefe Governours of those townes with them, to our Governour at Roanoak, or their answere. We also understood of the men of Croatoan, that our man Master Howe was slaine by the remnant of Winginos men dwelling then at Dasamonguepeuk, with whom Wanchese kept companie: and also we understood by them of Croatoan, how that the 15 Englishmen left at Roanoak

the yeere before, by Sir Richard Grinvile, were suddenly set upon, by 30 of the men of Secota, Aquascogoc, and Dasamonguepeuk, in manner following. They conveyed themselves secretly
behind the trees, neere the houses where our men carelesly lived:
and having perceived that of those fifteene they could see but
eleven only, two of those Savages appeared to the 11 Englishmen, calling to them by friendly signes, that but two of their
chiefest men should come unarmed to speake with those two Savages, who seemed also to bee unarmed. Wherefore two of the
chiefest of our Englishmen went gladly to them: but whilest one
of those Savages traiterously imbraced one of our men, the other
with his sworde of wood, which he had secretly hidden under his
mantell, strooke him on the head and slew him, and presently
the other eight and twenty Savages shewed them selves: the
other Englishman perceiving this, fled to his company, whom
the Savages pursued with their bowes, and arrowes, so fast, that
the Englishmen were forced to take the house, wherein all their
victuall, and weapons were: but the Savages foorthwith set the
same on fire: by meanes whereof our men were forced to take
up such weapons as came first to hand, and without order to
runne foorth among the Savages, with whom they skirmished
above an howre. In this skirmish another of our men was
shotte into the mouth with an arrow, where hee died: and also
one of the Savages was shot into the side by one of our men,
with a wild fire arrow, whereof he died presently. The place
where they fought was of great advantage to the Savages, by
meanes of the thicke trees, behinde which the Savages through
their nimblenes, defended themselves, and so offended our men
with their arrowes, that our men being some of them hurt,
retyred fighting to the water side, where their boat lay, with
which they fled towards Hatorask. By that time they had
rowed but a quarter of a mile, they espied their foure fellowes
comming from a creeke thereby, where they had bene to fetch
Oysters: these foure they received into their boate, leaving
Roanoak, and landed on a little Island on the right hand of our
entrance into the harbour of Hatorask, where they remayned a
while, but afterward departed, whither as yet we know not.

Having nowe sufficiently dispatched our businesse at Croatoan, the same day we departed friendly, taking our leave, and
came aboord the fleete at Hatorask.

The eight of August, the Governour having long expected the comming of the Wiroanses of Pomeiok, Aquascogoc, Secota, and Dasamonguepeuk, seeing that the seven dayes were past, within which they promised to come in, or to send their answeres by the men of Croatoan, and no tidings of them heard, being certainly also informed by those men of Croatoan, that the remnant of Wingina his men, which were left alive, who dwelt at Dasamonquepeuk, were they which had slaine George Howe, and were also at the driving of our eleven Englishmen from Roanoak, hee thought to deferre the revenge thereof no longer. Wherefore the same night about midnight, he passed over the water, accompanied with Captaine Stafford, and 24 men, whereof Manteo was one, whom we tooke with us to be our guide to the place where those Savages dwelt, where he behaved himselfe toward us as a most faithfull Englishman.

The next day, being the 9 of August, in the morning so early that it was yet darke, we landed neere the dwelling place of our enemies, & very secretly conveyed our selves through the woods, to that side, where we had their houses betweene us and the water: and having espied their fire, and some sitting about it, we presently set on them: the miserable soules herewith amazed, fled into a place of thicke reedes, growing fast by, where our men perceiving them, shot one of them through the bodie with a bullet, and therewith we entred the reedes, among which we hoped to acquite their evill doing towards us, but we were deceived, for those Savages were our friends, and were come from Croatoan to gather the corne & fruit of that place, because they understood our enemies were fled immediatly, after they had slaine George Howe, and for haste had left all their corne, Tobacco, and Pompions standing in such sort, that al had bene devoured of the birds, and Deere, if it had not bene gathered in time: but they had like to have payd deerely for it: for it was so darke, that they being naked, and their men and women apparelled all so like others, wee knew not but that they were al men: and if that one of them which was a Wiroances wife had not had a child at her backe, shee had bene slaine in stead of a man, and as hap was, another Savage knew master Stafford, and ran to him, calling him by his name, whereby hee was saved. Finding our selves thus disappointed of our purpose, we gathered al the corne, Pease,

Pompions, and Tabacco that we found ripe, leaving the rest unspoyled, and tooke Menatoan his wife, with the yong child, and the other Savages with us over the water to Roanoak. Although the mistaking of these Savages somewhat grieved Manteo, yet he imputed their harme to their owne folly, saying to them, that if their Wiroances had kept their promise in comming to the Governour at the day appointed, they had not knowen that mischance.

The 13 of August our Savage Manteo, by the commandement of Sir Walter Ralegh, was christened in Roanoak, and called Lord thereof, and of Dasamonguepeuk, in reward of his faithfull service.

The 18 Elenor, daughter to the Governour, and wife to Ananias Dare one of the Assistants, was delivered of a daughter in Roanoak, and the same was christened there the Sonday following, and because this child was the first Christian borne in Virginia, shee was named Virginia. By this time our ships had unladen the goods and victuals of the planters, and began to take in wood, and fresh water, and to new calke and trimme them for England: the planters also prepared their letters and tokens to send backe into England.

Our two ships, the Lion and the Flyboat almost ready to depart, the 21 of August, there arose such a tempest at Northeast, that our Admirall then riding out of the harbour, was forced to cut his cables, and put to sea, where he lay beating off and on six dayes before he could come to us againe, so that we feared he had bene cast away, and the rather for that at the time that the storme tooke them, the most and best of their sailers were left aland.

At this time some controversies arose betweene the Governour and Assistants, about choosing two out of the twelve Assistants, which should goe backe as factors for the company into England: for every one of them refused, save onely one, which all other thought not sufficient: but at length by much perswading of the Governour, Christopher Cooper only agreed to goe for England: but the next day, through the perswasion of divers of his familiar friends, hee changed his minde, so that now the matter stood as at the first.

The next day, the 22 of August, the whole company both of the Assistants and planters came to the Governour, and with one voice requested him to returne himselfe into England, for the better and sooner obtaining of supplies, and other necessaries for them: but he refused it, and alleaged many sufficient causes, why he would not: the one was, that he could not so suddenly returne backe againe without his great discredite, leaving the action, and so many whome hee partly had procured through his perswasions, to leave their native countrey, and undertake that voyage, and that some enemies to him and the action at his returne into England would not spare to slander falsly both him and the action, by saying, hee went to Virginia, but politikely, and to no other end but to leade so many into a countrey, in which hee never meant to stay himselfe, and there to leave them behind him. Also he alleaged, that seeing they intended to remove 50 miles further up into the maine presently, he being then absent, his stuffe and goods might be both spoiled, & most of them pilfered away in the cariage, so that at his returne he should be either forced to provide himselfe of all such things againe, or else at his comming againe to Virginia find himselfe utterly unfurnished, whereof already he had found some proofe, being but once from them but three dayes. Wherefore he concluded that he would not goe himselfe.

The next day, not onely the Assistants but divers others, as well women as men, began to renew their requests to the Governour againe, to take upon him to returne into England for the supply, and dispatch of all such things as there were to be done, promising to make him their bond under all their handes and seales for the safe preserving of all his goods for him at his returne to Virginia, so that if any part thereof were spoyled or lost, they would see it restored to him, or his Assignes, whensoever the same should be missed and demanded: which bond, with a testimony under their hands and seales, they foorthwith made, and delivered into his hands. The copie of the testimony I thought good to set downe.

May it please you, her Majesties subjects of England, we your friends and countrey-men, the planters in Virginia, doe by these presents let you and every of you to understand, that for the present and speedy supply of certaine our knowen and apparent lackes and needes, most requisite and necessary for the good and happy planting of us, or any other in this land of Virginia, wee all of one minde & consent, have most earnestly

intreated, and uncessantly requested John White, Governour
of the planters in Virgina, to passe into England, for the better
and more assured help, and setting forward of the foresayd
supplies: and knowing assuredly that he both can best, and wil
labour and take paines in that behalfe for us all, and he not
once, but often refusing it, for our sakes, and for the honour
& maintenance of the action, hath at last, though much against
his will, through our importunacie, yeelded to leave his governement, and all his goods among us, and himselfe in all our be-
halfes to passe into England, of whose knowledge and fidelitie
in handling this matter, as all others, we doe assure ourselves
by these presents, and will you to give all credite thereunto, the
25 of August 1587.

The Governour being at the last through their extreame intreating constrayned to returne into England, having then but
halfe a dayes respite to prepare himselfe for the same, departed
from Roanoak the seven and twentieth of August in the morning, and the same day about midnight, came aboord the Flieboat, who already had weyed anker, and rode without the
barre, the Admirall riding by them, who but the same morning was newly come thither againe. The same day both the
ships weyed anker, and set saile for England: at this weying
their ankers, twelve of the men which were in the Flyboate
were throwen from the Capstone, which by meanes of a barre
and brake, came so fast about upon them, that the other two
barres thereof strooke and hurt most of them so sore, that some
of them never recovered it: neverthelesse they assayed presently againe to wey their anker, but being so weakened with
the first fling, they were not able to weye it, but were throwen
downe and hurt the second time. Wherefore having in all but
fifteene men aboord, and most of them by this unfortunate
beginning so bruised, and hurt, they were forced to cut their
Cable, and leese their anker. Neverthelesse, they kept company with the Admirall, untill the seventeenth of September, at
which time wee fell with Corvo, and sawe Flores.

September

The eighteenth, perceiving of all our fifteene men in the Flyboate there remained but five, which by meanes of the former
mischance, were able to stand to their labour: and that the

Admirall meant not to make any haste for England, but to linger about the Island of Tercera for purchase: the Flyboate departed for England with letters, where we hoped by the help of God to arrive shortly: but by that time we had continued our course homeward about twenty dayes, having had sometimes scarse and variable windes, our fresh water also by leaking almost consumed, there arose a storme at Northeast, which for sixe dayes ceased not to blowe so exceeding, that we were driven further in those sixe then we could recover in thirteene daies: in which time others of our saylers began to fall very sicke and two of them dyed, the weather also continued so close, that our Master sometimes in foure dayes together could see neither sunne nor starre, and all the beverage we could make, with stinking water, dregs of beere, and lees of wine which remayned, was but three gallons, and therefore now we expected nothing but famine to perish at Sea.

October

The 16 of October we made land, but we knewe not what land it was, bearing in with the same land at that day: about sunne set we put into a harbour, where we found a Hulke of Dublin, and a pinnesse of Hampton riding, but we knew not as yet what place this was, neither had we any boate to goe ashore, untill the pinnesse sent off their boate to us with 6 or 8 men, of whom we understood wee were in Smerwick in the West parts of Ireland: they also releeved us presently with fresh water, wine, and other fresh meate.

The 18 the Governour and the Master ryd to Dingen a Cushe, 5 miles distant, to take order for the new victualing of our Flieboate for England, and for reliefe of our sicke and hurt men, but within foure daies after the Boatswain, the Steward, and the Boatswains mate died aboord the Flieboat, and the 28 the Masters mate and two of our chiefe sailers were brought sicke to Dingen.

November

The first the Governour shipped himselfe in a ship called the Monkie, which at that time was ready to put to sea from Dingen for England, leaving the Flyboat and all his companie in Ireland. The same day we set sayle, and on the third day we fell with the North side of the lands end, and were shut up the Severne, but the next day we doubled the same for Mounts Bay.

The 5 the Governour landed in England at Martasew, neere Saint Michaels mount in Cornewall.

The 8 we arrived at Hampton, where we understood that our consort the Admiral was come to Portsmouth, and had bene there three weekes before: and also that Ferdinando the Master with all his company were not onely come home without any purchase, but also in such weaknesse by sicknesse, and death of their chiefest men, that they were scarse able to bring their ship into harbour, but were forced to let fall anker without, which they could not wey againe, but might all have perished there, if a small barke by great hap had not come to them to helpe them. The names of the chiefe men that died are these, Roger Large, John Mathew, Thomas Smith, and some other saylers, whose names I knew not at the writing hereof. An. Dom. 1587.

The names of all the men, women and children, which safely arrived in Virginia, and remained to inhabite there. 1587. Anno regni Reginæ Elizabethæ. 29.

John White	Robert Wilkinson
Roger Baily	John Tydway
Ananias Dare	Ambrose Viccars
Christopher Cooper	Edmond English
Thomas Stevens	Thomas Topan
John Sampson	Henry Berry
Dyonis Harvie	Richard Berry
Roger Prat	John Spendlove
George How	John Hemmington
Simon Fernando	Thomas Butler
Nicholas Johnson	Edward Powell
Thomas Warner	John Burden
Anthony Cage	James Hynde
John Jones	Thomas Ellis
William Willes	William Browne
John Brooke	Michael Myllet
Cutbert White	Thomas Smith
John Bright	Richard Kemme

Clement Tayler
William Sole
John Cotsmur
Humfrey Newton
Thomas Colman
Thomas Gramme
Marke Bennet
John Gibbes
John Stilman

Thomas Harris
Richard Taverner
John Earnest
Henry Johnson
John Starte
Richard Darige
William Lucas
Arnold Archard
John Wright

33

A letter of M. John White to M. Richard Hakluyt
written in February 1593

TO the Worshipful and my very friend Master Richard Hakluyt, much happinesse in the Lord.

Sir, as well for the satisfying of your earnest request, as the
performance of my promise made unto you at my last being
with you in England, I have sent you (although in a homely
stile, especially for the contentation of a delicate eare) the
true discourse of my last voyage into the West Indies, and
partes of America called Virginia, taken in hand about the end
of Februarie, in the yeare of our redemption 1590. And what
events happened unto us in this our journey, you shall plainely
perceive by the sequele of my discourse. There were at the time
aforesaid three ships absolutely determined to goe for the
West Indies, at the speciall charges of M. John Wattes of London Marchant. But when they were fully furnished, and in readinesse to make their departure, a generall stay was commanded
of all ships thorowout England. Which so soone as I heard, I
presently (as I thought it most requisite) acquainted Sir Walter
Ralegh therewith, desiring him that as I had sundry times afore
bene chargeable and troublesome unto him, for the supplies
and reliefes of the planters in Virginia: so likewise, that by his
endevour it would please him at that instant to procure license
for those three ships to proceede on with their determined voyage, that thereby the people in Virginia (if it were God's pleasure) might speedily be comforted and relieved without further
charges unto him. Whereupon he by his good meanes obtained
license of the Queenes Majestie, and order to be taken, that the
owner of the 3 ships should be bound unto Sir Walter Ralegh
or his assignes, in 3000 pounds, that those 3 ships in considera-

tion of their releasement should take in, & transport a convenient number of passengers, with their furnitures and necessaries to be landed in Virginia. Neverthelesse that order was
not observed, neither was the bond taken according to the intention aforesaid. But rather in contempt of the aforesaid order,
I was by the owner and Commanders of the ships denied to
have any passengers, or any thing els transported in any of the
said ships, saving only my selfe & my chest; no not so much
as a boy to attend upon me, although I made great sute, &
earnest intreatie aswell to the chiefe Commanders, as to the
owner of the said ships. Which crosse and unkind dealing,
although it very much discontented me, notwithstanding the
scarsity of time was such, that I could have no opportunity
to go unto Sir Walter Ralegh with complaint: for the ships being then all in readinesse to goe to the Sea, would have bene
departed before I could have made my returne. Thus both
Governors, Masters, and sailers, regarding very smally the good
of their countreymen in Virginia; determined nothing lesse
then to touch at those places, but wholly disposed themselves
to seeke after purchase & spoiles, spending so much time
therein, that sommer was spent before we arrived at Virginia.
And when we were come thither, the season was so unfit, &
weather so foule, that we were constrained of force to forsake
that coast, having not seene any of our planters, with losse of
one of our ship-boates, and 7 of our chiefest men: and also
with losse of 3 of our ankers and cables, and most of our
caskes with fresh water left on shore, not possible to be had
aboord. Which evils & unfortunate events (as wel to their owne
losse as to the hinderance of the planters in Virginia) had not
chanced, if the order set downe by Sir Walter Ralegh had bene
observed, or if my dayly & continuall petitions for the performance of the same might have taken any place. Thus may
you plainely perceive the successe of my fift & last voiage to
Virginia, which was no lesse unfortunately ended then fro-
wardly begun, and as lucklesse to many, as sinister to my selfe.
But I would to God it had bene as prosperous to all, as noysome to the planters: & as joyfull to me, as discomfortable to
them. Yet seeing it is not my first crossed voyage, I remaine
contented. And wanting my wishes, I leave off from prosecuting that whereunto I would to God my wealth were answerable

to my will. Thus committing the reliefe of my discomfortable
company the planters in Virginia, to the merciful help of the
Almighty, whom I most humbly beseech to helpe & comfort
them, according to his most holy will & their good desire, I
take my leave: from my house at Newtowne in Kylmore the
4 of February, 1593.

Your most welwishing friend,

JOHN WHITE

34

The fift voyage of M. John White into the West
Indies and parts of America called Virginia, in
the yeere 1590

THE 20 of March the three shippes the Hopewell, the John
Evangelist, and the Little John, put to Sea from Plymmouth
with two small Shallops.

The 25 at midnight both our Shallops were sunke being
towed at the ships stearnes by the Boatswaines negligence.

On the 30 we saw a head us that part of the coast of Barbary, lying East of Cape Cantyn, and the Bay of Asaphi.

The next day we came to the Ile of Mogador, where rode,
at our passing by, a Pinnesse of London called the Mooneshine.

Aprill

On the first of Aprill we ankored in Santa Cruz rode, where
we found two great shippes of London lading in Sugar, of
whom we had 2 shipboats to supply the losse of our Shallops.

On the 2 we set sayle from the rode of Santa Cruz, for the
Canaries.

On Saturday the 4 we saw Alegranza, the East Ile of the
Canaries.

On Sunday the 5 of Aprill we gave chase to a double flyboat,
the which, we also the same day fought with, and tooke her,
with losse of three of their men slaine, and one hurt.

On Munday the 6 we saw Grand Canarie, and the next day
we landed and tooke in fresh water on the Southside thereof.

On the 9 we departed from Grand Canary, and framed our
course for Dominica.

The last of Aprill we saw Dominica, and the same night we
came to an anker on the Southside thereof.

May

The first of May in the morning many of the Salvages came aboord our ships in their Canowes, and did traffique with us; we also the same day landed and entered their Towne from whence we returned the same day aboord without any resistance of the Salvages; or any offence done to them.

The 2 of May our Admirall and our Pinnesse departed from Dominica leaving the John our Viceadmirall playing off and on about Dominica, hoping to take some Spaniard outwardes bound to the Indies; the same night we had sight of three smal Ilands called Los Santos, leaving Guadalupe and them on our starboord.

The 3 we had sight of S. Christophers Iland, bearing Northeast and by East off us.

On the 4 we sayled by the Virgines, which are many broken Ilands, lying at the East ende of S. Johns Iland: and the same day towards evening we landed upon one of them called Blanca, where we killed an incredible number of foules: here we stayed but three houres, & from thence stood into the shore Northwest, and having brought this Iland Southeast off us, we put towards night thorow an opening or swatch, called The passage, lying betwene the Virgines, and the East end of S. John: here the Pinnesse left us and sayled on the South side of S. John.

The 5 and 6 the Admirall sayled along the Northside of S. John, so neere the shore that the Spaniards discerned us to be men of warre; and therefore made fires along the coast as we sailed by, for so their custome is, when they see any men of warre on their coasts.

The 7 we landed on the Northwest end of S. John, where we watered in a good river called Yaguana, and the same night following we tooke a Frigate of tenne Tunne comming from Gwathanelo laden with hides and ginger. In this place Pedro a Mollato, who knewe all our state, ranne from us to the Spaniards.

On the 9 we departed from Yaguana.

The 13 we landed on an Iland called Mona, whereon were 10 or 12 houses inhabited of the Spaniards; these we burned & tooke from them a Pinnesse, which they had drawen a ground and sunke, and carried all her sayles, mastes, and rudders into the woods, because we should not take him away; we also chased the Spaniards over all the Iland; but they hid them in caves, hollow rockes, and bushes, so that we could not find them.

On the 14 we departed from Mona, and the next day after wee came to an Iland called Saona, about 5 leagues distant from Mona, lying on the Southside of Hispaniola neere the East end: betweene these two Ilands we lay off and on 4 or 5 dayes, hoping to take some of the Domingo fleete doubling this Iland, as a neerer way to Spaine then by Cape Tyburon, or by Cape S. Anthony.

On Thursday being the 19 our Viceadmirall, from whom we departed at Dominica, came to us at Saona, with whom we left a Spanish Frigate, and appointed him to lie off and on other five daies betweene Saona and Mona to the ende aforesaid; then we departed from them at Saona for Cape Tyburon. Here I was enformed that our men of the Viceadmirall, at their departure from Dominica brought away two young Salvages, which were the chiefe Casiques sonnes of that Countrey and part of Dominica, but they shortly after ran away from them at Santa Cruz Iland, where the Viceadmirall landed to take in ballast.

On the 21 the Admirall came to the Cape Tyburon, where we found the John Evangelist our Pinnesse staying for us: here we tooke in two Spaniards almost starved on the shore, who made a fire to our ships as we passed by. Those places for an 100 miles in length are nothing els but a desolate and meere wildernesse, without any habitation of people, and full of wilde Bulles and Bores, and great Serpents.

The 22 our Pinnesse came also to an anker in Aligato Bay at Cape Tyburon. Here we understood of M. Lane, Captaine of the Pinnesse; how he was set upon with one of the kings Gallies belonging to Santo Domingo, which was manned with 400 men, who after he had fought with him 3 or 4 houres, gave over the fight & forsooke him, without any great hurt done on eyther part.

The 26 the John our Vizadmirall came to us to cape Tyburon, and the Frigat which we left with him at Saona. This was the appointed place where we should attend for the meeting with the Santo Domingo Fleete.

On Whitsunday Even at Cape Tyburon one of our boyes ranne away from us, and at ten dayes end returned to our ships almost starved for want of food. In sundry places about this part of Cape Tyburon we found the bones and carkases of divers men, who had perished (as wee thought) by famine in those woods, being either stragled from their company, or landed there by some men of warre.

June

On the 14 of June we tooke a smal Spanish frigat which fell amongst us so suddenly, as he doubled the point at the Bay of Cape Tyburon, where we road, so that he could not escape us. This Frigat came from Santo Domingo, and had but 3 men in her, the one was an expert Pilot, the other a Mountainer, and the third a Vintener, who escaped all out of prison at Santo Domingo, purposing to fly to Yaguana which is a towne in the West parts of Hispaniola where many fugitive Spaniards are gathered together.

The 17 being Wednesday Captaine Lane was sent to Yaguana with his Pinnesse and a Frigat to take a shippe, which was there taking in fraight, as we understood by the old Pylot, whom we had taken three dayes before.

The 24 the Frigat returned from Captaine Lane at Yaguana, and brought us word to cape Tyburon, that Captaine Lane had taken the shippe, with many passengers and Negroes in the same; which proved not so rich a prize as we hoped for, for that a Frenchman of warre had taken and spoyled her before we came. Neverthelesse her loading was thought worth 1000 or 1300 pounds, being hides, ginger, Cannafistula, Copperpannes, and Casavi.

July

The second of July Edward Spicer whom we left in England came to us at Cape Tyburon, accompanied with a small Pinnesse, whereof one M. Harps was Captaine. And the same day we had sight of a fleete of 14 saile all of Santo Domingo, to whom we presently gave chase, but they upon the first sight of us fled, and separating themselves scattered here and there: Wherefore we were forced to divide our selves and so made after them untill 12 of the clocke at night. But then by reason of the darkenesse we lost sight of ech other, yet in the end the Admirall and the Moonelight happened to be together the same night at the fetching up of the Vizadmirall of the Spanish fleete, against whom the next morning we fought and tooke him, with losse of one of our men and two hurt, and of theirs 4 slaine and 6 hurt. But what was become of our Viceadmirall, our Pinnesse, and Prize, and two Frigates, in all this time, we were ignorant.

The 3 of July we spent about rifling, romaging and fitting the Prize to be sailed with us.

The 6 of July we saw Jamayca the which we left on our larboord, keeping Cuba in sight on our starboord.

Upon the 8 of July we saw the Iland of Pinos, which lieth on the Southside of Cuba nigh unto the West end or Cape called Cape S. Anthony. And the same day we gave chase to a Frigat, but at night we lost sight of her, partly by the slow sayling of our Admirall, & lacke of the Moonelight our Pinnesse, whom Captaine Cooke had sent to the Cape the day before.

On the 11 we came to Cape S. Anthony, where we found our consort the Moonelight and her Pinnesse abiding for our comming, of whom we understood that the day before there passed by them 22 saile, some of them of the burden of 300 and some 400 tunnes loaden with the Kings treasure from the maine, bound for Havana; from this 11 of July untill 22 we were much becalmed: and the winde being very scarse, and the weather exceeding hoat, we were much pestered with the Spaniards we had taken: wherefore we were driven to land all the Spaniards saving three, but the place where we landed them was of their owne choise on the Southside of Cuba neere unto the Organes and Rio de Puercos.

The 23 we had sight of the Cape of Florida, and the broken Ilands therof called the Martires.

The 25 being S. James day in the morning, we fell with the Matanças, a head-land 8 leagues towards the East of Havana, where we purposed to take fresh water in, and make our abode two or three dayes.

On Sunday the 26 of July plying too and fro betweene the Matanças and Havana, we were espied of three small Pinnasses of S. John de Ullua bound for Havana, which were exceeding richly loaden. These 3 Pinnasses came very boldly up unto us, and so continued untill they came within musket shot of us. And we supposed them to be Captaine Harps pinnesse, and two small Frigats taken by Captain Harpe: wherefore we shewed our flag. But they presently upon the sight of it turned about & made all the saile they could from us toward the shore, & kept themselves in so shallow water, that we were not able to follow them, and therefore gave them over with expence of shot & pouder to no purpose. But if we had not so rashly set out our flagge, we might have taken them all three, for they would not have knowen us before they had bene in our hands. This chase brought us so far to leeward as Havana: wherfore not finding any of our consorts at ye Matanças, we put over again to the cape of Florida, & from thence thorow the chanel of Bahama.

On the 28 the Cape of Florida bare West of us.

The 30 we lost sight of the coast of Florida, and stood to Sea for to gaine the helpe of the current which runneth much swifter a farre off then in sight of the coast. For from the Cape to Virginia all along the shore are none but eddie currents, settings to the South and Southwest.

The 31 our three ships were clearely disbocked, the great prize, the Admirall, and the Mooneshine, but our prize being thus disbocked departed from us without taking leave of our Admirall or consort, and sayled directly for England.

August

On the first of August the winde scanted, and from thence forward we had very fowle weather with much raine, thundering, and great spouts, which fell round about us nigh unto our ships.

The 3 we stoode againe in for the shore, and at midday we tooke the height of the same. The height of that place we found to be 34 degrees of latitude. Towards night we were within three leagues of the Low sandie Ilands West of Wokokon. But the weather continued so exceeding foule, that we could not come to an anker nye the coast: wherefore we stood off againe to Sea untill Monday the 9 of August.

On munday the storme ceased, and we had very great likelihood of faire weather: therefore we stood in againe for the shore: & came to an anker at 11 fadome in 35 degrees of latitude, within a mile of the shore, where we went on land on the narrow sandy Iland, being one of the Ilandes West of Wokokon: in this Iland we tooke in some fresh water and caught great store of fish in the shallow water. Betweene the maine (as we supposed) and that Iland it was but a mile over and three or foure foote deepe in most places.

On the 12 in the morning we departed from thence and toward night we came to an anker at the Northeast end of the Iland of Croatoan, by reason of a breach which we perceived to lie out two or three leagues into the Sea: here we road all that night.

The 13 in the morning before we wayed our ankers, our boates were sent to sound over this breach: our ships riding on the side thereof at 5 fadome; and a ships length from us we found but 4 and a quarter, and then deeping and shallowing for the space of two miles, so that sometimes we found 5 fadome, and by & by 7, and within two casts with the lead 9, & then 8, next cast 5, & then 6, & then 4, & then 9 againe, and deeper; but 3 fadome was the last, 2 leagues off from the shore. This breach is in 35 degr. & a halfe, & lyeth at the very Northeast point of Croatoan, wheras goeth a fret out of the maine Sea into the inner waters, which part the Ilandes and the maine land.

The 15 of August towards Evening we came to an anker at Hatorask, in 36 degr. and one third, in five fadom water, three leagues from the shore. At our first comming to anker on this shore we saw a great smoke rise in the Ile Raonoak neere the place where I left our Colony in the yeere 1587, which smoke put us in good hope that some of the Colony were there expecting my returne out of England.

The 16 and next morning our 2 boates went a shore, & Captaine Cooke, & Cap. Spicer, & their company with me, with intent to passe to the place at Raonoak where our countreymen were left. At our putting from the ship we commanded our Master gunner to make readie 2 Minions and a Falkon well loden, and to shoot them off with reasonable space betweene every shot, to the ende that their reportes might bee heard to the place where wee hoped to finde some of our people. This was accordingly performed, & our twoe boats put off unto the shore, in the Admirals boat we sounded all the way and found from our shippe untill we came within a mile of the shore nine,

eight, and seven fadome: but before we were halfe way betweene our ships and the shore we saw another great smoke to
the Southwest of Kindrikers mountes: we therefore thought
good to goe to that second smoke first: but it was much further
from the harbour where we landed, then we supposed it to be,
so that we were very sore tired before wee came to the smoke.
But that which grieved us more was that when we came to the
smoke, we found no man nor signe that any had bene there
lately, nor yet any fresh water in all this way to drinke. Being
thus wearied with this journey we returned to the harbour
where we left our boates, who in our absence had brought their
caske a shore for fresh water, so we deferred our going to
Roanoak untill the next morning, and caused some of those
saylers to digge in those sandie hills for fresh water whereof
we found very sufficient. That night wee returned aboord with
our boates and our whole company in safety.

The next morning being the 17 of August, our boates and
company were prepared againe to goe up to Roanoak, but Captaine Spicer had then sent his boat ashore for fresh water, by
meanes whereof it was ten of the clocke aforenoone before we
put from our ships which were then come to an anker within
two miles of the shore. The Admirals boat was halfe way
toward the shore, when Captaine Spicer put off from his ship.
The Admirals boat first passed the breach, but not without
some danger of sinking, for we had a sea brake into our boat
which filled us halfe full of water, but by the will of God and
carefull styrage of Captaine Cooke we came safe ashore, saving
onely that our furniture, victuals, match and powder were much
wet and spoyled. For at this time the winde blue at Northeast
and direct into the harbour so great a gale, that the Sea brake
extremely on the barre, and the tide went very forcibly at the
entrance. By that time our Admirals boate was halled ashore,
and most of our things taken out to dry, Captaine Spicer came
to the entrance of the breach with his mast standing up, and
was halfe passed over, but by the rash and undiscreet styrage of
Ralph Skinner his Masters mate, a very dangerous Sea brake
into their boate and overset them quite, the men kept the boat
some in it, and some hanging on it, but the next sea set the boat
on ground, where it beat so, that some of them were forced to
let goe their hold, hoping to wade ashore; but the Sea still beat

them downe, so that they could neither stand nor swimme, and the boat twise or thrise was turned the keele upward, whereon Captaine Spicer and Skinner hung until they sunke, & were seene no more. But foure that could swimme a litle kept themselves in deeper water and were saved by Captain Cookes meanes, who so soone as he saw their oversetting, stripped himselfe, and foure other that could swimme very well, & with all haste possible rowed unto them, & saved foure. They were a 11 in all, & 7 of the chiefest were drowned, whose names were Edward Spicer, Ralph Skinner, Edward Kelley, Thomas Bevis, Hance the Surgion, Edward Kelborne, Robert Coleman. This mischance did so much discomfort the saylers, that they were all of one mind not to goe any further to seeke the planters. But in the end by the commandement & perswasion of me and Captaine Cooke, they prepared the boates: and seeing the Captaine and me so resolute, they seemed much more willing. Our boates and all things fitted againe, we put off from Hatorask, being the number of 19 persons in both boates: but before we could get to the place, where our planters were left, it was so exceeding darke, that we overshot the place a quarter of a mile: there we espied towards the North end of the Iland ye light of a great fire thorow the woods, to the which we presently rowed: when wee came right over against it, we let fall our Grapnel neere the shore, & sounded with a trumpet a Call, & afterwardes many familiar English tunes of Songs, and called to them friendly; but we had no answere, we therefore landed at daybreake, and comming to the fire, we found the grasse & sundry rotten trees burning about the place. From hence we went thorow the woods to that part of the Iland directly over against Dasamongwepeuk, & from thence we returned by the water side, round about the North point of the Iland, untill we came to the place where I left our Colony in the yeere 1586. In all this way we saw in the sand the print of the Salvages feet of 2 or 3 sorts troaden ye night, and as we entred up the sandy banke upon a tree, in the very browe thereof were curiously carved these faire Romane letters C R O: which letters presently we knew to signifie the place, where I should find the planters seated, according to a secret token agreed upon betweene them & me at my last departure from them, which was, that in any wayes they should not faile to write or carve on the trees or posts of the dores the name of the place where they should be seated; for at my comming away they were prepared to remove from Roanoak 50 miles into the maine. Therefore at my departure from them in An. 1587 I willed them, that if they should happen to be distressed in any of those places, that then they should carve over the letters or name, a Crosse ✠ in this forme, but we found no such signe of distresse. And having well considered of this, we passed toward the place where they were left in sundry houses, but we found the houses taken downe, and the place very strongly enclosed with a high palisado of great trees, with cortynes and flankers very Fortlike, and one of the chiefe trees or postes at the right side of the entrance had the barke taken off, and 5 foote from the ground in fayre Capital letters was graven CROATOAN without any crosse or signe of distresse; this done, we entred into the palisado, where we found many barres of Iron, two pigges of Lead, foure yron fowlers, Iron sacker-shotte, and such like heavie things, throwen here and there, almost overgrowen with grasse and weedes. From thence wee went along by the water side, towards the poynt of the Creeke to see if we could find any of their botes or Pinnisse, but we could perceive no signe of them, nor any of the last Falkons and small Ordinance which were left with them, at my departure from them. At our returne from the Creeke, some of our Saylers meeting us, tolde us that they had found where divers chests had bene hidden, and long sithence digged up againe and broken up, and much of the goods in them spoyled and scattered about, but nothing left, of such things as the Savages knew any use of, undefaced. Presently Captaine Cooke and I went to the place, which was in the ende of an olde trench, made two yeeres past by Captaine Amadas: wheere wee found five Chests, that had bene carefully hidden of the Planters, and of the same chests three were my owne, and about the place many of my things spoyled and broken, and my bookes torne from the covers, the frames of some of my pictures and Mappes rotten and spoyled with rayne, and my armour almost eaten through with rust; this could bee no other but the deede of the Savages our enemies at Dasamongwepeuk, who had watched the departure of our men to Croatoan; and assoone as they were departed, digged up every place where they suspected any thing to be buried: but although it much grieved me to see such spoyle of my goods, yet on the other side I greatly joyed that I had safely found a certaine token of their safe being at Croatoan, which is the place where Manteo was borne, and the Savages of the Iland our friends.

When we had seene in this place so much as we could, we returned to our Boates, and departed from the shoare towards our Shippes, with as much speede as wee could: For the weather beganne to overcast, and very likely that a foule and stormie night would ensue. Therefore the same Evening with much danger and labour, we got our selves aboard, by which time the winde and seas were so greatly risen, that wee doubted our Cables and Anchors would scarcely holde untill Morning: wherefore the Captaine caused the Boate to be manned with five lusty men, who could swimme all well, and sent them to the little Iland on the right hand of the Harbour, to bring aboard sixe of our men, who had filled our caske with fresh water: the Boate the same night returned aboard with our men, but all our Caske ready filled they left behinde, unpossible to bee had aboard without danger of casting away both men and Boates: for this night prooved very stormie and foule.

The next Morning it was agreed by the Captaine and my selfe, with the Master and others, to wey anchor, and goe for the place at Croatoan, where our planters were: for that then the winde was good for that place, and also to leave that Caske with fresh water on shoare in the Iland untill our returne. So then they brought the cable to the Capston, but when the anchor was almost apecke, the Cable broke, by meanes whereof we lost another Anchor, wherewith we drove so fast into the shoare, that we were forced to let fall a third Anchor: which came so fast home that the Shippe was almost aground by Kenricks mounts: so that wee were forced to let slippe the Cable ende for ende. And if it had not chanced that wee had fallen into a chanell of deeper water, closer by the shoare then wee accompted of, wee could never have gone cleare of the poynt that lyeth to the Southwardes of Kenricks mounts. Being thus cleare of some dangers, and gotten into deeper waters, but not without some losse: for wee had but one Cable and Anchor left us of foure, and the weather grew to be fouler and fouler; our victuals scarse, and our caske and fresh water lost: it was therefore determined that we should goe for Saint John or some other Iland to the Southward for fresh water. And it was further purposed, that if wee could any wayes supply our wants of victuals and other necessaries, either at Hispaniola, Sant John, or Trynidad, that then wee should continue in the Indies all the Winter following, with hope to make 2. rich voyages of one, and at our returne to visit our countreymen at Virginia. The captaine and the whole company in the Admirall (with my earnest petitions) thereunto agreed, so that it rested onely to knowe what the Master of the Moone-light our consort would doe herein. But when we demanded them if they would accompany us in that new determination, they alledged that their weake and leake Shippe was not able to continue it; wherefore the same night we parted, leaving the Moone-light to goe directly for England, and the Admirall set his course for Trynidad, which course we kept two dayes.

On the 28. the winde changed, and it was sette on foule weather every way: but this storme brought the winde West and Northwest, and blewe so forcibly, that wee were able to beare no sayle, but our fore-course halfe mast high, wherewith wee ranne upon the winde perforce, the due course for England, for that wee were driven to change our first determination for Trynidad, and stoode for the Ilands of Açores, where wee purposed to take in fresh water, and also there hoped to meete with some English men of warre about those Ilands, at whose hands wee might obtaine some supply of our wants. And thus continuing our course for the Açores, sometimes with calmes, and sometimes with very scarce windes, on the fifteenth of September the winde came South Southeast, and blew so exceedingly, that wee were forced to lye atry all that day. At this time by account we judged our selves to be about twentie leagues to the West of Cuervo and Flores, but about night the storme ceased, and fayre weather ensued.

On Thursday the seventeenth wee saw Cuervo and Flores, but we could not come to anker that night, by reason the winde shifted. The next Morning being the eighteenth, standing in againe with Cuervo, we escryed a sayle ahead us, to whom we gave chase: but when wee came neere him, we knew him to be a Spanyard, and hoped to make sure purchase of him: but we understood at our speaking with him, that he was a prize, and of the Domingo fleete already taken by the John our consort, in the Indies. We learned also of this prize, that our Viceadmirall and Pinnesse had fought with the rest of the Domingo fleete, and had forced them with their Admirall to flee unto Jamaica under the Fort for succour, and some of them ran themselves aground, whereof one of them they brought away, and tooke out of some others so much as the time would permit. And further wee understood of them, that in their returne from Jamaica about the Organes neere Cape Saint Anthony, our Viceadmirall mette with two Shippes of the mayne land, come from Mexico, bound for Havana, with whom he fought: in which fight our Viceadmirals Lieutenant was slaine, and the Captaines right arme strooken off, with foure other of his men slaine, and sixteene hurt. But in the ende he entred, and tooke one of the Spanish shippes, which was so sore shot by us under water, that before they could take out her treasure she sunke; so that we lost thirteene Pipes of silver which sunke with her, besides much other rich marchandize. And in the meane time the other Spanish shippe being pearced with nine shotte under water, got away; whom our Viceadmirall intended to pursue: but some of their men in the toppe made certaine rockes, which they saw above water neere the shoare, to be Gallies of Havana and Cartagena, comming from Havana to rescue the two Ships; Wherefore they gave over their chase, and went for England. After this intelligence was given us by this our prize, he departed from us, and went for England.

On Saturday the 19. of September we came to an Ancre neere a small village on the North side of Flores, where we found ryding 5. English men of warre, of whom wee understood that our Viceadmirall and Prize were gone thence for England. One of these five was the Moonelight our consort, who upon the first sight of our comming into Flores, set sayle and went for England, not taking any leave of us.

On Sunday the 20. the Mary Rose, Admirall of the Queenes fleete, wherein was Generall Sir John Hawkins, stood in with Flores, and divers other of the Queenes ships, namely the Hope, the Nonpareilia, the Rainebow, the Swift-sure, the Foresight, with many other good merchants ships of warre, as the Edward Bonaventure, the Marchant Royal, the Amitie, the Eagle, the

Dainty of sir John Hawkins, and many other good ships and pinnesses, all attending to meete with the king of Spaines fleete, comming from Terra firma of the West Indies.

The 22. of September we went aboard the Raynebow, and towards night we spake with the Swift-sure, and gave him 3. pieces. The captaines desired our company; wherefore we willingly attended on them: who at this time with 10. other ships stood for Faial. But the Generall with the rest of the Fleete were separated from us, making two fleetes, for the surer meeting with the Spanish fleete.

On Wednesday the 23. we saw Gratiosa, where the Admiral and the rest of the Queenes fleete were come together. The Admirall put forth a flag of counsel, in which was determined that the whole fleete should go for the mayne, and spred themselves on the coasts of Spaine and Portugal, so farre as conveniently they might, for the surer meeting of the Spanish fleete in those parts.

The 26. we came to Faial, where the Admiral with some other of the fleete ankred, othersome plyed up and downe betweene that and the Pico untill midnight, at which time the Antony shot off a piece and weyed, shewing his light: after whom the whole fleete stood to the East, the winde at Northeast by East.

On Sunday the 27. towards Evening wee tooke our leave of the Admirall and the whole fleete, who stood to the East. But our shippe accompanied with a Flyboate stoode in againe with S. George, where we purposed to take in more fresh water, and some other fresh victuals.

On Wednesday the 30. of September, seeing the winde hang so Northerly, that wee could not atteine the Iland of S. George, we gave over our purpose to water there, and the next day framed our due course for England.

October

The 2. of October in the Morning we saw S. Michaels Iland on our Starre board quarter.

The 23. at 10. of the clocke afore noone, we saw Ushant in Britaigne.

On Saturday the 24. we came in safetie, God be thanked, to an anker at Plymmouth.

35

The examination of the Masters and Pilots which
saile in the Fleetes of Spaine to the West Indies:
Written in the Spanish tongue by Pedro Dias a
Spanish pilot taken by Sir Richard Grinville 1585

FIRST they make suit unto the Pilot major (who at this
present is called Alonzo de Chiavez) that he would admit them
to examination, because they are naturall Spaniards, and sufficient for the same.

Hereupon the Pilot major commandeth the party to be examined, to give information that he is a mariner, and well
practized in those parts, about which hee desireth to be examined. And then immediately he bringeth five or six pilots
before examined to give testimonie that he is a good mariner,
and sufficient to become a pilot, that he is a Spaniard borne,
and that he is not of the race of the Moores, Jewes or Negros.

Having made this information, hee presenteth it unto the
Pilot major. And the Pilot major seeing the information to be
good, willeth the Kings publique reader of navigation (who is
now Roderigo Zamorano) to admit him to his lectures. Whither
there doe resort foureteene or fifteene persons that desire to be
examined: and they come to a certaine house which the kings
reader hath appointed unto him for the same purpose, at eight
of the clocke in the morning: and then they stay two houres,
and two houres likewise in the afternoone: in one of which
houres Zamorano readeth unto them, and in the other they aske
one another many particulars concerning the art of navigation
in the presence of the said kings reader: and him that answereth
not to the purpose the sayd reader instructeth more perfectly,
and telleth him how everything is. And this exercise continueth
two moneths, during which time the examinates must not faile
to bee present twise in a day, as is aforesaid.

And having heard the kings reader those two moneths, they resort then unto the hall of examination which is in the Contractation house, where there are assembled the Pilot major and divers other pilots, to the number of 25 at the least; who all sitting there in order, the Pilot major demandeth of him that would be examined, of what part of the Indies he desireth to be examined: Whereto the examinate answereth, that he would bee examined concerning Nueva Espanna, or of Nombre de Dios and Tierra Firma. And others that are not experienced in those partes, crave to be examined of Santo Domingo, Puerto rico, and Cuba.

Then the Pilot major commandeth the examinate to spread a sea-chart upon the table, and in the presence of the other pilots to depart or shewe the course from the barre of Sant Lucar to the Canarie-Islands, and from thence to the Indies, till he come to that place whereof he is to bee examined, and then also to returne backe to the barre of Sant Lucar in Spaine, from whence he departed. Also the Pilot major asketh him, if when he saileth upon the sea, hee be taken with a contrary wind, what remedie he is to use, that his ship be not too much turmoiled upon the sea? And the examinate answereth him aswell as he can.

Then one of the other pilotes opposeth him about the rules of the Sunne and of the North-starre, and how hee ought to use the declination of the Sunne at all times of the yeere: whom the examinate is bound to answere in every thing that hee demandeth. Then another asketh him of the signes and markes of those lands which lye in his way to that haven whereof he is examined. And then another demandeth, that if his mastes should be broken by tempest, what remedy hee would use? Others aske him, if his ship should take a leake, to the hazarding of the lives of himselfe and his company, what remedy he would find to stop the same with least danger? Others aske him, what remedy, if his rudder should chance to faile? Others oppose him about the account of the Moone and of the tides? Others aske him if a Pirate should take him and leave him destitute of his Chart, his Astrolabe, and his other instruments serving to take the height of the Sunne and of the starre, what course hee would take in that extremitie? Others demand other questions needfull for a mariner to know, which desireth to be a pilot. Unto all which the examinate is very attentive, and answereth to every particular.

After they have all asked him so much as they think expedient, they bid him depart out of the hall, to the ende that every one of them may severally bee sworne upon a booke, that they will speake the trueth. Then they put into a certaine vessell of silver standing there for the same purpose so many beanes, and so many peason as there are pilots within the hall: and every one putting his hand into the vessell in order, he that thinketh the partie examined to be sufficient, taketh up a beane, and he that thinketh him not sufficient, taketh up a pease. And after that all have taken out what they please, the Pilot major looketh what voyces the examinate hath: and if he finde him to have as many voyces for him as against him, he commandeth him to make another voyage: but if he hath more voyces for him then against him, then they give him letters testimoniall of his examination signed by the Pilot major, by the kings reader, and the secretary, and sealed with the seale of the Contractation house. And upon the receipt of these letters testimoniall, the new pilot giveth a present unto the Pilot major, and the kings reader, for their gloves and hennes, every one according to his abilitie, which is ordinarily some two or three ducats.

And then he may take upon him to be pilot in any ship whatsoever, unto that place for which he was examined: and if he finde in the Indies any ship under the charge of a pilot not before examined, hee may put him out of his office, and may himself take charge of that ship for the same wages that the other pilot agreed for.

The pilots wages for making a voyage outward and homeward is according to the burthen of the ship. If she be of 100 tunnes, hee hath 200 or 250 ducats: and if shee bee of 400 or 500 tunnes, he taketh for his wages 500 or 550 ducates: and if she be bigger, he hath a greater allowance: over and besides all which, he hath every day while he remaineth on land, foure reals for his diet. And the greater shippes are alwayes committed unto the more ancient pilots, because they are of greater experience and better skill, then the yonger sort which newly take upon them to be pilots.

The pilot undertaketh no farther travell nor care, but in directing the course of navigation: for the masters of the ships take charge of the freighting and preparing their ships, and to pay the mariners, and to doe all things needefull for the ship; for the pilot commeth not unto the shippe, untill the visitours come to visite the same, to see whether he hath all things necessary for the voyage.

The visitours are foure men which are appoynted by the king, and these are men of great understanding: and they come to visite the shippes before they take in their lading, to see whether they be well prepared to make the voyage. And after the ships bee laden, they returne againe to visite them the second time, to see whether they have all things necessary, according to the orders of the Contractation house: and whether they have all their mariners, victuals, pouder, shot, and ordinance, and all other things necessary for the voyage. And if they want any thing, they charge them upon grievous penalties, to provide the same before they set out of the haven.

The ships that goe to the Indies are wont eche of them to have with them a Notarie, whose charge is to keepe a note of remembrance of all the marchandize which is laden in the ship, and to take the marks thereof, therby to deliver the commodities in the ship to their particular owners, after they have finished their voyage, and he serveth likewise to make willes, and other instruments, which are wont to be made by a Notarie, if any man chanceth to fall sicke. And his wages in eche voyage is as much as the wages of two mariners.

The Generall of the fleetes useth continually, after hee is arrived in the Indies, to send into Spaine a barke of Aviso, to advertise the king of the state of his arrivall; And after the fleetes be ready to come home, he dispatcheth another pinnesse of Aviso to certifie them how the fleetes are now ready to set saile, with other particularities. There go with the fleetes two great ships, the one as Admirall, the other as Viceadmirall, of the burthen of 400 or 500 tunnes, which carry nothing but victuals and souldiers for the wafting of the rest of the fleete, and these are payd out of the marchandize which come in the fleete, after the rate of one in the hundred, and sometime at one and an halfe in the hundred.

There is in the Contractation house of Sivil a table which serveth for an Aranzel, or table of rate or taxation, written in letters of gold, wherein the values of all kind of marchandize, which are embarqued for the Indies, are set downe.

By this table a man may know how many Botijas or jarres make a tunne of wine, or how many packes, or how many quintals, or how many barrels, or how many chests make a tunne.

And all marchandize have their rates set downe, to pay the king his customes and the Master his due fraight.

And therein is set up in writing that no Master may carry any passenger to the Indies, without licence, especially no learned men, nor any fryer, or clergyman, nor any body else without licence of the king: nor any strangers not borne in the kingdomes of Spaine.

Moreover, that they may not carry away any marchandize not comprized in the foresaid orders, under paine of death: and that all goods which they carry with them, they ought to carry the same registred; under paine of death.

Furthermore, that no Master nor Pilot may carry any Chart, nor Astrolabe, nor Crosse-staffe, nor regiment, without they bee signed and sealed by the Pilot major Alonzo de Chiavez, and the Cosmographer the kings reader Rodrigo Zamorano.

Moreover, that going in company with the fleete, they doe and obey all such things, as their Generall shall command them, under paine of death.

> Written by me Pedro Dias borne in the Isle of Palma one of the Canaries, upon the request and gratifica-tion of M. Richard Hakluyt, in February 1586.

36

---◆◆---

An excellent ruttier for the Islands of the West Indies,
and for Tierra firma, and Nueva Espanna

I F a man depart from the barre of S. Lucar in Summer time,
hee must steere Southwest until hee hath sight of Punta de
Naga, which is in the Isle of Tenerif. The markes to know it be
these. An high point sloping to the sea, & at the Easter point it
hath two down falles like particions, and they shew to be
separated from the maine of the Island & stand in 28 degrees
& a halfe. And if thou wilt have sight of the Grand Canaria,
and findest thy selfe with Punta de Naga, thou shalt then steere
Southwest and by South, and so thou shalt have sight of Canaria
which standeth in 28 degrees. And thou must come to ankor
on the Southeast side of the Island. But I advise thee, if it be
in winter time, that thou keepe another course, and that as
followeth.

*The course that a man must keepe departing in winter for
the Indies from Sant Lucar*

Departing from Sant Lucar in winter thou shalt goe West and
by South keeping along the coast, because if thou goe farre from
the coast, thou shalt meete with the wind off the sea untill thou
be as high shot as Cape Cantin, which is a low flat cape with
the sea. And thou shalt see a great wood before thou come at
this cape, called Casa del Cavallero. And from thence thou
shalt steere thy olde course, that is Southwest and by South for
the Isles of Alegranza, and Lancerota; and when thou art
North and South with Alegranza, thou shalt steere thence
Southwest, and so thou shalt see the Canaria, which is a round
high land, and standeth in twentie eight degrees.

What thou must doe if a contrary wind take thee fiftie leagues off the shore

When thou art fifty leagues shot on thy way into the sea Southwest off, and there thou chance to meete with a contrary winde off the sea, and if it force thee to put roome, then thou shalt steere Northeast and by East, and shalt hall with sight of Cabos del Plata, which shew when thou art a seaboord so farre as thou mayest descrie them, to be like two points of white sand: and if it be cleere thou shalt see within the land certain high hilles lying Northwest and by West called las Sierras de Zahara, and being three leagues from land thou shalt have thirtie fadomes water, and sand: And from thence to the bay of Cadiz thou shalt goe along Northwest by the coast: and if thou be in thirtie or forty fadomes, thou shalt have oaze; but if thou bee in lesse then thirtie fadomes, thou shalt have other sounding; which if it chance, then thou art against S. Pedro. And if it bee by day thou shalt see the Ermitage of Sant Sebastian, which seemeth to be a shippe under sayle. And thou shalt goe into the bay taking heede of the Puercos, give them a good birth off. And if thou chance to bee benighted when thou fallest with the bay, and wouldest goe into the bay, thou shalt carie thy lead in thy hand, and be sounding: and finding thy selfe in rockie ground, thou shalt steere North because of shunning the Puercos: and yet give them not too great a birth because of The Diamant, and so thou mayest goe in, sounding when thou thinkest good. And being benighted and then not East and West with the bay, and if thou doest not goe into it, then make the largest boord thou canst keeping off till day.

If thou be at the Canaries and wouldest sayle to Nueva Espanna, thou shalt sayle foure and twenty houres South because of the calmes of Fierro. And from thence thou shalt goe Westsouthwest, untill thou finde thy selfe in twenty degrees. And then thou must goe West and by South, which is the course for the Isle Deseada. And from Deseada thou shalt goe West and by North, because of the variation of the compasse. And falling with Deseada, thou shalt finde it to rise low with the sea: and it standeth in 15 degrees. And the eastermost part is the sharpest, and smaller then the West point.

And if thou art going for Tierra firma, thou shalt goe West

and by South untill thou come to Dominica, and there on the Northwest side is a river, where thou mayest water. The marks to know it bee a certaine high land full of hilles. And seeing it when thou art farre off to the seaward, it maketh in the middest a partition; so that a man would thinke it devided the Island in two parts. And this Island standeth in 14 degrees and a halfe.

I advise thee that if thou wouldest goe for Nueva Espanna, and so doest passe betweene Guadalupe and Monserate to the Westward, that being thus open off the entrance betwixt them thou shalt go Westnorthwest, and so shalt have sight of Santa Cruz, which standeth in seventeene degrees and a halfe. And the markes to know it be these. It is an Island not very high, and lyeth East and West, and at the East end it is lower then at the West end.

And going forward on thy course thou shalt runne West-northwest, and so thou shalt goe to have sight of the Isle of San Juan de Puerto rico, which is an Island lying East and West, and standeth in eighteene degrees. And the markes be these. That on the West end it is lowest, and the Eastermost is the highest. And if thou fall with the middest of the Island, then thou shalt goe a long it to the West unto Cabo Roxo, which is the end of the Isle. And from thence the coast runneth North to Punta Aguada. Cape Roxo hath certaine red cliffes. Thou must steere West and by South from Cape Roxo to find Mona, and so thou shalt have sight of Mona. And the marks thereof be these, it is a low land lying East and West: and on the East end it is highest, it hath a slope towards the sea, and standeth in 18. degrees, rather lesse then more. And if it be by day, then thou shalt runne West and shalt see Saona: which is an Island lying without Hispaniola, and lyeth East and West, and is full of trees; and hath certaine sandy bayes. And if it bee cleere weather thou shalt see within the land of Hispaniola certaine hie hils called las Sierras de Yguey. And being benighted upon Mona, then thou shalt steere West and by South, because of certaine shoalds that lye off Saona: but having day light and no sight of land, thou shalt loofe up Northwest and so passe by it, and as thou goest along the coast of Hispaniola, and seest the sea to be cast up into the aire, then thou shalt be about 10 leagues off the harbour of Santo Domingo, and these mountings up are called The Spoutes.

But I advise thee, that if thou bee benighted when thou
fallest with Santo Domingo, then thou must keepe the hils called
Sierras de las minas viejas to the Northwest. And if thou
wouldest goe into Santo Domingo, and meetest there with a
forcible Northerly wind, then the best way is to runne East till
it be day. And having daylight thou shalt cast about, and so
thou must ply to wind-ward untill the Northerly wind be done:
and when it is past, make all the saile thou canst to hale with
the sight of Calle de las Damas: and when thou hast sight
thereof thou shalt lye with thy stemme with a sandie Bay,
which lyeth on the other side: and thou must take in thy maine
saile, and go so till thou bring thy selfe open with the midst of
the river; and so having opened the river, thou must go with
great care in the middest of the same, with all thy sailes up,
except thy maine saile, and thou must have thy boat out, if it
be needefull to sound or to tow thy ship, if she cast too much to
the loofe, for the currents will cast here to the loofe: wherefore
bee sure to have thy boat out to helpe thy steerage: and this is
the way whereby thou must worke.

The course from Santo Domingo to go for Nueva Espanna

I advise thee that if thou wilt goe from Santo Domingo for
Nueva Espanna, thou shalt goe Southwest and by South, and
so thou shalt have sight of Punta de Nizao, which is a low
point, and is the end of the hilles called Sierras de las minas
Viejas, and towards the Northwest of them thou shalt see a
lowe land, and to goe into Hocoa thou shalt stirre from this
poynt of Nizao Westnorthwest, and thou shalt see the point of
Puerto Hermoso, and the Bay that it maketh: and thou must
be sure to keepe neere the shore to find a good road, and feare
not to go neere the land: for all is deepe water, and cleare
ground, and let not fall thine anker til thou be past all the
rivers; and beware of the land, for if thou ride much without,
thy anker wil come home, because it is rocky and flatte ground.
And thou must be ready, that when thine anker commeth
home, thou have thy moarings readie in thy boat to carry on
shore with foure or five men, and if thou thinke good, thou
mayest let them fall on land with a rope. And when thou art
come to anker thou mayest send on shore to moare, so shalt
thou best be moared.

37

A summarie and true discourse of sir Francis Drakes
West Indian voyage, begun in the yeere 1585.
Wherein were taken the cities of Saint Iago, Santo
Domingo, Cartagena, and the towne of Saint
Augustine in Florida; Published by M. Thomas Cates

THIS worthy knight for the service of his Prince and countrey
having prepared his whole fleete, and gotten them downe to Plimmouth in Devonshire, to the number of five and twenty saile of
ships and pinnesses, and having assembled of souldiers and
marines, to the number of 2300. in the whole, embarked them
and himselfe at Plimmouth aforesaid, the 12. day of September
1585. being accompanied with these men of name and charge,
which hereafter follow:

Master Christopher Carleil Lieutenant general, a man of long
experience in the warres as well by sea as land, who had
formerly caried high offices in both kindes in many fights,
which he discharged alwaies very happily, and with great good
reputation.

Anthonie Powel Sergeant Major.

Captaine Matthew Morgan, and Captaine John Sampson,
Corporals of the field.

These officers had commandement over the rest of the landCaptaines, whose names hereafter follow.

Captaine Anthony Plat   Captaine John Merchant
Captaine Edward Winter   Captaine William Cecill
Captaine John Goring   Captaine Walter Bigs
Captaine Robert Pew   Captaine John Hannam
Captaine George Barton   Captaine Richard Stanton

Captaine Martine Frobisher Viceadmirall, a man of great experience in sea-faring actions, who had caried the chiefe charge of many ships himselfe, in sundry voyages before, being now shipped in the Primrose.

Captaine Francis Knolles, Reereadmirall in the Galeon Leicester.

Master Thomas Vennor Captaine in the Elizabeth Bonadventure under the Generall.

Master Edward Winter Captaine in the Aide.

Master Christopher Carleil the Lieutenant generall, Captaine of the Tygar.

Henry White Captaine of the sea Dragon.
Thomas Drake Captaine of the Thomas.
Thomas Seelie Captaine of the Minion.
Baily Captaine of the Barke Talbot.
Robert Crosse Captaine of the Bark Bond.
George Fortescue Captaine of the Barke Bonner.
Edward Carelesse Captaine of the Hope.
James Erizo Captaine of the White Lyon.
Thomas Moone Captaine of the Francis.
John Rivers Captaine of the Vantage.
John Vaughan Captaine of the Drake.
John Varney Captaine of the George.
John Martin Captaine of the Benjamin.
Edward Gilman Captaine of the Skout.
Richard Hawkins Captaine of the Galiot called the Ducke.
Bitfield Captaine of the Swallow.

After our going hence, which was the foureteenth of September, in the yeere of our Lord 1585. and taking our course towards Spaine, wee had the winde for a fewe dayes somewhat skant, and sometimes calme. And being arrived neere that part of Spaine, which is called the Moores, wee happened to espie divers sailes, which kept their course close by the shore, the weather being faire and calme. The Generall caused the Viceadmirall to goe with the pinnesses well manned to see what they were, who upon sight of the said pinnesses approching neere unto them, abandoned for the most part all their ships (being Frenchmen) laden all with salt, and bound homewards into France, amongst which ships (being all of small burthen) there was one so wel liked, which also had no man in her, as being brought unto ye general, he thought good to make stay of her for the service, meaning to pay for her, as also accordingly he performed at our returne: which barke was called the Drake. The rest of these ships (being eight or nine) were dismissed without any thing at all taken from them. Who being afterwardes put somewhat farther off from the shore, by the contrariety of the wind, we happened to meet with some other French ships, full laden with Newland fish, being upon their returne homeward from the said Newfoundland: whom the Generall after some speech had with them (and seeing plainly that they were Frenchmen) dismissed, without once suffering any man to go aboord of them.

The day following standing in with the shore againe, we discried another tall ship of twelve score tunnes or thereaboutes, upon whom Master Carliel the Lieutenant generall being in the Tygar, undertooke the chase, whom also anon after the Admirall followed, and the Tygar having caused the said strange ship to strike her sailes, kept her there without suffering any body to go aboord untill the Admirall was come up: who forthwith sending for the Master, and divers others of their principall men, and causing them to be severally examined, found the ship and goods to be belonging to the inhabitants of S. Sebastian in Spaine, but the mariners to bee for the most part belonging to S. John de Luz, and the Passage. In this ship was great store of dry Newland fish, commonly called with us Poore John, whereof afterwards (being thus found a lawfull prize) there was distribution made into all the ships of the fleet, the same being so new and good, as it did very greatly bestead us in the whole course of our voyage. A day or two after the taking of this ship, we put in within the Isles of Bayon, for lacke of favourable wind: where wee had no sooner ankered some part of the fleete, but the Generall commanded all the pinnesses with the shipboats to be manned, and every man to be furnished with such armes as were needful for that present service; which being done, the Generall put himselfe into his gallie, which was also well furnished, and rowing towards the city of Bayon, with intent, and the favour of the Almighty to surprise it, before we had advanced one halfe league of our way, there came a messenger being an English merchant from the Governour, to see what strange fleet we were, who came to our General, conferred a while with him, and after a small time spent, our Generall called for Captaine Sampson, and willed him to go to the Governour of the citie, to resolve him of two points. The first, to know if there were any warres betweene Spaine and England. The second, why our marchants with their goods were embarged or arrested. Thus departed captain Sampson with the said messenger to the citie, where he found the governour & people much amazed of such a sudden accident.

The Generall with the advise and counsell of M. Carleil his Lieutenant generall, who was in the galley with him, thought not good to make any stand, till such time as they were within the shot of the citie, where they might bee ready upon the returne of Captaine Sampson, to make a sudden attempt if cause did require before it were darke.

Captaine Sampson returned with his message in this sort. First, touching peace or warres the Governour said he knew of no warres, and that it lay not in him to make any, hee being so meane a subject as he was. And as for the stay of the merchants with their goods, it was the kings pleasure, but not with intent to endomage any man. And that the kings countercommandement was (which had bene received in that place some sevennight before) that English merchants with their goods should be discharged: for the more verifying wherof, he sent such merchants as were in the towne of our nation, who traffiqued those parts: which being at large declared to our General by them, counsell was taken what might best be done. And for that the night approched, it was thought needful to land our forces, which was done in the shutting up of the day, & having quartered our selves to our most advantage, with sufficient gard upon every strait, we thought to rest our selves for that night there. The Governour sent us some refreshing, as bread, wine, oyle, apples, grapes, marmalad and such like. About midnight the weather beganne to overcast, insomuch that it was thought meeter to repaire aboord, then to make any longer abode on land, and before wee could recover the Fleete, a great tempest arose, which caused many of our shippes to drive from their anker-hold, and some were forced to sea in great perill, as the barke Talbot, the barke Hawkins, and the Speedewell, which Speedewel was onely driven into England, the others recovered us againe: the extremitie of the storm lasted three dayes, which no sooner began to asswage, but M. Carleil our Lieutenant generall was sent with his owne shippe and three others: as also with the gallie and with divers pinnesses, to see what he might doe above Vigo, where hee tooke many boates and some caravels, diversly laden with things of small value, but chiefly with houshold stuffe running into the high countrey, and amongst the rest, he found one boat laden with the principal churchstuffe of the high Church of Vigo, where also was their great crosse of silver, of very faire embossed worke, and double gilt all over, having cost them a great masse of money. They complained to have lost in all kind of goods above thirty thousand duckets in this place.

The next day the Generall with his whole fleete went from up the Isles of Bayon, to a very good harbour above Vigo, where M. Carleil stayed his comming, aswell for the more quiet riding of his ships, as also for the good commoditie of fresh watering, which the place there did afourd full well. In the meane time the Governour of Galicia had reared such forces as hee might, his numbers by estimate were some two thousand foot, and three hundred horse, and marched from Bayon to this part of the countrey, which lay in sight of our fleete, where making a stand, he sent to parley with our Generall, which was granted by our Generall, so it might bee in boats upon the water: and for safetie of their persons, there were pledges delivered on both sides: which done, the Governor of Galicia put himselfe with two others into our Viceadmirals skiffe, the same having bene sent to the shore for him, and in like sort our Generall went in his owne skiffe; where it was by them agreed, we should furnish our selves with fresh water, to be taken by our owne people quietly on the land, and have all other such necessaries, paying for the same, as the place would affourd.

When all our businesse was ended, wee departed, and tooke our way by the Islands of Canaria, which are esteemed some three hundred leagues from this part of Spaine, and falling purposely with Palma, with intention to have taken our pleasure of that place, for the full digesting of many things into order, and the better furnishing our store with such severall good things as it affourdeth very abundantly, we were forced by the vile Sea-gate, which at that present fell out, and by the naughtinesse of the landing place, being but one, and that under the favour of many platformes well furnished with great ordinance, to depart with the receit of many of their Canon-shot, some into our ships, and some besides, some of them being in very deede full Canon high. But the only or chiefe mischiefe was the dangerous sea-surge, which at shore all alongst plainly threatned the overthrow of as many pinnesses and boates, as for that time should have attempted any landing at all.

Now seeing the expectation of this attempt frustrated by the causes aforesaid, we thought it meeter to fall with the Isle Hierro, to see if we could find any better fortune: and comming to the Island, we landed a thousand men in a valley under a high mountaine, where we stayed some two or three houres, in which time the inhabitants, accompanied with a yong fellow borne in England, who dwelt there with them, came unto us, shewing their state to be so poore, that they were all ready to starve, which was not untrue: and therefore without any thing gotten, we were all commanded presently to imbarke, so as that night wee put off to sea Southsoutheast along towards the coast of Barbary.

Upon Saturday in the morning, being the 13. of November, we fell with Cape Blanke, which is a low land and shallow water, where we catched store of fish, and doubling the Cape, we put into the Bay, where we found certaine French ships of warre, whom wee entertained with great courtesie, and there left them. This afternoone the whole fleet assembled, which was a little scattered about their fishing, and put from thence to the Isles of Cape Verde, sailing till the 16. of the same moneth in the morning, on which day we discried the Island of S. Iago, and in the evening we ankered the fleet between the towne called the Playa or Praya, and S. Iago, where we put on shore 1000. men or more, under the leading of M. Christopher Carleil Lieutenant general, who directed the service most like a wise commander. The place where we had first to march did affourd no good order, for the ground was mountainous & full of dales, being a very stony and troublesome passage; but such was his industrious disposition, as he would never leave, untill wee had gotten up to a faire plain, where we made stand for the assembling of the army. And when we were al gathered together upon the plaine, some 2 miles from the town, the lieutenant general thought good not to make attempt til daylight: because there was not one that could serve for guid or giving knowledge at al of ye place. And therfore after having wel rested, even halfe an houre before day, he commanded the army to be divided into 3 speciall parts, such as he appointed, wheras before we had marched by several companies, being therunto forced by the badnesse of the way as is aforesaid.

Now by the time wee were thus ranged into a very brave order, daylight began to appeare, and being advanced hard to the wall, we saw no enemie to resist, whereupon the Lieutenant generall appointed Captaine Sampson with thirtie shot, and Captaine Barton with other thirtie, to goe downe into the towne which stood in the valley under us, and might very plainely bee viewed all over from that place where the whole Army was now arrived: and presently after these Captaines was sent the great ensigne, which had nothing in it but the plaine English crosse, to be placed towardes the Sea, that our Fleet might see Saint Georges cross florish in the enemies fortresse. Order was given that all the ordinance throughout the towne and upon all the platformes, which were above fiftie pieces all ready charged, should be shot off in honour of the Queenes Majesties coronation day, being the seventeenth of November, after the yeerely custome of England, which was so answered againe by the ordinance out of all the ships in the fleete which now was come neere, as it was strange to heare such a thundering noyse last so long together. In this meane while the Lieutenant generall held still the most part of his force on the hill top, till such time as the towne was quartered out for the lodging of the whole Armie: which being done every captaine tooke his own quarter, and in the evening was placed such a sufficient gard upon every part of the towne that we had no cause to feare any present enemie.

Thus we continued in the citie the space of 14. dayes, taking such spoiles as the place yeelded, which were for the most part, wine, oyle, meale, and some such like things for victuall, as vineger, olives, and some such other trash, as merchandise for their Indians trades. But there was not found any treasure at all, or any thing else of worth besides.

The situation of S. Iago is somewhat strange, in forme like a triangle, having on the East and West sides two mountaines of rocke and cliffe, as it were hanging over it, upon the top of which two mountaines were builded certaine fortifications to preserve the towne from any harme that might bee offered, as in a plot is plainely shewed. From thence, on the South side of the towne is the maine sea, and on the North side, the valley lying betweene the foresayd mountaines, wherein the towne standeth: the said valley & towne both do grow very narrow, insomuch that the space betweene the two cliffes of this end of the towne is estimated not to be above 10. or 12. score over.

In the middest of the valley commeth downe a riveret, rill, or brooke of fresh water, which hard by the sea side maketh a pond or poole, whereout our ships were watered with very great ease and pleasure. Somewhat above the towne on the North side betweene the two mountaines, the valley waxeth somewhat larger then at the townes end, which valley is wholly converted into gardens and orchards well replenished with divers sorts of fruites, herbes and trees, as lymmons, orenges, sugarcanes, cochars or cochos nuts, plantans, potato-rootes, cucumbers, small and round onions, garlicke, and some other things not now remembered, amongst which the cochos nuts, and plantans are very pleasant fruites, the saide cochos hath a hard shell and a greene huske over it, as hath our walnut, but it farre exceedeth in greatnesse, for this cochos in his greene huske is bigger than any mans two fistes: of the hard shell many drinking cups are made here in England, and set in silver as I have often seene.

Next within this hard shell is a white rine resembling in shewe very much even as any thing may do, to the white of an egge when it is hard boyled. And within this white of the nut lyeth a water, which is whitish and very cleere, to the quantitie of halfe a pynt or thereaboutes, which water and white rine before spoken of, are both of a very coole fresh tast, and as pleasing as any thing may be. I have heard some hold opinion, that it is very restorative.

The plantan groweth in cods, somewhat like to beanes, but is bigger and longer, and much more thicke together on the stalke, and when it waxeth ripe, the meate which filleth the rine of the cod becommeth yellow, and is exceeding sweet and pleasant.

In this time of our being there hapned to come a Portugall to the Westerne fort, with a flag of truce, to whom Captaine

Sampson was sent with Captaine Goring, who comming to the
said messenger, he first asked them what nation they were, they
answered Englishmen, hee then required to knowe if warres
were betweene England and Spaine, to which they answered
that they knew not, but if he would goe to their Generall he
could best resolve him of such particulars, and for his assurance of passage and repassage, these Captaines made offer to
ingage their credits, which he refused for that he was not sent
from his Governor. Then they told him, if his Governor did desire to take a course for the common benefit of the people and
countrey, his best way were to come and present himselfe unto
our noble and mercifull Governour sir Francis Drake, whereby
hee might bee assured to find favour, both for himselfe and
the inhabitantes. Otherwise within three dayes wee should
march over the land, and consume with fire all inhabited places,
and put to the sword all such living soules as wee shoulde
chance upon: so thus much he tooke for the conclusion of his
answere, and departing, hee promised to returne the next day,
but we never heard more of him.

Upon the foure and twentieth of November, the Generall accompanied with the lieutenant generall and six hundred men
marched foorth to a village twelve miles within the land, called
Saint Domingo, where the Governour and the Bishoppe with
all the better sort were lodged, and by eight of the clocke wee
came to it, finding the place abandoned, and the people fled
into the mountaines: so we made stand a while to ease our
selves, and partly to see if any would come to speake to us.

After we had well rested our selves, the Generall commaunded the troupes to march away homewards, in which re-
treat the enemie shewed themselves, both horse and foote,
though not such force as durst encounter us: and so in passing
sometime at the gase with them, it waxed late and towards night
before we could recover home to S. Iago.

On Munday the sixe and twentieth of November, the Generall commaunded all the pinnesses with the boates, to use all
diligence to imbarke the Armie into such shippes as every man
belonged. The Lieutenant generall in like sort commanded Captaine Goring and Lieutenant Tucker, with one hundred shot to
make a stand in the market place, untill our forces were wholly
imbarked, the viceadmiral making stay with his pinnesse & cer-

taine boats in the harbour, to bring the sayd last companie aboord the ships. Also the Generall willed forthwith the gallie with two pinnesses to take into them the company of Captaine Barton, and the company of Captaine Bigs, under the leading of captaine Sampson, to seeke out such munition as was hidden in the ground, at the towne of Praya or Playa, having bene promised to be shewed it by a prisoner, which was taken the day before.

The Captaines aforesayd comming to the Playa, landed their men, and having placed the troupe in their best strength, Captaine Sampson tooke the prisoner, and willed him to shewe that hee had promised, the which he could not, or at least would not: but they searching all suspected places, found two pieces of ordinance, one of yron, an other of brasse. In the after noone the Generall ankered with the rest of the Fleet before the Playa, comming himselfe ashore, willing us to burne the towne and make all haste aboord, the which was done by sixe of the clocke the same day, and our selves imbarked againe the same night, and so we put off to Sea Southwest.

But before our departure from the towne of S. Iago, wee established orders for the better government of the Army, every man mustered to his captaine, and othes were ministred to acknowledge her Majestie supreme Governour, as also every man to doe his uttermost endevour to advance the service of the action, and to yeeld due obedience unto the directions of the Generall and his officers. By this provident counsell, and laying downe this good foundation before hand, all things went forward in a due course, to the atchieving of our happy enterprise.

In all the time of our being here, neither the Governour for the king of Spaine, (which is a Portugall) neither the Bishop, whose authoritie is great, neither the inhabitants of the towne, or Island ever came at us (which we expected they should have done) to intreate us to leave them some part of their needfull provisions, or at the least, to spare the ruining of their towne at our going away. The cause of this their unreasonable distrust (as I doe take it) was the fresh remembrance of the great wrongs they had done to old M. William Hawkins of Plimmouth, in the voyage he made 4. or 5. yeeres before, when as they did both breake their promise, and murthered many of his men, whereof I judge you have understood, & therefore it is needlesse to be repeated. But since they came not at us, we left written in sundry places, as also in the spittle house, (which building was only appointed to be spared) the great discontentment & scorne we tooke at this their refraining to come unto us, as also at the rude maner of killing, & savage kind of handling the dead body of one of our boyes found by them stragling al alone, from whom they had taken his head and heart, and had stragled the other bowels about the place, in a most brutish and beastly maner.

In revenge whereof at our departing we consumed with fire all the houses, aswell in the countrey which we saw, as in the towne of S. Iago.

From hence putting off to the West Indies, wee were not many dayes at Sea, but there beganne among our people such mortalitie, as in fewe dayes there were dead above two or three hundred men. And until some seven or eight dayes after our comming from S. Iago, there had not died any one man of sicknesse in all the fleete: the sicknesse shewed not his infection wherewith so many were stroken, untill we were departed thence, and then seazed our people with extreme hot burning and continuall agues, whereof very fewe escaped with life, and yet those for the most part not without great alteration and decay of their wittes and strength for a long time after. In some that died were plainely shewed the small spots, which are often found upon those that be infected with the plague: wee were not above eighteene dayes in passage betweene the sight of Saint Iago aforesaid, and the Island of Dominica, being the first Island of the West Indies that we fell withall, the same being inhabited with savage people, which goe all naked, their skinne coloured with some painting of a reddish tawney, very personable and handsome strong men, who doe admit litle conversation with the Spanyards: for as some of our people might understand them, they had a Spaniard or twaine prisoners with them, neither doe I thinke that there is any safetie for any of our nation, or any other to be within the limits of their commandement, albeit they used us very kindly for those few houres of time which wee spent with them, helping our folkes to fill and carry on their bare shoulders fresh water from the river to our ships boates, and fetching from their houses great store of Tabacco, as also a kind of bread which they fed on, called Cassavi, very white and savourie, made of the rootes of Cassavi. In recompence whereof, we bestowed liberall rewards of glasse, coloured beades, and other things, which we had found at Saint Iago, wherewith (as it seemed) they rested very greatly satisfied, and shewed some sorowfull countenance when they perceived that we would depart.

From hence wee went to another Island Westward of it, called Saint Christophers Island, wherein we spent some dayes of Christmas, to refresh our sicke people, and to cleanse and ayre our ships. In which Island were not any people at all that we could heare of.

In which time by the General it was advised and resolved, with the consent of the Lieutenant generall, the Vice-admiral, and all the rest of the Captaines to proceede to the great Islande of Hispaniola, aswell for that we knewe our selves then to bee in our best strength, as also the rather allured thereunto, by the glorious fame of the citie of S. Domingo, being the ancientest and chiefe inhabited place in all the tract of Countrey thereabouts. And so proceeding in this determination, by the way we mette a small Frigat, bound for the same place, the which the Vice-admirall tooke: and having duely examined the men that were in her, there was one found, by whom wee were advertised, the Haven to be a barren Haven, and the shore or land thereof to bee well fortified, having a Castle thereupon furnished with great store of Artillerie, without the danger whereof was no convenient landing place within ten English miles of the Citie, to which the sayd Pilot tooke upon him to conduct us.

All things being thus considered on, the whole forces were commaunded in the Evening to embarke themselves in Pinnesses, boats, and other small barkes appoynted for this service. Our souldiers being thus imbarked, the Generall put himselfe into the barke Francis as Admirall, and all this night we lay on the sea, bearing small saile untill our arrivall to the landing place, which was about the breaking of the day, and so we landed, being Newyeeres day, nine or ten miles to the Westwards of that brave Citie of S. Domingo: for at that time nor yet is knowen to us any landing place, where the sea-surge doth not threaten to overset a Pinnesse or boate. Our Generall having seene us all landed in safetie, returned to his Fleete, bequeathing us to God, and the good conduct of Master Carliell our Lieutenant Generall: at which time, being about eight of the clocke, we began to march, and about noone time, or towards one of the clocke, we approched the towne, where the Gentlemen and those of the better sort, being some hundred and fiftie brave horses or rather more, began to present themselves but our small shot played upon them, which were so susteined with good proportion of pikes in all parts, as they finding no part of our troope unprepared to receive them (for you must understand they viewed all round about) they were thus driven to give us leave to proceed towards the two gates of the towne, which were the next to the seaward. They had manned them both, and planted their ordinance for that present, and sudden alarme without the gate, and also some troopes of small shot in Ambuscado upon the hie way side. We divided our whole force, being some thousand or twelve hundred men into two partes, to enterprise both the gates at one instant, the Lieutenant Generall having openly vowed to Captaine Powel (who led the troope that entred the other gate) that with Gods good favour he would not rest untill our meeting in the market place.

Their ordinance had no sooner discharged upon our neere approch, and made some execution amongst us, though not much, but the Lieutenant generall began forthwith to advance both his voice of encouragement, and pace of marching: the first man that was slaine with the ordinance being very neere unto himselfe: and thereupon hasted all that hee might, to keepe them from the recharging of the ordinance. And notwithstanding their Ambuscados, we marched or rather ran so roundly in to them, as pell mell we entred the gates, and gave them more care every man to save himselfe by flight, then reason to stand any longer to their broken fight. Wee forthwith repayred to the market place: but to be more truely understood, a place of very faire spacious square ground, whither also came as had bene agreed Captaine Powel with the other troope: which place with some part next unto it, we strengthened with Barricados, and there as the most convenient place assured our selves, the Citie being farre too spacious for so small and weary a troope to undertake to guarde. Somewhat after midnight, they who had the guard of the Castle, hearing us busie about the gates of the said castle, abandoned the same: some being taken prisoners, and some fleeing away by the helpe of boates to the other side of the Haven, and so into the countrey.

The next day we quartered a litle more at large, but not into the halfe part of the towne, and so making substantiall trenches, and planting all the ordinance, that ech part was correspondent to other, we held this towne the space of one moneth.

In the which time happened some accidents, more then are well remembred for the present, but amongst other things, it chanced that the Generall sent on his message to the Spanyards a Negro boy with a flagge of white, signifying truce, as is the Spanyards ordinarie maner to doe there, when they approch to speake to us: which boy unhappily was the first mette withall by some of those, who had bene belonging as officers for the King in the Spanish Galley, which with the Towne was lately fallen into our hands, who without all order or reason, & contrary to that good usage wherewith wee had intertained their messengers, furiously strooke the poore boy thorow the body with one of their horsemens staves: with which wound the boy returned to the General, and after hee had declared the maner of this wrongfull crueltie, died foorthwith in his presence, wherewith the Generall being greatly passioned, commaunded the Provost Martiall, to cause a couple of Friers then prisoners, to be caried to the same place where the boy was stroken, accompanied with sufficient guard of our souldiers, and there presently to be hanged, dispatching at the same instant another poore prisoner, with this reason wherefore this execution was done, & with this message further, that until the party who had thus murdered the Generals messenger were delivered into our hands, to receive condigne punishment, there should no day passe, wherein there should not two prisoners be hanged, until they were all consumed which were in our hands.

Whereupon the day following, hee that had bene Captaine of the kings Galley, brought the offender to the townes end, offring to deliver him into our hands; but it was thought to be a more honourable revenge to make them there in our sight, to performe the execution themselves: which was done accordingly.

During our being in this towne, as formerly also at S. Iago there had passed justice upon the life of one of our owne com-

pany for an odious matter, so heere likewise was there an Irish-
man hanged, for the murthering of his Corporall.

In this time also passed many treaties betweene their Com-
missioners and us, for ransome of their Citie; but upon disagree-
ments we still spent the early mornings in fiering the outmost
houses: but they being built very magnificently of stone, with
high loftes, gave us no small travell to ruine them. And albeit
for divers dayes together we ordeined ech morning by day
breake, until the heat began at nine of the clocke, that two hundred Mariners did nought els but labour to fire and burne the
said houses without our trenches, whilst the souldiers in a like
proportion stood forth for their guard: yet did wee not, or could
not in this time consume so much as one third part of the
towne: which towne is plainely described and set forth in a certaine Map. And so in the end, what wearied with firing, and
what hastened by some other respects, wee were contented to
accept of five and twentie thousand Ducats of five shillings sixe
pence the peece, for the ransome of the rest of the towne.

Amongst other things which happened and were found at
S. Domingo, I may not omit to let the world know one very
notable marke & token of the unsatiable ambition of the Spanish
king and his nation, which was found in the kings house, wherein the chiefe governour of that Citie and Countrey is appoynted
alwayes to lodge, which was this: In the comming to the Hall
or other roomes of this house, you must first ascend up by a
faire large paire of staires; at the head of which staires is a
handsome spacious place to walke in, somewhat like unto a gal-
lery: wherein upon one of the wals, right over against you as
you enter the said place, so as your eye cannot escape the sight
of it, there is described & painted in a very large Scutchion the
armes of the king of Spaine, and in the lower part of the said
Scutchion, there is likewise described a Globe, conteining in it
the whole circuit of the sea and the earth wherupon is a horse
standing on his hinder part within the globe, and the other fore-
part without the globe, lifted up as it were to leape, with a scroll
painted in his mouth, wherein was written these words in Latin,
Non sufficit orbis: which is as much to say, as the world suf-
ficeth not. Whereof the meaning was required to be knowen
of some of those of the better sort, that came in commission to

treate upon the ransome of the towne, who would shake their heads, and turne aside their countenance in some smyling sort, without answering any thing, as greatly ashamed thereof. For by some of our company it was tolde them, that if the Queene of England would resolutely prosecute the warres against the king of Spaine, hee should be forced to lay aside that proude and unreasonable reaching vaine of his: for hee should finde more then inough to doe to keepe that which hee had alreadie, as by the present example of their lost towne they might for a beginning perceive well inough.

Now to the satisfying of some men, who marvell greatly that such a famous and goodly builded Citie so well inhabited of gallant people, very brave in their apparell (whereof our souldiers found good store for their reliefe) should afoord no greater riches then was found there: herein it is to be understood that the Indian people, which were the naturals of this whole Island of Hispaniola (the same being neere hand as great as England) were many yeeres since cleane consumed by the tyrannie of the Spanyards, which was ye cause, that for lacke of people to worke in the Mines, the golde and silver Mines of this Island are wholy given over, and thereby they are faine in this Island to use Copper money, whereof was found very great quantitie. The chiefe trade of this place consisteth of Sugar and Ginger, which groweth in the Island, and of Hides of oxen and kine, which in this waste countrey of the Island are bredde in infinite numbers, the soyle being very fertile: and the sayd beasts are fedde up to a very large grouth, and so killed for nothing so much, as for their Hides aforesayd. Wee found heere great store of strong wine, sweete oyle, vineger, olives, and other such like provisions, as excellent Wheate-meale packed up in winepipes and other caske, and other commodities likewise, as Woollen and Linnen cloth, and some Silkes: all which provisions are brought out of Spaine, and served us for great reliefe. There was but a little Plate or vessell of Silver, in comparison of the great pride in other things of this towne, because in these hotte Countreys they use much of those earthen dishes finely painted or varnished, which they call Porcellana, which is had out of the East India: & for their drinking, they use glasses altogether, whereof they make excellent good and faire in the same place.

But yet some plate we found, and many other good things, as their houshold garniture very gallant and rich, which had cost them deare, although unto us they were of small importance.

From Saint Domingo we put over to the maine or firme land, and going all alongst the coast, we came at the last in sight of Cartagena, standing upon the sea side, so neere, as some of our barks in passing alongst, approched within the reach of their Culverin shot, which they had planted upon certaine platformes. The Harbour mouth lay some three miles toward the Westward of the towne, whereinto wee entred about three or foure of the clocke in the afternoone without any resistance of ordinance, or other impeachment planted upon the same. In the Evening we put our selves on land towards the harbour mouth, under the leading of Master Carliell our Lieutenant Generall, who after hee had digested us to march forwarde about midnight, as easily as foote might fall, expresly commanded us to keepe close by the sea-wash of the shore for our best & surest way, whereby we were like to goe through, and not to misse any more of the way, which once wee had lost within an houre after our first beginning to march, through the slender knowledge of him that tooke upon him to be our guide, whereby the night spent on, which otherwise must have bene done by resting. But as we came within two miles of the towne, their horsemen which were some hundred, met us, and taking the alarme, retired to their townward againe upon the first volley of our shot that was given them: for the place where wee encountred being wooddy and bushy even to the water side was unmeete for their service.

At this instant we might heare some pieces of Artillerie discharged, with divers small shot towards the harbour, which gave us to understand, according to the order set downe in the Evening before by our Generall, that the Vice-admirall accompanied with Captaine Venner, Captaine White, and Captaine Crosse, with other sea Captaines, and with divers Pinnesses and boates should give some attempt unto the litle Fort standing on the entrie of the inner Haven, neere adjoyning to the towne, though to small purpose, for that the place was strong, and the entry very narrow was chained over: so as there could be nothing gotten by the attempt, more than the giving of them an alarme on that other side of the Haven being a mile and a halfe from the place we now were at. In which attempt the Vice-admirall had the rudder of his skiffe stroken through with a Saker shot, and a litle or no harme received elsewhere.

The troopes being now in their march, halfe a myle behither the Towne or lesse, the ground we were on grewe to bee streight and not above fiftie paces over, having the maine Sea on the one side of it, and the harbour-water or inner sea (as you may tearme it) on the other side, which in the plot is plainely shewed. This streight was fortified cleane over with a stone wall and a ditch without it: the sayd wall being as orderly built with flanking in every part, as can be set downe. There was onely so much of this streight unwalled, as might serve for the issuing of the horsemen, or the passing of caryage in time of neede: but this unwalled part was not without a very good Barricado of winebuts or pipes, filled with earth, full and thicke as they might stand on ende one by another, some part of them standing even within the maine sea.

This place of strength was furnished with six great peeces, Demi-culverins, and Sakers, which shotte directly in front upon us as wee approched. Now without this wall upon the inner side of the streight, they had brought likewise two great Galleis with their prowes to the shore, having planted in them eleven peeces of ordinance, which did beate all crosse the streight, and flanked our comming on. In these two Galleis were planted three or foure hundred small shot, and on the land in the guard onely of this place, three hundred shot and pikes.

They in this their full readinesse to receive us, spared not their shot both great and small. But our Lieutenant generall, taking the advantage of the darke (the day light as yet not broken out) approched by the lowest ground, according to the expresse direction which himselfe had formerly given, the same being the sea-wash shore, where the water was somewhat fallen, so as most of all their shot was in vaine. Our Lieutenant generall commanded our shot to forbeare shooting untill we were come to the wall side, and so with pikes roundly together we approched the place, where we soone found out the Barricados of pipes or buts, to be the meetest place for our assault, which, notwithstanding it was well furnished with pikes and shot, was without staying attempted by us: downe went the buts of earth, and pell mell came our swordes and pikes together, after our shot had first given their volley, even at the enemies nose. Our pikes were somewhat longer then theirs, and our bodies better armed; for very few of them were armed: with which advantage our swordes and pikes grew too hard for them, and they driven to give place. In this furious entry, the Lieutenant generall slew with his owne hands the chiefe Ensigne bearer of the Spaniards, who fought very manfully to his lives end.

We followed into the towne with them, and giving them no leasure to breath, we wanne the Market-place, albeit they made head, and fought a while before we got it, and so wee being once seazed and assured of that, they were content to suffer us to lodge within their towne, and themselves to goe to their wives, whom they had caryed into other places of the countrey before our comming thither.

At every streetes end they had raised very fine Barricados of earth-workes, with trenches without them, as well made as ever we saw any worke done: at the entring whereof was some litle resistance, but soone overcome it was, with few slaine or hurt. They had joyned with them many Indians, whom they had placed in corners of advantage, all bowmen, with their arrowes most villanously empoysoned, so as if they did but breake the skinne, the partie so touched died without great marvell: some they slew of our people with their arrowes: some they likewise mischieved to death with certaine pricks of small sticks sharply pointed, of a foote and a halfe long, the one ende put into the ground, the other empoysoned, sticking fast up, right against our comming in the way, as we should approch from our landing towardes the towne, whereof they had planted a wonderfull number in the ordinarie way: but our keeping the sea-wash shore missed the greatest part of them very happily.

I overpasse many particular matters, as the hurting of Captaine Sampson at sword blowes in the first entring, unto whom was committed the charge of the pikes of the Vantguard by his lot and turne; as also of the taking of Alonso Bravo the chiefe commander of that place by Captaine Goring, after the said captaine had first hurt him with his sword: unto which Captaine was committed the charge of the shot of the sayd Vantguard.

Captaine Winter was likewise by his turne of the Vantguard in this attempt, where also the Lieutenant generall marched himselfe: the said Captaine Winter through a great desire to serve by land, having now exchanged his charge by sea with Captaine Cecil for his band of footemen.

Captaine Powel the Sergeant major had by his turne the charge of the foure companies which made the battaile.

Captaine Morgan, who at S. Domingo was of the Vantguard, had now by turne his charge upon the companies of the Rereward.

Every man as well of one part as of another, came so willingly on to the service, as the enemie was not able to endure the furie of such hot assault.

We stayed here sixe weekes, and the sicknesse with mortalitie before spoken of still continued among us, though not with the same furie as at the first: and such as were touched with the sayde sicknesse, escaping death, very few or almost none could recover their strength: yea, many of them were much decayed in their memorie, insomuch that it was growen an ordinarie judgement, when one was heard to speake foolishly, to say he had bene sicke of the Calentura, which is the Spanish name of their burning Ague: for as I tolde you before, it is a very burning and pestilent ague. The originall cause thereof, is imputed to the Evening or first night ayre, which they tearme La serena, wherein they say and hold very firme opinion, that who so is then abroad in the open ayre, shall certainly be infected to the death, not being of the Indian or naturall race of those countrey people: by holding their watch, our men were thus subjected to the infectious ayre, which at S. Iago was most dangerous and deadly of all other places.

With the inconvenience of continuall mortalitie, we were forced to give over our intended enterprise to goe with Nombre de Dios, and so overland to Panama, where we should have strooken the stroke for the treasure, and full recompence of our tedious travailes. And thus at Cartagena wee tooke our first resolution to returne homewardes: the forme of which resolution I thought good here to put downe under the principall Captaines hands, as followeth.

A resolution of the Land-captaines, what course
they thinke most expedient to bee taken.
Given at Cartagena the xxvij. of Februarie 1585

Whereas it hath pleased the Generall to demaund the opinions
of his Captaines what course they thinke most expedient to be
now undertaken, the Land-captaines being assembled by themselves together, and having advised hereupon, doe in three
points deliver the same.

The first, touching the keeping of the towne against the
force of the enemie, either that which is present, or that which
may come out of Spaine, is answered thus.

We holde opinion, that with this troope of men which we
have presently with us in land-service, being victualled and
munitioned, wee may well keepe the Towne, albeit that of men
able to answere present service, we have not above 700. The
residue being some 150. men by reason of their hurts and sicknesse are altogether unable to stand us in any stead: wherefore hereupon the Sea-captaines are likewise to give their resolution, how they will undertake the safetie and service of the
Shippes upon the arrivall of any Spanish Fleete.

The second poynt we make to be this, whether it bee meete to
goe presently homeward, or els to continue further tryall of our
fortune in undertaking such like enterprises as we have done
already, and thereby to seeke after that bountiful masse of treasure for recompence of our travailes, which was generally expected at our comming forth of England: wherein we answere.

That it is well knowen how both we and the souldiers are
entred into this action as voluntarie men, without any imprest
or gage from her Majestie or any body els: and forasmuch as
we have hitherto discharged the parts of honest men, so that
now by the great blessing and favour of our good God there
have bin taken three such notable townes, wherein by the estimation of all men would have bene found some very great
treasures, knowing that S. Iago was the chiefe citie of all the
Islands and traffiques thereabouts, S. Domingo the chiefe citie
of Hispaniola, and the head government not only of that
Iland, but also of Cuba, and of all the Ilands about it, as also
of such inhabitations of the firme land, as were next unto it,
& a place that is both magnificently builded, and interteineth

great trades of marchandise; and now lastly the citie of Cartagena, which cannot be denied to be one of the chiefe places of most especiall importance to the Spaniard of all the cities which be on this side of the West India: we doe therefore consider, that since all these cities, with their goods & prisoners taken in them, and the ransoms of the said cities being all put together, are found farre short to satisfie that expectation which by the generality of the enterprisers was first conceived: And being further advised of the slendernesse of our strength, whereunto we be now reduced, as well in respect of the small number of able bodies, as also not a litle in regard of the slacke disposition of the greater part of those which remaine, very many of the better mindes and men being either consumed by death, or weakened by sicknes and hurts: And lastly, since that as yet there is not laid downe to our knowledge any such enterprise as may seeme convenient to be undertaken with such few as we are presently able to make, and withall of such certaine likelihoode, as with Gods good successe which it may please him to bestow upon us, the same may promise to yeeld us any sufficient contentment: We doe therefore conclude hereupon, that it is better to hold sure as we may the honour already gotten, and with the same to returne towards our gracious Soveraigne and Countrey, from whence if it shall please her Majestie to set us foorth againe with her orderly meanes and intertainment, we are most ready and willing to goe through with any thing that the uttermost of our strength and indevour shall be able to reach unto; but therewithal wee doe advise and protest that it is farre from our thoughts, either to refuse, or so much as to seeme to be wearie of any thing, which for the present shalbe further required or directed to be done by us from our Generall.

The third and last poynt is concerning the ransome of this citie of Cartagena, for the which, before it was touched with any fire, there was made an offer of some xxvij. or xxviij. thousand pounds sterling.

Thus much we utter herein as our opinions agreeing (so it be done in good sort) to accept this offer aforesayde, rather then to breake off by standing still upon our demaunds of one hundred thousand poundes, which seemes a matter impossible to bee performed for the present by them, and to say trueth, wee may now with much honour and reputation better be satis-

fied with that summe offered by them at the first (if they will
now bee contented to give it) then wee might at that time with
a great deale more, inasmuch as we have taken our full pleasure both in the uttermost sacking and spoyling of all their
householde goods and marchandize, as also in that we have
consumed and ruined a great part of their Towne with fire. And
thus much further is considered herein by us, that as there bee
in the Voyage a great many poore men, who have willingly
adventured their lives and travailes, and divers amongst them
having spent their apparell and such other little provisions as
their small meanes might have given them leave to prepare,
which being done upon such good and allowable intention as
this action hath alwayes caried with it, meaning, against the
Spanyard our greatest and most dangerous enemie: so surely
wee cannot but have an inward regarde so farre as may lye in
us, to helpe eyther in all good sort towards the satisfaction of
this their expectation, and by procuring them some little benefite to incourage them and to nourish this readie and willing
disposition of theirs both in them and in others by their example against any other time of like occasion. But because it
may bee supposed that heerein wee forgette not the private
benfite of our selves, and are thereby the rather mooved to in-
cline our selves to this composition, wee doe therefore thinke
good for the clearing of our selves of all such suspition, to declare heereby, that what part or portion soever it bee of this
ransome or composition for Cartagena, which should come
unto us, wee doe freely give and bestowe the same wholy upon
the poore men, who have remayned with us in the Voyage,
meaning as well the Sayler as the Souldier, wishing with all our
hearts it were such or so much as might seeme a sufficient re-
warde for their painefull indevour. And for the firme confirmation thereof, we have thought meete to subsigne these presents
with our owne hands in the place and time aforesayd.
CAPTAINE CHRISTOPHER CARLIELL LIEUTENANT GENERALL
CAPTAINE GORING   CAPTAINE SAMPSON
CAPTAINE POWELL &c.

But while wee were yet there, it happened one day, that our
watch called the Centinell, upon the Church-steeple, had discovered in the Sea a couple of small Barkes or Boates, making

in with the Harbour of Cartagena, whereupon Captaine Moone and Captaine Varney, with John Grant the Master of the Tyger, and some other Seamen, embarked themselves in a couple of small Pinnesses, to take them before they should come nigh the shore, at the mouth of the Harbour, lest by some stragling Spanyardes from the Lande, they might bee warned by signes from comming in: which fell out accordingly, notwithstanding all the diligence that our men could use: for the Spanish Boates, upon the sight of our Pinnesses comming towardes them, ranne themselves ashore, and so their men presently hidde themselves in bushes hard by the Sea side, amongst some others that had called them by signes thither. Our men presently without any due regard had to the qualitie of the place, and seeing no man of the Spanyards to shew themselves, aboorded the Spanish Barkes or Boates, and so standing all open in them, were suddenly shotte at by a troope of Spanyardes out of the bushes: by which volley of shotte there were slaine Captaine Varney, which dyed presently, and Captaine Moone, who dyed some fewe dayes after, besides some foure or five others that were hurt: and so our folkes returned without their purpose, not having any sufficient number of souldiers with them to fight on shore. For those men they caryed were all Mariners to rowe, few of them armed, because they made account with their ordinance to have taken the Barkes well enough at sea, which they might full easily have done, without any losse at all, if they had come in time to the harbour mouth, before the Spaniards boates had gotten so neere the shore.

During our abode in this place, as also at S. Domingo, there passed divers courtesies betweene us and the Spaniards, as feasting, and using them with all kindnesse and favour: so as amongst others there came to see the Generall, the Governour of Cartagena, with the Bishop of the same, and divers other Gentlemen of the better sort.

This towne of Cartagena we touched in the out parts, & consumed much with fire, as we had done S. Domingo upon discontentments, and for want of agreeing with us in their first treaties touching their ransome, which at the last was concluded between us, should be 100. and 10000. Ducats for that which was yet standing, the Ducat valued at five shillings sixe pence sterling.

This towne though not halfe so bigge as S. Domingo, gives as you see, a farre greater ransome, being in very deede of farre more importance, by reason of the excellencie of the Harbour, and the situation thereof, to serve the trade of Nombre de Dios and other places, and is inhabited with farre more richer Merchants. The other is chiefly inhabited with Lawyers and brave Gentlemen, being the chiefe or highest appeale of their suites in law of all the Islands about it, and of the maine land coast next unto it. And it is of no such accompt as Cartagena, for these and some other like reasons, which I could give you, over long to be now written.

The warning which this towne received of our comming towards them from S. Domingo, by the space of twentie dayes before our arrivall here, was cause that they had both fortified and every way prepared for their best defence. As also that they had caried and conveyed away all their treasure and principall substance.

The ransome of an hundred & ten thousand Ducats thus concluded on, as is aforesaid, the same being written, and expressing for nothing more then the towne of Cartagena, upon the payment of the sayd ransome, we left the said towne, and drewe some part of our souldiers into the Priorie or Abbey, standing a quarter of an English mile belowe the towne upon the harbour waterside, the same being walled with a wall of stone, which we told the Spaniards was yet ours, and not redeemed by their composition: whereupon they finding the defect of their contract, were contended to enter into another ransome for all places, but specially for the sayde house, as also the Blockehouse or Castle, which is upon the mouth of the inner harbour. And when wee asked as much for the one as for the other, they yeelded to give a thousand Crownes for the Abbey, leaving us to take our pleasure upon the Blockehouse, which they sayd they were not able to ransome, having stretched themselves to the uttermost of their powers: and therefore the sayd Blockehouse was by us undermined, and so with gunne powder blowen up in pieces.

While this latter contract was in making, our whole Fleete of ships fell downe towards the harbour mouth, where they anchored the third time, and imployed their men in fetching of fresh water aboord the ships for our voyage homewards, which water was had in a great well, that is in the Island by the harbour mouth: which Island is a very pleasant place as hath bene seene, having in it many sorts of goodly and very pleasant fruites, as the Orenge trees and others, being set orderly in walkes of great length together. Insomuch as the whole Island being some two or three miles about, is cast into grounds of gardening and orchards.

After sixe weeks abode in this place, we put to sea the last of March, where after two or three dayes a great ship which we had taken at S. Domingo, and thereupon was called The new yeeres gift, fell into a great leake, being laden with ordinance, hides, and other spoyles, and in the night she lost the company of our Fleete; which being missed the next morning by the Generall, hee cast about with the whole Fleete, fearing some great mischance to bee happened unto her, as in very deede it so fell out: for her leake was so great, that her men were all tyred with pumping. But at the last having found her & the Bark Talbot in her company, which stayed by great hap with her, they were ready to take their men out of her, for the saving of them. And so the Generall being fully advertised of their great extremitie, made saile directly backe againe to Cartagena with the whole Fleete, where having staied eight or ten dayes more, about the unlading of this ship, and the bestowing thereof and her men into other Ships, we departed once againe to Sea, directing our course towards the Cape S. Antony, being the Westermost part of Cuba, where wee arrived the seven and twentieth of April. But because fresh water could not presently be found, we weyed anchor, and departed, thinking in few dayes to recover the Matanças, a place to the Eastward of Havana.

After wee had sailed some fourteen dayes, wee were brought to Cape S. Anthony againe, through lacke of favourable wind: but then our scarcity was growen such, as neede made us looke a litle better for water, which we found in sufficient quantitie, being indeede, as I judge, none other than raine water newly fallen, and gathered up by making pits in a plot of marrish ground, some three hundred pases from the sea side.

I doe wrong if I should forget the good example of the Generall at this place, who to encourage others, and to hasten the getting of fresh water aboord the ships, tooke no lesse paine himselfe then the meanest; as also at S. Domingo, Cartagena, and all other places, having alwayes so vigilant a care and fore-sight in the good ordering of his Fleete, accompanying them, as it is sayde, with such wonderfull travell of body, as doubtlesse had he bene the meanest person, as hee was the chiefest, he had yet deserved the first place of honour: and no lesse happy doe we account him, for being associated with Master Carliel his Lieutenant generall, by whose experience, prudent counsell, and gallant performance he atchieved so many and happy enter-prises of the warre, by whom also he was very greatly assisted, in setting downe the needfull orders, lawes, and course of jus-tice, and the due administration of the same upon all occasions.

After three dayes spent in watering our Ships, wee departed now the second time from this Cape of S. Anthony the thir-teenth of May, and proceeding about the Cape of Florida, wee never touched any where; but coasting alongst Florida, and keeping the shore still in sight, the 28. of May early in the Morning wee descried on the shore a place built like a Beacon, which was in deede a scaffold upon foure long mastes raised on ende, for men to discover to the seaward, being in the lati-tude of thirtie degrees, or very neere thereunto. Our Pinnesses manned, and comming to the shore, wee marched up alongst the river side, to see what place the enemie held there: for none amongst us had any knowledge thereof at all.

Here the Generall tooke occasion to march with the com-panies himselfe in person, the Lieutenant generall having the Vantguard; and going a mile up or somewhat more by the river side, we might discerne on the other side of the river over against us, a Fort which newly had bene built by the Spaniards: and some mile or thereabout above the Fort was a little Towne or Village without walles, built of woodden houses, as the Plot doeth plainely shew. Wee forthwith prepared to have ordinance for the batterie; and one peece was a litle before the Evening planted, and the first shot being made by the Lieutenant gen-erall himselfe at their Ensigne, strake through the Ensigne, as wee afterwards understood by a French man, which came unto us from them. One shot more was then made, which strake the foote of the Fort wall, which was all massive timber of great trees like Mastes. The Lieutenant generall was determined to passe the river this night with 4. companies, and there to lodge himselfe intrenched as neere the Fort, as that he might play with his muskets and smallest shot upon any that should appeare, and so afterwards to bring and plant the batterie with him: but the helpe of Mariners for that sudden to make trenches could not be had, which was the cause that this determination was remitted untill the next night.

In the night the Lieutenant generall tooke a little rowing Skiffe, and halfe a dozen well armed, as Captaine Morgan, and Captaine Sampson, with some others besides the rowers, & went to view what guard the enemie kept, as also to take knowledge of the ground. And albeit he went as covertly as might be, yet the enemie taking ye Alarme, grew feareful that the whole force was approching to the assault, and therefore with all speede abandoned the place after the shooting of some of their peeces. They thus gone, and hee being returned unto us againe, but nothing knowing of their flight from their Fort, forthwith came a French man being a Phipher (who had bene prisoner with them) in a litle boate, playing on his Phiph the tune of the Prince of Orenge his song; and being called unto by the guard, he tolde them before he put foote out of the boate, what he was himselfe, and how the Spaniards were gone from the Fort, offering either to remaine in hands there, or els to returne to the place with them that would goe.

Upon this intelligence, the Generall, the Lieutenant generall, with some of the Captaines in one Skiffe, and the Vice-admirall with some others in his Skiffe, and two or three Pinnesses furnished of souldiers with them, put presently over towards the Fort, giving order for the rest of the Pinnesses to follow. And in our approch, some of the enemie bolder then the rest, having stayed behinde their company, shot off two peeces of ordinance at us: but on shore wee went, and entred the place without finding any man there.

When the day appeared, we found it built all of timber, the walles being none other but whole Mastes or bodies of trees set up right and close together in maner of a pale, without any ditch as yet made, but wholy intended with some more time; for they had not as yet finished al their worke, having begunne the same some three or foure moneths before: so as, to say the trueth, they had no reason to keepe it, being subject both to fire, and easie assault.

The platforme whereon the ordinance lay, was whole bodies

of long pine trees, whereof there is great plentie, layd a crosse one on another, and some litle earth amongst. There were in it thirteene or fourteene great peeces of Brasse ordinance, and a chest unbroken up, having in it the value of some two thousand pounds sterling by estimation of the kings treasure, to pay the souldiers of that place, who were a hundred and fiftie men.

The Fort thus wonne, which they called S. Johns Fort, and the day opened, wee assayed to goe to the towne, but could not by reason of some rivers and broken ground which was betweene the two places: and therefore being enforced to imbarke againe into our Pinnesses, wee went thither upon the great maine river, which is called as also the Towne, by the name of S. Augustin.

At our approching to land, there were some that began to shew themselves, and to bestow some few shot upon us, but presently withdrew themselves. And in their running thus away, the Sergeant Major finding one of their horses ready sadled and brideled, tooke the same to follow the chase; and so overgoing all his company, was (by one layd behind a bush) shotte through the head: and falling downe therewith, was by the same and two or three more, stabbed in three or foure places of his body with swords and daggers, before any could come neere to his rescue. His death was much lamented, being in very deede an honest wise Gentleman, and a souldier of good experience, and of as great courage as any man might be.

In this place called S. Augustin, we understood the king did keepe, as is before said, one hundred and fiftie souldiers, and at another place some dozen leagues beyond to the Northwards, called S. Helena, he did there likewise keepe an hundred and fiftie more, serving there for no other purpose, then to keepe all other nations from inhabiting any part of all that coast; the governement whereof was committed to one Pedro Melendez Marquesse, nephew to that Melendez the Admiral, who had overthrowen Master John Hawkins in the bay of Mexico some seventeene or eighteene yeeres agoe. This Governour had charge of both places, but was at this time in this place, and one of the first that left the same.

Heere it was resolved in full assembly of Captaines, to undertake the enterprise of S. Helena, and from thence to seeke out the inhabitation of our English countreymen in Virginia, distant from thence some six degrees Northward.

When wee came thwart of S. Helena, the sholds appearing dangerous, and we having no Pilot to undertake the entrie, it was thought meetest to goe hence alongst. For the Admirall had bene the same night in foure fadome and a halfe, three leagues from the shore: and yet wee understood by the helpe of a knowen Pilot, there may and doe goe in Ships of greater burthen and draught then any we had in our Fleete.

We passed thus alongst the coast hard aboord the shore, which is shallow for a league or two from the shore, and the same is lowe and broken land for the most part.

The ninth of June upon sight of one speciall great fire (which are very ordinarie all alongst this coast, even from the Cape of Florida hither) the Generall sent his Skiffe to the shore, where they found some of our English countreymen (that had bene sent thither the yeere before by Sir Walter Ralegh) and brought them aboord: by whose direction wee proceeded along to the place which they make their Port. But some of our ships being of great draught unable to enter, anchored without the harbour in a wilde roade at sea, about two miles from shore.

From whence the General wrote letters to master Ralfe Lane, being governour of those English in Virginia, and then at his Fort about six leagues from the Rode in an Island which they call Roanoac, wherein especially he shewed how ready he was to supply his necessities and wants, which he understood of, by those he had first talked withall.

The morrow after, Master Lane himselfe and some of his company comming unto him, with the consent of his captaines he gave them the choice of two offers, that is to say: Either he would leave a ship, a pinnesse, and certaine boates with sufficient Masters and Mariners, together furnished with a moneths victuall, to stay and make farther discovery of the countrey and coastes, and so much victuall likewise as might be sufficient for the bringing of them all (being an hundred and three persons) into England, if they thought good after such time, with any other thing they would desire, and that he might be able to spare.

Or els if they thought they had made sufficient discoverie already, and did desire to returne into England, he would give them passage. But they, as it seemed, being desirous to stay, accepted very thankfully and with great gladnesse, that which was offred first. Whereupon the ship being appointed and received into charge by some of their owne company sent into her by Master Lane, before they had received from the rest of the Fleete the provision appoynted them, there arose a great storme (which they sayd was extraordinary and very strange) that lasted three dayes together, and put all our Fleete in great danger, to bee driven from their anchoring upon the coast. For we brake many Cables, and lost many Anchors: and some of our Fleete which had lost all (of which number was the ship appointed for Master Lane and his company) was driven to put to sea in great danger, in avoyding the coast, and could never see us againe untill we mette in England. Many also of our small Pinnesses and boates were lost in this storme.

Notwithstanding after all this, the Generall offred them (with consent of his Captaines) an other ship with some provision, although not such a one for their turnes, as might have bene spared them before, this being unable to be brought into their Harbour. Or els if they would, to give them passage into England, although he knew we should performe it with greater difficultie then he might have done before.

But Master Lane with those of the chiefest of his company which hee had then with him, considering what should be best for them to doe, made request unto the General under their hands, that they might have passage for England: the which being graunted, and the rest sent for out of the countrey and shipped, we departed from that coast the 18. of June.

And so, God bee thanked, both they and wee in good safetie arrived at Portesmouth the 28. of July 1586. to the great glory of God, and to no small honour to our Prince, our Countrey, and our selves.

The totall value of that which was gotten in this voyage is esteemed at three score thousand pounds, whereof the companies which have travelled in the voyage were to have twentie thousand pounds, the adventurers the other fortie. Of which twentie thousand pounds (as I can judge) will redound some six pounds to the single share.

We lost some seven hundred and fiftie men in the voyage: above three parts of them onely by sicknesse. . . .

The ordinance gotten of all sorts Brasse and Iron, were about two hundred and forty peeces, whereof the two hundred and some more were brasse, and were thus found and gotten.

At S. Iago some two or three and fiftie peeces.

In S. Domingo about fourescore, whereof was very much great ordinance, as whole Cannon, Demi-canon, Culverins, and such like.

In Cartagena some sixtie and three peeces, and good store likewise of the greater sort.

In the Fort of S. Augustin were foureteene peeces.

The rest was Iron ordinance, of which the most part was gotten at S. Domingo, the rest at Cartagena.

38

The first voyage of M. John Davis, undertaken in June 1585. for the discoverie of the Northwest passage, Written by M. John Janes Marchant, sometimes servant to the worshipfull Master William Sanderson

CERTAINE Honourable personages and worthy Gentlemen of the Court & Countrey, with divers worshipful Marchants of London and of the West Countrey, mooved with desire to advance Gods glory and to seeke the good of their native Countrey, consulting together of the likelyhood of the Discoverie of the Northwest passage, which heretofore had bene attempted, but unhappily given over by accidents unlooked for, which turned the enterprisers from their principall purpose, resolved after good deliberation, to put downe their adventures to provide for necessarie shipping, and a fit man to be chiefe Conductour of this so hard an enterprise. The setting forth of this Action was committed by the adventurers, especially to the care of M. William Sanderson Marchant of London, who was so forward therein, that besides his travaile which was not small, hee became the greatest adventurer with his purse, and commended unto the rest of the companie one M. John Davis, a man very well grounded in the principles of the Arte of Navigation, for Captaine and chiefe Pilot of this exployt.

Thus therefore all things being put in a readines, wee departed from Dartmouth the seventh of June, towards the discoverie of the aforesayd Northwest passage, with two Barkes, the one being of 50. tunnes, named the Sunneshine of London, and the other being 35. tunnes, named the Mooneshine of Dartmouth. In the Sunneshine we had 23. persons, whose names are these following, M. John Davis Captaine, William

Eston Master, Richard Pope Masters mate, John Jane Marchant, Henry Davie gunner, William Crosse boatswayne, John Bagge, Walter Arthur, Luke Adams, Robert Coxworthie, John Ellis, John Kelley, Edward Helman, William Dicke, Andrew Maddocke, Thomas Hill, Robert Wats Carpenter, William Russell, Christopher Gorney boy: James Cole, Francis Ridley, John Russell, Robert Cornish Musicians.

The Mooneshine had 19. persons, William Bruton Captaine, John Ellis Master, the rest Mariners.

The 7. of June the Captaine and the Master drewe out a proportion for the continuance of our victuals.

The 8. day the wind being at Southwest and West southwest, we put in for Falmouth, where we remained untill the 13.

The 13. the wind blew at North, and being faire weather we departed.

The 14. with contrary wind we were forced to put into Silley.

The 15. wee departed thence, having the wind North and by East moderate and faire weather.

The 16. wee were driven backe againe, and were constrained to arrive at newe Grymsby in Silley: here the winde remained contrary 12. dayes, and in that space the Captaine, the Master and I went about all the Ilands, and the Captaine did plat out and describe the situation of all the Ilands, rocks and harboroughs to the exact use of Navigation, with lines and scale thereunto convenient.

The 28. in Gods name we departed the wind being Easterly but calme.

The first of July wee sawe great store of Porposes; The Master called for an harping yron, and shot twise or thrise: sometimes he missed, and at last shot one and strooke him in the side, and wound him into the ship: when we had him aboord, the Master sayd it was a Darlie head.

The 2. we had some of the fish sodden, and it did eat as sweete as any mutton.

The 3. wee had more in sight, and the Master went to shoote at them, but they were so great, that they burst our yrons, and we lost both fish, yrons, pastime and all: yet neverthelesse the Master shot at them with a pike, and had welnigh gotten one, but he was so strong that he burst off the barres of the pike and went away: then he tooke the boat-hooke, and hit one with that, but all would not prevaile, so at length we let them alone.

The 6. we saw a very great Whale, and every day we saw whales continually.

The 16. 17. and 18. we saw great store of Whales.

The 19. of July we fell into a great whirling and brustling of a tyde, setting to the Northwards: and sayling about halfe a league wee came into a very calme Sea, which bent to the Southsouthwest. Here we heard a mighty great roaring of the Sea, as if it had bene the breach of some shoare, the ayre being so foggie and full of thicke mist, that we could not see the one ship from the other, being a very small distance asunder: so the Captaine and the Master being in distrust how the tyde might set them, caused the Mooneshine to hoyse out her boate and to sound, but they could not finde ground in 300. fathoms and better. Then the Captaine, Master, and I went towards the breach, to see what it should be, giving charge to our gunners that at every glasse they should shoote off a musket-shot, to the intent we might keepe our selves from loosing them. Then comming nere to the breach, we met many Ilands of yce floting, which had quickly compassed us about: then we went upon some of them, and did perceive that all the roaring which we heard, was caused onely by the rowling of this yce together: Our companie seeing us not to returne according to our appoyntment, left off shooting muskets, and began to shoote falkonets, for they feared some mishap had befallen us, but before night we came aboord againe with our boat laden with yce, which made very good fresh water. Then wee bent our course toward the North, hoping by that meanes to double the land.

The 20. as we sayled along the coast the fogge brake up, and we discovered the land, which was the most deformed rockie and mountainous land that ever we saw: The first sight whereof did shew as if it had bene in forme of a sugar-loafe, standing to our sight above the cloudes, for that it did shew over the fogge like a white liste in the skie, the tops altogether covered with snow, and the shoare beset with yce a league off into the Sea, making such yrkesome noyse as that it seemed to be the true patterne of desolation, and after the same our Captaine named it, The land of Desolation.

The 21. the winde came Northerly and overblew, so that we were constrained to bend our course South againe, for we perceived that we were runne into a very deepe Bay, where wee were almost compassed with yce, for we saw very much toward the Northnortheast, West, and Southwest: and this day and this night wee cleared our selves of the yce, running South-southwest along the shoare.

Upon Thursday being the 22. of this moneth, about three of the clocke in the morning, wee hoysed out our boate, and the Captaine with sixe saylers went towards the shoare, thinking to find a landing place, for the night before we did perceive the coast to be voyde of yce to our judgement, and the same night wee were all perswaded that we had seene a Canoa row-ing along the shoare, but afterwards we fell in some doubt of it, but we had no great reason so to doe. The Captaine row-ing towards the shoare, willed the Master to beare in with the land after him, and before he came neere the shoare by the space of a league, or about two miles, hee found so much yce, that hee could not get to land by any meanes. Here our mariners put to their lines to see if they could get any fish, because there were so many seales upon the coast, and the birds did beate upon the water, but all was in vaine: The water about this place was very blacke and thicke like to a filthy standing poole, we sounded and had ground in 120. fathoms. While the Captaine was rowing to the shoare, our men sawe woods upon the rocks like to the rocks of Newfoundland, but I could not discerne them, yet it might be so very well: for we had wood floting upon the coast every day, and the Moone-shine tooke up a tree at Sea not farre from the coast being sixtie foote of length and foureteene handfuls about, having the roote upon it: After this the Captaine came aboord, the weather being very calme and faire we bent our course toward the South, with intent to double the land.

The 23. we coasted the land which did lie Eastnortheast and Westsouthwest.

The 24. the winde being very faire at East, we coasted the land which did lie East and West, not being able to come neere the shoare by reason of the great quantitie of yce. At this place, because the weather was somewhat colde by reason of the yce, and the better to encourage our men, their allowance was increased: the captaine and the master tooke order that every messe, being five persons, should have halfe a pound of bread and a kan of beere every morning to breakfast. The weather was not very colde, but the aire was moderate like to our April-weather in England: when the winde came from the land, or the ice, it was some what colde, but when it came off the sea it was very hote.

The 25 of this moneth we departed from sight of this land at sixe of the clocke in the morning, directing our course to the Northwestward, hoping in Gods mercy to finde our desired passage, and so continued above foure dayes.

The 29 of July we discovered land in 64 degrees 15 minutes of latitude, bearing Northeast from us. The winde being contrary to goe to the Northwestwards, we bare in with this land to take some view of it, being utterly void of the pester of yce and very temperate. Comming neere the coast, we found many faire sounds and good roads for shipping, and many great inlets into the land, whereby we judged this land to be a great number of Islands standing together. Heere having mored our barke in good order, we went on shoare upon a small Island to seeke for water and wood. Upon this Island we did perceive that there had bene people: for we found a small shoo and pieces of leather sowed with sinewes, and a piece of furre, and wooll like to Bever. Then we went upon another Island on the other side of our shippes: and the Captaine, the Master, and I, being got up to the top of an high rocke, the people of the countrey having espied us, made a lamentable noise, as we thought, with great outcries and skreechings: we hearing them, thought it had bene the howling of wolves. At last I hallowed againe, and they likewise cried. Then we perceiving where they stood, some on the shoare, and one rowing in a Canoa about a small Island fast by them, we made a great noise, partly to allure them to us, and partly to warne our company of them. Whereupon M. Bruton and the Master of his shippe, with others of their company, made great haste towards us, and brought our Musicians with them from our shippe, purposing either by force to rescue us, if need should so require, or with courtesie to allure the people. When they came unto us, we caused our Musicians to play, our selves dancing, and making many signes of friendship. At length there came tenne

Canoas from the other Islands, and two of them came so neere the shoare where we were, that they talked with us, the other being in their boats a prety way off. Their pronunciation was very hollow thorow the throat, and their speech such as we could not understand: onely we allured them by friendly imbracings and signes of curtesie. At length one of them pointing up to the Sunne with his hand, would presently strike his breast so hard that we might heare the blow. This hee did many times before he would any way trust us. Then John Ellis the Master of the Mooneshine was appointed to use his best policie to gaine their friendship; who strooke his breast, and pointed to the Sunne after their order: which when he had divers times done, they beganne to trust him, and one of them came on shoare, to whom we threw our cappes, stockings and gloves, and such other things as then we had about us, playing with our musicke, and making signes of joy, and dauncing. So the night comming, we bade them farewell, and went aboord our barks.

The next morning being the 30 of July there came 37 Canoas rowing by our ships, calling to us to come on shoare: we not making any great haste unto them, one of them went up to the toppe of the rocke, and leapt and daunced as they had done the day before, shewing us a seales skinne, and another thing made like a timbrell, which he did beat upon with a sticke, making a noise like a small drumme. Whereupon we manned our boats and came to them, they all staying in their Canoas: we came to the water side were they were: and after we had sworne by the Sunne after their fashion, they did trust us. So I shooke hands with one of them, and he kissed my hand, and we were very familiar with them. We were in so great credit with them upon this single acquaintance, that we could have any thing they had. We bought five Canoas of them: we bought their clothes from their backs, which were all made of seales skinnes & birds skinnes; their buskins, their hose, their gloves, all being commonly sowed and well dressed: so that we were fully perswaded that they have divers artificers among them. We had a paire of buskins of them full of fine wooll like bever. Their apparell for heat was made of birds skinnes with their feathers on them. We saw among them leather dressed like Glovers leather, and thicke thongs like white leather of a good length. We had of their darts and oares, and found in them that they would by no meanes displease us, but would give us whatsoever we asked of them, and would be satisfied with whatsoever we gave them. They tooke great care one of another: for when we had bought their boats, then two other would come and cary him away betweene them that had solde us his. They are very tractable people, void of craft or double dealing, and easie to be brought to any civility or good order: but we judge them to be idolaters and to worship the Sunne.

During the time of our abode among these Islands we found reasonable quantity of wood, both firre, spruse and juniper; which whether it came floting any great distance to these places where we found it, or whether it grew in some great Islands neere the same place by us not yet discovered, we know not; but we judge that it groweth there further into the land then we were, because the people had great store of darts and oares which they made none account of, but gave them to us for small trifles, as points and pieces of paper. We saw about this coast marveilous great abundance of seales skulling together like skuls of small fish. We found no fresh water among these Islands, but onely snow water, whereof we found great pooles. The cliffes were all of such oare as M. Frobisher brought from Meta incognita. We had divers shewes of Study or Muscovy glasse shining not altogether unlike to Christall. We found an herbe growing upon the rocks, whose fruit was sweet, full of red juice, and the ripe ones were like corinths. We found also birch and willow growing like shrubbes low to the ground. These people have great store of furres as we judge. They made shewes unto us the 30 of this present, which was the second time of our being with them, after they perceived we would have skinnes and furres, that they would go into the countrey and come againe the next day with such things as they had: but this night the winde comming faire, the captaine and the master would by no meanes detract the purpose of our discovery. And so the last of this moneth about foure of the clocke in the morning in Gods name we set saile, and were all that day becalmed upon the coast.

The first of August we had a faire winde, and so proceeded towards the Northwest for our discovery.

The sixt of August we discovered land in 66 degrees 40 minuts of latitude, altogether void from the pester of ice: we ankered in a very faire rode under a brave mount, the cliffes whereof were as orient as golde. This mount was named Mount Raleigh. The rode where our ships lay at anker was called Totnes rode. The sound which did compasse the mount was named Exeter sound. The foreland towards the North was called Diers cape. The foreland towards the South was named Cape Walsingham. So soone as we were come to an anker in Totnes rode under Mount Raleigh, we espied foure white beares at the foot of the mount: we supposing them to be goats or wolves, manned our boats and went towards them: but when we came neere the shore, we found them to be white beares of a monstrous bignesse: we being desirous of fresh victuall and the sport, began to assault them, and I being on land, one of them came downe the hill right against me: my piece was charged with hailshot & a bullet: I discharged my piece and shot him in the necke; he roared a litle, and tooke the water straight, making small account of his hurt. Then we followed him with our boat, and killed him with boare-speares, & two more that night. We found nothing in their mawes; but we judged by their dung that they fed upon grasse, because it appeared in all respects like the dung of an horse, wherein we might very plainly see the very strawes.

The 7 we went on shore to another beare which lay all night upon the top of an Island under Mount Raleigh, and when we came up to him he lay fast asleep. I levelled at his head, and the stone of my piece gave no fire: with that he looked up, and layed downe his head againe: then I shot being charged with two bullets, and strooke him in the head: he being but amazed fell backwards: whereupon we ran all upon him with boare-speares, and thrust him in the body: yet for all that he gript away our boare-speares, and went towards the water; and as he was going downe, he came backe againe. Then our Master shot his boare-speare, and strooke him in the head, and made him to take the water, and swimme into a cove fast by, where we killed him, and brought him aboord. The breadth of his forefoot from one side to the other was fourteene inches over. They were very fat, so as we were constrained to cast the fat away. We saw a raven upon Mount Raleigh. We found withies also growing like low shrubs & flowers like Primroses in the sayd place. The coast is very mountainous, altogether without wood, grasse, or earth, and is onely huge mountaines of stone; but the bravest stone that ever we saw. The aire was very moderate in this countrey.

The 8 we departed from Mount Raleigh, coasting along the shoare, which lieth Southsouthwest, and Eastnortheast.

The 9 our men fell in dislike of their allowance, because it was too small as they thought: wherupon we made a new proportion; every messe being five to a messe should have foure pound of bread a day, twelve wine quarts of beere, six Newland fishes; and the flesh dayes a gill of pease more: so we restrained them from their butter and cheese.

The 11 we came to the most Southerly cape of this land, which we named The Cape of Gods mercy, as being the place of our first entrance for the discovery. The weather being very foggy we coasted this North land; at length when it brake up, we perceived that we were shot into a very faire entrance or passage, being in some places twenty leagues broad, and in some thirty, altogether void of any pester of ice, the weather very tolerable, and the water of the very colour, nature and quality of the maine ocean, which gave us the greater hope of our passage. Having sailed Northwest sixty leagues in this entrance we discovered certaine Islands standing in the midst thereof, having open passage on both sides. Wherupon our ships divided themselves, the one sailing on the North side, the other on the South side of the sayd Isles, where we stayed five dayes, having the winde at Southeast, very foggy and foule weather.

The 14 we went on shoare and found signes of people, for we found stones layed up together like a wall, and saw the skull of a man or a woman.

The 15 we heard dogs houle on the shoare, which we thought had bene wolves, and therefore we went on shoare to kill them. When we came on land the dogges came presently to our boat very gently, yet we thought they came to pray upon us, and therefore we shot at them, and killed two: and about the necke of one of them we found a leatherne coller, whereupon we thought them to be tame dogs. There were twenty dogs like mastives with prickt eares and long bush tailes: we found a bone in the pizels of their dogs. Then we went farther, and found two sleads made like ours in England: the one was made of firre, spruse and oken boords sawen like inch boords: the other was made all of whale bone, & there hung on the tops of the sleads three heads of beasts which they had killed. We saw here larks, ravens, and partridges.

The 17 we went on shoare, and in a little thing made like an oven with stones I found many small trifles, as a small canoa made of wood, a piece of wood made like an image, a bird made of bone, beads having small holes in one end of them to hang about their necks, & other small things. The coast was very barren without wood or grasse: the rocks were very faire like marble, full of vaines of divers colours. We found a seale which was killed not long before, being fleane, and hid under stones.

Our Captaine and Master searched still for probabilities of the passage, and first found, that this place was all Islands, with great sounds passing betweene them.

Secondly, the water remained of one colour with the maine ocean without altering.

Thirdly, we saw to the West of those Isles three or foure whales in a skull, which they judged to come from a Westerly sea, because to the Eastward we saw not any whale.

Also as we were rowing into a very great sound lying Southwest, from whence these whales came, upon the sudden there came a violent counter-checke of a tide from the Southwest against the flood which we came with, not knowing from whence it was mainteined.

Fiftly, in sailing twenty leagues within the mouth of this entrance we had sounding in 90 fadoms, faire grey osie sand, and the further we ran into the Westwards the deeper was the water; so that hard aboord the shoare among these Isles we could not have ground in 330 fadoms.

Lastly, it did ebbe and flow sixe or seven fadome up and downe, the flood comming from divers parts, so as we could not perceive the chiefe maintenance thereof.

The 18 and 19 our Captaine and Master determined what was best to doe, both for the safegard of their credits, and satisfying of the adventurers, and resolved, if the weather brake up, to make further search.

The 20 the winde came directly against us: so they altered their purpose, and reasoned both for proceeding and returning.

The 21 the winde being Northwest, we departed from these Islands; and as we coasted the South shoare we saw many faire sounds, whereby we were perswaded that it was no firme land but Islands.

The 23 of this moneth the wind came Southeast, with very stormy and foule weather: so we were constrained to seeke harborow upon the South coast of this entrance, where we fell into a very faire sound, & ankered in 25 fadoms greene osie sand. Here we went on shore, where we had manifest signes of people where they had made their fire, and layed stones like a wall. In this place we saw foure very faire faulcons; and M. Bruton tooke from one of them his prey, which we judged by the wings and legs to be a snite, for the head was eaten off.

The 24 in the afternoone, the winde comming somewhat faire, we departed from this road, purposing by Gods grace to returne for England.

The 26 we departed from sight of the North land of this entrance, directing our course homewards untill the tenth of the next moneth.

The 10. of September wee fell with The land of desolation, thinking to goe on shoare, but we could get never a good harborough. That night wee put to sea againe thinking to search it the next day: but this night arose a very great storme, and separated our ships, so that we lost the sight of the Mooneshine.

The 13. about noone (having tried all the night before with a goose wing) we set saile, & within two houres after we had sight of the Mooneshine againe: this day we departed from this land.

The 27. of this moneth we fell with sight of England. This night we had a marveilous storme and lost the Mooneshine.

The 30. of September wee came into Dartmouth, where wee found the Mooneshine being come in not two houres before.

39

The second voyage attempted by M. John Davis with others, for the discovery of the Northwest passage, in Anno 1586

THE 7. day of May, I departed from the port of Dartmouth for the discovery of the Northwest passage, with a ship of an hundred and twentie tunnes named the Mermayd, a barke of 60. tunnes named the Sunneshine, a barke of 35. tunnes named the Mooneshine, and a pinnesse of tenne tunnes named the North starre.

And the 15. of June I discovered land in the latitude of 60. degrees, and in longitude from the Meridian of London Westward 47. degrees, mightily pestered with yce and snow, so that there was no hope of landing: the yce lay in some places tenne leagues, in some 20. and in some 50. leagues off the shore, so that wee were constrained to beare into 57. degrees to double the same, and to recover a free Sea, which through Gods favourable mercy we at length obtained.

The 29. of June after many tempestuous storms we againe discovered land, in longitude from the Meridian of London 58. degr. 30. min. and in latitude 64. being East from us: into which course sith it please God by contrary winds to force us, I thought it very necessary to beare in with it, & there to set up our pinnesse, provided in the Mermayd to be our scout for this discovery, and so much the rather because the yere before I had bene in the same place, and found it very convenient for such a purpose, wel stored with flote wood, & possessed by a people of tractable conversation: so that the 29. of this moneth we arrived within the Isles which lay before this land, lying North northwest, and South southeast, we know not how farre. This land is very high & mountainous, having before it on the West side a mighty company of Isles full of faire sounds, and harboroughs. This land was very litle troubled with snow, and the sea altogether voyd of yce.

The ships being within the sounds wee sent our boates to search for shole water, where wee might anker, which in this place is very hard to finde: and as the boat went sounding and searching, the people of the countrey having espied them, came in their Canoas towards them with many shoutes and cries: but after they had espied in the boat some of our company that were the yeere before here with us, they presently rowed to the boate, and tooke hold on the oare, and hung about the boate with such comfortable joy, as would require a long discourse to be uttered: they came with the boates to our ships, making signes that they knewe all those that the yeere before had bene with them. After I perceived their joy and small feare of us, my selfe with the Merchants & others of the company went a shoare, bearing with me twentie knives: I had no sooner landed, but they lept out of their Canoas and came running to mee and the rest, and embraced us with many signes of heartie welcome: at this present there were eighteene of them, and to eche of them I gave a knife: they offred skinnes to me for reward, but I made signes that they were not solde, but given them of courtesie: and so dismissed them for that time, with signes that they should returne againe after certaine houres.

The next day with all possible speede the pinnesse was landed upon an Isle there to be finished to serve our purpose for the discoverie, which Isle was so convenient for that purpose, as that we were very wel able to defend our selves against many enemies. During the time that the pinnesse, was there setting up, the people came continually unto us sometime an hundred Canoas at a time, sometime fourtie, fiftie, more and lesse, as occasion served. They brought with them seale skinnes, stagge skinnes, white hares, Seale fish, samon peale, smal cod, dry caplin, with other fish, and birds such as the countrey did yeeld.

My selfe still desirous to have a further search of this place, sent one of the shipboates to one part of the lande, and my selfe went to another part to search for the habitation of this people, with straight commandement that there should be no injurie offered to any of the people, neither any gunne shot.

The boates that went from me found the tents of the people made with seale skinnes set up upon timber, wherein they found great store of dried Caplin, being a litle fish no bigger then a pilchard: they found bags of Trane oyle, many litle images cut in wood, Seale skinnes in tan-tubs, with many other such trifles, whereof they diminished nothing.

They also found tenne miles within the snowy mountaines a plaine champion countrey, with earth and grasse, such as our moory and waste grounds of England are: they went up into a river (which in the narrowest place is two leagues broad) about ten leagues, finding it still to continue they knewe not howe farre: but I with my company tooke another river, which although at the first it offered a large inlet, yet it proved but a deepe bay, the ende whereof in foure houres I attained, and there leaving the boat well manned, went with the rest of my company three or foure miles into the countrey, but found nothing, nor saw any thing, save onely gripes, ravens, and small birds, as larkes and linnets.

The third of July I manned my boat, and went with fifty Canoas attending upon me up into another sound where the people by signes willed mee to goe, hoping to finde their habitation: at length they made signes that I should goe into a warme place to sleepe, at which place I went on shore, and ascended the toppe of an high hill to see into the countrey, but perceiving my labor vaine, I returned againe to my boat, the people still following me, and my company very diligent to attend us, and to helpe us up the rockes, and likewise downe: at length I was desirous to have our men leape with them, which was done, but our men did overleape them: from leaping they went to wrestling, we found them strong and nimble, and to have skil in wrestling, for they cast some of our men that were good wrestlers.

The fourth of July we lanched our pinnesse, and had fortie of the people to helpe us, which they did very willingly: at this time our men againe wrestled with them, and found them as before, strong and skilfull. This fourth of July the Master of the Mermayd went to certaine Ilands to store himselfe with wood, where he found a grave with divers buried in it, only covered with seale skinnes, having a crosse laid over them. The people are of good stature, wel in body proportioned, with small slender hands and feet, with broad visages, and smal eyes, wide mouthes, the most part unbearded, great lips, and close toothed. Their custome is as often as they go from us, still at their returne to make a new truce, in this sort, holding his hand up to the Sun with a lowd voice he crieth Ylyaoute, and striketh his brest with like signes, being promised safety, he giveth credit. These people are much given to bleed, and therefore stop their noses with deeres haire, or the haire of an elan. They are idolaters and have images great store, which they weare about them, and in their boats, which we suppose they worship. They are witches, and have many kinds of inchantments, which they often used, but to small purpose, thankes be to God.

Being among them at shore the fourth of July, one of them making a long oration, beganne to kindle a fire in this maner: he tooke a piece of a board wherein was a hole halfe thorow: into that hole he puts the end of a round stick like unto a bed-staffe, wetting the end thereof in Trane, and in fashion of a turner with a piece of lether, by his violent motion doeth very speedily produce fire: which done, with turfes he made a fire, into which with many words and strange gestures, he put diverse things, which wee supposed to be a sacrifice: my selfe and divers of my company standing by, they were desirous to have me go into the smoke, I willed them likewise to stand in the smoke, which they by no meanes would do. I then tooke one of them, and thrust him into the smoke, and willed one of my company to tread out the fire, & to spurne it into the sea, which was done to shew them that we did contemne their sorcery. These people are very simple in all their conversation, but marveilous theevish, especially for iron, which they have in great account. They began through our lenitie to shew their vile nature: they began to cut our cables: they cut away the Moonelights boat from her sterne, they cut our cloth where it lay to aire, though we did carefully looke unto it, they stole our oares, a caliver, a boare speare, a sword, with divers other things, wherat the company and Masters being grieved, for our better securitie, desired me to dissolve this new friendship, and to leave the company of these theevish miscreants: whereupon there was a caliver shot among them, and immediatly upon the same a faulcon, which strange noice did sore amaze them, so that with speed they departed: notwithstanding their simplicitie is such, that within ten houres after they came againe to us to entreat peace; which being promised, we againe fell into a great league. They brought us Seale skinnes, and sammon peale, but seeing iron, they could in no wise forbeare stealing: which when I perceived, it did but minister unto mee an occasion of laughter, to see their simplicitie, and I willed that in no case they should bee any more hardly used, but that our owne company should be the more vigilant to keepe their things, supposing it to be very hard in so short time to make them know their evils. They eate all their meat raw, they live most upon fish, they drinke salt water, and eate grasse and ice with delight: they are never out of the water, but live in the nature of fishes, save only when dead sleepe taketh them, and then under a warme rocke laying his boat upon the land, hee lyeth downe to sleepe. Their weapons are all darts, but some of them have bow and arrowes and slings. They make nets to take their fish of the finne of a whale: they do all their things very artificially: and it should seeme that these simple theevish Islanders have warre with those of the maine, for many of them are sore wounded, which wounds they received upon the maine land, as by signes they gave us to understand. We had among them copper oare, black copper, and red copper: they pronounce their language very hollow, and deepe in the throat.

The 7. of July being very desirous to search the habitation of this countrey, I went myselfe with our new pinnesse into the body of the land, thinking it to be a firme continent, and passing up a very large river, a great flaw of winde tooke me, whereby wee were constrained to seeke succour for that night, which being had, I landed with the most part of my company, and went to the top of a high mountaine, hoping from thence to see into the countrey: but the mountaines were so many and so mighty as that my purpose prevailed not: whereupon I againe returned to my pinnesse, and willing divers of my company to gather muscles for my supper, whereof in this place there was great store, my selfe having espied a very strange sight, especially to me that never before saw the like, which was a mighty whirlewinde taking up the water in very great quantitie, furiously mounting it into the aire, which whirlewinde, was not for a puffe or blast, but continual, for the space of three houres, with very little intermission, which sith it was in the course that I should passe, we were constrained that night to take up our lodging under the rockes.

The next morning the storme being broken up, we went forward in our attempt, and sailed into a mighty great river directly into the body of the land, and in briefe, found it to be no firme land, but huge, waste, and desert Isles with mighty sounds, and inlets passing betweene Sea and Sea. Whereupon we returned towards our shippes, and landing to stoppe a floud, wee found the burial of these miscreants; we found of their fish in bagges, plaices, and caplin dried, of which wee tooke onely one bagge and departed. The ninth of this moneth we came to our ships, where wee found the people desirous in their fashion, of friendship and barter: our Mariners complained heavily against the people, and said that my lenitie and friendly using of them gave them stomacke to mischiefe: for they have stollen an anker from us, they have cut our cable very dangerously, they have cut our boats from our sterne, and nowe since your departure, with slings they spare us not with stones of halfe a pound weight: and wil you stil indure these injuries? It is a shame to beare them. I desired them to be content, and said, I doubted not but al should be wel. The 10. of this moneth I went to the shore, the people following mee in their Canoas: I tolled them on shore, and used them with much courtesie, and then departed aboord, they following me, and my company. I gave some of them bracelets, & caused seven or eight of them to come aboord, which they did willingly, and some of them went into the top of the ship: and thus curteously using them, I let them depart: the Sunne was no sooner downe, but they began to practise their devilish nature, and with slings threw stones very fiercely into the Moonelight, and strake one of her men then boatswaine, that he overthrew withall: whereat being moved, I changed my curtesie, and grew to hatred, my self in my owne boate well manned with shot, and the barks boat likewise pursued them, and gave them divers shot, but to small purpose, by reason of their swift rowing: so smally content we returned.

The 11. of this moneth there came five of them to make a new truce: the master of the Admiral came to me to shew me of their comming, and desired to have them taken and kept as prisoners untill we had his anker againe: but when he sawe that the chiefe ringleader and master of mischiefe was one of the five, he then was vehement to execute his purpose, so it was determined to take him: he came crying *Iliaout, and striking his brest offered a paire of gloves to sell, the master offered him a knife for them: so two of them came to us, the one was not touched, but the other was soone captive among us: then we pointed to him and his fellowes for our anker, which being had, we made signes that he should be set at libertie: within one houre after he came aboord the winde came faire, whereupon we weyed and set saile, and so brought the fellow with us: one of his fellowes still following our ship close aboord, talked with him and made a kinde of lamentation, we still using him wel with Yliaout, which was the common course of curtesie. At length this fellow aboord us spake foure or five words unto the other and clapped his two hands upon his face, whereupon the other doing the like, departed as we suppose with heavie chere. We judged the covering of his face with his hands and bowing of his body downe, signified his death. At length he became a pleasant companion among us. I gave him a new sute of frize after the English fashion, because I saw he could not indure the colde, of which he was very joyfull, he trimmed up his darts, and all his fishing tooles, and would make okam, and set his hand to a ropes end upon occasion. He lived with the dry Caplin that I tooke when I was searching in the pinnis, and did eate dry Newland fish.

All this while, God be thanked, our people were in very good health, onely one young man excepted, who dyed at sea the fourteenth of this moneth, and the fifteenth, according to the order of the sea, with praise given to God by service, was cast overboord.

The 17 of this moneth being in the latitude of 63. degres 8. minuts, we fell upon a most mighty and strange quantitie of yce in one intire masse, so bigge as that we knew not the limits thereof, and being withall so very high in forme of a land, with bayes and capes and like high cliffe land, as that we supposed it to be land, and therefore sent our pinnesse off to discover it: but at her returne we were certainely informed that it was onely yce, which bred great admiration to us all considering

---

* I.e.: "I mean no harm" (ED.).

the huge quantitie thereof, incredible to be reported in trueth as it was, and therefore I omit to speake any further thereof. This onely I thinke, that the like before was never seene: and in this place we had very stickle and strong currents.

We coasted this mightie masse of yce untill the 30 of July, finding it a mighty barre to our purpose: the ayre in this time was so contagious and the sea so pestered with yce, as that all hope was banished of proceeding: for the 24 of July all our shrowds, ropes and sailes were so frosen, and compassed with yce, onely by a grosse fogge, as seemed to me more then strange, sith the last yeere I found this sea free and navigable, without impediments.

Our men through this extremity began to grow sicke and feeble, and withall hopelesse of good successe: whereupon very orderly, with good discretion they intreated me to regard the state of this busines, and withall advised me, that in conscience I ought to regard the saftie of mine owne life with the preservation of theirs, and that I should not through my overboldnes leave their widowes and fatherlesse children to give me bitter curses. This matter in conscience did greatly move me to regard their estates: yet considering the excellencie of the businesse if it might be attained, the great hope of certaintie by the last yeeres discovery, and that there was yet a third way not put in practise, I thought it would growe to my great disgrace, if this action by my negligence should grow into discredite: whereupon seeking helpe from God, the fountaine of all mercies, it pleased his divine majestie to move my heart to prosecute that which I hope shal be to his glory, and to the contentation of every Christian minde. Whereupon falling into consideration that the Mermaid, albeit a very strong & sufficient ship, yet by reason of her burthen was not so convenient and nimble as a smaller bark, especially in such desperate hazzards: further having in account her great charge to the adventurers being at 100.li. the moneth, and that in doubtfull service: all the premisses considered with divers other things, I determined to furnish the Moonelight with revictualling and sufficient men, and to proceede in this action as God should direct me. Whereupon I altered our course from the yce, and bare Eastsoutheast to recover the next shore where this thing might be performed: so with favourable winde it pleased God that the first of August we discovered the land in Latitude 66. degrees, 33. min. and in longitude from the Meridian of London 70. degrees voyd of trouble without snow or ice.

The second of August wee harboured our selves in a very excellent good road, where with all speed we graved the Moone-light, and revictualled her: wee searched this countrey with our pinnesse while the barke was trimming, which William Eston did: he found all this land to be onely Ilands, with a Sea on the East, a Sea on the West, and a Sea on the North. In this place wee found it very hot, and wee were very much troubled with a flie which is called Muskyto, for they did sting grievously. The people of this place at our first comming in caught a Seale, and with bladders fast tied to him sent him unto us with the floud, so as hee came right with our shippes, which we tooke as a friendly present from them.

The fift of August I went with the two Masters and others to the toppe of a hill, and by the way William Eston espied three Canoas lying under a rocke, and went unto them: there were in them skinnes, darts, with divers superstitious toyes, whereof we diminished nothing, but left upon every boat a silke point, a bullet of lead, and a pinne. The next day being the sixt of August, the people came unto us without feare, and did barter with us for skinnes, as the other people did: they differ not from the other, neither in their Canoas nor apparel, yet is their pronuntiation more plaine then the others, and nothing hollow in the throat. Our Savage aboord us kept himselfe close, and made shew that he would faine have another companion. Thus being provided, I departed from this lande the twelft of August at sixe of the clocke in the morning, where I left the Mermayd at an anker: the foureteenth sailing West about fiftie leagues, we discovered land, being in latitude 66. degrees 19 minuts: this land is 70. leagues from the other from whence we came. This fourteenth day from nine a clocke at night till three a clocke in the morning, wee ankered by an Iland of yce, twelve leagues off the shore, being mored to the yce.

The fifteenth day at three a clocke in the morning we departed from this land to the South, and the eighteenth of August we discovered land Northwest from us in the morning, being a very faire promontory, in latitude 65. degrees, having no land on the South. Here wee had great hope of a through passage.

This day at three a clocke in the afternoone wee againe discovered lande Southwest and by South from us, where at night wee were becalmed. The nineteenth of this moneth at noone, by observation, we were in 64. degrees 20. minuts. From the eighteenth day at noone unto the nineteenth at noone, by precise ordinary care, wee had sailed 15. leagues South and by West, yet by art and more exact observation, we found our course to be Southwest, so that we plainely perceived a great current striking to the West.

This land is nothing in sight but Isles, which increaseth our hope. This nineteenth of August at sixe a clocke in the afternoone, it began to snow, and so continued all night with foule weather, and much winde, so that we were constrained to lie at hull all night five leagues off the shore: In the morning being the twentieth of August, the fogge and storme breaking up, we bare in with the lande, and at nine a clocke in the morning wee ankered in a very faire and safe road and lockt for all weathers. At tenne of the clocke I went on shore to the toppe of a very high hill, where I perceived that this land was Islands: at foure of the clocke in the afternoone wee weyed anker, having a faire North northeast winde, with very faire weather; at six of the clocke we were cleare without the land, and so shaped our course to the South, to discover the coast, whereby the passage may be through Gods mercy found.

We coasted this land till the eight and twentieth of August, finding it still to continue towards the South, from the latitude of 67. to 57. degrees: we found marveilous great store of birds, guls and mewes, incredible to be reported, whereupon being calme weather, we lay one glasse upon the lee, to prove for fish, in which space we caught 100. of cod, although we were but badly provided for fishing, not being our purpose. This eight and twentieth having great distrust of the weather, we arrived in a very faire harbour in the latitude of 56. degrees, and sailed 10. leagues into the same, being two leagues broad, with very faire woods on both sides: in this place wee continued until the first of September, in which time we had two very great stormes. I landed, & went six miles by ghesse into the countrey, and found that the woods were firre, pineapple, alder, yew, withy, and birch: here wee saw a blacke beare: this place yeeldeth great store of birds, as fezant, partridge, Barbary hennes or the like, wilde geese, ducks, black birdes, jeyes, thrushes, with other kinds of small birds. Of the partridge and fezant we killed great store with bow and arrowes: in this place at the harborough mouth we found great store of cod.

The first of September at tenne a clocke wee set saile, and coasted the shore with very faire weather. The thirde day being calme, at noone we strooke saile, and let fall a cadge anker, to prove whether we could take any fish, being in latitude 54. degrees 30. minuts, in which place we found great abundance of cod, so that the hooke was no sooner overboord, but presently a fish was taken. It was the largest and the best fed fish that ever I sawe, and divers fisher men that were with me sayd that they never saw a more suavle or better skull of fish in their lives: yet had they seene great abundance.

The fourth of September at five a clocke in the afternoone we ankered in a very good road among great store of Isles, the countrey low land, pleasant and very full of fayre woods. To the North of this place eight leagues, we had a perfect hope of the passage, finding a mightie great sea passing betweene two lands West. The South land to our judgement being nothing but Isles: we greatly desired to goe into this sea, but the winde was directly against us. We ankered in foure fathome fine sand. In this place is foule and fish mightie store.

The sixt of September having a faire Northnorthwest winde, having trimmed our Barke we purposed to depart, and sent five of our sailers yong men a shore to an Island, to fetch certaine fish which we purposed to weather, and therefore left it al night covered upon the Isle: the brutish people of this countrey lay secretly lurking in the wood, and upon the sudden assaulted our men: which when we perceived, we presently let slip our cables upon the halse, and under our foresaile bare into the shoare, and with all expedition discharged a double musket upon them twise, at the noyse whereof they fled: notwithstanding to our very great griefe, two of our men were slaine with their arrowes, and two grievously wounded, of whom at this present we stand in very great doubt, onely one escaped by swimming, with an arrow shot thorow his arme. These wicked miscreants never offered parly or speech, but presently executed their cursed fury.

This present evening it pleased God further to increase our sorowes with a mighty tempestuous storme, the winde being Northnortheast, which lasted unto the tenth of this moneth very extreme. We unrigged our ship, and purposed to cut downe our masts, the cable of our shutanker brake, so that we onely expected to be driven on shoare among these Canibals for their pray. Yet in this deepe distresse the mightie mercie of God, when hope was past, gave us succour, and sent us a faire lee, so as we recovered our anker againe, and newe mored our ship: where we saw that God manifestly delivered us: for the straines of one of our cables were broken, and we only roade by an olde junke. Thus being freshly mored a new storme arose, the winde being Westnorthwest, very forcible, which lasted unto the tenth day at night.

The eleventh day with a faire Westnorthwest winde we departed with trust in Gods mercie, shaping our course for England, and arrived in the West countrey in the beginning of October.

40

Master Davis being arrived, wrote his letter to M. William Sanderson of London, concerning his voyage, as followeth

S I R , the Sunneshine came into Dartmouth the fourth of this moneth: she hath bene at Island, and from thence to Groenland, and so to Estotiland, from thence to Desolation, and to our Marchants, where she made trade with the people, staying in the countrey twentie dayes. They have brought home five hundred seale skinnes, and an hundred and fortie halfe skinnes and pieces of skinnes. I stand in great doubt of the pinnesse, God be mercifull unto the poore men, and preserve them, if it be his blessed will.

I have now experience of much of the Northwest part of the world, & have brought the passage to that likelihood, as that I am assured it must be in one of foure places, or els not at all. And further I can assure you upon the perill of my life, that this voyage may be performed without further charge, nay with certaine profite to the adventurers, if I may have but your favour in the action. I hope I shall finde favour with you to see your Card. I pray God it be so true as the Card shal be which I will bring you: and I hope in God, that your skill in Navigation shall be gaineful unto you, although at the first it hath not proved so. And thus with my humble commendations I commit you to God, desiring no longer to live, then I shall be yours most faithfully to command. Exon this fourteenth of October. 1586.

Yours to command   JOHN DAVIS

41

The relation of the course which the Sunshine a barke of fiftie tunnes, and the Northstarre a small pinnesse, being two vessels of the fleete of M. John Davis, helde after hee had sent them from him to discover the passage betweene Groenland and Island, written by Henry Morgan servant to M. William Sanderson of London

THE seventh day of May 1586. wee departed out of Dartmouth haven foure sailes, to wit, the Mermaid, the Sunshine, the Mooneshine, & the Northstarre. In the Sunshine were sixteene men, whose names were these: Richard Pope Master, Marke Carter Masters mate, Henry Morgan Purser, George Draward, John Mandie, Hugh Broken, Philip Jane, Hugh Hempson, Richard Borden, John Philpe, Andrew Madock, William Wolcome, Robert Wag carpenter, John Bruskome, William Ashe, Simon Ellis.

Our course was Westnorthwest the seventh and eight dayes: and the ninth day in the morning we were on head of the Tarrose of Silley. Thus coasting along the South part of Ireland the 11. day, we were on head of the Dorses: and our course was Southsouthwest untill sixe of the clocke the 12. day. The 13. day our course was Northwest. We remained in the company of the Mermaid and the Mooneshine until we came to the latitude of 60. degrees: and there it seemed best to our Generall M. Davis to divide his fleete, himself sayling to the Northwest, and to direct the Sunshine, wherein I was, and the pinnesse called the Northstarre, to seeke a passage Northward betweene Groenland and Island to the latitude of 80. degrees, if land did not let us. So the seventh day of June wee departed from them: and the ninth of the same we came to a firme land of yce, which we coasted along the ninth, the tenth, and the eleventh dayes of June: and the eleventh day at sixe of the clocke at night we saw land which was very high, which afterward we knew to be Island: and the twelft day we harboured there, and found many people: the land lyeth East and by North in 66. degrees.

Their commodities were greene fish, and Island lings, and stockfish, and a fish which is called Scatefish: of all which they had great store. They had also kine, sheep and horses, and hay for their cattell, and for their horses. Wee saw also their dogs. Their dwelling houses were made on both sides with stones, and wood layd crosse over them, which was covered over with turfes of earth, and they are flat on the tops, and many of these stood hard by the shore. Their boates were made with wood and yron all along the keele like our English boates: and they had nayles for to naile them withall, and fish-hookes and other things for to catch fish as we have here in England. They had also brasen kettles, and girdles and purses made of leather, and knoppes on them of copper, and hatchets, and other small tooles as necessary as we have. They drie their fish in the Sun, and when they are dry, they packe them up in the top of their houses. If we would goe thither to fishing more then we doe, we should make it a very good voyage: for wee got an hundreth greene fish in one morning. Wee found heere two English men with a shippe, which came out of England about Easter day of this present yeere 1586, and one of them came aboord of us, and brought us two lambs. The English mans name was M. John Roydon of Ipswich marchant: hee was bound for London with his ship. And this is the summe of that which I observed in Island. We departed from Island the sixteenth day of June in the morning, and our course was Northwest, and we saw on the coast two small barkes going to an harborough: we went not to them, but saw them a farre off. Thus we continued our course unto the end of this moneth.

The third day of July we were in betweene two firme lands of yce, and passed in betweene them all that day untill it was night: and then the Master turned backe againe, and so away we went towards Groenland. And the seventh day of July we did see Groenland, and it was very high, and it looked very blew: we could not come to harborough into the land, because we were hindered by a firme land as it were of yce, which was along the shoares side: but we were within three leagues of the land, coasting the same divers dayes together. The seventeenth day of July wee saw the place which our Captaine M. John Davis the yeere before had named The land of Desolation, where we could not goe on shore for yce. The eighteenth day we were likewise troubled with yce, and went in amongst it at three of the clocke in the morning. After wee had cleared our selves thereof, wee ranged all along the coast of Desolation untill the ende of the aforesayd moneth.

The third day of August we came in sight of Gilberts sound in the latitude of 64. deg. 15. min. which was the place where wee were appoynted to meete our Generall and the rest of our Fleete. Here we came to an harborough at 6. of the clocke at night.

The 4. day in the morning the Master went on shore with 10. of his men, and they brought us foure of the people rowing in their boats aboord of the ship. And in the afternoone I went on shore with 6. of our men, and there came to us seven of them when we were on land. We found on shore three dead people, and two of them had their staves lying by them, and their olde skinnes wrapped about them and the other had nothing lying by, wherefore we thought it was a woman. We also saw their houses neere the Sea side, which were made with pieces of wood on both sides, and crossed over with poles and then covered over with earth: we found Foxes running upon the hilles: as for the place it is broken land all the way that we went, and full of broken Islands.

The 21. of August the Master sent the boate on shore for wood with six of his men, and there were one and thirtie of the people of the countrey which went on shore to them, & they went about to kill them as we thought, for they shot their dartes towards them, and we that were aboord the ship, did see them goe on shore to our men: whereupon the Master sent the pinnesse after them, and when they saw the pinnesse comming towards them, they turned backe, and the Master of the pinnesse did shoote off a caliver to them the same time, but hurt none of them, for his meaning was onely to put them in feare. Divers times they did wave us on shore to play with them at the football, and some of our company went on shore to play with them, and our men did cast them downe as soone as they did come to strike the ball. And thus much of that which we did see and do in the harborough where we arrived first.

The 23. day wee departed from the Merchants Isle, where wee had beene first, and our course from thence was South & by West, and the wind was Northeast, and we ran that day and night about 5. or 6. leagues, untill we came to another harborough.

The 24. about eleven of the clocke in the forenoone wee entred into the aforesayd new harborow, and as wee came in, we did see dogs running upon the Islands. When we were come in, there came to us foure of the people which were with us before in the other harborough, and where we rode, we had sandie ground. We saw no wood growing, but found small pieces of wood upon the Islands, & some small pieces of sweete wood among the same. We found great Harts hornes, but could see none of the Stagges where we went, but we found their footings. As for the bones which we received of the Savages I cannot tell of what beasts they be.

The stones that we found in the countrey were black, and some white, as I thinke they be of no value, neverthelesse I have brought examples of them to you.

The 30. of August we departed from this harborough towards England, & the wind tooke us contrary, so that we were faine to go to another harborough the same day at 11. of the clocke. And there came to us 39. of the people, and brought us 13. Seale skins, and after we received these skins of them, the Master sent the carpenter to change one of our boates which wee had bought of them before, and they would have taken the boate from him perforce, and when they sawe they could not take it from us, they shot with their dartes at us, and stroke one of our men with one of their dartes, and John Filpe shot one of them into the brest with an arrow. And they came to us againe, and foure of our men went into the shipboate, and they shot with their dartes at our men: but our men tooke one of their people in his boate into the shipboate, and he hurt one of them with his knife, but we killed three of them in their boates: two of them were hurt with arrowes in the brests, and he that was aboord our boat, was shot in with an arrow, and hurt with a sword, and beaten with staves, whome our men cast overboord, but the people caught him and carried him on shore upon their boates, and the other two also, and so departed from us. And three of them went on shore hard by us, where they had their dogs, and those three came away from their dogs, and presently one of their dogs came swimming towards us hard aboord the ship, whereupon our Master caused the Gunner to shoote off one of the great pieces towards the people, and so the dog turned backe to land and within an houre after there came of the people hard aboord the ship, but they would not come to us as they did come before.

The 31. of August we departed from Gylberts sound for England, and when we came out of the harborough there came after us 17. of the people looking which way we went.

The 2. of September we lost sight of the land at 12. of the clocke at noone.

The third day at night we lost sight of the Northstarre our pinnesse in a very great storme, and lay a hull tarying for them the 4. day, but could heare no more of them. Thus we shaped our course the 5. day Southsoutheast, and sayling untill the 27. of the sayd moneth, we came in sight of Cape Clere in Ireland.

The 30. day we entred into our owne chanell.

The 2. of October we had sight of the Isle of Wight.

The 3. we coasted all along the shore, and the 4. and 5.

The 6. of the said moneth of October wee came into the river of Thames as high as Ratliffe in safetie God be thanked.

42

The third voyage Northwestward, made by M. John Davis Gentleman, as chiefe captaine & Pilot generall, for the discovery of a passage to the Isles of the Moluccas, or the coast of China, in the yeere 1587. Written by M. John Janes

May

THE 19. of this present moneth about midnight wee weyed our ankers, set sayle, and departed from Dartmouth with two Barkes and a Clincher, the one named the Elizabeth of Dartmouth, the other the Sunneshine of London, and the Clincher called the Helene of London: thus in Gods name we set forwards with the wind at Northeast a good fresh gale. About 3. houres after our departure, the night being somewhat thicke with darknesse, we had lost the pinnesse: the Captaine imagining that the men had runne away with her, willed the Master of the Sunshine to stand to Seawards, and see if we could descry them, we bearing in with the shore for Plimmouth. At length we descried her, bare with her, and demanded what the cause was: they answered that the tiller of their helme was burst. So shaping our course Westsouthwest, we went forward, hoping that a hard beginning would make a good ending, yet some of us were doubtfull of it, falling in reckoning that she was a Clincher; neverthelesse we put our trust in God.

The 21. we met with the Red Lion of London, which came from the coast of Spaine, which was afrayd that we had bene men of warre, but we hailed them, and after a little conference, we desired the Master to carie our letters for London directed to my uncle Sanderson, who promised us a safe deliverie. And after wee had heaved them a lead and a line, whereunto wee had made fast our letters, before they could get them into the ship, they fell into the Sea, and so all our labour and theirs also was lost; notwithstanding they promised to certifie our departure at London, and so we departed, and the same day we had sight of Silley. The 22. the wind was at Northeast by East with faire weather, and so the 23. and 24. the like. The 25. we layd our ships on the Lee for the Sunneshine, who was a romaging for a leake, they had 500. strokes at the pumpe in a watch, the wind at Northwest.

The 26. and 27. wee had faire weather, but this 27. the pinnesses foremast was blowen overboord. The 28. the Elizabeth towed the pinnesse, which was so much bragged off by the owners report before we came out of England, but at Sea she was like a cart drawen with oxen. Sometimes we towed her because she could not saile for scant wind.

The 31. day our Captaine asked if the pinnesse were stanch, Peerson answered that she was as sound and stanch as a cup. This made us something glad, when we sawe she would brooke the Sea, and was not leake.

June

The first 6. dayes wee had faire weather: after that for 5. dayes wee had fogge and raine, the winde being South. The 12. wee had cleare weather. The Mariners in the Sunneshine and the Master could not agree: the Mariners would goe on their voyage a fishing, because the yeere began to waste: the Master would not depart till hee had the companie of the Elizabeth, whereupon the Master told our Captaine that hee was afrayd his men would shape some contrary course while he was asleepe, and so he should lose us. At length after much talke and many threatnings, they were content to bring us to the land which we looked for daily.

The 14. day we discovered land at five of the clocke in the morning, being very great and high mountaines, the tops of the hils being covered with snow. Here the wind was variable, sometimes Northeast, Eastnortheast, and East by North: but we imagined ourselves to be 16. or 17. leagues off from the shore.

The 16. we came to an anker about 4. or 5. of the clocke after nonne, the people came presently to us after the old maner, with crying Ilyaoute, and shewing us Seales skinnes.

The 17. we began to set up the pinnesse that Peerson framed at Dartmouth, with the boords which hee brought from London.

The 18. Peerson and the Carpenters of the ships began to set on the plankes. The 19. as we went about an Island, were found blacke Pumise stones, and salt kerned on the rockes, very white and glistering. This day also the Master of the Sunneshine tooke of the people a very strong lusty yoong fellow.

The 20. about two of the clocke in the morning, the Savages came to the Island where our pinnace was built readie to bee launched, and tore the two upper strakes, and carried them away onely for the love of the yron in the boords. While they were about this practise, we manned the Elizabeths boate to goe a shore to them: our men being either afrayd or amazed, were so long before they came to shore, that our Captaine willed them to stay, and made the Gunner give fire to a Saker, and layd the piece levell with the boate which the Savages had turned on the one side because wee should not hurt them with our arrowes, and made the boate their bulwarke against the arrowes which we shot at them. Our Gunner having made all things readie, gave fire to the piece, and fearing to hurt any of the people, and regarding the owners profite, thought belike hee would save a Sakers shot, doubting wee should have occasion to fight with men of warre, and so shot off the Saker without a bullet: we looking stil when the Savages that were hurt should run away without legs, at length wee could perceive never a man hurt, but all having their legges could carrie away their bodies: wee had no sooner shot off the piece, but the Master of the Sunneshine manned his boate, and came rowing toward the Island, the very sight of whom made each of them take that hee had gotten, and flee away as fast as they could to another Island about two miles off, where they tooke the nayles out of the timber, and left the wood on the Isle. when we came on shore, and saw how they had spoiled the boat, after much debating of the matter, we agreed that the Elizabeth should have her to fish withall: whereupon she was presently caryed aboord, and stowed.

Now after this trouble, being resolved to depart with the first wind, there fell out another matter worse then all the rest, and that was in this maner. John Churchyard one whom our Captaine had appoynted as Pilot in the pinnace, came to our Captaine, and master Bruton, and told them that the good ship which we must all hazard our lives in, had three hundred strokes at one time as she rode in the harbour: This disquieted us all greatly, and many doubted to goe in her. At length our Captaine by whom we were all to be governed, determined rather to end his life with credite, then to returne with infamie and disgrace, and so being all agreed, wee purposed to live and die together, and committed our selves to the ship. Now the 21. having brought all our things aboord, about 11. or 12. of the clocke at night, we set saile and departed from those Isles, which lie in 64. degrees of latitude, our ships being all now at Sea, and wee shaping our course to goe, coasting the land to the Northwards upon the Easterne shore, which we called the shore of our Marchants, because there we met with people which traffiqued with us, but here wee were not without doubt of our ship.

The 24. being in 67. degrees, and 40. minutes, wee had great store of Whales, and a kinde of sea birds which the Mariners call Cortinous. This day about sixe of the clocke at night, we espied two of the countrey people at Sea, thinking at the first they had bene two great Seales, untill wee sawe their oares glistering with the Sunne: they came rowing towardes us, as fast as they could, and when they came within hearing, they held up their oares, and cryed Ilyaoute, making many signes: and at last they came to us, giving us birdes for bracelets, and of them I had a darte with a bone in it, or a piece of Unicorns horne, as I did judge. This dart he made store of, but when he saw a knife, he let it go, being more desirous of the knife then of his dart: these people continued rowing after our ship the space of 3. howres.

The 25. in the morning at 7. of the clocke we descried 30. Savages rowing after us, being by judgement 10. leagues off from the shore: they brought us Salmon Peales, Birdes, and Caplin, and we gave them pinnes, needles, bracelets, nailes, knives, bels, looking glasses, and other small trifles, and for a knife, a naile or a bracelet, which they call Ponigmah, they would sell their boate, coates, or any thing they had, although they were farre from the shore. Wee had but few skinnes of them, about 20. but they made signes to us that if wee would goe to the shore, wee should have more store of Chichsanege: they stayed with us till 11. of the clocke, at which time wee went to prayer, and they departed from us.

The 28. and 29. were foggie with cloudes, the 30. day wee tooke the heigth, and found our selves in 72. degrees and 12 minutes of latitude both at noone and at night, the Sunne being 5. degrees above the Horizon. At midnight the compasse set to the variation of 28. degrees to the Westward. Now having coasted the land, which wee called London coast, from the 21. of this present, till the 30. the Sea open all to the Westwards and Northwards, the land on starboord side East from us, the winde shifted to the North, whereupon we left that shore, naming the same Hope Sanderson, and shaped our course West, and ranne 40. leagues and better without the sight of any land.

July

The second of July wee fell with a mightie banke of yce West from us, lying North and South, which banke wee would gladly have doubled out to the Northwards, but the winde would not suffer us, so that we were faine to coast it to the Southwards, hoping to double it out, that wee might have run so farre West till wee had found land, or els to have beene thorowly resolved of our pretended purpose.

The 3. wee fell with the yce againe, and putting off from it, we sought to the Northwards, but the wind crossed us.

The 4. was foggie: so was the 5. also with much wind at the North.

The 6. being very cleare, we put our barke with oares through a gap in the yce, seeing the Sea free on the West side, as we thought, which falling out otherwise, caused us to returne after we had stayed there betweene the yce. The 7. and the 8. about midnight, by Gods helpe we recovered the open Sea, the weather being faire and calme, and so was the 9. The 10. we coasted the yce. The 11. was foggie, but calme.

The 12. we coasted againe the yce, having the wind at North-northwest. The 13. bearing off from the yce, we determined to goe with the shoare and come to an anker, and to stay 5. or 6. dayes for the dissolving of the yce, hoping that the Sea continually beating it, and the Sunne with the extreme force of heat which it had alwayes shining upon it, would make a quicke dispatch, that we might have a further search upon the Westerne shore. Now when we were come to the Easterne coast, the water something deepe, and some of our companie fearefull withall, we durst not come to an anker, but bare off into the Sea againe. The poore people seeing us goe away againe, came rowing after us into the Sea, the waves being somewhat loftie. We truckt with them for a few skinnes and dartes, and gave them beads, nailes, pinnes, needles and cardes, they poynting to the shore, as though they would shew us some great friendship: but we little regarding their curtesie, gave them the gentle farewell, and so departed.

The 14. wee had the wind at South. The 15. there was some fault either in the barke, or the set of some current, for wee were driven sixe points beyond our course West. The 16. wee fell with the banke of yce West from us. The 17. and 18. were foggie. The 19. at one a clocke after noone, wee had sight of the land which we called Mount Raleigh, and at 12. of the clocke at night, we were thwart the streights which we discovered the first yeere. The 20. wee traversed in the mouth of the streight, the wind being at West, with faire and cleare weather. The 21. and 22. wee coasted the Northerne coast of the streights. The 23. having sayled threescore leagues Northwest into the streights, at two a clocke after noone wee ankered among many Isles in the bottome of the gulfe, naming the same The Earle of Cumberlands Isles, where riding at anker, a Whale passed by our ship and went West in among the Isles. Heere the compasse set at thirtie degrees Westward variation. The 23. wee departed, shaping our course Southeast to recover the Sea. The 25. wee were becalmed in the bottome of the gulfe, the ayre being extreme hot. Master Bruton and some of the Mariners went on shoare to course dogs, where they found many Graves and Trane spilt on the ground, the dogs being so fat that they were scant able to run.

The 26. wee had a pretty storme, the winde being at Southeast. The 27. and 28. were faire. The 29. we were cleare out of the streights, having coasted the South shore, and this day at noone we were in 62. degrees of latitude. The 30. in the afternoone wee coasted a banke of yce, which lay on the shore, and passed by a great banke or Inlet, which lay between 63. and 62. degrees of latitude, which we called Lumlies Inlet. We had oftentimes, as we sailed alongst the coast, great ruttes, the water as it were whirling and overfalling, as if it were the fall of some great water through a bridge.

The 31. as we sayled by a Headland, which we named War-wicks Foreland, we fell into one of those overfals with a fresh gale of wind, and bearing all our sailes, wee looking upon an Island of yce betweene us and the shoare, had thought that our barke did make no way, which caused us to take markes on the shoare: at length wee perceived our selves to goe very fast, and the Island of yce which we saw before, was carried very forcibly with the set of the current faster then our ship went. This day and night we passed by a very great gulfe, the water whirling and roaring as it were the meetings of tydes.

August

The first of August having coasted a banke of ice which was driven out at the mouth of this gulfe, we fell with the Souther-most cape of the gulfe, which we named Chidleis cape, which lay in 61 degrees and 10 minutes of latitude. The 2 and 3 were calme and foggie, so were the 4, 5, and 6. The 7 was faire and calme: so was the 8, with a litle gale in the morning. The 9 was faire, and we had a litle gale at night. The 10 we had a frisking gale at Westnorthwest. The 11 faire. The 12 we saw five deere on the top of an Island, called by us Darcies Island. And we hoised out our boat, and went ashore to them, thinking to have killed some of them. But when we came on shore, and had coursed them twise about the Island, they tooke the sea and swamme towards Islands distant from that three leagues. When we perceived that they had taken the sea we gave them over because our boat was so small that it could not carrie us, and rowe after them, they swamme so fast: but one of them was as bigge as a good prety Cow, and very fat, their feet as bigge as Oxe feet. Here upon this Island I killed with my piece a gray hare.

The 13 in the morning we saw three or foure white beares, but durst not go on shore to them for lacke of a good boat. This day we stroke a rocke seeking for an harborow, and received a leake: and this day we were in 54 degrees of latitude.

The 14 we stopt our leake in a storme not very outragious, at noone.

The 15 being almost in 52 degrees of latitude, and not finding our ships, nor (according to their promise) any kinde of marke, token, or beacon, which we willed them to set up, and they protested to do so upon every head land, Island or cape, within twenty leagues every way off from their fishing place, which our captaine appointed to be betweene 54 and 55 degrees: This 15 I say we shaped our course homewards for England, having in our ship but litle wood, and halfe a hogshead of fresh water. Our men were very willing to depart, and no man more forward then Peerson, for he feared to be put out of his office of stewardship: but because every man was so willing to depart, we consented to returne for our owne countrey: and so we had the 16 faire weather, with the winde at Southwest.

The 17 we met a ship at sea, and as farre as we could judge it was a Biskaine: we thought she went a fishing for whales; for in 52 degrees or thereabout we saw very many.

The 18 was faire, with a good gale at West.

The 19 faire also, with much winde at West and by South.

And thus after much variable weather and change of winds we arrived the 15 of September in Dartmouth anno 1587, giving thanks to God for our safe arrivall.

43

A letter of the sayd M. John Davis written to
M. Sanderson of London concerning
his forewritten voyage

G O O D M. Sanderson, with Gods great mercy I have made
my safe returne in health, with all my company, and have sailed
threescore leagues further then my determination at my departure. I have bene in 73 degrees, finding the sea all open, and
forty leagues betweene land and land. The passage is most
probable, the execution easie, as at my comming you shall
fully know.

Yesterday the 15 of September I landed all weary; therefore
I pray you pardon my shortnesse.

Sandridge this 16 of September anno 1587.

Yours equall as mine owne, which
by triall you shall best know,
JOHN DAVIS

44

The miraculous victory atchieved by the English Fleete, under the discreet and happy conduct of the right honourable, right prudent, and valiant lord, the L. Charles Howard, L. high Admirall of England, &c. Upon the Spanish huge Armada sent in the yeere 1588. for the invasion of England, together with the wofull and miserable successe of the said Armada afterward, upon the coasts of Norway, of the Scottish Westerne Isles, of Ireland, of Spaine, of France, and of England, &c. Recorded in Latine by Emanuel van Meteran in the 15. booke of his history of the low Countreys

HAVING in part declared the strange and wonderfull events of the yeere eightie eight, which hath bene so long time foretold by ancient prophesies; we will now make relation of the most notable and great enterprise of all others which were in the foresaid yeere atchieved, in order as it was done. Which exploit (although in very deed it was not performed in any part of the low Countreys) was intended for their ruine and destruction. And it was the expedition which the Spanish king, having a long time determined the same in his minde, and having consulted thereabout with the Pope, set foorth and undertooke against England and the low Countreys. To the end that he might subdue the Realme of England, and reduce it unto his catholique Religion, and by that meanes might be sufficiently revenged for the disgrace, contempt and dishonour, which hee (having 34. yeeres before enforced them to the Popes obedience) had endured of the English nation, and for divers other injuries which had taken deepe impression in his thoughts. And also for that hee deemed this to bee the most readie and direct course, whereby hee might recover his heredetarie possession of the lowe Countreys, having restrained the inhabitants from sayling upon the coast of England. Which verily, upon most weighty arguments and evident reasons, was thought would undoubtly have come to passe, considering the great aboundance and store of all things necessary wherewith those men were furnished, which had the managing of that action committed unto them. But now let us describe the matter more particularly.

The Spanish King having with small fruite and commoditie, for above twentie yeeres together, waged warre against the Netherlanders, after deliberation with his counsellers thereabout, thought it most convenient to assault them once againe by Sea, which had bene attempted sundry times heretofore, but not with forces sufficient. Unto the which expedition it stoode him nowe in hand to joyne great puissance, as having the English people his professed enemies; whose Island is so situate, that it may either greatly helpe or hinder all such as saile into those parts. For which cause hee thought good first of all to invade England, being perswaded by his Secretary Escovedo, and by divers other well experienced Spaniards and Dutchmen, and by many English fugitives, that the conquest of that Iland was lesse difficult then the conquest of Holland and Zeland. Moreover the Spaniards were of opinion, that it would bee farre more behoveful for their King to conquere England and the lowe Countreys all at once, then to be constrained continually to maintaine a warlike Navie to defend his East and West Indie Fleetes, from the English Drake, and from such like valiant enemies.

And for the same purpose the king Catholique had given commandement long before in Italy and Spaine, that a great quantitie of timber should be felled for the building of shippes; and had besides made great preparation of things and furniture requisite for such an expedition; as namely in founding of brasen Ordinance, in storing up of corne and victuals, in trayning of men to use warlike weapons, in leavying and mustering of souldiers: insomuch that about the beginning of the yeere

1588. he had finished such a mightie Navie, and brought it into Lisbon haven, as never the like had before that time sailed upon the Ocean sea.

A very large and particular description of this Navie was put in print and published by the Spaniards; wherein were set downe the number, names, and burthens of the shippes, the number of Mariners and souldiers throughout the whole Fleete; likewise the quantitie of their Ordinance, of their armour, of bullets, of match, of gunpoulder, of victuals, and of all their Navall furniture was in the saide description particularized. Unto all these were added the names of the Governours, Captaines, Noblemen and gentlemen voluntaries, of whom there was so great a multitude, that scarce was there any family of accompt, or any one principall man throughout all Spaine, that had not a brother, sonne or kinseman in that Fleete: who all of them were in good hope to purchase unto themselves in that Navie (as they termed it) invincible, endlesse glory and renowne, and to possesse themselves of great Seigniories and riches in England, and in the lowe Countreys. But because the said description was translated and published out of Spanish into divers other languages, we will here onely make an abridgement or briefe rehearsall thereof.

Portugal furnished and set foorth under the conduct of the duke of Medina Sidonia generall of the Fleete, ten Galeons, two Zabraes, 1300. Mariners, 3300. souldiers, 300. great pieces, with all requisite furniture.

Biscay, under the conduct of John Martines de Ricalde Admiral of the whole Fleete, set forth tenne Galeons, 4. Pataches, 700. mariners, 2000. souldiers, 250. great pieces, &c.

Guipusco, under the conduct of Michael de Oquendo, tenne Galeons, 4. Pataches, 700. mariners, 2000. souldiers, 310. great pieces.

Italy with the Levant Islands, under Martine de Vertendona, 10. Galeons, 800. mariners, 2000. souldiers, 310. great pieces, &c.

Castile, under Diego Flores de Valdez, 14. Galeons, two Pataches, 1700. mariners, 2400. souldiers, and 380. great pieces, &c.

Andaluzia, under the conduct of Petro de Valdez, 10. Galeons, one Patache, 800. mariners, 2400. souldiers, 280. great pieces, &c.

Item, under the conduct of John Lopez de Medina, 23. great Flemish hulkes, with 700. mariners, 3200. souldiers, and 400. great pieces.

Item, under Hugo de Moncada, foure Galliasses containing 1200. gally-slaves, 460. mariners, 870. souldiers, 200. great pieces, &c.

Item, under Diego de Mandrana, foure Gallies of Portugall, with 888. gally-slaves, 360. mariners, 20. great pieces, and other requisite furniture.

Item, under Anthonie de Mendoza, 22. Pataches and Zabraes, with 574. mariners, 488. souldiers, and 193. great pieces.

Besides the ships aforementioned there were 20. caravels rowed with oares, being appointed to performe necessary services unto the greater ships: insomuch that all the ships appertayning to this Navie amounted unto the summe of 150. eche one being sufficiently provided of furniture and victuals.

The number of Mariners in the saide Fleete were above 8000. of slaves 2088. of souldiers 20000. (besides noblemen and gentlemen voluntaries) of great cast pieces 2650. The foresaid ships were of an huge and incredible capacitie and receipt. For the whole Fleete was large ynough to containe the burthen of 60. thousand tunnes.

The Galeons were 64. in number, being of an huge bignesse, and very stately built, being of marveilous force also, and so high, that they resembled great castles, most fit to defend themselves and to withstand any assault, but in giving any other ships the encounter farre inferiour unto the English and Dutch ships, which can with great dexteritie weild and turne themselves at all assayes. The upperworke of the said Galeons was of thicknesse and strength sufficient to beare off musketshot. The lower worke and the timbers thereof were out of measure strong, being framed of plankes and ribs foure or five foote in thicknesse, insomuch that no bullets could pierce them, but such as were discharged hard at hand: which afterward prooved true, for a great number of bullets were founde to sticke fast within the massie substance of those thicke plankes. Great and well pitched Cables were twined about the masts of their shippes, to strengthen them against the battery of shot.

The Galliasses were of such bignesse, that they contained within them chambers, chapels, turrets, pulpits, and other commodities of great houses. The Galliasses were rowed with great oares, there being in eche one of them 300. slaves for the same purpose, and were able to do great service with the force of their Ordinance. All these together with the residue aforenamed were furnished and beautified with trumpets, streamers, banners, warlike ensignes, and other such like ornaments.

Their pieces of brasen ordinance were 1600. and of yron a 1000.

The bullets thereto belonging were 120. thousand.

Item of gun-poulder 5600. quintals. Of matche 1200. quintals.

Of muskets and kaleivers 7000. Of haleberts and partisans 10000.

Moreover they had great store of canons, double-canons, culverings and field-pieces for land services.

Likewise they were provided of all instruments necessary on land to conveigh and transport their furniture from place to place; as namely of carts, wheeles, wagons, &c. Also they had spades, mattocks and baskets to set pioners on worke. They had in like sort great store of mules and horses, and whatsoever else was requisite for a land-armie. They were so well stored of biscuit, that for the space of halfe a yeere, they might allow eche person in the whole Fleete halfe a quintall every moneth; whereof the whole summe amounteth unto an hundreth thousand quintals.

Likewise of wine they had 147. thousand pipes, sufficient also for halfe a yeeres expedition. Of bacon 6500. quintals. Of cheese three thousand quintals. Besides fish, rise, beanes, pease, oile, vineger, &c.

Moreover they had 12000. pipes of fresh-water, and all other necessary provision, as namely candles, lanternes, lampes, sailes, hempe, oxe-hides and lead to stop holes that should be made with the battery of gunshot. To be short, they brought all things expedient either for a Fleete by sea, or for an armie by land.

This Navie (as Diego Pimentelli afterward confessed) was esteemed by the King himselfe to containe 32000. persons, and to cost him every day 30. thousand ducates.

There were in the said Navie five terzaes of Spaniards, (which terzaes the Frenchmen call Regiments) under the commaund of five governours termed by the Spaniards, Masters of the field, and amongst the rest there were many olde and expert souldiers chosen out of the garisons of Sicilie, Naples, and Terçera. Their Captaines or Colonels were Diego Pimentelli, Don Francisco de Toledo, Don Alonço de Luçon, Don Nicolas de Isla, Don Augustin de Mexia; who had eche of them 32. companies under their conduct. Besides the which companies there were many bands also of Castilians and Portugals, every one of which had their peculiar governours, captaines, officers, colours and weapons.

It was not lawfull for any man, under grievous penaltie, to cary any women or harlots in the Fleete: for which cause the women hired certaine shippes, wherein they sailed after the Navie: some of the which being driven by tempest arrived upon the coast of France.

The generall of this mightie Navie, was Don Alonso Perez de Guzman duke of Medina Sidonia, Lord of S. Lucar, and knight of the golden Fleece: by reason that the Marques of santa Cruz appointed for the same dignitie, deceased before the time.

John Martines de Ricalde was Admirall of the Fleete.

Francis Bovadilla was chiefe Marshall: who all of them had their officers fit and requisite for the guiding and managing of such a multitude. Likewise Martin Alorcon was appointed Vicar generall of the Inquisition, being accompanied with more then a hundreth Monkes, to wit, Jesuites, Capuchines, and friers mendicant. Besides whom also there were Phisitians, Chirurgians, Apothecaries, and whatsoever else perteined unto the hospitall.

Over and besides the forenamed governours and officers being men of chiefe note, there were 124. very noble and worthy Gentlemen, which went voluntarily of their owne costs and charges, to the ende they might see fashions, learne experience, and attaine unto glory. Amongst whom was the prince of Ascoli, Alonzo de Leiva, the marques de Pennafiel, the marques de Ganes, the marques de Barlango, count de Paredes, count de Yelvas, and divers other marqueses and earles of the honourable families of Mendoza, of Toledo, of Pachieco, of

Cordova, of Guzman, of Manricques, and a great number of others.

While the Spaniards were furnishing this their Navie, the duke of Parma, at the direction of king Philip, made great preparation in the low Countreys, to give ayd & assistance unto the Spaniards; building ships for the same purpose, and sending for Pilots and ship-wrights out of Italy.

In Flanders hee caused certaine deepe chanels to be made, and among the rest the chanell of Yper commonly called Yper-lee, employing some thousands of workemen about that service: to the end that by the said chanel he might transport ships from Antwerp and Ghendt to Bruges, where hee had assembled above a hundreth small ships called hoyes being well stored with victuals, which hoyes hee was determined to have brought into the sea by the way of Sluys, or else to have conveyed them by the saide Yper-lee being now of greater depth, into any port of Flanders whatsoever.

In the river of Waten he caused 70. ships with flat bottomes to be built, every one of which should serve to cary 30. horses, having eche of them bridges likewise for the horses to come on boord, or to goe foorth on land. Of the same fashion he had provided 200. other vessels at Neiuport, but not so great. And at Dunkerk hee procured 28. ships of warre, such as were there to be had, and caused a sufficient number of Mariners to be levied at Hamburgh, Breme, Emden, and at other places. Hee put in the ballast of the said ships, great store of beames of thicke plankes, being hollow and beset with yron pikes beneath, but on eche side full of claspes and hookes, to joyne them together.

Hee had likewise at Greveling provided 20. thousand of caske, which in a short space might be compact and joyned together with nailes and cords, and reduced into the forme of a bridge. To be short, whatsoever things were requisite for the making of bridges, and for the barring and stopping up of havens mouthes with stakes, posts, and other meanes, he commanded to be made ready. Moreover not farre from Neiuport haven, he had caused a great pile of wooden fagots to be layd, and other furniture to be brought for the rearing up of a mount. The most part of his ships conteined two ovens a piece to bake bread in, with a great number of sadles, bridles, and such other like apparell for horses. They had horses likewise, which after their landing should serve to convey, and draw engines, field-pieces, and other warlike provisions.

Neere unto Neiuport he had assembled an armie, over the which he had ordained Camillo de Monte to be Camp-master. This army consisted of 30. bands or ensignes of Italians, of tenne bands of Wallons, eight of Scots, and eight of Burgundians, all which together amount unto 56. bands, every band containing a hundreth persons. Neare unto Dixmud there were mustered 80. bands of Dutch men, sixtie of Spaniards, sixe of high Germans, and seven bands of English fugitives, under the conduct of sir William Stanlie an English knight.

In the suburbes of Cortreight there were 4000. horsemen together with their horses in a readinesse: and at Waten 900. horses, with the troupe of the Marques del Gwasto Captaine generall of the horsemen.

Unto this famous expedition and presupposed victorie, many potentates, princes, and honourable personages hied themselves: out of Spaine the prince of Melito called the duke of Pastrana and taken to be the sonne of one Ruygomes de Silva, but in very deed accompted among the number of king Philips base sonnes. Also the Marques of Burgrave, one of the sonnes of Archiduke Ferdinand and Philippa Welsera. Vespasian Gonsaga of the family of Mantua, being for chivalry a man of great renowne, and heretofore Vice-roy in Spaine. Item John Medices base sonne unto the duke of Florence. And Amadas of Savoy, the duke of Savoy his base sonne, with many others of inferiour degrees.

Likewise Pope Sixtus quintus for the setting forth of the foresaid expedition, as they use to do against Turkes & infidels, published a Cruzado, with most ample indulgences which were printed in great numbers. These vaine buls the English and Dutchmen deriding, sayd that the devill at all passages lay in ambush like a thiefe, no whit regarding such letters of safe conduct. Some there be which affirme that the Pope had bestowed the realme of England with the title of Defensor fidei, upon the king of Spaine, giving him charge to invade it upon this condition, that hee should enjoy the conquered realm, as a vassal and tributarie, in that regard, unto the sea of Rome. To this purpose the said Pope proffered a million of gold, the

one halfe thereof to be paied in readie money, and the other
halfe when the realme of England or any famous port thereof
were subdued. And for the greater furtherance of the whole
businesse, he dispatched one D. Allen an English man (whom
hee had made Cardinall for the same ende and purpose) into
the Low countries, unto whom he committed the administration
of all matters ecclesiasticall throughout England. This Allen
being enraged against his owne native countrey, caused the
Popes bull to be translated into English, meaning upon the
arrival of the Spanish fleete, to have it so published in England.
By which Bull the excommunications of the two former Popes
were confirmed, and the Queenes most sacred Majestie was by
them most unjustly deprived of all princely titles and dignities,
her subjects being enjoined to performe obedience unto the
duke of Parma, and unto the Popes Legate.

But that all matters might be performed with greater secrecie,
and that the whole expedition might seeme rather to be intended
against the Low countries, then against England, and that the
English people might be perswaded that all was but bare words
& threatnings, and that nought would come to effect, there was
a solemne meeting appointed at Borborch in Flanders for a
treatie of peace betweene her majestie and the Spanish king.

Against which treatie the united provinces making open pro-
testation, used all meanes possible to hinder it, alleaging that
it was more requisite to consult how the enemie now pressing
upon them might be repelled from off their frontiers. Howbeit
some there were in England that greatly urged and prosecuted
this league, saying, that it would be very commodious unto the
state of the realme, as well in regard of traffique and navigation,
as for the avoiding of great expenses to maintaine the warres,
affirming also, that at the same time peace might easily and
upon reasonable conditions be obtained of the Spaniard. Others
thought by this meanes to divert some other way, or to keepe
backe the navy now comming upon them, and so to escape
the danger of that tempest. Howsoever it was, the duke of Parma by these wiles enchanted and dazeled the eyes of many English & Dutch men that were desirous of peace: whereupon it
came to passe, that England and the united provinces prepared
in deed some defence to withstand that dreadfull expedition and
huge Armada, but nothing in comparison of the great danger

which was to be feared, albeit the constant report of the whole
expedition had continued rife among them for a long time
before. Howbeit they gave eare unto the relation of certaine
that sayd, that this navie was provided to conduct and waft
over the Indian Fleets: which seemed the more probable because the Spaniards were deemed not to be men of so small
discretion as to adventure those huge and monstrous ships
upon the shallow and dangerous chanel of England.

At length when as the French king about the end of May
signified unto her Majestie in plaine termes that she should
stand upon her guard, because he was now most certainly enformed, that there was so dangerous an invasion imminent upon
her realme, that he feared much least all her land and sea-
forces would be sufficient to withstand it, &c. then began the
Queens Majestie more carefully to gather her forces together,
& to furnish her own ships of warre, & the principall ships of
her subjects with souldiers, weapons, and other necessary provision. The greatest and strongest ships of the whole navy she
sent unto Plimmouth under the conduct of the right honorable
Lord Charles Howard, lord high Admirall of England, &c.
Under whom the renoumed Knight Sir Francis Drake was appointed Vice-admiral. The number of these ships was about an
hundreth. The lesser ships being 30. or 40. in number, and
under the conduct of the lord Henry Seimer were commanded
to lie between Dover and Caleis.

On land likewise throughout the whole realme, souldiers were
mustered and trained in all places, and were committed unto
the most resolute and faithfull captaines. And whereas it was
commonly given out that the Spaniard having once united himselfe unto the duke of Parma, ment to invade by the river of
Thames, there was at Tilburie in Essex over-against Gravesend,
a mightie army encamped, and on both sides of the river fortifications were erected, according to the prescription of Frederike
Genebelli an Italian enginier. Likewise there were certaine ships
brought to make a bridge, though it were very late first. Unto
the sayd army came in proper person the Queens most roiall
Majestie, representing Tomyris that Scythian warlike princesse,
or rather divine Pallas her selfe. Also there were other such
armies levied in England.

The principall catholique Recusants (least they should stirre

up any tumult in the time of the Spanish invasion) were sent
to remaine at certaine convenient places, as namely in the Isle
of Ely and at Wisbich. And some of them were sent unto other
places, to wit, unto sundry bishops and noblemen, where they
were kept from endangering the state of the common wealth,
and of her sacred Majestie, who of her most gracious clemencie
gave expresse commandement, that they should be intreated
with all humanitie and friendship.

The provinces of Holland and Zeland, &c. giving credite unto
their intelligence out of Spain, made preparation to defend
themselves: but because the Spanish ships were described unto
them to be so huge, they relied partly upon the shallow and
dangerous seas all along their coasts. Wherfore they stood
most in doubt of the duke of Parma his small and flat-bottomed ships. Howbeit they had all their ships of warre to the
number of 90. and above, in a readinesse for all assayes: the
greater part whereof were of a small burthen, as being more
meete to saile upon their rivers and shallow seas: and with
these ships they besieged all the havens in Flanders, beginning
at the mouth of Scheld, or from the towne of Lillo, and holding on to Greveling and almost unto Caleis, & fortified all their
sea-townes with strong garrisons.

Against the Spanish fleets arrivall, they had provided 25.
or 30. good ships, committing the government of them unto
Admirall Lonck, whom they commanded to joine himselfe
unto the lord Henry Seymer, lying betweene Dover and Cales.
And when as the foresaid ships, (whereof the greater part
besieged the haven of Dunkerke) were driven by tempest into
Zeland, Justin of Nassau the Admiral of Zeland supplied that
squadron with 35. ships being of no great burthen, but excel-
lently furnished with gunnes, mariners and souldiers in great
abundance, and especially with 1200. brave Musquetiers, having
bene accustomed unto sea-fights, and being chosen out of all
their companies for the same purpose: and so the said Justin of
Nassau kept such diligent ward in that Station that the duke
of Parma could not issue foorth with his navy into the sea
out of any part of Flanders.

In the meane while the Spanish Armada set saile out of the
haven of Lisbon upon the 19. of May, An. Dom. 1588. under
the conduct of the duke of Medina Sidonia, directing their

course for the Baie of Corunna, aliâs the Groine of Gallicia,
where they tooke in souldiers and warlike provision, this port
being in Spaine the neerest unto England. As they were sailing
along, there arose such a mightie tempest, that the whole Fleete
was dispersed, so that when the duke was returned unto his
company, he could not escry above 80. ships in all, whereunto
the residue by litle and litle joyned themselves, except eight
which had their mastes blowen over-boord. One of the foure
gallies of Portingal escaped very hardly, retiring her selfe into
the haven. The other three were upon the coast of Baion in
France, by the assistance and courage of one David Gwin an
English captive (whom the French and Turkish slaves aided in
the same enterprise) utterly disabled and vanquished: one of
the three being first overcome, which conquered the two other,
with the slaughter of their governours and souldiers, and among
the rest of Don Diego de Mandrana with sundry others: and
so those slaves arriving in France with the three Gallies, set
themselves at libertie.

The navy having refreshed themselves at the Groine, & receiving daily commandement from the king to hasten their
journey, hoised up sailes the 11. day of July, and so holding
on their course till the 19. of the same moneth, they came then
unto the mouth of the narow seas or English chanel. From
whence (striking their sailes in the meane season) they dispatched certaine of their smal ships unto the duke of Parma.
At the same time the Spanish Fleete was escried by an English
pinasse, captaine whereof was M. Thomas Fleming, after they
had bene advertised of the Spaniards expedition by their scoutes
and espials, which having ranged along the coast of Spaine,
were lately returned home into Plimmouth for a new supply of
victuals and other necessaries, who considering the foresayd
tempest, were of opinion that the navy being of late dispersed
and tossed up and downe the maine Ocean, was by no means
able to performe their intended voiage.

Moreover, the L. Charles Howard L. high admiral of England had received letters from the court, signifying unto him
that her Majestie was advertised that the Spanish Fleete would
not come foorth, nor was to be any longer expected for, and
therefore, that upon her Majesties commandement he must send
backe foure of her tallest and strongest ships unto Chattam.

The lord high Admiral of England being thus on the sudden, namely upon the 19. of July about foure of the clocke in the afternoone, enformed by the pinasse of captaine Fleming aforesaid, of the Spaniards approch, with all speed and diligence possible he warped his ships, and caused his mariners and souldiers (the greater part of whom was absent for the cause aforesayd) to come on boord, and that with great trouble and difficultie, insomuch that the lord Admiral himselfe was faine to lie without in the road with sixe ships onely all that night, after the which many others came foorth of the haven. The very next day being the 20. of July about high noone, was the Spanish Fleete escried by the English, which with a Southwest wind came sailing along, and passed by Plimmouth: in which regard (according to the judgement of many skilful navigators) they greatly overshot themselves, whereas it had bene more commodious for them to have staied themselves there, considering that the Englishmen being as yet unprovided, greatly relied upon their owne forces, and knew not the estate of the Spanish navy. Moreover, this was the most convenient port of all others, where they might with greater securitie have bene advertised of the English forces, and how the commons of the land stood affected, and might have stirred up some mutinie, so that hither they should have bent all their puissance, and from hence the duke of Parma might more easily have conveied his ships.

But this they were prohibited to doe by the king and his counsell, and were expressly commanded to unite themselves unto the souldiers and ships of the said duke of Parma, and so to bring their purpose to effect. Which was thought to be the most easie and direct course, for that they imagined that the English and Dutch men would be utterly daunted and dismaied thereat, and would each man of them retire unto his owne Province and Porte for the defence thereof, and transporting the armie of the duke under the protection of their huge navy, they might invade England.

It is reported that the cheife commanders in the navy, and those which were more skilfull in navigation, to wit, John Martines de Ricalde, Diego Flores de Valdez, and divers others found fault that they were bound unto so strict directions and instructions, because that in such a case many particular accidents ought to concurre and to be respected at one and the same instant, that is to say, the opportunitie of the wind, weather, time, tide, and ebbe, wherein they might saile from Flanders to England. Oftentimes also the darkenesse and light, the situation of places, the depths and shoulds were to be considered: all which especially depended upon the conveniencie of the windes, and were by so much the more dangerous.

But it seemeth that they were enjoined by their commission to ancre neere unto, or about Caleis, whither the duke of Parma with his ships and all his warrelike provision was to resort, and while the English and Spanish great ships were in the midst of their conflict, to passe by, and to land his souldiers upon the Downes.

The Spanish captives reported that they were determined first to have entred the river of Thames, and thereupon to have passed with small ships up to London, supposing that they might easily winne that rich and flourishing Citie being but meanely fortified and inhabited with Citizens not accustomed to the warres, who durst not withstand their first encounter, hoping moreover to finde many rebels against her Majestie and popish catholiques, or some favourers of the Scottish queene (which was not long before most justly beheaded) who might be instruments of sedition.

Thus often advertising the duke of Parma of their approch, the 20. of July they passed by Plimmouth, which the English ships pursuing and getting the wind of them, gave them the chase and the encounter, and so both Fleets frankly exchanged their bullets.

The day following which was the 21. of July, the English ships approched within musquet shot of the Spanish: at what time the lorde Charles Howard most hotly and valiantly discharged his Ordinance upon the Spanish Vice-admirall. The Spaniards then well perceiving the nimblenesse of the English ships in discharging upon the enimie on all sides, gathered themselves close into the forme of an halfe moone, and slackened their sailes, least they should outgoe any of their companie. And while they were proceeding on in this maner, one of their great Galliasses was so furiously battered with shot, that the whole navy was faine to come up rounder together for the safegard thereof: whereby it came to passe that the principall Galleon of Sivill (wherein Don Pedro de Valdez, Vasques de

Silva, Alonzo de Sayas, and other noble men were embarqued)
falling foule of another shippe, had her fore-mast broken, and
by that meanes was not able to keepe way with the Spanish
Fleete, neither would the sayde Fleete stay to succour it, but
left the distressed Galeon behind. The lord Admirall of England when he saw this ship of Valdez, & thought she had bene
voyd of Mariners and Souldiers, taking with him as many
shippes as he could, passed by it, that he might not loose sight
of the Spanish Fleet that night. For sir Francis Drake (who
was notwithstanding appointed to beare out his lanterne that
night) was giving of chase unto five great Hulkes which had
separated themselves from the Spanish Fleete: but finding them
to be Easterlings, he dismissed them. The lord Admirall all that
night following the Spanish lanterne in stead of the English,
found himselfe in the morning to be in the midst of his enimies
Fleete, but when he perceived it, hee cleanly conveyed himselfe
out of that great danger.

The day folowing, which was the two and twentie of July,
Sir Francis Drake espied Valdez his shippe, whereunto hee sent
foorth his pinnasse, and being advertised that Valdez himselfe
was there, and 450. persons with him, he sent him word that
he should yeeld himselfe. Valdez for his honors sake caused
certaine conditions to be propounded unto Drake: who answered Valdez that he was not now at laisure to make any long
parle, but if he would yeeld himselfe, he should find him
friendly and tractable: howbeit if he had resolved to die in
fight, he should proove Drake to be no dastard.

Upon which answere Valdez and his company understanding that they were fallen into the hands of fortunate Drake,
being mooved with the renoume and celebritie of his name, with
one consent yeelded themselves, and found him very favourable
unto them. Then Valdez with 40. or 50. noblemen and gentlemen pertaining unto him, came on boord sir Francis Drakes
ship. The residue of his company were caried unto Plimmouth,
where they were detained a yere & an halfe for their ransome.

Valdez comming unto Drake and humbly kissing his hand
protested unto him, that he and his had resolved to die in
battell, had they not by good fortune fallen into his power,
whom they knew to be right curteous and gentle, and whom
they had heard by generall report to bee most favourable unto

his vanquished foe: insomuch that he sayd it was to bee
doubted whether his enimies had more cause to admire and
love him for his great, valiant, and prosperous exploites, or to
dread him for his singular felicitie and wisedom, which ever
attended upon him in the warres, and by the which hee had
attained unto so great honour. With that Drake embraced him
and gave him very honourable entertainement, feeding him at
his owne table, and lodging him in his cabbin.

Here Valdez began to recount unto Drake the forces of all
the Spanish Fleet, and how foure mightie Gallies were separated by tempest from them: and also how they were determined first to have put into Plimmouth haven, not expecting to
bee repelled thence by the English ships which they thought
could by no meanes withstand their impregnable forces, perswading themselves that by means of their huge Fleete, they
were become lords and commaunders of the maine Ocean. For
which cause they marveled much how the English men in their
small ships durst approch within musket shot of the Spaniards
mightie woodden castles, gathering the wind of them with
many other such like attempts.

Immediately after, Valdez and his company, being a man of
principal authoritie in the Spanish Fleete, and being descended
of one and the same familie with that Valdez, which in the
yeere 1574. besieged Leiden in Holland, were sent captives into
England. There were in the sayd ship 55. thousand ducates in
ready money of the Spanish kings gold, which the souldiers
merily shared among themselves.

The same day was set on fire one of their greatest shippes,
being Admirall of the squadron of Guipusco, and being the
shippe of Michael de Oquendo Viceadmirall of the whole Fleete,
which contained great store of gunnepowder and other warrelike
provision. The upper part onely of this shippe was burnt, and
all the persons therein contained (except a very few) were
consumed with fire. And thereupon it was taken by the English,
and brought into England with a number of miserable burnt
and skorched Spaniards. Howbeit the gunpowder (to the great
admiration of all men) remained whole and unconsumed.

In the meane season the lord Admirall of England in his
ship called the Arke-royall, all that night pursued the Spaniards
so neere, that in the morning hee was almost left alone in the

enimies Fleete, and it was foure of the clocke at afternoone before the residue of the English Fleet could overtake him.

At the same time Hugo de Moncada governour of the foure Galliasses, made humble sute unto the Duke of Medina that he might be licenced to encounter the Admirall of England: which libertie the duke thought not good to permit unto him, because hee was loth to exceed the limites of his commission and charge.

Upon Tuesday which was the three and twentie of July, the navie being come over against Portland, the wind began to turne Northerly, insomuch that the Spaniards had a fortunate and fit gale to invade the English. But the Englishmen having lesser and nimbler Ships, recovered againe the vantage of the winde from the Spaniards, whereat the Spaniards seemed to bee more incensed to fight then before. But when the English Fleete had continually and without intermission from morning to night, beaten and battered them with all their shot both great and small: the Spaniardes uniting themselves, gathered their whole Fleete close together into a roundell, so that it was apparant that they ment not as yet to invade others, but onely to defend themselves and to make hast unto the place prescribed unto them, which was neere unto Dunkerk, that they might joine forces with the duke of Parma, who was determined to have proceeded secretly with his small shippes under the shadow and protection of the great ones, and so had intended circumspectly to performe the whole expedition.

This was the most furious and bloodie skirmish of all, in which the lord Admirall of England continued fighting amidst his enimies Fleete, and seeing one of his Captaines afarre off, hee spake unto him in these wordes: Oh George what doest thou? Wilt thou nowe frustrate my hope and opinion conceived of thee? Wilt thou forsake mee nowe? With which wordes hee being enflamed, approched foorthwith, encountered the enemie, and did the part of a most valiant Captaine. His name was George Fenner, a man that had bene conversant in many Seafights.

In this conflict there was a certaine great Venetian ship with other small ships surprised and taken by the English.

The English navie in the meane while increased, whereunto out of all Havens of the Realme resorted ships and men: for they all with one accord came flocking thither as unto a set field, where immortall fame and glory was to be attained, and faithfull service to bee performed unto their prince and countrey.

In which number there were many great and honourable personages, as namely, the Erles of Oxford, of Northumberland, of Cumberland, &c. with many Knights and Gentlemen: to wit, Sir Thomas Cecill, Sir Robert Cecill, Sir Walter Raleigh, Sir William Hatton, Sir Horatio Palavicini, Sir Henry Brooke, Sir Robert Carew, Sir Charles Blunt, Master Ambrose Willoughbie, Master Henry Nowell, Master Thomas Gerard, Master Henry Dudley, Master Edward Darcie, Master Arthur Gorge, Master Thomas Woodhouse, Master William Harvie, &c. And so it came to passe that the number of the English shippes amounted unto an hundreth: which when they were come before Dover, were increased to an hundred and thirtie, being notwithstanding of no proportionable bignesse to encounter with the Spaniards, except two or three and twentie of the Queenes greater shippes, which onely, by reason of their presence, bred an opinion in the Spaniardes mindes concerning the power of the English Fleet: the mariners and souldiers whereof were esteemed to be twelve thousand.

The foure and twentie of July when as the sea was calme, and no winde stirring, the fight was onely betweene the foure great Galleasses and the English shippes, which being rowed with Oares, had great vauntage of the sayde English shippes, which notwithstanding for all that would not bee forced to yeeld, but discharged their chaine-shot to cut asunder their Cables and Cordage of the Galleasses, with many other such Stratagemes. They were nowe constrained to send their men on land for a newe supplie of Gunne-powder, whereof they were in great skarcitie, by reason they had so frankely spent the greater part in the former conflicts.

The same day, a Counsell being assembled, it was decreed that the English Fleete should bee devided into foure squadrons: the principall whereof was committed unto the lord Admirall: the second, to Sir Francis Drake: the third, to Captaine Hawkins: the fourth, to Captaine Frobisher.

The Spaniards in their sailing observed very diligent and good order, sayling three and foure, and sometimes more ships in a ranke, and folowing close up one after another, and the stronger and greater ships protecting the lesser.

The five and twentie of July when the Spaniardes were come over-against the Isle of Wight, the lord Admirall of England being accompanied with his best ships, (namely the Lion, Captaine whereof was the lord Thomas Howard: The Elizabeth Jonas under the commandement of Sir Robert Southwel sonne in lawe unto the lord Admirall: the Beare under the lord Sheffield nephew unto the lord Admirall: the Victorie under Captaine Barker: and the Galeon Leicester under the fore-named Captaine George Fenner) with great valour and dreadfull thundering of shot, encountered the Spanish Admiral being in the very midst of all his Fleet. Which when the Spaniard perceived, being assisted with his strongest ships, he came forth and entered a terrible combate with the English: for they bestowed each on other the broad sides, and mutually discharged all their Ordinance, being within one hundred, or an hundred and twentie yards one of another.

At length the Spaniardes hoised up their sayles, and againe gathered themselves up close into the forme of a roundel. In the meane while Captaine Frobisher had engaged himselfe into a most dangerous conflict. Whereupon the lord Admirall comming to succour him, found that hee had valiantly and discreetly behaved himselfe, and that hee had wisely and in good time given over the fight, because that after so great a batterie he had sustained no damage.

For which cause the day following, being the sixe and twentie of July, the lord Admirall rewarded him with the order of knighthood, together with the lord Thomas Howard, the lord Sheffield, M. John Hawkins and others.

The same day the lord Admirall received intelligence from Newhaven in France, by certaine of his Pinnasses, that all things were quiet in France, and that there was no preparation of sending aide unto the Spaniards, which was greatly feared from the Guisian faction, and from the Leaguers: but there was a false rumour spread all about, that the Spaniards had conquered England.

The seven and twentie of July, the Spaniards about the sunne-setting were come over-against Dover, and rode at ancre within the sight of Caleis, intending to hold on for Dunkerk, expecting there to joyne with the duke of Parma his forces, without which they were able to doe litle or nothing.

Likewise the English Fleete following up hard upon them, ancred just by them within culvering-shot. And here the lord Henry Seymer united himselfe unto the lord Admiral with his fleete of 30. ships which road before the mouth of Thames.

As the Spanish navie therefore lay at ancre, the duke of Medina sent certaine messengers unto the duke of Parma, with whom upon that occasion many Noblemen and Gentlemen went to refresh themselves on land: and amongst the rest the prince of Ascoli, being accounted the kings base sonne, and a very proper and towardly yong gentleman, to his great good, went on shore, who was by so much the more fortunate, in that hee had not opportunitie to returne on boord the same ship, out of which he was departed, because that in returning home it was cast away upon the Irish coast, with all the persons contained therein.

The duke of Parma being advertised of the Spanish Fleetes arrivall upon the coast of England, made all the haste hee could to bee present himselfe in this expedition for the performance of his charge: vainely perswading himselfe that nowe by the meanes of Cardinall Allen, hee should be crowned king of England, and for that cause hee had resigned the governement of the Lowe countries unto Count Mansfeld the elder. And having made his vowes unto S. Mary of Hall in Henault (whom he went to visite for his blind devotions sake) hee returned toward Bruges the 28. of July.

The next day travelling to Dunkerk hee heard the thundering Ordinance of either Fleet: and the same evening being come to Dixmud, hee was given to understand the hard successe of the Spanish Fleete.

Upon Tuesday which was the thirtieth of July, about high noone, hee came to Dunkerk, when as all the Spanish Fleete was now passed by: neither durst any of his ships in the meane space come foorth to assist the sayd Spanish Fleete for feare of five and thirtie warrelike ships of Holland and Zeland, which there kept watch and warde under the conduct of the Admirall Justin of Nassau.

The foresayd five and thirtie shippes were furnished with most cunning mariners and olde expert souldiers, amongst the

which were twelve hundred Musketiers, whom the States had
chosen out of all their garisons, and whom they knew to have
bene heretofore experienced in sea-fights.

This navie was given especially in charge not to suffer any
shippe to come out of the Haven, nor to permit any Zabraes,
Pataches or other small vessels of the Spanish Fleete (which
were more likely to aide the Dunkerkers) to enter thereinto,
for the greater ships were not to be feared by reason of the
shallow sea in that place. Howbeit the prince of Parma his
forces being as yet unreadie, were not come on boord his
shippes, onely the English Fugitives being seven hundred in
number under the conduct of Sir William Stanley, came in fit
time to have bene embarked, because they hoped to give the
first assault against England. The residue shewed themselves
unwilling and loath to depart, because they sawe but a few
mariners, who were by constraint drawne into this expedition,
and also because they had very bare provision of bread, drinke,
and other necessary victuals.

Moreover, the shippes of Holland and Zeland stood continually in their sight, threatening shot and powder, and many
inconveniences unto them: for feare of which shippes, the
Mariners and Sea-men secretly withdrew themselves both day
and night, least that the duke of Parma his souldiers should
compell them by maine force to goe on boord, and to breake
through the Hollanders Fleete, which all of them judged to bee
impossible by reason of the straightnesse of the Haven.

But it seemeth that the Duke of Parma and the Spaniards
grounded upon a vaine and presumptuous expectation, that all
the ships of England and of the Low countreys would at the
first sight of the Spanish and Dunkerk Navie have betaken
themselves to flight, yeelding them sea roome, and endevouring
onely to defend themselves, their havens, and sea coasts from
invasion. Wherefore their intent and purpose was, that the
Duke of Parma in his small and flat-bottomed shippes, should
as it were under the shadow and wings of the Spanish fleet,
convey over all his troupes, armour, and warlike provision,
and with their forces so united, should invade England; or
while the English fleet were busied in fight against the Spanish,
should enter upon any part of the coast, which he thought to
be most convenient. Which invasion (as the captives afterward

confessed) the Duke of Parma thought first to have attempted by the river of Thames; upon the bankes whereof having at his first arrivall landed twenty or thirty thousand of his principall souldiers, he supposed that he might easily have woonne the Citie of London; both because his small shippes should have followed and assisted his land-forces, and also for that the Citie it-selfe was but meanely fortified and easie to overcome, by reason of the Citizens delicacie and discontinuance from the warres, who with continuall and constant labour might be vanquished, if they yeelded not at the first assault. They were in good hope also to have mette with some rebels against her Majestie, and such as were discontented with the present state, as Papists, and others. Likewise they looked for ayde from the favourers of the Scottish Queene, who was not long before put to death; all which they thought would have stirred up seditions and factions.

Whenas therefore the Spanish fleet rode at anker before Caleis, to the end they might consult with the Duke of Parma what was best to be done according to the Kings commandement, and the present estate of their affaires, and had now (as we will afterward declare) purposed upon the second of August being Friday, with one power and consent to have put their intended businesse in practise; the L. Admirall of England being admonished by her Majesties letters from the Court, thought it most expedient either to drive the Spanish fleet from that place, or at leastwise to give them the encounter: and for that cause (according to her Majesties prescription) he tooke forthwith eight of his woorst & basest ships which came next to hand, & disburthening them of all things which seemed to be of any value, filled them with gun-powder, pitch, brimstone, and with other combustible and firy matter; and charging all their ordinance with powder, bullets, and stones, he sent the sayd ships upon the 28 of July being Sunday, about two of the clocke after midnight, with the winde and tide against the Spanish fleet: which when they had proceeded a good space, being forsaken of the Pilots, and set on fire, were directly carried upon the King of Spaines Navie: which fire in the dead of the night put the Spaniards into such a perplexity and horrour (for they feared lest they were like unto those terrible ships, which Frederic Jenebelli three yeeres before, at the siege of Antwerpe, had furnished with gun-powder, stones, and dreadfull engines, for the dissolution of the Duke of Parma his bridge, built upon the river of Scheld) that cutting their cables whereon their ankers were fastened, and hoising up their sailes, they betooke themselves very confusedly unto the maine sea.

In this sudden confusion, the principall and greatest of the foure galliasses falling fowle of another ship, lost her rudder: for which cause when she could not be guided any longer, she was by the force of the tide cast into a certaine showld upon the shore of Caleis, where she was immediatly assaulted by divers English pinasses, hoyes, and drumblers.

And as they lay battering of her with their ordinance, and durst not boord her, the L. Admirall sent thither his long boat with an hundreth choise souldiers under the command of Captaine Amias Preston. Upon whose approch their fellowes being more emboldened, did offer to boord the galliasse: against whom the governour thereof and Captaine of all the foure galliasses, Hugo de Moncada, stoutly opposed himselfe, fighting by so much the more valiantly, in that he hoped presently to be succoured by the Duke of Parma. In the meane season, Moncada, after he had endured the conflict a good while, being hitte on the head with a bullet, fell downe starke dead, and a great number of Spaniards also were slaine in his company. The greater part of the residue leaping over-boord into the sea, to save themselves by swimming, were most of them drowned. Howbeit there escaped among others Don Anthonio de Manriques, a principall officer in the Spanish fleet (called by them their Veador generall) together with a few Spaniards besides: which Anthonio was the first man that carried certaine newes of the successe of the fleet into Spaine.

This huge and monstrous galliasse, wherein were contained three hundred slaves to lug at the oares, and foure hundred souldiers, was in the space of three houres rifled in the same place; and there were found amongst divers other commodities 50000 ducats of the Spanish kings treasure. At length when the slaves were released out of their fetters, the English men would have set the sayd ship on fire, which Monsieur Gourdon the governor of Caleis, for feare of the damage which might thereupon ensue to the Towne and Haven, would not permit them to do, but drave them from thence with his great ordinance.

Upon the 29 of July in the morning, the Spanish Fleet after the foresayd tumult, having arranged themselves againe into order, were, within sight of Greveling, most bravely and furiously encountered by the English; where they once againe got the winde of the Spaniards: who suffered themselves to be deprived of the commodity of the place in Caleis rode, and of the advantage of the winde neere unto Dunkerk, rather then they would change their array or separate their forces now conjoyned and united together, standing onely upon their defence.

And albeit there were many excellent and warlike ships in the English fleet, yet scarse were there 22 or 23 among them all which matched 90 of the Spanish ships in bignesse, or could conveniently assault them. Wherefore the English shippes using their prerogative of nimble stirrage, whereby they could turne and wield themselves with the winde which way they listed, came often times very neere upon the Spaniards, and charged them so sore, that now and then they were but a pikes length asunder: & so continually giving them one broad side after another, they discharged all their shot both great and small upon them, spending one whole day from morning till night in that violent kinde of conflict, untill such time as powder and bullets failed them. In regard of which want they thought it convenient not to pursue the Spaniards any longer, because they had many great vantages of the English, namely for the extraordinary bignesse of their ships, and also for that they were so neerely conjoyned, and kept together in so good array, that they could by no meanes be fought withall one to one. The English thought therefore, that they had right well acquited themselves, in chasing the Spaniards first from Caleis, and then from Dunkerk, and by that meanes to have hindered them from joyning with the Duke of Parma his forces, and getting the winde of them, to have driven them from their owne coasts.

The Spaniards that day sustained great losse and damage having many of their shippes shot thorow and thorow, and they discharged likewise great store of ordinance against the English; who indeed sustained some hinderance, but not comparable to the Spaniards losse: for they lost not any one shippe or person of account. For very diligent inquisition being made, the English men all that time wherein the Spanish Navy sayled upon their seas, are not found to have wanted above one hundreth of their people: albeit Sir Francis Drakes shippe was pierced with shot above forty times, and his very cabben was twise shot thorow, and about the conclusion of the fight, the bedde of a certaine gentleman lying weary thereupon, was taken quite from under him with the force of a bullet. Likewise, as the Earle of Northumberland and Sir Charles Blunt were at dinner upon a time, the bullet of a demi-culvering brake thorow the middest of their cabbin, touched their feet, and strooke downe two of the standers by, with many such accidents befalling the English shippes, which it were tedious to rehearse. Whereupon it is most apparant, that God miraculously preserved the English nation. For the L. Admirall wrote unto her Majestie that in all humane reason, and according to the judgement of all men (every circumstance being duly considered) the English men were not of any such force, whereby they might, without a miracle, dare once to approch within sight of the Spanish Fleet: insomuch that they freely ascribed all the honour of their victory unto God, who had confounded the enemy, and had brought his counsels to none effect.

The same day the Spanish ships were so battered with English shot, that that very night and the day following, two or three of them suncke right downe: and among the rest a certaine great ship of Biscay, which Captaine Crosse assaulted, which perished even in the time of the conflict, so that very few therein escaped drowning; who reported that the governours of the same shippe slew one another upon the occasion following: one of them which would have yeelded the shippe was suddenly slaine; the brother of the slaine party in revenge of his death slew the murtherer, and in the meane while the ship suncke.

The same night two Portugall galeons of the burthen of seven or eight hundreth tunnes a piece, to wit the Saint Philip and the Saint Matthew, were forsaken of the Spanish Fleet, for they were so torne with shotte, that the water entered into them on all sides. In the galeon of Saint Philip was Francis de Toledo, brother unto the Count de Orgas, being Colonell over two and thirty bands: besides other gentlemen; who seeing their mast broken with shotte, they shaped their course, as well as they could, for the coast of Flanders: whither when they could not attaine, the principall men in the ship committing themselves to their skiffe, arrived at the next towne, which was Ostend; and the ship it selfe being left behinde with the residue of their company, was taken by the Ulishingers.

In the other galeon, called the S. Matthew, was embarked Don Diego Pimentelli another camp-master and colonell of 32 bands, being brother unto the marques of Tamnares, with many other gentlemen and captaines. Their ship was not very great, but exceeding strong, for of a great number of bullets which had batterd her, there were scarse 20 wherewith she was pierced or hurt: her upper worke was of force sufficient to beare off a musket shot: this shippe was shot thorow and pierced in the fight before Greveling; insomuch that the leakage of the water could not be stopped: whereupon the duke of Medina sent his great skiffe unto the governour thereof, that he might save himselfe and the principal persons that were in his ship: which he, upon a hault courage, refused to do: wherefore the Duke charged him to saile next unto himselfe: which the night following he could not performe, by reason of the great abundance of water which entered his ship on all sides; for the avoiding whereof, and to save his ship from sincking, he caused 50 men continually to labor at the pumpe, though it were to small purpose. And seeing himselfe thus forsaken & separated from his admirall, he endevored what he could to attaine unto the coast of Flanders: where, being espied by 4 or 5 men of warre, which had their station assigned them upon the same coast, he was admonished to yeeld himselfe unto them. Which he refusing to do, was strongly assaulted by them altogether, and his ship being pierced with many bullets, was brought into farre worse case then before, and 40 of his souldiers were slaine. By which extremity he was enforced at length to yeeld himselfe unto Peter Banderduess & other captaines, which brought him and his ship into Zeland; and that other ship also last before mentioned: which both of them, immediatly after the greater and better part of their goods were unladen, suncke right downe.

For the memory of this exploit, the foresayd captaine Banderduess caused the banner of one of these shippes to be set up in the great Church of Leiden in Holland, which is of so great a length, that being fastened to the very roofe, it reached downe to the ground.

About the same time another small ship being by necessity driven upon the coast of Flanders, about Blankenberg, was cast away upon the sands, the people therein being saved. Thus almighty God would have the Spaniards huge ships to be presented, not onely to the view of the English, but also of the Zelanders; that at the sight of them they might acknowledge of what small ability they had beene to resist such impregnable forces, had not God endued them with courage, providence, and fortitude, yea, and fought for them in many places with his owne arme.

The 29 of July the Spanish fleet being encountered by the English (as is aforesayd) and lying close together under their fighting sailes, with a Southwest winde sailed past Dunkerk, the English ships stil following the chase. Of whom the day following when the Spaniards had got sea roome, they cut their maine sailes; whereby they sufficiently declared that they meant no longer to fight but to flie. For which cause the L. Admirall of England dispatched the L. Henrie Seymer with his squadron of small ships unto the coast of Flanders, where, with the helpe of the Dutch ships, he might stop the prince of Parma his passage, if perhaps he should attempt to issue forth with his army. And he himselfe in the meane space pursued the Spanish fleet untill the second of August, because he thought they had set saile for Scotland. And albeit he followed them very neere, yet did he not assault them any more, for want of powder and bullets. But upon the fourth of August, the winde arising, when as the Spaniards had spread all their sailes, betaking themselves wholly to flight, and leaving Scotland on the left hand, trended toward Norway, (whereby they sufficiently declared that their whole intent was to save themselves by flight, attempting for that purpose, with their battered and crazed ships, the most dangerous navigation of the Northren seas) the English seeing that they were now proceeded unto the latitude of 57 degrees, and being unwilling to participate that danger whereinto the Spaniards plunged themselves, and because they wanted things necessary, and especially powder & shot, returned backe for

England; leaving behinde them certaine pinasses onely, which they enjoyned to follow the Spaniards aloofe, and to observe their course. And so it came to passe that the fourth of August, with great danger and industry, the English arrived at Harwich: for they had bene tossed up and downe with a mighty tempest for the space of two or three dayes together, which it is likely did great hurt unto the Spanish fleet, being (as I sayd before) so maimed and battered. The English now going on shore, provided themselves foorthwith of victuals, gunne-powder, and other things expedient, that they might be ready at all assayes to entertaine the Spanish fleet, if it chanced any more to returne. But being afterward more certainely informed of the Spaniards course, they thought it best to leave them unto those boisterous and uncouth Northren seas, and not there to hunt after them.

The Spaniards seeing now that they wanted foure or five thousand of their people and having divers maimed and sicke persons, and likewise having lost 10 or 12 of their principall ships, they consulted among themselves, what they were best to doe, being now escaped out of the hands of the English, because their victuals failed them in like sort, and they began also to want cables, cordage, ankers, masts, sailes, and other naval furniture, and utterly despaired of the Duke of Parma his assistance (who verily hoping and undoubtedly expecting the returne of the Spanish Fleet, was continually occupied about his great preparation, commanding abundance of ankers to be made, & other necessary furniture for a Navy to be provided) they thought it good at length, so soone as the winde should serve them, to fetch a compasse about Scotland and Ireland, and so to returne for Spaine.

For they well understood, that commandement was given thorowout all Scotland, that they should not have any succour or assistance there. Neither yet could they in Norway supply their wants. Wherefore, having taken certaine Scotish and other fisherboats, they brought the men on boord their owne ships, to the end they might be their guides and Pilots. Fearing also least their fresh water should faile them, they cast all their horses and mules overboord: and so touching no where upon the coast of Scotland, but being carried with a fresh gale betweene the Orcades and Faar-Isles, they proceeded farre North, even unto 61 degrees of latitude, being distant from any land at the least 40 leagues. Heere the Duke of Medina generall of the Fleet commanded all his followers to shape their course for Biscay: and he himselfe with twenty or five and twenty of his ships which were best provided of fresh water and other necessaries, holding on his course over the maine Ocean, returned safely home. The residue of his ships being about forty in number, and committed unto his Viceadmirall, fell neerer with the coast of Ireland, intending their course for Cape Clare, because they hoped there to get fresh water, and to refresh themselves on land. But after they were driven with many contrary windes, at length, upon the second of September, they were cast by a tempest arising from the Southwest upon divers parts of Ireland, where many of their ships perished. And amongst others, the shippe of Michael de Oquendo, which was one of the great Galliasses: and two great ships of Venice also, namely, la Ratta and Belanzara, with other 36 or 38 ships more, which perished in sundry tempests, together with most of the persons contained in them.

Likewise some of the Spanish ships were the second time carried with a strong West winde into the chanell of England, whereof some were taken by the English upon their coast, and others by the men of Rochel upon the coast of France.

Moreover, there arrived at Newhaven in Normandy, being by tempest inforced so to doe, one of the foure great Galliasses, where they found the ships with the Spanish women which followed the Fleet at their setting forth. Two ships also were cast away upon the coast of Norway, one of them being of a great burthen; howbeit all the persons in the sayd great ship were saved: insomuch that of 134 ships, which set saile out of Portugall, there returned home 53 onely small and great: namely of the foure galliasses but one, and but one of the foure gallies. Of the 91 great galleons and hulks there were missing 58, and 33 returned: of the patches and zebraes 17 were missing, and 18 returned home. In briefe, there were missing 81 ships, in which number were galliasses, gallies, galeons, and other vessels both great and small. And amongst the 53 ships remaining, those also are reckoned which returned home before they came into the English chanell. Two galeons of those which were returned, were by misfortune burnt as they rode in the haven; and such like mishaps did many others undergo. Of 30000 persons which went in this expedition, there perished (according to the number and proportion of the ships) the greater and better part; and many of them which came home, by reason of the toiles and inconveniences which they sustained in this voyage, died not long after their arrivall. The Duke of Medina immediatly upon his returne was deposed from his authority, commanded to his private house, and forbidden to repaire unto the Court; where he could hardly satisfie or yeeld a reason unto his malicious enimies and backbiters. Many honourable personages and men of great renowme deceased soone after their returne; as namely John Martines de Ricalde, with divers others. A great part also of the Spanish Nobility and Gentry employed in this expedition perished either by fight, diseases, or drowning, before their arrival; & among the rest Thomas Perenot of Granduell a Dutchman, being earle of Cantebroi, and sonne unto Cardinall Granduell his brother.

Upon the coast of Zeland Don Diego de Pimentell, brother unto the Marques de Tamnares, and kinseman unto the earle of Beneventum & Calva, and Colonell over 32 bands with many other in the same ship was taken and detained as prisoner in Zeland.

Into England (as we sayd before) Don Pedro de Valdez, a man of singular experience, and greatly honoured in his countrey, was led captive, being accompanied with Don Vasquez de Silva, Don Alonzo de Sayas, and others.

Likewise upon the Scotish Westerne Isles of Lewis, and Ila, and about Cape Cantyre upon the maine land, there were cast away certaine Spanish shippes, out of which were saved divers Captaines and Gentlemen, and almost foure hundred souldiers, who for the most part, after their shipwracke, were brought unto Edenborough in Scotland, and being miserably needy and naked, were there clothed at the liberality of the King and the Marchants, and afterward were secretly shipped for Spaine; but the Scotish fleet wherein they passed touching at Yarmouth on the coast of Norfolke, were there stayed for a time untill the Councels pleasure was knowen; who in regard of their manifolde miseries, though they were enemies, wincked at their passage.

Upon the Irish coast many of their Noblemen and Gentlemen were drowned; and divers slaine by the barbarous and wilde Irish. Howbeit there was brought prisoner out of Ireland, Don Alonzo de Luçon, Colonell of two and thirtie bandes, commonly called a terza of Naples; together with Rodorigo de Lasso, and two others of the family of Cordova, who were committed unto the custodie of Sir Horatio Palavicini, that Monsieur de Teligny the sonne of Monsieur de la Noüe (who being taken in fight neere Antwerpe, was detained prisoner in the Castle of Turney) might be raunsomed for them by way of exchange. To conclude, there was no famous nor woorthy family in all Spaine, which in this expedition lost not a sonne, a brother, or a kinseman.

For the perpetuall memorie of this matter, the Zelanders caused newe coine of Silver and brasse to be stamped: which on the one side contained the armes of Zeland, with this inscription: GLORY TO GOD ONELY: and on the other side, the pictures of certeine great ships, with these words: THE SPANISH FLEET: and in the circumference about the ship: IT CAME, WENT, AND WAS. Anno 1588. That is to say, the Spanish fleet came, went, and was vanquished this yere; for which, glory be given to God onely.

Likewise they coined another kinde of money; upon the one side whereof was represented a ship fleeing, and a ship sincking: on the other side foure men making prayers and giving thanks unto God upon their knees; with this sentence: MAN PURPOSETH; GOD DISPOSETH. 1588. Also, for the lasting memory of the same matter, they have stamped in Holland divers such like coines, according to the custome of the ancient Romans.

While this woonderfull and puissant Navie was sayling along the English coastes, and all men did now plainely see and heare that which before they would not be perswaded of, all people thorowout England prostrated themselves with humble prayers and supplications unto God: but especially the outlandish Churches (who had greatest cause to feare, and against whom by name, the Spaniards had threatened most grievous torments) enjoyned to their people continuall fastings and supplications, that they might turne away Gods wrath and fury now imminent upon them for their sinnes: knowing right well, that prayer was the onely refuge against all enemies, calamities, and necessities, and that it was the onely solace and reliefe for mankinde, being visited with affliction and misery. Likewise such solemne dayes of supplication were observed thorowout the united Provinces.

Also a while after the Spanish Fleet was departed, there was in England, by the commandement of her Majestie, and in the united Provinces, by the direction of the States, a solemne festivall day publikely appointed, wherein all persons were enjoyned to resort unto the Church, and there to render thanks and praises unto God: and the Preachers were commanded to exhort the people thereunto. The foresayd solemnity was observed upon the 29 of November; which day was wholly spent in fasting, prayer, and giving of thanks.

Likewise, the Queenes Majestie herselfe, imitating the ancient Romans, rode into London in triumph, in regard of her owne and her subjects glorious deliverance. For being attended upon very solemnely by all the principall estates and officers of her Realme, she was carried thorow her sayd City of London in a tryumphant chariot, and in robes of triumph, from her Palace unto the Cathedrall Church of Saint Paul, out of the which the ensignes and colours of the vanquished Spaniards hung displayed. And all the Citizens of London in their Liveries stood on either side the street, by their severall Companies, with their ensignes and banners: and the streets were hanged on both sides with Blew cloth, which, together with the foresayd banners, yeelded a very stately and gallant prospect. Her Majestie being entered into the Church, together with her Clergie and Nobles gave thanks unto God, and caused a publike Sermon to be preached before her at Pauls crosse; wherein none other argument was handled, but that praise, honour, and glory might be rendered unto God, and that Gods name might be extolled by thanksgiving. And with her owne princely voice she most Christianly exhorted the people to doe the same: whereupon the people with a loud acclamation wished her a most long and happy life, to the confusion of her foes.

Thus the magnificent, huge, and mighty fleet of the Spaniards (which themselves termed in all places invincible) such as sayled not upon the Ocean sea many hundreth yeeres before, in the yeere 1588 vanished into smoake; to the great confusion and discouragement of the authours thereof. In regard of which her Majesties happy successe all her neighbours and friends congratulated with her, and many verses were penned to the honour of her Majesty by learned men, whereof some which came to our hands we will here annexe.

45

A letter of M. Thomas Candish to the right
honourable the Lord Hunsdon, Lord Chamberlaine,
one of her Majesties most honourable Privy Councell,
touching the successe of his voyage about the world

RIGHT honourable, as your favour heretofore hath bene
most greatly extended towards me, so I humbly desire a continuance thereof: and though there be no meanes in me to
deserve the same, yet the uttermost of my services shall not be
wanting, whensoever it shall please your honour to dispose
thereof. I am humbly to desire your honour to make knowen
unto her Majesty the desire I have had to doe her Majesty
service in the performance of this voyage. And as it hath
pleased God to give her the victory over part of her enemies,
so I trust yer long to see her overthrow them all. For the places
of their wealth, whereby they have mainteined and made their
warres, are now perfectly discovered: and if it please her Majesty, with a very small power she may take the spoile of them
all. It hath pleased the Almighty to suffer mee to circompasse
the whole globe of the world, entring in at the Streight of
Magellan, and returning by the cape de Buena Esperanza. In
which voyage I have either discovered or brought certeine intelligence of all the rich places of the world that ever were
knowen or discovered by any Christian. I navigated alongst the
coast of Chili, Peru, and Nueva Espanna, where I made great
spoiles: I burnt and sunke 19 sailes of ships small and great.
All the villages and townes that ever I landed at, I burnt and
spoiled: and had I not bene discovered upon the coast, I had
taken great quantitie of treasure. The matter of most profit unto
me was a great ship of the kings which I tooke at California,
which ship came from the Philippinas, being one of the richest

of merchandize that ever passed those seas, as the kings register and merchants accounts did shew: for it did amount in value to ————— in Mexico to be solde. Which goods (for that my ships were not able to conteine the least part of them) I was inforced to set on fire. From the cape of California, being the uttermost part of all Nueva Espanna, I navigated to the Islands of the Philippinas hard upon the coast of China; of which countrey I have brought such intelligence as hath not bene heard of in these parts. The stateliness and riches of which countrey I feare to make report of, least I should not be credited: for if I had not knowen sufficiently the incomparable wealth of that countrey, I should have bene as incredulous thereof, as others will be that have not had the like experience. I sailed along the Ilands of the Malucos, where among some of the heathen people I was well intreated, where our countrey men may have trade as freely as the Portugals, if they will themselves. From thence I passed by the cape of Buena Esperanza, and found out by the way homeward the iland of S. Helena, where the Portugals use to relieve themselves: and from that iland God hath suffered me to returne into England. All which services with my selfe I humbly prostrate at her Majesties feet, desiring the Almighty long to continue her reigne among us: for at this day she is the most famous and victorious prince that liveth in the world.

Thus humbly desiring pardon of your honour for my tediousnesse, I leave your lordship to the tuition of the Almighty. Plimmouth this ninth of September 1588.

Your honours most humble to command,

THOMAS CANDISH

46

A report of the trueth of the fight about the Isles of Açores, the last of August 1591. betwixt the Revenge, one of her Majesties shippes, and an Armada of the king of Spaine; Penned by the honourable Sir Walter Ralegh knight

BECAUSE the rumours are diversly spred, as well in England as in the Lowe countreis and elsewhere, of this late encounter betweene her Majesties ships and the Armada of Spaine; and that the Spaniards according to their usuall maner, fill the world with their vaine-glorious vaunts, making great apparance of victories, when on the contrary, themselves are most commonly and shamefully beaten and dishonoured; thereby hoping to possesse the ignorant multitude by anticipating & forerunning false reports: It is agreeable with all good reason, for manifestation of the truth, to overcome falshood and untrueth; that the beginning, continuance and successe of this late honourable encounter of Sir Richard Greenvil, and other her Majesties Captaines, with the Armada of Spaine; should be truely set downe and published without partialitie or false imaginations. And it is no marveile that the Spaniard should seeke by false and slanderous pamphlets, advisoes and Letters, to cover their owne losse, and to derogate from others their due honors, especially in this fight being performed far off: seeing they were not ashamed in the yeere 1588. when they purposed the invasion of this land, to publish in sundry languages in print, great victories in wordes, which they pleaded to have obteined against this Realme; and spred the same in a most false sort over all parts of France, Italy, and elsewhere. When shortly after it was happily manifested in very deed to al Nations, how their Navy which they termed invincible, con-

sisting of 140. saile of shippes, not onely of their owne kingdome, but strengthened with the greatest Argosies, Portugal
Caracks, Florentines, and huge hulks of other Countries, were
by 30. of her Majesties owne ships of war, and a few of our
owne Marchants, by the wise, valiant, and advantagious conduct
of the L. Charles Howard high Admirall of England, beaten
and shuffled together; even from the Lizard in Cornwall first
to Portland, where they shamefully left Don Pedro de Valdes,
with his mighty ship; from Portland to Cales, where they lost
Hugo de Moncado, with the Gallias of which he was Captaine,
and from Cales, driven with squibs from their anchors, were
chased out of the sight of England, round about Scotland and
Ireland. Where for the sympathie of their barbarous religion,
hoping to finde succour and assistance, a great part of them
were crusht against the rocks, and those that landed, being very
many in number, were notwithstanding broken, slaine, and
taken, and so sent from village to village coupled in halters,
to be shipped into England. Where her Majestie of her Princely
and invincible disposition, disdaining to put them to death, and
scorning either to retaine or entertaine them: they were all sent
backe againe to their countreys, to witnes and recount the worthy achievements of their invincible and dreadfull Navy: Of
which the number of Souldiers, the fearefull burthen of their
shippes, the commanders names of every squadron, with all
other their magasines of provisions, were put in print, as an
Army and Navy unresistable, and disdaining prevention. With
all which so great and terrible an ostentation, they did not in
all their sailing round about England, so much as sinke or take
one shippe, Barke, Pinnesse, or Cockbote of ours: or ever
burnt so much as one sheepecote of this land. Whenas on the
contrarie, Sir Francis Drake, with onely 800. souldiers not long
before, landed in their Indies, and forced Sant-Iago, Santo
Domingo, Cartagena, and the forts of Florida.

And after that, Sir John Norris marched from Peniche in
Portugall, with a handfull of souldiers, to the gates of Lisbone,
being above 40 English miles. Where the Earle of Essex himselfe and other valiant Gentlemen braved the Citie of Lisbone,
encamped at the very gates; from whence, after many dayes
abode, finding neither promised partie, nor provision to batter;
they made retrait by land, in despight of all their Garrisons,

both of horse & foote. In this sort I have a little digressed from my first purpose, onely by the necessarie comparison of theirs and our actions: the one covetous of honour without vaunt of ostentation; the other so greedy to purchase the opinion of their owne affaires, and by false rumors to resist the blasts of their owne dishonours, as they will not onely not blush to spread all manner of untruthes: but even for the least advantage, be it but for the taking of one poore adventurer of the English, will celebrate the victory with bonefires in every towne, always spending more in faggots, then the purchase was worth they obtained. When as we never thought it worth the consumption of two billets, when we have taken eight or ten of their Indian shippes at one time, and twentie of the Brasill fleete. Such is the difference betweene true valure, and ostentation: and betweene honorable actions, and frivolous vaineglorious vaunts. But now to returne to my purpose.

The L. Thomas Howard with six of her Majesties shippes, six victualers of London, the Barke Ralegh, & two or three other Pinnases riding at anker neere unto Flores, one of the Westerly Ilands of the Azores, the last of August in the afternoone, had intelligence by one Captaine Middleton of the approch of the Spanish Armada. Which Middleton being in a very good sailer had kept them company three dayes before, of good purpose, both to discover their forces the more, as also to give advise to my L. Thomas of their approch. Hee had no sooner delivered the newes but the fleete was in sight: many of our shippes companies were on shore in the Ilande; some providing balast for their ships; others filling of water and refreshing themselves from the land with such things as they could either for money, or by force recover. By reason whereof our ships being all pestered and romaging every thing out of order, very light for want of balast, and that which was most to our disadvantage, the one halfe part of the men of every shippe sicke, and utterly unserviceable: for in the Revenge there were ninety diseased: in the Bonaventure, not so many in health as could handle her maine saile. For had not twenty men beene taken out of a Barke of sir George Careys, his being commaunded to be sunke, and those appointed to her, she had hardly ever recovered England. The rest, for the most parte, were in little better state. The names of her Majesties shippes were these as followeth, the Defiance, which was Admiral, the Revenge Vice-admirall, the Bonaventure commaunded by Captaine Crosse, the Lion by George Fenner, the Foresight by M. Thomas Vava-sour, and the Crane by Duffild. The Foresight & the Crane being but smal ships; only the other were of the middle size; the rest, besides the Barke Ralegh, commanded by Captaine Thin, were victuallers, and of small force or none. The Spanish fleet having shrouded their approch by reason of the Island; were now so soone at hand, as our shippes had scarce time to way their anchors, but some of them were driven to let slippe their Cables and set saile. Sir Richard Grinvile was the last that wayed, to recover the men that were upon the Island, which otherwise had bene lost. The L. Thomas with the rest very hardly recovered the winde, which Sir Richard Grinvile not being able to doe, was perswaded by the Master and others to cut his maine sayle, and cast about, and to trust to the sayling of the ship; for the squadron of Sivil were on his weather bow. But Sir Richard utterly refused to turne from the enemie, alleaging that hee would rather choose to die, then to dishonour himselfe, his countrey, and her Majesties shippe, perswading his companie that hee would passe through the two squadrons, in despight of them, and enforce those of Sivil to give him way. Which hee performed upon divers of the formost, who, as the Mariners terme it, sprang their luffe, and fell under the lee of the Revenge. But the other course had beene the better, and might right well have bene answered in so great an impossibility of prevaling. Notwithstanding out of the greatnesse of his minde, he could not be perswaded. In the meane while as hee attended those which were nearest him, the great San Philip being in the winde of him, and comming towards him, becalmed his sailes in such sort, as the shippe could neither make way, nor feele the helme: so huge and high carged was the Spanish ship, being of a thousand and five hundreth tuns. Who after layd the Revenge aboord. When he was thus bereft of his sailes, the ships that were under his lee luffing up, also layd him aboord: of which the next was the Admiral of the Biscaines, a very mighty and puissant shippe commanded by Brittandona. The sayd Philip carried three tire of ordinance on a side, and eleven pieces in every tire. She shot eight forth right out of her chase, besides those of her sterne ports.

After the Revenge was entangled with this Philip, foure other boorded her; two on her larboord, and two on her starboord. The fight thus beginning at three of the clock in the afternoone, continued very terrible all that evening. But the great San Philip having received the lower tire of the Revenge, discharged with crossebarshot, shifted her selfe with all diligence from her sides, utterly misliking her first entertainement. Some say that the shippe foundred, but we cannot report it for truth, unlesse we were assured. The Spanish ships were filled with companies of souldiers, in some two hundred besides the mariners; in some five, in others eight hundreth. In ours there were none at all beside the mariners, but the servants of the commanders and some few voluntary gentlemen onely. After many enterchanged volies of great ordinance and small shot, the Spaniards deliberated to enter the Revenge, and made divers attempts, hoping to force her by the multitudes of their armed soulders and Musketters, but were still repulsed againe and againe, and at all times beaten backe into their owne ships, or into the seas. In the beginning of the fight, the George Noble of London having received some shot thorow her by the Armadas, fell under the lee of the Revenge, and asked Sir Richard what he would command him, being but one of the victuallers and of small force: Sir Richard bid him save himselfe, and leave him to his fortune. After the fight had thus, without intermission, continued while the day lasted and some houres of the night, many of our men were slaine and hurte, and one of the great Gallions of the Armada, and the Admirall of the Hulkes both sunke, and in many other of the Spanish shippes great slaughter was made. Some write that sir Richard was very dangerously hurt almost in the beginning of the fight, and lay speechlesse for a time ere hee recovered. But two of the Revenges owne company, brought home in a ship of Lime from the Ilandes, examined by some of the Lordes, and others, affirmed that hee was never so wounded as that hee forsooke the upper decke, till an houre before midnight; and then being shot into the bodie with a Musket as hee was a dressing, was againe shot into the head, and withall his Chirurgion wounded to death. This agreeth also with an examination taken by sir Francis Godolphin, of foure other mariners of the same shippe being returned, which examination, the said sir Francis sent unto master William Killegrue, of her Majesties privy Chamber.

But to returne to the fight, the Spanish ships which attempted to bord the Revenge, as they were wounded and beaten off, so alwayes others came in their places, she having never lesse then two mighty Gallions by her sides, and aboard her: So that ere the morning, from three of the clocke the day before, there had fifteene severall Armadas assayled her; and all so ill approved their entertainement, as they were by the breake of day, far more willing to harken to a composition, then hastily to make any more assaults or entries. But as the day encreased, so our men decreased: and as the light grew more and more, by so much more grewe our discomforts. For none appeared in sight but enemies, saving one small ship called the Pilgrim, commaunded by Jacob Whiddon, who hovered all night to see the successe: but in the morning bearing with the Revenge, was hunted like a hare amongst many ravenous houndes, but escaped.

All the powder of the Revenge to the last barrell was now spent, all her pikes broken, fortie of her best men slaine, and the most part of the rest hurt. In the beginning of the fight shee had but one hundreth free from sicknes, and fourescore & ten sicke, laid in hold upon the Ballast. A small troup to man such a ship, & a weake garrison to resist so mighty an army. By those hundred al was susteined, the voleis, boordings, and entrings of fifteen ships of warre, besides those which beat her at large. On the contrary, the Spanish were always supplied with souldiers brought from every squadron: all maner of Armes and powder at will. Unto ours there remained no comfort at all, no hope, no supply either of ships, men, or weapons; the Mastes all beaten over boord, all her tackle cut asunder, her upper worke altogether rased, and in effect evened shee was with the water, but the very foundation or bottome of a ship, nothing being left over head either for flight or defence. Sir Richard finding himselfe in this distresse, and unable any longer to make resistance, having endured in this fifteene houres fight, the assault of fifteene severall Armadas, all by turnes aboord him, and by estimation eight hundred shotte of great Artillerie, besides many assaults and entries; and that himselfe and the shippe must needes be possessed by the enemy, who were now all cast in a ring round about him. (The Revenge

not able to moove one way or other, but as she was moved with
the waves and billow of the sea) commaunded the Master gunner, whom hee knew to be a most resolute man, to split and
sinke the shippe; that thereby nothing might remaine of glory
or victory to the Spaniards: seeing in so many houres fight,
and with so great a Navie they were not able to take her, having had fifteene houres time, above ten thousand men, & fiftie
and three saile of men of warre to performe it withall: and perswaded the company, or as many as hee could induce, to yeelde
themselves unto God, and to the mercie of none else; but
as they had, like valiant resolute men, repulsed so many enemies, they should not nowe shorten the honour of their Nation,
by prolonging their owne lives for a few houres, or a fewe dayes.
The Master gunner readily condescended and divers others; but
the Captaine and the Master were of another opinion, and besought Sir Richard to have care of them: alleaging that the
Spaniard would be as ready to entertaine a composition, as
they were willing to offer the same: and that there being divers
sufficient and valiant men yet living, and whose wounds were
not mortal, they might do their Countrey and prince acceptable
service hereafter. And whereas Sir Richard had alleaged that
the Spaniards should never glory to have taken one shippe of
her Majestie, seeing they had so long and so notably defended
themselves; they answered, that the shippe had sixe foote water
in holde, three shot under water, which were so weakely
stopped, as with the first working of the sea, she must needs
sinke, and was besides so crusht and brused, as shee could
never be removed out of the place.

And as the matter was thus in dispute, and Sir Richard refusing to hearken to any of those reasons: the Master of the Revenge (while the Captaine wanne unto him the greater party)
was convoyd aboord the Generall Don Alfonso Baçan. Who
(finding none over hastie to enter the Revenge againe, doubting
least Sir Richard would have blowne them up and himselfe, and
perceiving by the report of the Master of the Revenge his
dangerous disposition) yeelded that all their lives should be
saved, the company sent for England, & the better sort to pay
such reasonable ransome as their estate would beare, and in the
meane season to be free from Gally or imprisonment. To this
he so much the rather condescended as wel, as I have said, for

feare of further losse and mischiefe to themselves, as also for the desire he had to recover Sir Richard Greenvil; whom for his notable valure he seemed greatly to honour and admire.

When this answere was returned, and that safetie of life was promised, the common sort being now at the ende of their perill, the most drew backe from Sir Richard and the Master gunner, being no hard matter to disswade men from death to life. The Master gunner finding himselfe and Sir Richard thus prevented and mastered by the greater number, would have slaine himselfe with a sword, had he not bene by force withheld and locked into his Cabben. Then the Generall sent many boates aboord the Revenge, and divers of our men fearing Sir Richards disposition, stole away aboord the Generall and other shippes. Sir Richard thus overmatched, was sent unto by Alfonso Baçan to remoove out of the Revenge, the shippe being marveilous unsavorie, filled with blood and bodies of dead, and wounded men like a slaughter house. Sir Richard answered that hee might doe with his body what he list, for hee esteemed it not, and as he was carried out of the shippe hee swounded, and reviving againe desired the company to pray for him. The Generall used Sir Richard with all humanitie, and left nothing unattempted that tended to his recoverie, highly commending his valour and worthinesse, and greatly bewailing the danger wherein he was, being unto them a rare spectacle, and a resolution sildome approoved, to see one shippe turne toward so many enemies, to endure the charge and boording of so many huge Armadas, and to resist and repell the assaults and entries of so many souldiers. All which and more is confirmed by a Spanish Captaine of the same Armada, and a present actor in the fight, who being severed from the rest in a storme, was by the Lion of London a small ship taken, and is now prisoner in London.

The generall commander of the Armada, was Don Alphonso Baçan, brother to the Marques of Santa Cruz. The admiral of the Biscaine squadron, was Britandona. Of the squadron of Sivil, the Marques of Arumburch. The Hulkes and Flybotes were commanded by Luis Coutinho. There were slaine and drowned in this fight, well neere one thousand of the enemies, and two speciall commanders Don Luis de sant John, and Don George de Prunaria de Mallaga, as the Spanish captaine confesseth, besides divers others of speciall account, whereof as yet report is not made.

The Admirall of the Hulkes and the Ascension of Sivil were both sunke by the side of the Revenge; one other recovered the rode of Saint Michael, and sunke also there; a fourth ranne her selfe with the shore to save her men. Sir Richard died as it is sayd, the second or third day aboord the Generall, and was by them greatly bewailed. What became of his body, whether it were buried in the sea or on the land we know not: the comfort that remayneth to his friends is, that hee hath ended his life honourably in respect of the reputation wonne to his nation and countrey, and of the same to his posteritie, and that being dead, he hath not outlived his owne honour.

For the rest of her Majesties ships that entred not so farre into the fight as the Revenge, the reasons and causes were these. There were of them but sixe in all, whereof two but small ships; the Revenge ingaged past recovery: The Iland of Flores was on the one side, 53 saile of the Spanish, divided into squadrons on the other, all as full filled with souldiers as they could containe: Almost the one halfe of our men sicke and not able to serve: the ships growne foule, unroomaged, and scarcely able to beare any saile for want of balast, having bene sixe moneths at the sea before. If all the rest had entred, all had bene lost: for the very hugenes of the Spanish fleete, if no other violence had beene offered, would have crusht them betweene them into shivers. Of which the dishonour and losse to the Queene had bene farre greater then the spoyle or harme that the enemie could any way have received. Notwithstanding it is very true, that the Lord Thomas would have entred betweene the squadrons, but the rest would not condescend; and the master of his owne ship offred to leape into the sea, rather then to conduct that her Majesties ship and the rest to bee a pray to the enemie, where there was no hope nor possibilitie either of defence or victory. Which also in my opinion had ill sorted or answered the discretion and trust of a Generall, to commit himselfe and his charge to an assured destruction, without hope or any likelyhood of prevailing: thereby to diminish the strength of her Majesties Navy, and to enrich the pride and glory of the enemie. The Foresight of the Queenes commaunded by M. Thomas Vavisor performed a very great

fight, and stayed two houres as neere the Revenge as the
weather would permit him, not forsaking the fight, till he was
like to be encompassed by the squadrons, & with a great difficultie cleared himselfe. The rest gave divers voleis of shot, and
entred as farre as the place permitted, and their owne necessities, to keepe the weather gage of the enemie, untill they
were parted by night. A fewe dayes after the fight was ended,
and the English prisoners dispersed into the Spanish and Indie
ships, there arose so great a storme from the West and Northwest, that all the fleete was dispersed, as well the Indian fleete
which were then come unto them, as the rest of the Armada
that attended their arrivall, of which 14. saile together with the
Revenge, and in her 200 Spaniards, were cast away upon the
Isle of S. Michael. So it pleased them to honor the buriall of
that renowmed ship the Revenge, not suffering her to perish
alone, for the great honour she atchieved in her life time. On
the rest of the Ilandes there were cast away in this storme, 15
or 16 more of the ships of warre: and of an hundred and odde
saile of the Indie fleete, expected this yeere in Spaine, what
in this tempest, and what before in the bay of Mexico, and
about the Bermudas, there were 70 and odde consumed and
lost, with those taken by our shippes of London, besides one
very rich Indian ship, which set her selfe on fire, beeing boorded
by the Pilgrim, and five other taken by master Wats his ships
of London, between the Havana and Cape S. Antonio. The
fourth of this moneth of November we received letters from the
Tercera, affirming that there are 3000 bodies of men remaining
in that Iland, saved out of the perished ships: & that by the
Spaniards owne confession, there are 10000 cast away in this
storme, besides those that are perished betweene the Ilands
and the maine. Thus it hath pleased God to fight for us, and
to defend the justice of our cause, against the ambicious and
bloody pretenses of the Spaniard, who seeking to devoure all
nations, are themselves devoured. A manifest testimony how
injust and displeasing, their attempts are in the sight of God,
who hath pleased to witnes by the successe of their affaires,
his mislike of their bloody and injurious designes, purposed
and practised against all Christian princes, over whom they
seeke unlawfull and ungodly rule and Empery.

One day or two before this wracke happened to the Spanish

fleete, when as some of our prisoners desired to be set on shore upon the Ilandes, hoping to be from thence transported into England, which libertie was formerly by the Generall promised: One Morice Fitz John, sonne of olde John of Desmond, a notable traytour, cousin german to the late Earle of Desmond, was sent to the English from shippe to shippe, to perswade them to serve the King of Spaine. The arguments hee used to induce them were these. The increase of pay which he promised to be trebled: advancement to the better sort: and the exercise of the true Catholique Religion, and safetie of their soules to all. For the first, even the beggerly and unnaturall behaviour of those English and Irish rebels, that served the King in that present action, was sufficient to answere that first argument of rich pay. For so poore and beggerly they were, as for want of apparell they stripped their poore Countrey men prisoners out of their ragged garments, worne to nothing by six months service, and spared not to despoyle them even of their bloody shirtes, from their wounded bodies, and the very shooes from their feete; A notable testimonie of their rich entertainment and great wages. The second reason was hope of advancement if they served well, and would continue faithfull to the King. But what man can bee so blockishly ignorant ever to expect place or honour from a forraine King, having no other argument or perswasion then his owne disloyaltie; to be unnaturall to his owne Countrey that bred him; to his parents that begat him, and rebellious to his true Prince, to whose obedience he is bound by oath, by nature, and by Religion? No, they are onely assured to be imployed in all desperate enterprises, to bee helde in scorne and disdaine ever among those whom they serve. And that ever traitour was either trusted or advanced I could never yet reade, neither can I at this time remember any example. And no man coulde have lesse becommed the place of an Orator for such a purpose, then this Morice of Desmond. For the Erle his cosen being one of the greatest subjects in that kingdom of Ireland, having almost whole Countreis in his possession; so many goodly Mannors, castles, and lordships; the Count Palatine of Kerry, five hundred gentlemen of his owne name and family to follow him, besides others (all which he possessed in peace for three or foure hundred yeeres) was in lesse then three yeeres after his adhering to the Spaniards and rebellion, beaten from all his holdes, not so many as ten gentlemen of his name left living, himselfe taken and beheaded by a souldier of his owne nation, and his land given by a Parliament to her Majestie, and possessed by the English: His other cosen Sir John of Desmond taken by Master John Zouch, and his body hanged over the gates of his native Citie to be devoured by ravens: the thirde brother Sir James hanged, drawne, and quartered in the same place. If hee had withall vaunted of his successe of his owne house, no doubt the argument would have mooved much, and wrought great effect: which because, hee for that present forgot, I thought it good to remember in his behalfe. For matter of Religion it would require a particuler volume, if I should set downe how irreligiously they cover their greedy and ambicious pretenses, with that veile of pietie. But sure I am, that there is no kingdome or common-wealth in all Europe, but if they be reformed, they then invade it for religion sake: if it bee, as they terme Catholique, they pretend title; as if the Kings of Castile were the naturall heires of all the world: and so be-tweene both, no kingdome is unsought. Where they dare not with their owne forces to invade, they basely entertaine the traitours and vacabonds of all Nations: seeking by those and by their runnagate Jesuits to winne parts, and have by that meane ruined many Noble houses and others in this lande, and have extinguished both their lives and families. What good, honour, or fortune ever man yet by them atchieved, is yet unheard of, or unwritten. And if our English Papists doe but looke into Portugall, against which they have no pretence of Religion, how the Nobilitie are put to death, imprisoned, their rich men made a praye, and all sorts of people captived; they shall finde that the obedience even of the Turke is easie and a libertie, in respect of the slaverie and tyrannie of Spaine. What have they done in Sicill, in Naples, Millaine, and in the Low countreis; who hath there bene spared for Religion at all? And it commeth to my remembrance of a certaine Burger of Antwerpe, whose house being entred by a company of Spanish souldiers, when they first sacked the Citie, hee besought them to spare him and his goods, being a good Catholique, and one of their owne partie and faction. The Spaniards answered, that they knew him to be of a good conscience for himselfe, but his

money, plate, jewels, and goods, were all hereticall, and therefore good prize. So they abused and tormented the foolish
Fleming, who hoped that an Agnus Dei had bene a sufficient
target against all force of that holy and charitable nation.
Neither have they at any time as they protest invaded the kingdomes of the Indies and Peru, and elsewhere, but onely led
thereunto, rather to reduce the people to Christianitie, then for
either gold or Emperie. When as in one onely Island called
Hispaniola, they have wasted thirtie hundred thousand of the
naturall people, besides many millions else in other places of
the Indies: a poore and harmelesse people created of God, and
might have bene wonne to his knowledge, as many of them
were, and almost as many as ever were perswaded thereunto.
The storie whereof is at large written by a Bishop of their
owne nation called Bartholomew de las Casas, and translated
into English and many other languages, intituled The Spanish
cruelties. Who would therefore repose trust in such a nation of
ravenous strangers, and especially in those Spaniards which
more greedily thirst after English blood, then after the lives
of any other people of Europe, for the many overthrowes and
dishonours they have received at our hands, whose weakenesse
wee have discovered to the world, and whose forces at home,
abroad, in Europe, in India, by sea and land, wee have even
with handfulles of men and shippes, overthrowen and dishonoured. Let not therefore any English man, of what religion
soever, have other opinion of the Spaniards, but that those
whom hee seeketh to winne of our Nation, he esteemeth base
and trayterous, unworthy persons, or unconstant fooles: and
that he useth his pretence of religion, for no other purpose but
to bewitch us from the obedience of our naturall Prince, thereby
hoping in time to bring us to slavery and subjection, and then
none shall be unto them so odious, and disdayned as the traitours themselves, who have solde their Countrey to a stranger,
and forsaken their faith and obedience contrarie to nature &
religion; and contrarie to that humane and generall honour,
not onely of Christians, but of heathen and irreligious nations,
who have alwayes sustayned what labour soever, and embraced
even death it selfe, for their countrey, Prince, or common-
wealth. To conclude, it hath ever to this day pleased God to
prosper and defend her Majestie, to breake the purposes of

malicious enemies, of forsworne traytors, and of injust practises and invasions. She hath ever beene honoured of the worthiest kings, served by faithfull subjects, and shall by the favour of God, resist, repell, and confound all whatsoever attempts against her sacred person or kingdome. In the meane time let the Spaniard and traytour vaunt of their successe, and wee her true and obedient vassals, guided by the shining light of her vertues, shall alwayes love her, serve her, and obey her to the end of our lives.

47

A voyage with three tall ships, the Penelope Admirall,
the Marchant royall Viceadmirall, and the Edward
Bonaventure Rereadmirall, to the East Indies, by the
Cape of Buona Speransa, to Quitangone neere
Mosambique, to the Iles of Comoro and Zanzibar on
the backeside of Africa, and beyond Cape Comori in
India, to the Iles of Nicubar and of Gomes Polo
within two leagues of Sumatra, to the Ilands of Pulo
Pinaom, and thence to the maine land of Malacca,
begunne by M. George Raymond, in the yeere 1591,
and performed by M. James Lancaster, and written
from the mouth of Edmund Barker of Ipswich,
his lieutenant in the sayd voyage,
by M. Richard Hakluyt

O U R fleet of the three tall ships abovenamed departed from
Plimmouth the 10 of April 1591, and arrived at the Canarie-
ilands the 25 of the same, from whence we departed the 29
of April. The second of May we were in the height of Cape
Blanco. The fift we passed the tropique of Cancer. The eight
we were in the height of Cape Verde. All this time we went
with a faire winde at Northeast, always before the winde untill
the 13 of the same moneth, when we came within 8 degrees of
the Equinoctiall line, where we met with a contrary winde.
Here we lay off and on in the sea untill the sixt of June, on
which day we passed the sayd line. While we lay thus off and
on, we tooke a Portugal Caravel laden by marchants of Lisbon
for Brasile, in which Caravel we had some 60 tunnes of wine,
1200 jarres of oyle, about 100 jarres of olives, certaine barrels

of capers, three fats of peason, with divers other necessaries fit for our voyage: which wine, oyle, olives and capers were better to us then gold. We had two men died before wee passed the line, and divers sicke, which tooke their sicknesse in those hote climates: for they be wonderful unholesome from 8 degrees of Northerly latitude unto the line, at that time of the yeere: for we had nothing but Ternados, with such thunder, lightning, and raine, that we could not keep our men drie 3 houres together, which was an occasion of the infection among them, and their eating of salt victuals, with lacke of clothes to shift them. After we passed the line, we had the wind still at Eastsoutheast, which caried us along the coast of Brasil 100 leagues from the maine, til we came in 26 degrees to the Southward of the line, where the wind came up to the North, at which time we did account, that the Cape of Buona esperansa did beare off us East and by South, betwixt 900 and 1000 leagues. Passing this gulfe from the coast of Brasil unto the Cape we had the wind often variable as it is upon our coast, but for the most part so, that we might lie our course. The 28 of July we had sight of the foresayd Cape of Buona esperansa: untill the 31 wee lay off and on with the wind contrary to double the Cape, hoping to double it, & so to have gone seventie leagues further to a place called Agoada de S. Bras, before we would have sought to have put into any harbour. But our men being weake and sicke in all our shippes, we thought good to seeke some place to refresh them. With which consent we bare up with the land to the Northward of the Cape, and going along the shore, we espied a goodly Baie with an Iland lying to Seawards of it, into which we did beare, and found it very commodious for our ships to ride in. This Baie is called Agoada de Saldanha, lying 15 leagues Northward on the hither side of the Cape. The first of August being Sunday we came to an anker in the Baie, sending our men on land, and there came unto them certaine blacke Salvages very brutish which would not stay, but retired from them. For the space of 15 or 20 dayes we could find no reliefe but onely foules which wee killed with our pieces, which were cranes and geese: there was no fish but muskles and other shel-fish, which we gathered on the rockes. After 15 or 20 dayes being here, our Admirall went with his pinnasse unto the Iland which lieth off this Baie, where hee found great store of Penguines & Seales, whereof he brought good plenty with him. And twise after that we sent certain of our men, which at both times brought their bots lading unto our ships. After we had bene here some time, we got here a Negro, whom we compelled to march into the country with us, making signs to bring us some cattell; but at this time we could come to the sight of none, so we let the Negro goe with some trifles. Within 8 dayes after, he with 30 or 40 other Negroes, brought us downe some 40 bullocks and oxen, with as many sheepe: at which time we bought but few of them. But within 8 dayes after they came downe with as many more, & then we bought some 24 oxen with as many sheepe. We bought an oxe for two knives, a stirke for a knife, and a sheepe for a knife, and some we bought for lesse value then a knife. The oxen be very large and well fleshed, but not fat. The sheepe are very big and very good meat, they have no woll on their backs but haire, and have great tailes like the sheepe in Syria. There be divers sorts of wild beasts, as the Antilope, (whereof M. Lancaster killed one of the bignes of a yong colt) the red & fallow Deere, with other great beasts unknowen unto us. Here are also great store of over-growen monkeis. As touching our proceeding upon our voyage, it was thought good rather to proceed with two ships wel manned, then with three evill manned: for here wee had of sound and whole men but 198, of which there went in the Penelope with the Admiral 101, and in the Edward with the worshipfull M. captaine Lancaster 97. We left behind 50 men with the Roiall marchant, whereof there were many pretily well recovered, of which ship was master and governour Abraham Kendal, which for many reasons we thought good to send home. The disease that hath consumed our men hath bene the skurvie. Our souldiers which have not bene used to the Sea, have best held out, but our mariners dropt away, which (in my judgement) proceedeth of their evill diet at home.

Six dayes after our sending backe for England of the Marchant Roiall from Agoada de Saldanha, our Admirall M. captaine Raimond in the Penelope, and M. James Lancaster in the Edward Bonaventure, set forward to double the Cape of Buona esperansa, which they did very speedily. But being passed as far as Cape dos Corrientes, the 14 of September we were encountred with a mighty storme and extreeme gusts of wind, wherein we lost our Generals companie, and could never heare of him nor his ship any more, though we did our best endevour to seeke him up and downe a long while, and staied for him certaine dayes at the Iland of Comoro, where we appointed to stay one for another. Foure dayes after this uncomfortable seperation in the morning toward ten of the clocke we had a terrible clap of thunder, which slew foure of our men outright, their necks being wrung in sonder without speaking any word, and of 94 men there was not one untouched, whereof some were striken blind, others were bruised in their legs & armes, and others in their brests, so that they voided blood two dayes after, others were drawen out at length as though they had bene racked. But (God be thanked) they all recovered saving onely the foure which were slaine out right. Also with the same thunder our maine maste was torne very grievously from the head to the decke, and some of the spikes that were ten inches into the timber, were melted with the extreme heate theereof. From thence wee shaped our course to the Northeast, and not long after we fell upon the Northwest end of the mighty Iland of S. Laurence: which one of our men espied by Gods good blessing late in the evening by Moone light, who seeing afarre off the breaking of the Sea, and calling to certaine of his fellowes, asked them what it was: which eftsoones told him that it was the breaking of the Sea upon the Shoulds. Whereupon in very good time we cast about to avoyd the danger which we were like to have incurred. Thus passing on forward, it was our lucke to over-shoote Mozambique, and to fall with a place called Quitangone two leagues to the North-ward of it, and we tooke three or foure Barkes of Moores, which Barkes in their language they call Pangaias, laden with Millio, hennes, and ducks, with one Portugall boy, going for the pro-vision of Mozambique. Within few dayes following we came to an Iland an hundred leagues to the Northeast of Mozam-bique called Comoro, which we found exceeding full of people, which are Moores of tawnie colour and good stature, but they be very trecherous and diligently to be taken heed of. Here wee desired to store our selves with water, whereof we stood in great need, and sent sixteene of our men well armed on shore in our boate: whom the people suffred quietly to land and water, and divers of them with their king came aboord our

ship in a gowne of crimosine Sattin pinked after the Moorish
fashion downe to the knee, whom we entertained in the best
maner, and had some conference with him of the state of the
place and marchandises, using our Portugall boy which we
had taken before for our interpreter, and in the end licensed
the king and his company to depart, and sent our men againe
for more water, who then also dispatched their businesse, &
returned quietly: the third time likewise we sent them for
more, which also returned without any harme. And though we
thought our selves furnished, yet our master William Mace of
Radcliffe pretending that it might be long before we should
finde any good watering place, would needes goe himselfe on
shore with thirtie men, much against the will of our captaine,
and hee and 16 of his company, together with one boat which
was all that we had, and 16 others that were a washing over-
against our ship, were betrayed of the perfidious Moores, and
in our sight for the most part slaine, we being not able for want
of a boat to yeeld them any succour. From hence with heavie
hearts we shaped our course for Zanzibar the 7 of November,
where shortly after wee arrived and made us a new boat of
such boards as we had within boord, and rid in the road untill
the 15 of February, where, during our aboad, we sawe divers
Pangaias or boates, which are pinned with woodden pinnes, and
sowed together with Palmito cordes, and calked with the huskes
of Cocos shels beaten, whereof they make Occam. At length a
Portugal Pangaia comming out of the harborow of Zanzibar,
where they have a small Factorie, sent a Canoa with a Moore
which had bene christened, who brought us a letter wherein
they desired to know what wee were, and what we sought. We
sent them word we were Englishmen come from Don Antonio
upon businesse to his friends in the Indies: with which answere
they returned, and would not any more come at us. Whereupon
not long after wee manned out our boat and tooke a Pangaia
of the Moores, which had a priest of theirs in it, which in their
language they call a Sherife: whom we used very curteously:
which the king tooke in very good part, having his priests
in great estimation, and for his deliverance furnished us with
two moneths victuals, during all which time we detained him
with us. These Moores informed us of the false and spitefull
dealing of the Portugals towards us, which made them beleeve

that we were cruell people and men-eaters, and willed them if they loved their safetie in no case to come neere us. Which they did onely to cut us off from all knowledge of the state and traffique of the countrey. While we road from the end of November until the middle of February in this harborough, which is sufficient for a ship of 500 tuns to ride in, we set upon a Portugall Pangaia with our boat, but because it was very litle, & our men not able to stirre in it, we were not able to take the sayd Pangaia, which was armed with 10 good shot like our long fouling pieces. This place for the goodnesse of the harborough and watering, and plentifull refreshing with fish, whereof we tooke great store with our nets, and for sundry sorts of fruits of the countrey, as Cocos and others, which were brought us by the Moores, as also for oxen and hennes, is carefully to be sought for by such of our ships, as shall hereafter passe that way. But our men had need to take good heed of the Portugals: for while we lay here the Portugall Admiral of the coast from Melinde to Mozambique, came to view and to betray our boat if he could have taken at any time advantage, in a gallie Frigate of ten tunnes with 8 or 9 oares on a side. Of the strength of which Frigate and their treacherous meaning we were advertised by an Arabian Moore which came from the king of Zanzibar divers times unto us about the deliverie of the priest aforesayd, and afterward by another which we caried thence along with us: for wheresoever we came, our care was to get into our hands some one or two of the countreys to learne the languages and states of those partes where we touched. Moreover, here againe we had another clap of thunder which did shake our foremast very much, which wee fisht and repaired with timber from the shore, whereof there is good store there-about of a kind of trees some fortie foot high, which is a red and tough wood, and as I suppose, a kind of Cedar. Here our Surgeon Arnold negligently catching a great heate in his head being on land with the master to seeke oxen, fell sicke and shortly died, which might have bene cured by letting of blood before it had bin setled. Before our departure we had in this place some thousand weight of pitch, or rather a kind of gray and white gumme like unto frankincense, as clammie as tur-pentine, which in melting groweth as blacke as pitch, and is very brittle of it selfe, but we mingled it with oile, whereof wee

had 300 jarres in the prize which we tooke to the Northward
of the Equinoctiall, not farre from Guinie, bound for Brasil.
Sixe dayes before wee departed hence, the Cape marchant of
the Factorie wrote a letter unto our capitaine in the way of
friendship, as he pretended, requesting a jarre of wine, and a
jarre of oyle, and two or three pounds of gunpouder, which
letter hee sent by a Negro his man, and Moore in a Canoa:
we sent him his demaunds by the Moore, but tooke the Negro
along with us because we understood he had bene in the East
Indies and knew somewhat of the countrey. By this Negro we
were advertised of a small Barke of some thirtie tunnes (which
the Moores call a Junco) which was come from Goa thither
laden with Pepper for the Factorie and service of that kingdome.
Thus having trimmed our shippe as we lay in this road, in
the end we set forward for the coast of the East India, the 15
of February aforesayd, intending if we could to have reached
to Cape Comori, which is the headland or Promontorie of the
maine of Malavar, and there to have lien off and on for such
ships as should have passed from Zeilan, Sant Tome, Bengala,
Pegu, Malacca, the Moluccos, the coast of China, and the Ile
of Japan, which ships are of exceeding wealth and riches. But
in our course we were very much deceived by the currents that
set into the gulfe of the Red sea along the coast of Melinde.
And the windes shortening upon us to the Northeast and Easterly, kept us that we could not get off, and so with the putting
in of the currents from the Westward, set us in further unto the
Northward within fourescore leagues of the Ile of Zocotora,
farre from our determined course and expectation. But here we
never wanted abundance of Dolphins, Bonitos and flying fishes.
Now while we found our selves thus farre to the Northward,
and the time being so farre spent, we determined to goe for the
Red sea, or for the Iland of Zocotora, both to refresh our
selves, and also for some purchase. But while wee were in
this consultation, the winde very luckily came about to the
Northwest and caried us directly toward Cape Comori. Before
we should have doubled this Cape, we were determined to
touch at the Ilands of Mamale, of which we had advertisement, that one had victuals, standing in the Northerly latitude
of twelve degrees. Howbeit it was not our good lucke to finde
it, which fell out partly by the obstinacie of our master: for

the day before we fell with part of the Ilands the wind came
about to the Southwest, and then shifting our course we missed
it. So the wind increasing Southerly, we feared we should not
have bene able to have doubled the Cape, which would have
greatly hazarded our casting away upon the coast of India,
the Winter season and Westerne Monsons already being come
in, which Monsons continue on that coast until August. Nevertheles it pleased God to bring the wind more Westerly, & so
in the moneth of May 1592. we happily doubled Cape Comori
without sight of the coast of India. From hence thus having
doubled this Cape, we directed our course for the Ilands of
Nicubar, which lie North and South with the Westerne part of
Sumatra, and in the latitude of 7 degrees to the Northward of
the Equinoctiall. From which Cape of Comori unto the aforesayd Ilands we ranne in six dayes with a very large wind
though the weather were foule with extreme raine and gustes of
windes. These Ilands were missed through our masters default
for want of due observation of the South starre. And we fell
to the Southward of them within the sight of the Ilands of
Gomes Polo, which lie hard upon the great Iland of Sumatra
the first of June, and at the Northeast side of them we lay two
or three dayes becalmed, hoping to have had a Pilote from
Sumatra, within two leagues whereof wee lay off and on. Now
the Winter comming upon us with much contagious weather,
we directed our course from hence with the Ilands of Pulo
Pinaou, (where by the way is to be noted that Pulo in the
Malaian tongue signifieth an Iland) at which Ilands wee arrived about the beginning of June, where we came to an anker
in a very good harborough betweene three Ilands: at which
time our men were very sicke and many fallen. Here we determined to stay untill the Winter were overpast. This place
is in 6 degrees and a halfe to the Northward, and some five
leagues from the maine betweene Malacca and Pegu. Here we
continued untill the end of August. Our refreshing in this place
was very smal, onely of oisters growing on rocks, great wilks,
and some few fish which we tooke with our hookes. Here we
landed our sicke men on these uninhabited Ilands for their
health, neverthelesse 26 of them died in this place, whereof
John Hall our master was one, and M. Rainold Golding another, a marchant of great honestie and much discretion. In

these Islands are abundance of trees of white wood, so right and tall, that a man may make mastes of them being an hundred foote long. The winter passed and having watered our ship and fitted her to goe to Sea, wee had left us but 33 men and one boy, of which not past 22 were sound for labour and helpe, and of them not past a third part sailers: thence we made saile to seeke some place of refreshing, and went over to the maine of Malacca. The next day we came to an anker in a Baie in six fadomes water some two leagues from the shore. Then master James Lancaster our captaine, and M. Edmund Barker his lieutenant, and other of the companie manning the boat, went on shore to see what inhabitants might be found. And comming on land we found the tracking of some barefooted people which were departed thence not long before: for we sawe their fire still burning, but people we sawe none, nor any other living creature, save a certaine kind of foule called oxe birds, which are a gray kind of Sea-foule, like a Snite in colour, but not in beake. Of these we killed some eight dozen with haile-shot being very tame, and spending the day in search, returned toward night aboord. The next day about two of the clocke in the afternoone we espied a Canoa which came neere unto us, but would not come aboord us, having in it some sixteen naked Indians, with whom nevertheles going afterward on land, we had friendly conference and promise of victuals. The next day in the morning we espied three ships, being all of burthen 60 or 70 tunnes, one of which wee made to strike with our very boate: and understanding that they were of the towne of Martabam, which is the chiefe haven towne for the great citie of Pegu, and the goods belonging to certaine Portugal Jesuites and a Biscuit baker a Portugal, we tooke that ship & did not force the other two, because they were laden for marchants of Pegu, but having this one at our command, we came together to an anker. The night folowing all the men except twelve, which we tooke into our ship, being most of them borne in Pegu, fled away in their boate, leaving their ship and goods with us. The next day we weighed our anker and went to the Leeward of an Iland hard by, and tooke in her lading being pepper, which shee and the other two had laden at Pera, which is a place on the maine 30 leagues to the South. Besides the aforesaid three ships, we tooke another ship of Pegu laden with pepper, and perceiving her to bee laden with marchants goods of Pegu onely, we dismissed her without touching any thing.

Thus having staied here 10 daies and discharged her goods into the Edward, which was about the beginning of September, our sicke men being somewhat refreshed and lustie, with such reliefe as we had found in this ship, we weighed anker, determining to runne into the streights of Malacca to the Ilands called Pulo Sambilam, which are some five and fortie leagues Northward of the citie of Malacca, to which Ilands the Portugals must needs come from Goa or S. Thome, for the Malucos, China, and Japan. And when wee were there arrived, we lay too and agayne for such shipping as should come that way. Thus having spent some five dayes, upon a Sunday we espied a saile which was a Portugall ship that came from Negapatan a towne on the maine of India over-against the Northeast part of the Ile of Zeilan; and that night we tooke her being of 250 tunnes: she was laden with Rice for Malacca. Captaine Lancaster commanded their captaine and master aboord our shippe, and sent Edmund Barker his lieutenant and seven more to keepe this prize, who being aboord the same, came to an anker in thirtie fadomes water: for in that chanell three or foure leagues from the shore you shall finde good ankorage. Being thus at an anker and keeping out a light for the Edward, another Portugall ship of Sant Thome of foure hundred tunnes, came and ankered hard by us. The Edward being put to Leeward for lacke of helpe of men to handle her sailes, was not able the next morning to fetch her up, until we which were in the prize with our boate, went to helpe to man our shippe. Then comming aboord we went toward the shippe of Sant Thome, but our ship was so foule that shee escaped us. After we had taken out of our Portugall prize what we thought good, we turned her and all her men away except a Pilot and foure Moores. We continued here untill the sixt of October, at which time we met with the ship of the captaine of Malacca of seven hundred tunnes which came from Goa: we shot at her many shot, and at last shooting her maine-yard through, she came to an anker and yeelded. We commaunded her Captaine, Master, Pilot and Purser to come aboord us. But the Captaine accompanied with one souldier onely came, and after certaine conference with him, he made excuse to fetch the Master and Purser, which he sayd would not come unlesse he went for them: but being gotten from us in the edge of the evening, he with all the people which were to the number of about three hundred men, women and children, gote a shore with two great boates and quite abandoned the ship. At our comming aboord we found in her sixteene pieces of brasse, and three hundred buts of Canarie wine, and Nipar wine, which is made of the palme trees, and raisin wine which is also very strong: as also all kind of Haberdasher wares, as hats, red caps knit of Spanish wooll, worsted stockings knit, shooes, velvets, taffataes, chamlets, and silkes, abundance of suckets, rice, Venice glasses, certaine papers full of false and counterfeit stones which an Italian brought from Venice to deceive the rude Indians withall, abundance of playing cardes, two or three packs of French paper. Whatsoever became of the treasure which usually is brought in roials of plate in this gallion, we could not find it. After that the mariners had disordredly pilled this rich shippe, the Captaine because they would not follow his commandement to unlade those excellent wines into the Edward, abandoned her & let her drive at Sea, taking out of her the choisest things that she had. And doubting the forces of Malaca, we departed thence to a Baie in the kingdom of Junsalaom, which is betweene Malacca and Pegu eight degrees to the Northward, to seeke for pitch to trimme our ship. Here we sent our souldier, which the captaine of the aforesaid galion had left behind him with us, because he had the Malaian language, to deale with the people for pitch, which hee did faithfully, and procured us some two or three quintals with promise of more, and certaine of the people came unto us. We sent commodities to their king to barter for Amber-griese, and for the hornes of Abath, whereof the king onely hath the traffique in his hands. Now this Abath is a beast which hath one horne onely in her forehead, and is thought to be the female Unicorne, and is highly esteemed of all the Moores in those parts as a most soveraigne remedie against poyson. We had onely two or three of these hornes which are of the colour of a browne gray, and some reasonable quantitie of Amber-griese. At last the king went about to betray our Portugall with our marchandise: but he to get aboord us, told him that we had gilt armour,

shirtes of maile and halberds, which things they greatly desire:
for hope whereof he let him returne aboord, and so he escaped
the danger. Thus we left this coast and went backe againe in
sight of Sumatra, and thence to the Ilands of Nicubar, where
we arrived and found them inhabited with Moores, and after
wee came to an anker, the people daily came aboord us in their
Canoas, with hennes, Cocos, plantans and other fruits: and
within two dayes they brought unto us roials of plate, giving
us them for Calicut cloth: which roials they finde by diving
for them in the Sea, which were lost not long before in two
Portugall ships which were bound for China and were cast
away there. They call in their language the Coco Calambe, the
Plantane Pison, a Hen Jam, a Fish Iccan, a Hog Babee. From
thence we returned the 21 of November to goe for the Iland of
Zeilan, and arrived there about the third of December 1592.
and ankered upon the Southside in sixe fadomes water, where
we lost our anker, the place being rockie and foule ground.
Then we ranne along the Southwest part of the sayd Iland, to
a place called Punta del Galle, where we ankered, determining
there to have remained untill the comming of the Bengala Fleet
of seven or eight ships, and the Fleete of Pegu of two or three
sailes, and the Portugall shippes of Tanaseri being a great Baie
to the Southward of Martabam in the kingdom of Siam: which
ships, by divers intelligences which we had, were to come that
way within foureteene dayes to bring commodities to serve the
Caraks, which commonly depart from Cochin for Portugall by
the middest of Januarie. The commodities of the shippes which
come from Bengala bee fine pavillions for beds, wrought quilts,
fine Calicut cloth, Pintados and other fine workes, and Rice,
and they make this voiage twise in the yeere. Those of Pegu
bring the chiefest stones, as Rubies and Diamants, but their
chiefe fraight is Rice and certaine cloth. Those of Tanaseri are
chiefly fraighted with Rice and Nipar wine, which is very strong,
and in colour like unto rocke water somewhat whitish, and very
hote in taste like unto Aqua vitæ. Being shot up to the place
aforesayd, called Punta del Galle, wee came to an anker in
foule ground and lost the same, and lay all that night a drift,
because we had nowe but two ankers left us, which were un-
stocked and in hold. Whereupon our men tooke occasion to
come home, our Captaine at that time lying very sicke more

like to die then to live. In the morning wee set our foresaile
determining to lie up to the Northward and there to keepe our
selves to and againe out of the current, which otherwise would
have set us off to the Southward from all knowen land. Thus
having set our foresayle, and in hand to set all our other sayles
to accomplish our aforesayd determination, our men made
answere that they would take their direct course for England
and would stay there no longer. Nowe seeing they could not
bee perswaded by any meanes possible, the captaine was constrained to give his consent to returne, leaving all hope of so
great possibilities. Thus the eight of December 1592. wee set
sayle for the Cape of Buona Speransa, passing by the Ilands
of Maldiva, and leaving the mightie Iland of S. Laurence on
the starreboord or Northward in the latitude of 26 degrees to
the South. In our passage over from S. Laurence to the maine
we had exceeding great store of Bonitos and Albocores, which
are a greater kind of fish: of which our captain, being now
recovered of his sicknesse, tooke with an hooke as many in
two or three howers as would serve fortie persons a whole day.
And this skole of fish continued with our ship for the space of
five or sixe weekes, all which while we tooke to the quantitie
aforesayd, which was no small refreshing to us. In February
1593. we fell with the Eastermost land of Africa at a place
called Baia de Agoa some 100 leagues to the Northeast of the
Cape of Good Hope: and finding the winds contrary, we spent
a moneth or five weekes before we could double the Cape. After
wee had doubled it in March folowing, wee directed our course
for the Iland of Santa Helena, and arrived there the third day
of Aprill, where wee staied to our great comfort nineteene
dayes: in which meane space some one man of us tooke thirtie
goodly Congers in one day, and other rockie fishe and some
Bonitos. After our arrivall at Santa Helena, I Edmund Barker
went on shore with foure or five Peguins or men of Pegu which
we had taken, and our Surgion, where in an house by the Chappell I found an Englishman one John Segar of Burie in Suffolke,
who was left there eighteene moneths before by Abraham Kendall, who put in there with the Roiall marchant, and left him
there to refresh him on the Iland, being otherwise like to have
perished on shipboord: and at our comming wee found him
as fresh in colour and in as good plight of body to our seeming

as might be, but crazed in minde and halfe out of his wits, as afterward wee perceived: for whether he were put in fright of us, not knowing at first what we were, whether friends or foes, or of sudden joy when he understood we were his olde consorts and countreymen, hee became idle-headed, and for eight dayes space neither night nor day tooke any naturall rest, and so at length died for lacke of sleepe. Here two of our men, whereof the one was diseased with the skurvie, and the other had bene nine moneths sicke of the fluxe, in short time while they were on the Iland, recovered their perfect health. We found in this place great store of very holesome and excellent good greene figs, orenges, and lemons very faire, abundance of goates and hogs, and great plentie of partriges, Guiniecocks, and other wilde foules. Our mariners somewhat discontented being now watered and having some provision of fish, contrary to the will of the capitaine, would straight home. The capitaine because he was desirous to goe for Phernambuc in Brasil, granted their request. And about the 12 of Aprill 1593. we departed from S. Helena, and directed our course for the place aforesayd. The next day our capitaine calling upon the sailers to finish a foresaile which they had in hand, some of them answered that unlesse they might goe directly home, they would lay their hands to nothing; whereupon he was constrained to folow their humour. And from thence-foorth we directed our course for our countrey, which we kept untill we came 8 degrees to the Northward of the Equinoctiall, betweene which 8 degrees and the line, we spent some sixe weekes, with many calme and contrary winds at North, and somtimes to the Eastward, & somtimes to the Westward: which losse of time and expense of our victuals, whereof we had very smal store, made us doubt to keepe our course: and some of our men growing into a mutinie threatned to breake up other mens chests, to the overthrow of our victuals and all our selves, for every man had his share of his victuals before in his owne custody, that they might be sure what to trust to, and husband it more thriftily. Our capitaine seeking to prevent this mischiefe, being advertised by one of our companie which had bene at the Ile of Trinidada in M. Chidleis voyage, that there we should be sure to have refreshing, hereupon directed his course to that Iland, and not knowing the currents, we were put past it in the night into the gulfe of Paria in the beginning of June, wherein we were 8 dayes, finding the current continually setting in, and oftentimes we were in 3 fadomes water, and could find no going out until the current had put us over to the Westernside under the maine land, where we found no current at all, and more deep water; and so keeping by the shore, the wind off the shore every night did helpe us out to the Northward. Being cleare, within foure or five dayes after we fell with the Ile of Mona where we ankred and rode some eighteene dayes. In which time the Indians of Mona gave us some refreshing. And in the meane space there arrived a French ship of Cane in which was capitaine one Monsieur de Barbaterre, of whom wee bought some two buts of wine and bread, and other victuals. Then wee watered and fitted our shippe, and stopped a great leake which broke on us as we were beating out of the gulfe of Paria. And having thus made ready our ship to goe to Sea, we determined to goe directly for New-found-land. But before wee departed, there arose a storme the winde being Northerly, which put us from an anker and forced us to the Southward of Santo Domingo. This night we were in danger of shipwracke upon an Iland called Savona, which is environed with flats lying 4 or 5 miles off: yet it pleased God to cleare us of them, & so we directed our course Westward along the Iland of Santo Domingo, and doubled Cape Tiberon, and passed through the old chanell betweene S. Domingo and Cuba for the cape of Florida: And here we met againe with the French ship of Caen, whose Captaine could spare us no more victuals, as he said, but only hides which he had taken by traffike upon those Ilands, wherewith we were content and gave him for them to his good satisfaction. After this, passing the Cape of Florida, and cleere of the chanell of Bahama, we directed our course for the banke of Newfound-land. Thus running to the height of 36 degrees, and as farre to the East as the Isle of Bermuda the 17 of September finding the winds there very variable, contrarie to our expectation and all mens writings, we lay there a day or two the winde being northerly, and increasing continually more and more, it grewe to be a storme and a great frete of wind: which continued with us some 24 houres, with such extremitie, as it caried not onely our sayles away being furled, but also made much water in our

shippe, so that wee had sixe foote water in holde, and having
freed our ship thereof with baling, the winde shifted to the
Northwest and became dullerd: but presently upon it the extremitie of the storme was such that with the labouring of the
ship we lost our foremaste, and our ship grewe as full of water
as before. The storme once ceased, and the winde contrary to
goe our course, we fell to consultation which might be our
best way to save our lives. Our victuals now being utterly spent,
& having eaten hides 6 or 7 daies, we thought it best to beare
back againe for Dominica, & the Islands adjoyning, knowing
that there we might have some reliefe, whereupon we turned
backe for the said Islands. But before we could get thither the
winde scanted upon us, which did greatly endanger us for lacke
of fresh water and victuals: so that we were constrained to
beare up to the Westward to certaine other Ilandes called the
Nueblas or cloudie Ilands, towards the Ile of S. Juan de porto
Rico, where at our arrivall we found land-crabs and fresh water,
and tortoyses, which come most on lande about the full of the
moone. Here having refreshed our selves some 17 or 18 dayes,
and having gotten some small store of victuals into our ship,
we resolved to returne againe for Mona: upon which our determination five of our men left us, remaining still on the Iles of
Nueblas for all perswasions that we could use to the contrary,
which afterward came home in an English shippe. From these
Iles we departed and arrived at Mona about the twentieth of
November 1593, and there comming to an anker toward two or
three of the clocke in the morning, the Captaine, and Edmund
Barker his Lieuetenant with some few others went on land to
the houses of the olde Indian and his three sonnes, thinking to
have gotten some foode, our victuals being all spent, and we not
able to proceede any further untill we had obteyned some new
supply. We spent two or three daies in seeking provision to
cary aboord to relieve the whole companie. And comming
downe to go aboord, the winde then being northerly and the
sea somewhat growne, they could not come on shore with the
boate, which was a thing of small succour and not able to rowe
in any rough sea, whereupon we stayed untill the next morning, thinking to have had lesse winde and safer passage. But
in the night about twelve of the clocke our ship did drive away
with five men and a boy onely in it, our carpenter secretly cut

their owne cable, leaving nineteene of us on land without boate
or any thing, to our great discomfort. In the middest of these
miseries reposing our trust in the goodnesse of God, which
many times before had succoured us in our greatest extremities,
we contented our selves with our poore estate, and sought
meanes to preserve our lives. And because one place was not
able to sustaine us, we tooke our leaves one of another, dividing our selves into severall companies. The greatest reliefe that
we sixe which were with the Captaine could finde for the space
of nine and twentie dayes was the stalkes of purselaine boyled
in water, and nowe and then a pompion, which we found in the
garden of the olde Indian, who upon this our second arrivall
with his three sonnes stole from us, and kept himselfe continually aloft in the mountaines. After the ende of nine and twentie
dayes we espied a French shippe, which afterwarde we understood to be of Diepe, called the Luisa, whose Captaine was one
Mounsieur Felix, unto whom wee made a fire, at sight whereof
he tooke in his topsayles, bare in with the land, and shewed
us his flagge, whereby we judged him French: so comming
along to the Westerne ende of the Island there he ankered, we
making downe with all speede unto him. At this time the Indian
and his three sonnes came done to our Captaine Master James
Lancaster, and went along with him to the shippe. This night
he went aboord the French man, who gave him good entertainement, and the next day fetched eleven more of us aboord
entreating us all very courteously. This day came another
French shippe of the same towne of Diepe which remayned
there untill night expecting our other seven mens comming
downe: who, albeit we caused certaine pieces of ordinance to
be shot off to call them, yet came not downe. Whereupon we
departed thence, being devided sixe into one ship, and sixe into
another, and leaving this Island, departed for the Northside of
Saint Domingo, where we remained untill Aprill following 1594,
and spent some two monethes in traffike with the inhabitants by
permission for hides and other marchandises of the Countrey.
In this meane while there came a shippe of New-haven to the
place where we were, whereby we had intelligence of our seven
men which wee left behinde us at the Isle of Mona: which was,
that two of them brake their neckes with ventring to take foules
upon the cliffes, other three were slaine by the Spaniards, which

came from Saint Domingo, upon knowledge given by our men which went away in the Edward, the other two this man of New-haven had with him in his shippe, which escaped the Spaniards bloodie hands. From this place Captaine Lancaster and his Lieutenant Master Edmund Barker, shipped themselves in another shippe of Diepe, the Captaine whereof was one John La Noe, which was readie first to come away, and leaving the rest of their companie in other ships, where they were well intreated, to come after him, on sunday the seventh of Aprill 1594 they set homewarde, and disbocking through the Cajicos from thence arrived safely in Diepe within two and fortie dayes after, on the 19 of May, where after we had stayed two dayes to refresh our selves, and given humble thankes unto God, and unto our friendly neighbours, we tooke passage for Rie and landed there on Friday the 24 of May 1594, having spent in this voyage three yeeres, sixe weekes and two dayes, which the Portugales performe in halfe the time, chiefely because wee lost our fit time and season to set foorth in the beginning of our voyage.

We understood in the East Indies by certaine Portugales which we tooke, that they have lately discovered the coast of China to the latitude of nine and fiftie degrees, finding the sea still open to the Northward: giving great hope of the Northeast or Northwest passage. Witnesse Master James Lancaster.

48

The voyage truely discoursed, made by sir Francis Drake, and sir John Hawkins, chiefly pretended for some speciall service on the Islands and maine of the West Indies, with six of the Queenes ships, and 21 other shippes and barkes, containing 2500 men and boyes, in the yeere 1595. In which voyage both the foresayd knights died by sicknesse

W E E brake ground out of the sound of Plimmouth on Thursday the 28 of August, and that night ankored againe in Causon bay, where we rode till Friday. Then we set sayle and stoode Southwest: and about three of the clocke the next morning the Hope, wherein sir Thomas Baskervil went, strake upon the Edy stone, and shot off a piece, but after cleared herselfe wel enough.

On Munday at sixe of the clocke in the morning the landes end bare Northwest and by North, and then we stoode away Southwest and by South for the coast of Spaine.

The 8 of September we tooke two small Flemish fliboats bound for Barbary; which we caried a while with us and afterward dismissed them without doing them any harme: only wee learned newes of them, and stayed them from discrying our fleete to the enemie.

The 26 we saw Forteventura, being one of the Islands of the Canaries.

The 27 being Saturday by breake of day we had over-shot the chiefe towne of Grand Canaria to the Northeast, and then stood about for it againe, and by nine of the clocke were at anker fayre before the fort to the Eastward of the towne some league. At one of the clocke wee offred to land one thousand and foure hundreth men in the sandie bay betwixt the fort and the towne: But by our detracting of the time they had made a bulwarke in the sandie bay and planted Ordinance: so that by reason thereof, and the great breach of the sea that went then on shore we were not able to land without endangering our whole forces, which our General would not doe. There were of Spaniards horsemen and footmen some 900, which played upon us out of their trenches, most of them being shot. At the time of our landing there went by commandement of our Generals within musket shot of the shore, & rode there at ankor some three hours, the Salomon, the Bonaventure, the Elizabeth Constance, the Phenix, the Juell, the Little John, the Delight, the Pegasus, the Exchange, the Francis, the caravell, and the two catches: But when the Generall sir Francis Drake gave over the landing being in his barge, the ships weighed being in some danger, and stoode off againe to the great ships. Then we went to the West end of the Island and there watered: where captaine Grimston going up the hill with 6 or 7 in his company was set upon by the herdmen, who with their dogs and staves killed the captaine and three or foure of his company: the rest were sore wounded: the Salomons Chirurgian taken prisoner, who disclosed our pretended voyage as much as in him lay: so as the Viceroy sent a caravel of adviso into the Indies, unto all such places as wee did pretend to goe to. Howbeit they had intelligence from the king of all our voyage the eight of August, which was three weekes before we set foorth of England: as also by a Fleming that had seene all our provision at London.

The 28 being Sunday at ten of the clocke at night wee set saile, and stood away Southwest and Southsouthwest some 200 leagues, untill we came in the height of the Islands of Cape Verde, and then more Westerly for Martinino, one of the Islands of the West Indies, which we saw the 27 of October: but the night before we had a storme, in which sir Francis with foure or five other ships bearing on head of the fleete was separated. Then we stood for Dominica, an Island full of inhabitants of the race of the Canibals, not past ten leagues distant from Martinino. In it groweth great store of Tabacco: where most of our English and French men barter knives, hatchets, sawes, and such like yron tooles in trucke of Tabacco.

Before we came to Dominica our Generall Sir Francis Drake altered his course, and went for Marigalante, which we had sight of the 28 day, and came to an anker on the Northeast

side a saker shot off the shore in 13 fathomes water faire sholding. There the Generall went on shore in his barge, and by
chance met a Canoa of Dominicans, to the people whereof he
gave a yellow wastcoate of flanell and an hankerchiefe; and
they gave him such fruits as they had, and the Dominicanes
rowed to Dominica againe. They came thither to fetch some
fruits which they sowe and plant in divers places of that Island,
which they keepe like gardens.

The next morning by breake of day we weyed and stoode
betweene the Todos Santos, which are 4 or 5 little Islands betweene Guadalupe and Dominica. There is nothing upon these
Islands but wood. We came to the Southeast side of Guadalupe
and there ankered hard aboord the shore: the Southwest side
of the Island is deepe water and good ankorage: where that
day sir John Hawkins came to us againe standing up from
the South side of Dominica. There we watered, washed our
ships, set up our pinnesses, and refreshed our souldiers on
shore.

The 30 captaine Wignol in the Francis, a barke of 35 tunnes,
being the sternmost of sir John Hawkins fleete was chased by
five of the king of Spaines frigats or Zabras being ships of 200
tunnes a piece, which came of purpose with 3. other Zabras
for the treasure of S. Juan de Puerto rico: The Francis going
roome with them, supposing they had bene our owne fleete,
was by them taken in sight of our caravel. They left the
Francis driving in the sea with 3 or 4 hurt and sicke men, and
tooke the rest of our men into their ships, as the prisoners which
wee tooke at S. Juan de Puerto rico told us.

The 4 of November we began to unlade the Richard, one of
our victuallers, which was by the next day unladen, unrigged
and then sunken. Then we stood Northwest & by North: and
the next morning saw the Ilands of Monserrata, Redonda,
Estazia, S. Christopher and Saba. The biggest of these Islands
is not past 8 leagues long. There is good ankorage in 8, 7, and
5 fadomes water faire white sand. Then we stood away Southwest, and on the 8 in the morning being Saturday came to an
anker some 7 or 8 leagues off within certain broken Ilands
called Las Virgines, which have bene accounted dangerous:
but we found there a very good rode, had it bene for a 1000
sails of ships in 14, 12, and 8 fadomes faire sand and good

ankorage, high Islands on either side, but no fresh water that
we could find: here is much fish to be taken with hookes and
nets: also we stayed on shore and fowled. Here sir John
Hawkins was extreme sicke; which his sicknes began upon
newes of the taking of the Francis. The 18 day wee weyed and
stoode North and by East into a lesser sound, which sir Francis
in his barge discovered the night before, and ankored in 13
fadoms, having hie steepe hils on either side, some league distant from our first riding.

The 12 in the morning we weied and set sayle into the sea
due South through a small streit but without danger, and then
stode West and by North for S. Juan de Puerto rico, and in
the after noone left the 3 small Islands called The passages to
the Southward of us, and that night came up to the Eastermost
end of S. John, where sir John Hawkins departed this life: upon
whose decease sir Thomas Baskervil presently went into the
Garland. At 2 of the clocke we came to anker at the eastermost
side of the chiefe towne called Puerto rico in a sandie bay 2
miles off: where we received from their forts and places where
they planted Ordinance some 28 great shot, the last of which
strake the admirall through the misen, and the last but one
strake through her quarter into the sterage, the Generall being
there at supper, and strake the stoole from under him, but hurt
him not, but hurt at the same table sir Nicholas Clifford, M.
Browne, captaine Stratford, with one or two more. Sir Nicholas
Clifford and master Browne died of their hurts.

Then wee set sayle and stood to the Eastward, and at midnight tacked about to the West, and in the morning came to an
anker before the point without the towne, a little to the Westwards by the 3 Islands.

The 13 we rode still untill night, when in the beginning with
twenty five pinnesses, boats and shallops manned and furnished
with fire-workes and small shot wee went into the rode within
the great castels, and in despite of them fired the five Zabras
of frigats, all ships of two hundreth tunnes the piece or more,
quite burning the Rearadmirall downe to the water, which was
the greatest shippe of them all, and also mightily spoiled the
admirall and viceadmirall, notwithstanding the castles and ships
gave us a hundreth eighty and five great shot, besides small
shot abundance. They had also sunke a great shippe in the

mouth of the chanell and rafted it over with her mastes almost to the very fortes and castles, so as they thought it impregnable. The frigats had in each of them twenty pieces of brasse, and a hundreth barrels of powder. Their chiefe lading that they brought thither was silke, oyle, and wine. The treasure which they went to fetch, which was brought thither in a ship called the Vigonia, was conveyed into the strongest and surest castell of defence; being, as one of the prisoners confessed, three millions of ducats or five and thirty tunnes of silver. Also they had sent all the women, children, and unable persons into the woods, and left none but souldiers and fighting men in the towne. The fight on our side was resolute, hote, and dangerous: wherein wee lost some forty or fifty men, and so many were hurt. There was also great death of the Spaniards aboord the frigats, with burning, drowning, and killing, and besides some taken prisoners.

The 14 we rode stil, being within shot of the uttermost castell: but they fearing the next night we would come in againe, began to warpe up the other 4 frigats, beginning first with the Admirall: which whether by chance or their owne willes wee saw to sinke; and as wee suppose so did they with all the rest, or else by stealth got up farther within their chiefest forces.

The 15 also we rode still, and at afternoone wee espied a caravell comming from the castell point: but before our pinnesses could fetch her up, she ranne on shore, where our boates could not come at her because of the breach, and also many of the Islanders came downe to guard her with shot. The beginning of this night we weyed, and stoode one houre to the East, and then tacked about to the West.

The 16 being Sunday, and the 17 also we were becalmed.

The 18 we ankered a little to the Southward of the Southwest point of the Island, giving the point a birth because of a shoald of sand that lieth some two cables length off: there we rode in foure, five, and sixe fadomes faire white sand, where wee set up more pinnesses, washed our ships, and refreshed our men on shore. Here the Generall tooke a pinnesse of Hispaniola with divers letters, signifying that two Englishmen of warre had done great hurt along their Island.

The 20 the Generall rowed to the Phenix, the Delight and

the caravell, and caused them to wey and anker right against the mouth of a fresh river in two fadomes water in ozie sand to the Southward of the other ships some league or more. The Generall went into this river three of foure leagues up, and tooke horses in the countrey. Sir Thomas Baskervil rowed up the river, and stayed there all night, and went up into the land three or foure leagues.

The 23 wee discharged a barke called the Pulpit and burnt her: and at three of the clocke that afternoone, when we were ready to set saile, there came aboord the Defiance our Admiral, a Spaniard with his wife, who feared some great torment for not having repaired to the towne according to the Generals commandement of that Island, who had commanded that all able men of the fleete should repaire to the towne to defend it against us. Then we stood againe West and by North because of a ledge of rocks that lie sunke 4 or 5 leagues off the Southside of the Island.

The 25 we stood away southwest, and saw Mona being a lowe flat Island between Hispaniola and S. Juan de Puerto rico. That day the Exchange of captaine Winter spent her boultsprite; and in the beginning of the night the Phenix was sent backe to seeke her: which by Gods help that night met with her, and kept her company until the next morning, then taking in a small cable from her for a towe: but by 9 that morning she spent her maine mast and split her foreyard, breaking also her tow: so as they were faine to save some trifles out of her and the men, and to sinke the hull. Then we stood away South and South and by West after the fleete: and the 26 in the morning had sight of the fleete againe.

The 29 we had sight of the Island called Curazao within eight leagues of the maine, and on the Northwest side came to an anker in very deepe water hard aboord the shore without any danger: but the Generall weyed presently and stoode away Northwest and by West, and Northnorthwest for the maine, and that night saw Aruba, being somewhat a lesse Island then the other: we left it some three leagues to the Southward of us.

On Sunday morning being the last of November wee saw three or foure little Islands called the Monjes, betwixt Aruba and the next North point of the maine. At 12 of the clocke we sawe the maine, where we saw a great current setting to the

Westward, and also the water changing very white. The Phenix, the caravell, and one of the catches kept within, and at midnight came under Cape de la Vela, and made a fire, whereby the rest of the fleete came to anker under the Cape, where is a very good rode, faire sholding and sandie ground, fourteene, twelve, and tenne fadoms neere the shore. The Cape is a bare land without trees or shrubs, and falleth in eight or ten leagues Southeast and Northwest: and a saker shot off the point standeth a little Island like Mewestone neere Plimmouth, but somewhat bigger. In the morning the first of December wee imbarked all our souldiers for Rio de la Hacha, which is a towne twenty leagues to the Westwards, one of the ancientest in all the maine, although not very bigge: but it standeth in a most fertile and pleasant soyle. Our men tooke it by ten of the clocke in the night. The ships bearing all that night and the day before in 5 and 6 fadomes, the lesser ships in two fadomes and an halfe water: the Phenix went so neere the shore by the Generals commandement, that shee strake on ground, but got off againe. There lieth to the Eastward of the towne a mile or thereabout a shold of sand: therefore give a birth some halfe league or more before you come right against the towne. There wee came to anker in two fadomes, but the great ships rode off in five and six fadomes. There is a fresh river about a bow-shot to the Eastward of the towne; whereinto our pinnesses could scarse enter by reason of a barre of sand in the rivers mouth, but within it is navigable for barkes of twenty or thirty tunnes some sixe or eight leagues up.

The sixth day the Spaniards came in to talke about the ransome of the towne, but not to the Generall his liking: and that night Sir Thomas Baskervil marched up into the countrey to over-runne those parts: and the Generall the same night with some hundreth and fiftie men went by water six leagues to the Eastward, and tooke the Rancheria a fisher towne, where they drag for pearle. The people all fled except some sixteene or twenty souldiers, which fought a little, but some were taken prisoners, besides many Negros, with some store of pearles and other pillage. In the houses we refreshed our selves, and were all imbarked to come away, and then had sight of a brigandine or a dredger, which the Generall tooke within one houres chase with his two barges: she had in her Indie-wheat, which we call Maiz, and some silver and pearle, but of small value.

On Saturday the seventh, master Yorke captaine of the Hope dyed of sicknes, and then master Thomas Drake the Generals brother was made captaine of the Hope, and master Jonas Bodenham captaine of the Adventure, and master Charles Cæsar captaine of the Amitie.

The tenth day the Spaniards concluded for the ransome of the towne for 24000 ducats, and one prisoner promised to pay for his ransome 4000 ducats.

The fourteenth day they brought in the townes ransome in pearles, but rated so deare as the Generall after conference with them, misliking it, sent it backe againe, giving them foure houres respite to cleere themselves with their treasure.

The sixteenth the governour came into the towne about dinner, and upon conference with the Generall told him plainely, that he cared not for the towne, neither would he ransome it: and that the pearle was brought in without his command or consent, and that his detracting of time so long was onely to send the other townes word, that were not of force to withstand us, whereby they might convey all their goods, cattell, and wealth into the woods out of danger. So the General gave the governour leave to depart according to promise, having two houres to withdraw himselfe in safety.

The seventeenth Sir Thomas Baskervil with the Elizabeth Constance, the Phenix, the caravel with foure or five pinnesses went some five leagues to the Westward, & landing, marched some foure leagues up into the countrey to a place called Tapia, which he tooke & burned certain villages and ferme houses about it. He had some resistance as he passed over a river, but had but one man hurt, which he brought aboord alive with him: he marched one league farther and burnt a village called Sallamca, and so returned with some prisoners, the souldiers having gotten some pillage.

The 18 the Rancheria, and the towne of Rio de la Hacha were burnt cleane downe to the ground, the Churches and a Ladies house onely excepted, which by her letters written to the Generall was preserved. That day wee set sayle and fell to lee-ward, to meete with Sir Thomas Baskervil.

The 19 we weighed and stood to leeward for Cape de Aguja, which the twentieth at sunne rising we saw. It is a Cape subject much to flawes, by reason it is a very hie land: and within the cape lieth an Island within the mouth of the sound, which hath a white cliffe or spot in the Westnorthwest part of the Island. The land all about the cape riseth all in homocks or broken steepie hils. A league Southwest within that, (for so falleth the land thereabout) there standeth on the top of a cliffe a watch-house: and a little within that a small Island: you may goe in betweene the maine and it, or to leeward if you lust: and hard within that is the rode and towne of Santa Martha, which at 11 of the clocke we tooke, the people all being fled, except a few Spaniards, Negros & Indians, which in a bravado at our land-ing gave us some 30 or 40 shot, & so ran away.

That night their Lieutenant generall was taken and some little pillage brought in out of the woods: for in the town noth-ing was left but the houses swept clean. In all the main is not a richer place for gold: for the hops were mixt with the earth in every place, and also in the sand a little to the leewards of the towne. In the bay wee had a bad rode by reason of a small moone, for every small moone maketh foule weather all the maine along.

The 21, the Generall caused the towne to be burnt, and all the ships to wey, and stood out, many of the souldiers being imbarked where the Generall had appointed, in the small ships which rode neerest the shore. We lost that night the company of the Phenix, captaine Austin, Peter Lemond, and the Gar-lands pinnesse, which stood along the shore, and being chased off by gallies out of Carthagena Peter Lemond with nine of our men was taken, the rest came safe to our fleete.

The 26 we saw the Ilands some twelve leagues to the East-ward of Nombre de Dios standing in toward the shore, but toward night we stood to the offin untill the next day.

The 27 we came into the mouth of Nombre de Dios, and by one of the clocke tooke the towne, the people being all fled except some 100 Spaniards, which kept the Fort, and played upon us, having in the fort some 3 or 4 small pieces of ordi-nance, and one of them brake in discharging at us. They gave us also a voley of small shot: but seeing our resolution in runn-ing upon them they all fled and tooke the woods.

The towne was bigge, having large streetes, houses very hie, all built of timber, but one Church very faire and large wrought all of timber likewise. Nothing was left in the towne of value: there was a shew in their shops of great store of marchandises that had bene there. There was a mill above the towne, and upon the toppe of another hill in the woods stood a little watch-house, where we tooke twentie sowes of silver, two barres of gold, some money in coyne, besides other pillage.

The towne was situated in a waterie soile, and subject much to raine, very unhealthy as any place in the Indies, having great store of Orenges, plantans, cassavy-roots, & such other fruits; but very dangerous to be eaten for breeding of diseases. To the Eastwarde of the towne within the bay runneth out a fresh river of excellent good water, with houses, and all about it gardens: halfe a league from hence due East into the countrey was an Indian towne, whither as we marched a little before our comming away with an hundred men they had broken downe a bridge to hinder our passage, where they lay in ambush with some twentie or thirtie small shot, and bowes and arrowes, set upon us, and killed Lieutenant Jones, hurt three or foure and so fled into the woods, ranne before us and fired their owne towne, and then fled farther into the woods: our men fired diverse other houses in pursuing them, and so returned againe: our Generall with Sir Thomas being in the Rivers mouth with thirtie or fortie men filling water about some myle from us.

The road of Nombre de Dios is a faire road: but on each side, as you come to ride before the towne, lyeth a ledge of rockes, but there is no danger because they are in sight. You may ride betweene them in three or foure fadome water, and without if you will in eight or ten fadomes, where neither Castle nor Fort can annoy you. The name of Nombre de Dios was greater then their strength. For they had no Castle nor Fort, but onely the little fort aforesaid standing on the top of an hill, although they might have made it stronger if they would.

The 29 sir Thomas Baskervil with 750 armed men, besides Chirurgians and provand boyes, went for Panama.

The last of December the Generall burned halfe the towne, and the first of Januarie burnt the rest, with all the Frigats, Barks & Galiots, which were in the harbour and on the beach on shore, having houses built over them to keepe the pitch from melting.

The second of January sir Thomas returned with his souldiers both weary and hungry, having marched more then halfe the way to the South sea. The Spaniards played divers times upon us both outward and homeward in the woods, the way being cut out of the woods & rockes both very narrow, and full of myre and water. The march was so sore as never Englishman marched before. Having marched some ten leagues in a marvellous straite way, upon the top of an hill, through which we must needes passe, the Spaniards had set up a Fort and kept it with some 80 or 90 men, who played upon us as we came up, before wee were aware of them, and so killed some twentie or more of us, amongst whom was Captaine Marchant quarter-master Generall, and Ensigne Sampson, Maurice Williams one of her Majesties guard, besides diverse were hurt, as M. Captaine Nicholas Baskervil a valiant gentleman, with divers others. Then sir Thomas had perfect knowledge that they must passe two such Forts more, if he got that, besides Panama to be very strong, the enemie knowing of our comming long before.

Also our souldiers had no victuals left, nor any meanes to get more: which considerations caused sir Thomas to returne and give over his attempt. As he marched thitherward he tooke an Indian and sent him to Nombre de Dios with letters of his returne and proceeding.

The 5 we set saile at 12 of the clocke, and stood to the Westward.

The 10 day we saw an Iland lying Westward some 30 leagues called Escudo, where wee came to anker on the Southside in 12 fadoms water, faire sand and good ankorage. If you come into the Easterne point, give it a birth, because of a ledge of rockes, that lyeth out there from the end of the Island: comming to anker we sawe a roader, who seeing us, set sayle, but that night with our Pinnesses we tooke him, he had nothing in him but a little maiz. The men being examined by the Generall confessed him to be an Advisor sent from Nombre de Dios to all the ports along the coast Westward. This Iland lyeth 9 or 10 leagues from the maine, & is not past two leagues long full of wood, and hath great store of fresh water in every part of the Iland, and that very good. It is a sickly climat also, and given to much raine: here we washed our ships, and set up the rest of our Pinnesses.

The 15 day Captaine Plat died of sicknesse, and then sir Francis Drake began to keepe his cabin, and to complaine of a scowring or fluxe.

The 23 we set saile and stood up again for Puerto Bello, which is but 3 leagues to the Westwards of Nombre de Dios.

The 28 at 4 of the clocke in the morning our Generall sir Francis Drake departed this life, having bene extremely sicke of a fluxe, which began the night before to stop on him. He used some speeches at or a little before his death, rising and apparelling himselfe, but being brought to bed againe within one houre died. He made his brother Thomas Drake and cap-taine Jonas Bodenham executors, and M. Thomas Drakes sonne his heire to all his lands, except one manor which he gave to captaine Bodenham.

The same day we ankored at Puerto Bello, being the best harbour we found al along the maine both for great ships and small. There standeth a saker shot off the shore at the Easterne point a little Iland: and there is betwixt the maine & that 5 or 6 fadomes: but the best comming in is the open mouth betwixt that Iland & another Iland that lyeth to the westward with a range of rocks.

In Puerto Bello were but 8 or 10 houses, besides a great new house which they were in building for the Governour that should have bene for that place: there was also a very strong Fort all to the waters side with flankers of great trees and stones filled with earth betweene: and had not our comming disap-pointed their pretence, they would have made it one of the strongest places in all the maine. There they ment to have builded a great towne. We found there three pieces of brasse ordinance sunke in the sea, which we weighed up, all the peo-ple were fled and their goods carried away.

Up within this bay there was a little village but of no force, where we found a great fresh river, our men rowing up some two leagues found pillage, as wine and oyle, and some small quantitie of yron. After our comming hither to anker, and the solemne buriall of our Generall sir Francis in the sea: Sir

Thomas Baskervill being aboord the Defiance, where M. Bride made a sermon, having to his audience all the captaines in the fleete, sir Thomas commanded all aboord the Garland, with whom he held a Councell, & there shewing his Commission was accepted for General, & captain Bodenham made captaine of the Defiance, & M. Savill captaine of ye Adventure.

The 27 died captaine Josias of the Delight, and captaine Egerton a Gentleman of the Foresight, and James Wood chiefe chirurgion of the fleete out of the Garland.

The 28 died Abraham Kendall out of the Saker. At this place we watered againe, washed our ships & made new sailes, it being by the Generall and all the captaines agreed, that if we could by any meanes turne up againe for Santa Martha, we should, if not, to goe directly for England. Here also we tooke in some balast as our neede required.

The 6 of Februarie the Elizabeth of M. Wattes was discharged and sunke, and that day the Pegasus jolly was going on shore for water, carying no guarde: The Spaniards perceiving it came downe upon them, killed two of them, and tooke 2 or 3 prisoners, and so ranne up into the woods againe.

The seventh the Delight and captaine Edens frigat were discharged and sunke because they were old and leaked, and the Queenes ships wanted saylers.

That day our men being mustered we had sicke and whole 2000. And the next day we set on shore all our prisoners as Spaniards and Negros. But before at our first comming to Puerto Bello sir Thomas sent two of those Spaniards to Nombre de Dios and to Panama to fetch ransome for some of the chiefest prisoners, but they never returned againe. As we were setting saile there came one with a flagge of truce, and told the General that they had taken 18 of our men, and that they were well used, adding that if he would stay 8 or 10 dayes longer they should be brought from Panama. We supposed this to have bene but a delay to have kept us there while the kings forces had come about by sea, as they dayly expected. We set saile the 8 of Februarie, turning up for Santa Martha, and the 14 day we saw the Ilands of Baru some 14 leagues to the Westward of Carthagena: The Generall that night told us he would stand in for the towne of Baru in the bay: but that night blew so much winde and continued that small moone, that the same night we lost the Foresight, and the next day standing againe to make the land which we had made, we lost companie of the Susan Parnel, The Helpe, and the Pegasus. Then the next day we put over for Cape S. Antonie, and gave over Santa Martha.

The 25 we saw the Iland of Grand Cayman some 30 leagues to the Northwestward of Jamaica, being a low sandie Iland, having many tortoyses about it.

The 26 we saw the hie land of Cuba to the Eastward of the broken Ilands, to the East of the Iland of Pinos, and were imbayed in among those dangerous places. But perceiving it, we stood out againe Southsoutheast and so got cleere, and then stood away West and by North for the Ile of Pinos, which we saw the first of March. It is a low land with wood and fresh water to the Western end. If you come in with the middest of it you shall see rise up above the rest of the land 8 or 9 round homockes, and the Westermost hath three in one.

Being shot foorth with the West end, and standing in for to water we espied 20 sayle of ships about one in the afternoone. This was a third part of the fleete which the king sent for Carthagena, the rest of the fleete being gone for the Honduras. They were in all 60 sailes sent onely to meete our fleete, being commanded wheresoever they heard we were, to come upon us with all their three forces. This fleete which we met withall came standing for Cape de los Corrientes, and had bene refreshed at Havana.

As soone as they discried us, they kept close upon a tacke, thinking to get the winde of us: but we weathered them. And when our Admirall with all the rest of our fleet were right in the winds eye of them, sir Thomas Baskervil putting out the Queenes armes, and all the rest of our fleete their braverie, bare roome with them, and commanded the Defiance not to shoot, but to keepe close by to second him. The Viceadmirall of the Spaniards being a greater ship than any of ours, and the best sayler in all their fleete loofed by and gave the Concord the two first great shot, which she repayed presently againe, thus the fight began. The Bonaventure bare full with her, ringing her such a peale of ordinance and small shot withall, that he left her with torne sides. The Admirall also made no spare of powder and shot. But the Defiance in the middest of the

Spanish fleete thundering of her ordinance and small shot continued the fight to the end. So that the Viceadmirall with 3 or 4 of her consorts were forced to tacke about to the Eastward, leaving their admirall and the rest of the fleete, who came not so hotly into the fight as they did. The fight continued two houres & better. At sunne set all the fleete tacked about to the Eastward, we continued our course to the Westward for cape de los Corrientes, supposing we should have met with more of their consorts. In this conflict in the Defiance we had five men slaine, three English men, a Greeke and a Negro. That night some halfe houre after, their fleete keeping upon their weather quarter, we saw a mightie smoke rise out of one of their great ships which stayed behind: which happened by meanes of powder as we thinke, and presently after she was all on a light fire, and so was consumed and all burnt, as we might well perceive.

The next day being the second of March in the morning by breake of day we were hard aboord Cape de los Corrientes, which is a bare low cape, having a bush of trees higher than the rest some mile to the Eastward of the cape. All Cuba is full of wood on the Southside. The Spanish fleete which then were but 14 no more than we were, kept still upon our weather quarter, but dared not to come roome with us although our Admirall stayed for them. Assoone as we had cleered our selves of the Cape 3 of their best saylers came roome with the Salomon, which was so neere the land that she could not double the Cape, but tacked about to the Eastward, & so was both a sterne and also to leeward of all our fleete: But when we saw the Spaniards working, the Defiance tacked about to rescue her: which the Spaniards seeing, and having not forgotten the fight which she made the night before, they loofed up into the middest of their fleete againe, and then all the fleete stayed untill the Salomon came up, and so stood along for Cape S. Antonio, which wee came in sight of by two in the after noone, being a low cape also, and to the Southwest a white sandie bay, where 3 or 4 ships may very well water. There is a good road for North & Easterly windes: there the Spaniardes began to fall a sterne. That night wee stood away a glasse or two Northwest, and Northnorthwest, and Northeast, and in the morning-watch South, and in the morning had sight of Cuba about the

East part of the Organes, which are dangerous rocks lying 8 leagues off upon the North part of Cuba, presently assoone as you passe Cape S. Anthonie: then we stood to the Eastward of the land, the winde at Southsouthwest, and at 6 at night had foule weather, but after were becalmed all night. The 5 the winde came scant. The 7 we sawe a hie land like a crowne, which appeareth so 13 or 14 leagues to the Westward of Havana, and another place in Cuba called The Table, 8 leagues to the Eastward of the crowne. The land over Havana maketh two small mountaines like a womans breasts or paps. Here we found no great current untill we came to the Gulfe of Bahama.

The 10 we saw the Cape of Florida being but a reasonable low land and broken Ilands to the Southward of the Cape. And at two in the afternoone we lost sight of the land 12 leagues to the Northward of the Cape. After we had disemboqued, we stood West till midnight, and were in 28 degrees, and then stood Northeast till the 13 at night, when we were in 31 degrees. And after the wind scanted with a great storme, in which we lost the Bonaventure, and the Little John, they bearing on head. Then we stood with our larbord tacked Eastsoutheast.

The 19 we were in 29 degrees our course Eastnortheast. The 21 we had a great stormie gale of winde and much raine but large. And then all the rest of our fleete fell a sterne except the Hope, which bare a head: so that there kept no more with the Admirall, but the Defiance, the Adventure, and the Phenix.

The 28 we were in 39 degrees, and stood away for Flores, which the 8 of Aprill we saw, and the 9 came to an anker on the Southside, where we watered because the Defiance when we came in had but two buts of water. We bartered with the Portugals for some fresh victuals, and set here on shore at our comming away out of the Admirall our two Portugall Pilots; which sir Francis Drake caried out of England with him.

The 10 being Easter-eve at night we set saile the winde serving us to lie some slent in our course. That night and Easter day we had much raine: the winde came up at Northeast, wee beate it up some 30 leagues to the Eastward, & then about to the West, and so againe to the East, and tryed, and the next boord to the West. On Thursday towards night, being the 16 wee had sight of Corvo againe, we tryed all that night: and on Friday towards night we came to an anker to the Westward of the point of Santa Cruz under Flores: but before midnight we drave, and set saile the next day standing away Northeast. About three of the clocke in the afternoone the winde came up againe at North. On sunday the 19 by two of the clocke in the afternoone we had made 20 leagues an East way: and then the winde came up a good gale at Northwest, and so Northeast with a flowne sheete we made the best way we could: but being dispersed by bad weather we arrived about the beginning of May in the West parts of England. And the last ships which came in together to Plimmouth were the Defiance, the Garland, the Adventure, and the Phenix.

49

A briefe and true report of the Honorable voyage
unto Cadiz, 1596. of the overthrow of the kings
Fleet, and of the winning, sacking, and burning
of the Citie, with all other accidents of
moment, thereunto appertaining

AFTER that the two most Noble and Renowmed Lords Gen-
erals: The L. Robert Earle of Essex, and the L. Charles Howard L. High Admirall of England, were come unto Plymmouth
(which was about the beginning of May last, 1596.) being there
accompanied with divers other noble Peeres, as the Earle of
Sussex, the L. Thomas Howard, the L. Harbert, the L. Warden
Sir Walter Raleigh: the L. Marshall Sir Francis Vere: the L.
Burk, Don Christopher young Prince of Portingall, young Count
Lodovick of Nassaw, and the Admirall of the Hollanders, Sir
John Vanderfoord: besides many other most worthy Knights
and Gentlemen of great woorth attending upon this most honorable Action: It pleased them, there to make their abode
for the time of that moneth, as well for the new furnishing
and revictualing of her Majesties Royall Navie: as also for the
expecting of some other ships, which were to come from divers
places of the Realme, and were as yet wanting: making that
place as it should seeme the Rendevous for all the whole Fleete,
thereto complete the full number of al such companies both for
sea and land: as was in their noble and deepe wisedomes
thought meete and agreed upon.

All the time of this their abode there, there was a most
zealous and diligent care had for the holy service of God, dayly
and reverently to be frequented: and also for other good and
civill orders of militarie discipline to be observed, to the ex-

ceeding great comfort and rejoycing of all the hearts of the godly and well disposed.

And for that it might the better appeare, that there was small hope of pardon to be expected of the offenders, if they did at any time neglect their duties, about due observation of matters of importance: Their orders, lawes, and decrees being once published: about the 8. or 9. of the same moneth, there were two offenders executed a little without the towne, in a very fayre pleasant greene, called the Ho: the one for beginning of a muteny in his company, the other for running away from his Colours.

And about the same time in the Dutch Regiment, an other for murthering of one of his companions, about a quarrell betweene themselves, rising as it was supposed, upon their drinke, was by order of Martiall law, presently tyed to the partie so murthered, and foorthwith both of them so cast into the sea.

Moreover, about the 28. of the same moneth, a certaine Lieutenant (whose name I will forbeare) was by sound of Drumme publikely in all the streetes disgraced, or rather after a sort disgraded, and cashierd for bearing any farther Office at that time, for the taking of money by way of corruption, of certaine prest souldiers in the Countrey, and for placing of others in their roomes, more unfit for service, and of lesse sufficiency and abilitie. This severe executing of justice at the very first did breed such a deepe terror in the hearts of the whole armie, that it seemed to cut off all occasion of the like disorder for ever afterwards to be attempted.

And here before their departure from Plymmouth, it pleased their Lordships to publish in print, and make knowen to all the world, especially to such as whom it concerned, and that both in the Latine, French, Dutch, English and Spanish tongue, what were the true, just, and urgent causes, that at this time provoked her Majestie, to undertake the preparing and setting forth of this so great a Navie, annexing thereunto a full declaration, what was their good will and pleasure should be done and performed of all them that ment not to incurre their owne private present daungers, or else were willing to avoyde her Majesties future indignation and displeasure.

Likewise now, at the same instant, their owne most provident and godly decrees, which they had devised for the honest cariage of every particular person in their degrees and vocation, were made knowen to all men, and published in sundry writings, with divers great punishments, set downe and appointed for the wilfull offenders and breakers of the same.

Thus then, all things being in very good order and well appointed, the most holy name of our Omnipotent God being most religiously and devoutly called upon, and his blessed and sacred Communion being divers times most reverently and publikely celebrated: These two most noble personages, with all their honorable Associats, and most famous worthy Knights, Gentlemen, Captaines, Leaders, and very willing and expert Souldiers, and Mariners, being furnished with 150. good sayle of shippes or thereabout: In the name of the most High & everliving God, and with all true and faithful obedience, to her sacred Majesty, to the infinite good and tranquillitie of our Countrey, and to the perpetuall glory, and triumphant renowme of the eternall memory of their honorable names to all posterity, the first day of June embarked themselves, weighed Ancre, and hoysed up sayle, and put to sea onward their journey from the Sownds of Plymmouth.

The winde, at the first setting foorth, seemed very favourable: but yet in the evening growing very scant, and all that night falling more and more against us, and we having sayled no further then to a certain place called Dodman head: we were constrained the next day, to make our returne to the road of Plymmouth againe, and there in the Sownds to lie at ancre for that night.

About this time, and in this very place, by good fortune there came to my handes a prayer in English, touching this present Action, and made by her Majestie, as it was voyced: The prayer seemed to me to be most excellent, aswell for the matter, as also for the manner, and therefore for certaine divers good motives which then presently came to my minde, and whereof hereafter in his more convenient time and place, I will make farther mention, I presumed at that very instant to translate it into Latine.

The Prayer is thus

Most Omnipotent maker and guide of all our worlds masse, that onely searchest and fadomest the bottome of all our hearts

conceits, and in them seest the true originals of all our actions
intended: thou that by thy foresight doest truely discerne, how
no malice of revenge, nor quittance of injury, nor desire of
bloodshed, nor greedinesse of lucre hath bred the resolution of
our now set out Army, but a heedful care, & wary watch, that
no neglect of foes, nor over-suretie of harme might breed either
daunger to us, or glory to them: these being the grounds wherewith thou doest enspire the mind, we humbly beseech thee with
bended knees, prosper the worke, and with best forewindes
guide the journey, speed the victory, and make the returne
the advancement of thy glory, the tryumph of their fame, and
surety to the Realme, with the least losse of the English blood.
To these devout petitions Lord thou thy blessed grant.

My homely translation is thus

Summè præpotens Deus, immensæ hujus totius nostri mundi
molis fabricator & Rector, qui solus perscrutaris intimos cordis
nostri sensus, & ad fundum usque nostrarum cogitationum ex-
plorando penetras, ac in eis, quid verè, & ex animo cogitemus,
& quæ sint actionum nostrarum rationes, ac fundamenta, cog-
noscis: Tu, qui ea, quæ in te est, ab omni æternitate præscientia,
vides, quòd nec aliqua ulciscendi malitiosa cupiditas, nec in-
juriarum referendarum, desiderium, nec sanguinis effundendi
sitis, nec alicujus lucri, quæstusve aviditus ad istam classem
præparandam, & emittendam nos commoverit: sed potiùs, quòd
provida quædam cura, solersque vigilantia huc nos impulerit:
ne vel inimicorum nostrorum neglectus, vel status nostri firmita-
tis nimium secura cogitatio, aut illis gloriam & honorem, aut
nobis damnum & periculum pariat: Cum, inquam, hæc sint
nostri, quicquid attentatur, negotii fundamenta: cumque tu hunc
nobis animum, mentemque injeceris, ut istud aggrederemur:
curvatis genibus a te humillimè petimus, ut velis hoc nostrum
incœptum secundissimè fortunare, totum iter prosperrimis flati-
bus dirigere, celerem & expeditam victoriam nobis concedere,
reditumque talem nostris militibus elargiri, qualis & nomini tuo
incrementum gloriæ, & illis famæ, laudisque triumphum, &
Regno nostro firmam tranquillitatem possit apportare: idque
cum minimo Anglorum sanguinis dispendio. His nostris re-

ligiosis petitionibus concede, Domine, sacrosanctam & annuentem voluntatem tuam.

After that we had anchored at Plymmouth that night, as I have said, the third of June very early in the morning, having a reasonable fresh gale of winde, we set sayle, and kept our course againe, and the ninth of the same moneth comming something neere to the North cape, in a maner in the same altitude, or not much differing, which was about xliii. degrees, and something more, yet bearing so, as it was impossible to bee descried from the land: There it pleased the Lords to call a select Councell, which was alwayes done by hanging out of a flagge of the armes of England, and shooting off of a great warning peece. Of this select or privie Councell, were no moe then these: The two Lords Generall, the Lord Thomas Howard, the Lorde Warden Sir Walter Raleigh, the Lord Martiall Sir Francis Vere, Sir George Cary master of the Ordinance, Sir Coniers Clifford, and Sir Anthony Ashley, Clarke of the sayde Counsell. And when it pleased the Lords Generall to call a common Counsell (as often times they did upon weightie matters best knowen to their honours) then they would cause an other kinde of flagge to be hanged out, which was the Redcrosse of S. George, and was very easie to be discerned from the other that appertained onely to the select Counsell, and so often as this flagge of Saint George was hanged out, then came all the Masters and Captaines of all the ships, whose opinions were to be demaunded, in such matters as appertayned unto this sayd select Counsell: It was presently concluded, that our course in sayling should foorthwith be altered, and that we should beare more into the West, for some purposes to them best knowen.

At that very instant many letters of instructions were addressed and sent to every particular Master and Captaine of the Ships: What the contentes of those letters of instructions were it was not as yet knowne unto any, neither was it held meet to be enquired or knowen of any of us. But under the titles and superscriptions of every mans particuler letter these words were endorsed. Open not these letters on pain of your lives, unles we chance to be scattered by tempest, and in that case open them, and execute the contents thereof: but if by mishap you fall into your enemies hand, then in any case cast them into the sea, sealed as they are. It should seeme that these letters did conteine in them the principall place and meaning of this entended action, which was hitherto by their deepe foresights kept so secret, as no man to my knowledge either did, or coulde so much as suspect it, more then themselves, who had the onely managing thereof. A conceite in my judgement of greatest moment in the world, to effect any matter of importance. I meane, to entertaine those two vertues, Fidem, & Taciturnitatem: so much commended by the old writers. And if there was ever any great designement, in this our age, and memorie, discreetly, faithfully, and closely caried, I assure my selfe it was this, and though it were but in respect of that poynt onely: yet for such faithfull secrecie, it deserveth immortall praise.

All this while, our ships, God be thanked, kept in a most excellent good order, being devided into five squadrons: that is to say, The Earle of Essex, the Lord Admirall, the Lord Thomas Howard, the Lord Warden Sir Walter Raleigh, and the Admirall of the Hollanders. All which squadrons, albeit they did every day separate themselves of purpose, by the distance of certaine leagues, as well to looke out for such shippes as were happily under sayle, as also for the better procuring of searoome: yet alwayes commonly eyther that day, or the next day, towarde evening, they came all together, with friendly salutations and gratulations one to an other: which they terme by the name of Hayling: a ceremonie done solemnly, and in verie good order, with sound of Trumpets and noyse of cheerefull voyces: and in such sort performed as was no small encouragement one to the other, beside a true report of all such accidents, as had happened in their squadrons.

Hitherto, as I sayde, our journey was most prosperous, and all our shippes in very good plight, more then that the Mary Rose, by some mischance, either sprang or spent her foreyarde, and two dayes after Sir Robert Crosse had in a manner the like mischance.

Nowe being thus betweene the North cape, and cape S. Vincent, and yet keeping such a course a loofe, that by no meanes, those from the shoare might be able to descrie us: The tenth of June, a French Barke, and a Fleming comming from the coast of Barbarie were brought in by some of our companie: but they were both of them very honourably and well used by the Lords Generall: and so after a fewe dayes tarrying, were peaceably sent away, after that they had conferred with them about such matters, as was thought good in their honorable wisedomes.

The twelfth of the same moneth, Sir Richard Levison Knight, assisted with Sir Christopher Blunt, fought with three Hamburgers, and in that fight slewe two of them, and hurt eleven, and in the ende brought them all three in: and this was the very first hansell and maydenhead (as it were) of any matter of importance, or exployt woorthy observation that was done in the way outward of this honorable voyage, and was so well perfourmed of those most worthy Gentlemen, as every man highly commended them for their great valure, and discretion, and no lesse rejoyced at this their fortunate successe.

The next day after, Sir Richard Weston meeting with a Flemming, who refused to vale his foretoppe, with the like good courage and resolution, attempted to bring him in. The fight continued very hot betweene them, for a good space: in the end the Swan, wherein the sayd Sir Richard was, had her forebeake strooken off: and having spent before in fight the one side of her tire of Ordinance, while she prepared to cast about, and to bestow on him the other side, in the meane time the Fleming taking this opportunity, did get almost halfe a league from him: and so for that time made his escape. And yet the next day after, the sayd Flemming being in a maner got to the very mouth of the River up to Lisbone, was taken, and brought in by M. Dorrell, being Captaine of the John and Francis of London. Thus by deviding their squadrons, and spreading the whole sea over a mighty way, there could not so much as the least pinke passe but she was espied and brought in.

The 13. 14. and 15. dayes, certaine little stragling Caravels were taken by certaine of the Fleete, and in one of them a young beggarly Fryer utterly unlearned, with a great packet of letters for Lisbon: the poore wretches were marvellously well used by the Lords Generall, and that Caravel, and the like still as they were taken were commaunded to give their attendance, and their Honors did understand what they might of these poore men, of the estate of Spaine for that present.

About this time and in this place it was, that first in all my life time I did see the flying fishes, who when they are hardly pinched and chased by the Bonitoes and other great fishes, then to avoyde the daunger, they presently mount up, and forsake the water, and betake themselves to the benefite of their winges and make their flight, which commonly is not above five or sixe score, or there about, and then they are constrayned to fall downe into the water againe, and it is the Mariners opinion that they can fly no longer then their wings be wet. The fish it selfe is about the bignesse of a Mackrell or a great white Hearing, and much of that colour and making, with two large wings shaped of nature very cunningly, and with great delight to behold, in all the world much like to our Gentlewomens dutch Fans, that are made either of paper, or parchment, or silke, or other stuffe, which will with certaine pleights easily runne and fold themselves together. One of these flying fishes was presented to my L. Admirall by a fisher man, and newly taken in his L. returne from Cadiz, and then I had good leasure and opportunitie to view it.

The 18. day early in the morning wee tooke an Irish man, and he came directly from Cadiz, having beene there but the day before at twelve of the clocke at high noone. This man being examined, told truely that there was now great store of shipping at Cadiz, and with them xviii. or xix. gallies in a readinesse, and that among those ships there were divers of the kings best: and namely, that the Philip of Spaine was amongst them, but what their intent was, hee could not tell. This man was commanded also to give his attendance.

The 20. of June being Sunday, we came before Cadiz very early in the morning, and in all this time as yet, the whole Navy had not lost either by sicknesse or by any other maner of wayes sixe men to my knowledge: as for the Dutch company, I am not able precisely to say what happened there, for that they were no part of our charge to be looked unto, but were a regiment entire of themselves, and by themselves to be provided for, either for their diet, or for the preservation of their healths by phisicke.

Thus then I say, being all in good plight and strong, the 20. of June wee came to Cadiz, and there very earely in the morning presented our selves before the Towne, ryding about a league or something lesse, from it. The sea at that instant went marvelous high, and the winde was exceeding large. Notwithstanding, a Councell being called, our Lords Generall foorthwith attempted with all expedition to land some certaine companies of their men at the West side of the Towne, by certaine long boats, light horsemen, pynnesses, and barges made for the purpose, but could not compasse it, and in the attempting thereof, they chanced to sinke one of their Barges, with some foure score good souldiers well appointed in her, and yet by good hap and great care, the men were all saved excepting viii. And therefore they were constrayned to put off their landing till an other more convenient time.

That morning very timely, there lighted a very faire dove upon the maine yard of the L. Admirals ship, and there she sate very quietly for the space of 3. or 4. houres, being nothing dismayed all that while, every man gazed and looked much upon her, and spake their minds and opinions, yet all concluding by no meanes to disquiet her: I for my part, tooke it for a very good omen and boading, as in trueth (God be thanked) there fell out nothing in the end to the contrary. And as at our very first comming to Cadiz this chanced, so likewise on the very last day of our departing from the same towne, another Dove presented her selfe in the selfe same order into the same ship, and presently grew wonderfull tame and familiar to us all, and did so still keepe us company, even till our arrivall here in England.

We no sooner presented our selves, but presently a goodly sort of tall Spanish ships came out of the mouth of the Bay of Cadiz, the Gallies accompanying them in such good order, and so placed as all of them might well succour each other, and therewithall kept themselves very close to their towne, the castle, and the forts, for their better guard and defence, abiding there still, and expecting our farther determination. All that day passed, being very rough and boysterous, and litle or nothing could be done, more then that about the evening there passed some friendly and kinde salutations sent one from the other in warlike maner, by discharging certain great peeces, but to my knowledge no hurt done at all, or else very litle.

A carefull and diligent watch was had all that night thorough out the whole armie, and on monday morning being the 21. day, the winde and weather being become moderate and favourable, betweene five and sixe of the clocke in the morning, our ships in the name of almightie God, and in defence of the honour of England, without any farther delay, with all speed, courage, and alacritie, did set upon the Spanish ships, being then under sayle, and making out of the mouth of the Bay of Cadiz, up toward Puente de Suaço on Granada side, being in number lix. tall ships, with xix. or xx. Gallies attending upon them, sorted in such good order, and reasonable distance as they might still annoy us, and alwayes relieve themselves interchangeably: having likewise the Castle, Forts, and Towne, continually to assist them and theirs, and alwayes readie to play upon us and ours.

In most mens opinions it seemed that the enemy had a wonderful advantage of us, all circumstances being well weighed, but especially the straightnesse of the place, and the naturall forme and situation of the Bay it selfe, being rightly considered. For albeit the very Bay it selfe is very large and exceeding beautifull, so that from Cadiz to Port S. Mary, is some vi. or vii. English miles over or there abouts, yet be there many rockes, shelves, sands and shallowes in it, so that the very chanell & place for sea roome, is not above 2. or 3. miles, yea and in some places, not so much, for the ships of any great burthen, to make way in, but that they must either be set on ground or else constrained to run fowle one on another. All this notwithstanding, with great and invincible courage, the Lords generall presently set upon them, and sorting out some such convenient ships, as to their honorable wisedomes seemed fittest for that times service, they were driven to take some other course then before had beene by them entended. Wherefore upon a grave consultation had by a select Counsell, what great dangers might ensue upon so mightie a disadvantage as appeared in all probability, if it were not by good and sound judgement prevented, & therwithall in their singular wisedomes foreseeing that some great stratageme might be practised by the enemy, either by fire-worke, or some other subtill politike devise, for the hazarding of her Majesties ships of honor in so narrow a place, thus with al expedition they concluded that the Vice-admirall, the L. Thomas Howard, that most noble L. Howard (whose exceeding great magnanimity, courage, &

wisedome, joyned with such an honorable kind of sweet courtesie, bountie, and liberalitie, as is not able by me & my
weakenes to be expressed, hath wonne him all the faithfull loving hearts of as many as ever have had any maner of dealing
with him) This L. Thomas, I say, in ye Non Pareille for that
time, & the Reare Admirall Sir Walter Raleigh (a man of marvelous great worth & regard, for many his exceeding singular
great vertues, right fortitude & great resolutenes in all matters
of importance) in the Warspight associated with divers most
famous worthy knights, namely, Sir Francis Vere the L. Martiall
in the Rainbow, Sir George Cary M. of the Ordinance, in the
Mary rose, Sir Robert Southwell in the Lyon, gentlemen for all
laudable good vertues, and for perfect courage & discretion in
all military actions, of as great praise & good desert as any
gentlemen of their degree whosoever, having with them some of
ye ships of London, and some of the Dutch squadron of reasonable burthen, should leade the dance, & give the onset, and
that the two most noble Lords generall with some others of
their companies, should in their convenient time & order, second
the maine battell. The fight being begunne and growen very
hot, the L. Generall the Earle of Essex, (whose infinite princely
vertues, with triumphant fame, deserve to be immortalized)
being on Port S. Mary side, upon a sudden & unlooked for
of others, thrust himselfe among the formost into the maine
battell. The other most honorable L. Generall (whose singular
vertues in all respects are of such an excellencie & perfection,
as neither can my praise in any part increase them, nor any
mans envy any whit blemish or diminish them) understanding,
the most noble Earle to be in fight among them, & perceiving
by the M. of his ship, the Arke royall, that for lacke of water,
it was not possible, that he might put any neerer, without
farther delay, called presently for his Pynnesse, and in the same
Pynnesse put himselfe, and his honorable son L. William Howard that now is, aboord the Honor de la mer, & there remained
in the fight till the battell was ended. The fight was very terrible, and most hideous to the beholder by the continuall discharging of those roaring thundering great peeces, on all sides,
and so continued doubtful till about one or two of the clocke
in the afternoone: about which time the Philip, whom in very
truth, they had all most fancie unto, began to yeeld and give

over, her men that remained alive shifting for themselves as they were able, and swimming and running a shoare with all the hast that they could possibly, & therewithall, at the very same instant themselves fired their ship, and so left her, & presently thereupon a great Argosie, with an other mighty great ship, fired themselves in ye like maner. Immediatly hereupon, the residue of the ships, ran themselves on ground, as farre from us as they could, and thereby purchased their owne safety, or rather breathing space for the time. Of them all two faire ships only were boorded and taken by our men with most part of their furniture in them, the one called S. Matthy, a ship by estimation of some xii. hundred tunne, and the other S. Andrew, being a ship of not much lesser burthen. The Gallies, seeing this suddaine great victorious overthrow, made all the hast they could toward the Bridge called Puente de Suaço, and there shrowded themselves in such sort as our shippes could not by any meanes possible come nigh them for lacke of water.

The Spanish ships in all were lix. & as is sayd, all tall ships & very richly furnished and well appointed, whereof some of them were bound for the Indies, and other fraighted and furnished for Lisbon, as themselves affirme: and had we not come that very time that we did, (which for my part, I do not attribute so much unto meere chance, as to some secret deepe insight and foreknowledge of the two most worthy Lords generall, who no doubt spared for no cost or labour for true intelligence) we had certainely mist of them all.

Of what great wealth and riches these ships were, that I leave to other mens judgement and report, but sure I am, that themselves offered two millions and a halfe of ducats for the redemption of the goods and riches that were in them: which offer of theirs, albeit it was accepted of the Lords Generall, and should have beene received, yet we were defeated of it, as hereafter shall be more at large declared.

What maner of fight this was, & with what courage performed, and with what terror to the beholders continued, where so many thundring tearing peeces were for so long a time discharged, I leave it to the Reader to thinke & imagine. Yet such was the great mercy & goodnes of our living God, that in all this cruell terrible fight, in the end, there were not either slaine or hurt by any maner of meanes (excepting one mischance that happened, whereof I will by & by make mention) many above the number of 100. of our men: notwithstanding divers of our shippes were many times shot thorow and thorow: yea and some of them no lesse then two and twentie times, as I was enformed by credible report of the Captaines and Masters themselves. I knowe not of any other hurt done, saving onely that Sir Robert Southwell, who alwayes shewed himselfe a most valiant resolute knight in all this action, making a litle too much haste with his Pinnesse to boord the Philip, had there his said Pinnesse burnt with the Philip at the same instant, and yet by good care and diligence his men were saved.

One other mischance (as I said) there happened, and it was thus: One of the Flemings flieboats, who had, in all the conflict before, caried himselfe very well and valiantly, about ten of the clocke while the fight continued sharpest, chanced by great negligence and misfortune, to be fired and blowen up by his owne powder, who could not have any fewer in him, then one hundred fighting men by all supposall, and so in the very twinckling of an eye, both shippe and men were all cast away, excepting vii. or viii. which by very good fortune, and great care and diligence of some of the other ships were saved.

Immediatly upon this notable victory without any farther stay in all the world, the Lord generall the Earle of Essex put to shore, and landed about 3000. shot, & pikemen: of the which number the one halfe was presently dispatched to the bridge Puente de Suaço, under the conduct of three most famous worthy knights, Sir Christopher Blunt, Sir Coniers Clifford, & Sir Thomas Gerard: with the other halfe, being about fifteene hundred, the most noble Earle of Essex himselfe, being accompanied with divers other honorable Lords, namely the Earle of Sussex, the Lord Harbert, the Lord Burk, Count Lodovick of Nassaw, the Lord Martiall Sir Francis Vere, with many other worthy Knights, and men of great regard, who all in that dayes service did most valiantly behave themselves, with all expedition possible marched on foote toward the towne of Cadiz, which was about three English miles march. That time of the day was very hot and faint and the way was all of dry deepe slyding sand in a manner, and beside that, very uneven, and by

that meanes so tiresome and painefull as might be. The enemie
having reasonable companie both of horse and footemen, stoode
in a readinesse some good distance without the towne to welcome us, and to encounter the Lorde Generall. But the most
famous Earle with his valiant Troopes, rather running in deede
in good order, then marching, hastened on them with such
unspeakeable courage and celeritie, as within one houres space
and lesse, the horsemen were all discomfited and put to flight,
their leader being strooken downe at the very first encounter,
whereat the footemen being wonderfully dismayed and aston-
ished at the unexspected manner of the Englishmens kinde of
such fierce and resolute fight, retyred themselves with all the
speede possible that they could, to recover themselves into the
Towne againe, which being done by them, with farre swifter
legges then manly courage, our men were enforced to skale the
walles: which thing in very deede, although it was not without
great danger and difficulty to be perfourmed: Yet such was
the invincible resolution, and the wonderfull dexterity of the
English, that in one halfe houre or thereabout, the enemie
was repulsed, and the towne wall possessed, by the noble Earle
himselfe, being in all this action, either the very first man or els
in a maner joined with the first.

The towne walles being then possessed, and the English
Ensigne being there displayed upon them, with all speede possible they proceeded on to march through the towne, making
still their waie with sworde and shot so well as they could,
being still fought withall at every turne.

Immediately upon this most famous entrie, the noble Earle,
(according to their resolutions, as I take it, put downe before)
was seconded by the noble L. Admirall in person, who was accompanied, with the noble L. Thomas Howard, the most worthy gentleman his sonne, now L. Howard, Sir Robert Southwell,
Sir Richard Levison, and with divers other gentlemen, his L.
followers of good account: his colours being advanced by that
valiant resolute gentleman, (a man beautified with many excellent rare gifts, of good learning and understanding) S. Edward
Hobby Knight. And thus he likewise marching with al possible
speede on foote, notwithstanding his L. many yeres, the intolerable heate for the time, and the overtiring tedious deepe

sands, with other many impediments: Yet in good time, joyned himselfe with the Earle and his companies, and gave them the strongest, and best assistance that he could.

Thus then the two Lords Generall with their companies being joyned together, and proceeding so farre as the market place, there they were hotly encountered, where and at what time, that worthy famous knight Sir John Winkfield, being sore wounded before on the thigh, at the very entry of the towne, and yet for all that no whit respecting himselfe, being caried away with the care he had to encourage and direct his company, was with the shot of a musket in the head most unfortunately slaine.

And thus before eight of the clocke that night were these two most noble Lords General, Masters of the market place, the forts, and the whole Towne and all, onely the Castle as yet holding out, & from time to time as they could, still annoying them with seven battering pieces. By this time night began to grow on, and a kind of peace or intermission was obtained by them of the Castle: to whome the Lords Generall had signified: that unlesse before the next day in the morning they would absolutely render themselves, they should looke for no mercy, but should every one be put to the sword: upon which message they tooke deliberation that night: but in the morning before breake of day they hanged out their flag of truce, and so without any further composition did yeeld themselves absolutely to their mercy, and delivered up the Castle.

And yet notwithstanding all this, in the night time while they had this respite to pause, and deliberate about the peace-making, there were divers great and suddaine alarms given: which did breed some great outrages and disorder in the towne. At every which alarme, the two Lordes Generall shewed themselves marvelous ready & forward, insomuch that at the very first alarme, skant wel furnished with any more defence then their shirts, hose, and dublets, & those too altogether in a maner untied, they were abroad in the streetes themselves, to see the uttermost of it. But for that it is not as yet very well knowen (or at the least not well knowen unto me) either wherfore, or by whom these alarmes were attempted: I am therefore to intreat, that a bare report, that such a thing was done, may suffice.

These things being done, and this surrender being made, present proclamation was published, that the fury now being past, all men should surcease from all maner of blood and cruell dealing, and that there should no kind of violence or hard usage be offered to any, either man, woman or child, upon paine of death: And so permitting the spoyle of so much of the towne as was by them thought meete, to the common souldiers for some certaine dayes, they were continually in counsell about other grave directions, best knowen to their honorable wisdomes.

This honorable and mercifull Edict I am sure was streightly and religiously observed of the English: But how well it was kept by the Dutch, I will nether affirme, nor yet denie. For I perceive betweene them and the Spaniards there is an implacable hartburning, and therefore as soone as the Dutch squadron was espied in the fight, immediatly thereupon both they of Sivil and S. Lucar and also some of some other places did not onely arrest all such Dutch ships, as delt with them friendly by the way of traffick & Merchandise, and so confiscated their goods, but also imprisoned the Marchants and Owners of the same, and, as the report goeth, did intreat many of them with extreme cruelty thereupon.

In the meane while the very next day being the two and twenty day of June, all the Spanish shippes which were left on ground in the Bay of Cadiz, where the great overthrowe had beene but the day before, were by the Spaniards themselves there set on fire, and so from that time forward they never left burning of them, till every one of them, goods and all, as farre as wee know were burnt and consumed. This their doing was much marvelled at of us, and so much the more, for that, as I sayd before, there had bene made some offer for the redemption and saving of the goods, and it was not to them unknowen that this their offer was not misliked, but in all probabilitie should have bene accepted. The common opinion was, that this was done either by the appointment of the Duke de Medina Sidonia, or els by expresse commandement from the higher powers.

Not long after the same time (three dayes as I remember) the gallies that were runne on ground, did quitte themselves also out of that place, and by the bridge of the Iland called Puente de Suaço made their way round about the same Iland,

and so by putting themselves to the maine sea, escaped to a towne called Rotta, not farre off, but something up towards the Towne of Saint Lucars, and there purchased their safety by that meanes.

Thus was this notable victorie, as well by sea as by land, both begunne and in effect perfourmed, within the compasse, in a maner, of fourteene houres: A thing in trueth so strange and admirable, as in my judgement will rather bee wondered at then beleeved of posteritie. And if ever any notable exploit in any age was comparable to Cæsars Veni, Vidi, Vici, certainely in my poore opinion it was this.

Here it is to be wished (and perchance of some too it is looked for) that every mans particular worthy acte in this dayes service, with the parties names also, should be put downe, that thereby both they and their good deserts might be registred to all posteritie: and for my part I would it were so, and wish I were able to doe it. But for that I confesse it is a matter that passeth my power, yea, and for that I thinke it also a thing impossible to be precisely perfourmed by any other, I am to crave pardon for that I rather leave it out altogether, then presume to doe it maymedly: and in this point I referre the Reader onely to the Mappe that is set foorth of this journey, where it is in some parte conveniently touched and specified.

The Towne of it selfe was a very beautifull towne, and a large, as being the chiefe See of the Bishop there, and having a goodly Cathedrall Church in it, with a right goodly Abbey, a Nunnery, and an exceeding fine College of the Jesuites, and was by naturall situation, as also by very good fortification, very strong, and tenable enough in all mens opinions of the better judgement. Their building was all of a kind of hard stone, even from the very foundation to the top, and every house was in a manner a kind of a fort or Castle, altogether flat-roofed in the toppe, after the Turkish manner, so that many men together, and that at ease, might walke thereon: having upon the house top, great heapes of weighty stoanes piled up in such good order, as they were ready to be throwen downe by every woman most easily upon such as passed by, and the streetes for the most part so exceeding narrow, (I thinke to avoide the intolerable great heat of the Sunne) as but two men or three at the most together, can in any reasonable sorte march thorough them, no streete being broader commonly then I suppose Watling streete in London to be.

The towne is altogether without glasse, excepting the Churches, yet with faire comely windowes, and with faire grates of iron to them, and have very large folding leaves of wainscot or the like. It hath very fewe Chimnies in it, or almost none at all: it may be some one chimney in some one or other of the lower out roomes of lest account, serving for some necessary uses, either to wash in, or the like, or els nowe and then perchance for the dressing of a dish of meate, having, as it should seeme unto me, alwayes a greater care and respect how to keepe themselves from all kind of great heat, then how to provide for any store of great roste. It had in it by report of them that should best know it, some foure thousand and moe, of very good able fighting men, and sixe hundred horsemen at the least. No question but that they were well furnished of all things appertaining thereunto, especially so many good ships lying there, and being so well stored with all manner of munition, shot, and powder, as they were.

Whether they had knowledge of our comming or no, I can say nothing to it: Themselves give it out that they understood not of it, but onely by a Caravel the Friday at evening before we came. But whether they knew it or no, thus much I dare boldly affirme, that if the English had bene possessed of that or the like Towne, and had bene but halfe so well provided as they were, they would have defended it for one two moneths at the least, against any power whatsoever in al Christendome. But surely GOD is a mighty GOD, and hath a wonderfull secret stroke in all matters, especially of weight and moment. Whether their hearts were killed at the mighty overthrow by sea, or whether they were amased at the invincible courage of the English, which was more then ordinary, caring no more for either small shot or great, then in a maner for so many hailestones, or whether the remorse of a guilty conscience toward the English nation, for their dishonorable and divelish practises, against her Sacred Majestie, and the Realme, (a matter that easily begetteth a faint heart in a guilty minde) or what other thing there was in it I know not, but be it spoken to their perpetuall

shame and infamie, there was never thing more resolutely perfourmed of the couragious English, nor more shamefully lost
of the bragging Spaniard.

Of what wealth this towne should be, I am not able to resolve the asker: for I confesse that for mine owne part, I had
not so much good lucke, as to be partaker so much as of one
pennie, or penny worth. Howbeit my ill fortune maketh that
towne never a whit the poorer. But as it should appeare by the
great pillage by the common souldiers, and some mariners too,
and by the goodly furnitures, that were defaced by the baser
people, and thereby utterly lost and spoyled, as not woorth the
carying away, and by the over great plenty of Wine, Oyle,
Almonds, Olives, Raisins, Spices, and other rich grocery wares,
that by the intemperate disorder of some of the rasher sort
were knockt out, and lay trampled under feete, in every common high way, it should appeare that it was of some very
mighty great wealth to the first owners, though perchance, not
of any such great commoditie to the last subduers, for that I
judge that the better part was most ryotously and intemperately
spent and consumed. A disorder in mine opinion very much
to be lamented, and if it might be by any good meanes remedied, in my conceit, it were a most honourable device.

The Wednesday, Thursday, and Friday following, the Lords
Generall spent in counsell, about the disposing of all matters,
aswell touching the towne and prisoners, as also concerning
all other matters, thought meete of them in their honourable
wisedomes, and in all that meane while did shew such honourable bounty and mercy, as is not able to be expressed. For
not onely the lives of every one were spared, but also there
was an especial care had, that al the Religious, as wel men as
women, should be well and favourably intreated, whom freely
without any maner of ransome or other molestation, they caused
to be safely transported over to Port Saint Marie, a towne in a
manner as fayre as Cadiz: but at that time, as the case did
stand, certainely knowen to be of no wealth in the world, and
it was some six or seven miles distant over against Cadiz, in
a maner as Paules is against Southwarke, on the other side of
the Bay, in a part of Andaluzia, subject to the territory of the
Duke de Medina Sidonia.

Moreover, at the same instant they did appoint that worthy

knight Sir Amias Preston, and some others in some convenient Barkes, to transport over to the sayd Towne safely and in good order, a hundred or moe of the better sort of ancient gentlewomen, and marchants wives, who were suffered to put upon themselves, some of them two, yea, some three sutes of apparell, with some convenient quantitie of many Jewels, Chaines, and other ornaments belonging to their estate and degree. Such was the heroicall liberality, and exceeding great clemencie, of those most honourable Lords Generall, thereby, as it should seeme unto mee, beating downe that false surmised opinion, which hath bene hitherto commonly spread abroad, and setled among the Spaniards: which is, That the English doe trouble them and their countries, more for their golde, riches and pearle &c. then for any other just occasion. Whereas by these their honourable dealings it is manifest to all the world, that it is onely in respect of a just revenge for the manifolde injuries, and most dishonourable practises that have beene from time to time attempted by them against us and our nation, and also in the defence of the true honour of England: which they have sought, and daylie doe seeke, by so many sinister and reprochfull devices, so much as in them lieth, to deface.

Upon Saturday being the 26. Sir John Winkfield knight was buried, in honourable and warlike manner, so farre foorth as the circumstances of that time and place could permit. At whose funerals the Navie discharged a great part of their Ordinance, in such order, as was thought meete and convenient by the Lords Generals commandement. . . .

I spake in ye beginning of her Majesties praier, which I presumed (though unworthy) to translate into Latine: and nowe at this very time, there was some opportunity offered, for to make some use of that translation. For nowe being in Cadiz, attending upon my most honourable good Lord, I talked with certaine of the Religious men, such as I found learned, whereof indeed there were some, though not very many. I talked also with the Bishop of Cusco there, a grave aged comely man, and being of late chosen to that Bishopricke, he was as then to have gone to the Indies, had not we then taken him prisoner, and so stayed his journey for that time. With these men ever as occasion did serve, I did seeke nowe and then to spende some speech, and to entertaine time withall, I would breake with them of this our victorie, and of the injuries and bad dealings of their Prince and Countrey offered to her Majestie, whereby she was provoked, and in a manner drawen to this action: though otherwise of her own most excellent princely good nature, she was altogether given to peace, and quietnes. And alwayes in some part of our conferences, I would shew them a copie of her Majesties praier in Latine, which I had alwaies of purpose ready about me, whereby it might the better appeare unto them, how unwillingly, and upon how great & urgent occasions her Majesty was, as it were enforced to undertake this action: and therewithall I did use now and then to bestow upon them a copy of the same in writing. They seemed in all outward shew to allow of my speeches, and to praise her Majesties good inclination, and earnestly to wish that there might be a firme concord and peace againe.

It pleased the Lords general to deale exceeding favourably with this said Bishop of Cusco: for it was their good pleasure to give him his free passage without any ransome, and therewithal to let him to understand, that they came not to deale with Church-men, or unarmed men, or with men of peace, weaklings & children, neither was it any part of their meaning to make such a voyage for gold, silver, or any other their wealth and riches, &c. But that their only comming was to meet with their dishonorable practises, and manifold injuries, & to deale with men of warre and valour, for the defence of the true honour of England: and to let them to understand, that whensoever they attempted any base-conceited & dishonorable practise to their soveraigne Queene, their Mistresse, that it should be revenged to the uttermost, &c.

In this meane space, while the Lords general continued at Cadiz, there came to them certain poore wretched Turks, to the number of 38, that had bin a long time gally-slaves, and either at the very time of the fight by sea, or els immediately thereupon, taking the opportunity, did then make their escape, and did swim to land: yeelding themselves to the mercy of their most honorable Lordships. It pleased them with all speed to apparel them, and to furnish them with money, and all other necessaries, and to bestow on them a barke, and a Pilot, to see them freely and safely conveied into Barbary, willing them to let the countrey understand what was done, and what they had seene. Whereby I doubt not, but as her Majesty is a most admirable Prince already, over all Europe, all Africk, and Asia, and throughout Christendome: so the whole worlde hereafter shall have just cause to admire her infinite Princely vertues, and thereby bee provoked to confesse, that as she hath bin mightily protected from time to time, by the powerful hand of the almighty, so undoubtedly, that she is to be judged and accounted of us, to be his most sacred handmaide, and chosen vessel. And therefore, whatsoever wicked designement shalbe conspired and plotted against her Majesty hereafter, shalbe thought to be conspired, plotted, and intended against the almighty himselfe: and for that cause, as I trust, shalbe by the infinite goodnes and mercy of that almighty, mightily frustrate and overthrowen.

The 28. day being Munday, the L. Admiral came aboord the Arke againe, minding there to remaine for a space, as indeed he did, and upon the advise of his Phisition, to deale something in physicke, for that his L. found his body something out of frame. At that time it pleased his L. to write certain letters to the Duke of Medina Sidonia, for the deliverance of English captives, who were remaining in the gallies. For by this time, it was reported, that the saide Duke was come downe in person with some power, and that he was either at Port S. Mary, or els at Rotta, or thereabout. His L. did endite the letters himselfe, but his pleasure was, they should be turned into Latine by another: and so to be sent (as indeed they were) in the latine tongue unto the Duke. . . .

These letters were sent by a Spaniard, and an answere was brought from the Duke with al convenient speed, and as it should seeme by the L. Admirals next answere returned to him in writing. . . .

The next day after, being the 4. of July, the LL. general caused the town of Cadiz to be set on fire, and rased & defaced so much as they could, the faire cathedral Church, and the religious houses only being spared, and left unblemished. And with the town al such provision for shipping, & other things, as were serviceable for ye K. use, & yet were not either so convenient for us to be caried away, or els such as we stood no whit at all in need of, were likewise at the same instant consumed with fire. And presently thereupon, their Lordships, with as convenient speed as they could, and the whole army in such good order and leisure, as they thought best, came aboord.

The next day being the 5. of July, the LL. general with all the armie being under saile, & now making for England, & but as yet passing the very mouth of the bay of Cadiz, a galley ful of English prisoners, with a flag of truce, met us from Rotta, sent by the D. of Medina Sidonia, & sent as it should seeme, one day later then his promise: but yet their flag being either not big enough, or not wel placed in the galley, or not wel discerned of our men, or by what other mischance I know not: but thus it was: by one of our smallest ships y^t sailed formost, assoone as the said galley came within gunshot, there was a great peece discharged upon her, & at that instant there was one man slaine outright, and 2. other grievously hurt. The error being espied and perceived, our ship gave over immediatly from any farther shooting. Assoone as the galley came neere us, my L. Admiral caused a gracious salutation to be sounded with his trumpets, & willed the captains forthwith to come aboord his ship: which they did, and then he feasted them with a very fine and honorable banket, as the time and place might serve. And then by them understanding of that unfortunate mischance that had hapned by the shot of the said ship, he was very sory for the same, and yet such was the merciful providence of almighty God, that even in this mischance also, he did hold his holy hand over the English. And al the harme that was done did light only upon the poore Turk, and the Spaniard himselfe. When this Lorde had well banqueted them, hee presently called for his barge, and did accompany the said galley to the Lorde general the Earle of Essex, who then did ride with his ship a good distance off: and there they being in like maner most honorably received, and intertained, the Spanish gentlemen delivered up their prisoners the English captives, of whom some had bin there 6 yere, some 8, or ten: yea, and some 22. yeere, and upward, and some of them but lately taken in S. Francis Drakes last voiage to the Indies. The number of the prisoners delivered were but 39. and no mo, and were brought in, and delivered by Don Antonio de Corolla and his brother, and by Don Pedro de Cordua, and certaine others. If you demaund why, of one and fiftie Captives, there were no moe delivered then was, I presuppose, (and I thinke it true to) that at that time the residue were farther off in some remote places of Spaine bestowed, and so by that meanes, not able at this time to bee in a readinesse, but yet like enough that there is some good order taken for them hereafter, to be redeemed, and sent over into England.

If any man presume here so farre, as to enquire how it chanced, that the Lords generall rested so long at Cadiz, and went no farther, and why Port S. Mary being so faire a towne, and so neere to them, was forborne? and why Sheres aliâs Xeres? And why Rotta and the like? And why this or that was done? And why that or this left undone? I will not answere him with our common English proverbe, as I might, which is: That one foole may aske moe questions in one houre, then ten discrete men can wel answere in five dayes.

But that grave auncient writer, Cornelius Tacitus, hath a wise, briefe, pithy saying, and it is this: Nemo tentavit inquirere in columnas Herculis, sanctiúsque ac reverentius habitum est de factis Deorum credere, quàm scire. Which saying, in my fancy, fitteth marveilous well for this purpose: and so much the rather, for that this Cadiz is that very place, (at least by the common opinion) where those said pillers of Hercules were thought to be placed: and, as some say, remaine as yet not farre off to be seene. But to let that passe, the saying beareth this discrete meaning in it, albeit in a pretty kind of mystical maner uttered: That it befitteth not inferiour persons to be curious, or too inquisitive after Princes actions, neither yet to be so sawcy and so malapert, as to seeke to dive into their secrets, but rather alwayes to have a right reverend conceite and opinion of them, and their doings: and theron so resting our inward thoughts, to seek to go no further, but so to remaine ready alwaies to arme our selves with dutiful minds, and willing obedience, to perform and put in execution that which in their deepe insight and heroicall designements, they shall for our good, and the care of the common wealth determine upon.

This, and much lesse to, might suffice to satisfie any honest minded man. But yet if any will needs desire to be a little farther satisfied, albeit it neede not, yet then, thus much I dare say and affirme, that upon my knowledge, the chiefest cause why Port Saint Mary, and the rest were left untouched, was this: For that it was most certainly knowen, that they were townes not woorth the saluting of such a royal companie, in which there was no maner of wealth in the world left, more then bare houses of stone, and standing walles, and might well have served rather as a stale, perchance, to have entrapped, then as a meanes to have enriched. And it had bin more then a suspition of follie, for such an army as this, to have sought to fight with the aire, and to have laboured with great paine and charges, yea, and with some evident danger too, to have overthrowen that, which could very litle or nothing have profited, being destroyed: and yet nowe, can doe as little harme being left, as it is, untouched.

And thus much for our journey to Cadiz: for the accidents that happened by the way, for the winning, spoiling, and burning of the said towne, for the overthrowe of the Spanish Fleet there, and for al other by-matters that happened, as appendances to the same, both in the time of our abode there, as also at the very last houre of our comming from thence.

As for our returne home, and our entrance into a part of Portingal by the way, with the taking, spoyling, and burning of the towne of Faraon there, and marching into the Spanish confines thereabouts, &c. I minde to leave it to some other, whose chance was to be present at the action, as my selfe was not, and shalbe of more sufficient ability to performe it.

Bibliography

Hakluyt, Richard. *The Principal Navigations Voyages Traffiques and Discoveries of the English Nation.* 12 vols. Glasgow: 1903–1905. Includes the prefaces and introduction of the 1589 edition with the prefaces and text of the 1598–1600 edition. A definitive and masterful reprint. Vol. 12 is an index and includes an essay on English seamen of the 16th century by Sir Walter Raleigh.

————. *Hakluyt's Voyages.* Everyman edition. Introduction by John Masefield. 8 vols. London and New York: 1908 and 1927. An abridgment.

————. *Principall Navigations.* London: 1964. A facsimile reprint of the 1589 edition.

————. *The Original Writings and Correspondence of the Two Richard Hakluyts.* Introduction and notes by E. G. R. Taylor. 2 vols. London: 1936. A collection of miscellaneous papers in most instances not previously published.

Lynam, Edward, ed. *Richard Hakluyt and His Successors: a volume issued to commemorate the centenary of the Hakluyt Society.* London: 1947. Contains an article on Hakluyt by geographer J. A. Williamson. The Society, founded in 1846, published 100 volumes in its first series (1847–1898), has published 125 volumes in Series II. A Hakluyt Handbook is planned for publication. The Society has re-edited in its volumes most of the papers to be found in the *Voyages,* with supplementary original documents as well as commentaries. The object of the Society is to continue the tradition of Richard Hakluyt by publishing "original narratives of important voyages, travels, expeditions, and other geographical records."

Parks, George Bruner. *Richard Hakluyt and the English Voyages.* New York: 1928. The first definitive study of the two Richard Hakluyts, of their interrelationship, and of the *Voyages.* Intelligent, scholarly, and unlikely to be superseded.

Purchas, Samuel. *Hakluytus Posthumus or Purchas His Pilgrimes.* 4 vols. London: 1625. Reprinted in 20 vols., Glasgow: 1905–1907. Purchas was heir to Richard Hakluyt's papers and endeavored without much success to continue Hakluyt's work. Lacking his predecessor's judgments, insights, and over-all perspective, Purchas's work is valuable only in that it rescued some papers which might otherwise have been lost.

Taylor, E. G. R. *Late Tudor and Early Stuart Geography 1583–1650*. London: 1934. Places Hakluyt's work in perspective and includes a list of his published work as well as of all English geographical works of the period.

Watson, Foster. *Richard Hakluyt*. London: 1924. A slight, popular biography of limited value.